AF606017

Belief and its Neutralization

SUNY series, in Contemporary Continental Philosophy
Dennis J. Schmidt, editor

Belief and its Neutralization

Husserl's System of Phenomenology in Ideas I

Marcus Brainard

State University of New York Press

Cover image: "Husserl's last manuscript page." From Hans Rainer Sepp, ed., *Edmund Husserl und die phänomenologische Bewegung* (Freiburg/Munich: Alber, 1988), p. 412. Permission to reproduce it was granted by the Husserl Archive in Leuven, Belgium.

p. vii. Albrecht Dürer, "Knight, Death, and the Devil" (1513). From the Konrad Liebmann-Stiftung in the Stiftung Niedersachen at the Kulturgeschichtliches Museum Osnabrück.

p. viii. Rembrandt, "Jacob Wrestling with the Angel" (ca. 1659/60). From the Staatliche Museen zu Berlin Preussischer Kulturbesitz, Gemäldegallerie.

Published by
State University of New York Press, Albany

Printed in the United States of America

For information, address State University of New York Press,
90 State Street, Suite 700, Albany, NY 12207

Production by Judith Block
Marketing by Michael Campochiaro

Library of Congress Cataloging-in-Publication Data

Brainard, Marcus.
Belief and its neutralization : Husserl's system of phenomenology in Ideas I / Marcus Brainard.
p. cm. —(SUNY series in contemporary continental philosophy)
Includes bibliographical references (p.) and indexes.
ISBN 0–7914–5219–0 (alk. paper) — ISBN 0–7914–5220–4 (pbk. : alk. paper)
1. Husserl, Edmund, 1859–1938. Allgemeine Einfèhrung in die reine Phènomenologie. 2. Phenomenology. I. Title. II. Series.

B3279.H93 A3333 2002
142′.7—dc21

2001049416

10 9 8 7 6 5 4 3 2 1

For my parents

". . . nihil esse perniciosius quam quicquid ibi est accipi ad litteram, id est ad verbum, nihil autum salubrius quam spiritu revelari."

(". . . nothing is more pernicious than that whatever is there be taken by the letter, that is, literally, but nothing is more salubrious than that it be revealed through the spirit.")

— Augustine, *De utilitate credendi*

S.1513
AD

Contents

Preface

Edmund Husserl was not a philosopher, nor was his thought philosophy. He himself makes this quite clear, and repeatedly so. It is not, however, hubris that motivates his rejection of these titles, but rather his understanding of the philosophical tradition on the one hand and his high esteem of the idea of philosophy on the other. In fact it is his experience of the dissonance between the two sides, between the reality and the ideality of philosophy, that leads him to turn away from the former. Husserl sees himself forced to break completely with "the" tradition—thereby attesting his modernity—because he regards philosophy as having consistently failed to make good on its claim to be rigorous science and provide humanity with the ground and guidance it so desperately needs. Time and again, philosophy had fallen short of the realization of its ownmost idea, for it had not gotten sufficiently clear on that idea and therefore on what is required before all else. It is this twofold failure that has given rise to the said dissonance, which makes itself felt as the vital distress of humanity, its thoroughgoing crisis. If it is to be overcome, Husserl contends, one must start anew, one must set out on a path of thought that accords with the idea of philosophy and thus leads towards the fulfillment of the intention to be rigorous science.

As a consequence of his insight into the task of thinking, Husserl denies himself the title of philosopher. For him philosophy is and remains the highest vocation, but the one thing needful is far more basic, and it must be attended to first. Namely, a foundation must be secured on which all subsequent knowledge and every human endeavor can be based. This is the principial requirement. Fulfilling it is what alone makes philosophy possible as rigorous science. In light of philosophy's failure, however, it itself cannot achieve this end. Rather, a new discipline is called for that, though in spirit one with philosophy, is not itself philosophy, but prior to philosophy. Needed is the most radical discipline, one that finally understands "the seriousness of the beginning," one that is fully cognizant of and prepared to carry out its function as the archontic discipline. Needed, according to Husserl, is none other than phenomenology, and ultimately transcendental phenomenology.[1] It is to be the beginning science. And as its founder, Husserl is and remains the "eternal beginner," nothing more and nothing less. It is precisely the sense of the seriousness of the beginning, of finding the root of everything, that informs the entire movement of his thought. This radicality is what binds together each of its moments into one whole.

Husserlian thought is borne by an ethos of striving. It is the response to a vital need, which itself indicates how it is to be overcome: "And our age yearns for nothing so much as that the true origins might finally come to word and only then that they come, in the higher sense, to their Word, to the Logos."[2] Origins and Logos—these are the poles of all striving. In seeking to accord with the order of inquiry they dictate, Husserl's proves to be a faithful response to the things themselves: it is literally an endeavor. The task of thinking therefore requires that he strive first to find the absolute ground and then to climb up into the heights. And yet it is not enough that he find the ground; he must also bring it to word and to intuition for others. Hence, his task also entails a twofold struggle: first against himself, his inclinations, and then against the habits of thinking that hold sway within humanity. In thus striving and struggling, Husserl is Dürer's Knight who must pass between Death and the Devil, he is Rembrandt's Jacob wrestling with the angel. He must overcome great obstacles, he must purify himself and others, so as to move from what is first for us to what is first by nature.[3] In the service of this task, Husserl strives to make himself new, to become a transcendental phenomenologist, while also endeavoring to initiate the striving of others, leading them from the ground up into the heights. Properly understood, this amounts to awakening the naive from their dogmatic slumber, awakening them to their essence and thus to a new life lived in accordance with that essence, which is to say, with reason. He thereby hastens the natural, unconscious life processes, though necessarily so, for without such hastening what is initially only latent could never become fully patent: "Life is in itself striving and is as human [striving] an ascent from passivity to activity, from letting-oneself-go-and-be-carried-along, from a life according to inclination, to a considered choosing, to a critical, more highly valued, preferring life. That which is known to be of lesser value is no longer the good, but rather is bad. The better is the enemy of the good. Man necessarily lifts himself up to a valuation of life in view of the best, of that which is mostly to be preferred, but as something that is good and can satisfy, as that which satisfies best, which satisfies fully, because nothing better is practically possible."[4] On Husserl's view life in the best sense, thus ideally, is that which subjects itself wholly to the norm of reason. In its most authentic manifestation, then, life is "rational striving." It is a striving "to give one's personal life the form of perspicuity or that of legitimacy or rationality with respect to each of its judging, valuing, and practical position-takings [*Stellungnahmen*]."[5] Striving is never aimless, but has a *sense*. Its sense as directedness is to move from lower to higher, from unconscious to conscious, from irrational to rational. Its sense as meaning or telos is absolute rationality or harmony. The span of striving extends from the origins ultimately from *the* origin—up to the Logos, which for Husserl is the Word, but also absolute reason. The sense of this striving is the sense of his thought; it is captured in the system of transcendental phenomenology.

In order to grasp his thought completely, one must first grasp its sense. Such requires that one focus not only on his "words," but also and especially on the intention or sense informing them, which is to say, one must attend not only to the letter of his thought, but also to its spirit. Not just in recent times, but even in Husserl's day it was common to overlook the sense of his words, as he himself complained.[6] As for why, at least two possible explanations suggest themselves. On the one hand, the difficulty of seeing this sense would seem to stem from Husserl himself: at first glance, his works look to be little more than whirlwinds of distinctions (with distinction following upon distinction, though lacking any obvious direction or point save the simple possibility of making them).[7] In addition, his ever changing (so it seems) approaches to phenomenology—which are visible not only in the move from the descriptive psychology of the first *Logical Investigations* to the transcendental phenomenology of the first book of *Ideas Pertaining to a Pure Phenomenology and to a Phenomenological Philosophy*, but even in the subsequent "introductions" to phenomenology—give the impression that his thought is in constant flux. Yet Husserl himself asserts the unity of his thought. He himself speaks increasingly often of his task, the firmer his grasp of the idea of phenomenology becomes. In other words, he himself sees the abiding sense of his endeavor. Thus, although the difficulty may be said to stem from him to some extent—especially because he is often more concerned with doing the work he deems necessary than with explaining why he is doing it, but also because he did not always show himself to be the most gifted writer, so the complaint goes—its source must ultimately lie elsewhere. If it does not lie with the thinker, then it seems clear that it must lie with his readers, who have perhaps been blinded by the "prevailing habits of thinking" rather than achieving the requisite openness to the spirit of Husserl's writings.

Indeed, although there are important exceptions, and these should become clear in the course of the present study, two predominant tendencies may be discerned in Husserl scholarship that have served more to conceal than to reveal the decisive sense of Husserlian thought. Wherever the unity of his thought has been noted, the tendency has been either to reduce it to the accidental unity of his life and then to discount it in favor of the seeming multiplicity of his approaches,[8] or to regard its various phases as being unified by a central problem or constellation of problems.[9] From the latter standpoint, one might investigate Husserl's various approaches to a problem, e.g. that of intentionality, over the course of his career, whereby one solution is regarded as naturally leading to another related problem, and so on. On the other hand, one might want to take Husserl as part of a tradition: his answers to the problem of intentionality would accordingly be considered in the context of answers before and after him. By embedding him in "the" tradition in this way, he would become but one link in the endless chain of the history of philosophical problems,[10] and the difference he makes would be quashed. Neither of these approaches, however, would do justice to Husserl's self-understanding—which he made evident in each of his published works and which has since become even clearer in light of posthumous publications. Such a lack of justice would prevail so long as one failed to cultivate a radical reticence with respect to thought, to say nothing of effecting the epoché that Husserl himself demanded repeatedly.[11] The remedy for this situation is simply to take him at his word, listening all the while for its sense. That this has not been common practice should be obvious from the fact that hardly any of the proponents of the aforementioned approaches has inquired into the normative moment that unifies the various phases of Husserl's work and determines his choice of problems. That moment is itself not just one problem among others, but precisely a task, which alone determines what counts as a problem for a thought.[12] To discern it in the case of Husserl's endeavor, it is necessary to ask not only what phenomenology is but also why. It is to ask about the *sense* of phenomenology.

Again, while the difficulties involved in coming to terms with a thought may have any number of sources, primary among them is the failure to listen to *what* has been said just *as* it has been said. The aim of the present study is precisely to make the obvious visible, to make the sense of Husserl's words audible. In order to do so, one must pass, as it were, from what is merely first for us to what is first by nature, in this case to the task guiding the expression of Husserlian thought in its various forms. To succeed in making this passage, as Husserl himself notes, "one must simply have the courage here as everywhere in phenomenology to take what is actually to be seen in the phenomenon precisely as it gives itself instead of reinterpreting it, and to describe it *honestly*."[13] This is attempted in what follows under the scope of a new epoché, which may be called the 'logotectonic epoché'.[14]

By its intention, this epoché departs decisively from the horizon of Husserlian thought. Rather than excluding the general thesis as Husserl's epoché does in order to enter the sphere of phenomenological inquiry, or pure consciousness, the new "method" is meant to exclude all idiosyncrasies on our part, specifically our own desires with respect to his thought, thereby enabling us to approach that thought itself and to enter a sphere that has long been neglected, that of pure thought.[15] The new epoché proves to be "more radical" than Husserl's insofar as it does something Husserl's did not do—and necessarily could not do given his understanding of his task: It redirects the regard not to phenomena but to thought as such, in isolation from every influence and taken on (and in) its own terms, and so allows the thought itself to come to the fore.[16] In effecting this epoché, thinking discloses the finitude not only of Husserlian thought, but also of any thought to which it turns. The focus is accordingly on what Husserl wants, within the bounds of his task, and not on what we want from him. Hence we have sought to let Husserl "speak for himself" as far as possible.[17] Interventions on our part have been made only so as to make the "hidden sense" of his thought more perspicuous.

The logotectonic epoché allows the integrity of a thought to come into view by detemporalizing or denaturalizing thought, by wresting it from all temporal and natural continua. The modern assertion of the priority of Being over thinking is denied, which enables the disclosure of a thought as a static whole. In other words, the thought is viewed, to speak in Husserlian terms, solely as the unity of a preceding, regulative intention and the thinker's attempt—no matter how numerous the approaches involved therein—to fulfill it. Such can come to light only insofar as thought is not taken as primarily changing or in flux, nor as continuous with other thoughts, but as an identity of intention, and as such singular.

Insofar as it reduces thought to the *nunc stans* (standing now) or the "living present," without reference to prior or posterior temporal modes, the logotectonic epoché may be said to resemble Husserl's "apodictic reduction."[18] The aim of the new reduction, however, is to reveal thought, as it were, for thought's sake. Thinking under the scope of this epoché therefore focuses on it as a static, self-contained whole, and thus neither calls the thought into account nor asks what it is good for. Thus, the only critique in play here is critique that aims at distinction (κρινεῖν)—not at a reckoning. This may strike the reader as odd or even irresponsible insofar as we seek to let the thought be rather than making it answer to the demands or exigencies of contemporary thought. And such an objection to our approach may be warranted, but whether it is can be determined only after the necessary first step has been taken: only after the thought under consideration has first been understood as fully as possible, as a whole—which need not mean mastering all its problems. Critique in the sense of calling into account is justified and, more important, fruitful only where like criticizes like.

Because it is meant to provide the basis for such critique, the present study is intended to be an introduction to Husserlian phenomenology, to its sense and ethos.[19] It is a meditation on the task of thinking. To this end, we have undertaken a structural analysis of and commentary on the first book of *Ideas Pertaining to a Pure Phenomenology and to a Phenomenological Philosophy*, thus the *General Introduction to Pure Phenomenology*, with a view to showing the essential features of the whole of Husserlian thought.[20] Under the scope of the aforementioned epoché, Husserl's presentation will be traced step by step so as to draw out the logic of the development of his task, its movement, its unfolding. This means accounting for Husserl's "construction of the *idea* of a pure phenomenology" (*Ideas I*, 33) or his system. Since in pursuing this idea it is not our task—much as it was not Husserl's own—"to solve phenomenological problems, but rather to work out scientifically the main problems of phenomenology, or to predelineate the directions of investigation connected with them, it has to be enough for us to have taken things this far" (252). The task here is therefore not to solve his problems, but, in light of them, to trace the contours of the task, the lines along which Husserl's endeavor unfolds.[21]

In doing so, we seek to fulfill three interrelated intentions. The first is precisely to demonstrate the systematic character of the *whole* of his work—on the example of *Ideas I*. The unfolding at issue is not a genetic development, but rather the articulation and concretization of the task in and by the thought. The movement of phenomenology that thereby comes into view entails the following steps: (1) the establishment of the priority of essence over fact; (2) the location of and entry into the a priori, phenomenological sphere; (3) the explication of intentionality in terms of the noetic-noematic correlation; (4) the identification of the doxic "underground" of noetic activity; (5) the explication of the "objectual" underground or reference in the noema; and (6) the explication of reason or rationality. The second guiding intention arises out of the first and forms the heart of this study: to elaborate Husserl's "doctrine of the neutrality modification." The aim thereby is to demonstrate the significance of this modification within Husserlian thought, a significance that can be seen only in relation to his system. Otherwise, there is no apparent difference—and Husserl scholars have done much to strengthen this appearance—between that modification and the epoché. The present "forked" analysis is thus a double argument: for the systematic character of Husserlian thought and for the centrality of the neutrality modification therein. It is central not for what it contributes to Husserl's system, but for how it obstructs the latter's fulfillment. Determining how it is obstructive, however, reveals the basis of conscious life: belief. To exhibit this basis as such forms the third and unifying intention of the present study.

In keeping with these intentions, this book is divided into five chapters. In Chapter I, the task of Husserlian thought is outlined. Here it is shown not only why phenomenology comes into being, namely in response to a crisis, but also how Husserl intends to overcome the prevailing crisis. It is in this connection that the practical impulse of his work comes into view, but also the projective character of phenomenology. In constructing the idea of phenomenology, Husserl projects the lines along which phenomenology is to develop: from the ground up into the heights, or from the pure ego up to absolute reason or God. These are the limits of his system and as such frame the striving peculiar to phenomenology. After their centrality to his thought as a whole has been established, they and the trajectory they delimit are traced out in the next three chapters in the form of a commentary on *Ideas I*. In Chapter II, steps 1 and 2 just mentioned are addressed. First the systematic significance of Husserl's distinction between essence and fact is developed, and then the nature and effect of the phenomenological method, the epoché, is elucidated. By means of the latter, access to the ground and the field of inquiry it represents is given. It is in Chapter III that this new field is addressed (steps 3 and 4), specifically Husserl's analysis of the universal structures of consciousness, its noetic-noematic structures. Of particular importance here are the modifications that consciousness can undergo, and it is in this connection that both the prerequisite of all productive conscious life—belief—and its (debilitating) neutralization are elaborated; here only does the unique status of the universal neutrality modification become visible, but also what is required in order to ascend to reason. In Chapter IV, Husserl's understanding of reason is investigated (steps 5 and 6). Chapter V returns to the topic of the task of phenomenology as Husserl understands it, and indicates the way in which his undertaking remains paradigmatic for all other positions that would make their appearance as phenomenology. These concluding considerations appeal to the sense of Husserl's endeavor and what it requires of thought.

To ask after the Why of phenomenology is to seek to grasp the sense, the task of Husserlian thought. Because we intend to answer this question in what follows by drawing out the abiding sense, the present study may be considered a static analysis, though one that departs from Husserl's own in essential respects. Wherever the various phases of his development are addressed as such, then only insofar as they contribute to the understanding of his task and what he considers necessary for its fulfillment. In other words, given the kind of analysis undertaken here, any appeal to chronology cannot play a principial role, but serves only to make visible what is identical, though initially hidden, within the multiplicity, and thus to confirm by "natural" means the singularity of Husserl's mission. The "hidden sense" of a thought will remain hidden so long as one regards that thought as part of a continuum or as in flux. The key is to take the thought on its own and seek the invariant among the variations, whether they be of Being or time. For sense is unchanging. Thus, applying Frege's remark on number to thought, we can say: "Every change takes place in time. Therefore, analysis would have to occupy itself with a temporal event were it to consider what changes. And yet analysis has nothing to do with time; for the fact that it can be applied to temporal occurrences is beside the point."[22] Change is not the issue here, but rather that which abides.

Chapter I. Introduction

The Task of Thinking

Time is not of the essence. Essences are nothing in time, although their instantiations occur in time. Essences are idealities, not realities; formal, not material; universal, not individual. An essence or idea regulates the becoming of its corresponding individuals, which is to say, it sets the goal, the telos, of their becoming. The essence binds together every changing moment into a whole of becoming and thereby gives unity to multiplicity. It remains constant in the midst of change. Everything essential is fixed a priori, outside of time. Everything in time is regulated by essence. Every possibility, every contingency, has its basis in necessity, in essence. Outside of time while regulating all becoming in time, essence entails both the beginning and the end of the becoming of its corresponding individuals. In this way it sets the parameters of an individual system of becoming. As a consequence, essence proves to have priority over each of its individuals. It is first by nature, whereas individuals are only first for us, but second by nature.—Thus read the most fundamental insights that guide Edmund Husserl in the articulation of his thought.[1]

The priority of essence is not only drawn out by Husserl, but is also reflected in his thought in two possible modes of eidetic analysis: static and genetic. Genetic analysis focuses on the twists and turns in the becoming or constitution of individuals in time and thereby on the "'history' of consciousness" (SGM, 339/137).[2] It is still eidetic analysis, but one nevertheless focused on becoming. Static analysis, by contrast, is concerned with constituted individuals or with essences, without regard to time. Husserl sharpens the distinction between these two modes by noting that genetic analysis is "explicative," whereas static analysis is purely "descriptive" (340/138). The latter accesses essences, their structures and relations, directly; it focuses on them primarily in isolation and describes them with a view to completeness. Genetic analysis, on the other hand, accesses them only secondarily or derivatively insofar as it is concerned to explain how something becomes constituted. In doing so, it takes its bearings by the essence of what is constituted, the insight into which is first yielded, once again, by static analysis. Hence genetic analysis presupposes static analysis; they are connected in a hierarchy in which the former is founded on the latter. Husserl draws this out as follows: "It is clear that one will initially start out from individual fundamental types, some of which will . . . occur necessarily, while others will offer themselves as possibilities. The question is about the guiding threads of the system. The types of objects offer themselves as such, thus as guiding threads with respect to ontology. And thereby the constitutive teleologies. In this connection, ideal possibilities of harmonious givens are spun out, ideal possibilities of monadic streams in which the unity of a product [*Leistung*] is constituted, and, in addition, other possibilities are considered as counterforms" (344/141). Static analysis describes the fundamental types (and countertypes) and thereby provides genetic analysis with the guiding threads or parameters for the explication of the teleologies that are rooted in those types. In other words, static analysis describes the end of genesis, whereas genetic analysis explicates the means thereof. Together with a third, mediating mode, these two modes of analysis form a hierarchical progression. Phenomenology begins with the "universal phenomenology of the universal structures of consciousness" and proceeds up to "constitutive phenomenology" and beyond to the "phenomenology of genesis."[3] Each mode is integral to phenomenology taken as a whole, but for Husserl it is static analysis that is decisive, for it marks the beginning on which the other modes are founded and so in a certain sense already entails what follows.

These insights not only form the basis of phenomenological inquiry as a whole, but they also provide the key to Husserl's own self-understanding; they indicate the guiding threads, the tracing of which enables the determination of what phenomenology is for him. In this connection, the pivotal insight is into the normative function of essence. Namely, just as each individual is governed by an essence, likewise Husserl regards thought itself as having an essence, one that is bound up with the essence of human being, with humanness (*Menschentum*) in general. Thus phenomenology not only discloses essences but itself has an essence.[4] He refers to this essence differently—at times expressly as 'essence', 'idea', or 'norm', at others as 'concept', 'sense', or 'telos', and at still others as 'task'—but in each case he means the same.[5] In light of what was said at the outset about essence, it follows here that whereas a thought unfolds in time, specifically in the thinker's attempt to fulfill his task, that task itself is atemporal. It does not change, even though the thinker may get clear on it only over time, step by step. Insofar as the task fixes the norm of the thought's development, insofar as it is the unifying center amidst the myriad twists and turns of the thought's unfolding, that development proves to be subordinate to the task. It determines not just the end, but the beginning as well, and in so doing binds together the multiple phases into a singular unity.

Furthermore, just as it sets the parameters of that development, it also fixes the problems to be addressed in seeking to fulfill the task.[6]

Husserl himself repeatedly asserts the unity of his thought; he believes himself to be in pursuit of one task—it is literally his *idée fixe*.[7] This is in no way contradicted by the various approaches he undertakes over the course of his career, for, as should become clear below, they simply mark alternative attempts to fulfill the same task.[8] If one starts with what these attempts most obviously have in common, Husserl's task is at first glance best captured by the epithet 'theory of knowledge' or 'epistemology'. Accordingly, his primary intention would be to explain knowledge, both what it is and how it comes to pass. This would require, first of all, the establishment of the foundation of knowledge—whence the epithet 'foundationalist', which also may be used to describe his task.[9] It is due to his pursuit of the foundation that essence takes on and retains such prominence in Husserlian thought.[10]

In accordance with the insight into the aforementioned priority, phenomenology is centered on essence—from start to finish. It aims at being not just one eidetic science among others, but rather *the* eidetic science, the science on which all others are founded—initially in the form of "pure logic," then expressly as radical eidetics. As such it is intended to be the science of all sciences, that is, the first or archontic science, which discloses the norms for the others.[11] Furthermore, in performing its foundational function, it is intended to do nothing less than save humanity, and in fact precisely by giving it, just as in the case of the sciences, a new orientation. Especially in this regard theory proves to be thoroughly practical for Husserl.[12] To establish phenomenology as just this science is the intention that guides his analyses no later than as of his "breakthrough into phenomenology" in the *Logical Investigations*[13] and it continues to do so up through his final work, *The Crisis of the European Sciences and Transcendental Phenomenology*.[14]

But whereas the insight into the fundamental role of pure logic remains operative throughout this span,[15] the nature of the foundation sought undergoes a radicalization upon the discovery of the epoché. This method enables the disclosure of the Archimedean point on which all else rests: the pure ego.[16] In radicalizing phenomenology, the epoché ushers in the much discussed "transcendental turn."[17] Contrary to first appearances, however, this turn does not mark a break with the inaugural work of phenomenology, but is instead a progressive deepening of the fundamental insights gained there, region by region[18]—hence the talk of radicalization.[19] Even if it is "a long and thorny road"[20] that leads from the *Logical Investigations* to his first mature work of transcendental phenomenology, namely the first book of *Ideas Pertaining to a Pure Phenomenology and to a Phenomenological Philosophy*, it is nevertheless one continuous, which is not to say seamless, road.[21]

However, this talk should not be misconstrued. Although it involves a progression, the movement of phenomenology is not dialectical but more recursive in character, that is, it unfolds by way of zigzagging or a reflective spiral from the heights down to the ground of conscious life and then, from that ground, back up into the heights—at least that is Husserl's abiding intention.[22] If the talk can be of dialectic at all, then it must first be of an inverse dialectic, which is to say, not one primarily of sublation and synthesis, but rather of boring and laying foundations.[23] It is incipiently a drive to reach the absolute ground, the Archimedean point. Only after reaching it can there be any construction of a "system of doctrine [*Lehrsystem*]."[24]

Although it may not be obvious on the surface, especially due to its founder's own seemingly boundless productivity,[25] the entire movement of phenomenology is regulated by one task, one "purposive sense [*Zwecksinn*]" (see *FTL*, 8 and 5). As Husserl says: "There is no 'royal road' into phenomenology and therefore none into philosophy. There is only the *one* road prescribed by phenomenology's own essence" (*Ideas I*, 201). The movement is *pre*-scribed by its essence—which is *one* essence—or in other words, the teleology of the thought is predelineated by its telos. Only by coming to terms with this essence or task will it become possible to understand fully the whole it prescribes, and this holds no less for the parts it comprises.

In order to penetrate to the core of this whole, in order to disclose "its inner sense, its hidden teleology" (*Crisis*, 16/18), one might wish to follow a directive that Husserl himself gave in 1933, and thus relatively late in his career. He says that "a genuine elucidation of the historical development of a philosophy (*in* the philosopher) can be given only in light of its mature sense-formation [*Sinngestalt*]; only then does one understand the structure of the *dynamis* in each lower level."[26] Proceeding in this way would mean engaging in a "dynamic" or genetic analysis.[27] And yet, as seen above, it is first and foremost the static analysis that yields the guiding insight into the *dynamis* of a thought, which is to say, into its task. Thus an alternative and literally more radical approach would be to look to the "mature sense-formation" for confirmation of what is discerned in the beginning, at the root of his thought. This is not to say, however, that in proceeding in this way the concern would lie with a natural beginning and end, such as those bounding the span of a life. Rather, it is crucial that one discern the *sense* of the structure and movement of the "decisive phases" of the particular thought, or the telos after which the thought strives in each of its phases.[28] This requires that one ask not only 'What is phenomenology?'[29]—in answer to which 'epistemology' might count as a satisfactory answer—but also, and more important, 'Why phenomenology?' This is the more radical question. For it is the Why (here the *dynamis*) that lends unity and thus determinacy to the What (Husserl's thought as a whole) and thereby makes clear its singularity amidst the multiplicity of other thoughts, to say nothing of other "phenomenologies."

The present study aims at nothing more and nothing less than fixing the essence, the idea of phenomenology. This calls for the explication of both what moves Husserlian thought and the parameters within which it moves. However, they cannot be grasped immediately. Instead, the task of thinking that guided Husserl's articulation of phenomenology, and most fundamentally of transcendental phenomenology, must be approached by way of a new "method," specifically by means of what above was referred to as the logotectonic epoché.[30] Under its scope, thought is detemporalized, denaturalized. It is wrested thereby from the temporal continuum of thought largely presumed to exist today, as well as from a nature, or Being and becoming, that gives rise to thought. In this way it becomes possible to take thought—in this case Husserl's—on its own terms. This is the decisive step to be taken if an answer is to be given to the question 'What is phenomenology?' For it is a question about essence. Contrary to Husserl and the moderns, however, the answer to it is not *the* answer to the question 'What is called thinking?' but one that goes towards answering it. The difference here lies in the insight that thinking is not only of one kind, that it does not have only one task, but that it is differentiated by virtue of its—different but finite—tasks.[31] Husserl strove to fulfill his task, one that distinguishes his position from other positions that, together with his, are constitutive of modernity. It can be grasped only by excluding time, by denying time, as well as Being in time, any priority. Time is not of the essence. Time is beside the point as long as the concern lies with what is unchanging. Time contributes nothing essential to the consideration. To inquire into what thought is and, prior to that, why it is, is not to ask after time.

1. The Idea of Phenomenology

If one were to apply the aforementioned directive to Husserl's own thought, that is, if one were to seek to grasp the *dynamis* uniting its several phases so as to be in a position to elucidate "the historical development of a philosophy (in the philosopher)," then one would have to turn to *The Crisis of the European Sciences and Transcendental Phenomenology*, assuming, of course, that the final phase of Husserlian thought coincides with its "mature sense-formation."[32] As the title of that work suggests, Husserl sees the European sciences in crisis. Yet the crisis thematized there is not confined to them, but rather, as the heading of the work's first part indicates, theirs is but a symptom of a deeper-lying, far more perilous crisis, one that actually poses the greatest danger since it strikes at the very root of European culture and thus of humanity.[33] Husserl notes that "the crisis of a science means nothing less than that its genuine scientific character, that the whole manner in which it has set its task and developed a methodology for it, has become questionable" (*Crisis*, 1/3). The scientific character—that is, the essence—of a science is expressed precisely in the science's task and its corresponding method. It is only when they no longer provide sufficient guidance that a science can fall into crisis. This failing guidance is signaled by the questionableness of science's essence, or more precisely of the proper understanding of that essence and, by extension, the task and method it prescribes. This is no local disturbance, however. Rather, since the destinies of the sciences and man are inextricably interwoven, the crisis of concern here proves to be rooted not only in the questionableness of the sciences, but also of man himself—in their uniquely European manifestations—and in fact first and foremost in the questionableness of the essence of each.

Yet none of this is to say that the crisis marks an end. Instead, it indicates an impending shift or cut: insofar as being in crisis means being essentially in question, the crisis itself is the expression of a vital tension, of an Either-Or that demands decision. It is a decision about the proper understanding of the essence of science and, prior to that, of man. As the right decision, it depends on the crucial insight into the one thing needful, into both the task and the method of its fulfillment. It alone can bring about the end of the "present" crisis; and made rightly, it will result in a beginning, in a new life for the "new man."[34] It is precisely this decision that Husserl seeks to hasten by means of his reflections in the *Crisis*.[35]

1.1 The Crisis, its Source and Dimensions

Husserl considers the source of the crisis to be positivism, which came to power after the conclusion of Hegelian philosophy.[36] With its virulent skepticism, positivism has caused everything essential to become questionable. It is not the question itself, of course, but rather its character that is responsible for the crisis. And this is what receives Husserl's scrutiny. It is the skeptical ingredient in the questionableness that makes all the difference here. Its dominance not only signals but, prior to that, contributes to a loss that literally undermines European humanness and threatens it with "the greatest danger of drowning in the skeptical deluge" (12/14), for positivism's inherent skepticism helps pull the ground or the Apriori out from under humanity and its sciences.[37]

He pinpoints the loss as follows: "Skepticism about the possibility of a metaphysics, the collapse of the belief in a universal philosophy as the guide of the new man, means precisely the collapse of the belief in 'reason'" (10/12), and thus of "the belief in an 'absolute' reason through which the world has its sense, the belief in the sense of history, the sense of humanness, in its freedom, namely as man's capacity to provide his individual and universal human existence with rational sense" (11/13). In light of this, it becomes clear that whereas the crisis of concern to him in his last phase is ultimately and eminently a crisis of sense and so of reason, at base it is one of belief. That is the deepest point of tension as Husserl sees it; that is what must be decided. It is on account of this that Husserl calls it a vital crisis. He regards it as nothing less than a life-or-death struggle[38] between belief and unbelief, between universal philosophy and skepticism.[39] It is precisely this loss of belief in reason that Husserl seeks to remedy by means of phenomenology.[40] It is the Why, the motivation of his quest for a new foundation.

Phenomenology not only ends in crisis, but is born in crisis as well—in both individual and universal crisis.[41] To the extent that they are explicitly thematized, the crisis of European culture, as well as the philosopher's personal responsibility in redressing it, are concerns that are confined to Husserl's "phenomenological period," which stretches roughly from 1900 to his death in 1938.[42] Yet, although his thought culminates in reflections on these concerns and although his first writings, as he notes in retrospect, were "born of distress [*Not*], of unspeakable mental distress, of a complete 'collapse,'" it is in fact not until after the completion of the *Logical Investigations* in 1900–01 that he begins to grow aware of the crisis as such. It is only later that he begins to develop "an eye for practical and cultural realities" and thus to sense the "intrinsic hollowness" of the intentions that prevailed in that culture during the 1890s, the germinal phase of phenomenology.[43] Up until the turn of the century, he says, he had focused almost exclusively on "theoretical" issues.[44] Eventually, however, he came to understand the theoretical as being bound up with the practical, and in fact as being preliminary to it since the solutions of the problems found in the former sphere were to provide the basis on which those in the latter can be addressed.[45] It is precisely from this juncture that pure, transcendental phenomenology springs.[46] The deepening sense of the crisis goes hand in hand with the deepening sense of his task. In an "instinctive" response to the questionableness not only of the sciences in general and of philosophy in particular, but also of the whole of humanity, Husserl's intention to establish an ultimate foundation already guided his efforts in his *Investigations*. But it is not until his discovery of the epoché in 1905 that the "idea of phenomenology"[47] begins to become explicit. It sets the most radical phase of phenomenology in motion, for in it phenomenology becomes "critically" aware of the crisis and its source, and of what is needed to overcome it. In ever deepening cognizance of the loss of the ground of European humanness, Husserl's task must be to restore precisely that ground; he must begin anew. This calls for the reinstitution of the Apriori—or rather the first radical institution thereof, since Husserl views the whole of the philosophical tradition as having struggled towards it only naively. He considers himself the first to have gained insight into the true ground; and so it is his responsibility to bring this light to humanity.[48] It is this conviction that gives rise, on the one hand, to what he calls the "non-platitudinous sobriety and radical objectivity" of his writings from the *Investigations* on. They are "borne by a personal ethos," which he hopes to reawaken in European humanness.[49] But, on the other hand, it is also the source of the pathos[50] that occasionally erupts in his appeals to himself and to humanity, to the "self" that binds the one to the other.[51] His "exhortations" are not just to a philosophical life, but, prior to that, to a transcendental-phenomenological life.[52]

1.2 Natural Order and Critique

Although Husserl was aware of having a task already in 1896,[53] it is only after the discovery of the epoché in 1905 that its contours become more determinate.[54] For it alone is what enables Husserl to secure the absolute ground, the lost Apriori.[55] This discovery ushers in the "turn" to transcendental phenomenology, precisely because it is what makes everything possible. In it he sees the ultimate starting point, the true beginning. However, the insight into this ground is not enough. Husserl is obliged to bring it to intuition, to make it visible to others. And this is what occupies his reflections throughout his "transcendental" period. His sense of obligation, of responsibility, accounts for his unflagging preoccupation not only with the order of his presentation, but, first and foremost, with the beginning. For without the right beginning, there can be no right order; regardless of how well one builds one's edifice, it will be but a "castle in the clouds" (*Wolkenschloß*) as long as the proper beginning has not been made. Given this emphasis, Husserl is justified in calling himself "an actual beginner."[56] He is nothing more and nothing less—in complete compliance with his task.

Soon after the discovery of the epoché, and thus of the means for the most radical beginning, Husserl determines his task to be "a *critique of reason*," and in fact "of logical and practical reason, of any valuing reason whatsoever" (*PN*, 297).[57] For him this is not just one among other possible tasks, but rather the "general task that I must solve if I am ever to be able to call myself a philosopher." There are indeed other tasks, but they are encompassed by the critique of reason. Insofar as they are at all worth pursuing, they fit within that general task. As subtasks their solution contributes to its solution. And everything depends on its solution: "Without getting clear in general terms on the sense, essence, methods, main points of a critique of reason, without having thought out, drafted, established, and founded a general outline for them, I cannot live truly and truthfully." This task is of vital importance to him—from at least 1906 on. As a personal task, its solution will not only enable him to live, but also to become a philosopher, a hope he harbors until his dying day.[58]

Whereas the critique of reason is the task he sees for himself in 1906, and thus after his so-called transcendental turn, it is nevertheless of a piece with the task that guided his earlier work: "Since the publication of the *Logical Investigations*, my life has gained inner firmness. And from now on it shall and must show inner unity. Unfortunately, my personality can no longer become full and complete" (296). This unity is gained above all, he then notes, by disclosing the unity of the phenomenological and the psychological.[59] His entire Being is wrapped up in his work. He is literally fighting for his life, because he is fighting for his "self": "But I must live for my tasks and seek my value and my inner certainty in their fulfillment. You shall know them by their fruits.[60] And by my fruits I will know myself; I will be able to respect myself if I ripen them in myself through hard work and in a well-ordered sequence" (297). Again, these tasks are situated within the general task of a critique of reason. And yet this task is not just Husserl's personal task; he does not consider it something peculiar to himself, but rather something that bears upon others: "But thank heavens, there has been no lack of fruit, and more fruit is ripening. The proper values that were able to thrive on this trunk,[61] which—alas! [*Gott sei's geklagt!*]—is broken and malformed in so many places, must now be ripened. That will be my life henceforth; that is the field of my life's proper tasks. I do not want to despair, but to hope; I want to be content when I do work that will actually benefit my successors" (296–97). It is to be the trunk of a "sound tree," in this case the tree of knowledge, which is rooted in the Archimedean point and which is transcendental phenomenology, while also being cultivated by this phenomenology.[62] The critique called for is precisely the establishment of the proper order, from the root up into the heights.[63]

Husserl's drive for clarity—which is the drive for unity—not only concerns his personality, his self, but also the problems he deals with. This drive leads him first into the depths and, after he has reached the bottom, then up into the heights: "In devoted work, in purely objective engrossment, I want to and must approach the high goals" (297). Below and above are bound together into one whole. To get clear on this whole, he must fight against the temptations of skepticism: "I am fighting for my life, and that is why I confidently believe that I shall be able to progress. The most severe vital distress, the self-defense against the dangers of death, gives undreamt-of, unmeasured strength." The source of the danger is also the source of his strength for overcoming that danger.[64] It compels Husserl to achieve clarity where there is otherwise only darkness. The clarity he aims at is not partial, but is about the whole. Hence, his life-or-death struggle is an all-or-nothing struggle: "Only one thing can fulfill me: I must gain clarity, otherwise I cannot live; I cannot bear life if I cannot believe that I shall gain the ability to look actually into the promised land, on my own and with clear eyes." Husserl regards himself as wandering through the desert of skepticism (and dogmatism). He is at once Moses and Columbus: he is seeking the way into the "new world."[65] And only clarity will grant him safe passage.

To fulfill his intention, it is not enough, he says, to have "knowledge of the goals, guidelines, standard measures, methods, and position taken on other knowledge and sciences. We also need the actual work. We have to pursue the paths ourselves. We must solve the individual problems step by step. Thus, what is needed here is above all a treatment of the phenomenology of reason, step by step, and on the basis of that the actual elucidation of logical and ethical reason in the form of the principles and fundamental concepts proper to each" (298). He must actually work, which requires that he proceed "step by step." The sequence of inquiry is not arbitrary; there is an ideal order, which is set in advance by the things themselves (*die Sachen selbst*).[66] The deed called for in each case is guided by the insight into this order.

Thus, to reach the "promised land," he must be true to the things themselves. They alone provide the sole hope: "Pure reflection, pure inner life, absorbing the problems into myself and being turned purely and only to them—that is the hope of my future. If I do not succeed in this, then I may only live a life that is much more a death. I still may hope. But the hour has sounded in which I must reach *the* decision. The mere 'will' as a single resolution is not sufficient. Needed is inner renewal or inner purification and firmness. Against all externalities, against all the temptations of Adam, I must arm myself with nine layers of bronze" (300).[67] The decision called for is made once;[68] it initiates the would-be philosopher into the ethos that will bear him along the road to the "promised land." But his resolve must be continually renewed: this is the critical or rigorous attitude that animates pure phenomenology. One must purify oneself (and repeatedly so) of the "prevailing habits of thinking," of skeptical and dogmatic temptations. These are the extremes through which the phenomenological ethos safely guides one: "I must go my way as confidently, as firmly resolved, and as seriously as Dürer's Knight, despite Death and the Devil. O, my life has been serious enough. The cheerfulness of the sensuous enjoyment of life has become foreign to me and must remain foreign to me. I may not be passive (and enjoyment is passivity); I must live in work, in battle, in the passionately serious struggle for the wreath of truth. There will be no lack of cheerfulness: there will be clear sky[69] above me if I progress courageously and confidently, just as it is above Dürer's Knight! And God be with me as with him, although we are ever sinners."[70] That is to say, although we all stray repeatedly from the path set by the things themselves.

Precisely because it is so difficult to continue on this path, to abide by the things themselves, to proceed with the proper rigor, Husserl needs more than inner conviction: "More than anything else,[71] I need divine assistance [*himmlische Mithilfe*]. Good working conditions and inner concentration, inner oneness with the problems." But he also needs the aid of others who, on his view, have sought to move along the same path as that on which he is moving in his work: "How weak I am: I need the assistance of great souls. From the fullness of their strength and their pure will, they must fortify me. I suckle from them until I am full, and learn to divert my gaze from the hustle and bustle of everyday life that pulls me down." He needs them not for their problems, not for their various approaches to the "eternal problems" of philosophy—this could not be the case precisely because, in beginning for the first time, Husserl necessarily breaks with all pre-phenomenological disciplines, including every philosophy—but rather for his ethos: they lend him, literally, the "ethical" strength required for the passage between Death and the Devil to his goal.[72] He therefore desires strength both from within and from above.

In another diary entry, dated November 11, 1907, Husserl gives further insight into his understanding of the relation of his present inquiry to his earlier work: "How my heart swelled with pride as they [i.e., the *Logical Investigations*] began to have a prompt and strong effect—something I had never dared hope for—especially on the young generation; how the hope that this generation now placed in me elevated me, how close I seemed to be to reaching the great goal of gaining actual insight into logic, into the critique of knowledge, and into the critique of all reason, to fixing the natural order of the problems, to finding the natural order of the investigations, to raising the problems themselves to the greatest level of precision, to working out the methods to the point of purity and complete certainty, and then, with this clarity of the goal set and of the method, of doing—step by step—the one thing needful in each case" (300–1).[73] Can phenomenology be reduced to epistemology? If so, then what of logic and the critique of reason? What determines the natural order of the problems and the investigations? What counts as precision with respect to the problems? And, then, after Husserl has achieved clarity in all the areas listed here, what is the goal set? What is the method and why? And what is the one thing needful in each case? The answer to each of these questions is rooted in Husserl's task, and in it alone. It defines the natural order, which has an end, the ultimate aim, but above—or rather: below—all, one beginning. Getting clear on this is the work called for by the insight into the goal: "Now my passionate endeavor is first of all none other than to get on an absolutely firm track. At the moment, all my striving revolves around the question of the natural order of the investigations and around the way in which the fundamental investigations themselves are again to be begun and ordered" (301). The firm track is one of naturally *ordered* problems and corresponding investigations. They are bound together in a hierarchy, which is based on a firm, definite beginning. Husserl's interest in the problems is not a matter of fancy; on the contrary, it is dictated solely by the things themselves. To be faithful to them and to win over others to such faithfulness is his task. That is why he is concerned with the "natural order," and especially with the beginning. Everything depends on it.

1.3 System and Norms

By the time he published his manifesto, "Philosophy as Rigorous Science," thus by 1911, Husserl had come to regard the prevailing crisis no longer as merely a personal affair,[74] but as affecting the entire age: "The spiritual distress [*geistige Not*] of our age has indeed become unbearable" (*PRS*, 336). It has its source in the failure of philosophy: Despite the fact that since its "earliest beginnings philosophy has claimed to be rigorous science, and in fact the science that satisfies the highest theoretical needs and that enables, from an ethico-religious point of view, a life governed by pure rational norms" (289), despite the fact that philosophy has never given up this claim entirely, it was nevertheless "unable to satisfy the claim . . . in any of the epochs of its development"—not in Greek antiquity, not in the modern era, and not in Husserl's day. The distress to which this failure gave rise is unbearable not only because it "leaves no part of our lives untouched" (336), but especially because it strikes at the very root of all life. And precisely for this reason it proves to be "the most radical vital distress [*die radikalste Lebensnot*]." Because this distress threatens its ground, the whole of human life is in jeopardy.[75] This distress manifests itself in different ways but in all quarters as a "crisis of foundation," a rootlessness, a directionlessness. Husserl is convinced that the "highest interests of human culture demand the development of a rigorously scientific philosophy," which secures the ground of those "high interests"; furthermore, that for "a philosophical revolution [*Umwendung*]" to succeed—and that means here: in order to regain the ground, or gain it for the first time—"it must in any case be animated [*beseelt*] by the intention to found philosophy anew in the sense of rigorous science" (293). The insight into what is needful is not enough, then; one must also be imbued with the right ethos and will in order to reach one's goal. For the afflictions of his age there is "only one remedy": "scientific critique and in addition a radical science, rising from below [*von unten anhebend*],[76] grounded in sure fundaments, and progressing in accordance with the most rigorous method" (337)—in other words: "philosophy as rigorous science," both as program and as ethos. This is the discipline that is to pursue the "general task" of a critique of reason.

Because no one has succeeded in establishing philosophy as a rigorous science, Husserl's new science must make an absolute beginning, a clean break with all that has come before, to the extent that such a break is possible. This means that phenomenology must part with every previous philosophy and science. The rigorous scientist can have recourse to nothing save the things themselves and the intuition in which they are given immediately (see 340–41). As noted above, however, the things themselves prescribe an order of inquiry, in other words, a system. But of what kind? Not a "philosophical 'system' in the traditional sense" that is imposed upon the things from "on high"; thus not a system that, as a kind of "Minerva," "springs from the head of a creative genius" already completed and then is "preserved in the silent museum of history alongside other such Minervas" (291–92). Rather, the kind of system at which Husserl aims represents, at most, an inversion of such a Minerva, for it grows out of the things themselves; it accords with the order they prescribe. He introduces it by way of a question: "Or is it to be a philosophical system of doctrine that, after the colossal preparatory work of generations, actually begins from below [*von unten her*] with a fundament free of doubt and rises up like any sound edifice, in which stone is set upon stone, each as solid as the other, in accordance with guiding insights? On this question minds [*die Geister*] and paths must part" (292). Step by step, stone by stone, the edifice is constructed. But the first order of business is to secure the ground on which that edifice is to be built. This is the path Husserl will take, leaving all those behind who are unable to persist in the radicality such a system demands.

Husserl's system has two extremes, first the lowermost limit and finally the uppermost limit.[77] The philosophy he seeks to establish is the most rigorous because it is the most radical. It is, as he will later say, a "beginning science," and in two senses of the word. First and foremost, because it focuses principially on *the* beginning, on the lowermost limit: "But by its essence, philosophy is the science of true beginnings, of origins, of the ῥιζώματα πάντων [roots of everything]. The science of the radical must itself be radical in its procedure—and in every respect. Above all it must not rest until it has obtained its own absolutely clear beginnings, that is, its absolutely clear problems, the methods prescribed by the proper sense of these problems, and the lowermost field of work wherein the things are given with absolute clarity" (340–41).[78] But it is also a "beginning science" because it intends to reorient and reorder all aspects of human culture from this ground up and thereby to usher in a genuine renaissance or renewal of human life.[79] This is the ground from which alone one can rigorously and "ethically" work up into the heights, and in fact asymptotically up towards the uppermost limit, which is God, or "absolute reason."[80]

The will to rigorous science, and in fact to philosophy as rigorous science, is bound up with a specific ethos, which was touched on above in the form of Husserl's personal ethos. The will is one's personal commitment to the ethos. One must maintain this will, persist in the ethos, and do the work it demands if there is to be any hope of freeing oneself and humanity from the prevailing crisis. The practical intention of Husserlian thought comes to the fore here as well: "However, the question is to be asked not only from the standpoint of the individual, but also from that of humanity and of history, namely insofar as we consider what it means for the development of culture, for the possibility of a constantly progressive realization of the eternal idea of humanity—not of man *in individuo*—that the question be decided predominantly in one or the other sense" (334). For Husserl the answer to this question decides what kind of philosophy is called for. It is thus not only a theoretical, but also and ultimately a practical decision. Either rigorous science or crisis—there is no middle ground and no higher third. For this reason, once one has gained "the will to rigorous science," one must make a total break with all other disciplines, as well as with every philosophy. There can be "no attempt at mediation" between phenomenology and another position, there can be "no compromises" whatsoever (337). The claim of phenomenology is total; it is the first First Philosophy and, prior to that, the first First Science because it is the first genuinely rigorous science.[81] And necessarily so, for every other position has failed to attain sufficient rigor, that is, to be "true to the roots [*wurzelecht*]."[82] Precisely due to their failure to secure an absolute foundation, he says: "Not philosophies but the things and the problems are the point from which the impulse to inquiry must issue" (340).[83] On his view, then, Husserl does not and, for principial reasons, cannot stand in any tradition.[84] This is ruled out by his constant reference to the standard-setting character of the things themselves, or his invocation of what he will soon refine into the "principle of all principles": we can reach the great goal only "if with the radicalism that belongs to the essence of genuine philosophical science we accept nothing given in advance, allow nothing that has been handed down to us to pass as a beginning [or principle], nor ourselves to be dazzled by any name however great, but rather seek to gain the beginnings in a free devotion to the problems themselves and to the demands that issue from them."[85] If one abides by this demand, then Husserl's question about the proper path to be taken turns out to be only rhetorical. He does not see a true option here, but only one path, the one leading to the "roots of everything." For the same reason he sees only one task and only one will to one philosophy extending through history.[86] To stray from this path, after having seen its necessity, would mean plunging into countersense—or sin.[87] On the other hand, to fail to bring others to the insight into the proper road would be to fail to do one's duty to humanity, which he considers no less sinful.

In this regard, Husserl remarks that our personal goals are bound up with eternal ones, just as our responsibility to ourselves is bound up with a responsibility to others: "our ethical responsibilities . . . extend to the utmost reaches of the ethical ideal, up to the point denoted by the idea of human development" (334). We must never lose sight, he says, of "the responsibility with respect to humanity" (337). This duty issues not from the priority of intersubjectivity over subjectivity so much as from that of essence over the individual or factual entity. Our responsibility, then, is to the eternal in the sense of the essence or idea of humanity.[88] Doing our duty thus entails not losing sight of the priority of the eternal over individual, temporal concerns: "For the sake of time we must not sacrifice eternity; in order to alleviate our distress, we must not bequeath to our descendants distress upon distress as an ultimately ineradicable evil. The distress here stems from science. But only science can definitively overcome the distress that stems from science."[89] Only like can overcome like. Therefore, since the distress issues from the discord of past and present philosophy with its essence, the only remedy is philosophy as rigorous science, which accords fully with that essence.

1.4 Ethos, Ought, Teleology

As a consequence of both his rejection of the traditional system and of the infinity of the phenomenological system, Husserl asserts that "science can never again be the perfected creation of the individual"; instead each individual must work "in co-operation with those imbued with the same ethos [*Gleichgesinnten*] to help a scientific philosophy make its breakthrough and to develop further, step by step" (333), stone by stone, in the eternal work on the tower of phenomenology and the universal philosophy it founds. But precisely because this work cannot be done alone, the ethos must be passed on to others. New strength must be harnessed for rigorous science: "Whoever is capable of awakening belief"—both in himself and in others—"whoever is capable of arousing understanding of and enthusiasm for the greatness of a goal, will easily find the strength that is devoted to that goal" (340). By the same token, whoever is called is devoted to the eternal. But: "Those who set the goal in the finite, who want to have their system, and who want soon enough to be able to live by it, are in no way called to this task" (338). The construction of phenomenology is never-ending.

As always in Husserlian thought, however, this construction is not capricious, but proceeds according to eidetic norms. Each stone, as it were, must be scrutinized before it is added to the tower: "All life is position-taking [*Stellungnehmen*], all position-taking is subject to an ought [*Sollen*], to a verdict concerning validity or invalidity according to claimed norms that carry absolute weight. So long as these norms were not disputed, were not threatened and ridiculed by any skepticism, there was only one vital question: how best to satisfy the norms in practice" (336). These norms are rational norms; the "ought"[90] determines what is valid and what is not, which is to say, what is rational and what is not. And the verdict is reason or unreason. Thus the question 'How am I to satisfy these norms in practice?' is a question of reason, namely: How am I to live a rational life? How am I to act rationally? This, again, is the juncture of theory and praxis in Husserlian thought. All roads save one lead up to reason.

The critique of reason, which again is the task of tasks for Husserlian phenomenology, has two analogously related sides: that concerning the individual subject and that concerning humanity. Both sides are to be taken not as facts but as essential determinations. Thus, on the one hand, the task is to describe the universal eidetic structures of subjectivity, above all its intentionality, and to account for reason. On the other hand, the task is to explicate the teleology of humanity, or the senseful, intentional, historical becoming of man—according to his essence—in other words, the teleology that entails his rationalization.[91] The former side calls for static analysis; the latter, for genetic analysis. As noted at the outset of this introduction, the latter presupposes the former. The beginning is to be made with static analysis. It discloses the Archimedean point and its essential structures of individual consciousness, which then act as guiding insights for the explication of the collective consciousness, that is, of the becoming not only of man but also of humanity in history. All with a view to the verdict of reason.

Since the static analysis is the most radical of the two, and since the beginning is of the greatest importance to Husserl's endeavor, it constitutes the focal point of the present study. Prior to addressing it, however, it is necessary to complete our account of Husserl's understanding of the idea of phenomenology and the whole it defines. This requires that the second direction of the critique of reason, that of the rationalization of humanity, be considered. It is the primary concern of the so-called genetic phase of Husserlian thought, which culminates in his *Crisis*. There it becomes particularly audible what he has been fighting against since the birth of phenomenology, as well as how it is that he can describe philosophizing as a fight for life—for both his own and humanity's. In taking up this work, we come full circle, though not in order to fulfill Husserl's "genetic" directive, but to demonstrate that the unity of his thought derives from the singularity of his task. Again, despite every reference to chronology in the foregoing and in what is to come, the sole concern is with the detemporalized task. It is what makes the difference in the whole; it is the point of unity of the whole of Husserlian thought in its multiplicity.

The crisis of the European sciences brought about by skepticism was seen to be more fundamentally a crisis of European humanness. It is at bottom a crisis of essence or rather of the belief in essence. That is, the essence of man has grown questionable. And that questionableness signals the faltering of belief in his self, in himself as a rational being. Hence, it is a crisis of reason. It calls for decision.

Were they to succumb to skepticism, were they to cease to believe in reason, Husserl tells his fellow Europeans, they would "renounce [their] own truth" (*Crisis*, 12/14). As for what this truth is, the traditional definition of man (*Bestimmung des Menschen*) provides Husserl with the decisive clue: man is the *animal rationale*, the rational being (*Vernunftwesen*).[92] It is of his essence (*Wesen*) to *be* rational. And that is why the skeptical obfuscation is so dangerous: "If man loses this belief [in reason], then that means nothing less than: he loses the belief 'in himself,' in the true Being proper to him that he does not always already have, not already with the evidence of the 'I am,' but only has and can have in the form of a struggle for his truth, to make himself true. Everywhere true Being is an ideal goal, a task of *epistêmê*, of 'reason,' as opposed to Being that is unquestioningly 'taken for granted,' merely thought to be in *doxa*" (11/13).[93] Pivotal here (and for the whole of his thought) is, on the one hand, Husserl's revaluation of the sense of human Being: it is strictly becoming.[94] On the other hand, his binding of becoming to a goal, a telos, that always remains ideal. Accordingly, Husserl regards the designation '*animal rationale*' less as a description of man as actualized—that is, of how he is and remains—

than as a specification of his ownmost possibility, his *dynamis*—that is, of how he ought to be. He sees in it first and foremost man's destiny (*Bestimmung*), the *pre*scription of his proper vocation, of his task: to strive to actualize his *self*, to fulfill his essence, in short: "to make himself true." The telos at which all his striving is aimed is true Being, which is "absolute reason" or God.[95] It "alone can satisfy him, make him 'blessed' ['*selig*']" (275/341). But although it is proper to him, the desired actualization or entelechy[96] necessarily remains denied to him, for true Being as idea lies in the infinite.[97] Consequently, man's struggle for his telos—or his teleology as Husserl also refers to it—is an endless, "a constant becoming in a constant intentionality of development" (272/338); it "proceeds in stages of self-reflection and self-responsibility," from the ground of his *dynamis* upwards towards his entelechy, thereby moving always only step by step from lower to higher, latent to more manifest levels of self-understanding, from *doxa* to *epistêmê*.[98] Human life is essentially this teleology: "being human is a being teleological and being what one ought to be [*Sein-Sollen*]" (275/341); whether man knows it, whether he intends it or not, "this teleology holds sway in each and every activity and project of an ego" (276/341)—even when he is wholly submerged in *doxa* or under the spell of skepticism, it works latently. But it is only to the extent that he is conscious of and wills his telos, only to the extent that he reflects upon and is responsible to his self, that he is able to achieve greater self-understanding and move closer to his actualization; for otherwise he merely takes Being for granted and moves merely blindly towards his ownmost goal. And this is where the belief Husserl calls for, as well as the danger of skepticism, comes in. When man truly believes in reason, he believes in himself; when he so believes, he wills his actualization; and when he so wills, he struggles to make himself true. On account of this, Husserl says that in wanting to be rational, man is already rational.[99] Yet the belief on which this will to rationality and man's consequent becoming are based is not to be confounded with religious faith,[100] or in more Husserlian terms: with a belief bound by dogma;[101] rather, it springs solely from man's "free" intuition of his essence, that reason not only gives sense to his life but *is* his sense, his truth, his task. For Husserl, belief—in the active and not the passive sense, which is peculiar to unreflective modes of human life—is a "presentiment" (*Vorahnung*),[102] an anticipation of one's essence. It provides an "intentional guide" for the struggle to fulfill that essence, just as in sensory perception, for example, we have a presentiment of an object prior to having it adequately, one that points us in the direction of adequacy, even if such adequacy is ultimately unattainable.[103] What begins as the consciousness of one's essence is thereby transformed into deed: it becomes a "practical goal" that compels the will ever onward and upward (see *VL*, 321/275). Skepticism (no less than dogmatism) causes man to lose sight of his telos and thereby impedes his becoming, his teleology.

In its present crisis, as Husserl experiences it, European humanness stands to perish in a "conflagration of unbelief" (348/192).[104] If man is to be saved from this fate, he must be set back on his proper course, and knowingly so; and that requires that his ears be opened to the call to a "life of apodicticity" (*Crisis*, 275/340). Just this is Husserl's intention in the *Crisis*, as in all of his "introductions" to pure phenomenology.[105] To succeed in this endeavor, he regards it as imperative that the belief be restored, the faltering of which marked the end of metaphysics and the rise of positivism. However, this cannot be achieved simply by pitting the desired belief against the prevailing unbelief, for the one belief need not be any more convincing than the other. Rather, it must be made intuitively perspicuous which of them possesses such apodictic force that man cannot but believe in the ground.[106]

To shed light on this ground, Husserl turns from the present destitute state of European humanness to its history, where the desired belief still played an animating role. In fact he turns to the history of philosophy—of universal philosophy in its exclusively European manifestation—since he sees in it "the functioning brain on whose normal functioning genuine, healthy European spirituality depends" (*VL*, 338/290–91): philosophy has demonstrated repeatedly that it has an "archontic function"[107] with regard to the development of European science and culture; its generations have been "the bearers of this spiritual development" (*Crisis*, 273/339). By extension, European humanness is also considered to have had and still have such a function with regard to humanity as a whole. For this reason the crisis addressed here is not confined to Husserl's Europe but is actually of global proportions—as would be its resolution. Thus there is a telescopic, founded relationship: from (European) philosophy to European humanness to humanity as a whole; the first is to lead the next and it in turn is to lead humanity. (This, of course, mirrors the telescopic or analogous relationship between the individual subject and the community of egos or between subjectivity and intersubjectivity. These founding relationships are rooted in Husserl's understanding of essence, specifically of the self.)

In fact Husserl finds the ground, the disclosure of which is to enable such a resolution, in the unifying sense of the history of philosophy; it is simultaneously the origin and the end of this history, and as such binds together all of its moments: "We gain self-understanding and thereby inner support only by elucidating [history's] unifying sense, which, from its origin on, has been inborn in history with the newly established task, which moves [all] philosophical endeavors as a driving force [*Triebkraft*]" (12/14).[108] The history Husserl has in view is a continuum: it is *one* progression, *one* teleology, which has *one* underlying, unifying sense, and is directed towards and guided from beginning to end by *one* telos.[109] Yet the unity of history cannot be discerned, and thus the desired self-understanding and inner support not gained, so long as one allows oneself to be distracted by superficial differences in that history; instead, one must "break through the crust of the externalized 'historical facts' of the history of philosophy, interrogating, exhibiting, testing its inner sense, its hidden teleology" (16/18). In other words, it is necessary to pinpoint philosophy's abiding task, what it sought to achieve but did not: "through inquiry into what was originally and always wanted as philosophy and was wanted continually by all philosophers and philosophies that have communicated with one another throughout history," we gain access to the said ground, "that ultimate genuineness of the origin [*Ursprungsechtheit*], which, once seen, conquers the will apodictically." The apodictically conquered will is the one that has been awakened to the one thing needful and consequently strives to fulfill that abiding task, which is to say, to realize the essence of philosophy.

Having penetrated its outer crust, Husserl finds that what philosophy has always wanted was to be rigorous science, that is, universal philosophy, which is directed towards, guided by, and in the service of the proper, the "apodictic" telos of man and thus of history: namely absolute reason. As noted, such philosophy was to establish the foundation for and hierarchy of all human endeavor, in one teleological progression, from the ground up. In view of this inner, unifying sense it becomes evident that, "although it itself was not conscious of this" (17/18), from its ancient beginnings on all genuine philosophy, in its quest to become rigorous science, has been (latently) directed towards the "final form of transcendental philosophy—as phenomenology" (71/70).[110] Thus throughout its long history, genuine philosophy has harbored phenomenology as its "secret desire."[111] Not unlike the philosophy of the modern era, as whose heir Husserl regards himself, the institution of his phenomenology proves to be "at once a repetition and a universal transformation of sense. In this it considers itself to have been called to begin a new age, completely sure of its idea of philosophy and of its true method" (12/14).[112] Husserl understands himself as continuing the radical ethos of modern philosophy while also having to break with his predecessors, namely "to transform fundamentally and essentially [*grundwesentlich*] the total sense of philosophy" (16/18); this he intends to do by first getting clear on the requirements of rigorous science, laying a new foundation that does not suffer from the lack of clarity that had led to the dissolution of philosophy formerly, and so preparing the way for a possible metaphysics. All this promises to bring about the renewal of European humanness, which is to lead in turn to the renewal of humanity as a whole. On Husserl's view, it is through phenomenological philosophy, and it alone, that the crisis can be resolved.

And yet in the midst of the prevailing lack of belief in philosophy, the will to philosophy as the source and means of man's salvation from this present crisis has to seem paradoxical, if not plain absurd. This accounts for the "painful existential contradiction" into which Husserl notes he and his audience have fallen "as philosophers of this present" (15/17). But despite this state of affairs, as philosophers they have come to see that the possibility of a metaphysics means the possibility of a true humanity and that as a consequence it is their responsibility not to give up in the face of the foundering of belief; they "cannot let go of the belief in the possibility of philosophy as a task, thus in the possibility of a universal knowledge." To do so would be to renounce not just their personal truth, not just that of European humanness, but also humanity's, and that would spell the end of man: "The entirely personal responsibility for our own true Being as philosophers, our inner-personal vocation, bears within itself at the same time the responsibility for the true Being of humanity; this Being exists only as being directed towards a telos and can come to actualization, if at all, only through philosophy—through us, if we are philosophers in all seriousness."[113] For philosophers to proceed in seriousness, they must "maintain the belief that has sense only in relation to the one goal, the sole goal that is common to us all, to *the* philosophy."[114] As has been seen, this philosophy is first and foremost philosophy as rigorous science, which is to say: pure, transcendental phenomenology. Thus it is the task, the responsibility of phenomenologists, who in Husserl's eyes are the preeminent "functionaries of humanity,"[115] to reawaken man's belief in himself and thereby his will to reason as his ownmost telos. To do so is to reestablish the philosophical form of life, an ethos that formed the basis of Greek humanness in antiquity as well of European humanness in the modern era. In accordance with it, man struggles endlessly for self-understanding, for his sense. His ideal is a life based on autonomous rather than "blindly traditionalistic" inquiry; he lives by the maxim that one "freely give oneself, one's entire life, its *rule* based on pure reason, on philosophy" (5/8). This ethos is not just any form of life among others; rather, it is *the* form of life; it has, as it were, an archontic function since it grounds all other human endeavors. Husserl sees himself and his contemporaries on the brink of a new age, though one they can inaugurate only if they are serious philosophers who work together in community—who philosophize together, or συμφιλοσοφεῖν,[116] as Husserl is also wont to say—and cultivate a *philosophia perennis*.[117] Called to be the "functionaries of humanity" and, by extension, of the absolute, and bound together by their will to rigorous science and thus to rationality, they must take up the fight that will decide everything: the "vitality [of true philosophy in contrast to its skeptical adversary], however, consists in its struggle for its own genuine and true sense and thus for the sense of a genuine humanness. To bring latent reason to the understanding of its own possibilities and to make the possibility of a metaphysics evident as a true possibility—that is the sole way in which to set a metaphysics or a universal philosophy on its work-filled course to actualization. This alone will decide whether the telos inborn in European humanness with the birth of Greek philosophy, namely the telos of wanting to be a humanness based on philosophical reason and to be able to exist only as such—in the infinite movement from latent to manifest reason and in infinite striving for selfnormation [*Selbstnormierung*] through this, its human [*menschheitlich*] truth and genuineness—is merely a historical-factual delusion, the accidental acquisition of one accidental humanity among many other humanities and histories; or whether instead in Greek humanness that which is contained essentially [*wesensmäßig*] as entelechy in humanness as such burst forth for the first time" (13/15). As will become evident, this "infinite movement from latent to manifest reason" is precisely the movement of phenomenology. It is the task of the critique of reason to elucidate the structure or system of this movement, whether considered genetically or statically. It charts the path from below to above along which the properly phenomenological task is to be fulfilled, namely its calling to lead upwards (*Emporleiten*).[118]

2. The System of Husserlian Phenomenology: *Ideas I*

The beginning is everything to Husserl. One cannot simply begin wherever one likes if one is to begin rightly. Rather, one must find and set out from the absolute beginning. Otherwise all is for naught—since one will simply end up back where one started: in crisis. Husserl considers himself the first to have fathomed the seriousness of the beginning, which is what severs him from the entire philosophical tradition: "If the philosophical projects of the tradition lacked a feeling for the seriousness of the beginning, then they lacked what is first and most important: the originally and properly philosophical ground that is acquired through self-activity and therefore that steadfastness or trueness to the roots that alone makes actual philosophy possible" (Afterword, 569). It is because of their failure in this respect that the philosophies of the past likewise failed to make good on their claim to be rigorous science. For only to the extent that it secures the ground is a philosophy truly philosophy. Until then, it hangs in the air, problem-ridden: "A philosophy with problematic foundations, with paradoxes due to the lack of clarity of its fundamental concepts, is not philosophy; such contradicts its *sense* as philosophy. *Philosophy can be rooted only in radical reflections on the sense and possibility of its intention.* By means of such reflections, it must appropriate *first of all* its proper absolute ground of pure experience through self-activity, *then* establish original concepts through self-activity that adequately correspond to this ground, *and so*, in general, progress by absolutely transparent methods" (568).[119] The tradition had not achieved this, but phenomenology has done so—according to Husserl. It makes the right, because absolute, beginning: "Phenomenology is presented in our expositions as a *beginning* science. How many of the results of the analyses attempted here are definitive, only the future can tell. Certainly much of what we have described will have to be described otherwise *sub specie aeterni*. But there is one thing we may and must strive for: that at each step we faithfully describe what we, from our viewpoint and after the most serious study, actually see" (*Ideas I*, 201 n.).[120] Although the subsequent findings may be in need of revision, the beginning remains intact, just as an explorer's descriptions may require modification or supplementation, although the "new world" he has discovered stands firm. "Our procedure is that of an explorer journeying through an unknown part of the world who carefully describes what offers itself to him along his unbeaten paths, which will not always be the shortest."[121] Husserl's own journey into the transcendental sphere is labyrinthine and long, but the terrain itself through which he travels, he contends, is unimpeachable. Such an explorer "can rightfully be filled with the sure confidence that he gives utterance to what, at the time and under the circumstances, *had* to be said—something that, because it is the faithful expression of something seen, will always retain its value—even if new explorations may require new descriptions with manifold improvements. With a like ethos, in what follows we want to be faithful describers of phenomenological structures and, moreover, to preserve the habitus of inner freedom even with respect to our own descriptions." Faithfulness is the sole guarantee of value, come what may. All this Husserl says before penetrating to the heart of his analyses in the first book of *Ideas Pertaining to a Pure Phenomenology and to a Phenomenological Philosophy* (1913). He is convinced that in this work especially he has achieved everything necessary in order to institute philosophy as rigorous science,[122] for in *Ideas I* he locates the absolute ground, which is the first requirement for every true philosophy.[123] With this ground comes the right path, which accords with the things: "The fact that, in progressing, these reflections [on what is required to institute "the *One* Philosophy"[124]] become ever more complex and ultimately lead to a whole science, to a science of the beginning, to a 'first' philosophy, the fact that all philosophical disciplines, indeed the foundations of any science whatsoever, spring from its root-ground [*Wurzelboden*]—all this had to remain hidden because the radicalism was lacking without which philosophy cannot at all be, cannot even begin" (Afterword, 569). The radical ethos required for such a beginning could arise only in Husserl's day,[125] in the midst of the most extreme crisis.[126]

The beginning is everything, for it entails everything and so determines the whole. It is the ground from which every right path issues. It prescribes the course of every path leading from it and up into the heights.[127] It is the origin in which every sense is rooted.[128] These basic insights have guided Husserl from at least his "transcendental turn" on (and continue to do so up through the *Crisis*), but they take on determinacy for him only in the course of his investigations. Thus, in 1922 he writes: "It has become ever clearer to me . . . that one of the greatest tasks of a system of philosophy lies here: the task of the right beginning, the leading of the knower from the level of natural knowledge-naiveté up [!] to the level of the beginning of 'absolutely justified science,' of that of 'philosophy'"—of philosophy as rigorous science. "The establishment of the correct motivation, making clear the necessity of 'beginning' with the *ego cogito*, of giving the ego the sense of the phenomenological reduction, of passing from transcendental consciousness and the I to the eidetics of the transcendental sphere, of widening the ego, the I, to the 'I-all,' of also taking up 'empathy,' and so on—[all that] makes for a great many headaches and is nothing for idlers."[129] The insight into the seriousness of the right beginning entails the insight into the "system of philosophy." This system is nothing but the trajectory just outlined: from the ground of the *ego cogito* up into the heights, from subjectivity to intersubjectivity, "and so on." This is, of course, the same system he pits against the traditional system already in 1911 in "Philosophy as Rigorous Science."[130] It is a building upon the solid foundation, stone by stone, ever higher—but always with reference to that foundation. It is a building, a progression, a becoming, but never a fixed structure, never mere Being. What is more, after having established the ground and gained insight into the trajectory, or into the "natural order" or "sense" of the problems, phenomenology is in a position to lead other disciplines up into the heights.[131] In this sense it is "first philosophy," but also a "philosophy of ascent,"[132] and in fact towards the upper limit of the system, which again is God.[133]

In light of the foregoing, does it make sense to deny that Husserlian thought forms a system?[134] It is true, of course, that Husserl explicitly rejects the system in the traditional sense, which he understands to be something finished. In view of the significance of becoming to his thought, specifically the ethos of striving, he is entirely consistent in disapproving of any privileging of (mere, static) Being or a so-called Minerva. Perhaps the systematicity of Husserlian thought is generally denied by scholars because they attend too much to his denial of the system, while overlooking his continual, positive use of the term—at least in its adjectival and adverbial forms—or dismissing it as a mere metaphor. Perhaps they have assumed, strange though it may be, the singular reference of the word 'system', that is to say, perhaps they have been fixated on the meaning 'system' was given in metaphysics, especially by Hegel—while simultaneously denying the singularity of other names, such as, for example, 'phenomenology'. For systems along the lines of Hegel's are certainly what Husserl has in mind when he protests against the applicability of the term to his thought.[135] Such a system, on his understanding, would mean completion, which would mean the attainment of the idea, which he regards as a priori impossible, or it would mean a "finitizing of phenomenology,"[136] which would run against its essence and cause one to fall into countersense.[137] As is clear already in "Philosophy as Rigorous Science," however, Husserl does not reject the idea of a system outright, but only its traditional formulation. His is certainly not a deductive system—it is not derived from any first principles in the classical sense—but is rather an intuitive system—which is built upon the givenness of the things themselves. It takes its bearings by these things alone. Husserl's system is precisely a *hierarchy* wherein the highest is the ground, the root of everything.

2.1 Polarities

After the transcendental turn, after Husserl has gained a deeper understanding of his task, the contours of his system assume their final form. Again, pure consciousness or the pure ego is seen to be the absolute foundation, and absolute reason, or God, forms the uppermost limit.[138] They are the alpha and omega, which are "brought together" as the bounds of an intentional hierarchy. For Husserl it is these extremes that are decisive, and not their *center* or intermediate stages. On his self-understanding, there is no definitive middle term mediating between the extremes[139]—this in itself shows the radical difference of his position from those constitutive of metaphysics. But not even the limits of his system are treated equally. Whereas the uppermost limit is to orient all striving and so charges the ethos of such importance to him, Husserl focuses almost exclusively on the beginning (*Anfang*) or the ground (*Grund, Boden, Fundament, Basis*), which the pure ego is. It alone receives his undivided attention; the treatment of the uppermost limit, as he says repeatedly, must be postponed until he has climbed, step by step, stone by stone, up into the heights.[140]

Although Husserl never works out his system in its entirety—nor can he *per definitionem*—he does make express use of microsystems, as it were, which replicate the "macrosystem" in most essentials and thereby give a sense of the larger whole.[141] Like this all-encompassing system, they too are bipolar in structure. Unlike this system, however, they are not only analogously intentional, but are intimately bound up with the polarity Husserl discloses as the defining feature of consciousness: intentionality.[142] In his investigations, then, he makes use of two types of system: what might be called 'antipodal systems', the poles of which are either contradictories or contraries, and 'founded systems', in which one pole is founded on the other. The system of Husserlian thought is of the latter type, whereas the majority of the microsystems he explicates are of the former type. Whatever the character of their relation, the poles are inextricably linked together: wherever one is present, the other must stand in the wings, as it were, as a possibility—one that can break onto the scene, can become an actuality, at any time under the right circumstances. Each pole is accompanied by its opposite, in other words, like its shadow or mirror image. Considered statically, the antipodal systems are binary: the zero-pole forms the lowermost limit, and the one-pole, the uppermost limit; the former is the minimum and the latter, the maximum. Within his incipient static analyses, Husserl takes these pairs "absolutely," that is, he operates in terms of a radical Either-Or: either maximum or minimum, but no mixture, no gradation thereof. Even where a gradation is posited between the two extremes, it is a gradation within which the extremes are privileged. Examples of such systems, which are found throughout Husserl's corpus, include: fulfillment–nonfulfillment, clarity–obscurity, truth–falsehood, positionality–neutrality, and reason–unreason.[143] In a sense, these systems are constitutive of Husserl's system, since their explication contributes to its explication.

In the case of the latter system, which is of central concern here, at issue is not a pair of antipodes, as already indicated, but rather a founded hierarchy. Its lower limit is the pure ego. It founds the upper limit, which is reason. By extension, the so-called solipsistic ego forms the lower limit with respect to humanity, which is the upper limit. In other words, subjectivity founds intersubjectivity. Still another founded system consists of humanity on the one side and absolute reason or God on the other. Reducing the extremes of these nested or telescoped systems yields the pure ego as the lowermost limit and absolute reason as the uppermost limit. Here, too, the middle term plays next to no role—despite the existence of nested systems—for Husserl regards them as a rule as separate, if related, wholes.

A remarkable feature of all the bipolar systems described by Husserl—and especially in the case of the system consisting of subjectivity and reason, that is, *the* system of phenomenology—is that, in a special sense, each pole harbors its opposite within itself. Thus, for example, reason entails unreason, albeit as a possibility and never as an actuality—Husserl abides by the principle of noncontradiction. In the case of founded systems, the upper limit coincides with the lower limit. This becomes quite conspicuous in a terminological note: "Here, as throughout this writing, we are using the word *prinzipiell* [principial] in a rigorous sense, with reference to highest and *thus* most radical essential universalities or essential necessities" (*Ideas I*, 77 n.).[144] The *thus* shows that he thinks the two extremes together, and in fact as being two sides of the same coin. The highest is the most radical (the root of everything). A parallel case of coincidence is Husserl's occasional reference in his correspondence to the source of his task: it has been bequeathed to him "from within and from above."[145] With respect to subjectivity and reason, as will be seen, there is a sense in which reason is "latent" in all subjectivity, as Husserl claims in the *Crisis*.[146]

This mutual reference and coincidence of a system's extremes is in fact the expression of a still more fundamental common thread that runs through the bipolar systems employed or analyzed by Husserl, regardless of whether they are antipodal or founded. Namely, they are all intentional structures. They are such in analogy to and based upon the intentionality most proper to consciousness, as "consciousness *of* something."[147] These systems are intentional insofar as they are not only relational, but also directional: each side of a given system points in the direction of its opposite or counterpart as an essential possibility—such reference is the "special sense" in which each includes its opposite. The uppermost and lowermost limits are regulated entirely by the essence of the structure in question. This essence determines what counts, for example, as fulfillment and what does not, as well as what kind of fulfillment is at all possible in a given case. For fulfillment is not necessarily automatic. To know what is possible for the thing in question is to know what is essential to it. Furthermore, it is to know what one ought to strive for and how one is to strive. Thus, for example, expectation has two possibilities: fulfillment or disappointment. In the case of the former, Husserl notes: "All progressive fulfillment is thus effected in the normal case as the fulfillment of expectations. They are systematized expectations, ray-systems of expectations that, in being fulfilled, are also enriched, that is, the empty sense becomes richer in sense, which fits into the prescription of sense" (*Hua* XI, 26). This prescription, however, also includes the possibility of disappointment, which can manifest itself as either a complete lack of or only partial fulfillment. Both possibilities fall within what Husserl refers to as the "general parameters of sense [*Sinnesrahmen*]." Each process of fulfillment, or its corresponding disappointment, occurs within these parameters. It determines the ideal range of movement, as it were, within each process, and this holds for each of the aforementioned bipolar systems as well.

2.2 The Order of Critique

If the critique of reason is Husserl's general task, then intentionality is the central "problem" for this critique.[148] In fact, the critique turns out to be at bottom a critique of intentionality. As noted above, the critique of reason has two levels: that which proceeds by way of static analysis and that which proceeds by way of genetic analysis, whereby the latter presupposes the former. In view of the major work at the beginning (*Ideas I*) and that at the end (*Crisis*) of Husserl's transcendental phase, two principal types of intentionality present themselves for explication, namely that involved in subjectivity and that involved in humanity and its history. The inquiry into the former is concerned to grasp reason as it bears on a one solitary ego; the inquiry into the latter aims at showing how humanity can—and why it must—be rationalized as a whole. However, as was noted at the outset, since it is the static analysis that provides the guiding threads for the genetic analysis, the former may be said to include the latter. In this sense, then, the structure of an individual subject, of subjectivity, entails that of the whole of history. The history of humanity is the history of individual subjectivity writ large, for both are governed mutatis mutandis by the same essential structures.[149] Analytically, at least, it is subjectivity that has priority over intersubjectivity, for the latter is grounded in the former. The end is in the beginning, the upper limit is included in the lower insofar as the latter presupposes the former.[150] This is supported by a remark Husserl reportedly made: "Only when the nature of transcendental consciousness is understood, can the transcendence of God be understood. . . . The ethical-religious questions are the last questions of phenomenological constitution."[151] The first questions, by contrast, concern the universal structures of consciousness. The answers to them found the higher level questions. The lower level questions and their answers give the higher level questions sense, for they are integrated into the whole that the former define.

The beginning is everything. The path from the bottom to the top is a trajectory predelineated by the bottom, the beginning. In the beginning is the end. In the smallest part is the whole. The one points the way to the other, gives it sense. Thus, where there is no beginning, there is no end—and most certainly no whole. This accounts for Husserl's preoccupation with the beginning of the system and his relative theoretical neglect of its end.

2.3 The Whole and its Parts

Husserl's focus helps to explain why it has become commonplace to speak of him as a foundationalist, but not why it is less common that attention be paid to the role the foundation plays within his system.[152] His positive grasp of the system is evident, for example, in his talk of *First* Science or Philosophy and its relation to the other (second) sciences. This alone should make it clear that his thought forms a hierarchical system.[153] On the other hand, the fact that the presence of an uppermost limit—as such—has generally been overlooked by Husserl scholars may be explained variously.[154] Firstly, whereas Husserl's notion of God has been discussed in several studies, it has been treated in large part as a mere *problem*, with little if any connection to the *whole* of Husserlian thought.[155] Secondly, and perhaps the most important reason for the neglect of this feature of his thought—beyond the inattention to the fact that Husserlian thought is conceived of by its founder *as a whole*, albeit as an infinite whole, which is to say: beyond the general inattention to the demonstrable systematicity of his endeavor—is the unpopularity of what Husserl has actually thought: both his foundational intention and his principial focus on the pure ego and on pure consciousness, thus on subjectivity rather than on intersubjectivity. The abhorrence of such an approach is audible, however, not only in the neglect of Husserl's talk of God as he bears on the beginning, but also in the charges of solipsism brought against him.[156] Whatever the causes, the whole of Husserlian thought and the role the task plays in fixing that whole have as a rule been neglected. The reason for the neglect boils down to a lack of radicality among scholars, and in fact to a lack of the most genuine radicality—that impels one to attend not simply to origins, but to beginnings, to beginnings that for their part are determinative of the whole of a thought. Without having grasped the whole as such, one has nothing, or at best only something, which could just as easily be otherwise.

To grasp the structure and movement of Husserlian thought, it is not enough to be critical. But neither is it enough to speak of the unity of his thought, to speak of it as a whole, without determining its structure. And that means without discerning its bounds, where it begins and where it ends. Rather, one must have the courage that Husserl himself demands,[157] the courage that his thought supports with regard to the things themselves insofar as they are "phenomena," but that it cannot support—as Husserl's treatment of the philosophical tradition attests—with respect to thought itself, to thought taken as a discrete position or as a tectonic of such positions. Enabling one to do just this is the merit of the "logotectonic epoché."

If one is to begin at the beginning, if one is to begin with a view to the whole, then one must turn to Husserl's *Ideas Pertaining to a Pure Phenomenology and to a Phenomenological Philosophy*, the first book of which is a *General Introduction to Pure Phenomenology*. Husserl notes some seventeen years later that it remained a "fragment," and yet a careful analysis reveals that it contains everything essential to Husserlian thought. This work is first and foremost an introduction to and of pure phenomenology, not to philosophy, for phenomenology has yet to reach the level of philosophy (just as Husserl himself has yet to become a philosopher, as he often says). Since philosophy is possible on his view only on the basis of phenomenology and since philosophy is his ultimate goal, it follows that it is precisely the task of the inaugural volume of *Ideas* to prepare the way to philosophy, which means laying the foundation, but first of all locating the Archimedean point from which everything issues.[158]

The fragmentary character of *Ideas I* does not impinge upon the importance of this work, for Husserl calls it a "fragment" only in view of his original plan to write three books: the first elaborates "the most universal structures" of pure consciousness along with the method of its purification; the second was to "treat in depth some particularly significant groups of problems" on which the clarification of phenomenology's relationship to the other sciences depends; and the third was to be "devoted to the idea of philosophy" and show that phenomenology is the ground of every "genuine philosophy," of "every metaphysics and other philosophy"—and here he alludes to Kant's *Prolegomena*—"'that will be able to make its appearance as a science'" (*Ideas I*, 5). The fulfillment of this plan would have required extending the results of the first book to higher levels. Therefore the first book already entails everything needed, for it sets phenomenology on its way to the whole, it begins. Insofar as it is a reflection of the whole *in nuce*, when taken on its own it becomes clear that *Ideas I* is not a fragment—but a whole. On the other hand, given the infinite scope of Husserlian phenomenology, every one of his works was destined to be a fragment from the start—that is, in view of the projected whole in the idea of phenomenology. Such is the nature of phenomenological inquiry: to remain ever partial, and never achieve completion or perfection. It is, as it were, "the dream of phenomenology" to finally secure the foundation so as then to become philosophy—which was the intention behind the original plan for the "complete" *Ideas*.

Ideas I is not only the first full-fledged (published) work of transcendental phenomenology, but the only one in which Husserl lays out his *whole* system. It is here that he makes the first and the last attempt at a complete, systematic presentation of phenomenology itself, and in fact in the form of a critique of reason. As Walter Biemel notes, in *Ideas I* "Husserl realizes in a certain way his old plan of a critique of reason."[159] Likewise, Oskar Becker notes that this work has "remained until this day [1930] Husserl's most comprehensive philosophical work . . . regarding the breadth of the problem framed and the depth of philosophical foundation."[160] No subsequent work supersedes its systematicity; rather, each fits into the "general parameters of sense" it establishes. The works of transcendental philosophy that follow *Ideas I*—thus *Formal and Transcendental Logic, Cartesian Meditations,* and *Crisis*—are concerned principally with finding better ways to introduce the reader to the system outlined here for the first time and, in so doing, to "exhort" that reader to pursue the philosophical life, but, prior to that, to adopt the properly phenomenological ethos and the project it entails. If Husserl made his "breakthrough into phenomenology" in his *Logical Investigations*, then the thought born there—to borrow a phrase from Heidegger—"has swung into its tectonic"[161] only in *Ideas I*.

Husserl's intention in this work is to "construct the idea of a pure phenomenology" (*Ideas I*, 33), which means to articulate the essential features of and point the way to the whole. But to do so, he must bring the system to intuition—for others. And this he does by focusing on individual subjectivity and reason, which, once again, give the whole *in nuce*. Thus, if Husserl said in 1931 that the order of problems addressed in *Ideas I* is "fortuitous,"[162] this can only have concerned the steps leading from the ground up into the heights, but not the limits themselves. And if he later gives preference to more recent works as "introductions to phenomenology," if he suggests that one begin first with the *Cartesian Meditations*, then turn to the *Formal and Transcendental Logic*, and only thereafter take up *Ideas I*,[163] then it is because Husserl is convinced that these other works lead more "naturally," that is to say, more accessibly, to the beginning made in *Ideas I*,[164] and not that he has in any way dispensed with this first full work of transcendental phenomenology. On the contrary, in having disclosed and secured the roots of everything, it is and remains the beginning on which all else is built. In his 1930 Afterword to *Ideas*, Husserl makes this abundantly clear: "What the *Ideas* report is—as I am still convinced—a beginning piece of work done, which in the meantime I have endeavored to carry ever further" (Afterword, 551). The beginning remains in place. He continues writing "introductions" not in order to replace *Ideas I*, but rather in the service of his overriding concern: to save humanity from the prevailing crisis by leading it from the ground up into the heights. This requires that he win humanity over to his cause, or rather to the one cause, but not that he begin anew—that is, not after he has already begun in *Ideas I*.

Since the confrontation with this work opens up the horizon of Husserlian thought in all its essentials and as a whole, the core of the present study is focused on it. It not only provides the best test case for the foregoing account of Husserl's task and how it structures his thought. But also, when one traces the development of *Ideas I* step by step, from start to finish, rather than attending to the isolated problems that pop up in it, one becomes able to grasp the full sense of the phenomenological epoché, as well as the ground of productive conscious life—belief. Since it is this ground (which forms the heart of the pure ego) that enables consciousness to rise up to the level of reason and thereby fulfill its essence, it follows that whatever threatens the achievement of reason also has to pose the greatest danger for humanity, on Husserl's view. And whatever threatens the ground of possibility for such ascent has to give rise to the severest crisis. This is where Husserl's confrontation with skepticism comes in, but even more radically, with the universal neutrality modification. In what follows, it is shown that the latter poses the greatest danger since it can expunge each and every belief and thereby obstruct every ascent to reason. It is these two—belief and neutrality—that name the tension intrinsic not only to transcendental phenomenology, but to all human endeavor. Once one has grasped the role each plays or can play in individual consciousness, it becomes clear, by analogy, what significance they must have for humanity. Together they provide the key to Husserlian phenomenology, yet it is a key that can be gained only by passing through the whole of *Ideas I*. As a consequence, the account of this book given here proves to be an introduction not only to one work in the Husserlian corpus, but to the whole, the system of transcendental phenomenology.

Belief and its neutralization. Or rather: belief *or* its neutralization, since for Husserl there can be no conjunction of the two—at least not without the neutralization of belief. The *and* in this study's title thus marks the place of an exclusive disjunction. Either-Or. There is no middle ground between them, and no higher third. They are separated by an abyss. In fact, for Husserl neutrality is the abyss. It is belief alone that confers and maintains life.[165] Hence belief and neutrality are diametrically opposed, though not negatively. They are pitted against one another in a life-or-death struggle.

As for what belief is as Husserl understands it, that should become clearer in the course of what follows. But what was said in the foregoing should be borne in mind: despite his talk of God and his use of religious "symbols," the belief at issue in Husserlian thought is primarily not religious belief, not faith, but one more fundamental than such belief. Rather, it is *doxa*. It becomes visible as a characteristic of certain acts. On the other hand, its neutralization is not equivalent to unbelief. Neutralization is not negation, but annihilation, expunction.

The decisiveness of belief, on Husserl's view, was already indicated in the foregoing in connection with the crisis of European humanness. Although he warns about skepticism, although from at least 1910 on he holds skeptical positivism responsible for the state of European culture, the crisis in which he finds Europe in the mid-1930s is in fact not one in which unbelief prevails—Husserl does not speak of 'unbelief' in the *Crisis*, but of the 'loss', 'collapse', and 'fall' of belief,[166] which are not equivalent to *un*belief—but of the *lack* of belief. Unbelief is certainly of concern to Husserl inasmuch as skepticism gives rise to it, on account of which he regards skepticism as representing a grave danger, one against which he tirelessly fights. But unbelief is still belief, albeit with a changed sign. The true source of the crisis he addresses in his final phase is that resulting upon the *neutralization* of belief—even if he does not name it as such. For where belief has been lost, has collapsed, or has fallen, no belief remains, neither negative nor positive. The crisis is indeed one of belief, but not because it has been merely negated (though, again, this is no small matter to Husserl); rather, it is because it has been quashed altogether (which skepticism may or may not have helped to bring about due to its virulent negativity). It thereby obstructs the essential pursuit of man's teleology, and thus the fulfillment of the system of Husserlian phenomenology, more than any skepticism ever could. Hence it is the deepest responsibility of the philosopher—and of the phenomenologist before him—as the "functionary of humanity" to *reawaken* the belief in reason, to reinstill it. His task would be another were that belief to have been simply negated. The belief must be reawakened since it is of vital importance to European culture and, by extension, to all extra-European humanities. The danger of neutrality far outweighs that of unbelief. And this holds no less for the individual pure ego than for humanity as a whole. On the contrary, what Husserl shows with regard to the pure ego will hold for all of humanity as well.

Husserl's express task is a critique of reason. Although he envisions the structure of his system—and thus the path to be taken—as extending from the ground of absolute subjectivity up into the heights of absolute reason, he finds his age sunk in a state of neutrality, that is, in a state in which European humanness has grown indifferent to reason and its guiding function. This gives rise to a crisis not only for Europe, but also for phenomenology itself, since such indifference obstructs the fulfillment of its "God-given task." And since the value of his life has its source in his work, where Husserl's work threatens to become sense-less as a result of the prevailing indifference, it is obvious that the crisis turns into a vital crisis, a personal life-or-death struggle.

Already in 1922–23 Husserl pointed to what is at stake for humanity when such belief is lost, but this also shows, by analogy, the affect of such loss on the individual: "If the belief in all-governing reason has *failed* that in humanity's philosophical struggle could achieve ever purer self-consciousness and could transform it into a humanity of the children of God, its environing-world [*Umwelt*] into a Kingdom of God on Earth, [if this belief] has *lost its force*, then man throws himself into the arms of egoism and politically [into the arms] of the Moloch of the idea of power and dresses up his idol (especially in its nationalistic form) with idealistic phraseologies that, according to their original sources of sense, stem from the welding shop of eternal ideas, which in their unadulterated form stand in total opposition to every form of egoism. Just as skepticism passes itself off in academic and fictional philosophy as philosophy, as positive truth (this skepticism that, according to its principial sense, according to its presuppositions and theses, negates the very possibility of positive truth) under the rubric of positivism or fictionalism (Philosophy of the As-if)[167] or philosophy of overhumanness [*Übermenschentum*], likewise the practical skepticism of the 'Realpolitik' of political and scientific men of power passes off its goals, its means, its works as rational and laudable—that skepticism which slaps all reason, all categorical imperatives that have sprung from reason, in the face."[168] Again, skepticism negates reason, but such negation does not bring about the *loss* of belief, at least not immediately. Rather, a neutralization has to occur. The immediate danger of skepticism is that it causes humanity to stray from its proper path, which leads up to absolute reason and thereby to the ultimate achievement of humanity's truth. Wherever skepticism prevails, this cannot be achieved: "European humanity has strayed from its inborn telos. It has fallen prey to a sinful degeneration insofar as it had already become aware of this telos (had already tasted of the tree of knowledge), but had neither raised this telos to the fullest consciousness nor continued to implement it rigorously as the practical sense of its life, but instead became unfaithful to this sense."[169] It is precisely in the service of the life based on the belief in reason, which for him is the only genuine life, that Husserl seeks to establish phenomenology as the first science. Because he has fathomed the "seriousness of the beginning," he sees himself invested with the mission to reorient humanity, to set it back on its proper path. To do so, he must begin at the beginning: with the pure ego and its universal essential structures. Therefore, to the extent that one wishes to grasp the whole of Husserl's thought, one must follow his lead, one must begin at the beginning, one must engage Husserl where he is most radical, which is to say: one must begin with *Ideas I*.

Chapter II

Phenomenological Propaedeutics

By seeking to establish pure phenomenology as First Philosophy and, prior to that, as First Science, Husserl intends to make a radical beginning, one that is simultaneously to found and reorient not only the sciences but all human endeavor. However, because it is "remote from natural thinking," it is "only in our days" that *pure* phenomenology "presses towards development" (1),[1] the first and decisive fruits of which are presented systematically in *Ideas I*.

Unlike the familiar sciences, which have their proper abode in natural thinking, phenomenology is not to be a "science of realities." It, too, is concerned with phenomena, but "in a wholly different attitude whereby every sense of phenomenon that we find in the long-familiar sciences is modified in a definite way. Only as thus modified does that sense enter the phenomenological sphere." The key to this new, unheard-of science lies therefore in the new attitude in which it functions. Precisely because it is so radically different, it could only come to the fore "now"—in the center of modernity and thus in Husserlian thought.[2] But also on account of its newness, Husserl must take pains to introduce it properly. In this connection he sets his first task as follows: "To understand these modifications or, to speak more precisely, to effect the phenomenological attitude and, through reflection, to elevate its specific peculiarity and that of the natural attitudes to scientific consciousness," which is imbued with a radically new sense.[3] This enables Husserl to "gain the *ground* of phenomenology and scientifically assure ourselves of the peculiar *essence* of phenomenology." Gaining the ground is in fact separate only analytically from gaining insight into the essence of phenomenology. In deed they are the same.

In *Ideas I* Husserl seeks to give access to pure phenomenology rather than to the descriptive psychology of his "breakthrough" work. Nevertheless, he says, it is "the same phenomenology"—in other words, the new work shares the same essence with the first work of phenomenology—"that first made its breakthrough in the *Logical Investigations*, and whose sense disclosed itself to me ever more deeply and richly in the further work of the past decade" (2). Noteworthy is that Husserl sees no break between the phenomenology of the *Investigations* and that which has occupied him in the years since its publication, the first account of which he publishes in *Ideas I*. They are bound together by the same task.[4]

Phenomenology is a "science of ideas," not of nature. But again, in a radically new sense. In order to see phenomenology in the proper light, in order to grasp its uniqueness over against and its import to the familiar sciences—both natural and eidetic—Husserl sees it necessary to overcome the "prevailing habits of thinking." This entails a redefinition of science, which itself marks a differentiation of science—science is, after all, not only the natural sciences, not only the humanities, not only the known eidetic sciences. The first task in the service of the new science reads: "That all former habits of thinking be excluded"—literally: switched off[5]—"that the spiritual barriers [*Geistesschranken*] with which they confine the horizon of our thinking be discerned and torn down, and that now, with complete freedom of thought, the genuine philosophical problems be seized upon that are to be set completely anew, problems made accessible to us only by the horizon de-limited [*entschränkt*] on all sides—those are hard demands. But nothing less is required" (3). It is necessary to de-limit the horizon in order to attain the unlimited, universal horizon that is phenomenology's proper field of inquiry. Prior to Husserl's breakthrough into pure phenomenology, the habits of thinking have held sway over thinking—hence, also in the *Logical Investigations*, even if to a lesser extent than elsewhere. There was only natural thinking. The habits of thinking are thus ingrained in the whole of humanity, particularly in European humanity. They are deep-seated. Slipping from their grasp means nothing less than shedding the more than two-millennia-long philosophical tradition, but also the traditions of the individual sciences, which had broken free from philosophy over the centuries, that is to say, shedding such traditions insofar as they are bastions of "blinding" theory. Again, it is precisely because it is so difficult to overcome those habits that it is "only in our days" that pure phenomenology "presses towards development" (1): "Indeed, what makes so extraordinarily difficult the acquisition of the essence of phenomenology, the understanding of the peculiar sense of its problems and of its relationship to all other sciences (and particularly to psychology), is, moreover, that a new style of attitude is needed that is completely altered in contrast to the natural attitudes of experiencing and thinking. To move freely in [the new attitude] without relapsing into the old attitudes, to learn to see, distinguish, and describe what lies before one's eyes, requires, furthermore, special and arduous studies" (3).

The "chief task" of *Ideas I* is "to seek ways by which the enormous difficulties of penetrating into this new world can be overcome, so to speak, piece by piece." In this respect phenomenology is propaedeutic[6] in a twofold sense.

To prepare the way for the preparation of the way, as it were, Husserl must first clarify both the sense of 'phenomenology' and its method for entry into its proper field of inquiry, for especially in this case science and method are inextricably linked. But again, in view of the present in which he finds himself and the radical newness of phenomenology, the preparation called for must be tailored to the climate in which phenomenology is born. Thus Husserl cannot proceed simply "positively," but must do so proleptically. His propaedeutic expositions are accordingly advanced from out of a defensive stance, in anticipation of the skeptical and dogmatic objections likely to be raised against phenomenology and its method.[7] And this means that the negative beginning must precede the positive.

The path leading to the true beginning has its starting point in things as we usually find them in our everyday dealings or in received opinions concerning them. By focusing initially on what is familiar, Husserl proceeds "naturally," and thereby in accordance with the basic Aristotelian distinction between what is first for us and what is first by nature.[8] Radical analysis—and Husserl seeks to engage in it alone—aims at the latter, since it is the root of the former. Hence, although the truly first is concealed by the familiar, the investigator is not cut off from it, for it is always operative within the familiar. The order of inquiry must respect the things themselves. Were Husserl to begin his presentation with what is first by nature, and thus from the standpoint he has reached by respecting the things themselves, he would not only go against the nature of those things, but would fail to win over anyone to the cause of phenomenology.[9] The requisite legitimizing force of his endeavor is gained only to the extent that the intuitions are grounded in the things themselves. Precisely on account of this, radical analysis, which is simultaneously its presentation, must begin with the familiar in order to clear away the layers of sedimentation that naturally conceal the origin.[10] Only after having reached that origin, the true ground, does it become possible for phenomenological inquiry to climb up into the heights towards its goal.

Once the contours of natural consciousness have been sketched, Husserl elaborates the method of phenomenological reductions, which is then employed in order to switch off this kind of consciousness, that is to say, the natural attitude. By means of this method "we can do away with the barriers to cognition [*Erkenntnisschranken*] that belong to every natural style of inquiry, we can divert the one-sided orientation of regard proper to such inquiry until we have finally gained the free horizon of 'transcendentally' purified phenomena and thus the field of phenomenology in our special sense" (3). This new field is one of essences as opposed to facts.

In order to enter onto the threshold of pure phenomenology, Husserl employs the first of two kinds of reduction: the eidetic reduction. It "leads from the psychological phenomenon to the pure 'essence' or, in the case of judicative thinking, from factual ('empirical') universality to 'eidetic' universality"

(4)—in short, from an instance to its essence. The phenomena attended to under the scope of this reduction are "irreal." It enables the acquisition of fundamental insights that will be of use to the properly phenomenological analyses, which also focus on "irrealities," though in a radically different mode. Once those insights have been gained, the second reduction can be effected, namely the transcendental reduction or the epoché. It is more radical than the eidetic reduction inasmuch as it purifies phenomena of all reality, that is, of their embeddedness in the (real) world, in order to uncover the origin and thus the very possibility of eidetic cognition. This reduction is to sever all ties to the world: "Our phenomenology is to be a doctrine of essence, not of real, but of transcendentally reduced phenomena."[11] It is precisely at this reduction that Husserl's initial eidetic analyses are aimed.

The need for the second reduction; which discloses what is by nature first, becomes clear in light of the fact that whereas the eidetic reduction can be employed to disclose indefinitely many essences, the essences gained thereby are, as it were, of equal rank: none has immediately objective or absolute priority over any other. Consequently, there is no nonarbitrary direction of inquiry. This is changed, Husserl contends, by the epoché. Its principal achievement is nothing less than to *orient* eidetic inquiry, and hence ultimately all inquiry: in the purifying reduction to consciousness, a point is found relative to which eidetic findings gain importance; only relative to this point does the exposition of a hierarchy of essence become possible. Yet this does not mean that the epoché renders the eidetic reduction superfluous; it cannot do so precisely because the latter reduction remains the main tool of phenomenological inquiry.[12] Rather, the epoché provides eidetic inquiry with its absolute ground, its direction, its sense. Together, then, the two types of reduction are meant to secure the beginning of the actual introduction to pure phenomenology: the analysis of the universal structures of consciousness. And once the beginning has been won, they continue to be employed by the investigator as he strives to move up into the heights towards the other extreme.[13]

First of all, however, Husserl considers it is necessary to differentiate the eidetic spheres if phenomenology's proper domain is to be fixed: "It will become apparent that the concept of reality requires a fundamental restriction by means of which a distinction between real and individual Being (unqualifiedly temporal Being) must be established. The transition to pure essence yields, on the one hand, eidetic cognition of the real; on the other hand, with respect to the remaining sphere, it yields eidetic cognition of the irreal. Furthermore, it will become apparent that all transcendentally purified 'lived experiences' [*Erlebnisse*][14] are irrealities *posited* outside any integration in the 'actual world.' It is precisely these irrealities that phenomenology investigates, though not as singulars, but in 'essence.'" These distinctions point the way to be taken in order to establish phenomenology as an a priori, eidetic science, and in fact as the preeminent eidetics.

The steps of this founding begin with a consideration of "essence and eidetic science" (5) in contradistinction to facts and factual science, respectively. This is then followed by a "defense of the original legitimacy of eidetic cognition against naturalism." The final two steps of Husserl's phenomenological propaedeutics consist in differentiating the principal attitudes of consciousness and elaborating the method of epoché, which alone makes possible the entry into the proper sphere of phenomenological inquiry. This path leads from the familiar down to the "roots of everything." Under the scope of the eidetic reduction, these four steps make up the first two divisions of *Ideas I*. It is only upon effecting the epoché at the conclusion of the second division that the proper field of phenomenological inquiry is entered. This is where the properly transcendental analyses begin;[15] and they continue—ever under the scope of the epoché—throughout the last two divisions of this work.

1. Logical Considerations: Fact and Essence

The "logical considerations" with which Husserl opens *Ideas I* appear at first glance merely to continue the work he began in the *Logical Investigations*. This impression would seem to be supported not only by thematic kinships existing between that work and the first part of *Ideas I*, but even more so by Husserl's several references there to the *Investigations*. However, whereas an obvious continuity exists between the two works, *Ideas I* is not a mere continuation of the "breakthrough into phenomenology" he achieved in the *Investigations*, but a deepening and thus a radicalization of the insights gained in that first work of phenomenology.[16] The continuity between the two works proves to be first and foremost one of intention and only secondarily one of theme, that is, of problems and the approach to their solution. As is well known, both works are linked by a foundationalist intention, but they differ on where the foundation is located. It is precisely this difference that forces Husserl to radicalize his earlier work. In *Ideas I* his overriding concern is to establish phenomenology as First Science by showing not only the priority of essence over facts or experience, not only that facts are grounded in essences, but that the essences themselves are ultimately grounded.[17] The radicalization consists precisely in seeking out the source of this grounding, that is, the absolute ground or the so-called Archimedean point. Especially because Husserl seeks to disclose this point—on which all knowledge is based—*Ideas I* marks the breakthrough into pure, transcendental phenomenology.

This radicalization requires Husserl to reorient the course he began in the *Investigations*, as well as to revise the means he uses to achieve his new goal.

Because he aims at the ultimate ground, his "logical considerations" must motivate, or bring to intuition, the necessity of the ground, which means that he must penetrate the surface concealing it. The radicalization thus begins with that surface, which is the familiar, both in the sense of the everyday and, in the present context, in the sense of what was achieved in the *Logical Investigations*. From the familiar he seeks to descend to the ground, though here he cannot reach it, but only lay the groundwork for doing so. His intention in this first propaedeutic step is to point to the way to the absolute ground.

1.1 The Realm of the Natural

For Husserl, beginning with the familiar means beginning with the natural. His focus, however, is not on just any mode of being-in-the-world, but rather, due to his intention to found science in general, on what he considers the decisive mode: cognition. It is in this respect that he circumscribes the sense of 'natural': "Natural cognition," he says, "begins with experience and remains within experience" (7). 'Natural' denotes a stance or attitude towards things. For the natural attitude, experience is the measure of all things—which is why, as just noted, it begins with and remains within experience, never exceeding it. The realm of natural experience constitutes the "total horizon" (it is held to encompass *all* that is), which is called "the world." In its naturalness this attitude is not "innocent" or somehow pretheoretical. On the contrary, and this is Husserl's pivotal discovery, it is nothing less than a "theoretical attitude."[18] As the "original attitude,"[19] the natural attitude stamps every mode of natural Being, not just those modes typically taken to be theoretical, namely those of the various sciences. In fact, all the known sciences are grounded in this attitude and hence are literally "natural" sciences. As such they are "sciences of the world."[20]

All of this is reflected in speech. Husserl points out that "as long as it is the exclusively dominant attitude, the concepts 'true Being', 'actual Being', that is, real Being, and—since everything real combines to form the unity of the world—'Being in the world' coincide." In other words, for this attitude 'truth', 'actuality', 'reality' are synonymous with 'world'. These terms and their relation to Being will undergo a distinction in the course of Husserl's analyses, but in the meantime they are taken to be naturally equivalent. For his first task is not to criticize but to describe the natural "theoretical" attitude "as it is," which means allowing its fundamental lack of distinction to come into view. Of course, his descriptions are not aimless, but are designed to thwart the dominance of the natural attitude. This becomes manifest already in view of the way in which he proceeds—as it were, taxonomically. Namely, he seeks to combat the natural attitude's characteristic lack of distinction by entering onto a seemingly endless path of distinction and classification—it only seems to be endless, however, for all the while he aims at a definite target.

Regarding the sphere of "natural" science, he begins by noting that each science is a regional ontology: "To each science there corresponds an object-province [*Gegenstandsgebiet*] as the domain of its inquiries; and to all its cognitions, and that means here all its correct statements, there correspond, as primal sources [*Urquellen*] of the founding that demonstrates their legitimacy, certain intuitions in which objects [*Gegenstände*] from the province are brought to self-givenness and, at least partially, to originary givenness." The cognitions proper to each object-province are legitimated by that province's own mode of intuition, the greatest degree of legitimacy being accorded to the originary intuition of what is given.

Generally speaking, the legitimizing intuition of the sciences rooted in the natural attitude is experience: "The giving intuition of the first, the 'natural' sphere of cognition and of all its sciences is natural experience, and the originarily giving experience is perception, this word being understood in the ordinary sense. To have something real given originarily and 'to notice' [*gewahren*] and 'to perceive' [*wahrnehmen*] it in a simple intuiting are one and the same" (7–8).[21] Experience is, properly speaking, outwardly directed. It takes its bearings by, responds to, is involved in, the world "out there." Consequently, the most originary mode of experience and the givenness it affords is external perception: "We have originary experience of physical things in 'external perception,' but no longer in memory or forward-looking expectation"; in addition, as natural beings, as members of the world, we can also experience ourselves: "we have originary experience of ourselves and our states of consciousness in so-called internal or self-perception, but not of others and of their lived experiences in 'empathy'" (8). Experience, then, clearly has its limitations; it is not absolute, it cannot be of just anything, but rather the possibilities pertaining to experience in each case are fixed by the province within the world to which one seeks access. Nevertheless, such limitations do not lessen the value of experience, but indicate distinctions within the whole, distinctions that are bound together in a founded hierarchy. To begin with, these determinations and the limitations they bring to light show that among all the possible experiences, the intuition with the greatest legitimizing force is perception, for in it its object is given originarily, that is, actionally, here and now. Furthermore, the originary founds the non-originary, immediacy founds all mediacy.

For those living in the natural attitude, the world is all that is the case: "The world is the sum-total of the objects of possible experience and experiential cognition, of the objects that, on the basis of actional [*aktuell*] experiences, are cognizable in correct theoretical thinking." But whereas the natural theoretical attitude posits this whole always already, it does not typically investigate this total horizon as such. Rather, just as the foregoing consideration of experience showed both that not all experiences are equally originary and that there are fundamental distinctions between modes of experience, likewise the theoretical investigation of the world is not homogeneous, but is divided into various disciplines according to the overriding concern in each case. In this connection, Husserl identifies two main groups of sciences: the natural sciences, which include the sciences of physical and psychophysical nature, and the humanities (*Geisteswissenschaften*), the sciences of spirit and its products. Each group has its own region of inquiry (the region of nature and of spirit, respectively, which, of course, have undergone further distinction into ever more specific subregions over time), but whatever their differences, they are nevertheless unified: because they all are grounded in the natural attitude, these sciences remain sciences of the world.

Given their preoccupation, the members of these groups are called 'experiential sciences'. But due to the nature of experience, they are more accurately termed 'factual sciences'.[22] They focus entirely on individuals: "The founding cognitive acts of experiencing posit something real individually; they posit it as existing spatiotemporally," in this particular place and at this particular moment. What distinguishes the fact is precisely its contingency: "Individual Being of every kind is, put quite generally, 'contingent.' It is thus; by its essence, it could be otherwise" (9). Contingency is essential to the possibility proper to experience. Therefore the sciences of experience or facts are sciences of contingencies, although this would seem to be contradicted by their establishment of laws of nature. Yet, as Husserl emphasizes, even they are contingent: "for such laws express only de facto rules that could read quite otherwise and that already presuppose, as something proper from the start to the essence of objects of possible experience, that such objects that are governed by them are, considered in themselves, contingent"—again, they could be otherwise; their essence allows of this possibility.[23]

1.2 Individual and Essence, Possibility and Necessity

Husserl's account has employed a distinction that must now be made explicit, namely that between possibility and necessity. This distinction proves to entail a hierarchical relationship: the possibility proper to experience, which is always contingent, is bound up with a necessity. Husserl draws this out as follows: "But the *sense* of this contingency, which is called factualness here, is limited in that it is correlatively related to a necessity that does not signify the mere factual existence[24] of an obtaining rule of coordination among spatiotemporal facts, but rather has the character of eidetic necessity and thus a relation to eidetic universality. When we said that any fact could be otherwise 'by its own essence,' we were already saying that it belongs to the *sense* of anything contingent to have an *essence* and therefore an *eidos* that can be apprehended *purely*;[25]

and this *eidos* falls under eidetic truths belonging to *different levels of universality*." Thus contingency is an essential determination, which is to say that what it is is fixed by its essence, which itself is not contingent, but rather pure and thus universal to some degree.

Each individual is therefore bound to a determinate essence; the former may be said to participate in the latter. However, such participation is not restricted to one individual, but is an essential possibility of each individual of its kind: "An individual object is not merely an individual object as such [*überhaupt*], a 'This-here!', a unique object; as an object composed thus and so 'within itself,' it has its own specific character, its stock of essential predicables that *must* belong to it (as 'a being such as it is within itself') so that other, secondary, relative determinations can belong to it." Decisive for any individual object are not its contingent, but rather its essential determinations—for even contingencies are rooted in essential determinations, as is the distinction between essence and contingency in the first place. Each individual is governed by an essence. And precisely because an essence is not restricted to just one individual, but can bear on many individuals, it is universal: "Everything belonging to the essence of the individuum can also be had by another individuum; and highest eidetic universalities of the kind just indicated in our examples [i.e., tone as such, material thing as such] delimit 'regions' or 'categories' of individua." Just as the individua are not all of the same kind, likewise the regions or categories are not all of equal rank, but have—according to their essence—different degrees of purity and thus different degrees of universality. The differences in degree determine in turn the place of each region within the hierarchy of regions, which extends from the least to the greatest purity and universality.

Given the essential relationship between individual and essence, it must be possible—and that it is possible is one of Husserl's key insights already in the *Investigations*[26]—to perceive not only an individual but an essence as well.[27] And a move can indeed be made from the former to the latter: "Individual or experiencing intuition can be transformed into eidetic seeing [*Wesensschauung*] (ideation)—a possibility that is itself to be understood not as empirical but as essential. What is seen thereby is the corresponding pure essence or *eidos*, whether it be the highest category or a particularization thereof, down to full concretion" (10). Here the essence lies at first in the individual; through eidetic seeing it is, so to speak, freed from its concrete manifestation and raised to the level of pure essence—that is, our gaze is freed from its fixation on the individual and directed to the essence. The extent of such liberation determines its place in the aforementioned hierarchy.[28]

Husserl characterizes the seeing that gives an essence—whether originarily or not—as either adequate or inadequate. Adequate givenness is perfect givenness, whereas inadequate givenness is "more or less imperfect." Such imperfection, Husserl notes, is not only a matter of "a greater or lesser clarity and distinctness," but is fixed in each case by the essence of the object perceived. Thus no reality—nor an essence related to a reality—can ever be given adequately: "the spatial shape of the physical thing," for example, "can be given principially only in one-sided adumbrations" and no amount of experience will overcome this essential determination. There will always be a remainder; some part of the shape will have yet to be grasped or will have slipped from one's grasp. All of its sides can never be given at once. Because every determination of the physical thing leaves something open, Husserl says it draws us into "infinities of experience." By contrast, a pure essence or *eidos* can be given adequately and so does not entail such infinities.

Just as individual objects can be intuited, likewise each individual intuition can be transformed into an eidetic intuition: "Of whatever kind an individual intuition[29] may be, whether adequate or inadequate, it can take the turn into eidetic seeing; and this seeing, whether it be correspondingly adequate or not, has the characteristic of a giving act." The object of this act is now of a different kind: "The essence (*eidos*) is a new kind of object. Just as what is given in individual or experiencing intuition is an individual object, likewise what is given in eidetic intuition is a pure essence" (10–11). Husserl points to the "radical community" that obtains, not only between individuum and essence as objects, but also between the intuition proper to each: "The seeing of essences [*Wesenserschauung*] is also precisely intuition, just as an eidetic object is precisely an object" (11). Here 'intuition' and 'object' are the highest categories; the eidetic and the individual, their particularizations. Their "radical community" is precisely a community of essence. Despite their community, however, essential differences are maintained. The possibilities of intuition proper to each object are fixed by its essence: "Every possible object—logically speaking: 'every subject of possible true predications'—has precisely its ways, prior to all predicative thinking, of becoming the object of an objectivating, intuiting regard that perhaps hits upon it in its 'bodily selfhood,' that 'seizes upon' it." These ways of becoming an object of acts are predetermined essentially, a priori. They are not imposed by thinking, but inhere in the things themselves, that is, in their essences.

Concerning the aforementioned radical community, Husserl says: "no eidetic intuition is possible without the free possibility of turning one's regard to a 'corresponding' individual and forming a consciousness of an example—just as, conversely, no individual intuition is possible without the free possibility of effecting an ideation and, in it, directing one's regard to the correspond ing essence that is exemplified in what is sighted individually; but this in no way changes the fact that the two kinds of intuition are principially different" (12); nor does it change the fact that a hierarchy exists between the two sides. This community of kinds of intuition holds generally for the respective regions: "To the essential differences between the intuitions there correspond the essential relations between 'existence' (here obviously in the sense of some factually existent individual) and 'essence,' between fact and *eidos*." Both spheres are related as possibility to necessity.

Eidetic intuition has an advantage over its experiential counterpart inasmuch as, unlike the latter, it is not bound to experience for its examples, but can also make use of what is given in fantasy: "The *eidos*, the pure essence, can be exemplified intuitively by what is given in experience, by what is given in perception, memory, etc., but just as well by what is given in mere fantasy."[30] This suggests a sense in which fantasy has priority over experience. In fact the insight relayed here will prove crucial for Husserl's move away from the empirical to the essential in order to found the empirical anew. While he does admit the interdependence of the essential and the empirical-experiential, it nevertheless holds that the former is necessary, whereas the latter is only contingent. This is the pivotal distinction for Husserl's presentation; it alone can ground the said priority. The insight into this distinction ultimately provides the justification of his so-called transcendental turn, which Husserl makes no later than in the present work.

Whatever is regarded in free fantasy is fabricated; fantasy is concerned with fictions. And yet this does not mean that the fictions are "mere" fictions, mere fancy, which have no relevance; such is a bias proper to the natural attitude, which privileges the real. Again, essence is the sphere of necessity, whereas existence is the sphere of contingency. Because the former sphere is in no way dependent upon the latter in its actuality, "it does not matter whether anything of the kind [that is, a fiction generated in fantasy] has ever been given in actional experience or not. If, by some psychological miracle or other, free fantasy were to result in the imagination of a principially novel kind of data (for example, sensuous data) that have never occurred and will never occur in any experience, that would in no way alter the originary givenness of the corresponding essences—though imagined data are never ever actual data" (13). They are not actual (which in this context means not real) though the data are essential. This sheds light on the foregoing remark on the interdependence of individual and eidetic intuition. It need not be the case that the individual intuition is of something factually existent, something real, but can also be of something given in fantasy and thus beyond all (real) existence.[31] Again, the spheres are interdependent in the manner in which necessity and possibility are, not in that of necessity and actuality.

Essence and existence are separate, though related, spheres of Being. Contrary to the natural attitude, however, it is not existence that is decisive here, but rather essence. It has priority over factual existence. Only because this holds can Husserl say that the "positing [*Setzung*] of and, to begin with, intuitive seizing upon essences does not in the least imply the positing of any individual factual existence; pure eidetic truths do not contain the slightest assertion about facts, and thus not even the most insignificant factual truth can be deduced from pure eidetic truths alone." Simply put, necessity cannot be deduced from contingency, nor can contingency be deduced immediately from necessity. The justification of assertions or thoughts about either sphere can occur only by means of the intuition proper to the respective sphere. To seek to justify or found essential truths through empirical or experiencing intuition would generate countersense, for the attempt would entail a *metabasis eis allo genos*.[32]

To reinforce the insight into the independence of the eidetic from the experiential sphere, Husserl considers judgment: "Judging about essences and essence-complexes [*Wesensverhalte*] is not the same as eidetic judging of whatever kind," for "eidetic cognition does not have essences in all of its propositions as 'objects-about-which' [*Gegenstände-worüber*]. . . ." Thus, while it is possible to judge about essences, it is also possible to judge about an individual "purely as a singularity of an essence in the mode of Any-whatsoever [*Überhaupt*]" (14). Husserl's example of such judgment is drawn from geometry: one does not judge "as a rule about the *eidos* straight line, angle, triangle, conic section, etc., but about any straight line and any angle whatsoever, or about a straight line and an angle 'as such,' about any individual triangle, any conic section whatsoever." Not even in judgments of this kind, which are each eidetic universalities, does the positing of existence play a role; eidetic seeing need not be based on anything empirical, but rather is grounded in the eidetic itself, a state of affairs that becomes particularly evident in view of axioms or "immediately evident judgments." Husserl notes that they "require for their noetic founding [*Begründung*], that is, in order to make them matters of insight, a certain eidetic seeing that one could also designate (in a modified sense) as a seizing upon essences; and this seeing, too, like the eidetic intuition that makes essences objectual [*gegenständlich*], is based on a sighting of the individual particulars of the essences, but not on experiencing them." Because founding occurs by means of the kind of seeing proper to each sphere, the eidetic and the experiential spheres always retain their integrity. But even more important here is that the eidetic sphere is not "conditioned" by experience and so has "unconditional universality."

Within the eidetic sphere, certain "universal" correlations are to be found that Husserl fixes as follows: "It is now clear that the following ideas belong together: eidetic judging, eidetic judgment or eidetic proposition [*Satz*],[33] eidetic truth (or true proposition); as the correlate of the latter idea: the simple eidetic affair-complex [*Sachverhalt*] (as what obtains in eidetic truth); finally, as the correlate of the first ideas: the eidetic affair-complex in the modified sense of mere meantness, in the sense of the judged as such, which can either obtain or not obtain" (15). In fact, the idea 'eidetic judging' has the 'eidetic judgment or proposition' as its correlate. 'Eidetic truth' will be seen to issue from the perfect correspondence of these two sides, which is why Husserl calls its correlate the simple eidetic affair-complex; in the case of truth, it is given completely. Mere meantness as the correlate of the relation between judging and the proposition marks the situation in which such meantness has yet to be confirmed or denied.[34]

Beyond these correlations, the distinction is made between universality and necessity. Whatever is derived from a universality is a necessity: "Every eidetic particularization and singularization of an eidetically universal affair-complex, insofar as it is such, is called an eidetic necessity. Eidetic universality and eidetic necessity are thus correlates." But they are not synonyms; *universality is the source of and thus has priority over necessity.* This is evident in view of which of the two founds apodicticity: "The consciousness of a necessity, more precisely a judging consciousness in which there is consciousness of an affair-complex as a particularization of an eidetic universality, is called an apodictic consciousness, the judgment itself, the proposition, is called an apodictic (also an apodictically 'necessary') consequence of the universal proposition to which it refers." This hierarchy is not confined to the eidetic sphere, however, but holds for experience as well. An eidetic universality can be applied to some existent individual, in which case the resultant complex is a mixture of the contingent and the necessary: "The affair-complex that is posited as actual is then a fact insofar as it is an actuality-complex [*Wirklichkeitsverhalt*], but it is an eidetic necessity insofar as it is the singularization of an eidetic universality" (15–16). It is obvious that the necessity pertaining to the "real" affair-complex is distinct from the universality of which it is a particularization.

1.3 Factual and Eidetic Sciences

The distinctions drawn thus far between facts and essences, all of which were essential distinctions, carry over to and found the relationship between factual and eidetic sciences.[35] The pure eidetic sciences are "pure of all positings of facts; or, equivalently, in them no experience, as experience, that is, as a consciousness that seizes upon or posits actuality, factual existence, can assume the function of founding. Where experience functions in them, it does not function *as* experience" (16–17). This is why, Husserl says, it does not matter whether the investigator of essences, such as a geometer, hallucinates or operates in fantasy in the course of his inquiry. What is decisive is not the reality of what is given, but its essentiality and the originariness of its givenness. By contrast, for the investigator of nature experiencing is a "founding act, which could never be replaced by a mere imagining" (17). And on that account, "factual science and experiential science are equivalent concepts. But for the geometer, who explores not actualities but 'ideal possibilities,' not actuality-complexes but essence-complexes, the ultimately founding act is not experience but rather the seeing of essences." This seeing alone confirms its positings or judgments.

Since seizing upon an essence is the ultimately founding act for all eidetic sciences, it follows that all related acts subsequent to it can be traced back to it, for all mediate founding is based on immediate founding. Such immediate insight provides the guarantee for all mediate insight: "Every step of mediate founding is therefore apodictically and eidetically necessary." This founded relationship suggests "the practical ideal of exact eidetic science," which, though yet to be realized, promises to be if one follows the directive that, according to Husserl, modern mathematics was the first to provide: "to bestow the highest degree of rationality on each eidetic science by reducing all its mediate steps of thinking to mere subsumptions under the axioms of the particular eidetic province, axioms that have been systematically combined once and for all, and, provided that 'formal' or 'pure' logic (in the broadest sense of *mathesis universalis*) is itself not of concern from the start, reinforced with all the axioms of the latter." The ideal calls for the reduction of all mediacy to immediacy, and ultimately of all necessary deductions to the universal axioms on which they are based. Clearly, the reduction is not to be equated with a rejection of mediate steps; on the contrary, it aims at revealing the ground of those steps so as to secure them. Although Husserl is speaking here of mathematics in particular and eidetic science in general, in the ideal he does not see the demand to continue the modern project of mathematizing the sciences or even to improve mathematics or one of the other eidetic sciences somehow so as to guarantee the realization of that ideal. Rather, for reasons that will become clearer in the course of his analyses, he sees in the ideal solely the directive for the establishment of a new eidetic science as the eidetic science of all eidetic sciences, thus the most radical eidetics. As such phenomenology is to bestow "the highest degree of rationality" on every science—and precisely by means of the reduction to the absolute ground.[36] A science is rational to the extent that it discerns, acknowledges, and abides by the norms governing it, the "most universal and principial grounds."

In light of the founded relationship and the practical ideal to which it gave rise, Husserl turns to the relationship—rather than, as earlier, the distinction—obtaining between factual and eidetic sciences. The latter have to do with essences and essence-complexes alone. From the ground up, they make no use of any thesis about existence: "the sense of eidetic science principially precludes any incorporation of cognitive results of empirical sciences" (18). By contrast, the latter sciences are founded entirely on such theses: "After all, the theses about actuality that occur in the immediate findings of these sciences extend throughout all mediate findings. Nothing ever follows from facts but facts." There is an absolute division between these two groups of sciences that centers on the thesis about existence: a science is either factual or eidetic, but never both. Either the thesis about existence is present or it is absent. Were it to be introduced into an eidetic science, that science would lose its purity; it would be transformed into a factual, contingent science.

But although these sciences are separated in this respect, their separation is in a sense one-sided, for it is actually the eidetic sciences that are independent of factual sciences, since they make no use of cognitions gained by the latter. By contrast, the factual sciences are dependent upon the eidetic sciences: "There is no [factual science] that, were it fully developed as a science, could be pure of eidetic cognitions and therefore could be independent of the eidetic sciences, whether formal or material." Husserl cites two ways in which the factual sciences rely on the eidetic sciences: firstly, every factual science must make use of formal principles when it seeks to found its judgments mediately; secondly, insofar as it "entails a material eidetic composition," every fact is governed by eidetic laws, laws that determine the truth of any factual singularity of an essence. In light of this dependence, a hierarchy becomes visible that has two main tiers and in which the higher-order sciences are clearly the eidetic sciences. However, 'higher-order' does not mean that these sciences are situated somewhere in the heights—as it were, in the clouds—but rather, as noted above, it means that they form the ground of the factual sciences. The eidetic sciences are the most radical and so the most universal.

The hierarchy entails a kind of encasement or nesting wherein the factual is enclosed in the eidetic, the founded in the founding, the lower in the higher, the particular in the universal. Husserl elaborates this relationship, starting out from the empirical object: "Every concrete empirical objectuality [*Gegenständlichkeit*] finds its place within a highest material genus, a 'region,' of empirical objects. To the pure regional essence then corresponds a regional eidetic science or . . . a regional ontology" (19). Just as the empirical objectuality is the object of an empirical science, likewise the region to which it belongs is the object of a regional ontology. Furthermore, the cognitions gained in the latter must be applicable in their universality to the particular objects of that region and thus be of use to their corresponding empirical sciences. Because the reverse does not hold of empirical sciences, Husserl can speak of the latter as founded on eidetic sciences: "Every factual science (experiential science) has essential theoretical fundaments in eidetic ontologies."

The aforementioned practical ideal therefore cannot be achieved by a factual science, since its cognitions prove to be mediate and thus founded: "If we form the *idea* of a perfect, rationalized experiential science of nature, that is, of one that is so advanced in its theorizing that every particular included in it has been traced back to that particular's most universal and principial grounds, then it is clear that the realization of this idea is essentially dependent upon the elaboration of the corresponding eidetic sciences," that is, upon the formal *mathesis* as well as, in this case, the ontology of nature corresponding to the whole range of natural sciences. Husserl at once draws out the hierarchy of the sciences and points to the ideal as follows: "Also with regard to cognitive practice it is to be expected from the start that the closer an experiential science comes to the 'rational' level, the level of 'exact,' nomological science—thus the higher the degree to which an experiential science is provided with developed eidetic disciplines as its foundations and utilizes them for its foundings—the greater will become the scope and force of its cognitive-practical achievements [*Leistungen*]" (20). Like the mathematical sciences of the modern era, Husserl's aim is the "rationalization of the empirical." However, he does not stop there, but intends to rationalize all sciences. To win the world, the normative must first be won, that is, the eidetic ontologies must first be elaborated, but also and ultimately the ontology of these ontologies, in other words: the fundamental ontology. This science is to be none other than phenomenology.[37] It adopts the practical ideal as its task.[38]

2. Between Scylla and Charybdis: The Principle of All Principles

Husserl's expositions on essence, on its distinction from and relation to facts, as well as the differentiation of the sciences, have laid "the essential foundations for our *construction* of *the idea* of *a* pure phenomenology" (33).[39] Laying those foundations is the inaugural step of his phenomenological propaedeutics. At first glance, this step seems to have involved only "positive" work; there is, after all, scarcely a trace of defensiveness or "negativity" in the analyses encountered thus far, which would seem to refute the claim made at the outset of this chapter that Husserl's expositions are proleptic in character. And the claim would indeed be unjustified were it not for the second step of his preparatory studies. Here it becomes clear in what way Husserl has advanced the foregoing positive expositions so as to defuse the anticipated rejection of his chief concerns. It is this negativity, and it alone, that motivates the course he takes in constructing the idea of a pure phenomenology.[40] It also brings him to introduce the supreme principle of phenomenological inquiry, which itself cuts both ways: it is explicitly positive, but implicitly negative. On the one hand, it is to guide both the further construction of the said idea and all future phenomenological inquiry, as well as enable the reorientation of the sciences. But on the other hand, the principle excludes every form of inquiry, and its findings, that does not abide by it. In this way, it marks Husserl's first cut, which becomes particularly clear from the context in which the principle is first formulated.

2.1 Phenomenology and Philosophy

Pure phenomenology is to be an eidetic science. In order to establish it as such, Husserl finds it necessary to begin by rejecting all theories, including those advanced within the philosophical tradition. He has done just that from the start. Instead of relying on "philosophical doctrines," he has "carried out some, in the most rigorous sense, principial demonstrations, that is, we have brought only those distinctions to faithful expression that are directly given to us in intuition. We have *taken* them precisely *as they give themselves* there, without any hypothetical or interpretative exegesis, without reading into them anything that may be suggested to us by traditional theories of ancient or modern times"—without imposing any (preconceived) thought on them, but rather letting them, as it were, speak for themselves.[41] "Findings made in this way are actual 'beginnings' [cf. ἀρχαί]; and if, like ours, they have a universality related to the comprehensive regions of Being, then they are surely principial in the philosophical sense and themselves belong to philosophy" (33). Yet insofar as they are principial, they come before philosophy; properly speaking, they are not the province of philosophy. By contrast, phenomenology's concern lies with precisely such beginnings. It follows, then, that it cannot be philosophy, but must be prior to all philosophy.[42] What is more, because those beginnings bear on all regions, phenomenology proves to be prior even to every other eidetic science. As such it must be regarded as the highest, because most radical (eidetic) science.

Although he has excluded all theories, including all philosophies, Husserl nevertheless finds it necessary to consider a philosophical position that threatens to jeopardize his endeavor—not in and of itself, but rather its reception in "present" thought. Contrary to first appearances—after all, he does claim to have excluded every philosophy along with every theory—there is nothing contradictory about this, he notes, for he is not addressing the position on the level of its own claims, not as a philosophy per se; he does not meet it with acknowledgment, but instead considers it in conjunction with the beginnings that precede and thus ground that position, all the while giving pride of place to those beginnings. The justification for this approach lies, once again, in the things themselves: "If philosophy has any stock whatsoever of 'principial' foundings in the genuine sense that, according to their essence, can therefore be founded only by immediately giving intuition, then a conflict over them is decided independently of every philosophical science, of the possession of the idea of the latter and its allegedly founded theoretical content" (34). Again, philosophy is dispensable when at issue are the first things, which it presupposes. If a position is principled, then it is possible, and indeed necessary, to begin with those principles and work one's way upward only thereafter.

It is noteworthy that Husserl does not enter into the fray of his own accord, but sees himself compelled to do so: "The situation that forces the conflict upon us is that 'ideas,' 'essences,' 'eidetic cognitions,' are denied by empiricism."[43] What motivates him, then, is at bottom the rejection of the legitimacy of his entire endeavor. By confronting that denial, Husserl seeks to defuse a mentality that stamps his age: "In any case, in these circles [of empirical investigators], and therefore among psychologists as well, a hostility towards ideas [*Ideenfeindschaft*] is alive that ultimately must endanger the progress of the experiential sciences themselves; but that is because this hostility inhibits the eidetic founding of these sciences, which is by no means complete, and the perhaps necessary constituting of new eidetic sciences indispensable to their progress." The new eidetics Husserl has in view is, of course, none other than phenomenology. It was for its sake that he began *Ideas I* with a consideration of essence, but he also did so in order to lay the groundwork for his refutation of empiricism. In its skepticism Husserl sees his Charybdis;[44] his Scylla lies elsewhere, though not far away, namely in dogmatism. It is through them that he must steer his endeavor, and in fact with the aid of the aforementioned principle.

2.2 Empiricism, Naturalism, Skepticism

The first extreme taken up, and in fact the only one Husserl addresses at length here, is represented by empiricistic naturalism, his Charybdis. It enters onto the scene in opposition to dogmatism, which is actually the first, the "natural" extreme of this pair. Because the empiricist takes a stand "against all 'idols,' against the powers of the tradition and superstition, of crude and sophisticated prejudices of every kind," Husserl says he is to be commended. Even more praiseworthy is that in taking this stand, the empiricist asserts "the right of autonomous reason as the sole authority in questions of truth." The methodical principle that is to guide empiricistic inquiry reads, according to Husserl, as follows: "Judging rationally or scientifically about things means, however, taking one's bearings by the things themselves, or going back from talk and opinions to the things themselves, consulting them in their self-givenness, and disposing of all prejudices alien to them" (35). With this much Husserl agrees. The problems begin with the empiricist's restriction of the mode of givenness of the things to experience. For him experience is the measure of all things; it is regarded as the solely legitimate starting point of science: "All science, he contends, deals only with experienceable, real actuality. Whatever is not actuality is imagination, and a science based on imaginings is just an imagined science." Since ideas and essences are not actualities, the empiricist must reject them as mere imaginings. For him an eidetics is no better than the superstitions he rejected in the first place. Furthermore, the desire to establish an eidetics, and especially one such as Husserl aims at, has to strike the empiricist as a "return to scholasticism."

Husserl refutes this position by showing that it is self-contradictory in two respects. First of all, despite its denial of all prejudices, the empiricistic position is itself based on "misunderstandings and prejudices." They are rooted in the assertion of the exclusivity of experience: "The principial mistake of the empiricistic argumentation consists in identifying or confusing the fundamental demand for a return to the 'things themselves' with the demand that all cognition be justified by experience." The empiricist considers those things given by experience, which is to say, realities, to be the only things that are knowable. "But," Husserl retorts, "things are not simply things of nature, nor is actuality in the usual sense simply all of actuality, and that originarily giving act that we call experience is related only to the actuality of nature." Privileging the things of nature and experience proves to be no less justified than the dogmatic tenets empiricism itself rejects as "speculative constructions." To see that his position is based on prejudice, however, the empiricist must first see the essential distinctions between regions and the modes of intuition proper to each. And this presupposes the insight into the role essence plays in each region and, by extension, in each fact. It is precisely this insight that grounds the second and decisive refutation Husserl brings against empiricism.

The empiricist begins and remains with the obvious in his privileging of experience. He falls prey to the obvious because he lacks the requisite radicality: "Genuine presuppositionlessness does not demand the rejection of 'judgments alien to experience' absolutely, but only when the proper sense of the judgments demands founding by experience" (36). The talk of sense points to essence in this case, for, as seen above, the intuition required to found a judgment is determined by the essence of what is judged about. The basic requirement is therefore not the dogmatic rejection of one kind of intuition in favor of another, but the determination of the kind of intuition demanded by the essence of the thing in question: "Genuine science and the presuppositionlessness proper to it demands, as the basis of all proofs, immediately valid judgments as such that draw their validity directly from originarily giving intuitions. But these are of such a character as the sense of these judgments or the proper essence of the objects and judgment-complexes [*Urteilsverhalte*] *prescribes*." The things themselves set the standard for judgment, for all statements about them, and thus for all reason, evidence, truth, and knowledge. But whereas only originary, immediate intuition provides the most complete access to the things as they give themselves and thus itself plays a fundamental role in the achievement of truth, originarily giving intuition is not of just one kind; rather, it must be differentiated, which is precisely what the empiricist fails to do: "Immediate 'seeing,' not merely sensory, experiential seeing, but rather seeing in general as the originarily giving consciousness of whatever kind, is the ultimate source of legitimacy of all rational claims. It has a legitimizing function only because and to the extent that it is an originarily giving source." Intuition therefore plays a key role since the thing is given in it with more or less immediacy, that is, its self is received more or less fully, but the thing clearly remains decisive. It is the ground; one cannot get behind it. On account of this, Husserl points out that it is countersensical to question the "I see it." That is not to say, however, that two instances of seeing cannot conflict, but only that one cannot give the ground of originary seeing, for it is itself in essence the ultimate ground. The possible differences proper to a certain mode of seeing do not call the status of seeing in general into question, but rather inhere already in the category or essence of the thing seen. The different possibilities pertaining to sensuous and eidetic intuition, for example, are essential differences. Yet both remain modes of originary seeing—each in its own way.

Husserl's insight into the essential differences between things and the modes of intuition in which they are given enables him to refute both the empiricistic account of legitimacy and its source, as well as the consequent claim that experiential science is the only legitimate form of science. In fact, his refutation does not arise from some preference on his part, but is instead motivated by empiricism itself, since it refutes itself. His insight shows this to be the case not only because the empiricistic standpoint is prejudiced—contrary to the demands it itself places on science—but especially because it makes use of eidetic cognitions while contesting "the validity of purely eidetic thinking" (37). In this respect, empiricistic naturalism proves to be a radical form of skepticism, which—as Husserl showed already in his *Prolegomena to Pure Logic*[45]—is necessarily self-refuting because it leads to countersense. He illustrates this as follows: "One need only ask the empiricist about the source of the validity of his universal theses (for example, 'all valid thinking is grounded in experience as the solely giving intuition'), and he gets entangled in demonstrable countersense. For direct experience gives only singulars and no universalities; thus it is insufficient." By virtue of its own claims, empiricism cannot account for itself. And the attempt to do so forces the empiricist to fall into countersense because he commits a *metabasis*: he appeals to things in regions to which he has denied himself access.

Husserl is able to avoid such countersense by substituting 'intuition' taken generally for 'experience' as the true source of legitimacy for every judgment or claim. This requires, however, that one always attend to the distinctions between essences and their respective regions. To do so, one must first rid oneself of all presuppositions, all thought, and to take one's bearings by the things themselves: "Whereas [the empiricists], as genuine standpoint-philosophers and in obvious contradiction of their principle of freedom from prejudice, start from unclarified and unfounded preconceived opinions, we start out from that which is prior to all standpoints: from the total realm of what gives itself intuitively and prior to all theorizing thinking, from all that which one can see and seize upon immediately" (38)—in short, from Being as opposed to thinking.

Because he takes this new starting point, which lies before all theory, Husserl's rejection of empiricism proves to be not a mere negation of empiricism, but the disclosure of that position's self-nullification. Strictly speaking, because empiricism negates itself—albeit unwittingly—it neutralizes its own claims and thus itself. Once Husserl has gotten to the bottom of things, there is no way he can take the empiricistic position seriously as such. He therefore does not take a stand in opposition to empiricism, but rather outside it, and in fact prior to it.

2.3 Idealism

On the other hand, there is a position that opposes empiricism, and that is idealism. Although it itself is not exactly skeptical, the exclusivity of the idealist focus on the Apriori likewise fails to do justice to the things themselves. For by rejecting the skeptical position, idealism also rejects all experience. As a result, idealism remains one-sided no less than does empiricism. It fails to see the community of essence between eidetic and experiential intuition: "reflectively it is not brought to clear consciousness that there is something such as pure intuiting as a kind of givenness in which essences are given originarily as objects entirely in the same way as individual realities are given in experiential intuition; nor is it recognized that every judicative having of insight—such as, in particular, insight into unconditionally universal truths—also falls under the concept of giving intuition, which has many differentiations, above all, those that run parallel to the logical categories" (39). Although the idealist does speak of evidence, he does so "without bringing it, as a having of insight, into essential relations with ordinary seeing," but instead appeals to something on the order of a "feeling of evidence." The consequence is not only that idealism, on Husserl's account, gets lost in "mysticism," but also that it remains one-sided and so unable to contend with realities. As with empiricism, idealism also makes visible the vagaries of theorizing from "on high" (*von oben her*) and thus the importance of turning away from theory to the things themselves, or from thought to Being as it gives itself to thought.

2.4 The Blindness of Theory

Theoretical prejudices of whatever kind, whether those of empiricism, idealism, or some other ism, inhibit the proper grasp of the things themselves. This is no small matter, for, on Husserl's view, such inhibition ultimately cripples every endeavor aimed at knowledge: "Blindness to ideas [*Ideenblindheit*] is a kind of blindness of the soul [*Seelenblindheit*]; through prejudices one has become incapable of bringing what one has in the field of intuition into the field of judgment" (41).[46] Despite first appearances, which in fact are the result of empiricistic prejudices, essences are nothing mystical, but common currency, as it were, in one's everyday dealings: "In truth everyone sees 'ideas,' 'essences,' and does so, so to speak, continuously; they operate with them in thinking, they also effect eidetic judgments—except that from their epistemological standpoint they interpret them away." The things themselves are in no way affected by such disregard by theory. It in no way impinges upon their fundamental status: "Evident givens are patient; they let theories talk on by them, but remain what they are." Since the things are what remain constant, while theories are typically in flux, it is "the business of theories to take their bearings by the givens," but prior to that it is "the business of theories of knowledge to distinguish fundamental kinds of givens and describe such kinds with respect to their proper essences." It is not enough, then, to focus on the things themselves, whether they be experiential or essential; one must also take cognizance of the essences, that is, the norms, regulating those things. The two concerns go hand in hand. In truth they are only analytically two concerns; practically they are one and the same.

2.5 The First Principle

Husserl is able to steer clear of every theoretical position, whether dogmatic or skeptical, not by actually confronting it, not by arguing with it,[47] but rather by abiding by his supreme methodical principle, the first commandment of phenomenology, as it were: the "principle of all principles."[48] In it he fixes the priority of the things themselves over thinking, of respect for them over the disrespectfulness of traditional theory: "every originarily giving intuition is a legitimizing source of cognition . . . everything that offers itself to us in 'intuition' originarily (so to speak, in its 'bodily' actuality) is to be accepted simply as what it gives itself as being, but also only within the limits in which it gives itself there" (43–44).[49] This principle not only guarantees the intuition, but also every attempt to give faithful expression to what is seen, which makes it suitable not only as the basis of science, but, prior to that, of the theory of knowledge on which every science rests: "Every statement that *does no more than* confer expression on such givens by simple explication and by means of significations precisely conforming to them is thus actually . . . an *absolute beginning*, called in the genuine sense to serve as a foundation, a *principium*" (44). The statements advanced by theory, however, do more than this; in them theory imposes its opinions, its desires,[50] on the things from on high rather than starting out from the things. As a result it hangs in the air. And precisely on account of this, nothing essential is to be gained by entering into a discussion with theory on its level—again, such could be fruitful only if the opposing positions had a common ground.

There is no need to argue with the theoretician, then, since for the phenomenologist he is not a true adversary. Rather, on Husserl's view, the only recourse can be to the things themselves, for they alone offer a firm footing. In fact Husserl's only reason for addressing a theory is to defuse a prevailing "habit of thinking" and thus ease the return to the ground. His refutation of empiricism, for example, was not strictly speaking a refutation; it did not hinge on an argument—at least not in the form of a deduction—but on the disclosure of empiricism's failure to see the ground on which it actually rests, a failure that renders its constructions mere "castles in the clouds." Thus, Husserl's refutation consisted in the disclosure of empiricism's self-refutation. The phenomenological refutation and subsequent dismissal of theoretical positions is not the result of a deduction, but of a reduction, a *reductio*, that is, a return to and restoration of the ground the things themselves offer.

Clearly Husserl has made use of this principle from the start of his analyses. The fact that he formulates it only at this point might seem to plunge him into a vicious circle, in which case his analyses would be only question-begging. But no such problem arises here, and for two reasons. Firstly, the principle of all principles is employed as just that: a *principle*. Husserl's introductory remarks in no way seek to justify it by appealing to the principle itself. In fact no attempt is made to justify it at all; that is, no deductive argumentation is undertaken so as to prove its firstness. There is no getting behind it since it marks the starting point; and this rules out its derivation from other principles. The only way in which Husserl might be said to justify it is by clearing away any obstacles to its immediate intuition.

It is exactly his response to such obstacles that forms the second reason why Husserl has not proceeded circularly. Whereas the principle of all principles is a reduction and thereby effects, in a qualified sense, a modification of consciousness, it does not bring about a change of attitude.[51] This principle is rooted in the natural attitude, and remains entirely within this attitude. It does not arise first within the transcendental-phenomenological attitude, which is entered only by means of the epoché,[52] but is a *natural* response to the dilemmas generated by the "prevailing habits of thinking," specifically by skepticism and dogmatism of every kind.[53] That it is not a transcendental principle in the sense proper to *Ideas I* is further confirmed by the fact that the principle of all principles is a translation of what is advanced in the *Logical Investigations* as the "principle of presuppositionlessness."[54] It is in this respect that the two works are linked methodically, and not with respect to the epoché,[55] which is a discovery that belongs exclusively to the so-called transcendental turn secured in *Ideas I*. Furthermore, it should be clear that, due to its naturalness, the principle of all principles cannot be justifiably equated with the epoché. Although both must be willed, although both may be said to bring about "modifications of consciousness," whereby thinking is made to "hold itself back" so as to allow the things themselves to reveal themselves "on their own terms," and although both go against the tendency of natural thinking to subject Being to thinking, the decisive point of difference lies in the attitude in which each holds sway. As will be seen, this difference is underscored by the fact that the principle of all principles takes on a new function within the phenomenological attitude, namely that of a phenomenological reduction.[56]

2.6 Dogmatism

In concluding the second step of his propaedeutics, Husserl returns briefly to the prevailing habits of thinking, this time to dogmatism, his Scylla. Like everyone else, the positivist sees ideas and essences and thinks by means of them. He does so dogmatically, which is to say, uncritically or naively.[57] Such dogmatism is not immediately harmful, Husserl says, but in fact has proven quite productive within the history of science. A change occurs, however, as soon as philosophy enters the picture: the positivist "rejects eidetic cognitions only when he reflects 'philosophically' and allows himself to be deceived by the sophistries of empiricistic philosophers; but he does not do any of this when, as an investigator of nature, he thinks and founds in the normal, natural scientific attitude" (44). And yet, even when he ignores the skeptical dilemmas, his dogmatism nevertheless continues to harbor the seeds of skepticism within itself, namely in the form of reflections that inhibit his "possibilities for work" (46).[58] The skeptical reflections at first bear only on essence—"due to the devotion to empiricistic prejudices, skepticism now remains out of action only with respect to the sphere of experience, but no longer with respect to the sphere of essence"—yet given the connections between essence and existence, they are bound to affect experience as well. Although such skepticism may not affect the familiar eidetic sciences, it does, Husserl stresses, obstruct the establishment of new eidetic sciences, particularly pure phenomenology—which, again, is why he has taken pains to disclose the countersense of skepticism.

Once again, the other side of skepticism and every attempt to solve the problems posed by it is dogmatism.[59] Together they mark the two extremes through which phenomenology must negotiate its path. In this context Husserl mentions only the immediately less harmful dogmatism proper to the natural sciences that are "turned to the things, unconcerned with any epistemological or skeptical problems." They take originary givenness as the ultimate measure of their cognitions. However, this form of dogmatism is related to that other, more virulent form to which the empiricistic naturalists originally responded, namely the dogmatism enthralled with "idols" and under the spell of "tradition and superstition, of crude and sophisticated prejudices." This is the dogmatism that for Husserl was responsible for the "dark ages" and from which Descartes freed himself with his "attempt at universal doubt," that is, the Middle Ages, which find next to no mention in Husserl's work.[60] His concern lies instead with the philosophies of Greek antiquity and the early modern era, in which he sees kindred spirits. In his treatment of the philosophical tradition, he springs from the one epoch to the other, without mention of any interim.[61] But regardless of his subsequent preferences concerning the epochs of philosophy, what is decisive is his incipient rejection of all philosophy, whether it be dogmatic or skeptical. It is rejected as theory, just as all pre-phenomenological thought is rejected. Again, this is not to say it is negated, but rather it is left to its own devices.

Neither skepticism nor dogmatism can be eliminated by means of argument, whether deductive or inductive, but must be passed over.[62] Ignoring them in favor of an immediately intuitable principle is the only answer: "We exclude these obstacles in the form of natural 'dogmatic' science . . . by making clear to ourselves and vividly bearing in mind only the most universal principle of all methods, the principle of the original legitimacy of all givens, whereas we ignore the contentual and multiform problems concerning the possibility of different kinds and correlations of cognitions" (47–48). In a way, then, Husserl himself might be said to proceed dogmatically, though in the positive sense he noted in connection with the positivist. The difference of his dogmatism, however, lies in the fact that since he is armed with the principle of all principles, "the most universal principle of all methods," he has divested himself of all the latent skeptical tendencies harbored by natural dogmatic science. His dogma is that of the *doxa* that in each case meets the things themselves just as they give themselves originarily. This *doxa*, or belief, manifests itself in the acknowledgment of the priority of the things themselves, which is the acknowledgment of the priority of Being over thinking. The principle of all principles is nothing but the requirement that thinking not assert itself against the things (as it does in constructing theories), but rather exercise reticence with respect to them, wait upon the things as they give themselves. This is the belief that grounds every intuition.

3. The Epoché and the Phenomenological Reductions

Husserl's next propaedeutic step is to prepare the way to the epoché by demonstrating both its possibility and its necessity. The first task in this connection is to effect a cut, that is, to differentiate consciousness into attitudes. Only by means of it does phenomenology gain its proper field of inquiry, only thus does it become transcendental. Hence, Husserl's entire enterprise depends upon it. Far more crucial to his thought than this cut, however, is one that centers on belief and thus penetrates deeper than any attitude, precisely to the core of consciousness. It is this core at which he aims, but because the cut that reveals it becomes comprehensible only after the sense of the attitudinal cut has been grasped, it is necessary to start with the latter—which is precisely what Husserl does here.

It is the "entrance-gate of phenomenology" (52) Husserl seeks, and it is in the "Fundamental Phenomenological Consideration" that he finds it, thus in the second division of *Ideas I*, after having established in the first division the primacy of essence over facts and thus of necessity over contingency. The consideration is fundamental for two reasons: insofar as he starts at the beginning for us, "from the natural standpoint, from the world as it is about us, from consciousness as it offers itself in psychological experience" in order to "lay bare the presuppositions essential to that consciousness" (3)—and in fact *the* presupposition that forms the ground of this standpoint—but also insofar as he then intends to disclose the foundation on which knowledge can be firmly based and thus be knowledge *sensu stricto*. He has not yet officially entered into the field of inquiry proper to phenomenology, but remains on its threshold; both of the first two divisions contain preliminary reflections that are decisive for the establishment and advancement of phenomenology. Although these divisions lie outside the formal parameters of Husserl's system, they nevertheless provide the necessary tools for the final two divisions of *Ideas I*, which form the systematic core of that work.

As noted, Husserl's chief aim is to establish a "new eidetics" (58), the key to which is the modification he terms 'epoché'. Yet as long as he has not yet officially effected this modification, his reflections must proceed in the mode of mere eidetic analysis, that is, initially along the lines of the "old" eidetics of the *Logical Investigations*. He is, of course, aware of the epoché from the outset, but he has had to bar himself access to it until the foundation for its performance has been laid. This he does with the aid of a kindred modification of consciousness, the eidetic reduction; within it he gives an account of "natural" consciousness. Since this reduction was already a mainstay of the *Logical Investigations*, one is justified in viewing the epoché, as Husserl himself does, as marking an all-important advance over the methodology employed in that work. From the standpoint of Husserlian phenomenology, three levels of inquiry may be discerned, which are related to one another in an ascending order and which are entailed in this advance: the natural or naive level, the eidetic (which can be permeated by a certain "naturalness"), and the transcendental-phenomenological.[63] Methodologically speaking, Husserl does not progress beyond the version of the phenomenological reduction presented in *Ideas I*. He does, of course, seek to improve his "introduction" into phenomenology repeatedly in his subsequent writings, yet none of his attempts to do so is for its part a "breakthrough" as the discovery of the epoché is, but only a refinement, modification, or supplementation of his original doctrine. The epoché advanced in *Ideas I* is and remains paradigmatic for all other versions of it.[64] It is Husserl's long-sought method; this is the unnamed method he had continually emphasized was needed from the *Prolegomena* until his discovery of the epoché in 1905 and to which he adheres from no later than *The Idea of Phenomenology* and up to the *Crisis*. For him the method is everything, and it is precisely on account of this that he says in his 1930 Afterword to *Ideas* that those who view the phenomenological reduction as "a philosophically irrelevant eccentricity . . . abolish the entire sense of the work and of my phenomenology."[65]

3.1 The Attitudes of Consciousness

Husserl's first achievement on the path to the epoché is to reveal consciousness as consisting of many possible attitudes, which fall into two main groups: natural and pure or transcendental-phenomenological. Both the performance of the epoché and the very possibility thereof are premised on this distinction of consciousness. Whether Husserl actually saw the possibility of the epoché or rather this distinction of consciousness first is not important here—genesis always remains secondary. Procedurally, what comes first is the distinction of consciousness and thus of its particular possibilities. This insight is translated in turn into the modifiability of consciousness. Two types of modification may be discerned provisionally at this point: that of acts and that of attitudes. The latter type is of interest to us here; the former will be addressed in the next chapter.

Possible attitudes correspond to possible worlds. The move from one to the next is the result of the redirection of the ego's attentive gaze (51), which is possible based on "the complexes of my manifoldly changing spontaneities of consciousness" (50). Consciousness, or the ego, is distinct from and yet not independent of every attitude: whereas every attitude is situated within consciousness, none is identical with it; furthermore, the ego stands in a reciprocal relation with its possible and actual attitudes; neither side of this relation can exist without the other. Each attitude determines both *how* consciousness can relate to the world or sphere of activity and *what* world or sphere will be found in the first place. The attitude is, as it were, the lens through which a given world is viewed, though it is more than that.

The predominant attitude, the one that forms the "background" of all other attitudes, the one in which we always already find ourselves as natural beings, is the natural attitude. It stamps our encounter of the "natural" world, in all our acts and comportments in and towards it: all acts—"including the simple ego-acts in which I, in spontaneous advertence and seizing, am conscious of the world as immediately on hand—are embraced by the one Cartesian expression: cogito" (50). This attitude is at base unreflective; in all its dealings, even where it does reflect, an ego in this attitude remains unaware of its ground: "Living along naturally, I live continually in this fundamental form of all 'actional' living, whether I thereby state the cogito, whether I am directed 'reflectively' to the ego and the cogitare, or not. If I am directed to them, then a new cogito is alive, one that for its part is not reflected on and thus is not objectual for me" (50–51). But, as noted, the natural attitude is not the sole attitude; one is not always related only "naturally" to "the" world.[66] Husserl exemplifies this by distinguishing between the natural and the "arithmetical" attitudes: "I busy myself, say, with pure numbers and their laws: nothing like that is on hand in the environing-world, this world of 'real actuality.' The world of numbers is likewise there for me precisely as the Object-field [*Objektfeld*] of arithmetical busiedness . . . but obviously this being-there-for-me [in this attitude], like that which is itself there factually, is of a different kind" (51) than the world and things with which one busies oneself while in the natural attitude.

Viewed individually these attitudes and their respective worlds are completely separate; their only point of contact is in consciousness, for it houses all possible attitudes. Nevertheless, there is a sense in which a kind of hierarchy of attitudes may be said to exist. Namely, the natural attitude remains the predominant attitude; even if one enters into another attitude, one always returns to the natural attitude. Thus: "The arithmetical world is there for me only if, and as long as, I am in the arithmetical attitude. The natural world, however, the world in the usual sense of the word is constantly there for me as long as I live along naturally," that is, in the natural attitude. "None of this need be altered in any way if I appropriate to myself the arithmetical world or other similar 'worlds' by effecting the corresponding attitudes. In that case the natural world remains 'on hand'; I am still in the natural attitude, undisturbed in it by the new attitudes. If my cogito moves only in the worlds proper to these new attitudes, then the natural world remains out of consideration; it is the background for my act-consciousness, but it is not a horizon within which an arithmetical world is situated." All of these "worlds" and their corresponding attitudes, whether arithmetical, natural scientific, psychological, or some other kind, may be reached from the natural attitude. Although they do not lie within it, such attitudes are in a sense rooted in the natural attitude, for with it they share the same basic presupposition.

3.2 The General Thesis

The target of the epoché is nothing less—and nothing more—than *the* fundamental presupposition, or what Husserl terms the 'general thesis' (*Generalthesis*), of the natural attitude. The thesis is the posit of or belief in the existence of the world (*Weltglaube*); it is the defining feature of the natural attitude. In this attitude and thus living in its thesis, we always already move about in the world, with its myriad things, situations, moods, and values: "As my vis-à-vis, I continually find the one spatiotemporal actuality to which I myself belong like all other human beings who are found in it and are related to it like I am. I find this 'actuality,' the word already says it, as a *factually existent* actuality and also accept it as it gives itself to me *as factually existing*. Any doubt about or rejection of givens belonging to the natural world" (52–53) has no affect on this thesis, which always already forms the basis of one's natural approach to such givens.[67] Hence, despite any local disturbances, such as illusion or hallucination, the existence of the world as such never comes into doubt—and never can do so—as long as one is in the natural attitude, which is to say: in a thoroughly pretheoretical, which means here prephilosophical, attitude.[68] Husserl points, for instance, to sophistry, which places the existence of the world in doubt, and to skepticism, which denies the existence of the world (56); they represent positions based on the natural attitude, but are themselves by no means "natural." Such doubt and denial issues entirely from "theory." By contrast, the general thesis is always operative as long as one lives along in the natural attitude, and yet, as Husserl points out, it "does not consist in a particular act, in an articulated judgment about existence" (53), but accompanies "everything that issues from the natural world and of which there is consciousness, experientially and prior to any thinking";[69] everything of which one is conscious in this attitude "bears, in its total unity and with respect to all articulated prominent features in it, the characteristic 'there', 'on hand'."

As long as one lives in the natural attitude, or in the mode termed 'original experiencing', the general thesis remains an "unthematic, unthought, unpredicated" characteristic of all consciousness, and this holds as well for those attitudes that start out from the natural attitude and so participate in the general thesis. This thesis can be raised to the level of an explicit, i.e., predicative, existential judgment, thereby providing a basis for further acts, such as judgment, but originally it is prepredicative, thus potential, inexplicit, and purely experiential. In this way the natural attitude is fundamentally unreflective, for it does not thematize its ground. And yet by means of the eidetic description carried out here—which is reflective in this way and consequently already marks a departure from the natural attitude—Husserl is able to disclose the thetic underpinnings not just of the natural attitude but of consciousness as a whole.[70]

The general thesis is in fact not simply a special case of belief, not merely one among other kinds, but is unique and decisive.[71] The general thesis is distinguished from every other thesis first of all by its scope: it is the belief in the existence of the *world* and thus of all it includes; it is not a specific thesis, but rather a *general* thesis; it does not have one object in view, but rather the world in its entirety, which is to say: in all its indeterminacy. It is just this indeterminacy that distinguishes it from other possible theses, which are always related to something specific.[72] Another main, distinguishing feature of the general thesis is, as has been noted, that it is "unthematic, unthought, unpredicated." As soon as it has been thematized, thought, predicated of *as* a thesis, it ceases to be the "general" or "natural thesis," for reflection upon it necessarily revalues it; as a result of such reflection, it is no longer what it was originally.

Once he has exhibited the attitudinal diversity of consciousness, Husserl's next concern is to demonstrate that it is *possible* to perform the epoché, which excludes, "switches off," or "brackets" the "natural thesis" (53). Only after that *possibility* has been established will Husserl be in a position to make the *necessity* of that cut perspicuous. Thus at the start of the pivotal paragraph (§31) he says: "Now instead of remaining in this [natural] attitude, we want to alter it radically." The change he *wants* to make, the one of whose possibility he wants to convince his readers, is an act of the will. The change to be effected is nothing less than a modification of consciousness—*by* consciousness.[73] The modification in question here is *radical* since it cuts down to the roots. Hence this modification cuts more deeply than other possible modifications of consciousness, such as, for example, representiation, recollection, fantasy. In each of the latter an original act of perception is modified along with the belief peculiar to it. But with the epoché the decisive cut bears on attitudes, not merely on acts, which always take place within a particular attitude. This new cut is made *away* from the natural attitude with the result that access to the phenomenological attitude is gained. However, this move away is not negative, as Husserl is careful to point out: it is not negativity but rather a kind of neutrality that is the motor of his thought.[74] By means of the epoché, he severs consciousness. In doing so, this modification comes into view as a reduction, one that purifies. The severance it effects is one between contingency and necessity, which is mirrored in Husserl's demonstration of the epoché's possibility, followed by that of its necessity. By purifying consciousness of contingency, it wrests (pure) consciousness from the grips of its natural counterpart.

3.3 The Instrumentalization of Cartesian Doubt

Husserl's exposition of the epoché begins with a brief look at the general thesis, since the possibility of the epoché is bound up with its nature. Originally the general thesis is a "potential and inexplicit thesis" (53), one that accompanies every experience, every consciousness-of. But whereas it can be transformed into an actual thesis, it need not be; the explicitness or lack thereof does not affect it in its essence. However, whenever a thesis is thematized, for example by making it the object of a judgment, it undergoes a modification, so that it is no longer effective in the same way it was originally. Since Husserl has already demonstrated the ground of the natural attitude to be an inexplicit *thesis*, he is able to assert of it characteristics that pertain to explicit theses. For, he notes, one can treat such inexplicit theses just as one can treat explicit, judicative theses. It is in this connection that Husserl first appeals to Descartes's attempt to doubt universally; here he sets out on what he will later call the 'Cartesian way to the epoché'.[75]

Cartesian doubt is "one" example of a procedure that can be applied to any thesis, at any time.[76] Descartes's intention, according to Husserl, was to establish "a sphere of absolutely *indubitable* Being" (53); Husserl's intention is a "completely different" one. Nevertheless, this attempt to doubt is to serve Husserl in making his case for the possibility of the epoché, if "only as a methodical expedient for drawing out certain points that, as included in its essence, can be brought to light and made evident by means of it" (54). With the aid of this universal doubt, Husserl is able to discern the limits of our freedom, which are always grounded in essence.[77] We are free to attempt to doubt "anything and everything." What is doubted thereby is, according to the essence of this act, "some 'Being' or other—or predicatively explicated: a 'That exists!', a 'That is how it is!', or something like that." Such doubt bears upon a thesis; at issue in it is not the "way of Being" thematized in the thesis, not *how* something is, but rather *that* it is, *that* it exists—even in the case of an attribute of some thing, say that X 'is red', what is doubted is not that attribute as such but as a Being, namely as being-red. Even the attempt to doubt itself can be doubted—again, as a "Being."[78] Thus acts can be doubted just as easily as "things," for in each case what is doubted is a thesis of Being or existence, whether it is explicit or not.

To this point Husserl has spelled out what we can do, what we are free to do. A limit is set to this freedom, however, by a version of the principle of noncontradiction: "We cannot simultaneously doubt the same material of Being and hold it to be certain." From this limit follows an insight that is decisive for Husserl's entire endeavor: "the attempt to doubt anything of which we are conscious as on hand necessarily causes a certain annulment of the thesis." The attempt to doubt, according to his reading of Descartes, does not lead to "a transformation of thesis into antithesis, of position into negation," nor to "a transformation into presumption, deeming possible, into undecidedness, into a doubt (in whatever sense of the word): nor indeed is anything like that within the realm of our free choice [*Willkür*]." We are not free to subject the thesis of or belief in the Being of whatever it is we are presently conscious of to any modification that effectively negates it, whether outright (as in negation) or potentially (as, for example, in presumption, undecidedness, or doubt), for such a modification would generate an inadmissible contradiction—as long as the fundamental belief has not been annulled, it remains the ground of every modified thesis.[79] And this points to a modification to which, as he stresses, we are indeed free to subject the thesis: "We do not give up the thesis we effected; we do not in any way alter our conviction, which remains in itself as it is as long as we do not introduce any new judicative motives—which we by no means do. And yet the thesis undergoes a modification: while in itself it remains what it is, we, as it were, 'put it out of action,' we 'switch it off,' we 'bracket it.' It is still there, like the bracketed in the brackets, like what has been switched off outside of the context of switching."[80]

The modification effected here is not a further judgment, but an alteration of a thesis founding a (prior) judgment. This modification becomes possible only after that thesis has been thematized, thought, predicated; this itself marks a modification of the thesis, one that identifies the latter precisely *as* a thesis. Thus it is a conscious manipulation of consciousness itself, which always entails reflection.[81] The will is operative here, which Husserl indicates by pointing out that "we can" effect this modification. "We can also say: The thesis is lived experience but we make 'no use' of it, and this of course is not taken as a privation . . . rather, in the case of this expression and all parallel expressions it is a matter of allusive designations of a definite, specifically peculiar mode of consciousness that is added to the simple original thesis (whether it is an actional and even a predicative positing of existence or not) and, likewise in a specifically peculiar manner, revalues it. This revaluation is a matter of our perfect freedom and stands over against all cogitative position-takings coordinate with the thesis and incompatible with the thesis in the unity of the 'simultaneous,' as well as over against all position-taking in the proper sense of the word" (54–55). The "specifically peculiar mode of consciousness" that is *added* to the thesis is the mode that enables phenomenology and is first brought about by the epoché. The epoché is possible precisely because such a mode is possible.

Beyond the modifiability of consciousness it presupposes, what interests Husserl about the attempt to doubt is above all this added mode of consciousness. Insofar as it is "added" to the thesis, the new mode proves to be different than that resulting from modifications such as negation or supposition. Negation changes the sign, as it were, of the thesis and thus of the act, but retains the thesis as its substrate and so does not result in an additional mode of consciousness. Consequently, when one negates in the natural attitude, one remains in the natural attitude. But because the bracketing or exclusion aimed at here *neutralizes* and does not merely negate the general thesis of the natural attitude, it gives rise to a new attitude, specifically the transcendental-phenomenological attitude. Unlike the negated thesis, the neutralized thesis is retained (in brackets) but no use is made of it. It is precisely on account of this fundamental difference that Husserl sets the epoché apart from Descartes's attempt to doubt universally.[82]

But in fact that difference entails two reasons for dispensing with the Cartesian attempt and not simply one: firstly, since Husserl's express intention is to enter into a new field of inquiry, any method that does not bring about the desired entry must be dispensed with; negation does modify consciousness but, as noted, always leaves consciousness in the same attitude; insofar as Descartes's attempt to doubt universally is an attempt to negate universally, it cannot be productive of the desired attitude, leaving the investigator always only in the natural attitude; hence, Descartes's attempt is inadequate for Husserl's purposes. The second reason centers on Husserl's version of the principle of noncontradiction cited above, the corollary of which reads: "we cannot doubt a Being and, in the same consciousness (with the form of unity proper to the simultaneous), grant the substrate of this Being the thesis, thus being conscious of the substrate as 'on hand'" (54). As has been seen, it is precisely the general thesis at which the epoché aims, the thesis that founds the natural world. To negate it would be to fall into countersense. On Husserl's account, Descartes's attempt to doubt universally is an attempt to negate universally, that is, to negate the world and everything in it. However, this is inadmissible on the grounds just cited. The general thesis is not subject to any modalization, such as negation[83]—the modalization of this thesis does not lie within our power[84]—but only to one modification: *neutralization*. As a consequence, Husserl must abandon Descartes's attempt, while nevertheless retaining the exclusion to which it pointed. It is for these reasons that Husserl must begin and proceed *neutrally*, not negatively.[85] Such neutrality constitutes one of the most fundamental traits of his thought, and it alone should already make perspicuous a crucial difference that separates him not only from Descartes but from all of the philosophy of the modern era,[86] for the motor of the latter is negativity whereas in Husserl negativity comes into play only second to neutrality.

The neutralization peculiar to the epoché lies entirely within the limits of our freedom: "With regard to any thesis, we can exercise in complete freedom this peculiar ἐποχή, a certain refraining from judgment[87] that is compatible with the unshaken—and perhaps even unshakable, because evident—conviction of truth" (55). The scope of the possible application of the epoché is limitless; not only can it be applied to *any* thesis, regardless of the degree of certainty ascribed to it, but also: "nothing prevents speaking correlatively of bracketing with respect to a positable objectuality belonging to no matter what region and category. When speaking in this way, we mean that every thesis related to this objectuality is to be switched off and converted into its bracketing modification" (56). Although the possible application is limitless, the aim of its application will determine its actual scope. This is not without its dangers, however, which is why Husserl will find it necessary to restrict the scope of the epoché, a deed also within our power.

3.4 The Attitudinal Leap

The distinction between this modification and those mentioned earlier, that is, negation, supposition, indecision, and doubt, lies in the effect each has on the thesis. In negation, for example, the thesis is still "on hand" *as* negated and can still be used or appealed to, albeit in modified form. By contrast, the neutralized thesis has been bracketed, and as a result we are barred access to it; only by removing the brackets, as it were, can we once again make use of it, for only a "positional" thesis can play a role in consciousness. A further distinction of the epoché from other possible modifications turns on the difference between acts and attitudes. Whereas within one attitude an act and its thesis can be modified indefinitely, presuming it is not neutralized, and whereas one can, as it were, transit from one act to another via such modification, there is no "natural" transition between attitudes, even if between "naturally based" attitudes. Rather, a method is required in each case in order to move between them, a method that always bears upon the underlying thesis of each attitude and performs a cut with respect to that thesis. This is evident from the fact that, as noted above, the general thesis that stamps the natural attitude, both in its potentiality and its actuality, is not an act but a characteristic that accompanies all acts effected in this attitude.

Of primary interest here, however, is the move from the natural to the phenomenological attitude. It is a cut that compels a leap from the one to the other.[88] The leap is based on the intuition of necessity. One has to be brought to the point of seeing not just the *possibility* of effecting the epoché but also the *necessity* of doing so. Possibility is a feature of thought, of its freedom. Necessity precedes thought, determining it and thus the will; it establishes the goal thought aims to fulfill. It is this necessity that motivates Husserl's introductions into phenomenology. Precisely because of the impossibility of making a smooth transition from the natural attitude to the new attitude, he says of his enterprise: "The pure phenomenology to which we want to find the way here, whose unique position with regard to all other sciences we want to characterize, and which we want to demonstrate to be the science fundamental to philosophy, is an essentially new science, one that, due to its principial peculiarity, is remote from natural thinking and *therefore* presses towards development only in our days" (1). This 'therefore' is of central importance, for it points to Husserl's understanding of and relation to the philosophical tradition on the one hand and to the natural attitude on the other. In so doing, it indicates the difference Husserl is convinced his phenomenology makes to life and thought.

He is seeking the path into pure phenomenology—or more precisely: he intends to guide the reader along the path into pure phenomenology—for there is no immediate shift between the natural and the phenomenological attitudes. That is the sense of the 'therefore' above; that is also why Husserl speaks of the "effort" required in order to see the position of phenomenology, and its difference from the other sciences, the effort demanded in order to overcome the "prevailing habits of thinking." An introduction is necessary precisely because of those habits, which are run through with the general thesis, as well as being clouded by theory. Husserl must first open his reader's eyes to the *possibility* of just such a modification of attitude, so that the leap into the phenomenological attitude can be made and the path into phenomenology finally traversed. For this leap a method is required that "defuses" the prevailing attitude.

The method he employs is the "universal 'ἐποχή.'" However, its universality must be restricted, for otherwise everything would be "bracketed," everything "excluded," "no province would be left for unmodified judgments" and theses—there would be nowhere to leap to—which would mean that Husserl's endeavor would be over before it started. To avoid this, to save the domain he is seeking, he must restrict the scope of the epoché: although it *can* be applied to any and every thesis, Husserl singles out *one and only one* thesis: "We put out of action the *general thesis*, which belongs to the essence of the natural attitude; we bracket anything and everything that this thesis encompasses in an ontic respect: thus the whole natural world that is continually 'there for us,' 'on hand,' and that will always remain there for consciousness as an 'actuality' even if we choose to bracket it" (56). The epoché retains its universality since it bears upon the most general thesis. And therein lies the peculiar force of the epoché; it surpasses the effect of negation insofar as the modification brought about by means of the epoché no longer makes use of the modified thesis. In this sense the epoché is a refraining, a kind of abstinence: in excluding the general thesis, it "completely denies me every judgment about spatiotemporal existence," from any judgment about the natural world, including any by or about its sciences, religions, cultures, etc.—but prior to such explicit judgments, it even denies me any inexplicit belief in all of this.

Nothing that has the general thesis as its basis, thus nothing lodged in the natural attitude and its world, survives this cut; nothing is granted its former validity any longer, nor can it now be laid claim to as a foundation. Absolutely "no use" is made of any such validity. Only after the epoché has been performed, after the thesis has been bracketed, and thus only in modified consciousness, can anything from that world be "accepted." Yet the character of such acceptance is radically different from its natural counterpart. In accepting the bracketed world, nothing from that world is retained with its former validity; for the general thesis, which formerly founded everything and guaranteed its validity, has been excluded: "The whole world posited in the natural attitude, actually found in experience, taken in perfect 'freedom from all theory' as it is actually experienced, as it clearly shows itself in the concatenation of experiences, is now entirely without validity for us; without being scrutinized, but also without being contested, it shall be bracketed" (57). Although the epoché thereby puts the belief in the existence of the world out of action, this is but one thesis among others, albeit the most fundamental.

The wish to restrict the scope of the epoché, however, points to the importance of not excluding *all* belief: "But it is with good reason that we limit the universality of this [universal] ἐποχή. For if it were as comprehensive as possible—since every thesis or every judgment can be modified with complete freedom, since every judgeable objectuality can be bracketed—then no province would be left any longer for unmodified judgments, to say nothing of [a province for] science" (56). The negation proper to the Cartesian attempt to doubt universally negates the world. But the thesis remains, specifically as an antithesis. Husserl has revealed here a modification of consciousness that does not actively retain the thesis but "puts it out of action." That is what is radical about his phenomenology and what separates him from Descartes, despite all appearances of kinship, despite Husserl's own appeals to him.[89]

3.5 The Family of Reductions

The epoché belongs to a class of modifications of consciousness Husserl terms 'reduction'. It has two types: natural, as we may call those that in some way bear on natural actuality, and phenomenological reductions. Those belonging to the former type—for example, the arithmetical, geometrical, and physicalistic reductions—give rise to new attitudes on which individual fields of inquiry or sciences are based—in this case, those of arithmetic, geometry, and physics, respectively. They do so by restricting the investigator's regard to some part of actuality, and as a consequence each new field of inquiry continues to be based upon the general thesis, or the belief in the existence of the world. By contrast, the first phenomenological reduction Husserl introduces, the epoché, aims precisely at that thesis and thus bears on the whole of natural actuality. It sets this thesis and it alone out of action, thereby giving rise to the phenomenological attitude. In this the epoché proves to be a reduction that is literally a world apart from the others. And yet Husserl also says that the epoché can be applied to *any* thesis, which would seem to suggest that its scope of application can extend beyond the general thesis—would each application then produce a new phenomenological attitude? Or should this perhaps be taken to mean that there are multiple epochai, each of which may give rise to a new attitude? This would seem to be confirmed by Husserl's remark that the method or operation of the epoché has "different steps of 'excluding,' 'bracketing'" and as a result assumes "the character of a step-by-step reduction" (59).

It is in view of these different steps that Husserl speaks of a multiplicity of phenomenological reductions. They are transcendental and as such bear on a field that lies beyond or beneath—insofar as it is more original than—the actuality of concern to the individual, nonphenomenological sciences. Whereas both types of reduction seek to reduce to what is necessary, only the phenomenological reductions reduce to what is absolute, thus enabling a mode of inquiry free of the contingency that besets the sciences arising from what we have referred to as the natural reductions. On account of this, the field of phenomenological inquiry is said to encompass every other field. But the questions remain: What is the effect of the multiplicity of phenomenological reductions?

Are there multiple phenomenological attitudes? The answer to these questions is to be gained only by way of an explication of the sense in which the method of epoché represents a step-by-step reduction, which first requires the ascertainment of both the relation of the epoché to the other phenomenological reductions and the scope of the epoché.

The epoché is a unique reduction over against every other. To underscore its radicality, Husserl says that the epoché "annihilates" the world.[90] After effecting this reduction, the world is no longer there for us as it was in the natural attitude; strictly speaking, it no longer exists. However, the target of this reduction is primarily not the spatiotemporally, psychophysically, or physicalistically existent world, not some thing-in-itself, but rather the *thesis* of or the *belief* in the Being of the natural world. The talk of 'annihilation' or 'exclusion' tends to conceal not only this, but especially that the epoché's principal sense is not simply negative but rather neutralizing: it is our belief in the existence of the world that is annihilated insofar as it is neutralized. On account of this, its effect is at once purifying and inaugural: "The exclusion of nature"—that is, the natural world—"was for us the methodical means for making it at all possible to turn the regard to transcendentally pure consciousness" (108). This sphere, or rather the belief in it,[91] is excluded as a transcendence with the result that the wholly new sphere of consciousness comes into view; the epoché reduces thereby from a transcendent to an immanent sphere, and in fact to the absolute sphere of pure consciousness, which is pure precisely because it has been freed of any dependence on transcendencies. As a consequence, the scope of this epoché extends beyond the natural world to all that it includes. It puts out of action "all individual objectualities that are constituted by valuing and practical functions of consciousness . . . all the kinds of cultural formations, all works of the technical and fine arts, of the sciences (insofar as they come into question as cultural facts rather than as unities of validity), aesthetic and practical values in every form. Likewise, of course, such actualities as the state, custom, law, religion. Hence, all the natural sciences and humanities, with their total stock of cognitions, undergo exclusion precisely *as sciences that require the natural attitude*." In other words, all of these are excluded precisely because they are transcendencies based on the *general thesis*. The epoché is applied to this thesis and it alone; the world, and all it includes, is excluded all at once.

The talk of a step-by-step reduction, and thus of a multiplicity of phenomenological reductions, becomes relevant only after Husserl has effected the epoché and gained access to pure consciousness. They become important relative to transcendencies that are not affected by the epoché; in this connection he asks what must be excluded beyond the general thesis in order to retain consciousness in its purity as a field of inquiry.[92] This already indicates the chief distinction between the epoché and the other phenomenological reductions:

the former opens up the pure field of inquiry, whereas the latter are to preserve this field in its purity. Like the epoché, however, they are reductions from transcendence to immanence and thus, in a certain sense, from impurity to purity, from contingency to necessity and absoluteness. Each reduction effects the exclusion of a thesis pertaining to some transcendency. But what could possibly remain after the general thesis has been excluded? To answer this question is to clarify "what must remain excluded for the purpose of an investigation of pure consciousness and whether the necessary exclusion concerns only the sphere of nature." This clarification will in turn fix the sense in which the talk can be of a multiplicity of phenomenological reductions and further confirm what has been said about the epoché's scope.

3.5.1 The Pure Ego. Husserl notes a "limit-point [*Grenzpunkt*]" in the application of the epoché, namely the human being: it is excluded "as a natural being and as a person in personal association" just as is "every other animal being" (109). But by reducing to the "stream of pure consciousness," not only the stream remains but also reflection upon its lived experiences, where "each effected cogitatio has the explicit form cogito." The pure ego is active in each cogito,[93] even though it can be found nowhere in the stream itself, "in the flux of manifold lived experiences that remains as a transcendental residuum—neither as one lived experience among others, nor as a proper part of a lived experience, arising and then disappearing with the lived experience of which it were a part. The ego seems to be continuously, even necessarily, there and this continuousness is obviously not that of a stupidly persistent lived experience, a 'fixed idea.' Rather, the ego belongs to each lived experience as it comes and flows away; its 'regard' is passes 'through' each actional cogito to the objectual item. This ray of regard changes with every cogito, shooting forth anew with each new cogito and vanishing with it. The ego, however, is identical. At least, considered principially, every cogito can change, can come and go, even though one may doubt whether every cogito is necessarily transitory and not merely, as we find it, factually transitory. By contrast, however, the pure ego seems to be principially necessary; and, as absolutely identical throughout every actual or possible change in lived experiences, it cannot in any sense be regarded as a really inherent [*reell*] part or moment of the lived experiences themselves." The reduction to immanence is a reduction to the stream of lived experiences, which is also to say, to real inherence. And anything that is not really inherent in that stream is transcendent to it, although not necessarily in the same sense in which the natural world is transcendent.

The ego is therefore transcendent to the stream, but necessarily "involved" with it: "If we retain a pure ego (and then a principially different one for each stream of lived experiences) as a residuum of the phenomenological exclusion of the world and the empirical subjectivity included in it, then there is presented in the case of that ego a transcendency of a peculiar kind—

one that is not constituted—a transcendency within immanence" (109–10). The life of the ego is lived in the continual shift of regard, from one actional cogito to another, in which one lived experience is singled out while another allowed to fall back into the background that always belongs to the ego, the background that the stream of lived experiences is. The ego is not excluded, although in many cases "the questions of the pure ego can remain *in suspenso*" (110), for example when of concern is the object regarded or the regard itself but not the source of the ray of regard. Although it is possible to do so, the pure ego, as an immanent transcendence, may not be excluded, for doing so would eliminate the phenomenological enterprise. The pure ego thus marks the sole exception to every phenomenological reduction. Everything beyond it and its consciousness is excluded: "But we want to count the pure ego as a phenomenological datum only as far as its immediate, evidently ascertainable essential peculiarity and its givenness along with pure consciousness extends, whereas all doctrines [*Lehren*] about it that exceed those limits are to undergo exclusion." (Such doctrines about the ego are excluded precisely because they are grounded in the natural thesis and consequently treat the ego as a component part of the natural world.)

3.5.2 The Preliminary Exclusion of God. Beyond the pure ego, Husserl considers three other transcendencies: God, as well as the formal-eidetic and the material-eidetic spheres. Unlike that of the pure ego, the transcendence proper to God is "not given immediately in union with reduced consciousness but comes to be known in a highly mediated fashion, it being, as it were, *the polar opposite* of the transcendence proper to the world." Because this "extra-worldly" divine being in no way has its basis in the general thesis, the epoché does not touch the thesis pertaining to it. Nevertheless, although it would transcend both the world and absolute consciousness, although this being "would therefore be an 'absolute' in a totally different sense than that in which consciousness is an absolute, just as it would be transcendent in a totally different sense than that in which the world is transcendent" (111), it must be excluded here, for it lacks the requisite immediacy of the kind of transcendence proper to the pure ego: "Of course, we extend the phenomenological reduction to include this 'absolute' and 'transcendent' [being]. It shall remain excluded from the new field of inquiry that is to be established, since this shall be a field of pure consciousness itself." Husserl does not want to rule out the existence of God; he does not negate the belief in the same—note the subjunctive mood in his circumscription of the pertinent sense of absoluteness and transcendence. On the contrary, he says repeatedly in his correspondence, for example, that the "problem of God" is what he most yearns to deal with. But it lies in the heights, and he must begin with the ground.[94] The absoluteness of consciousness, of its stream, is the measure here; this is the foundation on which he must build. Anything that transcends it, and does not have the immediate relation to it that the pure ego has, must be subjected to a phenomenological reduction.

Before proceeding, however, Husserl once again voices a concern about the scope of reduction: "As in the case of individual realities in every sense, we now attempt to exclude all other kinds of 'transcendencies' as well. This concerns the series of 'universal' objects, of essences. After all, they too are 'transcendent' to pure consciousness in a certain manner; they are not to be found as really inherent within it. Nevertheless, we cannot go on excluding transcendencies without limit; transcendental purification cannot mean the exclusion of all transcendencies, since even though a pure consciousness would remain, no possibility of a *science* of pure consciousness would remain." His expression of concern points to a qualification. Husserl cannot exclude everything if he wishes to retain a region for his new science. So nothing can be excluded at the expense of that science. Thus far, in addition to absolute consciousness, only the pure ego in its immanent transcendence has been retained. Both of them are necessary for that science. Essences would also seem necessary, but for the same reason, in view of the same measure as in the case of the transcendence of God, Husserl sees himself bound to subject a certain kind of essence to a further reduction.

3.5.3 The Exclusion of the Formal-Eidetic Disciplines. Already as a result of the epoché, all the regional ontologies concerned with individual Being were excluded. And now beyond these, "formal logic and consequently all the disciplines of formal mathesis" must be excluded. Although they may at first seem indispensable to any science, those formal disciplines prove superfluous wherever the problems that phenomenology sets for itself in investigating pure consciousness do not exceed "those of descriptive analysis that are to be solved in pure intuition" (112–13). The formal-eidetic disciplines are all mediate, whereas intuition is immediate. Wherever the principle of all principles is in force, thus wherever it is the things themselves that provide the guidelines for description, a formal eidetics is unnecessary. To appeal to any such discipline would be to violate the principle. Therefore the exclusion of those disciplines does not impair in any way the science Husserl wishes to establish: "Now phenomenology is indeed a purely descriptive discipline that explores in pure intuition the field of transcendentally pure consciousness. The only propositions of logic to which phenomenology might ever have occasion to refer would therefore be simply logical axioms, like the principle of noncontradiction, axioms the universal and absolute validity of which it would be able to bring to insight, however, by means of examples provided by its own givens" (113)—they can be demonstrated in an original manner, and without recourse to those disciplines. "Thus we can include in the explicitly excluding ἐποχή formal logic and mathesis in its entirety"—however, this epoché is not to be confounded with the incipient epoché that bears solely on the general thesis; rather, what Husserl at this point refers to as an epoché is such by analogy to the first. Here he effects a phenomenological reduction that excludes specifically the thesis pertaining to the formal-eidetic disciplines and, by extension, their objects. The justification Husserl provides for this exclusion is in fact a corollary of the principle of all principles: "To lay claim to nothing except what we can bring essentially to insight with respect to consciousness itself in pure immanence." Phenomenology in Husserl's sense must therefore be independent of any discipline that does not abide by this principle.[95]

3.5.4 The Exclusion of the Material-Eidetic Spheres. The final phenomenological reduction discussed in this context excludes the material-eidetic spheres—that is, all of them except for one: "the eidetic sphere of phenomenologically purified consciousness." It is, after all, Husserl's express intention to found phenomenology itself as an eidetic science.[96] Yet it is distinguished from other eidetic sciences in that it is concerned solely with immanent essences; not all essences are immanent, but some are transcendent. Once again, the reduction is to immanence: "If we want to develop a phenomenology as a purely descriptive eidetic doctrine of the immanent formations of consciousness, the occurrences in the stream of lived experiences that can be seized upon within the parameters of the phenomenological exclusion, then nothing that is transcendently individual, and therefore none of the 'transcendent essences,' belong within those parameters. Such essences would instead have their logical place in the eidetic doctrine of the relevant transcendent objectualities" (114). What is excluded by this phenomenological reduction is precisely the thesis pertaining to transcendent essences: "in its immanence" the new eidetics at which Husserl aims "in no way posits the Being of *such* essences, makes no statements about their validity or invalidity, or about the ideal possibility of objectualities corresponding to them, and establishes no eidetic laws relating to them." As in the case of the formal essences, Husserl "broadens the phenomenological reduction" here also to include all provinces of transcendent, material essences along with all the ontologies, and so the sciences, pertaining to them (114–15). By means of the repeated reduction to immanence, to absolute consciousness, which is its proper field of inquiry, Husserl has sought to show phenomenology to be independent of every science, not just of the natural sciences, but also of the formal-eidetic and material-eidetic sciences. The result of the foregoing treatment of the reductions is thus threefold: the specification of the scope of the incipient epoché, a first indication of the sense and effect of the additional phenomenological reductions, and finally the first determination of the sense in which phenomenology is First Science, a topic that will be developed in greater detail in the final section of this chapter.

3.6 The Primacy of the Universal Epoché

From Husserl's analyses the relation between the epoché and the other reductions becomes clear: "The foregoing extensions of the phenomenological reduction obviously do not have the fundamental significance that attaches to the original exclusion merely of the natural world and the sciences related to it. It is, after all, *this first reduction* that *makes it possible in the first place* to turn the regard to the phenomenological field and seize upon what is given there. Because they presuppose the first, *the other reductions are secondary;* but that does not mean that they have less significance" (115). The epoché is fundamental because it opens up the new field; the other reductions are secondary since they are effected from within that field. They are no less important because they help keep this field free of impurities, of illegitimate borrowings or importations from other fields: "Their explicit 'bracketings' have the methodical function of continually reminding us that the spheres of Being and cognition in question lie principially outside those that, as transcendental-phenomenological, are to be explored, and that any intrusion of premises from those bracketed provinces is an indication of a countersensical confusion, a genuine μετάβασις." The boundaries between the various regions must be kept intact; and just that is the function of the post-epoché reductions. They are reminders that there can be no smooth transition from one attitude and its corresponding region to the next, for example from the natural to the phenomenological attitude; there is no possibility of a more or less immediate transition between them.

In fact it is the phenomenological field that is the most difficult to see, according to Husserl; and that is why the method of epoché is so important to his enterprise: "Were the province of phenomenology to present itself with such immediate obviousness as do the provinces proper to the attitude of natural experience, or were it to arise through a mere transition from the latter to the eidetic attitude, as, for example, the province of geometry does when one sets out from the empirically spatial, then there would be no need of involved reductions with the difficult deliberations they involve. Nor would there be any need to take pains to differentiate the individual steps were it not for the constant temptations to [commit] a fallacious *metabasis*, particularly in the interpretation of objectualities proper to the eidetic disciplines. They are such strong temptations that they threaten even him who has freed himself from generally prevalent misconceptions with regard to individual provinces" (115–16). Hence the need to remind oneself over and over again. One is always in danger of falling out of the phenomenological attitude and committing a *metabasis*. It is only with the greatest effort that one can free oneself of one's in-born dogmatism—which is to say, naturalness—and begin living in the phenomenological attitude. And yet even after one has taken on this new life, the threat of falling back into naturalness always remains. The multiplicity of phenomenological reductions are meant to preserve the effect of the original epoché and assure continued inquiry in the new attitude.

The path Husserl has followed in the foregoing analyses has two stages: "first of all a universal legitimization of the eidetic as such and then, in the context of the doctrine of phenomenological reduction, the specific exclusion of the eidetic," that is, of "the eidetics of transcendent individual objectualities in every sense" (116). This reiterates the operation employed throughout the development of those chapters of *Ideas I* meant to demonstrate the possibility of the epoché, and it will be employed in those chapters aimed at demonstrating its necessity. It is the repeated distinction between transcendence and immanence, and then the reduction from the former to the latter. This marks the breakthrough peculiar to *Ideas I*: "another great step forward is taken—one that by no means occurs automatically with the first—when the momentous differentiation that we briefly designated as that between immanent and transcendent essences, is recognized and consistently taken into consideration everywhere. On the one hand, essences of formations belonging to consciousness itself; on the other, essences of individual occurrences transcendent to consciousness, thus the essences of what is only 'manifested' in formations proper to consciousness, of what is 'constituted' in the manner peculiar to consciousness, for example, by means of sensuous appearances" (116–17). In reducing to absolute consciousness, Husserl is first able to account for the constitution of transcendent objectualities, something, as he notes, he had difficulties seeing in the *Logical Investigations* (117). The epoché is instrumental in bringing the relation of the two spheres to light. The struggle to keep this insight in view is one even the experienced phenomenologist cannot avoid. Only by means of the practical consciousness effected by the phenomenological reductions, namely an awareness of what does not belong in the field of phenomenological inquiry, can "we protect ourselves methodically against these confusions [between different regions], which are so deeply rooted in us as born dogmatists that we could not otherwise avoid them" (117). The insight into the absoluteness of consciousness, as well as into how it is to be demonstrated, points to the sense in which phenomenology is First Science: "It is the distinctive peculiarity of phenomenology to encompass within the scope of its eidetic universality all cognitions and sciences and in fact with respect to everything in them that is a matter of immediate insight, or at least would have to be such if they were genuine cognitions" (118). Phenomenology has this status only as a result of the universal epoché.

4. The Field of Phenomenological Inquiry: Pure Consciousness

After having established the *possibility* of performing the epoché, which is to say, after having elucidated its sense, it remains for Husserl to elucidate its "possible effect [*mögliche Leistung*]" (57) and thereby its *necessity*. He already indicated the direction his analyses must take when he restricted the scope of the epoché; this he did expressly so as to save pure consciousness as the region of phenomenological inquiry. It is precisely the "residuum" of this restriction that he pursues in his subsequent analyses. In clarifying the sense of that restriction and the residuum to which it gives rise, Husserl seeks to motivate the necessity of the epoché. This methodical device proves to be more than a mere possibility—and for Husserl it is *the* possibility—as soon as the weight of its effect or achievement is grasped.

4.1 The Phenomenological Residuum

To begin with, Husserl approaches the "residuum" from the standpoint of the natural attitude, which may seem surprising at first given that, on the one hand, his stated goal is "the acquisition of a new region of Being never before delimited in its own peculiarity, a region that, like every other genuine region, is a region of individual Being" (58), while, on the other hand, the natural attitude allows of no immediate access to the new region: "In the natural attitude nothing but the natural world can be seen" (59). If this apparent shift back to the natural attitude seems surprising, then it is because Husserl has just shown the epoché to be possible. The epoché does indeed provide him with the method he needs in order to enter that new region of Being; the purity achieved by means of the epoché is the dividing line between the natural attitude and the new one he seeks. On account of this, Husserl initially designates the Being ultimately of concern to phenomenology, "for essential reasons, as 'pure lived experiences,' 'pure consciousness' with its pure 'correlates of consciousness,' and on the other hand its 'pure ego'" (58). Yet the renewed emphasis of the natural attitude does not mark a regression, for thus far in his analyses Husserl has never left the standpoint of the natural attitude, even while explicating the sense of the epoché.

In fact, due to the primacy of the principle of all principles in his thought and his related intention to avoid all theory, Husserl is obliged to begin his analyses *outside* the epoché, and he must remain outside of it until he has made its necessity evident. Thus—beginning with what is first for us, as it gives itself to us—he approaches "the ego, the consciousness, and the lived experiences that are given to us in the natural attitude." Here he proceeds "by direct demonstration," all the while abiding by the "universal principle that every individual occurrence has its essence, which can be seized upon in eidetic purity and, in this purity, must belong to a field of possible eidetic inquiry" (60). Although Husserl begins his investigations from the standpoint of the natural attitude, he does not proceed entirely naturally—already the thematization of consciousness in this attitude shows it to be un-natural. He undertakes an eidetic analysis that still rests on the general thesis and so in this sense is permeated by naturalness; as a result, he may be said to proceed here in the mode of the "old" eidetics. However, such an analysis is pure—thereby testifying to its un-naturalness—to the extent that it considers consciousness *immanently* and with a view to ascertaining its *essence*. This is possible within the natural attitude, but it nevertheless remains bound up with the latter.

These analyses are preparatory for the entrance into the new region of Being, that is, pure consciousness, and thus for the establishment of a "new eidetics," one that differs radically from its predecessor. An understanding of its newness, and thereby of the radicality of Husserl's enterprise, cannot be gained immediately, for there is no "natural" transition between the two regions in question here. Rather, the foundation must be laid in the natural attitude for the necessary leap from it into the new region.

In the natural attitude, Husserl notes, I find myself and others as objects in the natural world. And I even consider my acts of consciousness and any other lived experiences to be "occurrences within the same natural actuality" (58). I one-sidedly view the "real world" as the sole sphere of Being. "It is so natural for us to see [the findings of psychological reflection] only as [real worldly occurrences] that now, already acquainted with the possibility of an altered attitude"—the means of attaining which was, after all, introduced as a modification *of* and *by* consciousness—"and searching for the new Object-province, we do not even notice that it is from these very spheres of lived experiences that the new province springs by means of the new attitude." Instead, caught up in the one-sidedness of the natural attitude, we have been in the habit of looking beyond these spheres to others—he points to those of arithmetic and geometry as examples—and their objects. Husserl's resolution is to "keep our regard fixed on the sphere of consciousness and study what we find *immanently* within it" (59), thus without giving priority to "actuality," but rather starting from consciousness itself as it gives itself. Because the focus is to be on immanence, the first step required is a "systematic eidetic analysis" of consciousness: "What we need most is a certain universal insight into the essence of consciousness as such and especially of consciousness insofar as it becomes in itself, by its essence, conscious of 'natural' actuality." The goal of this analysis is to bring his readers to "the insight that consciousness has, in itself, a Being of its own"—contrary to the habits of thinking—"that in its own *absolute* essence is not affected by the phenomenological exclusion." As such it will prove to be the residuum of the epoché sought by Husserl as the field of inquiry proper to phenomenology. "The 'phenomenological' ἐποχή will earn its name only by means of this insight; the fully conscious effectuation of that ἐποχή will prove to be the operation necessary to make 'pure' consciousness, and subsequently the whole phenomenological region, accessible to us."

Husserl begins eidetically in order to demonstrate the epoché because the only compelling necessity is essential necessity.

4.2 The Modifiability of Consciousness I: Actionality and Inactionality

Still in the natural attitude, Husserl begins with "a psychological reflection on our ego and its lived experiencing [*Erleben*]" (60). His concern thereby is to elaborate "the essence of the 'consciousness of something'" in its purity. Because he seeks to do so by means of immanent or pure eidetic analysis, or what he also calls 'ideation', the natural world vanishes altogether, for it has no immediate bearing upon his considerations in this context. He is not interested in a specific kind of consciousness but in "any lived experience whatsoever of consciousness."[97] He takes the Cartesian term 'cogito', the 'I think', in the broadest sense as his starting point, while initially leaving aside the 'I' or ego of the 'I think', to which all the lived experiences encompassed by the latter are related.[98] Instead, the focus is on the 'think': "We consider the lived experiences of consciousness in the complete fullness of the concreteness within which they appear in their concrete concatenation—the stream of lived experiences—and that, by virtue of their own essence, they combine to make up" (61). Thus the inquiry here has two reciprocally related foci: the individual lived experience in its essence and the unity of consciousness, which is the unity of the stream of lived experiences, the stream from which the individual lived experience may be picked out by our attentive gaze.[99]

Husserl begins with the individual lived experience and its relation to the stream in which it belongs. He thereby draws out a fundamental distinction of consciousness, namely that between actionality (*Aktualität*) and inactionality (*Inaktualität*). It is a distinction of regard or attention. An example of such a lived experience is the "perceptual seeing and touching of a sheet of paper."[100] The seeing and touching of it is a cogitatio. But the sheet itself is not; rather, it is the cogitatum—that is, "it is not a lived experience of perception but something perceived" (62). Furthermore, this perception proves to be a unique kind of selection: "In authentic [*eigentlich*] perceiving, as an attentive perceiving, I am turned towards the object, for example, the sheet of paper; I seize upon it as this existent here and now. The seizing-upon is a singling out," thereby wresting the object from "an experiential background." Thus in perceiving the sheet of paper, the desk on which it is lying fades into the background, just as does the lamp lighting it, etc. "Every perception of a physical thing has, in this way, a halo of background-intuitions . . . and that is also a 'lived experience of consciousness' or, more concisely, 'consciousness,' and in fact 'of' everything that indeed lies in the objectual 'background' seen along with it." Consciousness is accordingly of the object on the one hand and of the "halo" on the other. This indicates a possible modification of consciousness: I am free to shift my regard from one object to another of which I was previously conscious, though only "implicitly" conscious of it insofar as it was part of the "halo"; in directing my gaze to it, in becoming "explicitly" conscious of it, I let the object to which I formerly attended fall back into the background from which it was originally singled out. This modification is not confined to objects of perception, however, but also holds for objects of other acts, such as those of recollection, representiation, and fantasy: "to the essence of all such lived experiences—these always taken in full concreteness—there belongs that noteworthy modification that converts consciousness in the mode of actional advertence into consciousness in the mode of inactionality, and vice versa. At one time the lived experience is, so to speak, 'explicit' consciousness of its objectual item, at another time it is implicit, merely potential" (63). That an actional lived experience is always surrounded by a halo of inactional (*inaktuell*) lived experiences is a principial feature of consciousness, for "the stream of lived experiences can never consist of just actionalities." Actionality is the defining feature of the cogito.

In this connection Husserl reintroduces the ego as the "wakeful ego." It is an ego "that, within its stream of lived experiences, continuously effects consciousness in the specific form of the cogito"—that is, as an actionality surrounded by a halo of inactionalities—"which, of course, does not mean that it constantly gives, or is at all able to give, predicative expression to these lived experiences. There are, after all, also bestial ego-subjects" (63–64). Especially this latter remark makes it quite clear that Husserl aims to describe the essence of consciousness in general, and not simply human consciousness. These features are constitutive of every wakeful ego, whether human or bestial. Even if they remain "unthematic, unthought, unpredicated," lived experiences remain lived experiences. As will become clear, predication always presupposes this founding level of nonpredication for Husserl, and in fact in a manner akin to the way in which an actionality presupposes inactionalities, and conversely.

Actional and inactional consciousness are bound together in a "significant community of essence"; they are both modes of consciousness and as such share the same basic essential determination: "Universally it belongs to the essence of every actional cogito to be consciousness of something. In its way, however . . . the modified cogitatio is likewise consciousness, and [consciousness] of the same thing as is the corresponding unmodified consciousness. Thus the universal essential property of consciousness is preserved in the modification" (64). Although priority is given to actional consciousness in this context, for it is referred to as unmodified consciousness whereas inactionality is deemed to be modified consciousness, these two modes are in fact reciprocally related. Neither has absolute priority over the other; rather, together they form an inseverable unity. And yet conceptually consciousness first gains its proper sense for us from actionality, although inactionality would seem to be first by nature insofar as the stream of lived experiences harbors any individual lived experience to be singled out by an actional cogito and insofar as we are always already conscious (inactionally) of that stream prior to effecting the cogito. We shall have occasion to discuss the relation between the cogito and its stream in greater detail below. For now it is sufficient to note that actional consciousness is the canonical (*maßgeblich*) but not the exclusive mode of consciousness.

4.3 The Modifiability of Consciousness II: Intentionality

Particularly in view of the canonical mode, it becomes most obvious what binds these two modes of consciousness together, namely a fundamental feature that Husserl terms 'intentionality'[101]: "All lived experiences that have these essential properties"—that is, those of actional and inactional consciousness as just elaborated—"in common are also called 'intentional lived experiences' (acts in the broadest sense of the *Logical Investigations*); insofar as they are consciousness of something, they are said to be 'intentionally referred' to this something." Here, too, a relation is crucial to Husserl's analyses of consciousness—his distinctions are always aimed at elucidating essential, fundamental relations, which is to say, he thinks, as it were, always "two-sidedly" or "correlatively," contrary to the habits of thinking with which he sees himself faced. The intentional reference of a lived experience marks one side of the relation; the other side is the something referred to: "In the essence of a lived experience itself lies not only that it is consciousness but also whereof it is consciousness, and in what determinate or indeterminate sense it is so." Such gradation of determinacy is an essential feature of consciousness, just as is the modifiability of consciousness, to which those gradations are intimately related; both the gradation and the modifiability have their source in the stream of lived experiences that is consciousness. "Therefore what kind of actional cogitationes inactional consciousness can be converted into by the modification . . . we characterize as a 'turning of heeding regard to the formerly unheeded' also lies implicit in the essence of inactional consciousness" (64–65). In fact, the essence of this consciousness entails a predelineation of what can be transformed from implicitness into explicitness, just as every essence necessarily predelineates what is possible for that of which it is an essence.

Extending the distinction between actionality and inactionality, between implicitness and explicitness, Husserl further refines his notion of lived experience: "By lived experience in the broadest sense we understand anything and everything to be found in the stream of lived experiences; thus not only the intentional lived experiences, the actional and potential cogitationes taken in their full concreteness, but also whatever is to be found in the way of really inherent moments in this stream and its concrete parts" (65). Intentionality is an essential possibility of consciousness, but just as no stream can be made up of actionalities alone, neither can it be made up of intentional lived experiences alone. Consequently, "not every really inherent moment in the concrete unity of an intentional lived experience itself has the fundamental characteristic of intentionality, thus the property of being 'consciousness of something.'" Rather, there are certain really inherent components of which there is no consciousness but are "bearers of an intentionality." Husserl points to such a bearer as the datum 'white' in the perceptual lived experience of the white sheet of paper. Nevertheless, anything and everything that is really inherent in the stream of consciousness can be transformed into an intentional lived experience by a shift of regard to it, such as from the sheet of paper to the datum 'white'.

The actionality proper to the cogito is the originally simple, immanent regard of an object. This regard "wells forth from the 'ego,' which therefore can never be lacking." And yet, although its regard takes on the character of the act that is the cogito (perception, fantasying, etc.), that regard is not itself an act of its own, not a perceiving, a heeding, or a seizing upon; it is the mere consciousness or awareness of something in which that something remains unthematized, unthought, unpredicated. Thus Husserl distinguishes the intentional object from the object seized upon. At the level of consciousness directed to an intentional object, this consciousness has not been made explicit as such, but in a sense remains implicit. However, the originary mode of consciousness can be modified, that is, a perceiving, heeding, or seizing regard can be directed to it as consciousness, in which case that consciousness and its object are objectified, wrested, as it were, from their originary context and thematized. This new act is founded on, added to the original act; to overlook these essential differences is to miss the crux of Husserl's eidetic analysis: the modifiability of consciousness by new acts that are always founded on certain original acts.

Husserl sums up the relations within such a modification as follows: "In each act a mode of heedfulness holds sway. But whenever the act is not a simple consciousness of a thing, whenever there is founded on such a consciousness a further consciousness in which 'a position is taken' with respect to the thing, then thing and full intentional Object [*Objekt*] (for example, 'thing' and 'value'), likewise heeding and having-the-mind's-eye-on, arise separately" (67).—The new level retains the former level as its foundation; as a consequence, there is a kind of split in the object: in this case, the perceived thing and the new valued thing or value.—"But at the same time the essence of these founded acts involves the possibility of a modification by which their full intentional Objects become heeded and, in this sense, 'objectivized' objects, which are then, for their part, capable of serving as substrates for explications, relations, conceptual apprehensions, and predications. Thanks to this objectivation, in the natural attitude, and therefore as members of the natural world, we stand opposite not mere things of nature but values and practical Objects of every kind"—*in infinitum*.

4.4 Immanent and Transcendent Perception

In the foregoing, Husserl presented the initial levels of a stratified consciousness, having begun with the original mode of regard shared by actionality and inactionality. It is noteworthy that in the modification of consciousness in which a shift between actional and inactional lived experiences continuously occurs, no change of level takes place, but essentially the same relation between the ego and its stream of lived experiences is maintained throughout. The effect of this modification is, so to speak, a "horizontal" move from one singled out lived experience to another. As just mentioned, however, new levels may be achieved by moving "vertically," that is, by seizing upon the cogito as intentional object, that is, through reflection: "While living in the cogito, we are not conscious of the cogitatio itself as an intentional Object, but at any time it can become such; to the cogitatio's essence belongs the principial possibility of a 'reflective' turning of regard and naturally in the form of a new cogitatio that is directed to it in the manner proper to a cogitatio that simply seizes upon" (67). To reflect on a cogito means that one no longer "lives" in that cogito; rather, it becomes the cogitatio of another cogito. One now lives in the reflection but not in what is reflected upon—for one can live only *in* the actional lived experience and not in the object of the lived experience (even if that object is itself a lived experience). Such reflection marks a modification of consciousness, of the way in which one is "conscious of" something; it is a modification that may be repeated—or as he later says: iterated—indefinitely. Thus a perception can become the object of the reflective act of recollection, which can itself become the object of a further recollection, fantasy, or some other act, and so on. Every reflection, or what Husserl refers to provisionally as 'internal perception', effects a modification of consciousness and only of consciousness.

The chief characteristics of reflection make it clear that it represents a kind of perception radically different from so-called external perception, which is dominant in the natural attitude. Husserl couches this distinction more fittingly in terms of immanent and transcendent acts. Of the former, he says: "By immanently directed acts, or more generally formulated: by intentional lived experiences referring to something immanent, we understand those to which it is essential that their intentional objects, if they exist at all, belong to the same stream of lived experiences to which they themselves belong" (68). This type of lived experience is distinguished by the fact that the "consciousness and its Object form an individual unity established purely by lived experiences." This does not hold for the intentional lived experiences of something transcendent, such as essences, "intentional lived experiences of other egos with different streams of lived experiences," or "physical things or realities of whatever kind." And yet, even though there is no unity in the manner proper to immanent perception, in transcendent perception there is nevertheless a certain community of essence between perception and the perceived. We shall address this shortly. For now it is important to note the uniqueness of immanent acts, but especially that among such acts, immanent perception holds a distinctive position: in it "perception and perceived form essentially an *unmediated* unity, that of a single concrete cogitatio." The lack of mediation will prove decisive in Husserl's motivation of the necessity of making the leap into pure consciousness, that is, of effecting the epoché. Crucial at this point is that what is perceived is "contained" in the perception: "This kind of really inherent 'includedness' (which is really only a metaphor) is a distinguishing characteristic of immanent perception and of the position-taking founded on such a perception" (69). Real inherence bespeaks an unequaled community of essence in which perception and perceived share the same kind of Being. This does not hold for transcendent perception: "Not only does the perception of the physical thing not contain the physical thing itself as part of its really inherent composition; the perception also lacks any essential unity with the latter, its existence being presupposed here, of course. The unity of the stream of lived experiences is the sole unity determined purely by the essences proper to the lived experiences themselves; or, equivalently, a lived experience can be combined only with lived experiences to form a whole whose total essence encompasses and is founded on the essences proper to these lived experiences."

4.5 Consciousness and the Natural World

Husserl's analyses thus far have been eidetic, but because he has remained in the natural attitude, the essences he has investigated have belonged to the natural world as occurrences in it. That is not to say, however, that his insights into "the essential characteristics of lived experience and consciousness" are of negligible importance; on the contrary, together they constitute the "necessary preliminary steps" on the way to achieving his ultimate goal: "the acquisition of the essence of that 'pure' consciousness by means of which the phenomenological field is to be determined." The initial distinction between immanent and transcendent perception marks the second step in Husserl's account, after having explicated the most basic sense of modification proper to consciousness. As the third main step in his analyses, Husserl takes up the relation between consciousness and the natural, material world, where the former is involved in the latter in two ways when viewed from the natural attitude: "it is the consciousness belonging to some human being or beast; and, at least in a large number of its particularizations, it is consciousness of that world" (69–70). Having touched on it only briefly in the foregoing, Husserl now returns to an apparent problem that centers on essence.

Since consciousness is to have an essence of its own, one different from that of the natural world, since for there to be any involvement of one with the other, there would have to be some community of essence between them,[102] and since the material world seems to be "the fundamental substratum of the natural world to which all other real Being is essentially related" for the "naive" human being, it is necessary to ask: "To what extent, first of all, is the material world to be something of a principially different kind excluded from the essentiality proper to lived experiences? And if it is such, if in contrast to all consciousness, and to the essentiality proper to consciousness, the material world is 'alien,' 'other,' then how can consciousness become involved with it—with the material world and consequently with the whole world that is alien to consciousness?" (70). How can they be related if their essences differ so radically? If Husserl is to establish the priority of immanence over transcendence, he must account for how it is that consciousness comes into contact with the material world and especially for how it is that this world receives its sense from consciousness. The latter issue will be the focus of Husserl's transcendental, constitutive analyses. The former issue can be addressed by means of eidetic analysis; it is crucial here if progress towards the insight into the necessity of the epoché is to be made.

The solution to this apparent dilemma lies in "the ultimate source from which the general thesis of the world, which I effect in the natural attitude, draws its sustenance," for it is this source that "makes it possible that I consciously find an existing world of physical things opposite me and that I ascribe to myself a body in this world and now am able to assign myself a place in it. Obviously this ultimate source is sensory experience." But instead of treating sensory experience in general, Husserl turns to the canonical, because it is the "original" experience "from which all other experiencing acts derive a major part of their founding force": sensory perception. He says: "Every perceiving consciousness has the peculiarity of being a consciousness of the 'bodily' self-presence of an individual Object, which, for its part, is either an individuum in the sense of pure logic or else a logico-categorial variant of the same" (70–71). Husserl takes the perception of the physical thing as paradigmatic for all other kinds of perception. The aforementioned questions about the community of essence between the material world and consciousness are now recast in terms of sensory perception: "Our natural wakeful ego-life is a continuous actional or inactional perceiving. The world of physical things and, in it, our body, are constantly there perceptually. How does, and how can, consciousness itself become singled out as a concrete Being in itself? And how does that of which it is conscious, the perceived Being, become singled out as 'over against' consciousness and as 'in and of itself'?" (71). These questions are asked from the standpoint of the natural attitude, as if by the naive human being. The things of the world that it perceives, it considers actual; the perceptions either are confirmed or prove illusory. The possibility of mistakes or deception always accompanies such perceptions. Nevertheless, the world continues to be privileged, whereas the naive human being views the perception itself as inessential when it is considered "purely as a consciousness" apart from the body; instead, it seems to be "an empty looking at the Object itself by an empty 'ego' that comes into contact with the Object in a remarkable way." It is remarkable, even puzzling, because the pivotal role of consciousness in its relation to the (physical) thing is not seen.

In order to evade such deception and establish a realm of indubitability, the natural sciences reject the naive human being's sensory experience. Instead, they appeal to what promises to be an ameliorative distinction between primary and secondary qualities and assert that "the specific qualities pertaining to the senses"—the secondary qualities—"are 'merely subjective' and only the qualities dealt with in geometry and physics"—the primary qualities—"are 'objective.'" On this view, whatever appears to sensory perception is "mere appearance," that is, a mere sign of true Being, which itself possesses primary qualities. Because the objectivity of the latter is to provide a guarantee for the knowledge based on them, it is the business of the scientist to abstract the primary from the secondary qualities. However that may be, this approach to perception does not explain what perception is in itself; Husserl makes this clear by reformulating the view at issue here: "The 'true Being' would thus be something determined completely and principially differently than what is given in perception as 'bodily' actuality, given exclusively with sensuous determinations, to which sensorial-spatial determinations also belong" (72)—namely, differently than the Being perceived by the naive human being. "The authentically experienced physical thing provides the mere 'This,' an empty X, which becomes the bearer of mathematical determinations and corresponding mathematical formulae, and which exists, not in perceived space, but in an 'objective space' of which the former is merely a 'sign'—a three-dimensional Euclidean manifold that can be represented only symbolically."[103] On account of this, then, the true Being of the natural sciences would be transcendent to what is given "bodily" in perception; they would effectively belong to different regions, and in fact the "true Being" stands in a relation of dependence to the Being that gives itself in "mere appearances." Furthermore, the scientist would be guilty of a *metabasis* were he to seek to impose his natural scientific understanding of the "true Being" on the "naive" understanding of the beings that make up the material world. It should be noted at this point that, as so often in the course of his analyses, Husserl's critique is not meant to call into question the value of the object of critique. In other words, his aim in the foregoing was not to dispute the value of the sciences, not to privilege "naive" human experience over natural scientific experience, but to close off one avenue of explanation and thereby redirect his inquiry to what is most essential. His interest here is to ascertain what is really inherent in perception, and in fact in the perception of the naive human being. Since the sciences assert the transcendence of the "true Being" of interest to them, they already testify to its not being really inherent in such perception.

As a result Husserl must ask: "what belongs now to the concrete, really inherent composition of perception itself, as the cogitatio?" (73). From the aforementioned definition of real inherence, clearly neither the "physical thing as determined by physics" nor the "whole 'world of appearances'" themselves are really inherent in the perception of them, for both are transcendent. By ascertaining what is really inherent in the perception, Husserl is able to say "how the transcendent stands with respect to the consciousness that is conscious of it." By excluding everything that belongs to physics and theoretical thought in general, since they do not help answer his guiding question, and instead focusing on consciousness itself, Husserl stays "within the parameters of simple intuition and its accordant syntheses, parameters within which perception belongs." From the nontheoretical consideration of this sphere, it becomes "evident that although intuition and intuited, perception and perceived physical thing are essentially interrelated, they are not, as a matter of principial necessity, really inherently and essentially one and combined"—this reiterates the fundamental difference between transcendent and immanent perception.

In the perception of a physical thing—Husserl speaks of a table—the thing appears always as one and the same, while the perception of it constantly changes; in fact the one perception proves to be a continuous synthesis and therefore a continuity of varying perceptions of that thing: "The perception itself, however, is what it is in the continuous flux of consciousness and is itself a continuous flux: continually the perceptual Now of consciousness changes into the ensuing consciousness of the Just-Past and simultaneously a new Now lights up, etc." (74). The physical thing, along with all its various aspects, remains transcendent to the perception, but the point of contact between this thing and the perception of it lies in the manner in which the former gives itself in varying appearances to consciousness: "Of essential necessity there belongs to any 'all-sided,' continuously unitarily self-confirming experiential consciousness of the same physical thing a multifarious system of continuous manifolds of appearances and adumbrations in which all objectual moments falling within perception with the characteristic of 'bodily' self-givenness are presented or adumbrated by determinate continuities. Each determinacy has its system of adumbrations, and each of them, like the physical thing as a whole, stands there as the same for the seizing-upon consciousness that synthetically unites memory and new perception, despite any interruption of the continuity of actional perception" (74–75). Whereas the physical thing itself is not really inherent in the perception, "the perceptual manifolds themselves always have their determinate descriptive composition essentially coordinated with that [intentional] unity" which the physical thing is for transcendent perception.

Therein lie as really inherent moments "the data of sensation," which are "animated by 'interpretations' within the concrete unity of the perception and which in this animation exercise the 'presenting function,' or together with the animation they make up what we call 'appearings of' color, shape, etc." (75). These really inherent moments provide the points of contact; by virtue of them consciousness is related to the physical thing. They are related as coordinate but radically different regions of Being, which is reflected in their respective modes of givenness: "The adumbration, although called by the same name, is principially not of the same genus as the adumbrated. The adumbration is a lived experience. A lived experience is possible, however, only as a lived experience, and not as something spatial. But the adumbrated is principially possible only as something spatial (it is spatial precisely by its essence), and not as a lived experience" (75–76). The gap between these regions is unbridgeable but nevertheless mediable.

The demonstration of how consciousness and the "real world" are related establishes at the same time how they are different and, what is more, how each represents a different, autonomous region, contrary to the supposition of the "naive" human being. In addition, the demonstration marks an important step on the way to showing the priority of consciousness over that world.[104] Later it will be seen that and how it is just the generic or essential difference between them that makes their relation possible. Here (77) Husserl points to the gulf separating them as "the most cardinal distinctness"[105] there is between modes of Being: "with an absolutely unconditional universality or necessity, a physical thing cannot be given in any possible perception, in any possible consciousness, as something really inherently immanent. Thus a fundamentally essential difference emerges between Being as lived experience and Being as a physical thing. Principially it belongs to the regional essence 'lived experience' (specifically, to the regional particularization 'cogitatio') that it can be perceived in immanent perception; to the essence of a spatial thing, however, that it cannot be so perceived" (76). The differences between these modes do not amount to deficiencies or inadequacies, but simply reflect the characteristics of each; Husserl does not indulge in any valuation here, but seeks to engage in the pure eidetic description of affair-complexes.

The difference between the two regions rests on "a principial difference between kinds of givenness. Immanent and transcendent perception differ not merely because the intentional object, which stands there with the characteristic of a 'bodily' self, is really inherently immanent in the perceiving in one case but not in the other; rather, they differ with respect to a mode of givenness, which in its essential difference is carried over mutatis mutandis to all the representiational modifications of perception, to the parallel memorial intuitions and fantasy intuitions. We perceive the physical thing by virtue of its being 'adumbrated' with respect to all the determinations that, perhaps, 'actually' and authentically 'fall' within the perception. A lived experience is not adumbrated" (77).—Nor, incidentally, can a physical thing be modified, for modification in Husserl's sense is proper to consciousness alone.—What is more, the perception of a spatial thing can never reach an end; although the perception can become ever more complete—*in infinitum*—it is in keeping with its essence that it never can be had in its entirety, that is, adequately.[106] "It is inherent in the essential structure of [determinately ordered continuous manifolds of perception], then, that they produce the unity of a harmoniously giving consciousness, and in fact of the one perceptual physical thing that appears ever more perfectly, from ever new sides, with an ever greater wealth of determinations. On the other hand, the spatial thing is nothing but an intentional unity that can be given principially only as a unity of such modes of appearance" (78). These are essential and thus necessary determinations; Husserl stresses that there is nothing accidental or contingent about them. The lines separating the two spheres always remain intact. On account of this, he notes, it is "a principial error to contend that perception (and, after its own fashion, any other kind of intuition of a physical thing) does not reach the physical thing itself, that the latter is not given to us in itself or in its being-in-itself." As if we were to perceive something else in its stead, such as a sign or picture. Such a contention leads to the view that it is possible to get behind the sign, along with whatever limitations it imposes on consciousness, and intuit the physical thing adequately. Or even if in its finitude a human being cannot do so, then certainly God in his infinite knowledge can. "But this view is countersensical. It implies that there is no essential difference between the transcendent and the immanent," as if it were possible for God not to be bound by this difference.[107] By contrast, on the basis of the foregoing essential determinations Husserl is able to reassert of the perception of a physical thing: "In immediately intuitive acts we intuit a 'self'; interpretations of a higher level are not built on their interpretations; thus there is no consciousness of anything for which the intuited might function as a 'sign' or 'picture.' And precisely for that reason it is said to be immediately intuited as 'itself.' In perception the 'self' is further characterized in its peculiarity as 'bodily' [present] in contrast to its modified characteristic 'hovering,' 'representiated' in memory or in free fantasy. One falls into countersense if one confuses, in the usual fashion, these essentially differently structured modes of objectivation, and thus correlatively the givens corresponding to these modes, thereby confusing simple representiation with symbolizing (whether depictive or signitive) and—all the more—simple perception with both of them. The perception of a physical thing does not representiate something non-present, as if it were a memory or a fantasy; it presentiates, it seizes upon a self in its 'bodily' presence. Perception does this in keeping with its *own sense*, and to attribute something other than that to perception is precisely to violate its sense" (79–80). The confusions, and that includes all philosophical problems, arise from failing to observe essential differences.

4.6 Merely Phenomenal and Absolute Being

At this point in Husserl's analysis we reach another key step or turning point: the distinction between transcendence and immanence as that between "merely phenomenal Being" and "absolute Being." It is an essential necessity that "the perception of a physical thing involves a certain inadequacy. Principially, a physical thing can be given only 'one-sidedly'" (80), only presented by adumbration, which means that any perception, or synthesis of perceptions, of it will necessarily remain incomplete. This mode of givenness belongs essentially to the physical thing. It is "necessarily given in mere 'modes of appearance' in which necessarily a core of 'what is actually presented' is interpreted as being surrounded by a horizon of inauthentic [*uneigentlich*] 'co-givenness,' and of more or less vague indeterminacy."—It is never given all at once, never adequately; this is already the sense of the adumbration proper to it.—"And the sense of this indeterminacy is, again, prescribed by the universal sense of the perceived physical thing in general and as such, or by the universal essence of this type of perception, which we call physical-thing perception. After all, the indeterminacy necessarily signifies a determinableness in a rigorously prescribed style."—To say that it is indeterminate implies simply that there is some sense or presentiment of its determinacy; and it is of the essence of any essence to prescribe what is required for the achievement of determinacy, even if it can never be reached, which again is a feature determined by that essence.—"It points ahead to possible perceptual manifolds that, merging continuously into one another, join together to form the unity of one perception in which the continuously enduring physical thing always shows new 'sides' (or else old ones as returning) in a new series of adumbrations." These essential determinations, which are essential truths, cannot be altered: "To be *in infinitum* imperfect in this way is part of the indefeasible essence of the correlation between 'physical thing' and perception of a physical thing." Were this not to hold, the regional boundaries would fade between the immanent and the transcendent: "no matter what its genus may be, any transcendent Being whatsoever, understood as a Being for an ego, can be given only in a manner analogous to that in which a physical thing is given, thus only through appearances. Otherwise it would be precisely a Being that could also become immanent; but whatever is perceivable immanently is perceivable only immanently" (81).

The incompleteness or need of supplementation proper to transcendent Being does not obtain with respect to immanent Being: "Whereas it is essential to givenness through appearances that no appearance gives the thing as something 'absolute' instead of in a one-sided presentation, it belongs to the essence of immanent givenness precisely to give something *absolute* that can in no way be presented by means of sides or be adumbrated. It is, after all, also evident that though the adumbrative sensation-contents themselves—which belong really inherently to the lived experience of the physical-thing perception—may function as adumbrations of something, they are not themselves given in turn through adumbrations" (82). The absoluteness of immanent givenness is the crucial insight here. It severs the immanent from the transcendent and provides Husserl with the means for showing that the former sphere has priority over the latter. In its nonadumbrational givenness, in its absoluteness, however, there is nevertheless a sense in which it, too, involves a certain inadequacy: "Nor is a lived experience ever perceived completely; it cannot be adequately grasped in its full unity. By its essence, a lived experience is a flux that—in directing our reflective regard to it, starting from the Now-point—we can swim along after, while the stretches already covered are lost to our perception. Only in the form of retention do we have a consciousness of the phase that has just concluded, or else in the form of a retrospective recollection. And my whole stream of lived experiences is, finally, a unity of lived experiences that principially cannot be seized upon completely in a perceiving that 'swims along with it.' But this incompleteness or 'imperfection,' which belongs to the essence of the perception of a lived experience, is principially different from that which belongs to the essence of the 'transcendent' perception, perception by adumbrative presentation, by means of something such as appearance." A lived experience, say, a perception of something immanent, is absolute, although its necessary imperfection would seem to contradict Husserl's assertion. The sense in which it is absolute, however, must be traced back to the distinction between transcendence and immanence. Something transcendent is given through appearances, which allow of doubt. This is the pivotal difference. A lived experience cannot be doubted without leading to countersense. And this indubitability grounds its absoluteness. Its particular kind of inadequacy has significant implications for Husserl's phenomenology of reason, but, unlike in the case of the transcendent, it does not impinge upon its indubitability.

In view of these distinctions, Husserl returns to earlier distinctions so as to refine them. Unlike in transcendent perception, in immanent perception it holds that the perception and what is perceived form an immediate, absolute unity. It is by means of reflection that this unity arises: "The kind of Being proper to lived experiences is such that a regard of seeing perception can be directed quite immediately to any actual lived experience alive as an originary present. This occurs in the form of 'reflection,' which has the remarkable property that what is seized upon perceptually in it is characterized principially as something that not only exists and endures within the perceiving regard, but also already existed before this regard was turned to it" (83). The existence proper to what is perceived, both before, while, and after the regard is turned to it, is guaranteed by the existence of the stream of lived experiences. As noted above, it is this stream on which the reflective modification of consciousness from actionality to inactionality, and conversely, is possible. Before a lived experience is singled out by the reflective regard, it exists along with other lived experiences in the stream as a background. They are always there "ready to be perceived." An analogous possibility of perception pertains to physical things, but since they are given through appearances, they do not have the immediacy proper to lived experiences seized upon in reflection: physical things "can be ready [to be perceived] only insofar as there is consciousness of them already as unnoticed things, and with respect to them that means: only if they appear. Not all physical things fulfill this requirement: my 'field of attentive regard,' which embraces everything that appears, is not infinite" (84). But the field embracing all lived experiences is infinite.

Husserl's demonstration of the absoluteness of the immanent sphere, of the region of consciousness prepared the way to the insight into the necessity of performing the epoché. That sphere provides him with a heretofore unequaled foundation: "Every immanent perception necessarily guarantees the existence [*Existenz*] of its object. If a reflective seizing-upon is directed to my lived experience, then I have seized upon an *absolute* self, the existence [*Dasein*] of which is principially incapable of being negated, that is, the insight that it does not exist is principially impossible; it would be a countersense to consider it possible that a lived experience given in that manner did not in truth exist."—Thus he invokes once again the version of the principle of noncontradiction he advanced in his consideration of Descartes's attempt to doubt universally; the countersense here, as there, turns on belief and *not* on Being.—"The stream of lived experiences that is my stream, mine as the one who is thinking, may not have been grasped to some extent, may be unknown in the provinces of the stream that have run their course and that have yet to come, but as soon as I look at the flowing life in its actual present and, while doing so, grasp myself as the pure subject of this life . . . I say absolutely and necessarily: I am, this life is, I am living: cogito" (85). Here Husserl reverses the Cartesian formula—thus not *cogito ergo sum* but rather *sum ergo cogito*—and necessarily so, for in his thought Being has primacy and thinking comes always only second. (In view of this, can one reasonably claim that a continuum links Husserl to Descartes, or that Husserl continues the Cartesian "tradition"?[108])

It is the existence of the stream of lived experiences that is first, is absolute, and as such guarantees thought, not conversely. This primacy of existence, however, is followed by the primacy of belief over thought. The cogito is first and foremost belief; every consciousness-of is first belief in that of which there is consciousness. It is only on account of this that the aforementioned countersense could possibly arise, that is, it is such only because considering a lived experience given absolutely not to exist contradicts the preceding, necessary belief in that existence. On the other hand, the absoluteness of the stream of lived experiences is confined to each individual ego: "No countersense is implicit in the possibility that every alien consciousness that I posit in empathic experience does not exist. But my empathizing, my consciousness in general, is originarily and absolutely given not only with respect to its essence but also with respect to its existence. Only for an ego, or a stream of lived experiences, in relation to itself does this distinctive affair-complex [*Sachlage*] exist; only here is there, and must there be, such a thing as immanent perception" (85–86). Husserl's observations focus on the individual ego and its stream; he does not rule out a collectivity of egos, but the absoluteness of the stream and its lived experiences is confined to each individual ego and cannot be transferred to a collectivity—at least, not yet. Husserl begins in this way not because he is a naive solipsist but for systematic reasons. Whatever problems his incipient "solipsism" may pose for his thought, he must begin at the beginning, and that means with subjectivity—in its necessary individuality—before turning to intersubjectivity; the latter topic lies on a higher level of inquiry within the system of Husserlian thought.

Appealing once again to the contrast between transcendence and immanence, Husserl refines his understanding of the absoluteness of lived experiences, which comes to mean 'necessity' over against the contingency of the physical thing: "According to eidetic law it holds that material existence is never required as necessary by its givenness, but is in a certain way always contingent. That means: It can always be that the further course of experience will necessitate giving up what has already been posited with a legitimacy derived from experience" (86). By contrast, within consciousness itself there is no contingency: "In the absolute sphere there is no room for conflict, illusion, or being otherwise. It is a sphere of absolute *position*." In its absoluteness this sphere founds and demands a kind of belief that cannot be reasonably sustained towards the material world; the difference lies in the degree of indubitability accruing to each sphere: "Thus in every way it is clear that everything that is there for me in the world of physical things is principially only a presumptive actuality and, by contrast, that I myself, for whom it is there (when the 'part of me' belonging to the world of physical things is excluded), am absolute actuality, or that the actionality of my lived experience is an absolute actuality, given by an unconditional, absolutely indefeasible positing." The absoluteness of this belief is opposed to the contingency of the belief on which the natural attitude is based, the belief summed up in the general thesis: "Thus over against the thesis of the world, which is a 'contingent' thesis, there stands the thesis of my pure ego and ego-life, which is a 'necessary,' completely indubitable thesis. Anything physical that is given 'bodily' can also not exist; no lived experience that is given 'bodily' can also not exist: that is the eidetic law that defines the latter necessity and the former contingency." The thesis of my pure ego—that is, my belief in it—accompanies every act of consciousness, which, at its most fundamental level, is reflection: "The ideal possibility of a reflection having the essential characteristic of an evidently indefeasible thesis of factual existence is grounded in the essence of any pure ego whatsoever and of any lived experience whatsoever" (87). This thesis cannot be doubted, in contradistinction to the thesis of the existence of the world: "The world is dubitable not in the sense that rational motives were present that would have to be taken into consideration contrary to the tremendous force of harmonious experiences, but rather in the sense that a doubt is conceivable, and it is conceivable because the possibility of the nonexistence of the world is principially never excluded." Thus we return to Husserl's consideration of Descartes's attempt to doubt universally and of the general thesis. The epoché Husserl aims to effect will by no means exclude all belief, but only the general thesis. The thesis of my pure ego remains untouched.

4.7 The Destruction of Transcendence

By showing that "consciousness and natural actuality" represent autonomous regions on the one hand and that consciousness has priority over natural actuality (since immanence has priority over transcendence) on the other, Husserl has almost completely prepared the way for the move into pure consciousness. Like the priority pertaining to the immanence of consciousness, the priority of the sphere of pure consciousness lies in the absoluteness of the givenness proper to it, though its absoluteness is intensified, as it were, by an additional purification—precisely so that it become absolutely pure. Its absoluteness—in contrast to the contingency of natural actuality—attests the necessity of that sphere, which in turn translates into the necessity of the epoché. It is this operation that assures the sphere's absoluteness by ridding the latter of all naturalness, something of which the eidetic reduction is incapable of doing with the same radicality.

Although eidetic in character and thus imbued with a certain degree of purity, Husserl's reflections to this point have been carried out entirely in the natural attitude, and they will continue to be so until the epoché has been officially effected. But before that can occur, two further essential determinations must be made: he has to exhibit the character of the relation between consciousness and natural actuality—just this relation reveals the essentiality of consciousness as such—and thereafter the unique status of consciousness over against that actuality. In the natural attitude, predominant is none other than the experience of the world; experiential consciousness is thematized, if at all, only as part of that world. It is in terms of these, of the experiential world and consciousness, that Husserl accounts for the relation in question.

He proceeds "destructively," tracing every possibility back to its ground, that is, to the necessity from which it springs. Destruction in its peculiarly Husserlian sense means the reduction of whatever is in question to its essence, to the essential determinations that pertain to it. Here he begins by showing the contingency of a "truth of physics," under which we tend to subsume our experiences. Husserl notes that it is natural for consciousness to press beyond the "intuitively given things" and seek to explain them in terms of physics—in fact, he says, "our reason" is compelled to do so by our experiences (87–88). However, another experience is equally possible (88): It is also conceivable that "our intuited world were the ultimate one," that our "simple experience" of it would not allow of and thus not compel any explanation in terms of mathematics or physics, that our world were incompatible with the world of physics. Since something is contingent if it is conceivable that it be otherwise, this possibility attests the contingency or nonabsoluteness of the explanation offered by physics and the experience on which it is based; and this holds also of "simple experience." Because neither of these possibilities provides an absolute stopping point or foundation, the destruction must be carried further: "No limits check us in the destruction in thought [*gedankliche Destruktion*] of material objectivity—as the correlate of experiential consciousness." Noteworthy is that this destruction takes place *in thought* and in it alone—it is the methodical predecessor of what Husserl earlier called 'ideation' and soon will also call 'imaginative variation' or 'free fantasying'.[109] Both methods aim at bringing an Apriori to intuition.

Destruction aims in this context at transcendence; the mode of access to transcendent, physical things is experience: "It must always be borne in mind here that whatever physical things are—the only physical things about which we make statements, the only ones about whose Being or non-Being, being-thus or being-otherwise we can disagree and make rational decisions—they are such as things of experience. It is experience alone—and in fact, since factual physical things are at issue, actional experience in its definitely ordered experiential concatenations—that prescribes their sense to them." What in fact prescribes the sense of experienceable physical things is the *essence* of experience; it sets the norms and thus the parameters of possibility, of experienceability. What is here destructed is material objectivity as the *correlate* of experiential consciousness, and in fact as the necessary correlate of the latter. Only because it is the transcendent correlate of consciousness is its destruction conceivable—material objectivity as such is not destroyed thereby (which would be absurd); it is de-stuctured in thought. That is to say, the correlate is pared down to its essential features so as to ascertain its necessity, which is a feature of essence alone. Since the correlate in question is the thing given in experience, the possibilities of experience must be "destructed," their determinative essence, their hard core, must be distilled from them—again, in thought and thus with respect to consciousness.

The various possibilities pertaining to experience point back to just such an enabling essence: "But if we can subject the kinds of lived experience proper to experience, and especially the fundamental lived experience of perceiving physical things, to an eidetic examination, if we can discern essential possibilities and necessities in them (as we obviously can) and can therefore trace the essentially possible variations of motivated experiential concatenations eidetically, then the result is the correlate of our factual experience, called 'the actual world,' as one special case among manifold possible worlds and non-worlds, which for their part are nothing but the correlates of essentially possible variations of the idea 'experiencing consciousness', with more or less orderly experiential concatenations." The number of possible worlds corresponds to the number of attitudes. But regardless of the attitude, two sides may be discerned in the essence of experience: the experiencing consciousness and the experienced object.

The "actual world" encountered in the natural attitude represents but one possibility among others, none of which is any more necessary than the other possibilities. None is absolute. They have no senseful ground in themselves but only in consciousness; they remain possibilities *of* consciousness; it has ontological priority over them: "The genuine *concept*"—that is, the essence—"of the transcendence of something material that is the measure of any rational statement about transcendence, can itself be derived from nowhere else than from perception's own essential contents or from those concatenations of definite kinds we call demonstrative experience. The *idea* of such transcendence is thus the eidetic correlate of the *pure idea* of this demonstrative experience" (89). And yet, despite the priority of consciousness over the transcendent physical thing, in experience neither of them is conceivable without the other; it makes as little sense to speak of a thing-in-itself as it does to speak of a consciousness without relation to an object: "An object existing in itself is at no time such that consciousness or the ego proper to consciousness would be irrelevant to it." Every object, whether actionally or not yet perceived, is a correlate of consciousness; it is such by its essence. There is no thing-in-itself to which consciousness does not have access as that thing in its selfhood: "The physical thing is a thing belonging to the environing-world, even if it be an unseen physical thing, even if it be a really possible, unexperienced but experienceable, or perhaps experienceable, physical thing. Experienceability never means an empty logical possibility, but rather a possibility motivated in the experiential concatenation." The concatenation is itself necessarily determined by an essence: "It is an essential truth [*Im Wesen liegt es*] that anything that exists in reality but is not yet actionally experienced can be given and that this then means that the thing in question belongs to the undetermined but determinable horizon of my experiential actionality at the particular time. However, this horizon is the correlate of the components of indeterminacy essentially attached to experiences of physical things themselves; and those components—always essentially—leave open possibilities of fulfillment that are by no means arbitrary, but are motivated possibilities that are predelineated according to their essential types. Every actional experience points beyond itself to possible experiences, which themselves point to new, possible experiences, and so on *in infinitum*. And all of that is effected in accordance with essentially determined species and regulative forms that are bound up with a priori types" (89–90). The entire range of realizable possibilities are determined by the essence of experience.

One can posit all manner of "logical" possibilities—Husserl speaks of the possibility of a world existing outside of the actual world—but such can have validity only to the extent that they can be demonstrated by actual experience: "something transcendent must necessarily be *experienceable* and not merely by an ego conceived as an empty logical possibility but by some actional ego as a demonstrable unity relative to its experiential concatenations" (90)—and this holds for all egos: "what is cognizable by one ego must principially be cognizable by any ego."[110] The measure of sense here is thus experience; in its essence it prescribes what is possible, experienceable. While perhaps a legitimate logical possibility, anything posited as possible—for example, a possible world—but that is not experienceable is actually a countersense precisely because it is not experienceable, which is to say it can have no sense or meaning, and thus no validity, for us. Anything transcendent must be experienceable if it is to have any sense, for only in experience can its validity be demonstrated. Experienceability is always a feature of a transcendent object, and an object is as such only as a correlate of consciousness. By exhibiting this correlation and the hierarchy it entails, Husserl has cleared the way for the last step leading to the performance of the epoché.

4.8 *The Annihilation of the World*

Despite all that has been said, it is not the case that there must be a world or any physical thing. The existence of a transcendent world is not necessary; it is just "the correlate of manifolds of experience distinguished by certain essential formations" (91). As is made evident by the diverse formative possibilities pertaining to the world, it is conceivable that matters could be otherwise. The various positings bearing on it could prove illusory or untenable—so that the world would exist otherwise than we first thought. Furthermore, it is conceivable that the world could simply not exist. This all follows from the essential contingency of the transcendent as shown above. In addition, it follows that "although the Being of consciousness, of any stream of lived experiences whatsoever, would be necessarily modified by an annihilation of the world of physical things, its own existence would not be touched." That it is impervious to such operations is shown already by the foregoing considerations regarding possible worlds: the world of physics or the world in which physics had no place. In considering either possibility, consciousness remains intact, though it has been modified in conjunction with its altered correlate. What is annihilated is only the transcendent world of experience, the real world in all its contingency as opposed to the immanent stream of lived experiences in all its absoluteness—or rather, what is annihilated (and this cannot be stressed enough) is the *thesis* of the world, the annihilation of which Husserl speaks erases the *belief* in existence. It is precisely because such annihilation is effected in thought, in the immanent sphere, that the latter cannot be touched; any suggestion to the contrary would be sheer countersense: it would amount to the annihilation of thought in thought by thought.

The world is annihilated, the thesis of the world eliminated, in order to purify consciousness of all contingency: "no real Being, none that is presented and demonstrated *in* consciousness by appearances, is necessary to the Being of consciousness itself" (92). On the contrary: "Immanent Being is . . . indubitably absolute Being in the sense that it principially *nulla 're' indigit ad existendum* [needs no 'thing' in order to exist]." Its absoluteness indicates that the transcendent world is dependent upon it: "the world of the transcendent *res* is completely dependent on consciousness, and in fact not on some logically conceived consciousness but on actional consciousness." And yet this dependence is not based on a community of essence. Again, consciousness and the actual world represent interrelated but autonomous regions of Being; they "are anything but coordinate kinds of Being, which dwell peaceably side by side and occasionally become 'related to' or 'connected with' one another." They remain necessarily separate as two wholes; even though the world is related to consciousness, neither these regions nor any of their respective parts can be combined into one region, one whole, for: "Only things that are essentially akin, that have a proper essence in the same sense, can become connected in the true sense of the word, can make up a whole" (92–93).—This principle has been operative throughout Husserl's eidetic analyses to this point. It provides him with the means of assessing relations and making distinctions.—Dependence does not require real relation; and on account of this he can say, disregarding their empty logical, categorial points of contact (which do not interest Husserl here; rather, what does interest him is the distinction between the two spheres): "Between consciousness and reality yawns a veritable abyss of sense. Here, an adumbrated Being, incapable of ever being given absolutely, merely contingent and relative; there, a necessary and absolute Being, principially incapable of being given through adumbration and appearance" (93). The abyss separating them is the same as that yawning between necessity and possibility understood as contingency. It is an unbridgeable gulf: "consciousness, considered in 'purity,' must be regarded as a self-contained complex of Being, a complex of absolute Being into which nothing can penetrate and out of which nothing can slip, to which nothing is spatiotemporally external and which cannot be within any spatiotemporal complex, which cannot be causally affected by any physical thing and cannot exercise causation upon any physical thing. . . ." The spatiotemporal world is likewise self-contained and is available to consciousness as "a merely intentional Being, thus one that has the merely secondary, relative sense of a Being *for* a consciousness"—to be sure, not *in* consciousness. "It is a Being that consciousness posits in its experiences, one that principially can be determined and intuited only as something identical belonging to harmoniously motivated manifolds of appearances—beyond that it is nothing." The actual world is relative to absolute consciousness. The former, as the world encountered in the natural attitude, could easily be otherwise; consciousness, by contrast, cannot be otherwise. Consciousness is not just one among other "absolutes," among which a relative hierarchy of absoluteness would obtain. Rather, consciousness alone is absolute—or so it seems at this stage of Husserl's analyses. It is considered in general, in its essence. And as a consequence it is clear that the talk of absolute consciousness does not have one individual consciousness in view as absolute over against others; what holds of consciousness in its essence must likewise hold for all individual manifestations of consciousness.[111]

By showing the absoluteness of consciousness and the contingency of the actual world and furthermore the dependence of the latter on the former, Husserl turns the world of the naive human being on its head: "the usual sense of the talk of Being is reversed. The Being that is first for us is in itself second, that is, it is what it is only in 'relation' to the first." What in the natural attitude looks to be the priority of the world, proves to be secondary, and for essential reasons; consciousness is now seen to be primary: "Reality, both the reality of the physical thing taken individually and the reality of the whole world, lacks self-sufficiency by its essence (in our rigorous sense). The physical thing is not in itself something absolute that becomes linked secondarily to something else; rather, in the absolute sense, it is nothing at all; it has no 'absolute essence' whatever; it has the essentiality of something that is principially only intentional, only an object of consciousness, something presented or something apparent in the manner peculiar to consciousness" (93–94). In contrast to the reality of the physical thing, or simply reality, which is nothing of itself, consciousness need not have any relation to any possible real world—although it is the case that it must always have an object, whether actually or potentially. It is self-contained and is the source of the sense, not just of reality, but also of itself, of all it contains. The demonstration of the ontological priority of consciousness is the last requirement Husserl had to fulfill before effecting the epoché.

4.9 From the Natural to the Phenomenological Sphere

Each of the attitudinal modifications of consciousness discussed by Husserl thus far, including the epoché, takes place in the natural attitude, that is, each is effected on the ground of this attitude, the ground our naive existence is based on. Each modification results in a move away from the natural attitude and into another, but it is essential to every new attitude that it is possible to "fall" out of it and back into the natural attitude, which is the "background" of each attitude. The epoché is distinguished from the other modifications, however. Although each of the others brings about a new attitude, although as a result one lives in a new sphere, the new attitude continues to participate in the general thesis and consequently continues to be bound up with the natural attitude. By contrast, the epoché's uniqueness lies in the fact that it excludes the general thesis and thereby gives access to an absolute sphere, one radically severed from the natural attitude and all its contingency: "Instead of naively effecting the acts belonging to our nature-constituting consciousness with their transcendent theses and allowing ourselves to be induced, by motives implicit in them, to effect ever new transcendent theses—we put *all* of these theses 'out of action,' we do not 'participate in them'; we direct our seizing and theoretically inquiring regard to pure consciousness in its own absolute Being. That, then, is what is left over as the 'phenomenological residuum' sought after, left over despite the fact that we have 'excluded' the whole world along with all physical things, living things, and human beings, ourselves included" (94). This residuum is the new sphere of pure consciousness; the corresponding attitude in which one lives while in this sphere is the phenomenological attitude.

The epoché does not put an array of transcendent theses out of action individually, one by one, but *all* of them, as Husserl says, and all at once, by bracketing the one thesis on which all such theses are based: the general thesis. This is fundamental. The singularity of its target, however, implies that the epoché does not exclude every possible thesis; at least one sphere of belief must remain if there is to be a field for phenomenological inquiry.[112] It was precisely in order to save that field that Husserl had to establish the world and consciousness as two interrelated but autonomous regions of Being, and then show the priority of consciousness. In this connection the epoché is also called the 'phenomenological reduction'. It is not a reduction at the expense of comprehensiveness. On the contrary, it reduces to everything, which is to say: to the absolute sphere, by clearing away the barriers that have heretofore obstructed our access to it: "Actually, we have not lost anything but rather have gained the whole of absolute Being, which, rightly understood, contains within itself, 'constitutes' within itself, all worldly transcendencies." Only this modification makes that sphere visible; it is nothing natural and so could not be seen from the standpoint of the natural attitude.[113]

The new attitude retains access to the natural attitude, as well as to other attitudes based on the general thesis,[114] but it no longer lives in their theses: "In the phenomenological attitude we prevent, in principial universality, the effectuation of all such cogitative theses, that is, we 'bracket' the theses effected; in our new inquiries we do not 'participate in these theses.' Instead of living in them, instead of effecting them, we effect acts of reflection directed towards them; and we seize upon them themselves as the absolute Being they are. We are now living completely in such *acts of the second degree*, acts for which what is given is the infinite field of absolute lived experiences—the fundamental field of phenomenology" (94–95). By living exclusively in reflective acts, we are no longer living naturally, or naively. What previously was originally active as a thesis has been modified; within these acts of the "second degree" it is now the object of reflection and as an object has been rendered inactive; we have cut ourselves off from life within that thesis—at least as long as we remain in the phenomenological attitude, for it is always possible to return to the natural attitude by, so to speak, "letting go" or "falling out" of the phenomenological attitude, or in other words, by ceasing to effect the epoché, though never by willing the natural attitude. Reflection is possible in every attitude, but phenomenological reflection is distinguished from other varieties precisely by its radicality, which—based on the differentiation of regions of Being, on the demonstration that consciousness is a region of its own, that it is not "a component part of nature, and is so far from being such that nature is possible only as an intentional unity motivated in [transcendentally pure consciousness] by immanent connections" (95)—consists in the exclusion of the general thesis. As a consequence of that exclusion and thus of the reduction of everything to the absolute sphere, reflection always has its object as an absolute Being. And on the same grounds, the disregard of nature proper to the epoché cannot be equated with mere abstraction, for "through such 'abstraction' from nature, only something natural can be acquired, and never transcendentally pure consciousness." Nor is it a "restriction of judgment" to some part of reality. Rather, the epoché excludes everything natural and so every part of reality by bracketing the general thesis in which the naive human being encounters them. What is thereby excluded, however, is retained in a modified sense, as phenomenon, and it is on phenomena in the domain of absolute consciousness that phenomenological reflection bears. The domain of lived experiences "is a strictly self-contained domain, and yet without any boundaries that could separate it from other regions. For anything that could limit it would have to share a community of essence with it. It is, however, the All of absolute Being. . . . By its essence, it is independent of all worldly, all natural Being; nor does it need such Being for its existence. The existence of a nature cannot be the condition for the existence of consciousness, since, after all, nature itself turns out to be a correlate of consciousness: nature exists only insofar as it is constituted in regular concatenations of consciousness" (96). Since everything has been reduced to absolute consciousness, it contains everything. In phenomenological reflection there is always a community of essence between reflection and what is reflected upon, for both lie within the same region.

The rigid distinction between regions is a canonical insight in Husserlian thought. The phenomenologist works within the phenomenological attitude. His objects lie within the sphere of pure consciousness. And yet he still has access to other regions, including reality, albeit with a change of value. They have been freed from the general thesis and thereby absolutized—in a thoroughly Husserlian sense and contrary to what he considers the traditional philosophical sense—for now they exist only as objects in or members of the absolute sphere. As such they are revealed for the first time as unities of sense: "All real unities are 'unities of sense.' Unities of sense presuppose . . . a sense-bestowing consciousness that for its part exists absolutely and not by way of another sense-bestowal" (106). Husserl's assertion of the priority of consciousness finds its justification precisely in its sense-bestowing function—it can bestow sense only because it is absolute and provides the foundation on which all sense rests. The distinction between regional ontologies, which, again, is at base a distinction between essences, has been Husserl's guiding insight from the outset of *Ideas I*. While there are many senseful regions, there is only one region of sense, only one in which sense is bestowed, only one absolute region: the region of pure consciousness: "An absolute reality is just as valid as a round square. Here reality and world are precisely names for certain valid unities of sense, namely unities of 'sense' related to certain concatenations of absolute, pure consciousness that, by their essence, bestow sense and demonstrate sense-validity precisely in one way and not in another." Sense is not found in "the world" but is given to that world by consciousness. This holds for all regions that lie "outside" consciousness. By annihilating the world, the epoché presents it anew for thought; the world is originarily there, free of all confounding and obscuring theories: "Real actuality is not 'reinterpreted' or even denied, but rather what is done away with is a countersensical interpretation of the same, that is, an interpretation that contradicts its own sense as clarified by insight. That interpretation stems from a philosophical absolutization of the world that is completely alien to the natural way of considering the world. Such a consideration is just that, natural; it lives naively in the effecting of the general thesis . . . ; thus it can never become countersensical. The countersense only arises when one philosophizes and, while seeking ultimate information about the sense of the world, completely fails to notice that the world itself has its whole Being as a certain 'sense' that presupposes absolute consciousness as the field of sense-bestowal; and when, at the same time, one fails to notice that this field, this sphere of Being of absolute origins, is accessible to seeing inquiry and contains an infinite wealth of cognitions given in insight possessing the highest scientific dignity" (107).[115]

Husserl is not a philosopher but a phenomenologist. Only the phenomenologist is able to clarify the original states of affairs that are operative in natural, pretheoretical consciousness. Only by clarifying these in their originality, that is, from the ground up, is it possible to avoid falling into the countersense that plagues the age in which Husserl finds himself. On his view this intention is thoroughly nonphilosophical; it has guided his analyses thus far in *Ideas I*, and will continue to do so up through the *Crisis*: "That we have not ventured philosophical conceits from on high [*von oben her*] but, on the basis [*auf Grund*] of *fundamental systematic work* in this field, have condensed carefully acquired cognitions into descriptions [purposely] kept general, will be evident to the scientifically experienced reader from the conceptual determinacy of the exposition."[116] Husserl is seeking to establish the foundation of knowledge; he aims at a new beginning, which only the epoché makes possible: "It should be noted, however, that our aim here has not been to give a finished theory of such transcendental constitution and thereby to draft a new 'theory of knowledge' concerning the spheres of reality, but only to bring about insight into general thoughts that can be helpful for the acquisition of the *idea* of transcendentally pure consciousness. What is essential for us is the evidence that the phenomenological reduction, as the exclusion of the natural attitude or of the latter's general thesis, is possible and that, after the reduction has been effected, absolute or transcendentally pure consciousness remains as a residuum, to which it would be countersense to ascribe reality" (107–8). The insight at which he has aimed and to which his analyses thus far were designed to lead the reader, motivates the performance of the epoché and thereby the entry into the new field of inquiry. He has righted a formerly topsy-turvy world by bringing to light that what is first for us, that is, the world, is not what is first by nature but rather second, that this world derives its sense solely from this first, that is, pure consciousness. While in the epoché and thus by means of a transcendental phenomenological eidetics it remains for Husserl to investigate this first, by doing so, he aims to shore up the results of his "natural" eidetic analyses, which have led him to the present turning point.

Chapter III

The Disclosure of the System's Lowermost Limit: Subjectivity

Following the preliminary considerations that make up the first two parts of *Ideas I*, Husserl stands on the threshold to phenomenology's proper field of inquiry, pure consciousness. It is in his analyses of this field that the contours of the system of his thought first begin to take on determinacy. He starts with pure subjectivity and moves upwards towards reason—these are the extremes of his system. Yet before entering the field they mark out, Husserl looks back on the foregoing so as to account for the expositions there, as well as to specify further the nature of phenomenology and thereby point the ensuing path of thought. This is the last step before he engages in phenomenology proper, that is, before undertaking concrete, transcendental-phenomenological analyses.

1. The Science of Pure Phenomenology

To this point Husserl's account has been largely proleptic in character due to his expectation that his claims on behalf of phenomenology would be met with a "fundamental mood of skepticism," the natural response to the thoroughly disconcerting because paradoxical nature of phenomenology. Its paradoxicalness is most obvious in its express challenge to the prevailing habits of thinking.[1] The phenomenological attitude stands in an exclusive relationship to the natural attitude. Phenomenology asserts a radically new field of inquiry, which initially excludes the familiar fields in their naturalness so as to encompass all of them in a transformed sense; it encompasses them, namely, as their ground.[2] Yet it is not first and foremost phenomenology's challenge that threatens to hinder its success in breaking out of the confines of the natural attitude and establishing itself as a new science, but rather—and this is the primary respect in which phenomenology is paradoxical—its unnaturalness: both this science and its field are not merely new in the usual sense of supplementing existing fields of natural inquiry and thereby extending their scope; rather, phenomenology and its field are so new that they lie completely beyond everything that is familiar to the "naturally minded." On account of this, the relevance of phenomenology is not immediately apparent; it is not clear that the measures it calls for are at all necessary; and that generates resistance on the part of those living in the natural attitude. Consequently, if he is to dissolve the skeptical climate in which phenomenology is born and must establish itself, Husserl must become an intermediary. He is obliged to demonstrate not only the possibility but, more importantly, the necessity of phenomenology. That means that he must introduce the unfamiliar and make it familiar. This is the "most difficult" beginning, as Husserl says, but it must be undertaken if he is to help the uninitiated reader make the leap to phenomenology's radically new attitude from what is otherwise familiar. Husserl's guiding intention in the expositions making up the first two parts of *Ideas I* has been nothing but this, and it continues to guide him in his first thematization of phenomenology as a science to follow them.

This thematization has alternating negative and positive sides. Due to the radical unnaturalness of phenomenology over against the "natural" sciences, the negative account must come first in each instance—Husserl must make a case for the unfamiliar based upon his analyses of the familiar—so as to defuse the skeptical mood it anticipates. This means that he must say what phenomenology *is not* before he can specify what it *is*. In taking this path, Husserl abides by his requirement that one start out always only from the ground. Hence in the foregoing he began with what is first for us, with what is immediately familiar to us, and that means: on the one hand, with matters of fact and the experiential-factual sciences. From these he distinguished essence and the eidetic sciences, respectively; they proved to be more fundamental than the former. On the other hand, he began with the world as we encounter it in the natural attitude. Ultimately, however, this led to a differentiation of the ground, which entailed a differentiation of attitudes. For it turns out that the natural attitude, and thus what is first for us, only seems to give us access to the ground, to what is first by nature. By contrast, if we are to reach the true ground, we must move beyond this semblance, and that can be achieved only through phenomenology and its method, the epoché.

1.1 The First Negative Account: Phenomenological Method and its Dissenters

Accordingly, the first negative account begins with a retrospective justification of the elucidation of the epoché. Husserl's aim there is to make visible to the "naturally minded" just how this method can and why it must open a new field of inquiry—the absolute ground to which phenomenology alone has access, in contrast to the empirical and thus contingent ground attended to in the natural attitude. Every step of Husserl's exegesis of the epoché is pitted against the prevailing blindness to it and the field to which it gives access: "Thus this infinite field of the Apriori of consciousness, which has never been given its due—indeed, has actually never been seen— in its peculiar ownness, must be cultivated then and made to yield its fullest fruits" (120). Yet the desired cultivation is not enabled simply by correcting some mistake made by the naive; the fact that the new field had not been seen prior to its discovery by Husserl was not a mere shortcoming of the natural attitude, but rather a direct consequence of its essence. Two disparate spheres are at issue here, and for that reason the way of seeing proper to one cannot be sensefully called an error from the standpoint of the other. Any attempt to do so would be to ignore the essential autonomy and legitimacy of the other region, to cross the boundaries separating the two and thus to commit a countersensical *metabasis*.

The disparateness of these spheres is underscored by the fact that, unlike the "natural" sciences and their objects, phenomenology and its objects are not immediately familiar to us "because of continuous experience and ways of thinking that have been practiced for millennia." Even what is unknown in the natural sciences lacks the strangeness peculiar to phenomenology: "Anything unknown there is a horizon of something known. Every methodical effort starts from something given; every further development of the method starts from the method already on hand"—in the natural attitude, the familiar, the known always provides the basis for the explication of what remains unfamiliar, unknown; the former predelineates the halo made up of the latter.

The phenomenological field had not been seen, then, precisely because it is not a part of and so cannot be accessed by the natural attitude. The two regions do not stand in any immediate relationship to one another: "The new field does not lie spread out before our view with an abundance of prominent givens in such a way that we could simply take hold of them and be sure of the possibility of making them the Objects of a science, to say nothing of being sure of the method by which we ought to proceed here." Because there can be no natural transition from the natural to the phenomenological attitude, a leap away from the former must be made in order to enter the radically new attitude, a leap enabled by the epoché alone.[3] Such a leap is not made possible by correcting errors, however, but by overcoming the said blindness, by giving insight into the disparateness of the natural and phenomenological spheres.[4] By seeing and maintaining the distinction between them, it becomes possible to cultivate the field of phenomenological inquiry, to chart the field of the Apriori of consciousness, to explore this "new world."

Considered from the standpoint of the natural attitude, and thus outside its phenomenological counterpart, the purification effected by the epoché leads Husserl to make what is perhaps his most audacious claim on behalf of phenomenology, namely that phenomenology has primacy over every known science: "according to its essence, phenomenology must claim to be 'first' philosophy and to offer the means for carrying out every possible critique of reason; therefore, it demands the most perfect presuppositionlessness and, with respect to itself, an absolute reflective insight" (121). Since the epoché provides access to the absolute region, in which every other region is rooted, and phenomenology is the science of that first region, it is likewise the first science. It is to found every other science, and the results of its investigations are to provide the other, "second" sciences with the means of fulfilling their own tasks. Consequently: "It is of its own essence to realize the most perfect clarity about its own essence and therefore also concerning the principles of its method." If phenomenology is to justify its claim to the status of First Philosophy, it must gain clarity about itself and its method, which is to say that it must account for itself, it must demonstrate the "sense and validity" of its method—and thus far in *Ideas I* Husserl has sought to do just this. Only in achieving the most perfect clarity can it hope to eliminate the skeptical mood with which it is faced. And yet Husserl seems to fall victim to a vicious circularity here: on the one hand, in order to see the sense and validity of the phenomenological method one must already have made use of it and as a result be inside the new attitude.[5] Furthermore, as Husserl notes, it is of phenomenology's essence to gain clarity about its essence. Both of these observations give rise to objections that center on an apparent use of inadmissible circularity. Husserl seeks to dissolve the two main objections by clarifying the sense of reflection, or self-reference, and thereby to smooth the way for entry into the phenomenological sphere.

1.1.1 The First Objection: The Phenomenologist's Self-Exclusion. The first objection is bound up with an effect of the epoché that would seem to render phenomenology impossible almost from the start, namely the phenomenologist's exclusion of himself. Since as a result of the exclusion of the general thesis "the natural world and all transcendent-eidetic spheres" are also excluded, the same fate must of necessity befall every human being as a natural, empirical being—including the phenomenologist himself. However, pure or transcendental consciousness is retained. It is solely within and as such a consciousness that the phenomenologist carries out his inquiries. Nevertheless, he does not cease to be a natural being: "We can even go on speaking in the way we must as natural human beings, for as phenomenologists we are not supposed to stop being natural human beings or positing ourselves as such when we speak" (122). Again, the exclusion effected by the epoché is not an annihilation of Being—given his task, what sense would it make for the phenomenologist to do away with his own Being?—but a modification of thinking. That it is such is underscored by the fact that what is excluded thereby is precisely every "*validity* of Being" (*Seins*geltung) pertaining to the *omnitudo realitatis*; validity is after all nothing in the world, but issues wholly from consciousness. The modification first manifests itself as a radical distinction of regions—between transcendent and transcendental Being. By means of it, thinking is freed of its attachment to the transcendent and allowed to attend to the transcendental sphere alone. Within phenomenological praxis this distinction is reflected in a distinction of ways of speaking: "But as part of the method, regarding the findings that are to be entered into the registry book of phenomenology" no longer into the book of the world, as in Descartes, for it has been excluded—"we prescribe for ourselves *the norm of phenomenological reduction* that is also related to our empirical existence and prevents us from entering any proposition that contains, explicitly or implicitly, natural positings of that kind. Insofar as individual factual existence is at issue, the phenomenologist proceeds no differently than any other eidetic scientist, for example the geometer." Both the phenomenologist and the geometer maintain the distinction between regions of Being. And so long as each is careful to do so, he will not enter into countersense. Just this points the way out of the seeming countersense of the phenomenologist's exclusion of himself: the semblance is dissolved by attending to the pertinent regional distinctions and speaking accordingly.[6] One cannot stop speaking as a natural, empirical being—to require one to do so would be no less countersensical than the phenomenologist's self-annihilation mentioned above—but the propositions one expresses can be rid of all natural, empirical content. The phenomenologist is required simply to abide by the norm of the epoché—all the while abiding by the preceding principle of all principles—and thereby maintain the relevant regional distinctions.

1.1.2 The Second Objection: Self-Reference. Success in doing so depends on critical reflection, which is phenomenology's ownmost mode of inquiry. As a result, further objections, which center on an apparent vicious circularity in the self-reference of the phenomenological method, threaten to pull the rug out from under phenomenology. Husserl sums up the thrust of the objections as follows: "it might be found objectionable that in the phenomenological attitude we direct our regard to some pure lived experiences in order to inquire into them, but that the lived experiences of this inquiry itself, with this attitude and direction of regard, should, when taken in phenomenological purity, at the same time belong to the realm to be inquired into." Much like the objection to the phenomenologist's self-exclusion, this one has its source in a lack of distinction: it ignores the essential features of the structure of consciousness. Husserl retorts that such self-reference would pose a problem "only if the cognition of all the other things in the respective provinces of inquiry depended on the . . . cognition of the thinking currently done by the particular thinker — which is an obviously countersensical presupposition." Such countersense would arise from the failure to distinguish between the reflecting ego and the stream of lived experiences reflected upon, that is, between consciousness as reflecting act and consciousness as object of reflection. The endlessness of that stream provides for the essential disconnectedness of the individual lived experiences unified within it. Furthermore, in view of these basic distinctions, the presupposition would be countersensical precisely because the one asserting it would have to have made an observation about the sphere in question; in other words, he would have had to have availed himself of self-referential structures in attempting to deny the legitimacy of the very same structures.

1.1.3 The Third Objection: The Use and Justification of Concepts. A related objection confronts phenomenology, just as it does every self-referential science—and, strikingly, it at first seems to be one that Husserl cannot dispose of by pointing to its countersense. The "difficulty" that seems to place phenomenology in question is that it must work with concepts and methods that initially are not completely determinate and that can achieve determinacy only in the course of its inquiries, thus not in advance but only retroactively.[7] Examples of cases in which such reflective justification is required have already been touched on in the foregoing, specifically in Husserl's assertion that it is of phenomenology's "own essence to realize the most perfect clarity about its own essence," as well as in the implicit requirement that one must first effect the epoché before one can properly understand and evaluate it. Because phenomenology is based neither on induction nor on deduction, but on intuition alone, it cannot justify its concepts and methods by inference from axioms, unlike geometry or logic, for example. Husserl does, of course, employ one axiom, namely the principle of all principles; yet it has the status of a methodical and not of a logical axiom. Nothing can be inferred from it; nothing can be justified by means of it; rather, the principle merely sets the guideline for inquiry: one must take what is given as it presents itself to intuition and come to terms with it within the bounds of intuition. Consequently, the phenomenologist's initial employment of any conceptual or methodical determination can be only provisional, to be justified only by intuition in the course of inquiry.

Such provisionality is in fact unavoidable where thinking follows Being: "Without preliminary and preparatory deliberations on its subject matter and method, no new science is ever projected. But the concepts and the other elements of method with which an incipient psychology, phenomenology, etc. operates in such preparatory labors are themselves psychological, phenomenological, etc., and acquire their scientific stamp *only* within the *system* of the science that has *already* been justified" (123).[8] Any misgivings about proceeding in this way cannot be taken seriously, Husserl notes, for they will be dissolved through real phenomenological work, and, once again, that means: through intuition. No argument can or need be brought against an objection to the apparent circularity of an intuition-based science, such as phenomenology, and its reflective justificatory procedures, for at issue is really the ground of such a science, that is, its axioms, which one can neither get behind nor question in advance of any familiarity with them.[9] All Husserl need do in response to the said misgivings is appeal to his sole axiom, which amounts to a call for work:

"Now if phenomenology wants to be at all a science within the limits of mere immediate intuition, a purely 'descriptive' eidetic science, then what is universal of its procedure is already given as something completely obvious. It must bring into view occurrences of pure consciousness as examples, make them perfectly clear, analyze and seize upon their essences within the limits of that clarity, trace with insight the essential concatenations, capture what is seen in faithful [*getreu*] conceptual expressions that allow their sense to be prescribed purely by what is seen or what one gains general insight into, etc." This appeal to intuition as the starting point is not simply a matter of opinion or personal preference, but arises from insight into the essential features of reflection.

1.1.4 Reflection. Beyond its basis in intuition, phenomenology proceeds according to a fixed, unidirectional order of inquiry, which comprises two levels: first, one must proceed naively, abiding "blindly," as it were, by the principle of all principles; one must employ the corresponding procedure so as to become familiar with the new field of inquiry. Then, and only then, is one in a position to reflect upon the science and its results: "scientific reflection on the essence of the procedure itself, on the essence of the kinds of givenness operating in the latter, on the essence, effect [*Leistung*], and conditions of perfect clarity and insight, as well as of the perfectly faithful and fixed conceptual expression, and on other such things, now assumes the function of a general and logically rigorous justification of the method." Only by means of such reflection, thus by considering what one has done, does phenomenology become critical in the proper sense of the term; only then is the phenomenological method raised to a scientific method; and only on that basis can phenomenology achieve the status of science. Although reflection remains crucial to the further development of phenomenology as a science,[10] for essential reasons it must always alternate with "naive," that is un- or pre-reflective, inquiry. In each instance, reflective evaluation and justification presupposes the naive employment of the intuitive procedure. And it is precisely on account of this necessarily unidirectional order of intuition-based inquiry that the misgivings about the phenomenological procedure cannot be dispensed with in advance by means of arguments. Instead, Husserl must set them aside, for they violate the order on which any critique is necessarily based—because the initial "naive" work has not been done, there is nothing concrete on which such critique could be based. Those misgivings would be countersensical only if they were based on such work. As things stand, they arise from outside of the sphere in question.

1.2 The First Positive Account: The Aim and Method of Phenomenology

The recollection of the fundamental significance of intuition to phenomenological inquiry not only enables Husserl to bypass the last apparent obstacle to such inquiry, but it also provides him with the foundation for his first "positive" account of the new science in this context. This account centers on the aim and method of phenomenology. Whereas the order of actual inquiry proceeds from the ground up,[11] the account of phenomenology Husserl gives here is unfolded, as is customary, in the reverse order, thus beginning with the highest level of concern reached thus far (faithful conceptual expression) and moving down to the lowest level (what is given in pure intuition). This account consists of methodological considerations and as such takes place entirely in the mode of reflection; it draws on the results of previous eidetic analyses. By following the aforementioned order, Husserl puts himself in a position to begin immediately with the analysis of the structures of pure consciousness.

1.2.1 Doctrine of Predication. A doctrine of essences, such as phenomenology intends to be, can be effective only if its intuitions are brought to speech. In view of this, Husserl must develop a doctrine of predication, though at this point he can only sketch its basic features. First is the relation between the expression and what is expressed: "we thus perform acts of seeing essences immediately with respect to given examples of transcendentally pure consciousness and fix them conceptually or terminologically" (124). Implicit here is that there is no "natural" priority of the essence over its expression such that it would require a specific expression. Rather, it is consciousness that first decides on a term or phrase and imposes it on the essence; the expression *fixes* the essence. For this reason, neither the source of the words, whether they come from everyday or scientific or some other kind of speech, nor their initial degree of indeterminacy plays a role in such a decision. Any problems that might arise from a term's "original" significance are disposed of by means of this concrete reference: "As soon as [the words] 'coincide' with the intuitively given in the manner of an actional expression, they assume a definite sense as their sense which is actional and clear *hic et nunc*; and from here on out they can be scientifically fixed."[12] Only subsequent to such concretion may the essence expressed be said to take precedence over the expression. That is, the essence sets the standard by which the "faithfulness" of an expression is measured, and in fact as the latter's definite sense. It specifies the parameters of the expression's adequacy, which can range from emptiness to fullness. The more faithful the expression is, the greater its adequacy.

However, the faithfulness of individual expressions to what is given in a particular instance is but the starting point of Husserl's doctrine. The next step is to fix the expressions "scientifically," which is to say, to systematize the mass of statements accumulated through inquiry. They thereby gain scientific utility: "Science is possible only where the results of thinking can be stored up in the form of knowledge and used for later thinking in the form of a system of statements," and on account of the distinctness of their logical sense, the statements "can be understood without clarity in the underlying objectivatings—thus without insight—or, as the case may be, can be actionalized in judgments." Their logical sense stems, on the one hand, from the articulation of

HEIDEGGER ON TRUTH

Its Essence and Its Fate

New Studies in Phenomenology and Hermeneutics

Kenneth Maly, General Editor

New Studies in Phenomenology and Hermeneutics aims to open up new approaches to classical issues in phenomenology and hermeneutics. Thus its intentions are the following: to further the work of Edmund Husserl, Maurice Merleau-Ponty, and Martin Heidegger–as well as that of Paul Ricoeur, Hans-Georg Gadamer, and Emmanuel Levinas; to enhance phenomenological thinking today by means of insightful interpretations of texts in phenomenology as they inform current issues in philosophical study; to inquire into the role of interpretation in phenomenological thinking: to take seriously Husserl's term *phenomenology* as "a science which is intended to supply the basic instrument for a rigorously scientific philosophy and, in its consequent application, to make possible a methodical reform of all the sciences"; to take up Heidegger's claim that "what is own to phenomenology, as a philosophical 'direction,' does not rest in being *real*. Higher than reality stands *possibility*. Understanding phenomenology consists solely in grasping it as possibility"; to practise *phenomenology* as "underway," as "the *praxis* of the self-showing of the matter for thinking," as "entering into the movement of enactment-thinking."

The commitment of this book series is also to provide English translations of significant works from other languages. In summary, **New Studies in Phenomenology and Hermeneutics** intends to provide a forum for a full and fresh thinking and rethinking of the way of phenomenology and interpretive phenomenology, that is, hermeneutics.

For a list of books published in this series, see page 183.

Heidegger on Truth

Its Essence and Its Fate

GRAEME NICHOLSON

UNIVERSITY OF TORONTO PRESS
Toronto Buffalo London

Toronto Buffalo London
utorontopress.com
Printed in Canada

ISBN 978-1-4875-0441-0

Printed on acid-free, 100% post-consumer recycled paper with vegetable-based inks.

Library and Archives Canada Cataloguing in Publication

Title: Heidegger on truth : its essence and its fate / Graeme Nicholson.
Names: Nicholson, Graeme, author.
Series: New studies in phenomenology and hermeneutics (Toronto, Ont.)
Description: Series statement: New studies in phenomenology and hermeneutics | Includes bibliographical references and index.
Identifiers: Canadiana 20190137789 | ISBN 9781487504410 (hardcover)
Subjects: LCSH: Heidegger, Martin, 1889–1976. Vom Wesen der Wahrheit. | LCSH: Truth.
Classification: LCC B3279.H49 N52 2019 | DDC 121—dc23

This book has been published with the help of a grant from the Federation for the Humanities and Social Sciences, through the Awards to Scholarly Publications Program, using funds provided by the Social Sciences and Humanities Research Council of Canada.

University of Toronto Press acknowledges the financial assistance to its publishing program of the Canada Council for the Arts and the Ontario Arts Council, an agency of the Government of Ontario.

Canada Council for the Arts
Conseil des Arts du Canada

ONTARIO ARTS COUNCIL
CONSEIL DES ARTS DE L'ONTARIO
an Ontario government agency
un organisme du gouvernement de l'Ontario

Funded by the Government of Canada
Financé par le gouvernement du Canada
Canada

MIX
Paper from responsible sources
FSC
www.fsc.org
FSC® C016245

their systematic interconnections, but at bottom from the initial decision by which an expression fixes a given essence. Any attempt to get behind this decision, to lay bare its underpinnings, disregards the constitutive function of consciousness, and plunges one into the stream of lived experiences and thus into an infinite regress. What is important here is not the indeterminate background of some expression, but the clarity of its current reference. Hence, following the articulation of the systematic interconnections between statements, the next task is to assure that "the same words and sentences maintain an unambiguous relation to certain intuitively apprehensible essences, which constitute the words' and sentences' 'fulfilling sense.'" And that means that one must assure that any previous significance attached to the words and sentences prior to the said decision remain "crossed out."

1.2.2 Degrees of Clarity. Despite the great importance of expression to the science of phenomenology, in view of his guiding intention Husserl's account cannot stop at this level, but must descend to the next. The way was already pointed by the foregoing talk of expression. On the one hand, it is always the expression *of* some given, of an essence or essential concatenation seized upon, and so Husserl's primary concern here has to lie with this founding given. On the other hand, to the extent that it is faithful, an expression adequately renders what is given. This talk of faithfulness entails, in turn, a twofold distinction: not just between greater or lesser faithfulness to what is given, but also between greater or lesser clarity of the given itself. It is this distinction to which the said path leads. It especially is crucial to Husserl's endeavor precisely because of its implications for the clarification of the given, thus for the possibility of faithful expression, and ultimately for securing the status of science for phenomenology, which is based wholly on the knowledge contained in those expressions. Since the greater the degree of clarity, the more perfect the knowledge, phenomenology's objective has to be to obtain maximal clarity. But before pursuing this goal, Husserl must specify the general features of clarity. They pertain mutatis mutandis to the givenness of an essence and the seizing upon the essence, thus to both sides of the correlation between the objective and the subjective—though at this point the former is stressed, albeit in each case as *for* a seizing consciousness.

As always in Husserl, every predication necessarily implies its opposite; it carries the latter with it, so to speak, as its shadow; both are essential, inseparable possibilities. Hence, just as the talk of reason implies the possibility of unreason, likewise the talk of clarity implies a possible lack of clarity. When taken absolutely, both sides represent the extremes of a gradation (see 125ff.). The range of clarity for a given essence is bounded below by an absolute lack of clarity, or total obscurity, which may be denoted by the value '0'. Above it is bounded by absolute clarity, or the value '1'. In other words, the zero-limit is marked by complete "emptiness," or what Husserl also terms "vague remoteness," whereas the one-limit possesses complete fullness, or "absolute proximity." Such proximity is achieved only where an essence is present in "pure self-givenness." In which case: "We are conscious of something objectual not merely somehow or other as a 'self' standing in our view and as 'given,' but as a purely given self, completely as it is within itself [*in sich selbst*]" (126). Self-givenness is total, and as such is distinct from originary givenness, which is the mode of givenness proper to perception. Originary givenness can never be total givenness; nor can it orient further acts bearing on what it has been given. By contrast, insofar as self-givenness entails the upper limit of the said gradation, that self—which varies in accordance with the essence in question—sets the standard of clarity sought in each seizing upon an essence. Even where it is not given completely, that is, where there is a remainder of obscurity or emptiness, that self is determinative. On account of this, it holds that—at least where genuine degrees of clarity are in play—lesser degrees of clarity point to higher degrees, albeit not in the manner of a sign.[13] Husserl's emphasis on degrees here implies that the extremes of any gradation, self-givenness and complete emptiness, are relatively rare: "it is a rule that no pure intuitions be on hand, or that no pure empty objectivatings become pure intuitions; rather, impure intuitions play a major role—possibly as intermediate stages—in bringing the object of their concern to intuition in accordance with certain of its sides or moments, while objectivating it merely emptily in accordance with others" (128). Such incompleteness is compounded by the fact that whatever is given is "usually surrounded by a halo of indeterminate determinability, which is such that when it is brought closer 'explicatively,' it divides up into series of objectivatings—first of all perhaps again in obscurity, then afresh in the sphere of givenness, until what is intended enters into the brightly illuminated circle of perfect givenness" (129).

Since the acts founded upon self-givenness possess a certainty unequaled by other acts, it is only natural that phenomenology aims at the former degree of clarity. The objective of eidetic clarification is to bring the essence ever closer until absolute proximity is achieved. In keeping with the aforementioned characteristics of givenness, the phenomenologist must generally proceed step by step. But even here a distinction of levels or degrees must be borne in mind: absolute clarity, that is clarity on all levels, is rarely called for or even possible. Thus, in seizing upon essences, it is not always necessary that the clarity achieved on a higher level extend to its lower levels; the degree of clarity called for, as it were, how deep it runs, depends entirely on the aim or respect of clarification. Husserl illustrates this by pointing to the differences between the genera 'color' and 'tone'. Since of concern here would be the most general differences between essences, it would not be fruitful to press for clarity at a lower level—in fact it would lead to an infinite regress. The clarification involved in seizing upon essences is highly gradated, whereby the lower and upper limits of any given gradation depend upon both the givenness of the essence and the specific aim guiding the seizing-upon it.

1.2.2.1 PERCEPTION AND FANTASY. For the phenomenological method of eidetic clarification, for the effort to bring an essence to givenness and, where necessary, to bring it ever closer, two modes of intuitive consciousness are decisive: perception and fantasy. In certain respects, "originarily giving perception in general, and of course external perception in particular" has primacy over "all kinds of representiation," including fantasy, for in a unique way perception provides "a basis for phenomenological eidetic findings" (130).[14] The chief advantages of perception in this connection are that it possesses "perfect clarity with respect to all the objectual moments actually given in it in the mode of originariness" and that it offers, "perhaps with the cooperation of reflection referred back to it, clear and steady singularizations for universal eidetic analyses of a phenomenological kind, more precisely: even for act analyses." The unique clarity and constancy of its examples become evident when compared with other acts. Unlike anger, for instance, external perception is "not 'evaporated' by reflection; we can study its universal essence and the essence of its universally appurtenant components and essential correlates within the limits of originariness without any special effort to produce clarity." Aside from its possible deficient modes, such as perception in fog or darkness, these advantages generally derive from perception.

And yet despite the fundamental role played in eidetic analysis by perception, fantasy proves to have priority over it, a state of affairs Husserl makes abundantly clear when he points to the significance of fiction—which, of course, is fabricated in fantasy alone—to phenomenology: "one can . . . say in strict truth that 'fiction' makes up the vital element of phenomenology, as it does of every eidetic science, that fiction is the source from which the cognition of 'eternal truths' draws its sustenance" (132). The key to the hierarchy between the two lies in the distinction between the degrees of freedom each offers the eidetic investigator. This freedom is not arbitrariness, but rather the ability to gain maximal clarity on a definite essence.[15] It is precisely in this respect that the originariness of perception proves to be of lesser import. This has to be the case given the exclusion of the general thesis and thus of the natural world. Consequently, however helpful it may be, perception offers always only "restricted" clarity; by contrast, fantasy is the realm of absolute, eidetic freedom, for it is not bound to any actuality. Husserl illustrates this by way of the geometer, who works more in fantasy than in perception: "in actually sketching and building models, he is restricted; in fantasy he has incomparably more freedom reshaping fictitious figures at will, and in running through continuously modified possible formations, thus in generating a host of new constructions; a freedom that gives him access to the expanses of essential possibilities with their infinite horizons of eidetic cognitions for the very first time. That is why the sketches normally come after the fantasy-constructions and the eidetically pure thinking done on the basis of the latter and serve chiefly to fix certain stages in the previously performed process, thereby making it easier to representiate later" (131). What holds of the geometer holds also, generally, for the phenomenologist, "who deals with reduced lived experiences and the correlates belonging essentially to them. There are also infinitely many eidetic phenomenological formations. He, too, can make use of the resource of originary givenness only to a limited extent." The chief advantage of such givenness for eidetic clarification, then, is not that it provides "justifying validity"—this it cannot do once the epoché has been effected—but rather that it, so to speak, "fertilizes" fantasy by making available all manner of examples from the sphere of originary givenness. Thus the hierarchy between perception and fantasy is bidirectional: perception is first not only for us but also as the source of examples; on the other hand, free fantasy is first in that it plays a crucial role in seizing upon essences: through it, and not perception, one stands to gain maximal clarity. With this outline of the relation and distinction between perception and fantasy as the two primary modes of access to essences,[16] Husserl returns to the ground of phenomenology, namely intuition. It is at this ground that every negative account of phenomenology aims and with which every positive account begins.

1.3 The Second Negative and Positive Accounts: Intuition and First Science

This holds for the second negative account Husserl gives of phenomenology, with which the next positive account is intertwined. It centers on phenomenology's claim to be a science. Thus far Husserl has characterized it as an intuition-based, which is to say descriptive, science; and in fact, as an "eidetic doctrine of lived experiences" (133), it is to be a descriptive eidetics. Yet for those unfamiliar with phenomenology, this determination initially has to be disconcerting, since it seems to be countersensical. The consequent misgiving is expressed in the questions: How can an eidetics be descriptive? How can an a priori science describe anything? The misgiving has its source in the widespread prejudice that the mathematical disciplines provide the only legitimate model for any science that would be an eidetics—they are, Husserl notes, "the only ones that can at present represent the idea of a scientific eidetics in an effective manner" (133). Nevertheless, one who is practiced in phenomenology knows that for essential reasons they "cannot be called upon for guidance" (132) in evaluating phenomenology's claim. Consequently, if he is to establish the new eidetics as something other than a "mathematics of phenomena," his task here must be to dissolve the said prejudice, or the spell cast by the familiar eidetics. That requires that he first distinguish among the known eidetic sciences in order then to set phenomenology off from them—here the focus is on the "aims and method" of each discipline, but also and in fact primarily on the region that determines them. In this way it becomes clear how a nonmathematical discipline such as phenomenology can legitimately call itself an eidetics. Once again, Husserl's analyses start with what is first for us so as to introduce what is first by nature.

In order to determine the extent to which the mathematical disciplines may be taken as the standard by which to judge phenomenology's claim, Husserl must specify what mathematics is, which is to say, he must fix the sense in which the talk is of mathematics—for it is only after the concept has gained determinacy that he can use it as a standard. This he does by paring down the abstract general concept to a concrete, usable concept. The first step is to distinguish between material and formal essences and eidetic sciences. Because phenomenology is concerned with lived experiences, it cannot be a formal eidetic discipline, and so Husserl is justified in disregarding the latter. If mathematics is to be at all helpful in grasping phenomenology, then only in the form of a material discipline, such as geometry. The question is therefore "whether phenomenology must be, or can be, constituted as a 'geometry' of lived experiences." Before he answers, Husserl recalls that primary distinctions between sciences rest on distinctions between their respective regions: "To each region there corresponds a regional ontology with a series of regional sciences that are self-contained, or possibly based on one another, corresponding precisely to the highest genera that have their unity in the region" (134). In accordance with the character of the genera or the components thereof to which they attend, the material sciences may be further divided into concrete and abstract sciences. Geometry falls in the latter class; its genus and so its objects are abstract. The methodological consequence of this is that, like the other familiar eidetic sciences, geometry cannot proceed descriptively: "the lowest eidetic differences, thus the countless spatial shapes that can be sketched in space, are not seized upon in intuitions of singulars, described and organized into classes by geometry, as do the descriptive natural sciences with respect to the empirical formations of nature." Rather, it proceeds purely deductively: from its axioms it can derive "all the ideally possible spatial shapes and the eidetic relationships proper to them, in the form of exactly determinative concepts that stand in for the essences that generally remain alien to our intuition" (135). Geometry can and must proceed as it does precisely because it comprises a definite system of axioms, which is to say, it "'exhaustively defines' a manifold purely analytically" (136). Nothing treated by this discipline lies outside its system, that is, every new result is derived from and thus was already contained in its axioms.

This characterization indicates that the analogy suggested above between geometry and phenomenology is erroneous. First of all, the latter's objects are not abstract, but concrete: it inquires into the essences of lived experiences. Yet, Husserl notes, because lived experiences contain abstract moments, the question remains open whether their highest genera can be fixed in a definite system of axioms akin to that of geometry. Were this possible, phenomenological inquiry would proceed only by derivation, that is, by "a mediate logical determining, the results of which, even if they are 'sketched in a figure,' principially cannot be seized upon in immediate intuition" (137). This contrast in method, between derivation and intuition, already marks the second respect in which the said analogy is erroneous. It points to the unbridgeable gulf that separates material mathematical disciplines, such as geometry, and phenomenology. Their differences are by no means arbitrary, the result of idiosyncrasies on the part of investigators in each field, but are necessary consequences of their respective regions. Still, the question of the possible "definiteness" of phenomenology must be addressed. It can be answered by determining whether it is possible, to say nothing of necessary, that every science fulfill the ideal of material mathematical science, that is, whether the province of each can and must be a definite manifold. Generally speaking, this depends on the exactness of a science's concept formations, which itself depends on the exactness of the essences fixed by such concepts. In both cases the region, or province, is determinative: "But the extent to which 'exact' essences are to be found in an eidetic province, and whether exact essences at all undergird all the essences that can be seized upon in actual intuition, and therefore all their eidetic components as well, depends entirely upon the specific peculiarity of the province." The decisiveness of a given region for concept formation is shown by a consideration of descriptive and explicative, or exact, sciences. Husserl takes descriptive natural science, on the one hand, and geometry, on the other, as his examples.

The dangers of speaking "from on high" and not inquiring from "the ground up" become evident here. Namely, by accepting the authority of material mathematical eidetics in questions of exactness, the investigator is compelled to commit a *metabasis* and thereby plunges into countersense. This occurs because the assertion of such authority ignores the essential differences between regions, their unique requirements and possibilities. However, in accordance with his insight into such difference, Husserl is able to combat the threat of a *metabasis* by reiterating a form of the principle of all principles: he stresses that things "be taken as they are given" (138). Thus in the case of the descriptive natural scientist: because he attends to factual, sensuously intuitable shapes, he "forms morphological concepts of vague forms that are directly seized upon on the basis of sensuous intuition and that, however vague they are, are fixed conceptually or terminologically. The vagueness of such concepts, the circumstance that their spheres of application are fluid, does not make them defective; for in the sphere of knowledge in which they are used, they are absolutely indispensable, or in it they are the only legitimate concepts." Given the starting point of his inquiry (the sensuously intuitable), the natural scientist's concepts are necessarily "inexact and therefore nonmathematical"; geometry cannot "correct" this situation, even if it can be used as a tool in the investigation of nature. The difference between the starting points of the two sciences already renders the subsumption of one by the other impossible. This impasse becomes quite clear in view of the contrast between their respective concepts. Again, the natural scientist's concepts are necessarily morphological. The geometer's, on the other hand, are ideal: "they express something that one cannot 'see.'" Whereas "exact concepts have their correlates in essences that have the character of 'ideas' in the Kantian sense," descriptive concepts have their correlates in morphological essences. The differences between their essences, and thus their regions, is reflected in their respective methods; geometry proceeds nonintuitively and purely deductively, whereas descriptive science proceeds intuitively and inductively: "That ideation which yields ideal essences as 'ideal' limits that principially cannot be found in any sensuous intuition but that morphological essences 'approach' more or less, though without ever reaching them—this ideation is something fundamentally different in its essence from the seizing upon an essence by simple 'abstraction' in which a prominent 'moment' is raised into the region of essences as something principially vague, as something typical" (138–39). Failing to distinguish between these two types of concepts and their respective essences leads one into countersense.

Although the distinction between exact and descriptive science is instructive, it does not yet provide a positive definition of phenomenology. Like descriptive natural science, its field of inquiry (pure consciousness) is in constant flux. Therefore, its objects, the fluctuating lived experiences, cannot be fixed conceptually in an exact manner. "As for phenomenology, it intends to be a descriptive eidetic doctrine of transcendentally pure lived experiences in the phenomenological attitude; and, like every other descriptive, nonundergirding, and nonidealizing discipline, it has its legitimacy *within itself*. Whatever can be grasped eidetically in pure intuition as belonging to reduced lived experiences, whether as a really inherent component part or as an intentional correlate, properly belongs to phenomenology and is for it a great source of absolute cognitions" (139). Although phenomenology can and does make use of mediate inferences, such "nonintuitive procedures" have "only the methodical significance of leading us to the things that a subsequent direct seeing of essence must bring to givenness" (140). Actual seeing, immediate intuition, provides phenomenology with the absolute standard. Husserl ends this account by asserting that "as a descriptive science of essence, transcendental phenomenology belongs to a fundamental class of eidetic sciences that is totally different from the one to which the mathematical sciences belong" (141). As he showed in the foregoing, he cannot point to an example of the kind of eidetic science phenomenology wants to be. The limits of any analogy lie in the fact that phenomenology is a radically new science, one never before seen in the form Husserl is seeking to introduce in *Ideas I*.

2. First Categories: The Archimedean Point and its Other

After having discussed phenomenology as a science, Husserl next turns to the field of phenomenological inquiry itself. Although this has been his express goal from the outset of *Ideas I*, he initially had to postpone its investigation in order to clear the way into the new field. This required that he explicate the essential features of the phenomenological method, both the means for entering and then for describing pure or transcendental consciousness. Despite their inaugural function, however, those considerations had to remain largely provisional, since it is within this field alone that Husserl's claims for phenomenology find their justification. The analysis of pure consciousness therefore has a dual purpose: to shore up those claims by delineating the phenomenological system.

2.1 Phenomenology as Rigorous Science

Chief among his claims is that phenomenology is First Science with respect to every other science, but also First Philosophy with respect to every other thought that has laid claim to that status within the philosophical tradition. As the long-sought universal science, phenomenology is the first to set the sciences on their proper course, since it is the first to provide them with a firm foundation. In fact this claim is a corollary of that for the field's priority, and therefore is borne out only insofar as phenomenology's proper field of inquiry, its region, is shown to be the first. Husserl asserts its firstness in terms of absoluteness: "By means of the phenomenological reduction, the realm of transcendental consciousness had given itself to us as the realm of, in a determinate sense, 'absolute' Being." In one respect this sphere is absolute precisely because it has been purified of all transcendence and thereby freed of all the contingency that otherwise fetters consciousness. For example, when it is taken as the empirical entity investigated by psychology. Yet there is another, more decisive respect in which transcendental consciousness is absolute: "It is the primal category of all Being (or in our terminology, the primal region), the one in which all other regions of Being are rooted, to which they are related according to their essence, on which they are therefore all essentially dependent. The doctrine of categories"—that is, of regions, or more precisely: of regional ontologies—"must start out entirely from this most radical of all distinctions of Being: Being as consciousness and Being as something that 'manifests itself' in consciousness, 'transcendent' Being," a distinction that can be "gained and appreciated in its purity *only* through the method of phenomenological reduction" (141–42).[17] Phenomenology aims to be just such a doctrine. As its first category, transcendental consciousness accordingly forms the lower limit of the Husserlian system. It is, as it were, the "Archimedean point" from and with which phenomenology must start. By investigating the relationship between it and the corresponding categories of "transcendent" Being, Husserl abides by his own demand "that this affair-complex, with the various aspects peculiar to it, be understood from the ground up" (142).[18] It is by virtue of its radicality, its focus on that ground as the region in which all other regions are rooted, that his "doctrine of categories" proves to be the most fundamental ontology. Phenomenology is the first First Philosophy, because it makes the first absolute beginning—Husserl is, after all, the first to have seen this absolute sphere in all its purity, which is to say: he is the first to have seen it, for its Being is inseparable from its purity. And it is for this reason that he is the first to establish it as the absolute ground of all other spheres.

2.1.1 Region and Method. A point of tension makes itself felt here, however, when one recalls that this sphere is "gained and appreciated in its purity only through the method of phenomenological reduction." This would seem to call into question the source of phenomenology's firstness inasmuch as the primacy of its region looks to be dependent on its method for accessing the latter. Yet the tension dissolves as soon as the distinction between their respective modes of priority is considered: whereas the region of transcendental consciousness is first ontologically and thus by nature, the phenomenological method is first operationally and thus for us. The method is and remains dependent upon the region. This is not to say, however, that the method somehow becomes superfluous once phenomenology has attained its proper field of inquiry; on the contrary, the region can be accessed and investigated always only by means of the method. Both sides are bound together by a reciprocal relation, one so strong that there can be no thought of one without the other, even though the hierarchy between them remains intact. And this means that any discussion of one side of the pair necessarily sheds light on the other.

The nature of the reciprocity of method and region becomes particularly clear, for example, in view of one of the results of the epoché, namely the disclosure of the source of phenomenology's priority over all the other sciences, including psychology. Again, the epoché excludes the general thesis, and with it falls all transcendent Being. This exclusion proves to be an inclusion, however, insofar as transcendent Being is retained through its reduction to transcendental or immanent Being. At first glance this seems paradoxical: what is excluded is included. But whereas exclusion and inclusion are in one sense contrary moments, in this context they are ultimately complementary: they differ only in aspect; in effect they are simultaneous and indistinguishable. The semblance of paradox dissolves as soon as one sees that the epoché affects the sciences just as it does all transcendent Being, for they themselves are instances of transcendent Being on the one hand and they attend to regions of the same on the other. And yet: "it is inherent in the sense" of the relations between them that "the dominion [*Herrschaftsbereich*] of phenomenology encompasses in a certain remarkable way all the other sciences, which it after all excludes" (142). Here exclusion becomes inclusion solely on the basis of the modification it effects: "The exclusion has at the same time the character of a revaluing change of sign, and with this change what has been revalued once again fits into the phenomenological sphere." Exclusion and inclusion are thus two sides of one revaluation. As noted, it is not a modification of real things, but of consciousness—no real thing is excluded, but rather the *belief* in the real; and the corresponding revaluation shows them to be things *as* they are objects *of* consciousness. It is this relation that grounds phenomenology's priority over the other sciences. Although the sciences are excluded as transcendent entities (like their regions), they are reduced to immanencies and thereby included in transcendental consciousness as its objects. And these are considered, in turn, in one of two ways: "Everything transcendent, insofar as it is given in consciousness, is an Object of phenomenological investigation not only with respect to the consciousness of it—for example, the different modes of consciousness in which it is given as the same—but also, though this is essentially connected with the former, as what is given and accepted in the modes of givenness." The possibility of investigating these two sides of consciousness, the How and What of something given in consciousness, derives entirely from the said revaluation, which itself rests not only on the insight into the relation between both sides, but on the more radical insight into the primacy of consciousness insofar as it is the source of its object's sense.

That investigation amounts to an analysis of the newly won field of inquiry, the ascertainment of "its major themes, in particular which fundamental lines of description are prescribed by the most universal essential species of lived experiences" (143). However, given the aforementioned interdependence of field and method, Husserl's turn to this field cannot yield one-sided results; a consideration of the universal structures of consciousness necessarily entails the problems of method,[19] just as his "discussions of method thus far were already determined by the most universal insights into the essence of the phenomenological sphere" (144). Hence: "It is obvious that a more penetrating knowledge of the latter—not with respect to its particulars but with respect to the all-pervasive universalities—must also supply us with methodological norms that have a richer content and that at the same time are norms by which all specific methods will have to abide." Their interdependence, then, is not marked by equality so much as by hierarchy: Being as consciousness is first; thinking receives its norms from it. This accords fully with the principle of all principles, which privileges the thing, and thus Being, and places thinking in a position of dependence. At issue here, of course, is not just any thing, but rather the phenomenological sphere, pure consciousness. And it is to this sphere that thinking—and in the present context this means the method—is obliged to correspond: "A method is, after all, nothing that is, or can be, introduced from outside. Formal logic and noetics do not provide a method but only the form of a possible method; and no matter how useful a knowledge of form can be with respect to methodology, a determinate method . . . is a norm that arises *from* the fundamental regional specificity of the province and the latter's universal structures. Therefore, a cognitive seizing upon such a method depends essentially on the knowledge of these structures."[20] The method is unfolded in light of the work done in the particular region and not imported into it, not imposed upon the region from outside or on high.

And yet there is also a manner in which the field is dependent on the method: only by means of it can work be done in the field, which is to say: only by means of it can further, more adequate knowledge of the field be gained. The nature of field and method, as well as of their interdependence, becomes ever more evident only by means of reciprocal demonstration: the method is clarified through the articulation of the region, and the region through the articulation of the method; such clarification results in their mutual justification. Furthermore, because neither side can be accounted for without reference to the other, such demonstration cannot take place once and for all, but is a continual, reflective process, which entails an endless zigzagging or spiraling from one side to the other and back, ideally from the ground up into the heights. Precisely this process characterizes the phenomenological enterprise as such, the goal of which is a total elucidation of both its field and its method.

2.1.2 The Primacy of Reflection. If, as noted above,[21] fiction is the vital element of phenomenology, then reflection has to be even more vital to it since it names the class of acts to which the fiction-generating acts, that is, acts of fantasy, belong. The primacy of reflection[22] is attested in two ways, each of which corresponds to one of the two sides just touched on. On the one hand, reflection has a "universal methodological function: the phenomenological method moves entirely in acts of reflection" (144). Husserl's system is unfolded and justified from the start solely by means of reflective structures—the epoché itself is possible not only by virtue of but also as reflection, much the same as the eidetic reduction that precedes it. On the other hand, reflection marks one of the most fundamental traits of consciousness.[23] It is chiefly on these grounds that Husserl begins his investigation of the universal structures of consciousness by focusing on reflection. And yet he is compelled to do so also by "skeptical misgivings," which once again confront phenomenology. They peak in the denial of the efficacy of reflection for inquiry and, by extension, of the very possibility of phenomenology.[24] If Husserl is to save the new science from the danger posed by such misgivings, he must dispense with them entirely, and in fact by demonstrating the opposite of what they claim.

Characteristically, however, the misgivings themselves already testify to the efficacy of reflection, albeit unknowingly. And this provides Husserl with a foothold for his defense of reflection and phenomenology.[25] His guiding insight in this regard is that knowledge of consciousness—and thus of reflection—is possible only by means of reflection. Since the skeptic doubts precisely that which enables him to doubt, his misgivings about the cognitive significance of reflection prove to be countersensical and thus self-refuting, a state of affairs that, as Husserl notes, is consistent with the nature of skepticism: "All genuine skepticism, of whatever kind and orientation, gives itself away by the principial countersense that, in its argumentations, it implicitly presupposes as conditions of the possibility of their validity precisely what it denies in its theses" (155).[26] To refute such misgivings, Husserl must show how they refute themselves, which requires that he make explicit what remains implicit in them, that is, what they presuppose. Such showing indicates that what is decisive here is not Husserl's argument against skepticism so much as the intuition in which it is grounded. Consequently, the task at hand is to make visible the conditions of the skeptic's position, for without insight into them, into their source, the difficulties remain intact: "Here, as everywhere, skepticism is deprived of its force by going back from verbal argumentations to eidetic intuition, to originarily giving intuition and the legitimacy primally its own" (156). This is the *first rule of phenomenological inquiry*: wherever difficulties arise on the verbal level, the solution is to be found not in further argumentation, but rather at the intuitive level. Therefore, since the efficacy of reflection is in question, Husserl must make his guiding insight into the nature of consciousness clear to the skeptic, or to those placed in jeopardy by skepticism, which he can do only by looking directly at consciousness itself.[27]

At bottom there are two levels of consciousness: *Erleben* (living-in) and reflection upon what is lived-in (*Erlebtes*) or lived experience (*Erlebnis*).[28] Although intimately related, a hierarchy exists between them: "Every ego lives-in its lived experiences, and much is included in them really inherently and intentionally. It lives-in them: that does not mean that it has them *and* what they include 'in view,' and seizes upon them in the manner of immanent experiencing or of some other immanent intuiting or objectivating" (145). The *and* marks the point of scission between the two levels; it severs two kinds of "having." On the one hand, there is the living-in, which is always actional, always now. When it is originary, it is marked by immediacy. In it the ego "has" directly whatever it attends to, and in fact its attention is so intense that the ego is, as it were, unaware of or uninterested in anything beyond what it now "has." It is for essential reasons, then, that as long as it is living-in a lived experience the ego cannot simultaneously attend to that lived experience as such or to what it includes or to other lived experiences surrounding it. It has but one ray of regard, which can be directed only to one "object" at a given time. Yet the ego's regard is not confined to the lower level; rather, it may also be redirected at will to the living-in itself. Such redirection is reflection. At this second level of consciousness, the regard is also a lived experience, it has its object immediately, it lives-in it; but something new has occurred: it now has the object of the originary living-in only mediately.

On both levels, consciousness exhibits a peculiar pliability, an openness to varying directions of regard: the ego's regard can live-in one originary lived experience after another, but it can also be redirected in reflection to the living-in itself. Furthermore, because each lived experience includes components to which the ego does not attend immediately and is also surrounded by a halo of other lived experiences to which the ego's regard does not yet extend, each actionality of regard is accompanied by a range of possibilities for reflection: "Any lived experience that is not in view can—as an ideal possibility—become 'regarded'; a reflection of the ego is directed to it, it now becomes an Object for the ego. The same holds for the ego's possible regards directed to the components of the lived experience and to its intentionalities (to that of which the lived experience may be a consciousness)." In fact consciousness is so "pliable" that every lived experience can become the object of reflection, even reflections themselves "can become the substrates of new reflections; and so on *in infinitum*, in principial universality." But again, when one lives-in a lived experience, even if that lived experience is itself a reflection, there is no simultaneous reflection upon it: one lives-in always only immediately, actionally, now. The level of living-in can never be left behind, for it is the basis of all conscious life, whether this life is lived in originary *Erleben* (living-in or lived experiencing) or in reflection upon it. This is the source of the hierarchy between living-in and reflection; both levels are related insofar as each is a living-in and yet they remain distinct in view of their respective degrees of immediacy.

2.1.3 The Temporality of Reflection. The pliability of consciousness is evident in still another respect, one already intimated in the emphasis on actual living-in, on the ego's actional regard of a lived experience. Although it remains primary, such actionality—or the Now—is but one of three temporal modes of reflective access to lived experiences. The others are termed 'retention' and 'protention'. In the former, lived experiences are reflected upon as "having just been" or "having been earlier." They need not have been actually lived-in, for example perceived, but they must have been perceptible; they have to have belonged to the same stream—specifically, to the halo surrounding the originarily perceived lived experience—for it to be possible to live-in them "later." Likewise in the case of protention, which is "the precise counterpart of immediate retention,"[29] it does not bear on lived experiences that are actually lived-in, but on those that "will be" lived-in, that is, those one "expects" to live in. Each of the three temporal modes exhibits the nature of reflection: it is first and foremost an immanent "reference."[30] When the ego actually reflects on a lived experience, it actually refers to it. But in retention, the reference is a "reference back" (*Rückbezogenheit*) to what has been, and in protention a "reference in advance" (*Vorbezogenheit*) to what will be. It is significant to phenomenological inquiry that this reference is always a *self*-reference and, what is more, that the self in question has two sides: on the one side, the ego and, on the other, the stream of lived experiences, the infinite horizon of which extends in all directions. These essential features of reflection enable, but also justify, the "scientific eidetic study" of the "entire stream of lived experiences" (147). Yet although it aims at "systematic completeness," it should already be clear that the study of consciousness is an endless endeavor, and precisely because of the endlessness of its field, pure consciousness. This is further evidenced by Husserl's remark that the study is itself "carried out in various peculiarly structured reflective acts that themselves also belong in the stream of lived experiences and that, in corresponding higher level reflections, can and must be made the Objects of phenomenological analyses." *Despite its endlessness*, however, the field is neither groundless nor in flux in every respect; *such inquiry has a foundation, an Archimedean point from which every infinity of regard starts out*, and it is precisely this point that makes a phenomenological beginning possible.

2.1.4 The System of Reflections. Reflection alone enables that beginning, for through it alone "the stream of lived experiences, with all its manifold occurrences (moments of lived experience, intentionalia), becomes evidently apprehensible and analyzable."[31] Again, reflection is not only a fundamental trait of consciousness, but also "the method of consciousness for the cognition of any consciousness whatsoever," including reflection itself. And it is especially because of its methodological significance to phenomenology that reflection forms "one of the main chapters"—and in a sense the first—in the "book of phenomenology." Husserl begins with reflection. And since this book is to have "systematic completeness," he sees his present task in the complete differentiation and analysis of the diverse kinds of reflection "in systematic order" (148). Yet in view of the endlessness of the field of phenomenological inquiry, it is initially unclear as to how that order would look, to say nothing of how it could be systematic. The key lies in the effect of reflection, which was implicit in the foregoing: "every 'reflection' has the character of a modification of consciousness, and in fact a modification that principially any consciousness can undergo." The modification results in a change of attitude, of the comportment towards an "objectuality."[32] This talk is, of course, reminiscent of that of the epoché, which also introduces a change of attitude. But such change must be qualified in view of the scope of the modification in question, that is, whether it affects consciousness "globally" (as in the shift from the natural to the phenomenological attitude) or "locally" (as in the shift between individual acts). Of concern at the moment is a change of attitude not of the former type, which is effected by the epoché, but rather of the latter type. Furthermore, whereas reflection ultimately grounds the critical mode of phenomenology in which alone the critique of reason aimed at by Husserl can be carried out, that mode requires a much higher level of reflection, which is first reached through the epoché. By contrast, at the "local" level, the focus is on the shift from simple living-in to the consciousness of living-in or its components, and so on. Thus these analyses may be said to remain naive to a certain extent.[33] With this in mind, we may return to Husserl's account of reflection.

It is a modification to which any lived experience, as a "flux of becoming,"[34] may be subjected; and this indicates the manner in which consciousness is endless: "Since the modifications that we have fixed in view belong to every lived experience as ideally possible variations, and thus to a certain extent designate ideal operations that can be thought of as being performed on any lived experience, they can be repeated *in infinitum*; they can also be performed on the modified lived experiences" (149). What originally was not reflected upon, now becomes the object of reflection, and is thereby revalued. A change of sign occurs insofar as what was originarily lived-in is now present only mediately; the new, immediate object of regard is either the former lived experience as such or one of its components. Thus, for example, an originary perception, which is lived-in immediately, can become the object of remembering, in which case what was perceived is now had only mediately; this remembering can itself undergo a modification in recollection, and so on. Or a remembering can be modified in fantasy, and the fantasy, in turn, in another act of fantasy, and so on. Modifications can thus alternate between different kinds of acts or consist of iterations of the same act. Because such modification can be made of any lived experience at any time—albeit always in serial fashion, for each ray of regard can be trained on only one objectuality at a time—it is always possible to move to ever higher levels of reflection. Yet although such modifications can be iterated *without end, none is without a beginning*: "starting from any lived experience that has already been characterized as such a modification and that then is always characterized within itself as that modification, we are led back to certain primal lived experiences, to 'impressions' that represent the absolutely originary lived experiences in the phenomenological sense." Therefore the endlessness of the system of reflections is, as it were, an ascending order, but one that is always grounded in an originary lived experience. Husserl makes this point by recalling the primacy of both perception and actionality, each of which forms the basis for possible infinities of reflective modification: "Thus perceptions of physical things are originary lived experiences in relation to all rememberings, representiations in fantasy, etc. They are as originary as concrete lived experiences can ever be. For, considered precisely, they have in their concretion only one, but also always a continuously flowing, absolutely originary phase: the moment of the living Now." The absoluteness of any lived experience is proportional to the degree to which it is "alive" of its own and not founded on other lived experiences. It is this insight that guides Husserl's initial delineation of the "systematic order" of reflections.

Important, however, is to note that the order does not consist of actual—more precisely: real—but only of possible modifications. By sketching the possibilities, Husserl has made evident what is not merely possible, but rather absolutely necessary if there is to be any modification whatsoever; he has moved thereby from the heights down to their ground.[35]

2.2 The Pure Ego and its Lived Experiences

On this lowermost level, the relation between lived experiences and the pure ego is thematized. Both sides of the relation already played a role in the discussion of reflection, but there the ego was for the most part only visible in the form of acts. Husserl now makes it explicit: "Every 'cogito,' every act in a distinctive sense, is characterized as an act of the ego, it 'issues from the ego,' it 'lives' in the act 'actionally'" (159–60). After the exclusion of the general thesis, it is obvious that the talk here cannot be of a natural, empirical entity, but only of the *pure* ego. Like the transcendental sphere as a whole, it is impervious to the epoché: "no excluding can annul the form of cogito and cross out the 'pure' subject of the act: the 'being directed to,' the 'being busied with,' the 'taking a position on,' the 'undergoing,' the 'suffering from,'[36] necessarily harbors in its essence this: that it is precisely a ray 'emanating from the ego' or, in the reverse direction of the ray, 'towards the ego'—and this ego is the pure ego; no reduction can touch it" (160). And again, even those lived experiences that do not have the character of the cogito are nevertheless related to the ego: "they are its consciousness-background, its field of freedom." Although it is the ego's ray of regard that is always directed to a lived experience, this does not mean that the ego has primacy over any given lived experience; rather, they are of equal rank, which Husserl underscored above by noting that the ray emanates from the ego *or* towards it, thus from the lived experience. The sides are in fact complementary and inseparable: "Yet in these peculiar combinations with all of 'its' lived experiences, the ego living-in its lived experiences [*das erlebende Ich*] is nothing that could be taken on its own and made the Object of a separate investigation. Aside from its 'modes of relation' or 'modes of comportment,' the ego is completely lacking in eidetic components; it has no explicable content; it is indescribable in and of itself: it is the pure ego and nothing else." The ego *is* only by virtue of the relation.[37] But although they necessarily belong together, the pure ego and the lived experiences cannot be analyzed simultaneously. Each side must be addressed individually, which is to say, in terms of its role in the relation. As potentially misleading as it is, and Husserl points this out himself, he nevertheless avails himself of the traditional formulation of this relation so as to characterize roughly the direction of the ensuing phenomenological inquiry: "There is thus a certain, extraordinarily important two-sidedness in the essence of the sphere of lived experiences, of which we can also say that in lived experiences a subjectively-oriented side and an objectively-oriented side is to be distinguished" (161). Accordingly, Husserl's inquiry can take either of two directions: "one part of which is oriented towards pure subjectivity, the other part towards what belongs to the 'constitution' of objectivity for subjectivity." For the remainder of his present analyses, and thus until he begins his "phenomenology of reason," Husserl focuses on the side that is first for us: "the objectively-oriented side as the one that offers itself first when starting from the natural attitude." In light of the foregoing, it becomes clear that this commits him first to consider lived experiences, and in fact apart from the ego, the so-called subjective side of the relation.

2.2.1 Time, the Stream of Consciousness, and the Absolute. It is striking that before delving into those analyses, Husserl notes that—contrary to what was said previously about the transcendental absolute—the ego is "in truth" not ultimate: "it is something that constitutes itself in a certain profound and completely peculiar sense and that has its primal source in something ultimate and truly absolute" (see 162–63). Although he will not investigate this absolute in *Ideas I*, his remark proves significant to the present analyses insofar as it signals that Husserl is about to move down to a more fundamental level of inquiry—and thus, once again, from what is first for us down to what is first by nature. His remark alludes to the gravity of his initial analyses of the "objectively-oriented side." They point the way to the "ultimate and truly absolute."

While each lived experience can be discussed individually, each is thematized always against the background of other lived experiences; they are essentially bound together in a "stream," and in fact by phenomenological time. It is the "unitary form of all lived experiences in one stream of lived experiences (in the stream proper to one pure ego)" (161), and as such holds together the entire transcendental sphere. Husserl is careful to set phenomenological time off from the cosmic or objective time of the natural attitude, which was excluded by the epoché. But beyond the fact that one is excluded while the other is retained, the most obvious point of difference between cosmic and phenomenological time is that, unlike the former, phenomenological time cannot be measured. For it "belongs essentially to the lived experience as such, with its [i.e., time's] modes of givenness of Now, Before, After, with their modally determined simultaneity, succession, etc." (162). Time is nothing separate from lived experiences, but is bound up with them as the *form* of their givenness. The sense of this determination—that time is a unitary form—becomes clearer in light of the consideration of lived experiences solely in their primal unity in the stream, thus apart from the ego. The formal character of time will be seen to have important implications for the ascertainment of the "ultimate and truly absolute."

Within the isolated stream, every lived experience is equal to every other; there is no distinction between Now, Before, and After; and for this reason Husserl describes the stream here as a continuum or horizon and not as a gradation or hierarchy.[38] All lived experiences are, as it were, Now in the stream; they are radically simultaneous; each is just as actual as it is potential—which is to say: without an ego, they are neither—if it makes sense to speak in this way.[39] Husserl notes: "Every actual lived experience . . . is necessarily an enduring one; and with this duration it fits into an endless continuum of durations—in a fulfilled continuum. Of necessity it has a temporal horizon that is infinite [and] fulfilled on all sides. At the same time, this says: it belongs to one infinite 'stream of lived experiences'" (163). On all sides, in all directions, the continuum is always already fulfilled.[40] It lacks nothing in itself. What is more, it is eternal: "the stream of lived experiences cannot begin and end." Strictly speaking, then, the stream itself is nothing temporal—it is beyond time. For the same reason, the "duration" of lived experiences within the stream is, paradoxically enough, atemporal; the talk of their duration here merely indicates their limitless inherence in the stream. Although the lived experiences are discrete in a sense not yet specified by Husserl, in and of themselves they too are necessarily without beginning and end.[41] It is just this paradox that points to the sense in which the talk can at all be of temporality as a unitary form.

As form, time is expressly not an actuality, but rather a potentiality. But potential for what or whom? If one recalls that Husserl notes time's formal character above in connection with lived experiences and the ego, the answer is clear. He says that time is the form of "all lived experiences" and adds parenthetically that they are in the stream "proper to one pure ego." Time is therefore nothing in and of itself. Rather, it *is* only by virtue of the correlation of ego and stream, and in fact as the description of the former's traversal of the latter.[42] From this and the atemporality of lived experiences "in themselves," it follows that as soon as Husserl begins speaking of a distinction between lived experiences or their coming to be and passing away, the ego must have reentered the picture: "Every single lived experience—for example, a lived experience of joy—can begin as well as end and hence conclude its duration." Of course, in concluding, the lived experience does not cease to "exist," but only ceases to be regarded actionally by its ego. Were the lived experience to cease to exist altogether, the stream to which it belongs would of necessity collapse and itself cease to exist, for the stream is essentially a continuum; it is impossible that it contain any "gaps." A lived experience begins and ends only for an ego: "Every lived experience, as a temporal Being, is a lived experience that is proper to its pure ego. Of necessity this entails the possibility (which, as we know, is no empty logical possibility) that the ego direct its pure regard to this lived experience and seize upon it as actually existing or as enduring in phenomenological time." But it is equally possible that the ego divert its regard to another lived experience, in which case the duration of the former lived experience ends as soon as that of the new lived experience begins. Even where the ego attends to the "same" lived experience, it does so only in the succession of its temporal phases; the flow of the stream continues; the ego cannot hold fast to a lived experience or bring the flow of the stream to a standstill: "no enduring lived experience is possible unless it is constituted in a continuous flux of modes of givenness as something unitary pertaining to the event or the duration. . . ." And it is in this shift of regard and the consequent succession of lived experiences that time becomes actual, or rather, that its formal character comes into play: "The actional Now is necessarily and remains something punctual, a persisting form for ever new material. The same holds regarding the continuity of 'Just-Nows'; it is a continuity of forms of ever new content" (164).

Time is the unitary form of the stream insofar as it provides the possibility of actional regard in a continuous flow of temporal phases. Alternatively, time as form may be said to provide a succession of functions, such as a string of Nows, which are filled with arguments—the individual lived experiences—by the ego's regard. Thus, what was merely formal relative to the stream of lived experiences and without reference to the ego, becomes determinate or concrete as soon as both sides are considered together. For whereas time has its pure potentiality in the stream, it has its actuality in the necessary correlation of one pure ego and one stream of lived experiences. Time, in its linearity, springs from the ego's spontaneous movement through "the whole field of phenomenological time proper to the pure ego—a field that, [setting out] from any one of 'its' lived experiences, the ego can traverse according to the three dimensions of Earlier, Later, and Simultaneous" (165). In the actionality of its regard, the ego draws together lived experiences from the various dimensions into one seamless stream, "the whole, essentially unified and strictly self-contained stream of temporal unities of lived experiences."

Together the ego and the stream make up the "primal form of consciousness" (166), which is replete with infinite possibilities. Yet the spontaneity of the ego's regard of the stream is not without its limits. Whereas it can—as an "a priori possibility"—redirect its regard from any individual lived experience to another within the infinite stream of lived experiences, "principially this whole concatenation is never given nor can be given by a single pure regard"—there can be no lived experience and thus no intuition of the stream as a concrete whole. This limitation is already implicit in the fact that every lived experience is surrounded by a halo or is always regarded against a background. Because no lived experience is independent—"no concrete lived experience can be accepted as an independent one in the full sense" (167)—but is embedded in specific concatenations, which are themselves embedded in the stream, it must exceed the ego's regard: "Each is 'in need of supplementation' with respect to a concatenation that, according to its kind and form, is not arbitrary but rather determinate." That is, the supplementations of a lived experience are always regulated by its essence. They prove to be the key to how the stream can be grasped, and in fact by virtue not of their necessity so much as of their very possibility: it cannot be grasped after the manner of an individual concrete lived experience, but more as a sense of egoic motility, or as Husserl puts it: "after the manner of 'limitlessness in the progression' of immanent intuitions from a fixed lived experience to new lived experiences within its horizon of lived experiences, from fixing lived experiences to fixing their horizons, etc." (166). Despite its need of supplementation, each lived experience is seized upon in its concreteness, as the union of form and content. The ego has it, so to speak, extensionally. By contrast, the stream necessarily lacks the concreteness of its constituent lived experiences; it represents pure possibility for the ego and hence is not an extensional but rather an intensional infinity. To grasp the stream in its infinity is to grasp the promise of continuous movement, and in fact not only in the direction of the three temporal dimensions, but also in that offered by the diverse modes of consciousness, such as recollection or fantasy. Only through its involvement with these infinities, "in the continuous progression from seizing-upon to seizing-upon," can the ego "seize upon the stream of lived experiences as a unity," though again not as an actuality, not in its extension, "but rather in the manner of an idea in the Kantian sense," and so as a regulative concept.

The intuition of the stream's unity is imbued with a peculiar certainty: "It is not something posited or affirmed at random, but rather is something absolutely indubitably given—in a correspondingly broad sense of the word 'givenness'.[43] Even though it is also grounded in intuition, this indubitability has a source entirely different from that which obtains for the Being of lived experiences, thus for those that are given purely in immanent perception." There can be no perception of the stream as a whole, but only piecemeal. This is one reason for the difference between the intuition of a lived experience and that of its stream; the other lies in the difference between form and content: "It is precisely the peculiarity of the ideation that sees a Kantian 'idea' that it does not on that account, say, lose its character of insight because the adequate determination of its content, here the stream of lived experiences, is unattainable" (166–67). The "idea" of the stream is one of essence and thus of form as opposed to content. It is the form of the stream that is seized upon, the form as it necessarily exceeds all content and all concretion. The ego cannot seize upon the unity of the stream immediately, as it does a lived experience, but only mediately, and in fact by moving through the stream, from one concrete lived experience to another. And yet it should be noted that the fact that the ego "cannot" grasp the stream immediately, that it cannot intuit it adequately, is not due to any shortcoming of the ego, but to the essence of the stream. A form cannot be grasped in actuality, but only as potentiality. This recalls the nature of phenomenological time, which after all binds the lived experiences together into one stream.

Returning to Husserl's remark on the ultimate absolute, the question arises: Is time the absolute he has in view? If so, then the absolute would be a form. Or is the absolute to be found in the stream of consciousness, perhaps in its hyle, and thus in the content of that form? What is first, form or matter? On the other hand, it would be natural to equate this ultimate absolute with God, though this finds no support here. And even if Husserl were thinking of God, to name him in this context does not answer the question concerning the nature of the absolute. For what or who is God on Husserl's view? God remains a vague presentiment for him. Is God to be equated with time? Is God a form or an actuality? These and other related questions will have to be left open here.[44]

2.3 Intentionality and Constitution

Reflection, the correlation of the pure ego and the stream, phenomenological time—all of these eidetic peculiarities of consciousness are grounded in the relation of 'intentionality':[45] it "is what characterizes consciousness in the pregnant sense and justifies designating the whole stream of lived experiences at the same time as the stream of consciousness and as the unity of one consciousness" (168). This holds inasmuch as every lived experience, every mode of consciousness, is always a "consciousness *of* something." It is precisely due to this 'of' that intentionality counts "as virtually the general theme of 'objectively'-oriented," rather than subjectively-oriented phenomenology (167–68); for it points to the object to which the ego attends: "In every actional cogito a 'regard' that radiates *from* the pure ego is directed *to* the 'object' of the consciousness-correlate in question, to the physical thing, to the affair-complex, etc., and effects quite different kinds of consciousness of it" (168–69). Intentionality is in fact such a comprehensive concept in Husserlian thought that it characterizes not just actional lived experiences, but even the "inactional" lived experiences that make up the halo surrounding an actional lived experience, for each "inactionality," each lived experience not yet picked out by the ego's actional regard, "harbors intentionality within itself" insofar as each can become the object of regard (see 169). Although there are gradations of inactionality, which are distinguished in view of their proximity to or remoteness from the ego, inactionalities prove to be simply "special modalities" of intentionality by virtue of their openness to the ego's regard. And thus, because every lived experience possesses such openness, intentionality may be said to permeate all consciousness.

The regard essential to intentionality is not passive in the sense of merely contemplating the objects it happens upon. On the contrary, it is thoroughly active. What it touches, it changes, and in fact so much so that in picking a lived experience out of the stream, the ego creates or forms it.[46] In order to sketch the basic features of such formation, of the productivity peculiar to intentionality, Husserl need not delve into "the obscure depths of the ultimate consciousness, which constitutes all the temporality proper to lived experiences,"[47] but can instead remain on the level at which lived experiences are taken "as they offer themselves as unitary temporal events in immanent reflection" (171)—thus on the level of constituted temporality, specifically that on which the immediately preceding investigations took place. There Husserl discerns two basic strata of consciousness: sensuous ὕλη and intentional μορφή or, as he also says, "formless stuffs [*formlose Stoffe*]" and "stuffless forms [*stofflose Formen*]" (see 172–73).[48] Contrary to what natural experience reports, the regard does not find objects already composed of various sensuous stuffs; rather, objects or intentional lived experiences are present for consciousness as unities solely by virtue of the latter's bestowal of sense. By bestowing sense on what is originally sense-less, by imposing intentional form on sensuous stuffs (on lived experiences or components thereof), what is otherwise lifeless becomes animated.[49] Such animation is effected by noeses. As Husserl points out, they "make up what is specific to *nous*"—a term that for Husserl primarily does not recall the meaning 'reason' so much as 'sense', and only secondarily 'reason'—"in the broadest sense of the word; according to all its actional forms of life, it leads us back to cogitationes and then to intentional lived experiences in general, and therefore encompasses everything (and essentially only as much) that is the *eidetic presupposition of the idea of the norm*" (174). Although inquiry can proceed in the direction either of the stuffs (hyletic-phenomenological considerations) or of the intentional form and thus of sense-bestowal (noetic-phenomenological considerations), it is the latter direction that is most significant for Husserl's task of elaborating the general structures of consciousness (see 175). And yet of the greatest import to phenomenology are the problems harbored by the interaction of the two sides, namely those involved in the formation of senseful lived experiences just discussed. Husserl terms them 'constitutive' or 'functional problems'.

As problems of sense, specifically of how sense arises, the functional problems prove to be the core problems of phenomenology: "the investigations radiating from [the perspective of the function] encompass nearly the whole phenomenological sphere, and in the end all phenomenological analyses in some manner or other enter into its service as component parts or preliminary stages" (176). These problems are comprehensive precisely because knowledge, and thus science, is possible only on the basis of sense, which is to say: as a consequence of its evaluation. On account of this, Husserl says that the functional problems "concern the way in which noeses . . . by animating stuff and combining it into manifold-unitary continua and syntheses, bring about consciousness *of* something such that the objective unity of the objectuality can be harmoniously 'made manifest,' 'demonstrated,' and 'rationally' determined in" that consciousness. Precisely because the phenomenological function constitutes its objectualities, because it bestows sense on them, Husserl sets it off from the mathematical function.[50] Unlike in the latter, there is no equality between the two sides of this function; rather, consciousness has priority over its objectualities insofar as they depend on it, and in fact for their sense. The phenomenological function is "something wholly unique, grounded in the pure essence of the noeses. Consciousness is precisely consciousness 'of' something; it is of its essence to harbor 'sense' within itself, so to speak, the quintessence of 'soul,' 'spirit,' 'reason.'"[51] Consciousness is not just senseful, but the source of all sense.[52] And only on account of this is it "the source of all reason and unreason, all legitimacy and illegitimacy, all reality and fiction, all value and disvalue, all deed and misdeed"—not to mention all good and evil. These are through and through rational determinations. Since they presuppose sense in each case, it is obvious that sense and the consciousness that bestows it are themselves prerational. The functional problems therefore articulate the preconditions for rationality and thus knowledge. As a consequence, Husserl calls them the truly "transcendental problems." It is by virtue of its concentration on them that phenomenology "deserves the name of transcendental phenomenology" (177–78). This name sums up the foundational intention of Husserl's endeavor. If he can demonstrate the centrality of constitution, if he can show that pure, transcendental consciousness is first because it constitutes transcendent Being, then he will have secured phenomenology's place as First Science. Furthermore, he will have provided knowledge and all the sciences with a clear and distinct foundation unrivaled by any previous attempt to secure a foundation.

3. The Noetic-Noematic Correlation: Towards the Basis of Conscious Life

The functional or constitutive problems of such importance to phenomenology are problems of sense, specifically of how consciousness harbors sense within itself. Husserl's key insight in this connection is that such harboring is not a mere appropriation of some preexistent entity by consciousness, whereby consciousness would be dependent upon that entity. Rather, it is a creative relation of consciousness to that entity. Thus the functional problems concern how consciousness engenders, or constitutes, sense. To solve them, it is necessary to clarify the nature of intentionality, which means to determine more precisely what is involved in the expression 'consciousness of something'.

Intentionality, Husserl remarks, is generally familiar to everyone, yet in its specificity it has consistently eluded the grasp of traditional theories of consciousness. What makes it difficult "to seize purely and correctly upon the phenomenological eidetic peculiarities" of the intentional lived experience is precisely its seeming familiarity: the field of eidetic inquiry it designates is so obvious that it is not seen and so not grasped in its essence (see 179–80).

Phenomenology aims to correct this oversight. And yet its success in doing so is threatened by the general tendency to confound it with traditional theories, as well as by the skepticism to which the "labyrinthine wandering paths" followed in the first investigations of intentionality "easily give rise," "a skepticism that negates the entire sphere of unwieldy problems" (180). Husserl evades these dangers by abiding by the "principle of all principles": he takes "what is offered in immanent eidetic analysis just as it is given." This enables him to see both the one-sidedness and thus insufficiency of focusing solely on what is perceived, as his predecessors have done, and the necessity of considering perception itself: "Since they are living in the perception, adverted to the perceived in considering and theorizing about it, they do not manage to direct the regard instead to the perceiving, or to the peculiarities of the mode of givenness of the perceived. . . ." Thus, prior to Husserl, investigators have failed to engage in reflection on perception, having instead lived "blindly" in it. By contrast, Husserl reflects on it, which enables him to pass through the extremes of traditional theory and skepticism into the proper sphere of phenomenological inquiry. Because in reflecting he no longer lives in the perception, he is in a position to discern its essential features, which enables him to discover the creative role of consciousness in relation to its object.

Husserl is the first to make this move, for he is the first to adhere to the principle of all principles and abandon all theorizing from on high—an unheard of feat within the philosophical tradition, as he repeatedly points out, which speaks all the more for the newness, the radicality of phenomenology. It is the logical consequence of what Husserl elsewhere refers to as 'faithfulness', 'honesty', and '(self-) responsibility'. Here he emphasizes the need for courage precisely because the adherence to the principle of all principles requires that one abandon the abode afforded by received theory (whether positive or negative) and start at the beginning: "If one has gained the right attitude and fortified it by practice, but especially if one has gained the courage to obey the clear eidetic givens with a radical presuppositionlessness, unconcerned about all current and received theories, then firm results arise straightaway, and the same ones for everyone in the same attitude. . . . "[53] One must have the courage to trust in the things themselves, namely that they will show themselves as they are and that they provide the sole admissible standard for knowledge. It is Husserl's conviction that only on this basis will one be able to come to terms with the "most difficult problems," for it alone enables one to discern the "canonical fundamental distinctions" (179).

3.1 The Functionality of Intentional Reference

The pivotal distinction—one that is "determinative for all further methodical proceedings" (180) and therefore provides the underpinnings of the whole of phenomenology—lies within the traditional characterization of intentionality as 'consciousness of something'. Husserl's achievement—and he himself draws attention to it—is to have made the distinction explicit. To do so, he says, it is not enough to see that intentionality entails a relationship—this much was already obvious in the tradition. Rather, one must discern the nature of that relationship. The clue here is provided by the 'of' in the expression 'consciousness of something'. It not only links the two sides and, by extension, their respective regions, but thereby attests the functionality of their relationship. Thus consciousness and something are bound together not in just any relation, but in a functional correlation, and in fact one in which primacy is accorded to consciousness (which may be viewed as the function) over against its something (so to speak, the argument of the function). Armed with this insight, it becomes possible to fix the essence of each side, as well as the pivotal distinction between them. Only then does the first adequate description of the structures of consciousness become possible.

Husserl draws out the scission between the two sides in terms of real inherence, which means that he takes the first side of the pair as his starting point. Accordingly, the distinction is "between authentic," that is, really inherent, "components of intentional lived experiences and their intentional correlates or the components of the latter" (181). In addition to its really inherent moments, then, each intentional lived experience—which is, "thanks to its noetic moments, precisely a noetic lived experience" or, simply, noesis—"has" an object to which it intends and which itself is not really inherent in it: "it is of its essence to harbor within itself something like a 'sense' and possibly a manifold sense on the basis of these sense-bestowals [that is, by the noetic moments] and in unity with them to effect further productions [*Leistungen*] that become 'senseful' precisely through those sense-bestowals." Sense arises in each instance, regardless of the level in question, through the ego's direction of its regard to a given object; it bestows sense on that object, or what Husserl terms the 'noema'. Thus the noesis harbors sense insofar as the ego fixes its object in its gaze; only thereby can the sense or noema "exist" as such. But that is not to say that the noetic lived experience can "exist" apart from its noema. On the contrary, just as the noema depends on the lived experience for its Being, likewise the latter depends on the noema it has "in view" for its Being. Furthermore, the strength of the correlation between the two sides has its source not only in their existential interdependence, but also in their parallel structures: "Corresponding everywhere to the manifold data proper to the really inherent, noetic content, there is a manifold of data, demonstrable in actually pure intuition, in a correlative 'noematic content' or, more succinctly, in the 'noema'" (181–82).[54] The noetic-noematic correlation is therefore an isomorphic relationship: every part of one side corresponds to a part of the other. Husserl will express the existential and structural interdependence of the two sides in the form of an eidetic law: "no noetic moment without a noematic moment that specifically belongs to it" (193).[55] This means that any alteration of one side must of necessity result in an alteration of the other.

Hence in the case of perceiving a blossoming apple tree with pleasure, to use Husserl's example,[56] the intentional lived experience is the perception of or taking pleasure in the tree, whereas the noema is the perceived or pleasing tree.[57] In the natural attitude, the distinction, for example, between the perception of the tree and the perceived tree is acknowledged, but the two sides are regarded as standing in a real relation to one another, whereby the perceiver and the tree are held to be real, material entities. A problem arises for this attitude, however, as soon as the existence of the perceived tree becomes questionable, such as when it turns out to be a hallucination: the perceiver has been mistaken about the object's existence, which would seem to invalidate the perception. Yet, as Husserl indicates, this problem is spurious; it springs from the focus on real existence and the consequent neglect of essential relations. Considered more closely, it becomes clear that the relationship between the perceiving and the perceived remains intact even when the perceived is found not to exist; the perception of a hallucinated object is, after all, still a perception of an object.

3.2 The Discovery of the Noema

Husserl is able to dispense with this problem by directing the regard away from contingent existence to the previously neglected essential relations, and in fact by effecting the epoché. Once the general thesis has thereby been eliminated and the *omnitudo realitatis* annihilated, the question of reality can no longer play a meaningful role. This would seem to leave a void in its wake, and so the questions naturally arise: What could remain for the thematization of intentionality, that is, of consciousness as "consciousness of something," after the annihilation of the world? Of what could it be consciousness if not of something in the world? This is where the noema comes in. Its discovery as the correlate of the noesis, as the sense harbored by the latter, is enabled and even necessitated by the turn away from the "authoritativeness" of the "real" world to that of the "inner," immanent, absolute world. The noema is nothing but the reduced, purified objectuality, and as such may be said to take the place of what was formerly regarded as the real object. For this reason, the "purely phenomenological affair-complex" need not be troubled by the possible nonexistence of the perceived object—in this case, the apple tree. The epoché leaves things as they were,[58] for the essential relations between the perceiving and the perceived are maintained: "Even the phenomenologically reduced perceptual lived experience is a perceiving *of* 'this blossoming apple tree, in this garden, etc.,' and the same holds of the reduced taking pleasure in this same thing. The tree has not lost the least nuance of all these moments, qualities, characteristics with which it was appearing in this perception, with which it was 'lovely,' 'attractive,' and so forth in this taking pleasure" (183)—all that it has lost is the former posit of its reality.

But again, this loss, or rather the willed bracketing that brings it about, is no small matter. In fact it makes all the difference. It is what sets phenomenology apart. The loss proves to be a principial gain; it is the result of the move made from contingency to necessity by means of the epoché. Husserl illustrates the gulf between these two in terms of destructibility: "The tree plain and simple can burn up, be resolved into chemical elements, etc. But the sense—the sense of this perception, something belonging necessarily to its essence—cannot burn up; it has no chemical elements, no forces, no real properties" (184). By shedding the contingency proper to reality, Husserl discloses what is absolutely necessary: the sense harbored in the noetic lived experience. The sense, here the perceptual sense, is nothing that the phenomenologist has imported into the phenomenon; rather, it has always already belonged to the latter. The essential relations in which this sense has its place always already found all contingency, and every possible modification. As a consequence, Husserl's descriptions of the noetic lived experience and its noema also pertain to the unreduced perception and its object—provided, of course, that one attend faithfully, "in pure devotion," to what appears just as it gives itself.[59] Put in the most general terms: the eidetic findings secured in the phenomenological sphere therefore apply to all spheres, including that of the natural attitude. They are a priori.

3.2.1 Phenomenological Notation. However, despite the universal relevance of phenomenological findings, it must be borne in mind that the object of concern is not the real object, but rather the "reduced" object. In order to draw the reader's attention to the fact that a distinction of Being has taken place, or as Husserl says, that the object has undergone a "radical modification of sense"—and with it there has been a corresponding "modification of signification"—he introduces a distinction of speech, which he fixes by means of a notational device: he places the name of the object in quotation marks. They are to make manifest that the object under consideration is the noema and not the real object and, furthermore, that its proper place is not in the natural, but in the transcendental sphere. Yet, once again, this does not mean that the noema is contained really inherently in the intentional lived experience. The noema necessarily "transcends" the latter, albeit in a manner radically different from that in which the real object transcends consciousness for the natural attitude. Rather, since the noema is not part of reality but belongs to the transcendental sphere, it proves to be a transcendence within immanence. How it can be such forms the core of the functional or constitutive problems.

3.2.2 Real Inherence and its Counterparts. To begin to solve them, one must first distinguish between real inherence (in an intentional lived experience), the immanent object, and the real object. The failure to do so leads to a distortion of the essential relations and ultimately to countersense. Some of Husserl's predecessors, he notes, unwittingly fell into countersense because they did not attend to things as they give themselves, but instead imposed theory upon them; they sought to explain intentionality by means of a "picture theory" of consciousness. On this view, consciousness, or the intentional lived experience, is a real entity somehow related to another real entity, the object. To explain their relation, this theory posits the existence of a mediating picture of the object within consciousness. Husserl makes it clear, however, that, insofar as the two sides are real, the mediating picture will also be real. As a consequence, it is necessary to introduce another mediating image between consciousness and the first picture, and so forth. The resultant infinite regress makes manifest the countersense of the "picture theory." The only remedy for such confusions is to abide by the principle of all principles under the scope of the epoché, and to describe faithfully what is given just as it is given. According to Husserl, doing so reveals intentionality to be the unmediated correlation of a noesis with a noema, or of an intentional lived experience with an objectual sense.

Thus far the investigation of their correlation has been couched primarily in terms of perception, but again Husserl's findings here hold of all intentional lived experiences: "every intentional lived experience—precisely this makes up the fundamental part of intentionality—has its 'intentional Object,' that is, its objectual sense. Or in other words, to have sense or 'to have something in mind'[60] is the fundamental characteristic of all consciousness, which therefore is not just any lived experience whatsoever, but rather is a sense-having, 'noetic' lived experience" (185). And yet this correlation is more complex than has previously been indicated. Additional distinctions are required if a complete account is to be given of the myriad forms of consciousness.

3.2.3 Full and Core Noemata. The first distinction is made within the noema itself, namely between the full noema and the noematic core. The former "consists of a complex of noematic moments," whereas the latter is a singular, identical moment. That is to say, within the "noematic complex" there is a "specific sense-moment" that "forms only a kind of necessary core-stratum in which further moments are essentially founded." This pairing echoes the bipolar structures prominent throughout Husserlian thought, such as the gradations of fulfillment (ranging from 0 to 1) or the oppositional pairing of reason and unreason encountered above.[61] In this regard, the full noema may be viewed as the upper limit, or maximal sense, and the core noema as the lower limit, or minimal sense—though not as a zero-point. Accordingly, the distinction between the full noema and its core entails a necessary stratification, or even a gradation: "we must separate essentially different strata that are grouped around a central 'core,' around a pure 'objectual sense'—around that which in all our examples was describable with simply identical objective expressions because something identical can be in the different kinds of parallel lived experiences" (189). Thus a halo of sorts may be detected here that consists of possible intentionalities surrounding an identical core, for example the apple tree. The noematic correlate will be different for different noetic lived experiences—say, for a perception, a fantasy, a remembering, etc., of the tree, whereas the various correlates will all have one core noema in common. Each of the correlates making up a particular noematic complex, or the full noema, are founded on this shared core, and only because they are so founded can they be said to have sense (see 185).

3.2.4 Full and Core Noeses. In view of the aforementioned eidetic law that each noetic moment has a corresponding noematic moment, the structural features of the noema just sketched must have parallels on the noetic side; hence, it is to be expected that something like a noetic core and a full noesis may be discerned there as well, the former being a central moment of the latter and each of its additional moments. To characterize the noetic side of the correlation, Husserl recalls the metaphor of a "ray of regard" that can be turned towards or away from an object, a ray that emanates from the pure ego (189). This metaphor makes manifest the ego's directedness, that is, its *attention*, to its object. And on account of this, Husserl speaks of 'attentional changes' when referring to the redirection of the ego's ray of regard. It can be sent through diverse intentional strata—into different "worlds," as Husserl says—and trained on diverse intentional objects. Thus it can shift from one stratum or world to another, but also, within one stratum or world, from one level to another, for example from the world of perception to that of memory, or within the world of memory from one memory to another, and then back to the world of perception or over to that of fantasy (and within it, from fantasy to fantasy, etc.), etc. The diversity of possibilities pertaining to the ego indicates the aforementioned distinction: the noetic core is precisely the one ray of regard that emanates from one pure ego. Correspondingly, the "full noesis" may be said to be the full range of that ray's ideal possibilities of movement, that is, of attentional changes, pertaining to one noema. These can be viewed as "mere changes in the distribution of attention and its modes" (190); one ego attends thereby to one object, and yet in different acts it directs its ray of regard to different moments of that object, and in a sense even to a different object: "one objectual moment is 'favored' and, in another case, another"; or "one and the same moment is 'attended to primarily' at one time and only secondarily at another time, or is only 'just barely noticed still,' if not 'completely unnoticed,' although still appearing" (191). Such attention is what distinguishes the actionality of consciousness from inactionality, from "complete inattention, the mode that is, so to speak, the dead consciousness of something." And yet this is not to say that attention can be equated with life. As will be seen, mere attention alone does not make consciousness a living consciousness in the strict and decisive sense.

Just as an attentional change gives rise to a new lived experience while the noetic core remains the same, such changes likewise affect the noematic correlates of the lived experiences: new correlates are also generated, while the noematic core remains the same. To illustrate the kind of alterations that occur, Husserl extends the figure of the ray to a beam of light (*Lichtkegel*): "Attention is usually compared to a spot light. What is attended to, in the specific sense, lies in the cone of more or less bright light, but it can also move into the penumbra and into complete darkness. . . . This change in illumination does not alter what appears with respect to its own sense-composition, but brightness and darkness modify its mode of appearance; they are to be found and described when the regard is directed to the noematic Object." These alterations are in no way contingent, Husserl points out, but are "necessary modes proper to the mode in which the identical something is given." Every change in the noesis has its necessary counterpart in the noema. On the one side, an attentional change alters the lived experience as a whole while leaving the noetic core untouched. On the other, even though the noematic core remains constant throughout a series of attentional changes, the noema as a whole undergoes changes, namely in the way in which it is given in each lived experience: the apple in the ray of sunshine is given differently than the apple at dusk, although it is the "same" apple. The two aspects of both sides of the correlation—specifically, full and core—are what make it possible to speak of changes on the one hand and identity on the other; they provide the basis for all description, all comparison and differentiation. Nevertheless, whereas faithful description is Husserl's task here, in the present connection the acts and correlates under consideration are prepredicative: speech plays no role whatsoever at this level.

3.2.5 The Constituent Parts of Intentionality. In his first account of intentionality in terms of the noetic-noematic correlation, Husserl has focused on its most fundamental level. Although further refinements may be necessary, he says, he has nevertheless already pointed out the basic building blocks of all intentionality, regardless of its level. Consequently, his findings there will hold in turn for higher levels: "As modes of actionality, the attentional formations have the character of subjectivity to an outstanding degree, and this character is then acquired by all the functions that are modalized by these very modes or that, according to their specific kind, presuppose them. The ray of attention gives itself as radiating from the pure ego and terminating in the objectual item, as directed to it or being diverted from it. The ray does not become detached from the ego, but rather is itself and remains an ego-ray. The 'Object' is hit, it is the target, it has only been placed in relation to the ego (and by the ego itself), but itself is not 'subjective'" (192). The ego (with its ray) is constant throughout all attentional changes. Each instance of attention, each attentional moment can form the basis for attentional modifications. "A position-taking that bears the ego-ray within itself is thereby an act of the ego itself; the ego acts or suffers [i.e., is acted upon], is free or conditioned. The ego . . . 'lives' in such acts. This living does not signify the Being of some 'contents' or other in a stream of contents, but rather a manifold of describable modes in which the pure ego, as the 'free being [*Wesen*]' it is, lives in certain intentional lived experiences that have the universal mode of the cogito. However, the expression 'as the free being' means nothing but that such modes of living are involved in freely going out of itself or freely withdrawing into itself, in spontaneous acting, learning something from the Objects, suffering [or being acted upon by] them, etc. What goes on in the stream of lived experiences outside the ego-ray or the cogito is essentially characterized otherwise; it lies outside of the ego's actionality and yet . . . belongs to the ego insofar as it is the field of potentiality for the ego's free acts." Freedom and life are clearly interwoven; but both are still indeterminate at this point in Husserl's account.

The structural parallels between noesis and noema hold also in "'higher' spheres of consciousness," for example in the spheres of judgment, emotion, and volition. Husserl's analyses of them in this context are focused purely on the distinction and relation between the noesis and the noema. He is not yet concerned with the modifications that mark a move from one level to the next. This will be taken up in what follows. Here he is focused on the constituent parts of intentionality. The next section is concerned with modification because Husserl wishes to show how the move is made from the founding, prepredicative to the predicative level. He must reach the latter if he is to treat *reason*, which clearly has played no role thus far. Of course, he points to the modifiability of consciousness (at least implicitly) in the paragraphs on judgment, volition, and emotion, but it is not thematized.

Husserl characterizes his meditations on the noetic-noematic correlation—although the same holds for the whole of *Ideas I*—as "merely leading upwards [*bloß emporsteigend*]" (200). It is on account of this, he says, that he cannot elaborate all the details of each stage in the progression. In the case of this correlation, however, he has reached the fundamental distinction, "the seizing upon and mastery of which are of the greatest importance for phenomenology, are indeed decisive for its right foundation." Everything else depends on this distinction. And yet this is not the last word, for within this distinction a still more fundamental stratum awaits elaboration. Only thereafter will it be possible to begin moving upwards step by step, just as he has moved step by step down to the foundation, the basic features of subjectivity: "A rich idea of the fruitfulness of phenomenology, the magnitude of its problems, and the nature of its procedure is only gained by actually entering province after province and seeing the extent of the problems in each. But any such province is actually entered and can be sensed as [providing] the firm ground of work only when one carries out the phenomenological eliminations and clarifications by which the sense of the problems to be solved here can alone become understandable."

3.3 The Modifiability of Consciousness

In the foregoing analysis, Husserl advanced his first account of intentionality in terms of the noetic-noematic correlation and drew out the basic distinctions between both sides. He then indicated how those structures were present in higher level intentionalities, which are founded on "primal" or fundamental intentionalities. However, although he pointed to the possibility of such founded hierarchies, Husserl did not discuss how they arise, nor did he continue his analytical ascent to still higher levels of consciousness. These are the chief themes of the present analysis. But before he can begin to address them, he must first return to the fundamental distinction between noesis and noema. This he does in order to secure and deepen the results he has gained thus far, which will allow him in turn to account for the peculiar productivity of consciousness, but also, and most importantly, to reveal the basis of conscious life. Armed with these insights, he will be in a position to make his ascent into the heights of consciousness.

3.3.1 Multiplicity and Unity. The starting point for the further determination of the nature of the noesis and the noema is provided by sensory perception—for example, of a tree—as lived in the natural attitude (see 202–3).[62] In focusing on this example, Husserl attends once again to the lowest level of noetic lived experiences. He does so not only because the essential relations are easier—which is not to say easy—to discern there, but also because his findings on this level will hold on every higher level; for each higher-level act is founded on at least one lower-level act.

The relevant clue to the nature of the noesis and the noema lies in the distinction between the perceiver and the perceived as it is familiar to anyone living in the natural attitude. In naive perception, the same tree can appear in diverse states: it is still or moved by the wind; it is first in the sun, then in the shade. On the other hand, the tree appearing in these ways can be viewed by the perceiver from different positions, or various aspects of it can be regarded: the perceiver can see it from afar, then close up, then while moving about it, now looking at the top of the trunk, then at the bottom, etc. Husserl notes that in perceiving the same tree—itself a unity—the naive perceiver experiences "a unity of consciousness" that entails "a great multiplicity of modifications," which in turn are attributed variously—in some cases to the real object, in others to a real relationship between the perceived and the perceiver, in still others to the perceiver himself. Precisely this experience of the relationship of multiplicity to unity is decisive here. And yet the lack of certainty regarding the unity to which the multiplicity is to be attributed indicates that natural experience itself provides an insufficient basis for clarifying the essential relations between the perceiver and the perceived. Rather, the variability of attribution testifies to an aporia, one that inhibits the attempt to penetrate deeper here since it obscures the essential relations between the two sides. The source of this problem proves to be the posit of reality, or the general thesis. As long as the focus is on real relationships, as long as the real is privileged, what is essential to each side and to the relationship between them must of necessity remain obscure. To shed light on them, Husserl must effect the epoché. For only after transcendence has been reduced to "pure immanence" does it become possible to inquire into the perception and the object in their own right. And so to account for the relationship of multiplicity to unity at issue.

As above, the first order of business in this connection is to inquire into the noetic side, specifically into what is really inherent in a pure lived experience and what is not. Husserl recalls that whereas the "'perceived tree as such,' or the full noema," essentially belongs to the perceptual lived experience, it does not belong really inherently to it—an observation Husserl supports by appealing to the natural understanding of the relationship between the perceiver and the perceived: "this noema, with its 'tree' in quotation marks, is no more contained really inherently in the perception than is the tree belonging to actuality" (202). Really inherent in a pure lived experience are rather its hyletic (or stuff-) and noetic components. The counterparts of the former are the noematic moments. Thus, with respect to the color of a tree trunk, for example, the reduced color belongs to the noema, whereas the "sensed color" belongs really inherently to the perceptual lived experience: it is the "hyletic moment of the concrete lived experience, in which the noematic or 'objective' color is 'adumbrated.'"

The talk of adumbration provides the key to the aforementioned aporia of the relationship of multiplicity to unity. The solution lies in the distinction between adumbrating and what is adumbrated, each of which has its own continuity: "one and the same noematic color that is thus intended [*bewußt*] throughout the continuous unity of a changeable perceptual consciousness as an identical and, within itself, unchanged color, is adumbrated by a continuous multiplicity of sensed colors" (202–3). The adumbrations are *of* the noematic color, but *in* the sensed color. By reflecting on them, Husserl notes, it is possible to grasp them "as evident givens" and, what is more, to grasp "in perfect evidence" not only that the adumbrations correspond to objectual moments, but also that the unity of the latter founds the multiplicity of the former (203). Reflection reveals, then, "that here 'unity' and 'multiplicity' belong to totally different dimensions, and indeed that everything hyletic belongs to the concrete lived experience as a really inherent component, whereas what is 'presented,' 'adumbrated' in it as a multiplicity belongs to the noema." Although the structural parallels between noesis and noema specified by the aforementioned eidetic law—that there can be no noetic moment without a corresponding noematic moment—remain intact here, the law is sharpened in light of the new insights into the structure of the lived experience. Namely, the appearance of an object—that and how it appears to a consciousness[63]—is found to depend on the hyletic moments, such that "any change of the hyletic content of the perception, if it does not quite annul perceptual consciousness, must at least result in the appearing something's becoming objectively 'other,' whether within itself, in the orientation in which it appears, or in some other manner." This means that the isomorphic relationship between noetic and noematic moments discussed above proves to be at base a relationship between hyletic and noematic moments.

The said multiplicity is thus a function of the noesis, not of the noema. However, the determination of the role of the former's hyletic moments does not exhaust its features. While the multiplicity is indeed rooted in the hyletic moments, it arises by means of the specifically noetic moments. Both sides belong really inherently to the lived experience. But it is their interaction alone that generates the lived experience, namely insofar as the noetic moments "animate" the hyletic moments by bestowing sense on them—as long as "the ego is turned not to them but to the object." In this way the noetic moments shape, as it were, the hyletic moments, which is why Husserl terms such animations not only 'sense-bestowals' but also 'interpretations'. In the case of adumbration, the hyletic moments provide the stuff or material corresponding to the object, whereas noetic moments serve to shape the matter, stamp it with a specific "quality," reflecting the way it appears, in the adumbration.[64] These two sides, the hyletic and the noetic, are indispensable to a sufficient account of the noesis, of the lived experience in its unity, and without such an account none could be given of the relationship of consciousness to its objectuality—thus of consciousness *sensu stricto*. By the same token, however, such an account requires no less the reference to the noema itself. These sides are individual and yet form an inseparable unity. Consciousness is always consciousness of something; it always has an object. But again, the way in which the noema belongs to the noesis is different from the way in which the latter's moments belong to it. They belong really inherently—immanently, as it were—to the noesis, whereas the noema does not. From this it follows that the noesis and the noema belong to different dimensions, even though the noema is "something 'given'" to consciousness, something transcendentally constituted "'on the basis' of material [*stofflich*] lived experiences 'by' noetic functions," and is even "something evidently given," as long as "we faithfully describe in pure intuition the lived experience and the noema of which it is conscious" (204). Husserl has thereby established the difference between the noesis and the noema, as well as having indicated how the two sides are related to one another. To inquire further into their relationship is to return to the "greatest problems of phenomenology," the functional problems. And yet they cannot be meaningfully treated in abstraction beyond the outline already provided, one sketched, to be sure, on the basis of concrete, intuitable examples. Rather, Husserl must turn once again to concrete acts of consciousness and their objects in order to fill out the contours of the noetic-noematic correlation. In doing so, he begins his ascent to higher levels of consciousness, or so it seems.

Before engaging in further analyses, however, Husserl stops to survey the results of his investigations. By having found in the noesis and the noema the basic building blocks, as it were, of consciousness and thus of knowledge, he has taken a significant step towards solving the functional problems. It is precisely this step that justifies his use of the epithet 'transcendental' to describe phenomenology, its field of inquiry, and the method by which alone it is accessed and that thus enabled the foregoing eidetic insights: the epoché. Husserl says: "The characterization of the phenomenological reduction and, likewise, of the pure sphere of lived experiences as 'transcendental' is based especially on the fact that we discover in this reduction an *absolute sphere* of stuffs and noetic forms among the determinately structured combinations of which belong, of immanent eidetic necessity, this wonderful consciousness of something determinate or determinable, given thus and so, which is something over against consciousness itself, something principially other, not really inherent, transcendent; and [it is also based] on the fact that this [sphere] is the *primal source* in which is found the only conceivable solution of the deepest problems of knowledge, which concern the essence and possibility of objectively valid knowledge of something transcendent." Thus by excluding the general thesis, by reducing transcendence to immanence, Husserl has not cut himself off from the world; on the contrary, it is his conviction that he has finally found the means for regaining the world, and this time in the proper sense: "The 'transcendental' reduction exercises ἐποχή with regard to actuality: but among that which it retains from the latter belongs the noemata with the noematic unity that lies in them and therefore the way in which something real is precisely intended [*bewußt*] and specially given in consciousness itself." The present direction of inquiry is to lead towards a full account of transcendent givenness and thus of conscious life. While the foregoing explication of the noetic-noematic correlation provided the starting point for such an account, the last word about it has not been spoken. It remains open whether the correlation is itself the source of conscious life or if it provides the underpinnings of such life, much as a skeleton provides the structure of animal life. What if a further distinction were to be made, one that were even more fundamental, even if it did not lie deeper, than those touched on thus far? Would it not testify to the true basis of conscious life and thus of transcendental phenomenology? Might it not then be what ultimately justifies Husserl's use of the epithet 'transcendental'?

3.3.2 Reflection and the Productivity of Consciousness. The noetic-noematic correlation, and thus all the structural features proper to it that have been discerned to this point, is also in play on every higher level of consciousness—insofar as it is at all consciousness. This was already indicated above with respect to judicative, emotional, and volitional acts. But the way in which the higher levels of consciousness were reached had yet to be treated in these terms. In fact it is by means of reflection that the move is made from a lower to a higher level, which accords with the previous finding that it is by reflection alone that consciousness can access itself. What is new here, however, is the insight into the productivity of such access. In its light Husserl is careful to point out that the move between levels does not leave things as they were, at least not entirely. He stresses "that every transition from a phenomenon to a reflection that itself analyzes the former [in view of what belongs to it] really inherently, or to the quite differently articulated reflection that dissects the phenomena's noema, generates new phenomena, and that we would fall into error if we were to confuse the new phenomena—which in a certain way are transformations of the old—with the old phenomena, and were we to attribute to the old what belongs really inherently or noematically to the new" (205).[65] The talk of 'old' and 'new' underscores the productivity peculiar to consciousness with respect to itself, a productivity that is rooted entirely in the essential possibility of its reflective relation to itself.

Just as the ego's ray of regard may be directed in sensory or "external" perception, as it were, away from itself and to "physical objects," it likewise can be directed in reflection, or "inner perception," to itself—namely, either to the noesis or its components or to its noema. When the ego directs its ray of regard, say, to the really inherent moments of a noesis, they are transformed into noematic moments and are no longer really inherent: "in the analyzing lived experience they are objectual, targets of noetic functions that earlier were not present." By the same token, reflection on the noema of a previous noesis would generate a new noema. Thus it holds mutatis mutandis: the ego's regard, whether as sensory perception or reflection, generates a new objectuality—that is, the new noesis constitutes a new noema. In a sense the moments retain the functions they had on the previous level, but because the new regard has wrested them from the original context in which they were transparently at work, or alive, because they are now given differently, those functions, and thus the moments themselves, have taken on a new value. They have been put out of action in their original sense. Now they are considered on a new level, as it were, *in vitro*; they are embedded in a new dimension, a new intentional complex, and as a consequence are invested with a new role. In that sense they are new phenomena, albeit as modifications of lower level moments.

As has been noted of their basic noetic-noematic structures, here also the two new sides of the higher level complex are interdependent. And yet the reflectively produced noema proves to be wholly dependent upon the reflective regard, or noesis: "Its *esse* consists exclusively in its '*percipi*,'" whereby, of course, "the *percipi* does not contain the *esse* as a really inherent component" (206). These parallels are to be found not only in concrete noeses and their noemata, but in the essences of each as well: "the *eidos* of the noema points to the *eidos* of the noetic consciousness; both belong together eidetically. The intentional [object] as such is what it is as the intentional [object] of a consciousness structured thus and so, which is the consciousness of it [i.e., the object]." The noesis has priority over the noema, but it can exist without the noema no more than the noema can exist without it. Despite their interdependence, however, Husserl notes that it is nonetheless possible to study each side in (relative) isolation from the other and thereby work out a doctrine of forms for each. The articulation of such doctrines represents the next step towards the solution of the functional problems.

3.3.3 Noetic and Noematic Characteristics. In the foregoing, the focus has been on the objectuality as a noematic core on the one hand and on the ray of regard as the noetic core on the other. While they are integral to a proper grasp of the full noesis and the full noema, they by no means exhaust the latter. A complete account of them becomes possible only when the characteristics pertaining to each side of the correlation are considered. It is precisely this distinction that Husserl has in view when he expresses the following caveat: "We must impress upon ourselves in advance, however, that the parallelism between the unity of the object noematically 'meant' in such and such a way, of the object in 'mind' [*im 'Sinne'*], and the constituting formations of consciousness ('*ordo et connexio rerum – ordo et connexio idearum*') must not be confused with the parallelism between noesis and noema, particularly understood as the parallelism between noetic and corresponding noematic characteristics" (208). The focus of the remainder of *Ideas I*, insofar as the noetic-noematic correlation is addressed, is upon the parallelism of just these characteristics.

To account fully for their parallelism means to elaborate the aforementioned doctrines of forms, which will culminate in the attainment of "the full noema and the full noesis." Although the foregoing analyses have helped in this regard by exhibiting "parallel series of noetic and noematic occurrences," their findings are still in need of expansion. This is evident already in view of the talk of characteristics. Thus far only noetic characteristics have been thematized. Instead of investigating the noema's characteristics, the possible existence of which came to speech at best only marginally, the noema has been treated as if it were "only a central core," but even then it was not "unambiguously delimited" as such. This core became visible as the identical "objectual sense" "by comparing the noemata of various kinds of objectivation," such as perceptions, memories, and picture-objectivations (208–9). It provided the point of unity for the changing objectivations. And yet that sense—for example, an "apple tree"—is in fact given differently in each kind of objectivation: in perception the consciousness of it is "'originary'"; in memory, "memorial"; in the picture-objectivation, "pictorial." In each case, "characteristics—found when the regard is directed to the noematic correlate and not to the lived experience and its really inherent composition—are indicated in the 'appearing tree as such.' Here 'modes of consciousness' are not expressed in the sense of noetic moments, but rather modes in which that of which there is consciousness is itself and as such is given. As characteristics belonging to what is, so to speak, 'ideal' ['*Ideelles*'], they are themselves 'ideally inherent' and not really inherent" (209). Thus by attending to the mode of givenness, to *how* something is given, it is possible to discern the noematic characteristics. But to do so, one must take one's bearings by the act to which the noematic correlate is given, since such givenness is always for a consciousness, for an ego.

3.3.4 Presentiation and the Varieties of Representiation. The preceding talk of objectivations, but especially that of the corresponding noematic characteristics, employed a distinction between the kinds of objectivation and their correlates, though only implicitly. Husserl identifies two main classes of objectivation: presentiation (*Gegenwärtigung*), which gives its object originarily, and representiation (*Vergegenwärtigung*), which gives its object always only reproductively. Unlike presentiation, it is of the essence of representiation to be a modification of something else.[66] Whereas perception is the sole mode of presentiation, there are at least three kinds of representiation, all of which are modifications of something else.

The *first* is representiation as the basic reproductive modification of perception. Husserl illustrates this by means of the memory of something past, which refers to a perception, namely as "having perceived": "in a certain way there is consciousness of the 'corresponding' perception (perception of the same core-sense) in the memory, and yet it is not actually contained in it. Precisely by its own essence, memory is a 'modification of' perception." The memory does not "actually" contain the perception because the ego does not live in it; instead, it actually lives in the memory. The perception is had here only second-hand. Although formerly it was not an object, but the objectivating act itself with its own objectuality, now the perception has become the object of a new act. And in this way it is modified or revalued. However, the effects of this modification are not confined to the noetic side; they are mirrored in the noematic side as well: "Correlatively, what is characterized as past gives itself as 'has been present,' thus as a modification of 'present,' which as something unmodified is precisely the 'originary,' the 'bodily present' of the perception." Every modification, whether noetic or noematic, is ultimately the modification of perception or its originarily given object. And that means that every higher level act or correlate refers back to, in other words: is founded on, originariness.

The *second* kind of representiation specified by Husserl is the pictorializing modification. It, too, is the modification of something else, and in fact of something originary, but in a manner differing from that of simple representiation. The pictorializing modification "representiates 'in' a 'picture.'" Here Husserl notes two kinds of pictorial representiation. On the one hand, the picture can appear originarily, as *in* an etching, for instance Dürer's "Knight, Death, and the Devil,"[67] and be perceived. The picture cannot be reduced to the physical thing, the sheet of paper, ink, etc., though these physical aspects play an important role in its Being. On the other hand, a picture can appear reproductively, "as when we have picture-objectivations in memory or free fantasy" (210). Both kinds of picture have characteristics akin to those of the simple representiation, Husserl says, but they are different from the latter insofar as they presuppose "combinations." These are visible in the "distinction between 'picture' and 'depicted' that belongs noematically to the essence of consciousness." What sets this modification off from simple representiation is that "here the noema always includes a pair of characteristics that refer to one another even though they include differing Objects as Objects of objectivatings."

The *third* kind of representiation is closely related to the pictorializing modification, and yet distinct. It is the sign-objectivation. It is similar to the previous kind with respect to the pairing of characteristics in the noema, but instead of the picture and depictured, the sign-objectivation has the sign and the signified. The distinction between the latter two kinds of modification will be seen to lie in the way in which their objects are given, which, of course, will be reflected in the pairings of characteristics.

Since presentiation is not a modification, it remains simple, always on the same level, even if the various presentiations are linked in internal time consciousness. By contrast, representiations, which again are essentially modifications, are not bound to one level. The essence of modification already speaks against this. Rather, every kind of representiation can be iterated *in infinitum*: "All the types of objectivation-modification previously dealt with are always accessible for ever newer hierarchical formations of such a kind that the intentionalities in the noesis and noema are hierarchically built up on one another, or rather encased in one another in a unique way." Thus there are simple representiations, that is, modifications of perception; but representiations of representiations are also possible, for example rememberings in rememberings, and so on. By the same token, fantasies are generated by a "mere change of sign" in a presentiation or representiation. As a result, "fantasies in fantasies" become possible, "and this at any level of encasement" (211). Moreover, just as the levels of modification are unlimited, likewise such modifications are not limited to one kind; beyond the encasement of rememberings in rememberings, or fantasies in fantasies, mixtures are also possible, and on any level. Thus, whereas every representiation ultimately points back to an originary perception, representiations can also be of memories, anticipations, fantasies, etc., such that there are fantasies in rememberings or rememberings in fantasies, and so on.

Correlative possibilities of encasement and mixture are also to be found on the noematic side: "In all those kinds of hierarchical constructs that contain iterated representiation-modifications in their structures, noemata with a corresponding hierarchical formation are obviously constituted" (211–12). That is to say, there are noemata of noemata, such that each subsequent noema points back, as it were, to the previous noema. Each new noema sublates, as it were, the lower level noemata, which, again, retain their former characteristics, but now with a change in value. The reference to the ordinal sequence of levels naturally suggests the hierarchical classification of those levels. Husserl terms the number of each level its 'index': "To every noematic level belongs a characteristic proper to that level as a kind of index by means of which each thing characterized manifests itself as belonging to its level" (212), from the first level to the highest reached. The index is significant because, although it is possible to move upwards into ever higher levels, it is also possible to remain on one level and reflect within it. Husserl illustrates this by the memory of a visit to the Dresden Gallery (see 211–12). Walking through it, one encounters a painting. It is itself a painting of a gallery. By regarding it within memory, one enters into the picture-world and thus into picture-consciousness. Here one has entered onto a second level, but still within memory. On this level it is possible to engage in further reflections.

The talk of the noema of a noema, of one referring back to another, of hierarchical levels and indexes, suggests a kind of *noematic intentionality*: "Each noematic level is an 'objectivation' 'of' the givens of the next level down. However, 'objectivation' does not mean here the objectivational lived experience, nor does the 'of' here express the relation between consciousness and the Object of consciousness. It is, as it were, a noematic in contrast to a noetic intentionality. The latter bears the former within itself as its consciousness-correlate, and in a certain way its intentionality runs through the whole line of the noematic intentionality" (212). The line of so-called noematic intentionality leads from the present level back to the original noema. Each level down to the original level may be accessed by the ego's ray of regard. But again, the ray can be sent in virtually any direction: it can move, as it were, vertically through the levels of the hierarchy or horizontally, thereby remaining with one level and engaging in reflection on the various objectivations pertaining to the noemata of that level.

The chief advance made in the preceding analyses of objectivation-modifications lies in the demonstration of the existence of noematic characteristics as they are borne by the noematic core, the "intentional object as such" (see 213). These characteristics belong no more really inherently to the noesis than does the noematic core. They transcend the noesis just as does the core to which they are attached. Given the fundamental role this distinction plays for Husserl in solving the greatest, the epistemological problems, it is crucial that the distinction between the noetic and the noematic be kept in view. Armed with the new insights, Husserl is in a better position to give a balanced, "two-sided," and thus adequate account of consciousness than before.

To this point he has attended principally to the simplest of relationships, and he will continue to do so. And with good reason. Husserl's intention here, as everywhere, is to work from the ground up. He aims at fixing the beginning and, only on that basis, at moving up to higher levels. In this respect simplicity proves not to be a fault but a virtue, for whatever holds on the lower, simpler levels will also hold on higher, more complex levels. The complex is founded on the simple. While a discussion of higher-level relationships would no doubt be instructive, it would be most fruitful only after the basic relationships had been articulated. It is on account of this that Husserl focuses on the basic noetic-noematic structures; only after elucidating them does he indicate the essential possibility of further modifications, the employment of which would carry one up to higher levels. Due to the founding nature of those structures, he stresses "that all of the characteristics suggested here or still to be suggested . . . are of universal phenomenological scope" (213).

3.4 Belief- and Being-Characteristics

The noematic characteristics encountered in the foregoing are not the only ones; there are other, "quite different" characteristics, which "fit into fundamentally different genera, so to speak, into fundamentally different dimensions of characterization." Their investigation marks a shift of focus. Among the new genera are characteristics that lie deeper than any seen before and that found all the others in this series. Consequently, the shift in question is first a move downward so as to locate the founding characteristics and only thereafter a move upward by means of the modifications applicable to them. These are new characteristics, and as such are to be kept apart from those other, familiar ones. The new characteristics prove to be the simplest.

The structural features of the noesis and the noema sketched above presuppose another set of features; they underlie every act and its correlate. On the one hand, the noematic characteristics are bound up with "*Being-characteristics*, which are obviously of a totally different kind" (214). On the other hand: "As noetic characteristics—'*doxic*' or '*belief-characteristics*'[68]—which are related correlatively to modes of Being, *perceptual belief* and, moreover, sometimes *perceptual certainty* are contained really inherently in intuitive objectivations, for example in those of normal perception [*Wahrnehmung*] as 'noticing' [*Gewahrung*]; to it there corresponds the Being-characteristic *actual*, as the noematic correlate in the appearing 'Object.'"[69] The same parallels of characteristics are to be found in other kinds of objectivation, for example in memory, representiation, and anticipation, as long as they are "certain" or "sure" objectivations. In his characterization of such objectivations, Husserl captures succinctly the relation between the two sides of the parallel: "They are Being-'positing,' 'thetic' acts." On the noetic side, then, there is certainty, sureness, in short: belief or position without qualification. On the noematic side, there is Being, actuality, which is expressed in the predicate 'actual'. It should be noted, however, that these acts are not yet position-takings in the strict sense. In other words, the talk of 'act' should not be understood as meaning that the will is involved here. Husserl says that it can be ignored at this stage of the analysis since the lowest levels of belief and Being are of concern and the will enters onto the scene always only at higher levels. The positing in question takes place at the lowest level and is thoroughly passive—no decision is made to believe in any Being; it occurs, so to speak, without one's knowing it. This recalls, incidentally, the observation made above that attention entails a kind of position-taking, while not being a position-taking in the strict sense.[70] In that context, Husserl already alluded to the existence of a kind of thetic "stratum" that accompanies every attention to, every pointing of the ray of regard at something. The implication is that every directedness of consciousness, and thus all intentionality, already entails belief.

3.4.1 Modalizations of the Originary. Although the certainty of belief, the position of actuality, is the originary mode of belief, it is not the only mode possible. On the contrary, it can be modified, that is, modalized: "The mode of 'certain' belief can change into the mode of mere deeming possible or presuming, or questioning or doubting"—whereby the belief is not expunged, but merely weakened.[71] Correlatively, whatever modification occurs on the noetic side, it is answered on the noematic side: "that which appears (and regarding the first dimension of characterizations[72] is characterized as 'originary,' 'reproductive,' and the like) has now taken on the Being-modalities of 'possible,' 'probable,' 'questionable,' 'doubtful,' respectively." But again, at this point the will has no part in any of these modifications. Regardless of the kind of objectivation modified, whether it be perception, memory, or some other kind, the modifications take place passively, which is to say, "without the participation of any 'thinking' in the specific sense, without a 'concept' and predicative judgment" (215). These modifications simply happen, without any rational motivation, without any decision, and without being fixed in speech. They are prepredicative. A distinction of "thinking" lies at the root of these determinations, a distinction from the "natural" understanding of what thinking is. Husserl's remarks show that, at its most fundamental level, consciousness is not identical with thinking "in the specific sense," and so it is also not identical with "reason." Interestingly enough, because consciousness operates prepredicatively and prerationally here, no meaningful distinction between human beings and beasts can be made—both are merely animals at this stage. Only with the appearance of speech and then reason will such a distinction of conscious life prove possible within the system of phenomenology. For Husserl, the human being is first of all merely one conscious being among others, then the speaking being, and only thereafter the rational being.

Husserl's discovery of belief- and Being-characteristics, and especially their respective modalities, brings "the distinctive, specifically intentional sense of the talk of modification" into view. To begin with, every modification is *per definitionem* the modification of something else—and this phrase clearly entails an intentional reference; the 'of' indicates that the modification points to that "something else." Since on the simplest level a modification is of something unmodified, each modification may to be said to refer back to something unmodified or originary. This became clear in Husserl's earlier analyses of the varieties of objectivation and their correlates. On the noetic side, every representiation proved to point back ultimately to a presentiation. For example, on the lowest level, memory is the modification of perception; the former points back, refers "intentionally" to the latter, which means that in the end every memory is founded on a perception. The sphere of belief has analogous foundational concatenations, and in fact ones that found those seen in the sphere of objectivations. Like perception in the former series, here "belief-certainty obviously plays the role of the unmodified or . . . 'unmodalized' primal form of the mode of believing. Correspondingly, in the correlate: the unqualified Being-characteristic (the noematic 'certainly' or 'actually' existing [*seiend*]) functions as the primal form of all Being-modalities. Indeed, all of the Being-characteristics originating from it, the ones that are specifically to be called Being-modalities, refer in their own sense back to the primal form. In itself, 'possible' says as much as 'possibly existing', 'probable', 'doubtful', 'questionable' say as much as 'probably existing', 'doubtfully and questionably existing'," respectively (215–16). Hence there is a sense in which each side, the noesis as well as the noema, has its own peculiar kind of intentionality, for every modality, whether a belief- or Being-modality, points back mutatis mutandis to something more originary. And in fact, with respect to the modalizations touched on thus far at least, the originary proves to be the strongest instance of either series: certainty and actually, and certainly, surely existing, respectively. However, just as in the case of the previous reference to a kind of noematic intentionality in the objectivational sphere, Husserl is careful here to qualify the use of this phrase, for compared with noetic intentionality, the talk of 'noematic intentionality' is more metaphorical: "The intentionality of the noeses is mirrored in these noematic references, and one almost feels forced again to speak of a 'noematic intentionality' as a 'parallel' of noetic intentionality, which is intentionality properly so called" (216). The talk of intentionality is justified in both cases insofar as every modified noesis or noema points back to an unmodified predecessor.

Every line of "doxic" intentionality terminates in an originary term. In the case of the noema it is the characteristics 'actually' or 'certainly existing'. In that of the noesis, on the other hand, it is belief-certainty, which is "unqualifed belief in the pregnant sense." Husserl draws out its special founding role by renaming it. Due to its "highly remarkable special status in the multiplicity of acts, all of which are included under the title of belief—or 'judgment'," he terms it "primal belief or protodoxa [*Urglaube oder Urdoxa*]." Furthermore, because every modality is a modality of belief, he calls them 'doxic modalities', a term he will even apply—conscious of the consequent ambiguity—to Being-characteristics.

Husserl has shown the way in which each modality represents a modification of something else—at bottom: of an unmodified, originary modality. On account of this, he stresses that it is completely wrong to assert that "'belief' (or 'judgment') is only differentiated into certainty, uncertain presumption, etc., as though it were a matter there of a series of coordinate species (no matter where the series broke off)" (217), and not of modifications.

The talk of intentionality within the sphere of belief has centered on the way in which "secondary modes refer to a protodoxa." However, matters do not stop here. There is not always only one protodoxa with, so to speak, a straight line of intentionality leading back to it from the secondary mode. In other words, protodoxa do not belong to one level alone. Rather, a new protodoxa may be generated on higher levels by means of a redirection of the ray of regard, that is, by ceasing to live-in an act and instead reflecting on it or its correlate: "On the one hand, we can, for example, while living in probability-consciousness (in the presuming), look at what is probable; on the other hand, however, at the probability itself and as such, that is, at the noematic Object with the characteristic ascribed to it by the presumption-noesis. However, the 'Object,' with its sense-composition and with this probability-characteristic, is given in the second focusing of regard as existing: in relation to this Object, accordingly, consciousness is simple belief in the unmodified sense." This same possibility pertains to every modality. The modalization of primal belief is not final, therefore, but can itself be transformed into such belief. Of course, the protodoxa on the next level retains the founding intentionality, which led from probability back down to certainty, or to the original protodoxa. This possibility of redirecting the regard and thereby generating new protodoxa, which correspond to new Being-objects (*Seinsobjekte*) and their characteristics constituted by the new regard, reinforces the insight into the primacy of belief.

3.4.2 Negation and Affirmation. A new pair of belief-modifications presents itself[73] that, although akin to the series just seen, is distinct from them, a state of affairs Husserl indicates already by treating the new pair separately. It consists of rejection (*Ablehnung*), denial (*Verneinung*), or negation on the one hand and assent (*Zustimmung*) or affirmation (*Bejahung*) on the other. As in the previous series, here too peculiar intentionalities are in play: "Every denial is a denial of something, and this something points us back to some doxic modality or other. Noetically, negation is thus a 'modification' of some 'position' or other; that does not mean of an affirmation, but rather of a 'positing' in the broadened sense of some doxic modality or other" (218).[74] All of this holds of affirmation as well, of course, except that its effect lies in the opposite direction: "Just as negation, figuratively speaking, crosses out, likewise affirmation 'underscores,' it 'confirms' a position by 'assenting' instead of 'annulling' it as does negation" (218–19). This makes it clear that *all modification is at bottom a modification of belief* and, what is more, that all intentionality presupposes a "position" or "positing." In other words: *wherever there is intentionality, there is belief*.[75]

The primacy of *doxa* is emphasized in Husserl's qualification concerning the target of negation: not an affirmation but a *position* is negated. While an affirmation can itself be a position, it is not synonymous with belief. It is a *modification* of a preceding position and only as such does it become a position itself. For the same reason, Husserl has warned of the equivocation centering on the word 'certain'. It is not the correlate of affirmation; rather, 'yes' is. Affirmation can only be a modification of the protodoxa whose correlate is 'certain'. The latter lies therefore on a lower level. Were an affirmation to be negated, it would be negated as a position, just as it would be affirmed as a position.

The newness of the pair in question rests precisely in its affect on belief; each side generates a new product, a new Being-object that the previous series did not have. As the aforementioned qualification makes clear, there is no affirmation contained in—as it were, concealed beneath the surface of—the other belief-modifications, likewise no negation, but only belief and its modalities. Certainty is no more affirmation than doubt is negation. These new modifications are not modalizations, or if they are, then in a different sense than the foregoing series. Their difference resides in the fact that they do not weaken belief but, instead, either cancel it or confirm it. Or put differently, the other modalizations leave their correlate hanging in the balance, whereas affirmation and negation decide the matter—either yes or no, with no middle ground. Like the other modalizations, however, they point back to the primacy of belief, even while perhaps distancing themselves from an original belief.

This is visible not only on their noetic side, but on the noematic side as well. Thus in the case of negation: "Its new noematic product [*Leistung*] is the 'crossing out' of the corresponding positional characteristic, its specific correlate is the crossing-out characteristic, the characteristic of 'not'. Its negation-stroke goes through something positional, or more concretely: through a 'positum' ['*Satz*'], and in fact by virtue of the crossing out of its specific positum-characteristic, that is, its Being-modality. Precisely thereby this characteristic, and the positum itself, stands there as a 'modification' of something else. Put differently: by transforming the simple Being-consciousness into the corresponding negation-consciousness, in the noema the simple characteristic 'existing' becomes 'nonexisting'" (218). The same possibility of modification applies to the other doxic modalities: 'possibly existing' becomes 'impossibly existing'; 'probably existing' becomes 'improbably existing'; and so on. As with all modifications, likewise the effect of negation is by no means partial, but rather total: "the whole noema, the whole 'positum,' taken in concrete noematic fullness" is crossed out. According to Husserl, affirmation generates analogous correlates, but he does not pursue them here.[76] Nor, for that matter, does he investigate the peculiarities of negative and affirmative position-takings.[77]

He does make a remark in passing, however, that is of some interest. It concerns the possibility of redirecting the regard and rests on the distinction made above between living-in (*Erleben*) and reflection: "We can live in the negating consciousness, in other words, 'effect' the negation: the ego's regard is then directed to what gets crossed out" (219). This is "naive" regard in the lived experience; by contrast, the possibility of reflection always remains open to consciousness: "But we can also direct the regard as a seizing regard to the crossed out as such, to that which bears the negation-stroke: the crossed out is then there as a new 'Object,' and in fact it is there in the simple protodoxic mode as 'existing.'" This accords with what has been seen above. But Husserl continues with a remark that seems to deviate significantly from his earlier findings: "The new focus [*Einstellung*] does not generate the new Being-object; in the 'effectuation' of the rejection there is consciousness of the rejected as having the characteristic of crossed-out"—thus the reflection is itself not a modification of what it fixes in its gaze, at least not in the sense of the two groups just seen. From the above it is clear that reflection alters the object on which it focuses, but not in the sense of a modification. Rather, it wrests the Being-object, replete with its former functions, out of its former context; through reflection, the former living-in is cut off, put out of action. The gaze is directed to what was formerly lived-in while living-in the new reflective regard. Because such reflection does not create a Being-object in the sense of the foregoing modifications, it becomes possible to speak about the noema: "but it is only in the new focus that the characteristic becomes the predicable determination of the noematic sense-core." This holds likewise for affirmation, of course, but also of the other belief-modifications seen thus far.[78]

3.4.3 Iterability. Every modification of consciousness is of a Being-object. Every modification presupposes belief. Every modification produces a new

Being-object. This holds no less of belief-modifications, including negation. It does not annihilate a position but rather produces a new Being-object by effecting a change of sign in the former position—from + to –, as it were.[79] "Since every negatum and affirmatum is itself a Being-object, it can, like everything else of which there is consciousness in a mode of Being, be affirmed or denied. In consequence of the constitution of Being that is effected anew in every step, an ideally infinite chain of iterated modifications therefore results." For example, it is denied that it is denied that it is denied, etc. Or correlatively, 'nonexistent' is negated and becomes 'not nonexistent', etc. In each case, a new Being-object arises. Since each of the other modifications treated above produces a new Being-object, they are also iterable: "That something is possible, probable, questionable, etc., can itself be intended [*bewußt*] again in the mode of possibility, probability, questionability; to the noetic formations correspond the noematic Being-formations: it is possible that it is possible that it is probable, questionable; it is probable that it is possible that it is probable; and thus in all combinations. To formations on higher levels, then, correspond affirmata and negata, they being modifiable anew, and thus it continues, ideally stated, *in infinitum*" (220). Iteration is not, however, the continued modification of the same Being-object as such, but of the new Being-object. Nevertheless, this new object remains bound to the foregoing noema and so on, such that one can speak again of a so-called noematic intentionality in this connection. "But it should always be borne in mind that the talk of modifications here refers, on the one hand, to a possible transformation of the phenomena, thus to a possible actional operation; on the other hand, it refers to the much more interesting eidetic peculiarity of the noeses or noemata—in their own essence and without any consideration of their genesis—that they point back to something other, something unmodified." The prerequisite of iteration is the possibility that the ego redirect its ray of regard to the new Being-object. And that means that the ego must believe in the object it is to modify. What is "much more interesting" to Husserl is precisely the basis of all modification—which, in all but one case, is to say: of all production. His analyses turn now to this exception.

4. The Doctrine of the Neutrality Modification

After having disclosed the fundamental role of belief and Being, as well as the modifications applicable to the sphere of belief, Husserl's investigations of the noetic-noematic correlation literally reach a low point and, what is more, a potential impasse: he hits upon an "extremely important" modification, one that "occupies a completely isolated place, and thus by no means may be placed in the series of those modifications discussed above" (222).[80] It is a modification of belief, but in a totally different sense than the latter modifications. Its uniqueness is indicated by the fact that, while it is applicable within the sphere of belief, it does "not at all belong specifically" to that sphere—it does not modify acts of belief alone. Rather, it is, as Husserl himself emphasizes, "an extremely significant *universal* modification of consciousness," and so can be applied to any and every act, as well as to its correlate. Strangely enough, however—and this further underscores its uniqueness—although this new modification first comes into view in this sphere, Husserl implies that is not a "genuine modification of belief." The paradoxicalness of this observation will fade only after "the peculiar way it behaves towards doxic positings"[81] has been grasped, which requires that the decisive distinctions first be made.

As Husserl himself points out, he is the first to have seen this modification—it "has never been scientifically elaborated"—and in this sense it is new. On the other hand, it is not new, for it is and has always been operative in various modes of consciousness, including that effected by the epoché: "It is contained in every abstaining-from-producing, putting-something-out-of-action, 'bracketing'-it, 'leaving-it-undecided,' and then having-something-'undecided,' 'thinking-oneself-into-the-producing,' or 'merely thinking' what has been produced without 'joining in.'"[82] It is contained in, not identical with, them; it is not any one of these, but is all of them and more; it lies beneath their surface, that is, it founds them, and so is not obvious to the "unaided eye." Just this lack of obviousness is responsible for its oversight,[83] a lack attested and further strengthened by the fact that, prior to Husserl, there was no name for it, neither as a technical term—in previous inquiry, "wherever it had been touched upon, it had been confused with other modifications"—nor as a "univocal name . . . in ordinary language"—again, despite the role it plays in various modes of consciousness. Because it lies within those modes, a "deeper investigation" is called for, one more radical than any undertaken hitherto, in order to draw out the new modification's "own peculiarity."[84] And yet in view of the prevailing state of affairs, Husserl "can approach it only circumscriptively and step by step through a process of elimination," making his way down a *via negativa* from what is familiar to what is not.

Husserl began his account of the new modification, as it were, in the negative by asserting its uniqueness in contrast to all the modifications previously treated. However, before continuing in this direction, and thus before seeking to shore up that assertion, he gives a "positive" characterization of it: the new modification "completely annuls, completely debilitates in a certain way every doxic modality to which it is applied." It annuls, it debilitates, "but in a totally different sense than negation." What is distinctive about this modification is its negativity, a negativity that surpasses even that of negation itself. The gulf that in fact separates these two modifications first becomes visible in their respective results, in what each "produces." The "positive product" of negation is "the negatum"; it is positive insofar as it is "a non-Being that is itself again a

Being."[85] As such the product can again be subjected to any of the familiar modifications: it can be negated, doubted, affirmed, etc. Doing so generates a new product, which in turn can be modified, and so on. By contrast, the new modification "does not cross out, *it 'produces' nothing*; in consciousness it is the counterpart of all producing"—it is precisely the "neutralization" thereof.[86] It annuls, debilitates belief—completely. It leaves no doxic remainder, generates no product. The key difference between this modification and negation therefore lies already in the target of each operation: negation crosses out the belief in a Being, transforms it into the belief in a non-Being, whereas the new modification completely expunges the doxic modality pertaining to a given Being and thereby effectively annihilates both. In this sense it proves to be the "most original negation."[87] This characterization gives the first indication not only of why Husserl denies that such neutralization is a "genuine modification of belief," as well as of the way in which it marks a potential impasse, but also sheds light on what counts as a genuine modification and so points the way beyond that impasse. All of this is to become clearer by following the aforementioned negative path.

That this universal modification coincides with any of the specific modifications of belief treated thus far, including negation, has already been ruled out. It remains to be seen if this modification is related to or perhaps even identical with any others. Among the candidates in this connection are the epoché, assuming or supposing, fantasy, and picture-object or aesthetic consciousness. By elucidating them, Husserl seeks to draw out key features of the new modification, while also setting it off from all kindred modifications.

Beyond its unproductivity, Husserl discerns another feature of the new modification, one that concerns the will. He notes that in the foregoing the expressions for the modes of consciousness in which neutralization plays a role—such as abstaining-from-producing or bracketing something—include "a surplus of sense." They imply "a voluntary doing, whereas that should not matter at all. We therefore eliminate it."[88] As in the other modifications, the will is not essential to the universal neutrality modification and so can be ignored: "In any case, the result of this doing has a peculiar content, which . . . also can be considered on its own, as it is in fact also possible and does occur in concatenation of lived experiences without such volition." Instead, what is essential here is the modification's effect: "The positing characteristic has become powerless. Now belief is no longer *serious* belief, presuming no longer *serious* presuming, negating no longer *serious* negating, etc." (223). Seriousness depends on a positing, on belief, and as a consequence the neutralization of the latter must likewise result in the elimination of the former. Nevertheless, despite these losses, the neutralized act otherwise remains intact. Correspondingly, its correlate is the same in all points except for one: it "is there for consciousness, though not in the mode of 'actually', but rather as something 'merely thought of,' as 'mere thought.'" Everything is "bracketed" once the underlying belief has been "put out of action." With it fall seriousness, interest, and commitment—which is to say, the primary modes of the will.[89]

4.1 The Epoché and the Neutrality Modification

At this point in *Ideas I* Husserl alludes to the kinship of the neutrality modification with the epoché, for it too is in a sense universal, it too brackets everything.[90] And yet despite their superficial similarities (primary of which is the fact that both neutralize belief and that in doing so neither is productive), they are separated literally *toto coelo*—which should already be obvious in light of the difference in the role the will plays in each, and which should become even clearer once it has been specified just how the scope of each "neutralization" differs radically from that of the other modifications of belief.[91] In this connection it is once again necessary to underscore the effect of the neutrality modification: unlike in unneutralized positings, each of which has a positum as its correlate, the correlates of neutralized positings "do not contain anything positable, anything actually predicable; in no respect does neutral consciousness play the role of a 'believing' for that of which it is conscious." Although it should be clear from this and the foregoing that the particular intentional structure is not disrupted by the application—though, again, it need not be voluntary—of the neutrality modification, the fact that the underlying positing has been rendered powerless has grave implications for subsequent intentionalities, implications that center on the lack of anything positable or actually predicable. Decisive here, then, is the positing. Only where there is a positing can there also be actual predication. The elimination of the one means the elimination of the other. And it is in this respect that the neutrality modification would represent an impasse. By contrast, and this is the central point of difference, the epoché in no way threatens to obstruct the achievement of the telos of Husserl's system, to say nothing of that of humanity. Rather, it provides the means for entering onto the path leading to that telos. This is precisely because the epoché brackets but one thesis, one that had for its part blocked entry into the phenomenological sphere, namely the general thesis. By excluding the belief in the existence of the world (*Weltglaube*), not only does a whole new sphere of Being come into view, but also a new sphere of belief. After all, just as the world is not the only sphere of Being, likewise the belief in the world is not the only kind of belief. By making this visible, the epoché does not only allow of a description of the natural attitude, but of conscious life as a whole. This is the primary achievement of the epoché; in this way its unproductivity proves to be productive in an unequaled manner. The universal neutrality modification, on the other hand, is absolutely unproductive. Unlike the epoché, it leaves no remainder.

4.2 Neutrality and Reason

Husserl himself stresses that this modification marks "an incomparable peculiarity of consciousness"—it has no equal, not even in the epoché. Its incomparability springs from the fact that its noeses cannot be rationally scrutinized: "in accordance with their essence, the authentic, unneutralized noeses are subject to the 'verdict of reason,' whereas the question about reason and unreason makes no sense for neutralized noeses." The same holds for the corresponding noemata: "Everything characterized noematically as existing (certain), as possible, presumed, questionable, null, etc., can be so characterized in a 'valid' or 'invalid' way; it can be 'in truth,' be possible, be null, etc. By contrast, mere thinking-of 'posits' nothing; it is not a positional consciousness. The 'mere thought' of actualities, possibilities, etc., 'claims' nothing; it is neither to be admitted as correct nor rejected as incorrect." This is the crucial point in which neutral consciousness differs from its positional counterpart: because it posits nothing whatsoever, makes no claim, evades the Either-Or, merely entertains a thought, neutral consciousness gives nothing to be scrutinized, nothing to be decided. Where there are no actual predicates—and, on Husserl's understanding, there is actuality only where there is seriousness, interest, commitment, in short: belief[92]—there can be no scrutiny. And since reason can come into play only when such scrutiny is possible, this means that where the neutrality modification is in effect, there can be no reason.

But what is reason? Although this question is somewhat premature, at least in view of the development and structure of Husserl's system, a provisional answer may be given. It should already be clear from the foregoing, especially from Husserl's remark about "the question of reason and unreason," that reason is not identical with consciousness. On the contrary, consciousness has a prerational life of its own, one that the use of reason presupposes. The functional problems that are so important to phenomenology are, after all, not at base problems of reason, but of the productivity peculiar to consciousness—in general. Reason is what consciousness does—under the best circumstances. It is nothing in and of itself, but is a characteristic deriving from the scrutiny of the productions of consciousness, which is to say, of positional consciousness. Thus reason is, as it were, superadded to consciousness. The total lack of reason in neutral consciousness confirms this: it is still consciousness, even if a "deficient mode" thereof. On the other hand, reason is not the only possibility pertaining to positional consciousness; unreason is equally possible. Both extremes belong as essential possibilities to productive consciousness and to it alone: reason is the positive pole and unreason, the negative.[93] It is crucial that the latter not be confounded with neutral consciousness. Neutrality allows of no reason. But unreason is reason, albeit the negative mode thereof. It is related to reason just as disbelief is related to belief. Neither represents a lack in the sense of total absence or neutrality; rather, each is a negative mode of positionality. In view of the bipolar structures on which Husserlian thought is built, wherein every actuality is accompanied by a potentiality, namely that it will swing into its opposite, it is clear that for him there is no positive without the negative. This is the point at which the myriad distinctions come together: the insight into the productivity of consciousness enables Husserl to discover its counterpart: unproductive consciousness. Here the opposite of positional consciousness is not simply negative consciousness, however, but rather neutral consciousness. Whereas neutrality, so to speak, pulls the ground out from under reason and thereby obstructs the ascent to the latter, its discovery also discloses that ground as the basis of productive, more or less rational consciousness life. It is nothing other than belief.

4.3 Supposing and Neutrality

And yet neutrality need not be a dead end. There is a way in which a kind of neutral consciousness can be modified and thereby become productive. Namely, "every merely-thinking-of can be translated into an assuming [*Annehmen*], a supposing [*Ansetzen*]" (224). This, Husserl notes, is "subject to the unconditionally free will." By means of the modification, the merely-thinking-of becomes susceptible to scrutiny, though not as merely-thinking-of, but only as supposing. For supposing is, after all, "something like positing, what is supposed [*Ansatz*], in turn, a kind of 'positum' [*Satz*], except that it is a very peculiar modification of doxic positing that *stands over against and apart* from the principal series dealt with above." Supposing differs from the modifications making up the "principal series" in two respects: first of all, because it is a modification of a neutralized positing, but also because it depends on an unneutralized positing for its "actuality." Accordingly, this modification can be attached to an authentic positing as the latter's "hypothetical 'antecedent' or consequent." This is necessary, for on its own a supposing would be a merely-thinking-of and thus not susceptible to scrutiny and so could not receive the "verdict of reason": "It is not of a mere undecided thought, but rather of what is hypothetically supposed that it can be said that it is correct or not." It is literally hypo-thetical and therefore can be scrutinized. And precisely this susceptibility to scrutiny shows that assuming or supposing are not equivalent to the neutrality modification. Husserl stresses that it is "a fundamental error to confuse the one with the other, and to overlook the equivocation lying in the talk of merely-thinking-of or of the mere thought." A hypothesis is not equivalent to a quasi-thesis. It must be stressed that neutrality in and of itself represents a dead end for consciousness. "Merely-thinking-of" leads nowhere. However, one escape route—as will be seen, there is another—runs through supposing. By attaching what is "merely-thought-of" to a thesis, it becomes a supposition. On account of its new link to belief, it can now be scrutinized. This way out of neutrality, then, is not provided by neutrality itself, but by a subsequent, transforming belief. Without it, consciousness remains at a standstill.

Even the talk of 'thinking' harbors a possible equivocation one must be on guard against, Husserl stresses. Thinking must be distinguished; just as consciousness and reason are not identical, likewise consciousness is not identical with thinking in the specific sense: the word 'thinking' is "at one time related to the distinctive sphere of explicating, conceiving, and expressing thinking, to logical thinking in a specific sense; and at another time it is related to the positional as such, which, as we just had it in view, does not ask about any explicating or any conceiving predicating." This distinction is between reflective and unreflective or naive consciousness. Positional consciousness, taken in the most general sense, is not logical, that is, it is not expressive, but is sublinguistic. Logical consciousness is a very specific and higher form of merely positional consciousness.

4.4 Fantasy and the Neutrality Modification

Husserl warns that yet another "dangerous" equivocation of merely-thinking-of is possible, one that confuses the neutrality modification with fantasy. The source of this error lies in the fact that "fantasy itself is indeed a neutrality modification"; moreover, its scope looks to be the same as that of the latter: "despite the particularity of its type, it is of universal significance, it is applicable to all[94] lived experiences"; and it plays a "role in most formations of merely-thinking-of." However, like the epoché, fantasy is but *one*—not *the*—neutrality modification; while they are akin, Husserl stresses repeatedly that fantasy and the universal neutrality modification are not identical, and must be kept apart.[95] The necessity of doing so derives from the insight into the universal neutrality modification's result: it renders consciousness impotent; because neutral consciousness produces nothing, its noeses cannot be rationally scrutinized. One need only recall Husserl's remark that the vital element of phenomenology is fiction and, what is more, that the mode of phenomenological investigation is imaginative, eidetic variation or free fantasy, in order to see just how harmful the failure to maintain the distinction between the two modifications would be. Were fantasy equivalent to the universal neutrality modification, phenomenology could never succeed in securing the status of First Philosophy for itself; it could never engage in a fundamental critique of reason. For without the scrutiny of reason, there can be no science, no critique—no phenomenology. In light of Husserl's claims for phenomenology, then, the danger posed by the failure to make the requisite distinctions is not a particular danger, it is not confined merely to the viability of the phenomenological enterprise, but is universal: to confound fantasy with the neutrality modification endangers the whole of humanity.

The difference between the two modifications becomes apparent in light of Husserl's definition of fantasying: it is "the neutrality modification of 'positing' representiation, thus of memory in the broadest sense thinkable." Although fantasy is said to be applicable to *any* lived experience,[96] its universality is in fact restricted, for it can modify solely on the level of representiation, or memory, and not on that of, say, originary lived experiences; a representiation may itself be either a modification of an originary lived experience—for example, as the memory of a perception—or of another representiation, but by virtue of its essence it itself is never an originary lived experience. The restriction of its scope of application is what first distinguishes fantasy from the universal neutrality modification, "which we can contrast with every 'positing' lived experience" (225). Representiation, or memory, is just one among other positing lived experiences,[97] all of which may be subjected to the universal neutrality modification—"with its manifold formations that comply with all kinds of positing" (224)—whereas fantasy affects memory alone.

4.5 Fantasy, Aesthetic Consciousness, and the Neutrality Modification

To indicate the limits of fantasy and the extent of the universal neutrality modification, Husserl turns to perception: "the neutrality modification of normal perception, which posits in unmodified certainty, is the neutral picture-object consciousness [*Bildobjektbewußtsein*] that we find as a component in the normal consideration of a perceptually presented, depicted world" (226).[98] Already the possible directions of regard of each modification differ: as the neutrality modification of memory, fantasy can affect consciousness as it is always only directed towards immanencies; by contrast, whereas the neutrality modification can also affect this kind of consciousness, it can do more: it can affect consciousness as it is directed towards transcendencies. To illustrate an instance of the latter kind of neutralization, Husserl refers to Dürer's etching "Knight, Death, and the Devil." Essential here, of course, is not which etching is considered—though Husserl's choice of examples is never entirely arbitrary; their significance often lies beyond the immediate context—but rather the various levels of consciousness involved in the contemplation of any picture. The first level is the normal perception of the page on which the etching is printed. Then the regard, as perceptual consciousness, can be redirected from the page to the figures appearing on it. As soon as they are contemplated aesthetically, however, the viewer is not directed to them as objects in their own right, but rather as what is depicted "'in the picture,' or more precisely: to the 'depicted' realities, to the knight made of flesh and blood, etc." Since for aesthetic consciousness the concern lies with the depiction, the objects on the page are not the target of regard, not the terminus; rather, they point beyond themselves to what is depicted. This consciousness, which "mediates and enables the depiction," is "an example of the neutrality modification of perception." Aesthetic consciousness is therefore a form of neutral consciousness. The enabling neutralization is obvious from the fact that the aesthetic regard passes, as it were, through what is perceived to what it depicts. The perceived object itself may thus be said to be a matter of indifference to this consciousness; the "depicting picture-object stands before us neither as existing nor as not existing nor in any other positing modality; or rather, there is consciousness of it as existing, but as quasi-existing [*gleichsam-seiend*] in the neutrality modification of Being." The same holds of the correlate, of what is depicted, when it is regarded "purely aesthetically" as a "mere picture": no determination is made of whether it exists or not; such existence is of no concern to aesthetic consciousness. That no such determination is made, that it hangs in the air, as it were, does not mean that what is at work here is "a privation, but rather a modification—precisely that of neutralization." As was noted above, were this modification to effect a privation, it would just be negation, and the result would be a non-Being that would itself be a Being. By contrast, this neutralization does not result in a definitive Being, but only in a *quasi*-Being, one that lies beyond all immediate decision. In this connection Husserl adds a telling qualification, telling insofar as it gives a further indication of the nature of the universal neutrality modification: "We just must not think [*vorstellen*] of it as a transforming operation attached to a preceding position. It can also be such occasionally. But it need not be."[99] In this respect the neutrality modification differs radically from fantasy. As the account of picture-object or aesthetic consciousness makes clear, the neutralization of perceptual consciousness does not stay on the level of that perception, but instead proceeds to the level of what is depicted and thus to the level of quasi-existence. Only on this level can there be any talk of depiction—the simple perceived objects do not of themselves refer to anything beyond themselves.

Beyond the scope of application, the second index of their "radical difference" lies in iterability: "the fantasy modification as representiation is iterable (there are fantasies at any level: fantasies 'in' fantasies), whereas the repetition of the 'operation' of neutralization is, according to its essence, excluded" (227).[100] The significance of this observation becomes evident when one recalls the presupposition of all iteration. Namely, as noted above,[101] every iteration of a modification is based on a Being-object that is posited as existing. Since iteration presupposes Being and since Being presupposes belief, the fact that fantasy is iterable indicates that some mode of belief has not been neutralized, which is to say: that fantasying consciousness is still, in some as yet indeterminate sense,[102] positional consciousness. By contrast, the fact that the neutrality modification cannot be iterated follows from the fact that it eliminates every doxic modality, there is no belief and hence no Being left over to be modified.[103] Here it becomes especially clear that this modification stops consciousness, as it were, dead in its tracks. It marks an impasse. Fantasy does not do so. And yet there are limits to its hierarchical formations, or rather: while consciousness is free to a certain extent in fantasy to move through myriad levels, its spontaneity is still bound by essential determinations: "every fantasy of a higher level can be freely converted into a direct fantasy of what was mediately fantasied in it, whereas this free possibility does not take place in going over from fantasy to the corresponding perception. For spontaneity there is an abyss here that the pure ego can transcend only in the essentially new form of realizing action and creation," the nature of which will be addressed below. This abyss marks a limit of the pure ego's will.

4.6 *The Abyss between Positional and Neutral Consciousness*

Such limits have special significance with respect to egoic motility. The ego's regard may be either positional or neutral, a distinction that points in two directions of inquiry. Since the unmodified and thus originary form of regard is positional, Husserl begins with it; the contours of neutral regard become evident only in contrast to it. Positional consciousness has two sides: actional and potential positings. Although the distinction between them, he notes, is "closely related" to that between attention and inattention encountered above, the former "by no means coincides with" the latter (see 228). The source of their lack of identity will be seen to lie in the neutrality modification, specifically in a duality in the distinction between the actionality and inactionality of attentional regard that becomes visible in its light.

Again, actional positings ground the actual activity of consciousness. It is with respect to potential positings, however, that the distinction becomes evident between actionality and potentiality on the one hand and attention and inattention on the other: "From any 'actual' consciousness, various positings potentially inherent in it may be derived, and these are then actual positings: in everything actually intended thetically, there are actual predicables. But a neutral consciousness does not 'contain' within itself any 'actual' predicables whatsoever" (228–29).[104] Consequently, neutral consciousness does not include any potential positings, which means that nothing more may be actually predicated of it. This is not to say, however, that the corresponding ego cannot direct its ray of regard to predicates, but only that: "The explication through attentional actionalities, through advertences to the various predicates proper to the objectual item of which there is conciousness, yields[105] nothing but neutral acts or modified predicates" (229). Neutral consciousness is therefore no less attentive than positional consciousness, and for that reason attention cannot be equated automatically with positionality or belief, nor even with interest.[106]

But whereas both kinds of consciousness entail attentional potentialities—which is guaranteed already by the nature of original time-consciousness—they differ radically with respect to the potentiality of position. The difference is decisive, for the kind of potentiality determines the character of egoic motility and thus of conscious life itself. Here the distinction might be made between the (neutral) sub-sistence and the (positional) productive existence of consciousness. The danger of speaking in this way, however, lies in the possibility of overlooking the fact that neutrality *sensu stricto* contributes nothing to consciousness. It is in effect a parasitic mode, for it lives off a preceding positionality. Thus, neutral consciousness subsists, but not of its own doing; rather, it owes its continued existence to positional consciousness. In Husserlian thought, wherever the talk is of 'life' or of 'actuality' in connection with consciousness, belief is also always meant. It alone animates.

Husserl illustrates the differences between positional and neutral consciousness with respect to perception, in which perceptual belief (or a proto-doxa) posits its objectuality as 'certain', as 'actually existing'. He distinguishes between immanent and transcendent perception. In the latter a physical thing is seized upon or posited as 'actually existing'. When the regard is directed to another object, it is now posited as 'actually existing'; the former object slips into the background from which it came, although it remains accessible to the positing regard. By contrast, the actuality of such a perceptual object is neutralized in picture consciousness. There a picture is seized upon, it is a fiction, but nothing actual: "'Seizing-upon' has the actionality proper to advertence, yet it is not 'actual' seizing-upon, but mere seizing-upon in the modification 'quasi'; the positing is not actional[107] positing, but rather modified into 'quasi'-positing" (230). By diverting the regard from the picture, the neutral object slips into the background, that is, into inactionality or potentiality. The regard may be redirected to that object at another time, of course, but the seizing-upon proper to neutral consciousness will never generate a positional actionality—not on its own. The same state of affairs holds of immanent perception, say, of a memory. It posits its object originarily as "actually existing." When neutralized in fantasy, however, that object ceases to be actual, but is instead a phantasm. It is "quasi-existent." An abyss exists between the two sides, between 'actual' and 'quasi-', which cannot be bridged directly: "Mere advertence of the regard cannot do away with this neutrality, no more than it can generate the actionality of a positing in other cases." A seamless transition from neutrality to positionality is not possible. Rather, the only transition possible is one mediated by an additional actual thesis, as in the case of a supposition. And only after such a transition has been made will consciousness once again become productive in the authentic sense. Until then, everything is seized upon merely in the mode of 'quasi'. Consciousness runs, as it were, in idle.[108]

Perception, whether immanent or transcendent, is not the only mode of consciousness, however. And this compels Husserl to make explicit a distinction here that has already played a role in his previous analyses and that will later be of importance, namely the distinction between doxic and nondoxic theses. He draws out the distinction between the two classes with respect to the modalizations of "the specifically doxic theses (of the doxic primal theses)" on the one hand—for example, presuming, deeming possible, and questioning—and negation and affirmation on the other (231). He says: "The correlates in them of which there is consciousness (possibility, probability, non-Being, and the like) can undergo doxic positing and therefore at the same time specific 'objectualization.' But while we 'live in' the presuming, questioning, rejecting, affirming, and the like, we do not effect any doxic primal theses—though [we do effect] other 'theses,' in the sense of a necessary universalization of the concept, namely presumption-theses, questionability-theses, denial-theses, etc." Yet the fact that other theses may be effected, that they may be lived in, does not mean that the doxic disappears from the scene altogether when one effects a nondoxic thesis. On the contrary, the doxic founds those other theses; each of them harbors a doxic thesis within itself: "But we can effect the corresponding doxic primal theses at any time; grounded in the essence of the phenomenological affair-complexes is the ideal possibility of actionalizing the potential theses inherent in them." Such actionalization presupposes, of course, the presence of an actional actual thesis with its halo of potential actual theses. Only on that basis can other actual theses be "put into action," as it were. By contrast, wherever the neutrality modification has been effected, wherever a thesis has been "put out of action," its background of potential theses is also put out of action. Neutralized theses can be effected, but they remain ever neutral. They are principially unproductive. Neutral consciousness is stagnant without the aid of positional consciousness, a stagnancy that becomes visible solely with respect to the verdict of reason. And there it marks an impasse.

4.6.1 The Realm of Shadows. The neutrality modification is a *universal* modification of consciousness (232). It is applicable to every form of thetic consciousness, whether actional or potential, whether originary or modalized.[109] Neutrality is not a mere anomaly,[110] however, but is just as much an essential possibility of consciousness as is positionality, which clarifies the aforementioned duality: positionality is always accompanied by the possibility of neutrality. They are bound together in an exclusive relationship—"[c]onsciousness in general, of whatever kind or form it may be, is pervaded by a radical scission"—one that centers on their respective behavior towards positings. Both sides modify consciousness, but in contrary ways. On the first side, that of positionality, Husserl has shown that "there belongs to every consciousness in which the pure ego does not live from the outset as one that 'effects' the cogito, which thus does not have the form 'cogito' from the outset, the essentially possible modification that converts it into this form." The other side, the second relative to the first, is that of neutrality: "To every cogito there belongs a precisely corresponding counterpart such that its [the cogito's] noema has its precisely corresponding counter-noema in the parallel cogito" (233). Like reason and unreason, they belong together essentially; there cannot be the one without the other—not, of course, as an actually existent counterpart, but rather as an essential possibility of consciousness, of every cogito: "The relationship between the parallel 'acts' consists in the fact that one of the two is an 'actual act,' the cogito is an 'actual,' 'actually positing' cogito, whereas the other is a 'shadow'[111] of an act, an inauthentic, not actually positing act. The one produces actually, the other is the mere mirror-image of all production."[112] As everywhere, likewise here: what holds of the acts must also hold of their correlates: "To this there corresponds the radical distinction of correlates: on the one hand, the constituted noematic production, which has the characteristic of an unmodified, actual product; on the other hand, the 'mere thought' of the precisely corresponding product. The actual and modified [products] correspond to one another ideally with absolute precision and yet are not of the same essence." One is alive, while the other is in effect dead. On Husserl's analysis, the distinction between both sides is not merely superficial, but reaches down to their essence: "to the originary essence there corresponds its counter-essence as a 'shadow' of the same essence." They are related to one another much like Oldenburg's soft sculptures: the "original" and its ghost. Each "exists," but with a different "quality."[113]

4.6.2 Positionality or Neutrality. This indicates the nature of the exclusive relationship between positional and neutral consciousness. Whereas they belong together, they are not of equal rank. Actual positing has primacy over quasi-positing, the living cogito over its neutral counterpart: "The cases are now radically separated by the fact that the protodoxa in question is either an actual protodoxa, so to speak, an actually believed belief, or its powerless counterpart, the mere 'thinking of' (Being, possible Being, etc. without qualification)" (234). The shadow of neutrality is cast, so to speak, by positional consciousness; the shadow depends for its existence on that of which it is a shadow, just as the mirroring presupposes what is mirrored. Positional consciousness and neutral consciousness correspond exactly, except that in the latter the living positing has been expunged. Either positionality or neutrality—there is no middle ground.[114] Hence Husserl's talk of the scission of consciousness: "consciousness in general is such that it is of a double type: prototype and shadow, positional and neutral consciousness. The one is characterized by the fact that its doxic positionality leads to actually positing doxic acts; the other, by its allowing only shadow-images of such acts, only neutrality modifications of them, to emerge from itself; in other words, that neutral consciousness does not contain anything at all in its noematic composition that is doxically apprehensible or, equivalently, that it does not contain an 'actual' noema, but instead only a counter-image thereof" (234–35). The opposition is between actually living and living as-if, that is, virtually.

Since a positing is the prerequisite of iteration, of further modification, and thus of productivity, and since neutral consciousness has expunged the positing at hand, it would seem to represent a dead end. And yet while this is true of the neutral consciousness taken on its own, Husserl sees an escape route in internal time consciousness: "And merely one doxic positability remains for the neutral lived experiences: that belonging to them as data of immanent time consciousness, determining them precisely as the modified consciousness of a modified noema" (235).[115] Internal time consciousness is and remains the basis of all conscious life; it alone is impervious to the neutrality modification. Time consciousness, however, has two basic components: the infinite stream of lived experiences and the pure ego. The former is the Being to which the latter's belief is directed. And it is just this belief that keeps the stream flowing. Even when one positing has been neutralized, the ego continues to swim on in the infinite stream. It can sidestep the neutralized positing by retreating into the halo of positings surrounding it, and from there view that positing anew, thetically. This suggests the earlier remarks made on supposing, by means of which a neutralized positing became accessible to scrutiny. But this is not the only possibility: it can be transformed into a supposing, but need not be. The neutralized can also be regarded as such from the standpoint of a positional consciousness and that means insofar as the former belongs to the stream. These possibilities are guaranteed by the fact that the neutrality modification affects always only one positing "at a time," and not the entire stream, to say nothing of the pure ego, though it can affect any and every positing. The belief of the pure ego combined with the Being of the stream make up conscious life. Internal time is the basis of this life in the sense that it is the expression of the union of both sides: it arises from the movement of the ego through the stream. Even if the neutrality modification is able to stop the ego in its tracks, as it were, on one level, the stream—and thus time—continues to flow, which means that the ego continues to believe, if darkly. Yet, although this possibility of revitalizing belief is important, especially since it testifies once again to the fundamental role of belief, this escape route is significant for Husserl's endeavor and for his analyses at the point in *Ideas I* because it shows that and how it is possible to return to belief so as to begin the climb once again up to reason. That is the decisive point.

Because of the centrality of the distinction between positionality and neutrality, because "every lived experience, whether it has the form of the cogito, whether it is an act in some particular sense, or not, falls under this opposition," Husserl says that he is going to use the terms 'positional' and 'neutral' "from now on." As a consequence, this distinction is in effect in every analysis of consciousness, whether explicitly or not. Again, it plays a role not only in the sphere of belief; rather, the "distinction between positionality and neutrality" is a "universal distinction of consciousness"—it bears on every kind of consciousness. Therefore, wherever the talk is of positional consciousness or of any actuality of consciousness or its correlates, there too one must hear talk of its neutral counterpart; wherever the positional or actual is attended to, there too one must see its shadow.

4.7 *The Levels of Consciousness*

Consciousness, whether positional or neutral, may be seen to comprise three main levels of acts. *First*, and of primary interest here, are explicit acts. *Second* are inexplicit or implicit acts. And *third* are explicitly reflective, knowing, or predicative acts. Acts on this third level are a special class of the acts belonging to the primary level. Although it is admittedly problematic, the metaphor of levels makes visible the place of the various acts in relation to egoic regard. Explicit acts occupy the center of active conscious life. The predicative acts are added to them; the ego operates from a "higher level." On the other hand, the inexplicit acts may be said to lie below the primary level of egoic regard, so to speak, in the depths of the unconscious. Because Husserl is still concerned solely with the pre-"logical" and thus prerational, which is to say: with the foundation thereof, the predicative acts are excluded from the present analysis. The focal point here is accordingly the scission between the remaining two kinds of acts: between the explicit and inexplicit cogito, or between effected and uneffected acts, as they are also termed.

As usual, Husserl's analysis of such acts begins with the "positive" term: "The explicit intentional lived experience is an 'effected' 'I think'" (236), a cogito. It is *actional*. But it is always surrounded by a halo of potentiality, that is, of inexplicit or uneffected acts, which can in turn be made explicit or be effected through a redirection of regard. Potentiality goes in two directions: passing out of actionality into potentiality or entering into actionality from potentiality. Although the ego lives in only one cogito at a time, it has access to all those acts making up the halo. When it adverts its regard to another lived experience, the former "sinks" into the background, but does not thereby cease to exist. All that has changed here is that it is no longer lived in, no longer actional, but rather potential—ready to be lived in. As such it can be "reactivated" at any time.

4.7.1 *Passivity and Activity*. Whereas egoic activity has pride of place in the analysis of the relationship between the actionality and potentiality of acts, a peculiar form of passivity also plays a significant role in conscious life. Lived experiences that have not yet been attended to are also potential targets of regard. They are simply *aroused*: they come into Being for an ego prior to any engagement of the will. While this is correct in a certain sense, in another it is not. Namely, insofar as the aroused acts were already part of the background, they were, so to speak, "lying in wait." They exist beforehand, just as acts no longer effected continue to exist "after the fact." As Husserl says, "cogitationes break forth in the background of the lived experience, sometimes modified memorially or neutrally, sometimes even unmodified." Lived experiences or acts are alive "before we know it," and others are alive after we have known them. In both cases, *knowing* the act or its correlate means *living in* that act, and so must be distinguished from the knowing resultant upon predicative acts.[116] Because the uneffected acts exist always already beyond a particular effected act, and because they must "break forth" into consciousness before they can be effected, Husserl terms all such acts 'act-arousals'. They precede and follow every act-effectuation.

Because the "cogitationes force their way up in the background of lived experience, sometimes modified memorially or neutrally, sometimes even unmodified," it follows that they are constituted already before the ego's ray of regard has reached them. And it is on account of this that Husserl can remark that actionality has no affect on the "structure of the lived experience"—the move into or out of actionality from or into potentiality, respectively, does not add anything to or take anything away from that structure. Those structures are present at the most basic level of consciousness—before any awareness and especially before the will enters into the picture—as they will be once they have been effected. Furthermore, it is clear that the will has nothing to do with their constitution: it is nothing active or willed, but purely passive. And just as the presence of the will is not essential to the arousal of acts, likewise it plays no necessary role in the generation of positionality and neutrality. Even at the most basic level, the relationship between them holds—once again, before we know it: "It is now clear that acts in the broadest sense, just as in the case of specific cogitationes, bear within themselves the distinction between neutrality and positionality, that they are already productive noematically and thetically *prior* to their transformation into cogitationes; it is just that we see these products only through acts in the narrower sense, through cogitationes. The positings, or the positings in the mode of 'quasi,' are already actually present in them with all the noeses to which these positings belong: the ideal case being presupposed that at the time of the transformation they are not also intentionally enriched or otherwise altered" (237). The radical scission of consciousness into *either* positional *or* neutral consciousness is therefore literally radical: it reaches down to the very roots of every consciousness. Neither kind of consciousness need be the result of the will, for it presents itself (through arousal) already as it is. What is more, the fact that both precede every actionality not only underscores the fundamental role of belief in conscious life, but also the universal scope of the neutrality modification.

None of this is called into question, incidentally, by Husserl's restriction of his preference to doxic positionality, which was the "index" of every neutrality. He notes that such preference "rested on the fact that in its essence every thetic act-characteristic of whatever kind . . . harbors within itself a characteristic that 'coincides' with it in certain ways, [a characteristic] of the genus 'doxic thesis'. According as the act-intention in question is unneutralized or neutralized, so is the doxic thesis inherent in it—which was thought here as primal thesis." Preference will instead be given to doxic modalities in general and, furthermore, extended to all theses, whether doxic or not. Husserl's aim here is to broaden the scope of his analyses from the sphere of belief to all of consciousness. And yet such broadening changes nothing in the fundamental eidetic relationships discerned in the foregoing: "But within the general pride of place granted to doxic modalities, the doxic primal thesis, belief-certainty, is then singled out by the fact that the modalities are themselves to be transformed into doxic theses, so that once again all neutrality has its index in doxic potentiality in the distinctive sense that it refers back to the primal thesis. In this respect, the kind of 'coincidence' of the doxic factors with the thetic ones of every kind undergoes more precise determination" (237–38). The doxic is and remains the ground of conscious life, whether it be positional or neutral, whether generally thetic or specifically doxic.

4.7.2 Higher Level Features of Consciousness: Founded Positings. In his effort to articulate the universal structural features of the noesis and the noema, Husserl has thus far confined his analyses to "a mere substratum of the stream of lived experiences to which relatively simply structured intentionalities still belonged" (238). On this level preference was given to sensuous objectivations and their accordant phenomena. However, as he points out, since the validity of his findings there is universal; they are not restricted to that stratum, but hold for every higher, more complex level as well. On them "all the distinctions between the central core of sense . . . and the thetic characteristics grouped around it return and likewise all the modifications—such as those of representiation, attention, neutralization—that affect the core of sense in their own ways, while nevertheless leaving it its 'something identical'" (239). Husserl discerns two paths of inquiry, "both of which lead to intentionalities that are founded on objectivations: either in the direction of noetic syntheses or in the one that leads us up to novel but founded kinds of 'positing.'" He takes the second path first; the first path will not be entered onto until speech or Logos becomes thematic, thus not until after he has concluded his exposition of the doctrine of the neutrality modification. The second path is still free of all synthesis. It includes "feeling, desiring, volitional noeses that are founded on 'objectivations,' on perceptions, memories, sign-objectivations, etc., and that show in their structure obvious differences of stratified founding."

Before proceeding, however, Husserl first adds an important qualification to his present investigation. Just as all his findings on the lower levels also obtain on the higher levels, it likewise holds that what he says of positional consciousness will hold of neutral consciousness: "Regarding the total acts, we now give preference everywhere to the positional forms (thought they should not exclude neutral substrata) since what is to be said of them holds, when appropriately modified, of the corresponding neutralizations." In other words, since neutral consciousness is the shadow of positional consciousness, what is said of the latter will hold of both sides; to apply the findings in the investigation of positional consciousness to neutral consciousness, one need only bear in mind that whereas the latter mirrors the former in all respects, the two kinds of consciousness are by no means identical, for neutral consciousness lacks the actuality of position—that is the decisive difference. Thus, the modification that the application of those findings requires is that they be taken not as "actual" but rather as "quasi"-findings. The parallels between the modes of consciousness extend therefore from the roots into the heights of conscious. However, there need not be a straight line of positionality or of neutrality extending from bottom to top. On the contrary, the parallels indicate that neutral levels can found positional ones (Husserl's example is "an aesthetic liking founded on a neutral consciousness with a perceptual or reproductive content") and thus that neutrality need not mark a dead end for consciousness: it can be overcome by means of a new positionality.

The prerequisite for moving to a higher level is positionality. This becomes manifest in view of the productivity of such a move, on both the noetic and the noematic sides: "along with the new noetic moments, new noematic moments also appear in the correlates. On the one hand, there are new characteristics that are analogous to the modes of belief, but that at the same time themselves possess doxological positability in their new content; on the other hand, novel 'interpretations' are connected with the novel moments, a new sense is constituted that is founded on, while at the same time encompassing, that of the underlying noesis. The new sense brings in a totally new dimension of sense; with it no new determining parts of mere 'things' are constituted, but rather values of things, value-qualities, or concrete value-objects: beauty and ugliness, goodness and badness; the utensil, the artwork, the machine, the book, the action, the deed, etc." (239–40). On the higher level, "every full lived experience" has structural parallels in its "full correlate" much as in the case of noeses and noemata on lower levels. In this case, the noematic "core of sense is, for example, the valued as such, which is surrounded by new thetic characteristics" (240). Analogies therefore obtain between the new characteristics (valuable, pleasing, gratifying) and those seen previously on lower levels (possible, presumable, or null, yes indeed).

Like the latter characteristics, the new ones also can be modified. On the one hand, they can be modalized insofar as the consciousness of them is positional: "the 'valuable [*wert*]' is doxically positable as being valuable. Furthermore, the 'existing [*seiend*]' that belongs to the 'valuable' as its characterization can be thought as modalized like every 'existing' or 'certain': the consciousness is then consciousness of possible value; the 'thing' only suggests itself as valuable; or else there is consciousness of it as presumably valuable, as not valuable," etc. On the other hand, these new constellations are also open to attentional modifications, which, again, arise through the shift of regard. The movement of the ray of regard through manifold intentional levels is always bound by essential determinations. Thus the ray can be directed to the thing and its moments on a lower level, but then to the value, its constituting interpretations, to the noemata, their characteristics, or to the noeses, etc. Different modes of attention are possible in each case.

4.8 Detours and Direct Routes: The Universality of the Neutrality Modification

To conclude his exposition of the "doctrine of the neutralization modification," Husserl considers how this modification is effected at the higher levels of consciousness just touched upon. Thus far it has targeted explicitly doxic positionalities. But while they also play a role here, as at every level, they are not the only possible targets of neutralization, a fact that recalls Husserl's earlier remark that this modification does not belong specifically to the sphere of belief. Rather, another target may often be reached more directly on levels higher than those of doxic positionalities. On account of this Husserl says that "the relating of the neutrality modification to doxic positionality is . . . in a certain way a detour" (241). To be sure: in a certain way, not absolutely. The intention behind this observation is not to call the course of the foregoing analyses or their findings into question, but rather to indicate the need to extend them in two respects: on the one hand, the neutrality modification's scope of application; on the other, the sense of belief.

Insofar as the neutrality modification is a modification of belief, it is necessary to begin with the latter. But again, not merely as doxic positionality. The talk of the detour has already ruled this out. Nevertheless, that talk also points the direction in which the extension of the sense of belief must proceed, namely in that of positionality. This calls, therefore, for a distinction of the latter, one to which Husserl alludes in his description of the role doxic positionality plays in the higher levels of consciousness: "In the consciousness that presumes, the 'presumable,' the 'probable,' are positionally 'inherent'; likewise, however, in the consciousness that likes, the 'pleasing' is also 'inherent'; in the consciousness that is glad, the 'gladsome' is inherent; etc. It is inherent in it—that means it is accessible to doxic positing, *therefore* it is predicable. Accordingly, every emotional consciousness, along with its novel founded emotional noeses, falls under the concept of positional consciousness," though this holds, of course, not only for emotional consciousness, but mutatis mutandis for every higher-level, nonneutral consciousness. The characteristics of any such positional consciousness are *positionally inherent*, which means that while they are indeed positional, they are not doxic—not yet. They can become so only by being accessed by doxic positing. Only in this way does a doxic positing become actional, which is to say, explicit, and not merely inherent, or implicit, at higher levels. It is not actional from the start, but must be activated. Thus, although doxic positionality is determinative of the Being of consciousness, of its "quality" (a form of consciousness is positional only insofar as it is accessible to doxic positing, otherwise it is neutral), and although it alone makes predication possible (the characteristics of positional consciousness are predicable only insofar as this consciousness is accessible in that way), the key insight here is that positionality is not only doxic. It is in fact either doxic or nondoxic. Husserl noted as much above, of course, but without following up the implications of this insight.[117] In the present context, however, it is clear that if the application of the neutrality modification to doxic positionality is a "detour," then the more direct route will have to pass through nondoxic positionality.

Husserl points out that, "whether effected or not," all higher level acts—such as liking, emotional, and volitional acts—are "precisely 'acts,' 'intentional lived experiences,' and that to each belongs an *intentio*, a 'position-taking.'" Consequently, "they are 'positings' in a broadest, though essentially unitary sense, but just not doxic positings." This should be obvious already from the fact that not all acts are acts of belief. By the same token, act- or positing-characteristics, which Husserl also terms 'theses', are not exclusively of one kind: they are "theses in the extended sense, and only in particular, doxic theses or their modalities." This, then, provides the justification for referring to nonneutral consciousness most generally as either positional or thetic, and only more specifically as doxic consciousness, as well as for distinguishing between thetic and doxic positings. The descriptor 'thetic' is synonymous with 'nondoxic', though neither in the sense of a negative mode of belief nor in that of neutrality. After all, thetic consciousness is still believing consciousness, even if it is not explicitly doxic. Despite the division of positional consciousness into doxic and thetic positings, it is still a unity, and precisely because they are all just that: positings—no matter how different from one another they might otherwise be. It is for this reason that the investigation of the universal structures of consciousness is at all possible: "That is, after all, also the source of parallelizations between the various species of consciousness and all the classifications thereof: one actually classifies species of positing." Such classification is possible precisely because the "community of essence" of positing characteristics does not eliminate essential differences, but rather provides the basis for distinguishing between their kinds.

Among the various theses making up an intentional lived experience, a special thesis is always to be found that determines what might be called the "total thesis" and so enables its classification. As Husserl puts it: "in this plurality one is then necessarily the *archontic* thesis, so to speak, which unifies and governs all the others" (242). The archontic is the uppermost thesis; it is founded upon and so encompasses all of its lower level theses. It gives a thetic constellation its signature, as it were; it is what makes a given thesis what it is. Precisely because of its governing and unifying role, it can be classified and compared with other "archontic" or "total theses." In contrast to the uppermost thetic limit, the doxic positing may be said to form the lowermost thetic limit, and as such it provides the ground of the archontic thesis.[118] Again, a ground that is merely "inherent" so long as the archontic thesis is in power.

As everywhere in Husserl, where the talk is of the noesis, in this case of positings and their characteristics, the other side, that of the noema, must also play a role. Thus, correlatively speaking: "With the generic community of essence of all positing characteristics, that of their noematic positing correlates (of the 'thetic characteristics in the noematic sense') is *eo ipso* given, and if we take the latter [correlates] with their further noematic substrata, the community of essence of all 'posita' [*Sätze*] is *eo ipso* given" (242). As in the case of the positing characteristics, likewise in the case of the posita, essential distinctions are maintained that allow of classification: "Ultimately grounded in this, however, are the analogies that have always been felt to hold between universal logic, the universal doctrine of values and ethics, which, when pursued into their nether reaches, lead to the constitution of universal formal parallel disciplines, those of formal logic, formal axiology, and the theory of praxis." Whereas these three disciplines are of importance to him, Husserl's contention—and this guides his endeavor not only in *Ideas I*, but in every work of phenomenology from start to finish—is that the logical founds the axiological and the practical, or in other words, theory grounds praxis.[119] The sense of such grounding and thus the source of his contention will become evident once the "realm of Logos" has been reached.

After having extended the sense of belief, it is now possible to understand the "certain way" in which the focus on doxic positionality represents a "detour." Since "[e]very consciousness is either actionally or potentially 'thetic,'" every consciousness has its archontic thesis either actionally or potentially as well. It is just this thesis that is neutralized, regardless of whether it is doxic or not, regardless of whether it is actional or potential. Any thetic consciousness whatsoever can be subjected to the neutrality modification; it is therefore truly universal. As a consequence, the aforementioned scission permeates every kind of consciousness, whether explicitly doxic or not: "On the one hand, we have characterized the positional"—that is, authentic—"theses by [saying] that they are either actional theses or can be converted into actional ones; that they accordingly have 'actually' positable noemata—actionally positable in the extended sense. In contrast to these, there are the *inauthentic*, the 'quasi'-theses, the powerless mirrorings, incapable of taking up into themselves any actional-thetic effectuations with respect to their noemata, which are precisely neutralized noemata" (242–43).[120] The scission can set in on any level, no matter how far removed from the doxic primal positings, and precisely because each thesis is also belief, even if not in its originary form: "The distinction between neutrality and positionality has its noetic and noematic parallel; it concerns . . . all sorts of thetic characteristics *directly, without taking the detour* through the 'positions' in the narrow and solely common sense of the phrase 'doxic primal positings'—with respect to which *alone* [that distinction] can be demonstrated" (243). None of this contradicts the foregoing claim, however, that the doxic is the basis of conscious life. Nor does it place in question the significance of the doxic for the distinction of consciousness, since, as Husserl noted in the passage just cited, it is the doxic primal positings that enable the distinction of consciousness in the first place; without the doxic, there could be no neutral consciousness. The talk of the "detour" above concerned only the neutrality modification, in particular the extension of its scope—or rather the demonstration of its true scope. The doxic retains the status Husserl accorded it in his earlier analyses.

Thus the fact that the neutrality modification may be effected without taking a detour through doxic primal positings, or more generally the doxic modalities, does not at all mean that the latter are dispensable. On the contrary, "precisely the doxic modalities, and among them in a particular way the doxic primal thesis, that of belief-certainty, have the unique advantage that their positional potentiality encompasses the entire sphere of consciousness. By eidetic law, every thesis of whatever genus can be transformed into an actional doxic positing by virtue of the characterizations belonging inseparably to its essence." This is due to the aforementioned inherence of the doxic positing in every nondoxic positing. It is inherent in it, that is, the doxic modality is implicit, potential, inactional in the nondoxic or thetic positing: "A positional act posits, but in whatever 'quality' it posits, it also posits doxically; whatever is posited by it in other modes is also posited as existing: just not actionally." Precisely because the doxic positing is potential, it can be actionalized: "But, according to its essence, actionality can be generated in the manner of a principially possible 'operation.' Every 'positum'—for example, a wish-positum—can thus be transformed into a doxic positum, and it is then in a certain way both in one: simultaneously doxic positum and wish-positum." The relationship between the potential and the actional here echoes the one just touched upon between the doxic and the archontic, the lower and the upper limits of any thesis and its correlate. Transforming the potential or implicit into the actional or explicit doxic thesis is precisely explication, and in fact logical explication. By means of the transformation, the former affair-complex, the archontic thesis or its correlate, is grasped predicatively.

4.9 The Transition to the Logical and its Obstruction

Transformation, explication, predication. The actionalization of the doxic carries one across the threshold of and into the realm of Logos.[121] Here again the "inherent" is brought to light, the concealed is unconcealed: "Every act or every act-correlate harbors within itself something 'logical,' explicitly or implicitly. It is to be explicated always logically, namely by virtue of the essential universality with which the noetic stratum of 'expressing' can be conformed to all that is noetic (or the stratum of the expression can be conformed to all that is noematic). In this connection it is evident that with the transition to the neutrality modification, the expressing itself and what is expressed as such are also neutralized" (244). The explication involved here is fixed in expression. It literally expresses an affair-complex, and in fact just as that affair-complex gives itself. If it is positional, then this is reflected in expression, just as is neutrality, should the affair-complex have been neutralized. They differ, however, in that the neutral cannot be subjected to rational scrutiny, or at least not without first being attached to a position (such as occurs in supposing). This points to the distinguishing feature of the logical: it is authentic and as such can be scrutinized. By rendering an authentic expression inauthentic, neutralization detaches the expression from the realm of actual, logical, scrutinizable speech. Such expression remains logical, of course, though only as a shadow or ghost. It is now quasi-logical: one speaks "as if," with no commitment. The doxic and the genuinely logical are thus intertwined, but they are not of equal rank. Rather, the logical depends on the doxic. Its dependence will be seen to inhere in the fact that the logical or the expressive stratum itself is *not* productive, though unproductive in a manner radically different from the neutrality modification.

The doxic, however, is the basis of all production, which is nothing but objectivation: "all acts of whatever kind—the emotional and volitional acts as well—are 'objectivating' acts, which 'constitute' objects originally, [and] are necessary sources of diverse regions of Being and thereby also their appurtenant ontologies." Higher level acts thus produce new objectualities above and beyond those on which the acts are founded. Valuing, to use Husserl's example, constitutes an axiological objectuality in addition to the thing valued. But it is only the actional doxic thesis that brings this objectuality to the fore.

Expression is given to nondoxically posited objectualities by means of doxic theses: "In the emotional act they are meant as emotional; through the actionalization of the doxic content of these acts, they achieve doxic and, furthermore, logical-expressive meantness." Here it is clear that the logical is subsequent to and thus founded on the doxic.

This has important implications not only with regard to neutral consciousness, but also with regard to positional consciousness, specifically in view of the nature of conscious life. The prerequisite of production is belief, or a doxic thesis: "Every non-doxically effected act-consciousness is in this way potentially objectivating; the doxic cogito alone effects actional objectivation." A neutral cogito can never do so.[122] And it is just this distinction that once again underscores the basis of conscious life: belief. Only where it is alive, whether actionally or not, and so only where it has not been neutralized, is consciousness productive. Husserl testifies to just how significant the doxic is in a concluding remark in his "doctrine of neutralization." He says: "Here lies the deepest of the sources out of which the universality of the logical, ultimately that of the predicative judgment, is to be elucidated . . . and from there the ultimate ground of the universality of the reign of logic itself is also understood" (244–45). Thus, as was noted above, logic is the supreme discipline in Husserl's system. But this discipline is itself grounded in belief—"the deepest of the sources."[123] In neutral consciousness, belief has been eradicated. This not only makes logic impossible here, but every science, and precisely because it renders reason impossible. The neutrality modification obstructs the rise of consciousness to reason precisely by expunging belief and the interest it entails. For wherever interest is lacking, there can be no scrutiny and thus no reason.

5. The Realm of Logos

The analyses making up the "doctrine of the neutralization modification" did not lead to a dead end, but rather to the ground from which all else springs, namely belief. Husserl began with the most basic acts and their correlates. From there he then took up higher level and thus founded acts and their correlates. He did so along the first of two possible paths of inquiry. All of this was addressed, however, with next to no consideration of the logical. Yet there are systematic grounds for its having been neglected thus far. While the logical is universal, it is also situated in a higher stratum than anything treated in the foregoing. Only after climbing up the ladder of Husserl's analyses, that is, by penetrating to the ground of consciousness and then ascending into its heights, can the logical be thematized. In fact it is by pursuing the second of the aforementioned directions of inquiry, thus not into founded, thetic consciousness, but rather into "the forms of synthetic consciousness" (245), that Husserl is able to enter into the "realm of Logos."

5.1 Higher Level Features of Consciousness: Synthetic Consciousness

The focus here is on "the manifold modes of the formation of lived experiences through intentional connection," whereby one consciousness is combined with another, etc. into *one* consciousness—which means that one noesis is combined with another, etc. into *one* noesis and, correlatively, one noema with another, etc. into *one* noema. Each new consciousness, noesis, and noema is founded on the preceding consciousnesses, noeses, and noemata, respectively. Through such combinations, consciousness remains in itself singular, while embracing a plurality. Once again we have another instance in which the relation between unity and multiplicity proves fundamental.[124] Of course, at this point it is not the noetic multiplicity bearing on one noema, but rather one consciousness bearing on multiple instances of consciousness. The modes in question "pertain, as essential possibilities, partly to every intentional lived experience of whatever kind, partly to the peculiarities of their particular genera." In keeping with his aim to trace the universal features of consciousness, Husserl attends to the former modes.

He identifies two main kinds of synthesis: continuous and many-membered (*gegliedert*). The former comprises in turn two subdivisions. The first of these is the synthesis proper to internal time consciousness, whereby a lived experience is formed out of a continuous flow of constitutive segments "as a unity extended in phenomenological time." This holds of the stream of lived experiences as well: "No matter how alien in essence lived experiences can be with respect to one another, they are constituted altogether as one temporal stream, as members in the one phenomenological time." An example of the other, related form of continuous synthesis is the constitution of a spatial thing. While both of these kinds of continuous synthesis are significant to phenomenology, Husserl does not address them in this context. As for why not, he gives a clue when he says of the "primal synthesis of original time consciousness" that it "is not to be thought of as an active and discrete synthesis" (246): on the one hand, the lack of discreteness entails greater complexity; on the other, the lack of activity implies that such synthesis is passive, and as such is *prevolitional*. Consequently, Husserl engages in static rather than genetic analysis and so attends to "syntheses not within the parameters of time consciousness but instead within the parameters of time itself, of concretely fulfilled phenomenological time or, what is the same, of syntheses of unqualified lived experiences, taken . . . as enduring unities, as passing events in the stream of lived experiences, which is itself nothing but fulfilled phenomenological time." This means that he directs his attention to the second main division of syntheses mentioned above, namely to many-membered syntheses. His interest thereby is in "the peculiar ways in which *discrete* acts are combined into a many-membered unity, into that of a synthetic act of a higher hierarchical order." Continuous syntheses do not result in unities or acts of a higher order, he notes, but always belong to the same order or level as their constituent moments. The concern here lies with the synthesis of multiple intentionalities into one intentionality.

The topic is still constitution, of course, but now synthetic constitution. In the foregoing the talk was of the productivity of consciousness, which was considered on one level, specifically on that of thetic—or mono-thetic—productions. Now Husserl turns to syn-thetic productions. Such syntheses are polythetic. Thus "monothetic" acts, which have been of concern up to now, are combined into polythetic acts. Of the possible kinds of the latter, Husserl focuses on a group that "encompasses collecting (taking together), disjunctive (concerning the 'this or that'), explicating, relating syntheses, generally the whole series of syntheses that, according to the pure forms of synthetic objectualities being constituted in them, determine the formal-ontological forms and that, on the other hand, regarding the structure of the noematic constructs, are reflected in the apophantic significational forms proper to formal logic (to the logic of propositions [*Sätze*], which is completely noematic in orientation)" (246–47). This group, he notes, is closed on the one hand and has universal application on the other, so that it is not restricted to particular genera but concerns every kind of lived experience. This group is of syntactic forms. It is "in a certain way a universal group of syntheses" (246).

Every synthetic consciousness, insofar as it is a unity, has one object, a "total object," as Husserl terms it (247). It is singular, although it may be founded on or made up of the objects of the theses and syntheses underlying the synthetic consciousness in question. And yet due to the difference of the oneness or unity of its object, synthetic consciousness has its object "in view" differently than does monothetic consciousness: "Synthetic consciousness, or the pure ego 'in' it, is directed with many rays to something objectual; unqualified thetic consciousness, with one ray." Whereas monothetic consciousness has simply one ray directed to but one object, the many rays of a synthetic consciousness that are directed to *one* total object are in fact aimed at its constituent parts; the ego is aware of the object of each ray not individually, but together, in their plurality. "Thus synthetic collecting is a 'plural' consciousness; one and one and one are taken together. Likewise in a primitive relating consciousness the relation is constituted in a twofold positing." Each new moment in the synthetic object contributes to the latter's make up; and in doing so, it adds a new stratum to the object. However, the new stratum is nothing actually separate from the object; the ego does not have it as well as the object. On the contrary, the addition of the new stratum generates a new object, which is founded precisely on the former object—Husserl speaks of the act of valuing, which adds the stratum of "objectual value" to that of the consciousness of the object now valued. The same holds for the group of syntactic forms of primary interest to Husserl here.

Exactly because it has a total object, a many-rayed or polythetic consciousness may be converted into a single-rayed or monothetic consciousness. As a result of such a conversion, "the synthetically constituted collection becomes objectual in a distinctive sense; it becomes an object of a simple doxic thesis by referring a simple thesis back to the collection that was just constituted originally" (248). Monothetic consciousness is explicitly of *one* simple object (the collection taken as a unity) and no longer of the plurality of the collection (consisting of many parts). The same essential possibility pertains, of course, to the other members of the group of syntactic forms (disjunction, etc.).

The new unity owes its existence to a simple doxic thesis. Furthermore, it is only as a result of referring the thesis to a plurality that this plurality, for example a collection, "can be compared" with other pluralities. But even more significant here is that only in this way can the plurality be "employed as a subject of predicates." Thus, it is only through the simple doxic thesis that actual predication—or more generally: speech—becomes at all possible. The plurality cannot as such be the subject of predication, but only after it has been converted into a totality or unity. Despite the radicality of this conversion, however, it in fact adds nothing to the previous affair-complex; in other words, no new stratum is added to the object: "But here it must be made completely evident that what is simply objectualized and what is synthetically unitary are actually the same, and that neither the subsequent thesis nor its removal adds anything to the synthetic consciousness, but rather seizes upon *what it gives*. Evident also is clearly the essentially different mode of givenness." Precisely because this thesis and the subsequent predication add nothing,[125] because they leave everything as it was, just as it gives itself, phenomenological description is able to be faithful; otherwise the principle of all principles would make an impossible demand on the phenomenologist. For Husserl the sole respect in which the predicatively given differs from the prepredicatively given is in *how* it is given. And yet this How does not alter anything in the What.

5.2 Positional and Neutral Syntheses

Although Husserl concluded his treatment of neutrality in the foregoing, the topic has not ceased to play a role in his further investigations. This is necessarily the case, as he showed, for wherever the talk is of positional consciousness, neutral consciousness is also present—as its shadow. From his insight into the double nature of consciousness, as well as into the fact that "[a]ll *authentic* syntheses . . . are built on simple theses" and syntheses "themselves are theses, theses of a higher level," it follows that the "findings about actionality and inactionality, about neutrality and positionality" made above hold of syntheses as well (249). This is not to say, however, that "a positional thesis of a higher level presupposes nothing but positional theses on its lower levels." It can do so, but need not. Rather, the lower levels can also contain neutralized theses: "an actional seeing of an essence is, after all, a positional act and not a neutralized act founded on some exemplificative intuiting consciousness or other, which for its part can very well be a neutral, a fantasy consciousness." Matters are different, however, for the syntheses presently of interest (collection, disjunction, explication, and relation). In their case Husserl notes "that, with respect to its positional characteristic, every synthesis in the group is dependent upon the characteristic of the founding noeses; more precisely, that it is positional (and can only be so) when the complete subtheses are positional, and it is neutral when they are not" (249–50). There is no middle ground between positionality and neutrality. And this holds here for the distinction between the corresponding theses: "A collecting, for example, is either actually collecting or collecting in the mode of 'quasi'; it is actually or neutrally thetic" (250). For the synthetic forms, neutrality is, so to speak, infectious and even fatal since the mere presence of one neutral subthesis in a synthesis is enough to render the entire synthesis neutral. "*Pure* neutrality can never work for [*fungieren für*] positional syntheses; it must at least be transformed into 'suppositions,' say, into hypothetical antecedents or consequents, into hypothetically supposed nominatives, such as, for example, 'Pseudo-Dionysius' and the like." Whereas for a synthesis of this kind to be positional it may contain only actual theses, for the synthesis to be neutral it suffices that only one of its subtheses be neutral. For the "class of syntheses that are mirrored in the logical syntaxes," then, the presence of positionality decides everything.

5.3 *The Expression of Syntheses*

Mention was made in the foregoing of the actional doxic thesis as the prerequisite of predication. Husserl asks at this point how it is that the group of syntheses under consideration "come to be expressed in the syntactical forms of statements that the logical doctrine of propositional forms develops systematically." It does not suffice to say that they themselves are "doxic syntheses" or "doxic syntaxes"; even though this holds of them in a certain sense, the syntheses in question cannot be simply reduced to the doxic. Rather, because they play a role in theses that are not specifically doxic,[126] it is evident that: "These syntheses of 'and', of 'or', of 'if' or of 'because' and 'thus', in short: the syntheses that are given first of all as doxic, are by no means merely doxic syntheses." Thus, just as theses are not only doxic, likewise the synthetic forms, and the syntheses to which they give rise, are not only doxic. Although the doxic plays a central role here, it is not the only role. But to be appreciated, its role must be distinguished from those of the nondoxic, which requires that one make and maintain the relevant regional distinctions. Failing to do so—which is precisely what would occur were one to reduce everything to the doxic—would mean not being true to the things themselves and committing a *metabasis*. By contrast, Husserl indicates the heterogeneity of the synthetic forms: "in addition to the doxic (the logical) 'and', there is also an axiological and practical 'and'" (251). And the same holds, of course, of the other forms in the group under consideration as well. The forms of 'and', for example, are not identical, but instead make up a family—they are related, to borrow Wittgenstein's term, by "family resemblance." As will be seen, however, unlike in Wittgenstein, where there can be no "absolute" or a priori hierarchy among the "family members," in Husserl the hierarchy is indeed absolute at least with respect to its starting point, that is, insofar as it is founded always on the doxic.

Husserl illustrates the said heterogeneity with reference to "collective love." A mother "gazes lovingly upon her flock of children": "in one act of love she embraces each child individually and all of them together." She does not effect two separate acts thereby—an objectivating embracing *and* a loving—but only one, the loving embracing. Just as the object of her love is a collective, a "love collective" as Husserl says, the mother's love is likewise collective or plural, and immediately so, without any detour through the doxic sphere. This is possible precisely because the syntactical forms bear on all theses and not just on doxic these (see 251). And that means that these forms play a role in every stratum.

This recalls, of course—and Husserl himself draws attention to it—the earlier findings about the "essential kinship between doxic theses and theses in general." There a distinction was made between kinds of positionality, specifically between kinds of thesis. Again, what distinguishes a positional thesis from its neutral counterpart is its accessibility to a doxic thesis; the prerequisite of such access is precisely the inherence of the doxic in the nondoxic thesis. In the present context Husserl expresses the relationship in slightly different terms: "Hidden in every thesis whatsoever there lies . . . a parallel doxic thesis." This parallelism is operative in the syntactical forms as well, so that one can say that concealed in every syntactical form of whatever kind there lies a parallel doxic form. Furthermore, the parallelism is not one-sided, but holds mutatis mutandis for both the noesis and the noema: "The axiological 'and' harbors essentially within itself a doxic 'and'; every axiological syntactical form of the group considered here, a logical syntactical form: just as every simple noematic correlate includes within itself an 'existing' or another Being-modality and, as its substratum, the form of 'something' and the forms that otherwise belong to it" (252). Each side of the correlation has a substratum: belief underlies every noesis; Being, every noema. These substrata are always present, even where they are not explicit—which, Husserl notes, is usually the case.

It is precisely the doxic basis that provides the answer to the initial question about how the syntheses of the group of syntheses in question come to be expressed. Although one generally lives in emotional acts—like the mother loving her flock of children—without activating the underlying, "inherent" doxic theses, it is nevertheless always possible to do so. As soon as one makes a statement, say, about how well-behaved the flock of children is, one activates a doxic thesis, one turns an object—in this case the love collective—that was only the object of emotional acts into a doxic object or phenomenon. In a sense, then, the initial answer to the question, namely that those syntheses are themselves doxic syntheses or doxic syntaxes, was not entirely off the mark. Its inadequacy lay in its neglect of both the need for activating the doxic thesis, whereby the nondoxic thesis is converted into a doxic thesis (as has been seen, although the doxic thesis is always present, it is not always actional), and the distinction between synthetic forms.

5.4 The Directions of Synthesis

Syntheses, as well as simple theses, may be effected in two contrary directions. Each has its own modes. The *first*, and preferred, *direction* is marked by a clarity peculiar to actionality: "A synthesis can be effected step by step; it comes to be, it arises in original production" (253). The ego exhibits thereby a definiteness, a firmness of will: "The thesis and synthesis come to be insofar as the pure ego takes one step and each new step actionally; it itself lives in the step and 'steps forth' with it. The positing, positing-thereupon, positing antecedently and consequently, etc., is its free spontaneity and activity; it lives in the theses not as passively dwelling in them, but the theses are instead radiations from the pure ego as a primal source of generations." Such activity is marked by total commitment, which is synonymous with belief. When the ego begins, it begins purely and simply. Each beginning marks a cut; it breaks with what preceded it—despite the halo of inactionality surrounding it. Each beginning is absolutely certain: "Every thesis begins with a point of initiation, with a punctual, original positing; so it is with the first thesis, as with every one subsequent to it in the concatenation of the synthesis. This 'initiation' belongs precisely to the thesis as such, as a distinctive mode of original actionality. It is something like the *fiat*, like the point at which willing and acting are initiated"—the Archimedean point, as it were, on which all further synthesis builds in a given instance. In each new act, with each beginning, "the pure ego makes its entrance as the subject"—that is, the agent—"of the spontaneity." This subject is, however, a believing subject. Of course, it lies within its free will to put its belief out of action, to neutralize it. But this freedom, like all freedom in Husserl, is limited. Again, positionality encompasses the whole of consciousness; the universal neutrality modification, like the specific neutrality modifications (such as the epoché and fantasy), never targets the whole of consciousness, but always only particular positionalities, particular theses. The initiating actionality of consciousness is and remains positional.

The "mode of initiation" cannot be maintained with the same clarity, definiteness, or urgency it has at the outset, however, but of necessity is soon transformed into another mode, into a "having-been-initiated." Or: a perceptual seizing upon or taking hold of, to use Husserl's example, changes into "having in one's grip." This mode is transformed yet again when a new object is attended to. Here the former "thematic object" makes way for a new one. Whereas both may be members of the same "total theme," the "thematic grip" can hold only one "primary theme" at a time. The shift from one such theme to another does not result in the former thematic object's extinction; rather, as was seen above, it merely slips out of view and into the background.[127] It remains part of the total theme, even though it is not presently thematized. This becomes particularly clear in Husserl's example of carrying out a proof: one moves step by step through the premises towards the conclusion. Each premise is held in one's thematic grip and then released when the next premise is taken up into that grip. Each link in the chain of thought continues to "exist," although only one step is thematized at a time. This kind of attentional modification is to be distinguished, of course, from that in which the pure ego "lets the thetic correlates slip out of its 'grip,'" namely when "it 'turns to another theme,'" a new total theme. Although the two distinct total themes are bound together within the stream of lived experiences, as far as many-membered synthesis is concerned, they are distinct synthetic unities.

In contrast to the foregoing "modalities of effectuation," Husserl points to other modalities that make up the *second direction* in which syntheses can be effected. Whereas the first direction began with the actional grasping of one theme instead of another, and always with clarity, the present direction begins with confusion and proceeds ideally to clarity. In this case the ego has a thought vaguely; it has a presentiment that has yet to be filled out or realized. Husserl illustrates this by way of the thought that "pops up"[128] as a "'confused' thought" (255). At first the thought is there as "a simple objectivation without any actional-thetic articulation." It pops up in the background, it occurs to one. When the ego directs its ray of regard to this object and wrests it from the background, a new process of clarification and thus of synthesis can begin. This process can go in either of two directions, depending on what kind of thought it is. If the thought is a memory, for example, then the clarification is a reproduction of what has been. On the other hand, Husserl notes, a theoretical notion can occur to us that has never been thought through, has never been experienced in any way before. The insight lacks in total clarity. It is initially more of a presentiment. As such it gives the parameters of clarification; it points the direction in which the notion is to be filled out. The end product of such processes is a "synthetic actionality."

Husserl's intention in the present context is to elaborate the basic features of expression. The preceding distinctions between confusion and clarity are of key importance in this regard. He indicates their relevance to expression by appealing to the process of trying to understand a text: "One need only think of the way in which we are accustomed to seize upon the very complex, synthetic constructs making up the 'intellective content' of our reading at a given time, and consider what, in the understanding of what one has read, comes to actually originary actionalization with respect to the so-called intellective substratum of expressions."[129] The understanding of a complex text develops over time in a zigzag, much like the unfolding and justification of the phenomenological system itself. Implicit in the talk of understanding is the desire and attempt to be faithful to the text. Here, as in phenomenological expression or description, faithfulness is the key issue—as the principle of all principles already makes clear.

5.5 The Logical Strata

It is only at this point in his analyses that Husserl explicitly addresses the "noetic-noematic stratum of 'Logos.'"[130] This is because it is always higher than the strata seen previously. Yet, despite their being on a higher level, its acts have a unique relationship to those of other strata, one that differs from all other higher level acts: "Interwoven with all the acts considered thus far are the expressive act-strata, which are 'logical' in the specific sense" (256). Expressive acts do not modify other acts, say, as negation would; they do not add a new layer to the acts to which they give expression, but are "interwoven" with those acts. In a sense they merge with the latter.

When he turns to the "logical" strata, Husserl's interest is directed "exclusively to 'signifying' [*Bedeuten*] and 'signification' [*Bedeutung*]," that is, to the "mental" side of expression (the noesis) on the one hand and to what is expressed (the noema) on the other. In doing so, he frees the terms 'signifying' and 'signification' from their confinement to the linguistic sphere and extends them by making them applicable to all acts, to all noetic-noematic correlations. As a consequence, they can be used to account for intentionality in general.

To illustrate the effect of expression, Husserl considers an object present in perception. He notes that it is common to effect "an explicating of the given and a relating combining of the parts and moments singled out—say, according to the schema 'This is white'" (257). Here the signifying in question is the explicating and combining, whereas the signification is the resultant schema. Whatever else may occur on this level, Husserl notes, expression plays absolutely no role here; nor is there any need of it. This is the level of un-thinking, naively operative consciousness. Signifying and signification are therefore first and foremost sublinguistic, as their applicability to all acts already implies. That this is so is shown by the effect of thought or speech, which thematizes the signification: "But if we have 'thought' or stated, 'This is white,' then a new stratum is also there, united with what is purely perceptually 'meant as such.'" The thought or statement does not transform the affair-complex given expression, but rather exists alongside it. Although this requires further elucidation, it can be said at this point that thinking occurs wherever a doxic thesis is directed to an affair-complex. On the basis of this thesis, expression becomes possible. By extension, what holds of the perceived also holds of the correlates of other acts: "In this way anything remembered, anything fantasied, is also explicable and expressible as such. Anything 'meant as such,' any meaning [*Meinung*] in the noematic sense (and in fact as a noematic core) proper to an act of whatever kind, is expressible through 'significations.'" Again, the signification is incipiently sublinguistic, or better: prelogical. But, of course, it can be raised to the level of the logical, in which case it becomes an expression: "Logical signification is an expression." Decisive here, then, is not the verbalization of the affair-complex, but rather the signification itself; it is what enables expression: "The verbal sound can be called an expression only because the signification belonging to it expresses; expressing lies in [the signification] originally." For Husserl "'expression' is a distinctive form that can be adapted to every 'sense' (to the noematic 'core') and that raises it up into the realm of 'Logos,' of the conceptual, and therefore of the 'universal.'" The universality of expression will be seen to inhere in that of the doxic.

What distinguishes expressive acts from all those seen thus far is that they adapt themselves to what is to be expressed, rather than adapting their object to themselves, as it were. They do not modify their object in any way. In light of this, Husserl characterizes the realm of Logos as follows: "A peculiar intentional medium is present here that, by its essence, has the distinction of, so to speak, mirroring every other intentionality with respect to form and content, of depicting it in its own colors, and of thereby imprinting on it its own form of 'conceptuality.'" The expressing and what is expressed correspond to one another completely and of essential necessity with regard to their thetic characteristics. The essential correspondence is so complete, Husserl notes, that no distinction is usually made between expressing and expressed. Precisely because it mirrors intentionalities, because it adapts itself to them, nothing new arises in this medium. Expressive acts are held to have no effect on what is expressed through them. They merely relay what was already present in the signification. Hence: "Apart from the fact that it does just that, gives expression to all other intentionalities, the stratum of expression is—and this makes up its peculiarity—*not productive*. Or if one prefers: its productivity, its noematic production [*Leistung*], is exhausted in expressing and the form of the conceptual that is added in the [expressing]" (258). And precisely because of its essential unproductivity—or, as one is tempted say, because expression *is* what it expresses, no more and no less—it follows that "the distinction between positionality and neutrality also passes over into the expressive" (258–59), albeit in a qualified sense. In expressing, the expression mirrors what is expressed: "The expressive stratum cannot have a differently qualified positional or neutral thesis than the stratum that is given expression, and in the coincidence we find not two theses that are to be separated but only one thesis" (259). This does not contradict what has been said in the foregoing, however. Even though both positional and neutral expression are equally possible[131]—and necessarily so—it is positional expression that is of interest to Husserl, for it alone enables the scrutiny of statements and thus, ideally at least, the accumulation of knowledge, which in turn enables the unfolding of the desired "system of doctrine."

Despite the talk of mirroring, interweaving, and merging, despite its unproductivity, Husserl points out that "the expression is not something like a coat of varnish, or like a garment pulled over it"; rather, "it is a mental formation that exercises new intentional functions on the intentional substratum and that, correlatively, is subjected to the intentional functions of the substratum." This would seem to contradict Husserl's observation that expression is essentially unproductive. But this semblance dissolves as soon as one sees that he is referring to reflective formations, which are based on belief.[132]

The modalities of act-effectuation discussed above also have a bearing on expressive theses and syntheses. These modalities affect the latter "in a twofold way": "They concern, on the one hand, the signification-stratum, the specifically logical stratum itself; on the other hand, the founding substrata." Regarding the former, the example of reading a text is instructive. In moving through the text, one signification is combined with another and so on. One can thereby achieve the "perfect clarity of 'logical' understanding" (260). But as earlier, here too the clarity of one sentence can fade as soon as it slips from the thematic grip; the ego's regard shifts from one sentence to the next in a continuous chain. The whole remains intact, a synthetic whole emerges, but clarity pertains only to the sentence currently in its grip.

Such logical clarity must be distinguished, however, from that of its founding strata. In view of this distinction, Husserl says that the clarity of signification need not be total: "A clear understanding of word and proposition (or a clear, articulated effectuation of the acts of stating) is compatible with confusion in the substrata." Where the clarity of signification is at issue, it is not necessary to clarify the substrata; for it is not the substrata that express, but the signification: "The substratum can be something confusedly unitary (and it usually is) that does not bear its articulation actionally within itself, but that rather owes [its articulation] to [its] mere conformity to the stratum of the logical expression actually articulated and effected in original actionality." Of course, clarity may be sought in both directions, in that of either signification or its substrata. And such is ultimately required of phenomenology and science in general. But again, total clarity is not necessary in every case. Rather, as Husserl points out, the amount of clarity required is dictated by the kind of evidence sought. And when the concern lies with the purely logical, as is the case in phenomenology, the clarity of its substrata will not have any importance—which explains why Husserl is justified in sketching the contours of the phenomenological system, and thus of inquiry, without seeking to fill in those contours along the way. It is Husserl's task to point the way for future inquiries, not to carry them all out himself.

A further distinction, which has obvious parallels with that between clarity and confusion, is the distinction between the complete and incomplete expression. On the one hand, at issue are kinds of expression: "The expression is complete when it molds all of the substratum's synthetic forms and materials in a conceptual-significational way; it is incomplete when it does so only partially" (261), such as, for example, in an elliptical sentence. On the other hand, at issue is a kind of incompleteness that pertains to the universality of expression. It is impossible for an expression to exhaust the substratum it expresses: "It is inherent in the sense of the universality proper to the essence of expressing that all the particulars of the expressed can never be reflected in the expression. The stratum of signifying is not, and principially not, a kind of reduplication of the substratum" (261–62). The expression is necessarily selective. It cannot exhaust all of the founding substrata; it cannot capture all its qualities, its diverse dimensions; just as no one lived experience can exhaust the entire stream of lived experiences. It is essentially necessary that the basis of a given expressing always exceed the expression, that there always be a remainder.

5.6 Expression, Judgment, Belief

Clarification of the foregoing features of expression are required, Husserl notes, before "one of the oldest and most difficult problems in the sphere of signification" can be addressed, that is, "the problem of how stating as the expression of judging is related to the expressions of other kinds of acts" (262). This problem is, of course, bound up with the feeling that belief and judgment are one and the same, and so it proves to be a problem of the relationship between expression and belief. Hence Husserl's radicalization of the problem in the following questions: "Is the medium of expressive signifying, this peculiar medium of Logos, a specifically doxic one? In the conforming of the signifying to the signified, does [this medium] not coincide with the doxic itself inherent in all positionality?" (263). The conformity of the signifying to the signified must be faithful and complete if there is to be a contribution to knowledge, that is, if an expression is to be meaningful.[133] It is on account of this that Husserl sought to elucidate the noetic-noematic structures in the foregoing—again, to show what conforms to what, as well as what counts as complete. The "radical problem" to which his analyses ultimately lead, however, centers on the noetic side, specifically on the role of the doxic.

That the questions in which this problem was captured are to be answered affirmatively becomes evident in light of Husserl's distinction between direct and indirect modes of expression. In the former mode, the expression is adapted to the lived experience expressed. The prerequisite of such adaptation is the correspondence of their respective doxic strata. Husserl illustrates this by way of an emotional lived experience: "The doxic form inherent in all the components of the emotional lived experience would thus be what enables the conformability of the expression, as an exclusively doxothetic lived experience, to the emotional lived experience that, as such and with respect to all its members, is multi-thetic, but therein also necessarily doxo-thetic." Expression is "an exclusively doxic lived experience" that gives voice to the underlying doxic moment inherent in the lived experience expressed. But the character of the doxic is decisive here for expression: faithful and complete expression is possible only for "doxically unmodalized lived experiences." Expression requires definiteness, or certainty: "in the sense of the interpretation just advanced, all expressing is a doxic act in the pregnant sense, that is, a belief-certainty" (263–64). That means that a doxic primal thesis is pointed directly at what is to be expressed. It hits upon the doxic thesis concealed within the lived experience to be expressed, and without further ado where at issue is a doxically unmodalized lived experience. By contrast, whenever a doxically modalized lived experience is of concern, it must first be converted into belief-certainty in order to be expressed: "As soon as modalities appear, it is necessary to recur to the doxic theses with changed thetic material that lie, so to speak, hidden within them in order to gain the best conformed expression possible" (264). Such conversions result in indirect expressions. Whether an expression is direct or indirect depends, then, on the immediacy of the unmodalized doxic thesis. But whatever the distinctions involved in expression, the doxic plays a fundamental role in all expression and ultimately in all knowledge.

Yet in view of its role, a threefold distinction is called for: "Here one must always bear in mind that explicative or analytic synthesis (judgment prior to the conceptual-significational expression), then statement or judgment in the usual sense, and, finally, *doxa* (belief), are things that are to be kept well apart. . . . The eidetic clarification of the *idea* of *doxa* is something other than that of the statement or of explications" (264). *Doxa* is not to be equated, then, with judgment; it is something more fundamental than judgment. Furthermore, it is more fundamental than statement or explication. It is not to be equated with any of these, even though it plays a decisive role in each. In fact the doxic is, as has been seen, that which enables judgment, statement, and explication.

Chapter IV

Towards the System's Uppermost Limit: Reason

In the foregoing Husserl showed the scission between noesis and noema to be "a fundamental structure pervading all intentional structures, which consequently must form a dominant leitmotif of phenomenological methodology and determine the course of all inquiries into problems of intentionality" (265). His analyses of this structure culminated in a consideration of the role it plays in expression, especially in view of the latter's part in knowledge. There the expression of interest to him was not just any expression, but assertoric and thus positional expression. It is precisely the scrutiny of this kind of expression—never neutral expression—that can yield the verdict of reason. However, before such scrutiny can be carried out, it is necessary to establish the criteria by which each expression is to be weighed. To do so, the noetic-noematic structure must be reconsidered briefly; in particular, the findings concerning the noema must be deepened.

1. The Referentiality of the Noema

Again, the noesis and the noema mark two individual but inseparable regions of Being. The former is the region of consciousness; the latter, the region of its objectualities. The ground of every noesis was seen to be *doxa*, belief. This accorded with the fundamental determination of belief-characteristics made above. And yet there they were seen to be correlated with Being-characteristics. The question arises: if "every *infima species* on the noematic side points back to *infima species* on the noetic side," and conversely, and if the noesis is grounded in belief, in what then is the noema grounded? In light of Husserl's discovery that all belief corresponds to Being, it follows that the noema must for its part be grounded in Being. But in which? The noema is, after all, a reduced objectuality. It has been seemingly cut off from any relation to anything lying beyond the transcendental sphere; there would seem to be no outside and especially no world to which it might itself refer.

Husserl answers as follows: "The phenomenological problem of the reference of consciousness to an objectuality has especially its noematic side. The noema has an objectual reference within itself, and in fact through the 'sense' proper to it. If we then ask how the consciousness-'sense' gets hold of the 'object' that is its own and how that can be 'the same' in multiple acts with quite different noematic content, [if we ask] how we discern this in the sense, then new structures emerge the extraordinary significance of which is clear" (266). Each noesis is related to a noema; the noema contains a sense; and this sense is in turn related to an object. It is this object that will prove to ground the noema. Furthermore, it will be seen to provide the aforementioned criteria for the scrutiny of reason: "For, continuing on in this direction and, on the other hand, reflecting on the parallel noeses, we finally hit upon the question of what the 'pretension' of consciousness to 'refer' actually to something objectual, to be 'well-founded,' really means, how 'valid' and 'invalid' objectual references are phenomenologically elucidated in terms of noesis and noema—and with that we stand before the great problems of reason"; in fact, by following this route, not only will the question be hit upon, but, more important, the answer will be gained as well, namely that which has guided Husserl's inquiry from the start: the object.[1] In the noema it plays the role that belief plays in the noesis.

The noema has been shown to consist of a stable core and its changing characteristics. Given that the latter have not shed light on the noematic referentiality here in question, the key to it must lie in the core. Since he has largely neglected it in the foregoing, Husserl's present task is to characterize it. This requires him to get clear on what is involved in the talk of the content of consciousness. He begins not by speaking of the core, but of sense: "As content we grasp the 'sense,' of which we say that in or through it consciousness refers to something objectual as 'its own'" (267). However, the sense looks to be distinct in some way from the noema. And this would seem to complicate the mediation: "Each noema has a 'content,' namely its 'sense,' and refers through it to 'its' object." The noema harbors sense; sense is a moment within it. Through sense alone the noema gets hold of its object. The mediation would thus seem to have the following structure: noesis–noema–sense–object. The noesis is directed to the noema; the noema contains its sense; and it is linked to the object. Consciousness would therefore seem to be two steps away from its object.[2]

Despite appearances, however, there is not a twofold mediation here. Rather, the noema contains its sense as its core, so to speak, as its heart;[3] the sense is not separate from but an integral moment in the noema. Husserl recalls that "consciousness of something" as an intentional object is not identical to the relation of the full noesis to "the full noema as its intentional and full What" (268). The key to this difference lies in the structural parallels between the noetic and the noematic moments. Whereas each corresponds to the other, the latter are distinct from the noematic core: "to every noetic, specifically thetic-noetic, moment there corresponds a moment in the noema, and in the latter there is set apart from the complex of thetic characteristics the noematic core characterized by them." This core, however, is not the terminal point of the ray of regard. Rather it passes through the core to another point: "with the talk of the reference (and specifically of the 'directedness [*Richtung*]') of consciousness to its objectual item, we are pointed to an innermost moment of the noema. It is not the core itself just described but rather something that makes up, so to speak, the necessary central point of the core and functions as the 'bearer' of the noematic peculiarities that belong specifically to the core, namely the noematically modified properties of the 'meant as such'" (268–69). Consequently, as Husserl points out, it is necessary to distinguish between content and object not only in the noesis but also in the noema; both are related to the same object, but differently so, with the result that their content differs.

In order to specify what the "central point" is, Husserl must first delimit the sense of 'noematic sense'. This he does by way of a renewed consideration of what is involved in the "consciousness of something." Essential to each living cogito is its reference to an objectuality. It has a "'directedness' towards an objectuality. In other words, there belongs to its noema an 'objectuality'—in quotation marks—with a certain noematic composition, which is unfolded in a description of determinate delimitation, namely in such a description that, as a description of the 'meant objectual item as it is meant,' avoids all 'subjective' expressions" (269). By contrast, noetic description focuses on the "way in which something is intended" by a consciousness. Hence it is thoroughly "subjective," whereas noematic description is completely "objective." The recollection of this distinction at this point is necessary in order to guarantee the possibility of talking of the noema in its own terms. By cordoning off this talk from that of the noesis, it becomes clear what belongs properly to faithful noematic description: "Each consciousness has its What and each means 'its' objectual item; it is evident that, in the case of each consciousness, we must, speaking principially, be able to carry out such a noematic description of that [something] 'just as it is meant'; through explication and conceptual apprehension, we gain a closed total concept [*Inbegriff*] of formal or material, materially determinate or even 'indeterminate' ('emptily' meant) 'predicates,' and these in their modified significance determine the 'content' of the object-core of the noema under consideration here" (270). By determining the content, the predicates also determine the fullness of the core, a fact that later will be of importance in connection with reason.

Noematic description employs predicates that are always "predicates of 'something,' and this 'something' also belongs, and obviously inseparably, to the core in question: it is the central point of unity" that is contained in the sense. The central point, and not the core, binds all its predicates together within the core, while it itself is neither a predicate nor the sum total of predicates that apply to it: "It is the point of connection or the 'bearer' of the predicates, but by no means the unity of them in the sense in which some complex, some combination of the predicates would be called a unity. It must necessarily be distinguished from them, though not placed alongside them and separated from them; just as, conversely, they themselves are its predicates: unthinkable without it and yet distinguishable from it" (270–71). Thus in the case of an "apple tree," it is intended in continuous or actively synthetic acts perceived, say, from various positions, under various conditions, various aspects of it are focused upon (first the branches, then the trunk, etc.), and so on. Although it is given differently through the series of perceptions, although different predicates pertain to it in each case, although it has different contents, the object remains the same; amidst the variations, it is identical. Through adequate noematic description of the tree, it becomes evident that "the identical intentional 'object' is evidently separated from the changing and alterable 'predicates.' It is singled out as the central noematic moment: the 'object,' the 'Object,' the 'identical,' the 'determinable subject of its possible predicates'—the pure X in abstraction from all predicates—and it is separated off from these predicates or, more precisely, from the predicate-noemata" (271). This X is precisely the point of unity within each core; it is around the inalterable X that the changing predicates are gathered in each case.

Each noema has its X, its "pure object-something" (272). And yet not every X is unique to one noema. On the contrary, it is possible—and essentially so—for several noemata to share the same "something" and thereby form a unity, no matter how different they might otherwise be from one another. The relationship here between multiplicity and unity makes it clear that the talk of the object must be differentiated. To this end Husserl introduces a twofold distinction, namely between "this pure point of unity, this noematic 'object plain and simple,' and the 'object in the How of its determinations,'" as well as—in keeping with Husserl's bipolar architecture—any determinations that have yet to be made in it. The former object is constant, identical throughout the variations in the latter object. These variations, however, do not result in only one "object in the How," but in several such objects, which, again, are unified insofar as they have the object plain and simple in common. In fact the "noematic 'object in the How'" is nothing but the noematic sense. And so the distinction here is between the object as the X and that as the sense.

Husserl is careful to point out, however, that while this sense is not identical with the core, it is nevertheless "a fundamental piece of the noema." It is no less indispensable to a noema than the "determinable X." Just as the core is indispensable. The three moments—X, sense, and core—are essential to each noema: "No 'sense' without the 'something' and, again, without 'determinative content.'" This holds as much of the noemata of higher level acts as it does of the noemata of polythetic acts, albeit in both cases in a more complex manner.

Sense is neither content nor the point of unity.[4] It is "not a concrete essence in the total composition of the noema, but rather a kind of abstract form dwelling within the latter" (273). It is a kind of receptacle for content. As such it allows of degrees of fullness in how an object is given. That is, there can be varying degrees of clarity within a particular sense that range from total obscurity to total clarity, from minimal to maximal fullness. Such variability can, of course, pertain to the consciousness of something: one and the same thing can be intended obscurely in one instance and clearly in another. Husserl notes that it is possible to be conscious of both sides within a unitary consciousness, in which both are taken in one sense as two sides of the same thing. In view of this possibility, he expands the sense of 'sense': "As the full core we shall accordingly count precisely the full concretion of the noematic component in question, thus the sense in the mode of its fullness." The core and sense coincide with regard to fullness; otherwise they are distinct. Together they mediate between the noesis and the object.

The concept of sense is further refined in view of its relation to thetic moments. Unlike in the *Logical Investigations*, as Husserl notes, here he defines sense as 'material' and designates "the unity of sense and thetic characteristic as positum [*Satz*]" (274). Recalling that positings can be mono- or polythetic, it becomes clear that, correlatively, posita can have one or many members: "We then have one-membered posita (such as in the case of perceptions and other thetic intuitions) and many-membered, synthetic posita, such as predicative doxic posita (judgments), presumption-posita with predicatively membered material, etc. One-membered as well as many-membered posita are, moreover, liking-posita, wish-posita, command-posita, etc."

As he himself points out, Husserl has extended the sense of *Satz* here. But just how radical this extension is is not immediately apparent from the English text. For the translation of this term as 'positum' conceals the ambiguity of the German term. Without any qualification, *Satz* is most likely to be understood as 'sentence' or 'proposition'; 'positum' would suggest itself only in connection with positing (*Setzung*). It is with the latter term in mind that 'positum' was chosen. These comments are necessary in order to account for remarks Husserl makes here and elsewhere about *Sätze*, remarks that might otherwise remain unintelligible to the English-speaking reader. A case in point is his explanation of the extension of the sense of *Satz* in the preceding passages: "for us the concepts of sense and positum contain nothing of expression and conceptual signification, while, on the other hand, they encompass all expressive posita, or all positum-significations." Taken on its own, 'positum' need not have anything to do with expression or signification, but 'proposition' or 'sentence' clearly would.

By virtue of their extension, "these concepts [of sense and positum] mark an abstract stratum that belongs to the full web of all noemata" and so "has its place actually in all act-spheres." They belong as much to the sphere of simple intuition as to the realm of Logos. In fact, expression and conceptual signification are only special instances in which sense and positum play a role. But, as was seen above, they can do so only because they are at work on the lower levels to which expression is later given. In other words, for Husserl *Satz* means primarily 'positum' and only secondarily 'proposition'.

Precisely because these terms—but especially 'sense'—apply to every sphere, he regards the systematic classification of the fundamental kinds of sense as another important task for phenomenology. In pursuing this task, "we climb up to the idea of a systematic and universal doctrine of the forms of senses (significations). If in addition we take into consideration the systematic distinction between positing characteristics, then at the same time a systematic typology of posita is produced" (275). However, despite the importance of this task, it remains one to which Husserl can only allude here. For it lies outside of the scope of his present intention, which is to sketch the contours and point the trajectory of phenomenological inquiry.

By the same token, he is unable to undertake another task, one that, although more specific, nevertheless is of universal significance, namely the task of systematically elaborating the "doctrine of apophantic forms." This doctrine now "gains its home within the universal doctrine of the forms of senses in general—a doctrine conceived as an idea—and its ultimate place of origin in noematic phenomenology" (276). But like the more universal doctrine, in the present context the doctrine of apophantic forms (as well as related doctrines of forms) must remain an idea that will guide future inquiry. In fact, the articulation of these doctrines does not fall within the scope of phenomenological inquiry, for they require the deduction of "the systematic possibilities of all further formations from primitive axiomatic formations" (277–78), and phenomenology is not a deductive science. Rather, it is to provide the basis and the norms for all such sciences. Its chief concern must therefore be "the analysis of the Apriori, which is demonstrable in immediate intuition, the fixing of immediately evident essences and concatenations of essences and their descriptive cognition in the systematic combination of all strata in transcendentally pure consciousness" (278). The phenomenologist's task thereby is not one-sided, as is the logician's, but rather all-sided: "To investigate the phenomenological complex of essences on all sides"—and that means always the noetic and noematic concatenations—"is his great task." The phenomenologist cannot occupy himself with such derivative tasks as the elaboration of those doctrines, but must instead seek to lay the groundwork that will enable others to pursue them.

It is in view of just this Apriori that insights amassed in the foregoing gain their significance. The Apriori was seen to be none other than pure, transcendental consciousness. To gain access to it, the epoché had to be effected; it was then further secured through additional transcendental reductions. The seeming price of entering into this a priori sphere, however, was the loss of the world. For it was "annihilated" when all transcendence was reduced to immanence. And yet the course of analyses undertaken by Husserl since that loss has been aimed precisely at regaining the world. This is achieved by disclosing the fundamental features of intentionality: "Just as every intentional lived experience has a noema and therein a sense through which it refers to the object, likewise, from the other direction, everything that we call an object, that we talk about, that we have before our eyes as an actuality, that we regard as possible or probable, that we think of however indeterminately, is therefore already precisely an object *of* consciousness; and that means that whatever world and actuality may at all be and be called, they must be represented within the parameters of actual and possible consciousness by corresponding senses or posita filled with more or less intuitive content." Thus it is the discovery of the noema that restores the world to consciousness. It links the noesis to its object: "the real and ideal actualities that are excluded are represented in the phenomenological sphere by the total multiplicities of senses and posita corresponding to them" (279).

And yet, although the noema provides the means of explaining the relation between consciousness and the world, or actuality, there is no guarantee that its mediation is complete. Such always remains open to question: "Consciousness, or the consciousness-subject itself, judges about actuality, asks about it, presumes [that it exists], doubts it, resolves the doubt and thereby issues 'verdicts of reason'" (281). The result of such scrutiny, then, are verdicts of *reason*. It is—under the best circumstances—the last word on all acts of consciousness and their productions; it is the highest mark of distinction with respect to questions of actuality and identity: "Questions about actuality are contained in all cognitions as such, even in our phenomenological cognitions that bear upon the possible constitution of objects: after all, they all have their correlates in 'objects' that are meant as 'actually existing.' When is . . . the noematically 'meant' identity of an X 'actual identity' instead of 'merely' meant [identity], and what does this 'merely meant' entail in each case?" To ask this is to ask about how rational consciousness decides the question of actuality, of identity. And this amounts to asking about the essence of the verdict of reason. These questions are at once the ultimate and the highest questions within the system of phenomenology. They lead to the heart of the critique of reason, which has been Husserl's express aim from the very beginning.

2. The Verdict of Reason

Phenomenology is critique, and in fact radical critique inasmuch as it seeks always to get to the root of the matter at hand. In the foregoing Husserl has sought to explicate the "roots of everything" and so the fundamental structures of subjectivity. But although he is convinced he has located therein the Archimedean point on which all knowledge rests, such is not enough to secure the status of universal science for phenomenology. For even if all knowledge is based on those structures, of themselves they neither generate nor amount to knowledge; it—and thus the ultimate confirmation of phenomenology's claim—lies beyond them, on a higher level. The explication of knowledge forms the missing piece in the phenomenological puzzle, the keystone of the phenomenological edifice. Yet in its most radical form the explication of knowledge, specifically of how it arises, is nothing but the explication of reason. This calls for the "critique of reason" that is of central concern to Husserl. It makes its first explicit appearance as the "phenomenology of reason,"[5] but in fact Husserl has been engaged in this critique from the start.[6]

2.1 The Nature of Reason

Knowledge has its abode in the realm of Logos, which is to be understood not only as speech but also as reason.[7] By elucidating the basis of expression, Husserl indicated the nature of speech and the direction to be taken in order to develop it fully. But he has yet to do the same for reason, despite its occasional mention in the course of his analyses. He has instead left his goal indeterminate in the sense of an abstract general name, thereby allowing his reader to associate with it whatever he might wish. This was necessitated by his guiding maxims "to the things themselves" and "from the ground up." They prevent him from prematurely concretizing concepts. Such concretization must instead grow out of the analyses of the things themselves. Thus, while his goal has been reason, it can become the focus of attention only at the end of his analyses, and in fact on the highest level of consciousness. It crowns, as it were, the course of the analyses making up *Ideas I*, for reason presupposes speech, and speech presupposes the noetic-noematic structures that have occupied the core of this work.

Reason is inextricably linked to speech, or more specifically, to categorial speech or "speaking about." As seen above, the speech of concern to Husserl is first and foremost expressive or assertoric. It is always about something; it expresses something: "If one speaks simply of objects, one normally means actual, truly existing objects belonging to a particular category of Being" (282). Thus belief-certainty underlies the speaking.[8] But it remains mere belief so long as it has not been confirmed; this is where reason comes in: "Whatever one says about such objects, what is meant and stated thereby must—if one speaks rationally—be something that can be 'justified,' 'demonstrated,' directly 'seen' or [had] mediately 'through insight.'" Husserl's sole interest here is in *rational* speech. That is not to say, however, that reason's contrary—namely, unreason—is excluded from consideration in the phenomenology of reason. Rather, unreason always accompanies reason as a possibility; it too belongs to rationality, albeit as the pole at which it is completely lacking. Thus irrational speech is not what Husserl has in view here as the opposite of rational speech, but rather a-rational speech, that is, neutralized speech.[9] Rational speech is thoroughly positional. It alone allows of the justification, demonstration, seeing, or insight called for, and so of the establishment of knowledge. Positionality and rationality are therefore correlated, whereby the latter presupposes the former, but the former only implies the possibility of the latter: "In the logical sphere, in that of the statement, 'being truly' or 'actually' and 'being rationally demonstrable' are principially correlated; and this holds for all doxic modalities of Being or positing"—though, again, never for their neutralizations. However, the correlation between positionality and rationality need not be a real identity: "Of course the possibility of rational demonstration referred to here is understood not as an empirical, but rather as an 'ideal,' as an essential possibility." Reason is the highest ideal. It marks the upper limit of conscious life, that towards which each ego is to strive.[10]

Surprisingly, Husserl begins his phenomenology of reason not by asking what reason is, but rather "what rational demonstration means, that is, what rational consciousness consists in." The talk of 'reason' (*Vernunft*) is conspicuously infrequent here. As will become clear, however, this is because reason is nothing separate from consciousness; it is not a subject or substance, but rather something that belongs intimately to consciousness.[11] But then not as a faculty in the classical sense. Rather, as something predicated of a consciousness. Hence it is more appropriate to speak of 'rationality' (*Vernünftigkeit*) than of 'reason' inasmuch as the former term emphasizes the predicative nature of reason in *Ideas I*. This nature also accounts for the vacillation in the foregoing, and in what follows, between 'rationality' and 'reason'.[12]

Because reason is a predicate,[13] Husserl's analyses are focused not on reason so much as on *rational* consciousness. But even here, in seeking to characterize it, his aim is not at an exhaustive account. As throughout *Ideas I*, his intention is to specify the primary moments of reason qua rational consciousness, to map out the terrain and thereby sketch the contours that future inquiry is to fill out. This work is in all essentials a blueprint, a projection or project (*Entwurf*); Husserl reminds the reader of this repeatedly. The real work Husserl does is different from that expected of his successors. He is blazing the trail to the new world; it is up to those who follow to settle and civilize it.

2.2 Forms of Rational Consciousness and Evidence

Husserl discerns three fundamental forms of rational consciousness. In each case, a positive or maximal side is accompanied by a negative or minimal side; both contraries are equally possible, though preference is given always to the maximal side. The *first* form is captured in the distinction between *originary and nonoriginary givenness*, or "between positional lived experiences in which the posited is given originarily and those in which it is not so given: thus between 'perceiving,' 'seeing' acts—in the broadest sense—and non-'perceiving' acts" (282). In perception, for instance, a landscape is given originarily, it is actually seen, whereas in memory it is not; it is given only derivatively, as the represen-tiation of its perception. That is not to say that memory lacks its own legitimacy. Rather, it is simply not originary consciousness, and so does not share in the latter's primacy.

This distinction is in fact not restricted to external perception and related acts, but holds for all positional lived experiences. To illustrate this, Husserl appeals to "internal seeing," or insight, distinguishing between blind assertions and those based on insight. It is possible, he notes, to make the judgment that $2 + 1 = 1 + 2$ blindly or with insight. In the latter case, one actually sees the relevant relationships; in the former, one does not. The moment of insight has primacy over the insight that has ceased to be actually effected. And, as has become clear in the course of Husserl's analyses, every effecting must of necessity give way to a new effecting. So that what was once insight turns into blindness the farther it slips from actual effectuation.

But this scission between modes of givenness, between originariness and nonoriginariness of givenness, and the variability it entails clearly cannot "concern the *pure* sense or positum; for in the members of any such exemplary pair [the sense or positum] is identical and also can always be seized upon by consciousness as identical. The distinction concerns the way in which the *mere* sense or positum—which, as a mere abstractum in the concretion of the noema of consciousness, requires an increase in supplementary moments—is or is not a fulfilled sense or positum" (283). Decisive here are therefore the differences in the extent of fullness or fulfillment of sense. But "the How of fulfillment matters as well." It determines the maximum level of fulfillment possible. In the case of the aforementioned perceptual lived experience, the landscape intended is given "bodily." In the memorial lived experience it is not. In the former lived experience, the sense is perceptually fulfilled; in the latter, memorially. Originary givenness has greater fullness than does nonoriginary givenness. And on this account, it is accorded a greater amount of rationality: "But to the positing characteristic belongs a specific rational character as a mark of distinction accruing to it essentially if and only if it is a positing based on a fulfilled, originarily giving sense and not merely on just any sense." As will be seen, just as there are gradations of fulfillment, likewise there are corresponding gradations of rationality.[14]

In the case of a rational consciousness, the position or belief belongs inextricably to the rational act. Husserl's example is the appearing of a physical thing. When its appearing motivates—gives rise to—the position, that position is "rationally motivated." The maximal degree of such motivation issues from originary givenness: "The positing has its original legitimizing ground in originary givenness. In other modes of givenness, the legitimizing ground need not be lacking; lacking, however, is the priority of the original ground, which plays a distinctive role in the relative assessment of the legitimizing grounds" (284). The priority of originariness holds mutatis mutandis of both transcendent and immanent objectualities, though the latter are privileged over the former.

Because he has in view the perfect coincidence of positionality and what motivates it, Husserl is speaking in absolute terms. He calls the result of such coincidence 'evidence' (*Evidenz*): "Insight, evidence of any kind, is thus a highly distinctive occurrence; in its 'core'"—i.e., *in nuce*—"it is the unity of a rational positing with what essentially motivates the positing, whereby this entire situation can be understood noetically as well as noematically." Reason is nowhere to be found here in the sense of a faculty or a subject; it is a predicate, and as such a mark of distinction. Although not every position is rational, wherever there is evidence, the position is indeed rational. Evidence is a byproduct of the coincidence of belief and Being, of intentionality in its most fundamental respects. On the other hand, evidence is not a product in the sense in which a noema is the product of a positional noesis. Rather, as noted, it is a rational characteristic that is accorded to a distinctive affair-complex.

The *second* fundamental form of rational consciousness becomes visible in the distinction between *adequately and inadequately giving consciousness*. It is adequacy that marks maximal rationality in this case: "What we usually call evidence and insight (or having insight [*Einsehen*]) is a positional doxic and thereby adequately giving consciousness that 'excludes being otherwise'; the thesis is motivated in a wholly distinctive manner by the adequate givenness and is in the highest sense an act of 'reason'" (285). In the case of the aforementioned arithmetical example, one can have such insight; the objectuality is given adequately. The landscape, however, is given always only inadequately, and for essential reasons. There can be no insight within the sphere of experience, but only in that of essences. For in the former sphere, the objectuality is given always only as an individual, and contingently so; it can always be "otherwise." As was seen above, contingency always entails imperfection and changeability. In the eidetic sphere, by contrast, the objectuality given is universal, not contingent. It is immutable and perfect.

The *third* form of rational consciousness becomes visible in the distinction between *apodictic and assertoric seeing*: "the, so to speak, 'assertoric' seeing of something individual, for example the 'becoming aware' of a physical thing or of an individual affair-complex, differs essentially in its rational character not only from an 'apodictic' seeing, from the having insight into an essence or essence-complex; but it also differs from the modification of this having insight, which may arise through the mixture of the two, namely in the case of the application of insight to something seen assertorically and, generally, in the cognition of the necessity of the being-thus [*Sosein*] of a posited singular." Rational consciousness thus arises from apodictic seeing.[15]

Much like the second form of rational consciousness, the characterization of the third form does not distinguish it from its contrary: assertoric and apodictic seeing are not necessarily opposites. Apodicticity does mark a maximum, but the assertoric need not mark a minimum, even if it always requires some degree of supplementation. Both kinds of seeing belong essentially together: "It should be regarded as a phenomenological cognition of the greatest import that both [assertoric seeing and having apodictic insight] actually belong to one eidetic genus and that, put still more universally, any rational consciousness whatsoever marks a highest genus of thetic modalities in which the 'seeing' (in the extremely broadened sense) related to originary givenness is precisely a rigidly delimited species" (285–86). Generally speaking, then, 'evidence' denotes the highest genus, and so can be applied to both assertoric and apodictic seeing; wherever a position is motivated by originary givenness, Husserl speaks of 'originary evidence'. 'Insight', on the other hand, is reserved for apodictic seeing. Furthermore, Husserl notes that a distinction must be made between pure and impure insight, as well as between pure and impure evidence (see 286). Since these distinctions are not absolute, they entail the notion of gradations of insight and evidence in contrast to the talk of them thus far.

2.2.1 Adequacy and Inadequacy. Adequate and inadequate evidence are based on adequate and inadequate givenness, respectively. The latter can give rise only to a kind of "'impure' evidence"; it is always imperfect and so requires supplementation. Inadequate givenness is peculiar to the sphere of experience: "While the positing based on the bodily appearance of the physical thing is, of course, a rational positing, the appearance is always only a one-sided, 'imperfect' appearance; when there is consciousness of it as bodily present, what appears 'authentically' does not only stand there, but simply this physical thing itself, the whole in conformity with the total, though only one-sidedly intuited and, moreover, multifariously indeterminate, sense" (286). The inadequately given thing is a mixture of determinacies and indeterminacies, of full and empty components. It is impossible to derive the pure thing in its fullness in abstraction from its empty moments, for the latter belong as essentially to it as do the full moments. In other words, the inadequate givenness is no fault of the thing, nor is it a shortcoming on the part of the subject; rather, it is a function of its essence, which predelineates the possibilities of givenness pertaining to it.

Again, inadequacy belongs essentially to the sphere of experience: "Principially something physically real, a Being with such sense, can appear only 'inadequately' in a closed appearance." Such inadequacy can never be overcome completely, and so must always stamp givenness within this sphere: "Essentially connected with this is the fact that no rational positing based on such an inadequately giving appearance can be 'definitive,' 'inconvertible,' that no [such positing] is equivalent in its singularization to the simple 'The physical thing is actual,' but is equivalent only to 'It is actual'—assuming that the further course of experience does not give rise to 'stronger rational motives' that show the original positing to be one that is must be 'crossed out' in the broader context. Accordingly, the positing is rationally motivated only by the appearance (the imperfectly fulfilled perceptual sense) in and of itself, considered in its singularization" (286–87). A thing can be given more or less adequately, but in the sphere of experience there can be no transition from inadequate to adequate givenness. A remainder is always left over that escapes the subject's grip. No last word can be uttered here.

And yet, even if it is impossible to reach the upper limit of adequacy, it is nevertheless possible to gain greater adequacy. This possibility of increase is delineated a priori by the essence of the Being in question.[16] To clarify this state of affairs, the phenomenology of reason must study "how the consciousness of inadequate givenness, how the one-sided appearing is related to one and the same determinable X in the continuous progression to ever new appearances that continuously merge with one another, and which eidetic possibilities arise here; how, on the one hand, a progression of experiences is possible and always rationally motivated by continuously preceding rational positings: precisely the course of experience in which the empty spaces in the previous appearances are filled out, the indeterminacies are determined more precisely, and thus always in the manner of a thoroughly harmonious fulfilling with its steadily increasing rational force" (287). Such increase is of necessity always only asymptotic. For essential reasons, the goal of adequacy can never be reached in the case of transcendencies.

Increase in adequacy, however, is not the only possibility pertaining to the givenness of a transcendent being. A decrease may also occur. Hence, the phenomenology of reason must also seek to explicate "the cases of fusions or polythetical syntheses of discordance, the 'determination of otherwise' of the X always intended as the same—otherwise than it corresponded to the original sense-bestowal. In this connection it must be shown how the positing components of the earlier perceptual flow get crossed out along with their sense; how, under some circumstances, the whole perception, so to speak, explodes and disintegrates into 'conflicting interpretations of a physical thing,' into suppositions about a physical thing; how the theses of these suppositions are annulled and peculiarly modified in this annulment; or else how the one thesis, remaining unmodified, 'conditions' the crossing out of the 'counter-thesis'; and other such occurrences." Thus whereas it is impossible to achieve total fulfillment and thus adequacy within this sphere, it is possible—as when a perception "explodes"—to achieve total nonfulfillment or sheer emptiness, which is the ultimate form of inadequacy.

The distinction between adequacy and inadequacy, like that between apodictic and assertoric seeing, does not have the exclusiveness of other bipolar structures encountered thus far in Husserl's thought. Although they are mutually exclusive and although adequacy marks the upper limit, inadequacy need not be total inadequacy and thereby mark the lower limit of this pair. Rather, inadequacy allows of degrees extending from no adequacy in the direction of perfect adequacy, which, however, can never be reached in this case. Precisely such gradation distinguishes it from adequacy: "Every such [i.e., originary] evidence . . . is either adequate evidence, principially incapable of being further 'strengthened' or 'weakened,' thus without degrees of weight, or it is inadequate evidence and thus capable of being increased and decreased. Whether one or the other kind of evidence is possible in a given sphere depends on its generic type; it is therefore a priori preformed, and it is countersense to demand in one sphere the perfection proper to the evidence of another sphere (for example, that of eidetic relations) that essentially excludes it" (288). The possibilities of adequacy and inadequacy are fixed from the start, and in fact by the essence of the objectuality in question. The wish to contravene such predelineation must necessarily end in countersense.

2.2.2 Mediate Rationality. Thus far Husserl's focus has been on positings that are immediately, that is, in themselves, rational. They testify of themselves to their rationality: "as a positing of its sense, a positing—of whatever quality—has its legitimacy when it is rational; the rational characteristic is itself precisely the characteristic of legitimacy that it is 'due' essentially and thus not as a contingent fact under the contingent circumstances proper to a factually positing ego. Correlatively, the positum is also said to be legitimate" (289). But such immediacy is not the only possibility here; positings and posita may also be mediately rational: "it can also be that 'something speaks for the positum,' that it can still have a share in reason without 'itself' being rational." It has its legitimacy by virtue of something else. To illustrate this, Husserl recalls that, within the doxic sphere, each doxic modality refers back to a protodoxa, and he adds here that each modality has its own rational characteristic, which itself refers back, "so to speak, to a primal rational characteristic that belongs to the domain of primal belief: back to the case of originary and ultimately perfect evidence." The significant distinction centers on actionality. When a doxic modality is actional, it can be immediately rational; but in that case the protodoxa it harbors could only be mediately rational: "Within itself a presumption can be characterized as rational. If we follow the reference inherent in it back to the corresponding primal belief, and if we adopt this belief in the form of a 'supposing,' then 'something speaks for it.' It is not the belief itself, unqualifiedly, that is characterized as rational, although it has a share in reason." Rationality is primarily proper to the living, actional positing, regardless of its modality. That living speaks directly for the modality in question. The protodoxa harbored in the modality can, of course, be accessed, but because it is harbored and not lived in, because it is not actional, it can have only mediate rationality; it is actionality that determines the quality of rationality and thus of the legitimacy pertaining to a particular positing or its positum.

2.3 Hierarchies of Belief, Reason, Evidence, and Truth

But regardless of the character of legitimacy pertaining to a positing or its positum, in the end it is primal belief that is decisive: *"ultimately, all lines run back to primal belief and its primal reason or to 'truth'"* (290). Truth, or perfect evidence, consists in the correspondence of or harmony between belief and what motivates it. In other words, truth is "obviously the correlate of the perfect rational characteristic of protodoxa, of belief-certainty." Rationality therefore proves to be a feature of noeses, and truth, one of noemata.

Just as the neutrality modification can be effected without making a detour through doxic theses, likewise reason is not the property of doxic theses alone: "But evidence is by no means a mere name for those kinds of rational occurrences in the sphere of belief (and even less in that of predicative judgment), but rather for all thetic spheres and in particular also for the significant rational relations obtaining between them." Theses of every kind and level can in fact be rational or evident. Thus, for example, the spheres of theory, axiology, and praxis each has its own kind of truth or evidence: "'Theoretical' or 'doxological truth,' or evidence, has its parallel in 'axiological and practical truth, or evidence,' whereby the 'truths' referred to by the latter terms are expressed and known in doxological truths, namely in specifically logical (apophantic) truths" (290–91). This suggests that these spheres and their respective truths are not of equal rank, but instead make up a hierarchy in which the logical or theoretical is fundamental. It is on account of this that Husserl considers one of his chief tasks to be the clarification of "why belief-certainty and, correspondingly, truth play such a dominant role in all reason, a role that at the same time, incidentally, makes it understandable why, with respect to their solution, the problems of reason in the doxic sphere must take precedence over those of axiological and practical reason" (291). In solving these problems in the doxic sphere, then, those in the other spheres become solvable, which is why Husserl cannot be rightly accused of neglecting the practical sphere. For he regards his theoretical work as laying the foundation for all praxis. Phenomenology is accordingly thoroughly practical. It is to be a critique of all kinds of reason, beginning with logical reason.[17]

Another important area of investigation for the phenomenology of reason is that of the coincidence of acts. Husserl takes as an example of such acts those that have the same sense or positum, but that are not equally evident, or have different "rational values [*Vernunftwerte*]." In such cases, Husserl notes, it is possible for evident and nonevident acts to coincide. An act of the former kind then provides the standard for increase in evidence in the act of the latter kind: "in the transition from the latter to the former, this [evident act] takes on the character of the demonstrating act, [whereas the nonevident act] takes on the character of the act that is demonstrated. The insightful positing of the one functions as 'confirming' for the noninsightful positing of the other. The 'positum' is 'verified' or 'confirmed'; the imperfect mode of givenness is transformed into a perfect one." The possibilities of such transformation are, however, not the same for every act, but are predetermined by the essence of the act in question. Thus, for instance, a perception can undergo such transformation, but a recollection cannot. In keeping with its essence, it can never achieve "originary verification."

In this connection Husserl distinguishes between motivated and empty or unmotivated possibilities.[18] The former is specified by the given objectuality: "it is determinately motivated by that which the positum, which is fulfilled in the manner it is given, entails" (292). On the other hand, an empty possibility exceeds what is given and so unbinds itself from the standard set by the positum. Husserl illustrates the distinction between the two kinds of possibility with reference to his desk: "It is an empty possibility that the now unseen underside of this desk here has ten legs instead of four, which is actually the case. By contrast, the number four is a motivated possibility for the determinate perception I am now effecting." He further refines this distinction with respect to the spheres of experience and of essence. In the former sphere, "possibility coincides with actuality" insofar as actual experience verifies "positings bearing on something real"; this something gives itself originarily to perceptual consciousness, but never to the representiating consciousness in which, for example, one merely thinks up possible experiences, or, in this case, perceptions. In the eidetic sphere, matters are different. Here representiation does not generate empty possibilities, but rather fulfills possibilities by bringing them to intuition: "in each case of a positing of an essence, or else of a positum belonging to an essence, the intuitive representiation of its perfect fulfillment is equivalent to the fulfillment itself, just as a priori the intuitive representiation, indeed the mere fantasy, of an eidetic concatenation is 'equivalent' to the insight into that concatenation, that is, the one is converted into the other by means of a mere change of attitude; and the possibility of this reciprocal conversion is an essentially necessary, rather than an accidental, one" (293). Insight and fantasy are equivalent in the eidetic sphere. This is of special significance to phenomenology, since it intends to be an eidetic science on the one hand and its vital element is fiction, or fantasy, on the other. The fulfillment proper to fantasy indicates the manner in which fantasy can be productive, and, paradoxically enough, for the phenomenologist more so than any field of positional consciousness. What remains open, however, is how the results gained in fantasy can be made the subjects of positional consciousness, in other words: how insight, which presupposes a positional consciousness, can be gained by means of fantasy, which is generated by a neutral consciousness. Is there not a gulf between positionality and neutrality? There is, but, again, a bridge of sorts is provided by supposing.

2.4 The Animating Force of the Originary, Immediate, Direct

Verification, confirmation, legitimization, evidence—each can be achieved directly or indirectly, immediately or mediately. Directness or immediacy, of course, has primacy over indirectness or mediacy, since the former founds the latter: "As is well known, all mediate founding leads back to immediate founding. With respect to all object-provinces and positings related to them, the primal source of all legitimacy lies in immediate evidence, and more narrowly delimited, in originary evidence, or in the originary givenness motivating it." Originariness always provides the ultimate standard for anything derived from it. It is on account of this that perception, both external and internal, have primacy over their respective modifications. And yet even in the latter, originariness can mediately found the rational value of a positing.

Once again, even positings that lack originary evidence can have "original, immediate legitimacy," or as Husserl also says, they can have a peculiar kind of "weight." This holds, for instance, of the memory of something past. But because it does not have originary evidence, it has "only a relative and imperfect legitimacy." In order to achieve maximal clarity and strength for the memorial positing, then, it is necessary that the memory be traced back to a present, that is, this process of recovery "would terminate in actional perceptions, in the actional *hic et nunc*." The closer one comes to the present, the greater the legitimacy. The progression from memory to memory down to the present, forms a concatenation of memories. Together, Husserl notes, they are stronger than any individual memory in the series. But this concatenation does not disappear upon reaching the actional Now; rather, once it has been reached, "something of the light of perception and its evidence shines back onto the entire series" (294). The originary, immediate evidence thereby supports every nonoriginary, mediate, and thus relative evidence. Husserl underscores the support lent the nonoriginary by the originary, which is to say, by perception, by appealing to the figure of force, as in the vital force that courses through one's veins or an electric charge that drives a motor: "In a hidden way the rationality, the characteristic of legitimacy, pertaining to a memory springs from the force of perception—which is at work in all confusion and obscurity—even if the perception is 'not in effect.'" Although one sees the memory immediately, and this immediacy has its own legitimacy, ultimately its force derives from another source: its legitimacy is always "the mediate reflection of the legitimacy of perception." Here there are possibilities of "pure and impure" as well as "unmixed and mixed rational positings." Pure are those positings proper to acts centering on essences; impure, those proper to acts centering on experience; unmixed, a perception; mixed, any modification thereof.

2.5 Being and Thinking

The aim informing the foregoing "cataloging" of aspects of "reason" that phenomenology must investigate further is the achievement of a "universal understanding of the essence of reason" (295). But, again, reason is nothing in and of itself, but, like truth, has its source in a relationship, namely in that between objectual Being and consciousness. Accordingly, one of the chief results of the quest for such "universal understanding" is the "universal elucidation of the essential correlations linking the idea of true Being to the ideas of truth, reason, consciousness" (295–96). It is not by chance that the idea of true Being is first mentioned here. As prescribed by the principle of all principles, consciousness or reflection must always take its bearings by a preceding and thus standard-setting Being. Reason no less than truth necessarily has its ultimate standard in Being. As Husserl notes, a rational thesis has its "rational ground in the originary givenness of what is determinate in the full sense: The X is not only meant in full determinacy, but is given originarily in precisely this determinacy" (296). The rational ground by no means rests in "reason itself," nor in thought, but solely in Being.

The ideas of reason and truth depend upon an essential possibility of the correlation of objectual Being and consciousness: "Principially (in the Apriori of unconditioned eidetic universality) there corresponds to every 'truly existing' object the idea of a possible consciousness in which the object itself can be seized upon originarily and thereby with perfect adequacy. Conversely, if this possibility is guaranteed, then *eo ipso* the object truly exists." But whereas consciousness of an object given originarily and in perfect adequacy guarantees the true existence of the object, it is nevertheless the object that is decisive here. The guarantee and thus truth of its existence is found in consciousness, but the objectuality *always* precedes that consciousness. In other words: *Being has priority over thinking.*[19]

2.6 The Prescriptive Function of Essence

This is not contradicted by the seeming precedence of apprehension over givenness: "In the essence of every interpretation-category (which is the correlate of every object-category) the possible formations of the concrete, perfect or imperfect, interpretations of objects proper to such a category are determinately predelineated. Moreover, for each imperfect interpretation it is essentially prescribed how it is to be perfected, how its sense is to be completed, fulfilled by intuition, and how the intuition is to be further enriched." Some modes of interpretation have priority over others—for instance, perception has priority over memory—and how an object is apprehended does indeed determine the possibilities of truth and reason, but the latter are always grounded in the givenness of the object. Although they arise always only from the correlation of consciousness and its object, reason and truth are ultimately grounded in Being. For Husserl reason is no more autonomous than truth.

The essential possibilities of interpretation are established in each case by the category of the object in question. Before use can be made of it as a standard, however, each category must first be brought to adequate givenness, which is possible since it is an idea or essence: "In its adequate givenness it [i.e., an object-category] prescribes an evident *general rule* for every particular object of which there comes to be consciousness in multiplicities of concrete lived experiences (which lived experiences, of course, are to be taken here not as individual singularities but rather as essences, as ultimate concreta). It prescribes the rule for how an object subordinate to it would be made fully determinate with respect to sense and mode of givenness, how it would be brought to adequate, originary givenness; by which isolated or continuously serial concatenations of consciousness and by which concrete eidectic composition of these concatenations" (296–97). Each rule therefore determines the course to be taken in order to achieve adequacy as well as the degree of adequacy possible in each case. In this way it sets the requirements for rationality and truth.

Thus according to the essence of the transcendent object, it cannot be perceived adequately "in a closed appearance" (297). That is to say: "There are objects—and all transcendent objects, all 'realities' that fall under the names 'nature' and 'world', belong here—that cannot be given in complete determinacy and likewise in complete intuitiveness in a closed consciousness." Whereas this holds of each "reality," it does not hold of its essences, which can indeed be grasped adequately. Here Husserl distinguishes between the idea and its instantiation: "The idea of an essentially motivated infinity is not itself an infinity; the insight that this infinity principially cannot be given does not exclude but rather requires the evident givenness of the idea of this infinity" (298). Even if the physical thing cannot be perceived adequately, its idea can be, and this idea prescribes the course to be taken in seeking to achieve adequacy. Because this course is essentially asymptotic, because the idea sets an upper limit that can never be fully reached in reality, Husserl speaks of the idea "in the Kantian sense" (297). It is regulative and as such it specifies perfect givenness "as a system that, in its eidetic type, is an absolutely determinate system of endless processes of continuous appearing, or as a field of these processes, an a priori determined continuum of appearances with different but determinate dimensions, governed throughout by a fixed eidetic lawfulness." Once grasped, the idea can be employed as a standard to evaluate every "claim" to rationality or truth bearing on what is given.

2.7 Belief and Normativity

Although it has been Husserl's goal from the outset, reason could only enter into consideration at the end of his analyses, for "the phenomenology of reason, noetics in a pregnant sense, which intends to undertake an intuitive exploration not of just any kind of consciousness, but of rational consciousness, by all means presupposes universal phenomenology" (299), that is, the phenomenology of consciousness in general, of its universal structures. The universality attended to by phenomenology is precisely that pertaining to essence, and so the chief aim is systematically to bring to light the essential structures and the norms they entail, norms that govern all individuals.[20] Insofar as it is to yield firm results and thus knowledge, such inquiry takes place always within the realm of positionality: "That—in the realm of positionality—thetic consciousness of every genus is subject to norms, is itself a phenomenological fact; the norms are nothing but eidetic laws that refer to certain noetic-noematic concatenations, which must be strictly analyzed and described according to their kind and form" (299–300). It is only within this realm that the norms are in effect. They have no weight for neutral consciousness, which is why Husserl adds a note to 'positionality' here: "In the sphere of fantasy *and* neutrality, all thetic occurrences are carried over as 'mirrored' and 'powerless'; thus all occurrences of reason as well. Neutral theses are not to be confirmed, but to be 'quasi'-confirmed; they are not evident, but 'quasi'-evident; etc." (299 n.). No norms hold sway within the realm of neutrality; all are a matter of complete indifference to neutral consciousness. However, beyond pointing tacitly to the priority of positionality for the phenomenology of reason, Husserl's note has a twofold effect. Firstly, it reminds the reader that Husserl has not forgotten his exposition of the doctrine of the neutrality modification, a fact attested already by the mere mention of 'positionality' (one need only recall his earlier remark that wherever the talk is of positionality, neutrality is also present—as a possibility). But, secondly, it also draws attention once again to the centrality of bipolar structures in Husserlian thought. His express reference to neutrality is to the opposite—as it were, to the "dark side"—of positionality, which is the prerequisite of reason. As a consequence, the opposite of reason is not neutral reason—which is in fact an oxymoron—but unreason: "Of course, in this connection 'unreason' as the negative counterpart of reason is also to be considered everywhere, just as the phenomenology of evidence includes its counterpart, absurdity" (299). Phenomenology aims at the total explication of every essential structure, which always entails maximal and minimal phases. In order to achieve completeness, not only of foundation but also of all knowledge in every sphere based on it, the phenomenologist must explicate both sides in each case. However, this does not mean that the phenomenologist is indifferent to what he investigates. On the contrary, he privileges the maximal, positive modes, thus, for example, positionality, reason, evidence, and truth. Such privileging, Husserl would likely maintain, is not a mere prejudice, but rather springs from the insight into the essence of man and so of the human community and its sciences. But not only does eidetic insight guide the selection of the central topics of incipient phenomenological inquiry, it also fixes the order of that inquiry. Reason comes last due to its dependence upon the universal structures of consciousness. And evidence comes still later because it is of a piece with reason. This in no way impinges upon the significance of evidence: "The universal eidetic doctrine of evidence, along with its analyses related to the most universal eidetic distinctions, forms a relatively small, though fundamental piece of the phenomenology of reason." It is last not because it lacks primacy; on the contrary, it must be the supreme goal of all science on Husserl's view and so especially of the science of all sciences, universal phenomenology. Rather, it comes last because of the order of inquiry prescribed by eidetic insight.

Actual and not just quasi-evidence is the goal here. And such is possible only within the realm of positionality. It is, however, a realm correlated with objectual Being. Both, together and taken separately, are governed by essential determinations, which alone provide the standards for rational scrutiny: "Evidence is indeed not some consciousness-index pinned to a judgment (and one usually speaks of such evidence only in the case of judgment), calling to us like a mystical voice from a better world: Here is the truth!—as if such a voice would have anything to say to free spirits like us and would not have to demonstrate its title to legitimacy" (300). Evidence arises instead from the perfect correspondence of a "peculiar mode of positing" and the "eidetically determinate constitutions of the essence of the noema" to which the positing belongs.[21] On the level of the individual subject, which has been the sole object of investigation in the foregoing, rationality proves to be harmony, the total agreement of a positing and its objectuality or, more generally, between belief and Being.

2.8 Phenomenology and the Acquisition of the World

Transcendental phenomenology does not remain cut off from the world, consigned to some solipsistic purgatory, as a consequence of the epoché. Rather, just this modification is to enable the first authentic acquisition of the world. Because it works from the ground up, because it begins with the elucidation of the intentional structures that play a decisive role in every aspect of the life of consciousness, "phenomenology actually encompasses the whole natural world and all the ideal worlds it excludes: it encompasses them as the 'world sense' by virtue of the eidetic lawfulnesses connecting any object-sense and noema whatsoever with the closed system of noeses, and specifically by virtue of the rationally lawful eidetic concatenations the correlate of which is the 'actual object,' which thus, for its part, always represents an index for wholly determinate systems of teleologically unitary formations of consciousness" (302–3). The teleology of such formations is the trajectory set by the essential predetermination of what counts as the fulfillment of sense. The productivity of consciousness is therefore not aimless, nor is it random, but is ever directed towards the achievement of the telos in question. The journey towards such achievement is one supported and even driven by belief. In the end, belief proves to be not only the basis of conscious life, but also the source of all reason, truth, and evidence.[22]

3. Towards Absolute Reason

The analyses Husserl presents in his "phenomenology of reason" by no means mark the conclusion of the phenomenological enterprise. They are only the beginning, for the system of phenomenology must continue its movement beyond individual subjectivity and on up into the heights, towards its apogee in absolute reason. This reason has two senses: on the one hand, it is God as the ideal subject or, as Fink reported, the community of transcendental egos;[23] on the other hand, it represents the complete rationalization of every domain of human endeavor, the achievement of absolute harmony.[24] In seeking the latter, the former is also reached.

But a quandary makes itself felt here, namely one concerning the nature of God in Husserl.[25] If God is absolute reason and reason is a predicate, what does this say about God? Is 'God' a predicate?[26] If God is the community of transcendental egos, which is to say, maximally rational egos, is this community divine and therefore to be equated with God? And what if God founds conscious life; does that make "him" something prerational or, in other words, irrational? Is God to be identified with the hyletic stratum? But then there is the issue of essence and norms. Is God both the giver and instance of the maximal fulfillment of norms? It was noted above that rationality pertains to noeses. If this holds, what does it say about God as absolute reason? Husserl does not answer these questions, but he does make it clear that God is a "limit concept," and in fact the uppermost limit, as well as that it is the phenomenologist's task, as the "functionary of humanity," to set humanity on the path to reason and to keep it on that path. This path leads up towards absolute reason. It is thus the path of the rationalization of the human community, the achievement of which would be the fulfillment of Husserl's vision of a transcendental-phenomenological community or humanness.

The rationalization sought is founded on the analyses making up *Ideas I*. Because Husserl intends to make "eidetic beginnings," his analyses were carried out with the "greatest universality." This holds no less of his phenomenology of reason, the problems of which, he says, have been treated at "heights of universality, which did not allow the essential ramifications of the problems and their connections with formal and regional ontologies to emerge" (303). In order to reach absolute reason, the next step to be taken must be to pursue the ramifications of those problems and "disclose the full sense of the phenomenological eidetics of reason and the entire wealth of its problems."

The talk of the "heights of universality" would seem to contradict Husserl's foundationalist intention, just as would his remark on the proper sequence of eidetic inquiry: "In all eidetic spheres, the systematic path leads from higher to lower universality, even if the analyses tracing them out take up something particular." Yet this does not mean that Husserl is "philosophizing from on-high." On the contrary, the essential or universal founds the factual and particular. Thus in seeking the most universal, he has sought the "roots of everything," and so the deepest ground.

Before he elaborates the aforementioned ramifications, before he points the direction of ascent into the heights, Husserl returns briefly to a consideration of "the sources of the problems of reason." As has become clear, for him the source of all sources is intentionality: "The name of the problem that encompasses the whole of phenomenology is intentionality. It expresses precisely the fundamental property of consciousness; all phenomenological problems, even the hyletic ones, fall under this name. Therefore phenomenology begins with problems of intentionality; but first of all in universality and without drawing into its sphere questions of whether that of which there is consciousness actually (truly) exists. We shall not consider the fact that positional consciousness, with its thetic characteristics, can be designated in the most universal sense as 'meaning' [*Vermeinen*] and as such is necessarily subject to the rational opposition between validity and invalidity." Husserl's beginning is therefore to be nothing more than that: a beginning. And yet he regards it as one that provides a firm basis and points the way for all future inquiry. In fact such inquiry must be carried out, for Husserl has by no means sought to provide exhaustive analyses: "As everywhere, here too we pursued only the methodical intention to elaborate for every principially new stratum that may be described as a field of phenomenological investigations, as much firm ground for ourselves [as is necessary in order to be able to] assure ourselves of them, formulate the incipient and fundamental problems based on them, and cast our gaze freely in the horizon of problems surrounding them" (304). It remains for future phenomenologists, Husserl's co-workers, to fill out, revise, and secure his findings. He has been, as he says, an explorer in a strange land. In seeking to penetrate *terra incognita*, it was inevitable that he make errors; but his concern lay less with them than with making that land visible. It is easier, he notes, to come after and put everything in order.[27]

The course he projects for his successors at the conclusion of *Ideas I* involves pursuing the ramifications of the "universal phenomenology of reason." Future phenomenologists are to attend to the branching out of inquiry, which has its starting point in the ground of intentionality. Husserl himself began with the most universal problems. The next step is to take up the formal disciplines of logic, axiology, theory of praxis, followed by the unfolding of their respective formal ontologies. From there, phenomenologists would have to turn to the strictly material disciplines, beginning with regional ontologies, and in fact with the physical thing and its constitution. Husserl sketches here the "trajectory" or teleology of a complete phenomenology of reason, that is, he points the direction in which inquiry needs to be carried out. "Principially, phenomenology does not stop with vague talk, with obscure generalities; it demands systematically determinate clarification, analysis, and description that penetrates into the essential concatenations and down to their last reachable particularizations: it demands work that settles matters [*erledigende Arbeit*]" (314). Such work is to be carried out by a community of investigators.[28] It cannot be Husserl's concern. He is and remains, by his own testimony, the "eternal beginner." He did not conceive of himself as one who could complete his projections, nor could he have done so given his intention to provide humanity with a "new *orientation*."

Chapter V. Conclusion

The Phenomenological Movement

What is phenomenology? Is it a style, a trend, a school, or a movement of thought? Can it even be spoken of in the singular? Assuming that it makes sense to speak of "the" phenomenological movement, then the source of this sense is to be found in the movement of phenomenology as it is prescribed by the latter's task. This task is rooted, in turn, in the beginning of that movement, which is to be found nowhere else save in Husserlian thought.

By his own testimony, the most radical form of his phenomenology is transcendental phenomenology—the most radical because it unveils the lost Apriori, the root of everything, and in fact first by means of the epoché or phenomenological reduction. This achievement, however, does not mean the end of phenomenology, but rather brings its proper task into view for the first time with the greatest amount of determinacy, and in fact in *Ideas I*. Hence the unveiling actually means the beginning of a "long and thorny" journey in pursuit of the essence of man, that is to say, of the reason peculiar to him. In this sense it is the methodical attempt to comply with the Delphic imperative: γνῶθι σεαυτόν, "Know thyself!" which Husserl recasts in 1929 at the close of his *Cartesian Meditations*.[1] There, in a work widely praised for its thematization of intersubjectivity, he recalls the beginning and the movement it founds: The self, the essence of man, determines him to be a rational being, the *animal rationale*. In striving for his actualization, man seeks to become precisely that: rational. This striving has two principal stages: "The necessary path to a knowledge that is ultimately justified in the highest sense or, equivalently, to a philosophical knowledge, is that of a universal self-knowledge, *first* of a monadic, and *then* of an intermonadic self-knowledge." The proper beginning therefore lies in subjectivity and not in intersubjectivity—at least within the parameters established by Husserl's task. One cannot begin here immediately, however, due to the prevailing—and necessarily prevailing—natural habits of thinking. Rather, one must first effect the epoché. It alone grants access to the phenomenological sphere of inquiry, pure consciousness. Husserl is steadfast in asserting the decisiveness of this reduction.

His thought is focused on method in a twofold sense: both as the path and as the means for entering onto that path. It is directed from the start: first towards the beginning and then, after having secured that beginning by means of the epoché, towards the end of the system. In 1927 Husserl expresses the direction of the phenomenological movement as follows: "In its universal *self*-referentiality phenomenology knows its own function in a possible transcendental life of humanity. It knows the absolute norms that can be discerned in that life, but also life's original teleologically inclined structure in the direction of the unveiling of these norms and their practical, conscious effect. It knows itself then as a function of the universal *self*-reflection of (transcendental) humanity in the service of a universal rational praxis, that is, in the service of the striving, which has been freed by the unveiling, in the direction [*Richtung*] of the universal idea of absolute perfection, which lies in the infinite or, equivalently, in the direction of the idea—which lies in the infinite—of a humanity that would live and be in deed and completely in truth and genuineness. It knows its *self*-reflective function for the relative actualization of the correlative practical idea of a, in the *second* sense, genuine life of humanity (the essential forms and practical norms of which it is phenomenology's task to investigate), namely as a life directed consciously and willfully towards that absolute idea" (*EBA*, 299/177). The genuine life is the rational life. The fulfillment of the idea of humanity consists in the complete rationalization of humanity, just as the fulfillment of one's self consists in the rational self. It is phenomenology's task ultimately to bring about both—in an ordered sequence.

Husserl's system defines the "parameters of sense" within which phenomenology, or phenomenological inquiry, is to move. The lowermost limit is the pure ego and the uppermost is absolute reason. This span and the phenomenological reductions that give access to and secure it are constitutive of phenomenology. Both are essential to Husserl's attempt to establish philosophy as rigorous science and thereby to reorient the sciences and humanity as a whole. Looking back in 1930 on his own path, Husserl notes the price of his radicalism: "In the final clarification of their sense, my intentions have been confirmed wonderfully, and the project [*Entwurf*] of a 'philosophy as rigorous science' has come about thereby that secures philosophical communal work progressing to infinity and that has, so to speak, marked out for that work the first map and thus the systematic order of problems [*Problematik*]—a field of infinite, undreamt-of discoveries for future generations. Almost all of my students have gotten stuck in half-measures and have shied away from the radicalism that is essentially necessary to phenomenology, precisely that which makes up my vital element and to which I owe all of my insights. Almost everyone has finitized himself. . . ."[2] Husserl's radicalism is to be taken literally, as has been seen. It is the drive to secure the roots, even the root, of everything. It requires that one abide by the principle of all principles. It requires that one purify oneself by means of the epoché. It requires that one be steadfast in the will to pursue the task of establishing philosophy as a rigorous science. And it requires that one struggle to make the ascent to absolute reason and to lead others along this path. All this is predicated on making the right beginning: on summoning up the will to philosophy as rigorous science, as well as on continuously performing the epoché. Yet this is easier said than done,[3] as became increasingly clear to Husserl in view of his students.[4] Be that as it may, without the necessary will and method, there is no phenomenology. Without them, one necessarily strays from the all-important telos.

The loss of followers was nothing new to Husserl by 1930. Already at the time he fixed his task, that is, when he secured his "transcendental turn" in *Ideas I*, he effectively left behind the followers he had gained after the publication of the *Logical Investigations*.[5] There, too, the break resulted principally because of the introduction of the epoché or transcendental reduction, for his students failed to grasp it in its full significance. As a result, Husserl's radical ethos, his strong will to rigorous science, did not lead to the cultivation of the "community of investigators" he dreamed of. In 1934 this looks unexpectedly different: "It has grown quiet, almost eerily quiet around me. I had to part company in all sharpness with my philosophical 'school' to the extent that it had not already detached itself from me. I am quite alone—in the certainty of having brought about in my life and especially in my continued work in my old age a complete revolution of philosophy never dreamed of before, [a revolution] in which philosophy can have a future alone in the spirit of radical honesty, in sober scientificity, and will make possible the construction of a new humanness in genuine steadfastness. No one understands the deep, novel sense of the order of problems and methodology disclosed by me; everyone is blinded by the passions and prejudices of this age; there is a complete lack of interest in a radical philosophy that tries to get behind every prejudice."[6] What does this say about the so-called phenomenological movement?

While it may be that a rose by any other name would still be a rose, it is certainly not the case that anything called a rose is indeed a rose simply because it is so called. By the same token, phenomenology is not phenomenology simply because it bears this name. If at all, then because of essential determinations. Again, while it may hold—to borrow another poetic word, though this time from modernity—that a rose is a rose is a rose, it is certainly not the case that phenomenology is phenomenology is phenomenology, unless of course one fixes the sense of this term, and in the final analysis that means its essence, which in turn means its task.[7] One must keep one's terms straight. Not simply out of pedantry, but in order to preserve differences.[8] By denying the name 'phenomenology' to any position other than Husserl's, the intention is not to deny the value of that other position. On the contrary, by acknowledging the finitude of the Husserlian project—that is, the parameters it set for itself in its task—it becomes possible to free other positions from the academic continuum and approach them in their own terms, in their own right. This alone enables one to discern the difference they make and thereby to accord their achievements the respect they deserve.

But what about the phenomenological movement? Insofar as it does not seek to fulfill Husserl's task in Husserl's terms, it proves to be a movement *away* from phenomenology. It is precisely a "straying" from the path his task established.

To give an indication of what this means in the best sense, it is helpful to consider two examples from "the" phenomenological movement, which are more than examples, for each marks a limit of a different totality: Heidegger, whose thought concludes and thus marks the limit of modernity, and Merleau-Ponty, who inaugurates submodernity.[9]

Although his break with Husserl is much discussed, it is nevertheless not uncommon for Heidegger to be integrated into the continuum of the phenomenological movement.[10] He himself does not help in this regard, for he occasionally gives the impression of somehow continuing in the phenomenological "tradition." Thus, for example, in "My Way to Phenomenology."[11] However, if one considers his account of phenomenology in light of Husserl's task, it becomes clear that Heidegger's own thought has no place in such a tradition. In order to include him in the continuum of phenomenological inquiry, one would have to privilege similarities at the expense of decisive differences—as is the prevailing habit.[12]

Heidegger describes phenomenology as follows: "The age of phenomenological philosophy seems to be over. It is already regarded as a thing of the past that is only recorded historially alongside other trends [*Richtungen*] in philosophy. But in its ownmost, phenomenology is not a trend. It is the possibility of thinking, at times changing and only thus persisting, of corresponding to the claim of what is to be thought. If phenomenology is thus experienced and retained, it can disappear as a name in favor of the topic of thinking [*Sache des Denkens*] whose manifestness remains a mystery [*Geheimnis*]."[13] Although Heidegger clearly asserts a form of the "principle of all principles" here, that is about all this description has in common with Husserl's elaboration of (transcendental) phenomenology. There is, for instance, no trace of the epoché in Heidegger's positive accounts of phenomenology, and certainly not in accounts of his own thought; such an absence rules out the thematization of the subject from the start. But the most striking difference in this passage is made clear by his 1969 Postscript to this essay in which he cites a passage from *Being and Time* (p. 38): "what is essential to it (phenomenology) does not consist in being *actual* as a 'trend.' Higher than actuality stands *possibility*. The understanding of phenomenology consists solely in grasping it as possibility."[14] Heidegger denies not just that phenomenology is a school of thought, but also that it is a trend, or in other words, that it entails a direction. This is the crucial point of difference here. Whereas Husserl would certainly have agreed that phenomenology aims at grasping possibility, he would have meant *essential* possibility. And this would have entailed the thought of direction, of the direction towards the fulfillment of (the sense of) the essence in question. For him phenomenology has and is a direction insofar as it has an *idea*. But while this idea regulates the possibilities of becoming, it itself is never an actuality. Nor is phenomenology ever an actuality. Rather, it is a constant striving for actualization. Thus, not only does Heidegger implicitly deny the method, but he also denies the path of Husserlian phenomenology and so its proper "topic of thinking," which for Husserl is no "mystery," but at most the "enigma of the world [*Welträtsel*]." In doing so, Heidegger effectively expunges both. By focusing on possibility without direction, Heidegger is thrown out of Husserl's system and onto *Holzwege*—on which phenomenology would persist only in change. Such has its own necessity, its own dignity, but one radically different from that of Husserlian thought.

On this side of the limit of modernity, that is, within submodernity, Merleau-Ponty institutes a "phenomenology" that is expressly at odds with Husserl's endeavor. In his *Phenomenology of Perception* he clearly reformulates the task of phenomenology. He begins this work, appropriately enough, with the question 'What is phenomenology?' After nodding to Husserl's work, however, he says of this question: "The fact remains that it has by no means been answered."[15] But did Husserl not answer this question in each and every one of his works? Did he not establish the system of phenomenology within *Ideas I*? And did he not *live* it? Another text gives Merleau-Ponty's position quite succinctly: "The perceiving mind is an incarnated mind. I have tried, first of all, to re-establish the roots of the mind in its body and in its world, going against doctrines which treat perception as a simple result of the action of external things on our body as well as against those which insist on the autonomy of consciousness."[16] He dispenses with the epoché and all purification and turns back to the world, to the "natural attitude" in Husserl's terminology. This Merleau-Ponty does with the intention of being more radical. In perception he means to find something more original than the pure ego. Thus he says: "Perception is not a science of the world, it is not even an act, a deliberate taking up of a position; it is the background from which all acts stand out, and is presupposed by them. The world is not an object such that I have in my possession the law of its making; it is the natural setting of, and field for, all my thoughts and all my explicit perceptions. Truth does not 'inhabit' only 'the inner man,' or more accurately, there is no inner man, man is in the world, and only in the world does he *know himself*. When I return to myself from an excursion into the realm of dogmatic common sense or of science, I find, not a source of intrinsic truth, but a subject destined to the world."[17] Truth is no longer the correlate of reason, but has become the correlate of bodily being-in-the-world. Man now knows himself *in* the world, that is, he sees himself only in the world and its others. There is no room here for the self in Husserl's sense. There is no longer the prospect of a progression from subjectivity to intersubjectivity along the path leading up to absolute reason, but only intersubjectivity as intercorporeity. Here we are, and here we shall stay—among those of our kind: not like-minded, but rather like-bodied individuals who are individual thanks only to the others.

Not only does Merleau-Ponty reject the primacy of the ego, however, but also that of essence: "We find that perceived things, unlike geometrical objects, are not bounded entities whose laws of construction we possess a priori, but that they are open, inexhaustible systems which we recognize through a certain style of development."[18] Essences no longer play a normative role in Merleau-Ponty's world—not only with regard to the pure ego, but also to the things of this world. In this world of embodiment, not only the construction is ruled out, but the last reminiscence of the laws of construction as well. This results not in the "freedom of essence" that is so crucial to Husserl, but rather in the "freedom from essence," and thus from all constraints: "If we now wish to characterize a subject capable of this perceptual experience, it obviously will not be a self-transparent thought, absolutely present to itself without the interference of its body and its history. The perceiving subject is not this absolute thinker; rather, it functions according to a natal pact between our body and the world, between ourselves and our body. Given a perpetually new natural and historical situation to control, the perceiving subject undergoes a continued birth; at each instant it is something new."[19] Without eidetic norms, becoming continues aimlessly. Life is continuous rebirth, but never the striving for the fulfillment of an essence. This must be the case where not essences but the others are "normative" in their multifarious interactions with me as an embodied subject: "History is other people; it is the interrelationships we establish with them, outside of which the realm of the ideal appears as an alibi,"[20] or in Dummett's terms, a "promissory note."

Can there be any doubt that Husserl's thought has been expunged here in all essentials since its very beginning has been expunged? Can there be any doubt that 'phenomenology' does not name the same thing here as in Husserl's case? Or might one perhaps be able to trace the lines of the continuum leading, say, from Husserl to Heidegger and beyond to Merleau-Ponty? Such would be possible only by ignoring differences, and key differences at that. Neither Heidegger's nor Merleau-Ponty's thought marks a mere transformation of Husserlian phenomenology, that is to say, a mere modification or supplementation, but rather a decisive break with it. Both are quite insistent on this point.

Each breaks out of Husserl's and into his own respective horizon. And necessarily so, for the task proper to each requires it. Only in this way do they distance themselves from the vagaries of the schools and make a difference in the whole of thought.[21]

❦

If the dream of philosophy as rigorous science, if the "dream of phenomenology has been dreamed out,"[22] then only to the extent that Husserl's successors have been or are unable to abide by his task. This would either speak for the mere finitude of Husserlian thought or testify to its having fallen into oblivion. If this has occurred, then it would indicate a possible task: to rescue Husserlian thought from oblivion. This would in turn suggest a twofold possibility: either one is to acknowledge its finitude while giving it thought or one is to seek to resuscitate it in our present—and thus outside Husserl's own present. Pursuing the latter path would mean adopting his task and abiding by it wholly. But where would this task be rooted? Who experiences at all, let alone with the same intensity as did Husserl, the crisis in which he found himself and his fellow Europeans? And if no one, then what would motivate one to attempt to take up Husserl's task if not one's desire for the comfort lent by the illusion of tarrying in the abode of past achievements? By contrast, pursuing the former possibility means allowing what has passed to remain in the past, to let it be, which means approaching the thought in reticence, in full cognizance of its difference and thus honoring the difference it has made. This after having freed oneself from every imagining (*Vorstellung*), from every desire save one: the intention to listen in openness to what has been thought in order to learn from it. These are undoubtedly "hard demands. But nothing less is required" (*Ideas I*, 3).

Postscript

If there is to be a last word, then let it be one of thanks. Here I would like to express my gratitude to all those who have accompanied me through the various phases of this book's composition and have contributed to it in diverse ways, gratitude that will not end with these lines.

Among the friends with whom I have had the good fortune over the years to be able to discuss many of the topics addressed in this book and much else besides, I am indebted especially to Pierre Adler, Alexandre Costa, Friederike-Andrea Dorner, Elisabeth Harth, Guido Heinrich, Sean Leichtle, and Hans Ruin.

I cannot begin to express my gratitude to Heribert Boeder, my teacher and *Doktorvater*, in every sense of the word. It would not be an exaggeration to say that I owe him everything. It was under his direction that the first version of this text was written at the University of Osnabrück (Germany), and it has been his work by which I have taken and continue to take my bearings while seeking to come to terms with the epochally distinct forms and the systemic unity of philosophy. It is his emphasis on everything, that is, his bold appreciation of the whole, that has informed my engagement not only of Husserlian thought.

I should like to thank both the OLB-Foundation in Oldenburg (Germany) and the Lynne and Harry Bradley Foundation in Milwaukee for their generous support while writing the doctoral thesis on which this book is based. Furthermore, I am grateful to the Carl Friedrich von Siemens Foundation in Munich, particularly to its director, Heinrich Meier, and its Board of Directors, for awarding me a postdoctoral fellowship, which has allowed me to profit not only from the stimulating setting and exchanges at the Siemens Foundation, but also has enabled me to further my research and to revise the present work for publication. But my debt to Heinrich Meier does not stop there: he has been both a constant source of encouragement and a tireless practitioner of maieutics, providing me thereby with an unwavering example of what philosophy can be.

I should like to express my thanks also to the State University of New York Press's readers for their helpful remarks on an earlier version of this text, to Jane Bunker and Judith Block at the Press for their tireless assistance, and to Dennis J. Schmidt, not least for including this book in his series.

Munich/Frankfurt a. M., November 2000 M. B.

Notes

Preface

1. That phenomenology and philosophy do not name the same thing on Husserl's understanding is underscored by the title of the inaugural work of transcendental phenomenology, *Ideas Pertaining to a Pure Phenomenology and to a Phenomenological Philosophy*. Pure phenomenology comes first and then phenomenological philosophy. The former founds the latter, gives it its sense, its direction.

2. Letter to Rudolf Otto, dated March 5, 1919 (*BW* 7, 208). (For the conventions used here in citation, both in the body of the text and in the notes, see the prefatory note to the Bibliography. Abbreviations of Husserl's texts precede the titles listed there also.)

3. See II, n. 8.

4. Wert, 210. See "Fünf Aufsätze über Erneuerung" (1922–24), in *Hua* XXVII, 3–124, here 25.

5. See *Hua* XXVII, 26.

6. See, e.g., his Afterword, 549. And see esp. his Preface to Eugen Fink, "Die phänomenologische Philosophie Edmund Husserls in der gegenwärtigen Kritik," *Kant-Studien* 38 (1933), 321 (reprinted in E. F., *Studien zur Phänomenologie 1930–1939*, ed. H. L. van Breda et al. [The Hague: Nijhoff, 1966], vii): "All of the criticisms with which I have become familiar missed the fundamental sense of my phenomenology to such an extent that the latter was not affected in the slightest—despite the quotation of my words." Consider also the following: "No one understands the deep, novel sense of the order of problems and methodology disclosed by me; everyone is blinded by the passions and prejudices of this age; there is a complete lack of interest in a radical philosophy that tries to get behind every prejudice" (*BW* 7, 189). Where there is no interest in it, there can be no "dream of phenomenology." Such would no longer make or have any sense.

7. See Robert Sokolowski, "The Structure and Content of Husserl's *Logical Investigations*," *Inquiry* 14 (1971), 318–47. He notes that the *Investigations* "seem to be a loosely connected series of studies" and claims that this semblance is illusory (ibid.,

319). He supports his claim there by means of his structural analysis of the *Investigations*. Much in the same way, it is our intention here to dispel the cloud of confusion seemingly surrounding and pervading Husserlian thought by drawing out its *sense*, but also the *logic of development* entailed in that sense.

8. See, e.g., Herbert Spiegelberg, *The Phenomenological Movement: A Historical Introduction* (Dordrecht: Nijhoff, 3d rev. ed., 1982), xxviii. Spiegelberg goes so far as to deny the possibility of answering the question 'What is phenomenology?' (see xxvii and 69), for he does not wish to see anything decisive in Husserlian thought for the "movement" to which it gave rise (see xxviii and 69). Spiegelberg's aversion to the inaugural and thus (ideally) unifying character of Husserlian thought with respect to the "movement" is maintained in his "Movements in Philosophy: Phenomenology and Its Parallels," *Philosophy and Phenomenological Research* 43 (1983), 281–97. Particularly intriguing in the latter is his discussion of the affinities between the "phenomenological movement" and "nonphilosophical movements" in the first half of the twentieth century (see 293–94). Karl Schuhmann, in his "Markers on the Road to the Conception of the Phenomenological Movement: Appendix to Spiegelberg's Paper," *Philosophy and Phenomenological Research* 43 (1983), 299–306, here 300, notes that "an awareness of the peculiar status of phenomenology" played a central role in the formation of the "movement." He says in the same context: "The programmatic platform text published first as a flier and which headed the first volume [of the *Jahrbuch für Philosophie und phänomenologische Forschung*] in April 1913, seems especially to have acted as a catalyst in the rise of a feeling of solidarity among phenomenologists in view of a common task." The movement is infused with a sense of "the novelty of its message." The unifying moment in the movement would seem to be nothing less than the ethos that carried Husserl's thought from start to finish, though the movement in question here centers on pretranscendental phenomenology, namely that of the *Logical Investigations*.

9. See, e.g., William R. McKenna, *Husserl's "Introductions to Phenomenology": Interpretation and Critique* (The Hague: Nijhoff, 1982), 1–2 and 18–31.

10. Such a view is reflected, e.g., in A. J. Ayer, *Central Questions of Philosophy* (London: Weidenfeld & Nicolson, 1973) or in Bertrand Russell, *The Problems of Philosophy* (London: Oxford University Press, 1962). Of course, this approach is not restricted to the so-called analytic tradition. Heidegger views the history of philosophy as the history of one "problem," that is, of the Being of beings (see, e.g., the first chapter of *Sein und Zeit* [Tübingen: Niemeyer, 16th ed., 1986]/*Being and Time,* trans. John Macquarrie and Edward Robinson [New York: Harper & Row, 1962]), just as his teacher, Husserl, before him views the history of philosophy, to the extent that he considers it all, as the history of the longing for phenomenology, or for philosophy as rigorous science, hence of the attempt to achieve an ultimate foundation for all thought and knowledge (see *Ideas I*, 118 and *BW* 4, 185 n. 33). This is echoed in Husserl's view of "the spiritual form [*Gestalt*] of Europe": it is said to have one "single infinite task" (see *VL*, 336/299).

11. David Bell is, by his own testimony, not only unable to perform the Husserlian epoché, which for him is reason enough to reject it, but, what is more, he is also unable to perform the other, more radical epoché, namely, the epoché that enables one to approach Husserlian thought in reticence and let it speak for itself. Admirable as his honesty is, Bell's critical stance towards Husserl renders his "introductory" study only

limitedly useful—and certainly not useful to anyone unfamiliar with Husserl. By imposing his views on Husserl, Bell ends up concealing that thought, and ultimately strangling it. Husserl becomes a mere straw man. See David Bell, *Husserl* (New York: Routledge, 1990), 162 concerning Bell's personal difficulties with Husserl's epoché, or as he says, the "phenomenological reduction." Bell in fact confounds the epoché and the phenomenological reduction, and misconstrues their effects; see 164 and 166. See J. N. Mohanty's critique of Bell's book in "Husserl," *Journal of the British Society for Phenomenology* 23 (1992), 280–87.

12. Insofar as one views a thought or its task as the whole and the problems as its parts, one is tempted to borrow one of Robert Sokolowski's insights when describing the prevalent trends in scholarship: "In regard to wholes and parts, phenomenological analysis goes awry essentially by taking a moment for an independent part or for the whole. It takes an abstractum for a concretum." See his *Husserlian Meditations* (Evanston, Ill.: Northwestern University Press, 1974), 16.

13. *Ideas I*, 221; Husserl's emphasis. See also *PRS*, 341 and *Hua* II, 62: "And the whole art consists in purely giving the viewing eye the say [*das Wort lassen*] and excluding the transcending opinions [*Meinen*] that are intermixed with the seeing, [as well as excluding] the supposition of having something co-given, the co-thought, and perhaps that which is indicated by subsequent reflection."

14. For the "paradigm" that guides our reflections, see Heribert Boeder, *Das Vernunft-Gefüge der Moderne* (Freiburg/Munich: Alber, 1988), as well as his *Seditions: Heidegger and the Limit of Modernity*, ed. and trans. M. Brainard (Albany, N.Y.: State University of New York Press, 1997). Decisive here is, on the one hand, his emphasis on the importance of reticence with respect to thought, a reticence we have named the 'logotectonic epoché'. (Boeder's sense of 'epoché' and 'logotectonic' are discussed in *Seditions*. See the following note for references.) Pivotal is, on the other hand, the attention to thought as a whole, which requires that one discern its structure, how it is built. The structure of Husserlian thought is elucidated in what follows precisely as the system of phenomenology.

15. Namely, that of the logotectonic, a "sphere" in which thinking attends not to phenomena but to thought itself. Thought is pure to the extent that it is wrested from historical contingency, which is to say, causation and influence. For the characterization of the logotectonic, as well as of the sense of the epoché operative here, cf. my Introduction to Boeder, *Seditions*, ix–xlix, as well as Boeder's remarks in ibid., 3–4 and 11. For an extended discussion of Husserl's epoché, see II, 57–75, esp. 62–68.

16. It is pure, once again, insofar as it is taken on its own terms. Thought in this respect is nothing phenomenal, nothing dependent on a preceding Being, but belongs to a sphere separate from Being. From the standpoint of the present study, to reduce thought to phenomenon is to commit a *metabasis*. This is admittedly not Husserl's position, and therefore indicates that the framing considerations advanced here—and they are precisely that: framing—have their place outside the horizon of his thought. The advantage of approaching his thought from the outside (and that, among other things, is what we hope to demonstrate here) is that one is in a better position to account for that thought as it articulated itself—provided, of course, that one does not lose sight of what is and what is not properly Husserlian and so does not fall victim to another kind of

metabasis. The logotectonic epoché enables one to give each thought its due—in this case, Husserl's thought.

That we admit that this study is written from a standpoint outside of that proper to Husserlian phenomenology should not decrease the value of the account given here. Rather, this admission is but the responsible first step, we maintain, in engaging any thought—that is, insofar has one seeks to engage in thinking and does not merely take up the banner of this or that party out of mere preference or fancy, one must not only take one's distance from the thought under consideration but one must also recognize—to borrow one of Husserl's insights—that the reflective turn to a thought already implies that one is not living in that thought. Indeed until one has fully grasped the thought, which requires that one grasp its task, one necessarily remains outside the thought. The crucial first step in engaging any thought is to recognize that one is outside of its horizon. Only when armed with this insight into the alterity of the thought in question can one stop taking that thought for granted and ask the truly radical questions: What is it and why? Only after having answered these questions is one in a position to decide in a meaningful way whether it is possible, to say nothing of desirable or legitimate, to seek to continue that thought, even if the continuation in question is one of modification and supplementation (as it usually is in scholarship). It is within the horizon of these questions that the urgency of the issue of a thought's finitude makes itself felt most intensely. With respect to Husserl's endeavor, one then must ask: Is (Husserlian) phenomenology perennial or infinite? And if so, what would that mean? Or is it instead finite? And if so, what are the consequences of its finitude, not only for scholarship, but for thought taken as a whole?

17. See Walter Biemel, "Die entscheidenden Phasen in Husserls Philosophie," in his *Gesammelte Schriften* I: *Schriften zur Philosophie* (Stuttgart: frommann-holzboog, 1996), 59–95, here 60.

18. See *Hua* VIII, 80. Sokolowski describes it as follows: "It means limiting our phenomenological attention to the segment of consciousness actually at work, and 'shutting off' our intending the future and past that stretch beyond [the living present]. This maneuver is like the transcendental reduction in *Ideas I*, in which we bracket the world and its objects, then find them all again as phenomena inside the residue left by reduction; in the case of time, we bracket everything temporally outside the living present, then find it all again inside the present, since even the future and past, as well as forgetfulness, take place there" (*Husserlian Meditations*, 159). The apodictic reduction presupposes the epoché or transcendental reduction, since the field of "apodictic criticism" is that opened by the epoché. See ibid., §61.

19. Numerous introductions to Husserlian phenomenology have already been written, of course, and one specifically on the work in question here—I am thinking of Erazim Kohák's *Idea and Experience: Edmund Husserl's Project of Phenomenology in "Ideas I"* (Chicago: University of Chicago Press, 1978). However, Kohák's book neither treats the whole of this work, nor is he concerned to explicate the sense or task of Husserlian thought in its own terms. His approach lacks the rigor and reticence required especially of an introduction; instead he imposes his own originality, though not in Husserl's sense (see *BW* 7, 207), on *Ideas I*, which tends to obfuscate rather than elucidate the text. Two modes or stages of introduction seem admissible: either the attempt to elicit the task of the thought in question and thus to stay within the bounds it prescribes, or the

move out of the confines of that thought, taking the tools it offers so as to move forward in thought. In view of the stated intention of the present study, it may be said to follow the first approach, at least initially. The second approach is best exemplified by the work of Robert Sokolowski, esp. by his *Introduction to Phenomenology* (Cambridge: Cambridge University Press, 2000). On the basis of his careful exegesis of the Husserlian corpus over the years, he has worked himself free of Husserl's task and instead seeks to move phenomenology into a new horizon, much as did Merleau-Ponty. He makes no claim to present *Husserlian* phenomenology in the work cited, though his is definitely a phenomenology that has learned from Husserl especially.

20. Note that it is by no means an attempt to present a synthesis of Husserl's various introductions to phenomenology, as McKenna has done in *Husserl's "Introductions to Phenomenology."* While such an approach may be instructive, and McKenna's text certainly is, it seems unnecessary to seek to improve on Husserl's own introductions. *Ideas I* provides *the* introduction, and it is precisely on account of this that we shall focus on it here. It is Husserl's second "breakthrough" work. The first, as he never tired of saying, was the *Logical Investigations*. The centrality of *Ideas I* within this corpus becomes evident once the parameters of Husserl's system have been made evident.

21. Rather than become embroiled in the debates surrounding certain key issues in Husserlian thought, the most prominent of which is currently focused on the noema, we thus follow Husserl's example of not entering into the debate centering on epistemological or other problems for their own sake. In order to remain true to the course of *Ideas I*, he notes that he "must remain in a state of innocence." See *Hua* III/2, 279, as well as ibid., 559.4–6.

22. "Jede Veränderung geht in der Zeit vor sich. Danach müßte sich die Analysis mit einem zeitlichen Geschehen beschäftigen, indem sie Veränderliche ihrer Betrachtung unterwirft. Nun hat sie aber mit der Zeit nichts zu schaffen; denn daß sie auf zeitliche Vorgänge angewendet werden kann, tut nichts zur Sache." Gottlob Frege, "Was ist eine Funktion?" in *Kleine Schriften*, ed. I. Angelelli (Hildesheim: Olms, 1967), 273–80, here 273.

Chapter I. Introduction: The Task Of Thinking

1. See, e.g., Rudolf Bernet, Iso Kern, and Eduard Marbach, *Edmund Husserl. Darstellung seines Denkens* (Hamburg: Meiner, 1989), 83, where Husserl is cited on, among other things, the relationship between essence and time: "If through ideation 'only the universal essence itself, so to speak, the idea,' is brought out, then we have 'a unity that is not in any flux, that is only singularized in the flowing, but that thereby is not itself drawn into the flux. Ideas or essences are "supratemporal" objectualities, essences of phenomenological givens are free of the individuation through phenomenological temporality, of individualization in the change from Now to Has-been that belongs to the phenomenological individual as such' (Ms. F I 17, p. 140)." Contrary to first appearances, the claim made at the outset that essences are formal and not material is not contradicted by Husserl's thematization of formal and material essences, for these are simply essences that bear on the formal and material spheres, respectively. Nor does the constitution of essences call into question their atemporality. As the passage just

quoted suggests, such constitution consists in drawing them out by means of ideation. For discussions of the constitution of essences, which will not be addressed in the present study, see chapter 3 ("How to Intuit an Essence") of Robert Sokolowski, *Husserlian Meditations*, 57–85. Vincenzo Costa also discusses this topic briefly in his "Transcendental Aesthetic and the Problem of Transcendentality," in N. Depraz and D. Zahavi, eds., *Alterity and Facticity: New Perspectives on Husserl* (Dordrecht: Kluwer, 1998), 9–27, here 19.

2. On the systematic, rather than merely chronological, relationship between static and genetic analysis, see Donn Welton, "Der andere Husserl," *Phänomenologische Forschungen* 24/25 (1991), 116–48, here 124–37, esp. 126. See also his "Structure and Genesis in Husserl's Phenomenology," in F. A. Elliston and P. McCormick, eds., *Husserl: Expositions and Appraisals* (Notre Dame, Ind.: University of Notre Dame Press, 1977), 54–69, esp. 56–62.

3. See *SGM*, 340 n. 1/152 n. 28. See also *EBA*, 286.23ff./167.

4. See Husserl's Introduction to *FTL*, 1–15.

5. That is, they often mean the same when Husserl speaks of phenomenology or philosophy or man, but then he uses the terms in a less rigorous sense. Although the relationship between essence and sense, to mention only the two central members of the foregoing list, is an extremely complex issue in Husserlian thought, one still unclear in many respects, the following general observations can be made. Each belongs to a different sphere: essence, to the ontological; sense, to the semantic, linguistic. They are parallel, but not of equal rank. Namely, insofar as it delimits the possibilities that may be realized in its corresponding individuals, essence may be said to encompass sense, for the latter may be regarded as picking out one possibility among those defined by the relevant essence. Accordingly, sense would be subject to the norm of that essence or any constellation of essences of which it "makes use." The predelineation integral to a noema is made possible by the preceding predelineation of its corresponding essence. The analyses making up *Ideas I* suggest this hierarchy, which should become clearer in the course of the present study. On the relationship and distinction between sense, or noema, and essence, see *Ideas III*, § 16. See also J. N. Mohanty, "Noema and Essence," in J. J. Drummond and L. Embree, eds., *The Phenomenology of the Noema* (Dordrecht: Kluwer, 1992), 49–55, as well as his "Husserl's Transcendental Phenomenology and Essentialism," in *The Possibility of Transcendental Philosophy* (Dordrecht: Kluwer, 1985), 191–212, and "Husserl's Theory of Meaning," in F. A. Elliston and P. McCormick, eds., *Husserl: Expositions and Appraisals* (Notre Dame, Ind.: University of Notre Dame Press, 1977), 18–37, esp. 27–33. The normative function of essence with respect to sense has not been sufficiently addressed in the literature, though Mohanty has taken steps in this direction, esp. in his paper on Husserl's "essentialism," as has Sokolowski in *Husserlian Meditations*, § 23. See II, n. 11 for a sampling of the key contributions on essence in Husserl.

As for the relationship between essence and sense with regard to phenomenology and philosophy, Husserl's claim is that there is *one* essence of philosophy to which phenomenology alone has gained access in its purity. There have been many philosophies, all of which have striven after the same goal or telos, but which have failed to achieve the telos and thereby fulfill the essence of philosophy. Here it seems that the individual philosophies represented several of the possibilities prescribed by the essence of philosophy. And yet, not all these possibilities are of equal rank, as Husserl's remarks make clear. Namely, phenomenology alone has gained possession of the radical insight into both its own essence and that of philosophy; the former may be said to be the heart of the latter. And insofar as it has grasped this essence most adequately, it seems that telos, sense, idea, and essence coincide; they are ultimately synonymous in this context. The striving peculiar to phenomenology is a striving after these in their oneness. Similarly, man's striving to fulfill his essence or idea or sense, and to achieve his telos, is one and the same striving. But the coincidence of these terms seems to be restricted to certain "spiritual formations," such as phenomenology, philosophy, culture, humanity. They are distinct at the level of individual acts of consciousness. Concerning the foregoing sketch of Husserl's notion of the oneness of the telos and essence of philosophy, see esp. *Hua* XXIX, 406–12, as well as the remainder of this introduction. On the regulative function of the idea, see James G. Hart, "I, We, and God: Ingredients of Husserl's Theory of Community," in S. IJsseling, ed., *Husserl-Ausgabe und Husserl-Forschung* (Dordrecht: Kluwer, 1990), 125–49, here 125–27. See also Hans Rainer Sepp, *Praxis und Theoria. Husserls Transzendentalphänomenologische Rekonstruktion des Lebens* (Freiburg/Munich: Alber, 1997), 117.

6. See Eugen Fink, "Die Entwicklung der Phänomenologie Edmund Husserls," in *Nähe und Distanz* (Freiburg/Munich: Alber, 1976), 45–74, here 72 (his emphasis): "The fundamental problem of a philosophy is not only not a 'preliminary stage,' not a question that is related to an 'answer'; rather, it is, as the path of its [i.e., the fundamental problem's] inner unfolding, the *entire philosophy*, the horizon that comprehends all philosophical knowledge and the full thematic. The greatness of the problem's unfolding [*Problementfaltung*] as the true scope of the creative projection of the problem [*Problementwurf*] is the greatness of a philosophy." What Fink calls the 'fundamental problem' here is what is referred to within the present study as the 'task' of a thought.

7. The oneness of Husserlian thought is underscored, e.g., in a letter to Arnold Metzger, dated September 4, 1919, where Husserl says of his own thought that "no development has ever been straighter, more goal-oriented, more predestined, more 'daimonic'" (*BW* 4, 412). This contention is repeated some twelve years later to Dorion Cairns, as he reports in his *Conversations with Husserl and Fink* (The Hague: Nijhoff, 1976), 106 (June 27, 1931): "Nie vorher ist eine Wissenschaft von einem Mensch [*sic*] von einem Standpunkt aus so weit getrieben. ([Cairns's] Explanation: Never before has one man developed a science all alone and to such a high degree without changing his standpoint.)" A more literal translation of the German would read: "Never before has a science been carried so far by one man from one standpoint." See Ubaldo R. Pérez-Paoli, "Husserl und die Aufgabe der Philosophie," *Mitteilungen der TU Braunschweig* 24, no. 3 (1989), 46–50.

8. The manifold of particular approaches are gathered into the one thought: ξυμβάλλειν εἰς ἕν (see *Hua* XIX/1, 160).

9. In the Introduction to their edition of *The Cambridge Companion to Husserl* (Cambridge: Cambridge University Press, 1995), 1–44, here 13, Barry Smith and David Woodruff Smith claim that Husserl's various approaches "should lead us to view his philosophy as a unity and to avoid giving total precedence to any single element. To see his philosophy as having its foundations exclusively in either phenomenology or ontology or epistemology (the claims of each have been advanced) is to miss the mutual depen-

dence among the different aspects of his thinking." We would concur with this view, though with the qualification that the unity of various aspects of and approaches employed in Husserlian thought must not be seen as equivalent, but rather as related to one another in a hierarchy. No one of these approaches will tell the whole story, but one of them will provide the basis for the articulation of the others. And even if it is supplemented at some point by the results of the other two approaches, its founding role will not be compromised. See, e.g., the opening remarks above on the difference and relationship between static and genetic analysis. On a similar note, Dagfinn Føllesdal asserts that "Husserl never was a foundationalist," but instead "developed more and more in the direction of a quite extreme holism"; see his "Husserl on Evidence and Justification," in R. Sokolowski, ed., *Edmund Husserl and the Phenomenological Tradition* (Washington, D. C.: Catholic University of America Press, 1988), 107–29, here 107. The passage he cites (114 and 122) in support of his central claim is from the *Cartesian Meditations*, 62.9–10. There he considers Husserl to have cast doubt on the apodicticity of the pure ego by means of a 'perhaps'. But if one examines the context of the passage, one will see that it is not the apodicticity of the pure ego that is placed in question, but rather the extent to which it is apodictic. Husserl says: "Thus in a similar way the apodictic certainty of transcendental experience concerns my transcendental *I am* in the indeterminate universality attached to it of an open horizon. The being-actual of the in-itself-first ground of cognition accordingly stands absolutely firm, but not automatically what determines its Being more precisely, and what during the living evidence of the *I am* is not yet given itself but only presumed." That the pure ego is, is absolutely certain; what it is, however, can be known only more or less adequately. It is to the latter that the 'perhaps' pertains. If Husserl is a holist, then he is an oriented holist, for he is convinced he has located an absolute beginning. He aims at a whole in which all its aspects are in complete harmony, but the whole is hierarchically structured and extends from bottom to top.

10. Essence is an abiding concern for Husserl, contrary to the claims of Vincenzo Costa and Merleau-Ponty, whom Costa cites (see Costa, "Transcendental Aesthetic," 18).

11. Phenomenology is to be a normative discipline insofar as it brings to light the norms, which lie in essence. However, in doing so, it does not determine what is "best," or only in very few cases, specifically concerning the intertwined essences of thought and of man. The phenomenologist is first and foremost concerned with displaying the range of possibilities. In most cases, it is up to other, subsequent disciplines to determine what is best among the possibilities and so what is to be striven after. Herman Philipse sheds much light on phenomenology and normativity in his article "Psychologism and the Prescriptive Function of Logic," *Grazer Philosophische Studien* 29 (1987), 13–33. On Husserl's understanding of the firstness of phenomenology, see Jeffner Allen, "What is Husserl's First Philosophy?" *Philosophy and Phenomenological Research* 42 (1982), 610–20. The premise of Peter H. Spader's paper, "Phenomenology and the Claiming of Essential Knowledge," *Husserl Studies* 11 (1994), 169–99, is that Husserl failed to account for the normative function of essence and thus failed to develop phenomenology adequately as a normative discipline.

12. See, e.g., his remark to Winthrop Pickard Bell in a letter from August 11, 1920 (*BW* 3, 16.16–17): "all theory means nothing to me except [to bring about] a new world." See also *Hua* XXIX, 377 and Ms. K III 9, p. 64a, cited in Karl Schuhmann,

Husserls Staatsphilosophie (Freiburg/Munich: Alber, 1988), 176. In his Introduction to Edmund Husserl, *Phenomenology and the Crisis of Philosophy* (New York: Harper & Row, 1965), 1–68, here 7, Quentin Lauer notes the salvational character of Husserl's task. However, it should be noted that phenomenology is itself not primarily practical, but at base a theoretical enterprise, which *in turn* is to found all future practice. On the priority of theory over practice see, e.g., *Ideas III*, 80.26ff. Phenomenology is literally the beginning science, for it is to enable all other endeavors insofar as it dispenses with the "lack of clarity," which naturally hampers those endeavors; such is first and foremost a lack of clarity on their "beginnings." For a specification of what can count as phenomenology, see ibid., 81.

In recent years, increasing attention has been paid to the practical dimension or the "ethical impulse" of Husserlian thought. See the outstanding work of James G. Hart, esp. his *The Person and the Common Life: Studies in a Husserlian Social Ethics* (Dordrecht: Kluwer, 1992), and Hans Rainer Sepp, esp. his *Praxis und Theoria*. They confirm throughout our thesis of the practical intention of Husserlian phenomenology, while going beyond the parameters of the present study. Significant contributions in this connection have also been made by Ullrich Melle, G. Hoyos Vásquez, and Christine Spahn. Schuhmann's *Husserls Staatsphilosophie* also provides insight into this dimension of Husserlian thought.

13. See Husserl's preface to the second edition (*Hua* XVIII, B viii) concerning the inaugural character of this work. See also *Hua* XIX/1, A 4 [6.30ff.].

14. See, e.g., *Crisis*, 275/340. See also the supplementary material to *Hua* VI in *Hua* XXIX.

15. See, e.g., *FTL*, 1–15, esp. 11–12 and 7–8.

16. The status of this absolute, Archimedean point would seem to be placed in question by Husserl's remark in *Ideas I*, 162–63 (see III, 127–28) that the ego has "its primal source in the ultimate and truly absolute." This is consonant with the principle of all principles, of course. The ego as the source of sense is such "in response to" the preceding Being of the stream of lived experiences (*Erlebnisstrom*) and its temporality. However, this gives rise to an apparent tension in Husserlian thought, since it seems to undermine Husserl's endeavor by decentering it or depriving it of the absolute starting point or foundation Husserl was so certain he had found. Indeed this decentering of the absolute, and thus the seeming self-dissolution of Husserlian thought, has received increasing attention of late. The tendency has been to neglect the ego's primacy in search of that "ultimate and truly absolute," and in fact by pursuing either of two interrelated directions. On the one hand, the focus has been on the stream of lived experiences or the hyletic data that affect the ego (see, e.g., Sepp, *Praxis und Theoria*, 32–41; Liangkang Ni, "Urbewußtsein und Reflexion bei Husserl," *Husserl Studies* 15 (1998), 77–99; Sokolowski, *Husserlian Meditations*, 10; and Hart, *The Person and the Common Life*, 59ff.). On the other hand, stress has been laid on the horizon in which the ego finds itself, a horizon held to have priority over that ego insofar as it *affects* the ego (see, e.g., Denis Fisette, "The Horizon of the Self: Husserl on Indexicals," in D. Zahavi, ed., *Self-Awareness, Temporality, and Alterity* [Dordrecht: Kluwer, 1998], 119–35, and Dan Zahavi, "Horizontal Intentionality and Transcendental Intersubjectivity," *Tijdschrift voor Filosofie* 59 [1997], 304–21). Both directions focus, whether directly or indirectly, on a peculiar kind of egoic passivity—that is, the way in which the ego receives what is given and so is secondary to the preceding source of the given. Though important, nei-

ther of these directions of inquiry places the approach of the present study in question, for it is concerned with the beginning relative to the end, or with the sense-bestowing ego relative to reason. No matter how important the passive dimension of egoic life is, it is prespontaneous, which is to say, prior to the activity of the will. Only where the will is active, can there be reason. What is more, the ego's passivity gains its significance only in contrast to its activity. Whereas this passivity may naturally be first, systematically it is activity with which one must begin. The movement of phenomenology is possible only because it begins with such activity. The pivotal distinction is that between beginning and origin. The hyletic stratum may be the origin, but it is not the beginning, at least not in and of Husserlian phenomenology. What is more, in light of the necessary correlation between ego and stream, it is difficult to say which is first, since consciousness is nothing without both. The absoluteness of either is relative. The ego is first, or absolute, with regard to sense.

Incidentally, the thematization of the ego's passivity and affectivity goes hand in hand with that of instinct. The prevailing interest seems to be in how spontaneity grows out of passivity, which is of a piece with the question concerning how reason arises out of irrationality or instinct. Furthermore, this is connected with the question of the status of God in Husserlian thought. Some wish to see God in the hyletic stratum, thus the "source" of rationality in the irrational, or, in other, somewhat hyperbolic terms, that absolute reason is absolute unreason. On this and related issues see I, n. 51.

17. See, e.g., Roman Ingarden, *On the Motives which led Husserl to Transcendental Idealism*, trans. Arnór Hannibalsson (The Hague: Nijhoff, 1975). See also Ludwig Landgrebe, "Husserls Phänomenologie und die Motive zu ihrer Umbildung," in *Der Weg der Phänomenologie* (Gütersloh: Gerd Mohn, 1963), 9–39.

18. In his "Transcendental Idealism," in B. Smith and D. W. Smith, eds., *The Cambridge Companion to Husserl* (Cambridge: Cambridge University Press, 1995), 239–322, here 262, Herman Philipse rightly notes that it is difficult to trace the development of Husserl's transcendental idealism from the *Logical Investigations* to *Ideas I* because he "covers over the tracks of the genesis of this doctrine, which was born from tensions in the first edition" of the former. Hence, we suggest, the first rather than the second edition of the *Investigations* should be the center of attention, followed by *Ideas I*, and only then the second edition of the former work when seeking to grasp the said development, an undertaking that, in its particulars, exceeds the parameters of the present study. It is precisely in order to avoid the difficulties posed by Husserl's subsequent, often confusing clarifications that we shall focus on the first edition of *Ideas I*.

19. Were the "turn" a break, there would be little sense in Husserl's (positive) appeal to the *Logical Investigations* throughout the later phases of his thought.

20. See *Ideas I*, 179–80, where Husserl describes the path leading from the level of the *Logical Investigation* down to the level reached in *Ideas I*.

21. See I, nn. 5–7. See also Eugen Fink's "preliminary remarks" to Husserl's "Draft" ("Entwurf einer 'Vorrede' zu den *Logischen Untersuchungen* [1913]"), 107: "The inner unity of the 'three phases' [of Husserl's work], as the history of the radicalization of one problem, has yet to be grasped in most cases because the usual interpretations follow the chronology of the works instead of, conversely, starting out from the final form of the phenomenological problematic and interpreting the preliminary forms that are striving to reach it." Concerning the "usual account" of the three phases or stages of

Husserlian thought, see Barry Smith and David Woodruff Smith, Introduction, 1. They regard Husserlian thought as being a systematic unity, while also embedding it in the philosophical tradition and denying the distinction as a very modern position from contemporary, "postmodern" positions (2–3).

22. See *Hua* III/2, 569: "Phenomenological inquiry is moving in its beginnings, and it will remain at the stage of its beginnings for a long time yet, unavoidably in a zigzag." The nondialectical reading runs counter to Karl Schuhmann's main thesis in his "trilogy," *Die Fundamentalbetrachtung der Phänomenologie. Zum Weltproblem in der Philosophie Edmund Husserls* (The Hague: Nijhoff, 1971); *Die Dialektik der Phänomenologie* I: *Husserl über Pfänder* (The Hague: Nijhoff, 1973); and *Die Dialektik der Phänomenologie* II: *Reine Phänomenologie und phänomenologische Philosophie. Historisch-analytische Monographie über Husserls "Ideen I"* (The Hague: Nijhoff, 1973). Schuhmann implies, e.g., in his preface to the latter work that Husserl progressed along the lines of the Platonic dialectic (see ibid., viii), which in Husserlian thought is rooted in the tension between the "concept" of phenomenology and its "genesis" (see, e.g., ibid., 7). Informative as his "trilogy" is, Schuhmann's account of the dialectic "operative" in Husserlian thought remains unconvincing; it is incomplete because it misses what is essential and most radical in Husserl. This becomes clear when one sees that the development of Husserlian thought—so the guiding thesis of the present study—can be better elucidated with reference to Husserl's task, the system it prescribes, and the struggle to make his way down the path that that system is for him, which is to say, teleologically. The talk of dialectic adds nothing essential to one's understanding of Husserl so long as one has not fixed the telos towards which he strives. As for the "thematic" use of dialectic, Boyce Gibson records Husserl's ill regard of it (in W. R. Boyce Gibson, "From Husserl to Heidegger: Excerpts from a 1928 Freiburg Diary," ed. H. Spiegelberg, *Journal of the British Society for Phenomenology* 2 [1971], 58–81, here 66 col. 1): "Here Husserl was firm. Dialectic of all kinds is unnecessary, superfluous." On the other hand, Cairns (*Conversations*, 52; November 24, 1931) reports the following: "He described the teleological process as one of reconciliation of opposites, as a dialectic process." Again, it is first and foremost the telos that determines this process.

23. See *PN*, 296. See I, n. 26 for Cairns's report according to which Husserl describes the phenomenological method as a process of "dismantling" (*Abbau*) and reconstruction—again, one first moves down to the ground and only thereafter up into the heights.

24. See *PRS*, 290–91.

25. It has become almost a cliché to point to the more than 40,000 pages of Husserl's shorthand manuscripts as an excuse for not coming to terms with the whole of his thought. That such an account is nevertheless possible, however, is one of the principal theses of the present study. But it does not stand alone in this respect. Examples of valuable works that have sought to come to terms with the *whole* of Husserlian thought, despite the extent of his productivity, are provided by: Elisabeth Ströker, *Husserls transzendentale Phänomenologie* (Frankfurt a. M.: Klostermann, 1987); Biemel, "Die entscheidenden Phasen in Husserls Philosophie"; Boeder, *Das Vernunft-Gefüge der Moderne*, 135–87; Sepp, *Praxis und Theoria*; Hart, *The Person and the Common Life*; and James R. Mensch, *Intersubjectivity and Transcendental Idealism* (Albany, N.Y.: State

University of New York Press, 1988). Needless to say, each work determines this whole differently.

26. Letter to Daniel Martin Feuling, O.S.B., dated March 30, 1933 (*BW* 7, 89.26–30). See Cairns, *Conversations*, 65 (January 13, 1932): "By the method of *Abbau* <unbuilding> we are led not only to differentiate structural levels but also to 'reconstruct' an actual temporal process in which the lower levels preceded the higher ones." See *Hua* XXIX, 417.36ff. on 'turning points' (*Wenden*) and 'rupture points' (*Bruchstellen*) and their importance for discerning the motivation of a new movement. Husserl speaks of *Sinngestalt* in this context as well. Twenty years earlier he points to the relationship between teleology and clarification or justification (*Ideas III*, 94): "A strange teleology prevails in the development of human culture in general, and thus also in scientific culture, [such] that valuable products can arise without insight or through a mixture of insight and instinct in the workings of psychic forces. That they are valuable is shown, of course, by a subsequent justification, which proves the claims to validity, within the bounds of complete insight." This structure has counterparts, e.g., in the relationship between consciousness and the unconscious, as well as in that between reflection and lived experience and between ἐπιστήμη and δόξα. See I, 24–26 on such polarities.

27. See *PP*, 286.

28. See Ms. B I 5 V, p. 23 (cited in Costa, "Transcendental Aesthetic," 19): "I must first have the Apriori of the static correlation in order to inquire into the 'genesis of this Apriori,' as the genesis of concrete subjectivity and its correlative 'world'" (my translation).

29. For a historical account of the term 'phenomenology,' see Karl Schuhmann, "'Phänomenologie': Eine begriffsgeschichtliche Reflexion," *Husserl Studies* 1 (1984), 31–68.

30. See Preface, xv–xvi.

31. See Boeder, *Das Vernunft-Gefüge der Moderne*, 15–19 et passim.

32. Ernst Wolfgang Orth surveys the chief issues in the debate surrounding the *Crisis* in his *Edmund Husserls "Krisis der europäischen Wissenschaften und die transzendentale Phänomenologie". Vernunft und Kultur* (Darmstadt: Wissenschaftliche Buchgesellschaft, 1999), 9–28. At bottom, the debate centers on the makeup of the "real" text, the various parts of which are contained in *Hua* VI and *Hua* XXIX. Such questions cannot concern us here, especially as they in no way jeopardize the reading of the *Crisis* presented in what follows. Our focus is on the *intention* elaborated in that work, an intention that permeates each of its component parts.

33. See Husserl's remarks as recorded in Cairns, *Conversations*, 8 (August 13, 1931): "Our culture [has been] determined fundamentally by the ideal of science, which first appeared in Greece and continued, though mixed with other elements. Today the ideal has been lost, though the technic which is the result of science remains. But the culture itself must find its renewal in a rediscovery and thorough working out of the idea of science: phenomenology. The crisis, the impasse, of culture [is] shown by the fact that the *young* today are dissatisfied. Before it has been the old." J. N. Mohanty touches on the disharmony or rupture that results in a crisis of greater or lesser extent in his "Husserl on 'Possibility'," *Husserl Studies* 1 (1984), 13–29, here 23–24.

34. See *Hua* XXVII, 23.

35. In light of the guiding role Husserl accords phenomenology, it becomes clear as the work unfolds that the conjunction in the title of the *Crisis* actually marks the place of an exclusive disjunction, of a vital decision: *either* the crisis and the doom it entails if allowed to run its course *or* transcendental phenomenology. On this disjunction see *VL*, 347–48/299. That Husserl intended his "introductions to phenomenology" to lead to such a decision is evident from a letter he wrote to Dorion Cairns, who had informed Husserl of his plans to translate his *Formal and Transcendental Logic*: "for the guidance upward to the Gate to the Castle of the Grail, [which leads] to the reduction and to the compulsion [to make] a philosophical decision, this work is the best" (September 19, 1935; *BW* 4, 51: "zur Emporleitung bis an das Thor der Gralsburg zur Reduktion und zum Zwang einer philosophischen Entscheidung ist dieses Werk das Beste"). In what way it is the "best" remains unclear. On this point, see I, 29–30.

36. Husserl's estimation of the point at which the present crisis first arose—namely, after and in reaction to Hegel on the one hand and in the mid-nineteenth century on the other—is maintained from no later than "Philosophy as Rigorous Science" (see *PRS*, 292–93) and up through the *Crisis* (see 3/5–6). In view of a remark made on *Hua* XXIX, 228, it seems that Husserl regards his age, or modernity in our terms, as beginning with Schopenhauer.

37. For an alternative account of the source of the crisis in which not only Husserl, but the whole of modernity found itself, see Heribert Boeder, *Topologie der Metaphysik* (Freiburg/Munich: Alber, 1980), 701; *Das Vernunft-Gefüge der Moderne*, 16, 369, 375; and *Seditions*, 9, 15. In their light, it becomes clear that the skepticism Husserl blames for the crisis is actually a response to an absence that is brought about by the conclusion of metaphysics with Hegel.

38. See *Crisis*, 11/13: "Viewed from within, the history of philosophy takes on ever more the character of a fight for existence, namely as the fight of the philosophy that lives out its task directly—of philosophy invested with a naive belief in reason—against the skepticism that either negates it or devalues it empiricistically."

39. Husserl entered into this struggle already in his *Prolegomena zur reinen Logik* (1900). See Pierre Adler's insightful study on the context of Husserl's struggle with skepticism in the form of psychologism, as well as on the "weapons" Husserl employed in order to secure his first victory: "Prolegomena to Phenomenology: Intuition or Argument?" *Graduate Faculty Philosophy Journal* 16 (1992), 3–76, esp. 31–48. See also Walter Biemel, "Die Idee der Phänomenologie bei Husserl," in *Gesammelte Schriften* I, 147–71, here 153; he identifies Husserl's task as the "confrontation of skepticism, the fight against it."

40. In his 1935 Vienna lecture, entitled "The Crisis of European Humanness and Philosophy," Husserl says: "The European nations are ill; Europe is, they say, in crisis." And just prior to this observation, he asks: "How is it that . . . a scientific medicine, a medicine for nations and supranational communities has never been developed?" (*VL*, 315/270). For Husserl, the cause of this illness is a lack of belief in reason; the remedy for it is phenomenology. Five years before Husserl's lecture, Sigmund Freud asked a similar question, although he diagnosed the illness differently, as well as its remedy. For him its cure was not to be found in phenomenology, of course, but in psychoanalysis. See his *Das Unbehagen in der Kultur* (1930), in *Sigmund Freud, Fragen der Gesellschaft / Ursprünge der Religion*, Freud-Studienausgabe IX (Frankfurt a. M.: Fischer, 7th ed.,

1994), 191–270. Note that also in the account Husserl gives in his lecture, the crisis and philosophy are opposed, and that philosophy responds to a preceding crisis. Regarding Husserl's views on the source of crisis and its remedy, see a passage from Boyce Gibson's dairy, dated May 20, 1928 ("Freiburg Diary," 65 col. 1): "He has strong feelings, and it is chiefly—so I gather from his conversation—the tremendous effect of the war upon his Lebens and Welt-anschauung, his inability to see Reason at work in the world . . . that makes him regard all Lebens-and-Welt-anschauungen [life- and world-views] as *Privat*, and concentrate on the Pure *Apriori* Reason of Phenomenology as the sole field in which one's faith in Reason can have its perfect way."

41. Elisabeth Ströker provides an overview of the circumstances in which phenomenology emerged in the latter part of the nineteenth century in her and Paul Janssen's *Phänomenologische Philosophie* (Freiburg/Munich: Alber, 1989), 15–35. See also J. N. Mohanty, "The Development of Husserl's Thought," in B. Smith and D. W. Smith, eds., *The Cambridge Companion to Husserl* (Cambridge: Cambridge University Press, 1995), 45–77, as well as Christian Möckel, *Einführung in die transzendentale Phänomenologie* (Munich: Fink, 1998) and the essays and documents presented in Hans Rainer Sepp, ed., *Edmund Husserl und die phänomenologische Bewegung* (Freiburg/Munich: Alber, 1988).

42. Admittedly, the 1890s could be added to this period, especially as that decade was in effect the "incubation period" of the *Logical Investigations*. However, of concern here is principally the first point of "solidification" of phenomenology as such—that is, the point at which Husserl's thought gives definitive evidence of having come into its own. As a matter of convenience we take this point to be the publication dates of that first work of phenomenology (1900–01). Regarding the crisis of European culture, Husserl's earliest extended treatment of it, albeit less explicitly than in the *Crisis*, is found in "Philosophy as Rigorous Science" (1911); thereafter it becomes increasingly of concern to him. For instance, it is touched upon in his Fichte lectures of 1917 and is given considerable attention—couched in terms of the "renewal of humanity"—in his *Kaizo* articles. For the latter, see "Fünf Aufsätze über Erneuerung" (1922–24), in *Hua* XXVII, 3–124. On the topic of renewal in Husserl, see Hans Rainer Sepp, "Husserl über Erneuerung. Ethik im Schnittfeld von Wissenschaft und Sozialität," in H.-M. Gerlach and H. R. Sepp, eds., *Husserl in Halle. Spurensuche im Anfang der Phänomenologie* (Frankfurt a. M.: Peter Lang, 1994), 111–30. For the Fichte lectures, see "Fichtes Menschheitsideal (Drei Vorlesungen 1917)," in *Hua* XXV, 267–293; "Fichte's Ideal of Humanity (Three Lectures, 1917)," trans. James G. Hart, *Husserl Studies* 12 (1995), 111–133. On the latter, cf. Hart's "Afterword" to his translation: "Husserl and Fichte: With Special Regard to Husserl's Lectures on 'Fichte's Ideal of Humanity,'" ibid., 135–63.

43. See the letter to Arnold Metzger, September 4, 1919; *BW* 4, 408.11–20. In his talk of "practical and cultural realities" Husserl tacitly appeals to a key distinction in his thought, namely between realities (*Realitäten*) and actualities (*Wirklichkeiten*). The former is the sphere of facts, the latter that of ideas. Thus his theoretical work in the germinal phase of phenomenology was concerned almost exclusively with ideas; it is only later that he takes notice of the factual.

44. See *BW* 4, 407–14, esp. 408–9 and 412–13.

45. This becomes particularly clear in the final phase of Husserl's thought, well before the *Crisis*. For instance, in his *Conversations* (35–36) Cairns reiterates Husserl's remarks from September 22, 1931, on "the highest goals of life" and the unethical, both of which prove to be practical determinations based upon theoretical considerations: "Fink suggested that the individual still had to *live* in the world of naive *Geltung* <acceptance, position, validity>, as a practical being had to. Husserl replied that this was not true as regards the highest goals of life, which are the goals of the transcendental ego." "The whole of life and the activity of self-constitution and the constitution of objects, is guided by a telos, is directed toward the achievement of consistency or harmony. The unethical is that which is contrary to this telos. In the individual, *Ehrlichkeit* <honesty> is a characteristic of self-consistency. Acts of all sorts that I cannot affirm genuinely are unethical. This is applicable not merely to the individual but also to society. The harmony of monads is something to be striven towards. I must be able to affirm the acts of others as well as my own acts. Husserl quoted Dostoievsky as saying that each is guilty for the guilt of all [see ibid., n.]. There are various levels of *Einstimmigkeit* <harmony>. The ultimate goal may be called *Seligkeit* <bliss, blessedness>." "In addition to our common goal as human beings, we have, each of us, a special calling, *Beruf*, that we must hearken to. (Here and elsewhere the religious formulation is to be taken as a symbol.) The universal harmony reckons on me and on my freedom. It is easy to say, be *ehrlich* <honest>, but it is a frightening task to carry out the injunction."

46. At first glance, this would seem to be expressly contradicted by a remark Husserl made to Metzger in 1919 (*BW* 4, 409): "That which has been worked out by me theoretically, if I may say so, in the most passionate will to honesty and in the most fervently doubting self-criticism, requires your understanding study and then comes the powerful task originarily meant for you, the study of the realities of humanity and their philosophical elucidation and guidance. That is not my task; I am not called to be the leader of the humanity which struggles for the 'blessed life'—in the sorrowful distress of the war years I had to acknowledge that; my Daimonion warned me." On the other hand, he is providing the *theoretical* basis for praxis. And in that sense it is legitimate to see the juncture of the theoretical and the practical in his thought. In his book *Praxis und Theoria* Hans Rainer Sepp goes a long way in explaining the connection between theory and praxis in Husserl's thought.

47. In September 1917 Husserl makes the following note on the folder of the "Seefeld manuscript" (A VII 25): "In the Seefeld papers (1905) I already find the concept and correct use of the 'phenomenological reduction!'" Cited from Karl Schuhmann, *Die Dialektik der Phänomenologie* I, 168. Concerning the circumstances surrounding the "Seefeld manuscript" and the discovery of the epoché, see ibid., 128–83. See also *The Idea of Phenomenology* (*Hua* II), in which the first five lectures from a course taught during summer semester 1907 were posthumously published. As is well known, it is in them that the epoché receives its first extended elaboration.

48. See the "motto" Husserl prefaced to his "diary-like" entries published by Walter Biemel as "Persönliche Aufzeichnungen" (*PN*, 293). Rather than an Epimetheus, Husserl is through and through a Prometheus. Regarding the former, see Heinrich Meier, *The Lesson of Carl Schmitt*, trans. Marcus Brainard (Chicago: University of Chicago Press, 1998), esp. the final chapter.

49. See *BW* 4, 408.7–8.

50. See Biemel, "Die entscheidenden Phasen," 59. On pathos see also Cairns, *Conversations*, 51.

51. Gilbert Ryle notes that Husserlian phenomenology is an investigation of the I or ego, or more generally of the self: for phenomenology "all intentional experiences, whatever their 'accusatives', must belong to an experiencing ego. *Cogito ergo sum* is a cardinal proposition in Husserl's phenomenology. 'What is it to be an "I"?' is perhaps, the most general way of formulating the question of phenomenology—indeed Husserl coins the unattractive alternative title for phenomenology of 'descriptive transcendental egology'." (See Ryle's "Phenomenology" [1932], in *Collected Papers* I [New York: Barnes & Noble, 1971], 167–78, here 172.) See II, n. 93 for selected literature on the ego in Husserl. The self has been the subject, either directly or indirectly, of a number of illuminating phenomenological studies. See esp. Tom Nenon, "Husserl's Theory of the Mental," in T. Nenon and L. Embree, eds., *Issues in Husserl's "Ideas II"* (Dordrecht: Kluwer, 1996), 218–31, esp. 225 and 230–31; Robert Sokolowski, "Husserl's Protreptic," in L. Embree, ed., *Life-World and Consciousness* (Evanston, Ill.: Northwestern University Press, 1972), 55–82, here 62–67; and James R. Mensch, "Husserl's Concept of the Self," in *After Modernity* (Albany, N.Y.: State University of New York Press, 1996), 139–48, as well as his "Freedom and Selfhood," *Husserl Studies* 14 (1997), 41–59. In the latter, Mensch notes three Husserlian positions on the self (ibid., 42–43): (1) "the self is not a substance or a thing, but rather a process"; (2) the self 's "constitutive process is an instinct-driven one"; and (3) the self "is defined in terms of its environment." While all these features undoubtedly play an integral role in the self, the question remains open concerning the status of the telos of the process (1), the relation of instinct to that telos (2), and the bearing of the environment on that telos (3). The self in Husserl is first and foremost an essential determination. He adopts the classical definition of man as *animal rationale* or rational being. The telos guiding man's becoming is none other than this essence, or simply reason. All his striving, whether he knows it or not (thus whether reflected and willed or merely instinctual), is aimed at becoming rational. The self does the striving while also being the telos of the striving. That is the sense of Husserl's remarks in the *Crisis* that man is rational already by wanting to be rational (see *Crisis*, 275/340). By the same token, the self to which one is responsible in the self-responsibility thematized by Husserl is not an individual, contingent self so much as the self as the essence of man. Only if one reads Husserl's remarks on the self, esp. in his final period, in this way do they gain their full sense. By the same token, Husserl's understanding of freedom can be grasped completely only if one takes essence into consideration. Consider in this connection Sokolowski, *Husserlian Meditations*, 162: "The self is not a prepackaged whole; it is a constituted as an identity within differences." This points to the link between individual process and universal essence, esp. in light of the procedure of imaginative variation and its results.

The primacy of the twofold distinction of the self—both as individual and as essence—is underscored by Husserl's use of terms such as *Selbstvergessenheit*' (self-forgetfulness) and *Selbsterhaltung*. The latter may be translated by 'self-preservation', but also by 'self-obtainment'. The latter is supported by Mensch's argument for the processual character of the self. In "das Streben nach Selbsterhaltung" (see *EJ*, § 71), the ego strives not only for its preservation, but also and primarily for the obtainment of its self in all its fullness, thus to achieve its telos or fulfill its ownmost essence. Such striving on

Husserl's view is never aimed at maintaining the status quo, but only at the (asymptotic) movement towards the telos. On *Selbsterhaltung* see Sepp, *Praxis und Theoria*, 39, 45, 79–80, 86, 120–22, and 274–76.

In his article "Husserl's Complex Concept of the Self and the Possibility of Social Criticism" (in A. B. Dallery and C. E. Scott, eds., *Crises in Continental Philosophy* [Albany, N.Y.: State University of New York Press, 1990], 47–55, here 52–53), Charles Harvey identifies three senses of self in Husserlian thought: the naive or worldly, the empty or world-purified, and the transcendental self. Each of the former two is said to be one-sided and the polar opposite of the other. It is by means of the third, the transcendental self, that they are linked together. Each exists with the other—that is to say, each individual human being has the three, intertwined selves. Thus far, we can agree with Harvey. However, there is a problem, it seems, with his characterization of this mediating self. Insofar as it is "transcendental," we would expect the third self to be enabling—in other words, that it would not only mediate between the other two selves, but be their basis, the ground of their possibility. He characterizes "the transcendental sense of selfhood" as that in which "one is both connected and disconnected [from the social world], both constituted and constituting" (52), or as he also says: "The transcendental sense of self is the sense of oneself as a content-laden, spatial, and historical point of intentional interface with the world. To experience oneself in this way is to experience oneself as both a passive inheritor of a previously existing world, and an active point of transmission and transformation of the world. The sense of oneself as transcendental is the sense of oneself as a channel for the intentional re-formation of the meanings, values, and beliefs that the world has given to one" (53–54). It is the transcendental self that shows each of the two sides to be one-sided, to be forgetful of the other: each is an "achievement of forgetfulness" (54). Harvey maintains that Husserl came "to realize that the descriptive unity of the sense of self is approximated only when the socio-historical sources of these senses are recognized. And once these sources are made conscious, the 'self' is recognized to be the multifaceted living point of interaction between society, culture, history, and the present world" (55). The key aspect of the transcendental self is precisely its making the other selves aware of their one-sidedness and so of their respective contributions to the "whole" self. The transcendental self would thus seem to be a reflective moment that each "side" possesses, but does not activate. A question that Harvey does not address in his paper is what motivates a self to overturn its "achievement of forgetfulness" and thereby become transcendental in his sense. The answer to this question is bound up with a fourth sense of self in Husserl, which Harvey does not take into consideration—namely, Harvey considers the self primarily as an entity and not as an essential or normative determination. In the case of human beings, this means the self as essence, that is the essence of man, which is his rationality, according to Husserl. The answer to the question of what motivates the transcendental awakening, as it were, is to be found in a fundamental dissonance that Husserl terms 'crisis'. It is the crisis of reason, but prior to that the crisis of belief, and precisely due to the latter's failing.

The "transcendental self" has the task of awakening the "naive self" to its essential self, to motivate it to transform what is merely "latent reason" into actual reason (see *Crisis*, 13/15). This requires the move from *doxa* to *epistêmê*, from "dogmatic slumber" to lucid wakefulness, but also from "instinct" or drive to full awareness or will.

Mensch gives an intriguing account of this movement in his "Instincts – A Husserlian Account," *Husserl Studies* 14 (1998), 219–37. But again, he does not consider the role of telos or essence in the movement and its importance in the constitution of the self. James Hart takes steps in the latter direction in his *The Person and the Common Life*, 184–90. See also Nam-In Lee, *Edmund Husserls Phänomenologie der Instinkte* (Dordrecht: Kluwer, 1993) and Hart's discussion of this book, "Genesis, Instinct, and Reconstruction: Nam-In Lee's *Edmund Husserl's Phänomenologie der Instincte,*" *Husserl Studies* 15 (1998), 101–23.

52. See Sokolowski, "Husserl's Protreptic," 56.

53. On December 22, 1896, Husserl writes to his friend, Hans von Arnim: "Of course, I am not lacking in honest efforts to play out the role properly that has been entrusted to me in this enigmatic existence; but that I would comply with it, that I would live the life I ought to live—how far I am from doing so!" (*BW* 9, 135.)

54. See *BW* 9, 40–41 for Husserl's letter to his friend, Gustav Albrecht, dated July 1, 1908: "My life is the old one, it is just that I am growing ever older and sense ever more the seriousness of life's tasks that have not been taken on accidentally [*nicht zufällig*], but have come to me from within and from above [*von innen und oben her*]. Will I fulfill them and be able to fulfill them, that which indeed lies before my eyes so clearly and certainly as my cause [*Sache*], my goal, my duty, my destiny [*Bestimmung*]? I see golden fruits that no one else sees, and I have them within reach before my eyes. But I am Sisyphus, for whom they vanish again and again when he tries to grasp them. And this grasping is hard, the hardest work. I make constant progress, and great progress. But the scope of the investigations to be completed and the intricacy of the problems, none of which can be concluded and delimited in isolation, is unprecedented. Thus things are as they were for me during the previous decade, and with age I have not grown more comfortable; instead, I have almost lost all capacity for experiencing joy, except from these works. Of course, at issue are once again large publications with the ultimate goal of a completely new critique of reason, for which my *Logical Investigations* already contain the first fundaments." By 1916 Husserl becomes aware of having a "great mission"; see *BW* 3, 405. In 1919 he speaks of his "true God-willed mission" (*BW* 4, 412). See also the letter to his cousin, Flora Darkow, dated February 12, 1921 (*BW* 9, 163–64): "A great burden rests on my shoulders that I can never discharge—aware of a mission bestowed on me from above for the blessing of an ill-fated, confused humanity. Unfortunately, this burden has only increased as I have grown older, since I have yet to complete my main works or to fashion them out of colossal drafts." In 1934 Husserl makes a similar appeal to the source of his task: "I stand firm, and strive to continue to work productively and live up to the *task* that has been entrusted to me, I am certain, from above" (*BW* 7, 190; Husserl's emphasis). See also ibid., 217.8 and 218.28. Husserl is reported by Adelgundis Jaegerschmid, O.S.B. (in her "Gespräche mit Edmund Husserl 1931–1936," *Stimmen der Zeit* 199, no. 1 [1988], 48–58, here 55; henceforth referred to as "Conversations") to have said on September 4, 1935: "I have a task, a mission, that has been given to me by God. I must fulfill it—that is what I live for. Continuously and daily I work further and at new things, for thirty-five years now. I have not had any time to prepare my manuscripts for publication. . . . My mission is science alone. With it I want to serve both Christian confessions." In her account of her husband's life, Malvine Husserl sums up his ethos as follows: "His life was always subject

to the idea of infinity; he had into his last days of health an infinite temporal horizon for his infinite tasks. . . . His work on earth was for him a mission from above, the service of which made up his life, without concern for the future. Endlessly lay his task before him and endlessly was he striving to fulfill it." (Cited from Karl Schuhmann, "Malvine Husserls 'Skizze eines Lebensbildes von E. Husserl'," *Husserl Studies* 5 (1988), 105–25, here 118.) See also ibid., 111 ("but as so often in his life, a will decided that he was not aware of") and 114 ("his will was subject to a higher will he was unaware of").

55. See *EBA*, 297/176.

56. See Afterword, 569. Husserl makes this remark in 1930. Some eight years earlier he calls himself "the eternal beginner" (*BW* 3, 50.2). Note that, rather than 'actual beginner', the more natural translation of *wirklicher Anfänger* would be 'true beginner'. The literal translation preferred here is required, however, by his remarks on 'actual' (*wirklich*)—which is to be distinguished from 'real' (*real*) on the one hand and from 'neutral' on the other—in his explication of the "doctrine of the neutrality modification." See III, 157–80, esp. 161.

57. Entry dated September 26, 1906; Husserl's emphasis. See *FTL*, 8–9, e.g., for his understanding of 'critique'.

58. See Afterword, 569, where in 1930 Husserl speaks of himself as author: "He would almost like to hope—were he allowed to grow as old as Methuselah—still to be able to become a philosopher after all."

59. On September 25, 1906, Husserl looks back on his work in the *Philosophy of Arithmetic* (*PN*, 294): "And while I struggled with the drafts on the logic of mathematical thinking and, in particular, of mathematical calculus, inconceivably foreign worlds tormented me: the world of the purely logical and the world of act-consciousness, [or,] as I would say today, of the phenomenological and of the psychological. I didn't know to put them together, yet they had to have been related to one another and to have formed an inner unity."

60. See Mt. 7:16. See the context (Mt. 7:15–20) for the sense of his remark on the trunk. Husserl's metaphors are more than simply metaphors (see the following note)—that is, they are not merely decorative. In this connection, it reflects the ethos that carries his endeavors.

61. The image of the trunk makes visible Husserl's understanding of the "system" of phenomenology, as well as of all knowledge based upon it. Metaphor plays a central role in Husserl's intuitive method. In this regard, Manfred Sommer ("Husserl on 'Ground' and 'Underground'," *Phänomenologische Forschungen*, sup. vol. [1998], 131–49, here 139) is right in calling attention to the importance of metaphor in Husserlian thought: "Thus metaphors scattered through the text are not to be understood as isolated occurrences. Instead, one has to conceive of them as indications and parts of a whole pictorial structure." Despite the interest of his remarks, however, Sommer's reading proves inadequate since it fails to account for the *whole* picture; for that is the function of metaphor in Husserl: to point the way into the whole, or *up* to it, as the case may be. And the "Persönliche Aufzeichnungen," as well as every work of transcendental phenomenology Husserl penned after them, make it quite clear that he has a whole in view, even if it is a whole he can never achieve. Despite—or because of—his critical intention, Hans Blumenberg (*Paradigmen zu einer Metaphorologie* [Frankfurt a. M.: Suhrkamp, 1998], 80) regards Husserl's appeal to explorer metaphors as "ana-

chronistic." But this label only testifies to Blumenberg's failure to understand Husserl as he understood himself. Blumenberg's critical intention apparently blinded him to Husserl's self-understanding and thereby rendered him unable to see the *chronos* of Husserl's reflections. This explains why Blumenberg embeds Husserl in the modern era (*Neuzeit*), instead of according him his rightful place in modernity. James Hart has shown himself to have a rare ear for Husserl's metaphors and their significance to Husserlian thought. See, e.g., his *The Person and the Common Life*, 1–5 and 50–52.

62. This accords with the reflective structures of central importance to phenomenology. See, e.g., Husserl's remarks concerning the method and its justification as discussed, e.g., on III, 106 and 109.

63. Husserl notes that his "breakthrough into phenomenology" in the *Logical Investigations* followed upon "many years of unclear struggling and struggling [infused with the] burning desire to climb up to clarity" (*PN*, 300). But before he could climb up into the heights, he had to secure the ground, which, again, required the discovery and articulation of the epoché.

64. The positive effect of the "barb of skepticism" is elaborated on some eighteen years later in his 1923–24 lecture course First Philosophy. See *Hua* VIII, 27–29. Heidegger will echo his teacher's view about the relationship between danger and salvation by repeating what has subsequently become a famous passage from Hölderlin: "Wo aber Gefahr ist, wächst / Das Rettende auch" (But where danger is, grows / the saving power also). See Martin Heidegger, "Die Frage nach der Technik," in *Vorträge und Aufsätze* (Pfullingen: Neske, 6th ed., 1990), 39; "The Question Concerning Technology," trans. William Lovitt, in *The Question Concerning Technology and Other Essays* (New York: Harper & Row, 1977), 34. Unlike in Husserl, however, in Heidegger the danger does not give rise to a First Science as savior.

65. See, e.g., *Ideas I*, 3 and *Hua* II, 45–46. In 1930 he believes he has reached his goal: "The universal horizon of work for a phenomenological philosophy has disclosed its main geographic structures, so to speak; the essential layers of problems and the eidetically corresponding methods of access have been clarified. The author sees the infinitely open land of true philosophy, the 'Promised Land,' sprawled out before him, which he will no longer be able to experience [*erleben*] after it has been thoroughly cultivated" (Afterword, 569–70). That is to say, he will not grow as old as Methuselah and so not become a philosopher, for he will not be able to enter the Promised Land. One is tempted to say that Husserl simulates the reception of a revelation, in a manner that was unthinkable for metaphysics. See Heribert Boeder, "Die conceptuale Vernunft in der Letzten Epoche der Metaphysik," *Abhandlungen der Braunschweigischen Wissenschaftlichen Gesellschaft* 43 (1992), 345–60.

66. Adopting Cairns's convention (see his *Guide for Translating Husserl* [The Hague: Nijhoff, 1973]), 'physical thing' will render *Ding*. At times Husserl himself qualifies *Ding* as a 'physical thing', at others he does not. It is clear, however, that he uses this word always in contrast to thing as *Sache*. Hence, when unqualified, 'thing' will translate the more general *Sache*, just as 'the things themselves' will translate *die Sachen selbst*. For Husserl's distinction, see *Ideas I*, 35 (and II, 50), where he contests the empiricistic reduction of *Sachen* to 'things of nature', which are also 'physical things'.

67. Husserl's emphasis.

68. See *Hua* VIII, 19 and 6; also *EBA*, 293.33ff./173.

69. The German reads *heiterer Himmel*, which may be rendered literally as 'cheerful heavens' instead of 'clear sky'.

70. "Sinners" are those who do not accord with their telos; see I, n. 45, where Husserl speaks of 'the unethical', which is equivalent to 'sinful' in his usage. His occasional talk of 'sin' entails the notion of straying from one's essence or telos, from essential determinations, or from the things themselves. Error no less than sin arises from not being true to the things. See *Hua* VIII, 12: for the philosopher, "every straying [*Abirrung*] from the ultimate aim of his life [means] a straying from himself, a becoming-untrue-to-his-self [*Sich-selbst-untreu-werden*]." See *Hua* XXVII, 118 (quoted on the final page of this introduction). Consider also the thought of the *metabasis eis allo genos*, which is itself a kind of straying from the path; see II, n. 32.

See the letter to Eugen Fink, dated March 6, 1933 (*BW* 4, 91), in which Husserl, trying to encourage Fink, refers to Dürer's etching "Knight, Death, and the Devil" as a "great symbol" and to Rembrandt's Jacob-painting: "And then there is the symbol by Rembrandt, which truly does not just hang on my wall like a dead picture: Jacob's battle with God, 'til his ribs crack—and his God as the angel blesses him." See Gen. 32:26ff. for the account of Jacob's wrestling with God (or the angel) and the frontispieces provided above. The notion of struggle is central to Husserl's thought; it informs the ethos he aims to instill. Made visible in Rembrandt's painting, it is the struggle towards the ideal, towards absolute reason. At best this struggle points to a provisional distinction of man from himself. Very much akin in spirit to Husserl's understanding of the guiding function of the symbol is the following passage from Thomas Carlyle, *Sartor Resartus* (1832), bk. III, chap. iii: "In the Symbol proper . . . there is ever, more or less distinctly and directly, some embodiment and revelation of the Infinite; the Infinite is made to blend itself with the Finite, to stand visible, and as it were, attainable there . . . man . . . everywhere finds himself encompassed with Symbols, recognised as such or not recognised: the Universe is but one vast Symbol of God; nay if thou wilt have it, what is man himself but a Symbol of God; is not all he does symbolical; a revelation to sense of the mystic god-given force that is in him?" (Cited from Andrew Wilton, "Symbolism in Britain," in A. Wilton and R. Upstone, eds., *The Age of Rossetti, Burne-Jones & Watts: Symbolism in Britain 1860–1910* [London: Tate Gallery, 1997], 11–33, here 31.) See *Hua* XXVII, 65. On Dürer's etching, see Hart, *The Person and the Common Life*, 50–52.

71. In Biemel's edition of Husserl's "Personal Notes" this reads *Vor allen*, but in *Hua* XXIV, 447 it reads *Vor allem*.

72. Eduard Marbach stresses the stimulation Husserl received from the philosophical tradition, or certain of its key figures, in Rudolf Bernet, Iso Kern, and Eduard Marbach, *Edmund Husserl*, 63. He refers to *PRS*, 340, where Husserl speaks of letting the philosophies constituting that tradition "have a stimulating effect on us [*auf uns anregend wirken*]"; but just before saying this, Husserl had rejected the interest in the history of the development of philosophy. And immediately after the passage cited by Marbach, Husserl says: "But it is not through philosophies that we become philosophers." This is followed by: "Not philosophies but the things and the problems are the point from which the impulse to inquiry must issue." One must see the way in which those philosophies are supposed to be stimulating, and that is always in view of the *task*, of which Husserl is already aware and which he did *not* receive from the tradition. That is, all that Husserl gains from the tradition—he maintains—is the strength to continue

on in the all-important ethos towards the fulfillment of *the* task, the one task common to all genuine philosophy. Marbach's talk of 'influence' in this connection is out of place. The "ethical" function of the philosophical tradition for Husserl is underscored in *Hua* VIII, chap. 1. There it is quite clear that the will to pursue or the belief in the task is strengthened by various philosophies, whether they were right or wrong. He also speaks of the stimulation one gains from the New Testament or religion in general. Any thought can be stimulating for him only because he already has firm ground to stand on, ground provided by his task—or the projection thereof. Thus, one can speak of stimulation, of "influence," but one has to recognize in what way influence is had. It is always secondary and always in the service of further clarifying the—principial—task. In this sense, one cannot embed Husserl in an "effective history" (*Wirkungsgeschichte*); at most one can speak of an "appropriative history" (*Aneignungsgeschichte*), to which Husserl turns in order to gain his sustenance (see Cairns, *Conversations*, 22; August 22, 1931). The only other reason he has for addressing the philosophical tradition is to appeal to prevailing habits of thinking and show them that the tradition "really" wanted phenomenology. In that case it has a purely heuristic function for him. The problems pursued or generated by the tradition are ruled out for him from the start. This holds for his discussion of all philosophers, including Descartes and Kant. (On Husserl's relationship to these philosophers, see Dieter Henrich, "Über die Grundlagen von Husserls Kritik der philosophischen Tradition," *Philosophische Rundschau* 6 [1958], 1–26, here 7–9 and 12–17, respectively.) If Husserl stands in a continuum, then as he understands himself it is one of ethos, and of ethos only, not one of problems and certainly not of philosophy.

It is common practice to name Husserl and other, "similar" philosophers in the same breath. However, such an approach tends not to shed light on the difference of Husserlian thought, but rather absorbs it into a continuum of problems. Often this approach amounts to a projection of one's own agenda, instead of listening to Husserl himself. Gary Overvold's "Husserl and the Tradition," *Analecta Huserliana* 55 (1998), 13–23, is an example of the latter practice and thus of how *not* to read Husserl. By contrast, Klaus Erich Kaehler's work is exemplary for how one ought to approach the question of Husserl's relation to the tradition. See *Cognitio humana – Dynamik des Wissens und der Werte* (Berlin: Akademie Verlag, 1997), 423–32. Regarding Husserl and contemporary analytic thought, see Tom Nenon, "Husserls phänomenologischer Cartesianismus. Zum Verhältnis von Selbstbewußtsein und Selbstverantwortung in seiner phänomenologischen Transzendentalphilosophie," *Phänomenologische Forschungen* n.s. 2 (1997), 177–88.

73. The natural order of problems determines the course of inquiry, specifically the kinds of questions one asks and when one asks them. See, e.g., Cairns, *Conversations*, 58 (December 22, 1931): Husserl "said that ethical problems are not immediately approachable. There are only certain questions to which we have a right at any stage of our investigations."

74. Looking back on his beginnings, Husserl notes that it was the failure of philosophy that motivated his work beginning no later than in the 1890s; and yet, up until he began to fathom the "real" situation and the crisis as such, he experienced this failure as a personal failure: "In large part it [i.e., his depression and loss of self-confidence] was caused by my failure in philosophy, which I recognized only very late to have been a failure of contemporary philosophy, whose lack of clarity and illusory scientific character I

at first had to attribute to myself" (*BW* 4, 21–22). Out of what he took to be a purely personal crisis, then, his work arose: "there was but one single source of salvation [from it]: in desperate and dogged resoluteness, to begin a completely new life all over again and to continue in radical honesty and not to falter in the face of any consequence" (408). Such resoluteness initially entailed the restriction of the scope of his inquiry to modest problems: "In philosophical work I resolved to deny myself every grand goal and to be happy if in the bogs of the groundless lack of clarity I could work out here and there only the smallest [piece of] firm ground on which I could really stand, in the evidence provided by just this firm standing. Only what I can 'see for myself' again and again (can bring to 'self-givenness'), I said, will hold for me" (22). Whereas the discovery of its inadequacy compelled him to abandon philosophy in its contemporary and historical manifestations, he retained the *idea* of philosophy. This idea caused him to radicalize his initial intention, to move deeper and find the corresponding natural order of problems and investigations that led up from one "absolute" piece of firm ground.

75. See *FTL*, 3 concerning the "tragedy of modern scientific culture" in which "the principial rootedness of the sciences and their unification with respect to these roots" is endangered.

76. See Mohanty, "Husserl on 'Possibility'," 21–22.

77. See *Hua* XXVIII, 200. Heinz Hülsmann has noted the importance of the beginning to Husserl's system, as well as the interconnection of striving and responsibility therein, but he only sensed the importance of the upper limit at which such striving aims. See his "Der Systemanspruch der Phänomenologie E. Husserls," *Salzburger Jahrbuch für Philosophie* 7 (1963), 173–86, esp. 186. The title of Hart's *The Person and the Common Life* names two intermediate limits within the system we intend to explicate here. Hart certainly seeks to account for the whole spectrum of consciousness life, from hyletic data up to the achievement of the divine entelechy, but he does not consider the movement this entails as reflecting the very system of Husserlian thought, nor does he focus on the normative function of essence in conscious life according to Husserl's analyses, particularly the normative ideal of reason for man. In a similar vein, Mensch focuses expressly on intersubjectivity as opposed to subjectivity in his *Intersubjectivity and Transcendental Idealism.* He therefore focuses on higher level issues in Husserlian thought, tending towards the uppermost limit, while neglecting in large part the lowermost limit in its own right. This is not to deny the value of either of these works. On the contrary, the present study may be seen to complement them, for what it seeks to establish, they could not have undertaken, and necessarily so, given the concerns that guided the authors of each of these works, specifically their overriding concern with genesis rather than the stasis central to Husserl's inaugural work of transcendental phenomenology. No less than Husserl, the value of their works must be measured against the criteria of the tasks they have set for themselves, thus immanently.

78. See *Ideas I*, 201 n.

79. See the *Kaizo* articles on renewal in *Hua* XXVII; see also I, n. 42.

80. In a letter to William Ernest Hocking (July 7, 1912; *BW* 3, 160) in response to Hocking's gift of his book *The Meaning of God in Human Experience: A Philosophic Study of Religion* (New Haven 1912), Husserl writes: "'The meaning of God in human Experience'—what a beautiful topic, one that interests me inwardly! Even if I have made it my life's task to found a philosophy 'from below' at least for myself, to my satis-

faction (which is very difficult to gain!), I nevertheless strive unceasingly from this 'below' upwards into the heights. In the last years, metaphysical considerations, and especially the idea of God, have entered ever more powerfully into the horizon of my studies." See Cairns, *Conversations*, 23 (August 22, 1931): "However one must creep before one can fly; one must do a lot of dirty work (*schmutzige Arbeit*) on the ground before one can get into one's airplane and fly." In her "Conversations" (49; April 28, 1931), Sister Jaegerschmid reports Husserl as saying: "I have no access to this sphere [i.e., that of the religious life], although I have always been one of the most fervent seekers of God from my youth on." In *Ideas I* (157 n.; see also *Crisis*, 67/66) Husserl calls God a "limit concept," whose necessity not even the atheist can avoid. See *Hua* XXVII, 33–34: "The absolute limit, the pole that lies beyond all finitude, at which all genuine human striving aims, is the idea of God." See also *Crisis*, 7/9: "The problem of God obviously entails the problem of 'absolute' reason as the teleological source of all reason in the world, of the 'sense' of the world." This sense of God's limiting function for Husserl is recorded by Sister Jaegerschmid. He said to her: "Genuine science must be universal science, which comprehends the totality of all evidences [gained] on the basis of autonomy, [the totality] in which religion is also included. In this sphere Christianity has its place. Finally, by means of this universal science, as phenomenology has sought to articulate it, one begins a teleological development that ultimately leads to God, the absolute." See James G. Hart, "I, We, and God," 125–49, here 125–27, and *The Person and the Common Life*, passim, on the "divine entelechy." On reason see a passage from Ms. E III 4, p. 9b (cited from Schumann, *Husserls Staatsphilosophie*, 136): "Highest level of human practical autonomy the level of absolute reason or of life subject to the idea of absolute reason, the phenomenologically justified [*begründet*] life." See I, n. 133.

81. See *FTL*, 14. It is not, of course, *philosophy* as rigorous science, but phenomenology, that is to lay the groundwork for the former. See *EBA*, 519/150: "Accordingly, transcendental phenomenology is not a special science among others, but rather, thought in systematic exposition, the actualization of the idea of a universal science, and in fact as eidetic science. As such it must hold within itself all possible a priori sciences, and in fact by virtue of its all-sided consideration of a priori concatenations in absolute justification."

82. It was Karl Weierstrass—whose mathematics was "truest to the roots [*wurzelechtest*]"—who first exposed Husserl to the ethos called for here and who "trained him in intellectual clearness [*Reinlichkeit*]" (*BW* 4, 408; see *Hu-Chr.*, 6–11). But he was impelled to leave mathematics and take up philosophy as his vocation by what he describes as "overpowering religious lived experiences and complete reversals [*Umwendungen*]" (ibid.), specifically by his encounter with Christianity and with philosophy. Concerning their relationship in his thought, he says: "For the powerful effect of the New Testament on the 23-year-old did indeed turn into the drive [*Trieb*] to find the way to God and to a true life by means of a rigorous philosophical science" (*BW* 4, 408). Instead of *wurzelecht*, in 1930 Husserl speaks of *ursprungsecht* (true to the origin) in order to characterize the ethos or "spirit of the most radical scientific character" (see Afterword, 549). See Boyce Gibson, "Freiburg Diary," 70 col. 2 (July 25, 1928): "Husserl then replied. His main aim had been excellently indicated: *Strenge Wissenschaft* [rigorous science] and as regards Ethos, *absolute Redlichkeit, absolute Ehrlichkeit*

[absolute honesty] in all relations to life and of thought. Above all a strict intellectual conscience. These Ideals were of vital importance in these days of *Zusammensturz* [collapse] when all things seemed to be breaking up." "One thing he was perfectly convinced about and that was that Phenomenology was in its essentials absolutely valid, and that it marks the beginning of a new epoch in philosophy." See also ibid., 65 col. 1, quoted in IV, n. 28.

83. See I, n. 72.

84. Nor is he engaged in a "conversation" with the philosophical tradition here—or anywhere for that matter. If he "converses" with anyone, then it is with the natural scientists and mathematicians. For they have achieved in some measure what he aims at for philosophy. See in this connection Biemel, "Die Idee der Phänomenologie bei Husserl," 149. See also Cairns, *Conversations*, 22 (August 22, 1931): "in phenomenology one has to come to these questions from the bottom up, and is not impelled directly by an historical *Anregung* <suggestion, incitement>."

85. The "principle of all principles" demands a kind of "piety" of the phenomenologist. On this principle, see II, 54–56 (sec. 2.5). For a stimulating reading of piety in Husserlian thought, see James G. Hart, "A Précis of an Husserlian Philosophical Theology," in S. W. Laycock and J. G. Hart, eds., *Essays in Phenomenological Theology* (Albany, N.Y.: State University of New York Press, 1986), 89–168.

86 See I, 22 and I, nn. 105 and 114.

87. 'Countersense' translates *Widersinn*: it goes against or runs counter to the sense [*Sinn*]. Taken in the broadest terms, sense entails a direction, a reference, a norm. On straying from the path it prescribes, see I, n. 70.

88. This essence or idea is none other than the (essential) self—that is, the definition of man as rational being. It is precisely this determination that founds the analogies of fundamental importance to Husserlian thought, central among which is the analogy between subjectivity and intersubjectivity, or between the individual personality and the "personality of a higher order" (*Hua* XXVII, 22; see also "Wert des Lebens," 220: "We have, then, an ethical community—which is the analog of an ethical personality and which is a personality of a higher level—and the individual persons contained therein . . ."). For Husserl an analogy is in fact the expression of a "community of essence." It is based on such community that empathy, e.g., is possible: "Each human being – my equal. Each an 'other,' each is experienced with understanding as a variation of my self" (*Hua* XV, 622), and precisely due to a shared, essential self that exceeds each individual self. The universal structures of subjectivity, which are ultimately intentional structures, are mirrored in intersubjectivity, which is why Husserl feels justified in concentrating on the former in *Ideas I*. His is never a naive solipsism, but at most a systematic or methodical solipsism. That is, the analysis of subjectivity is the preliminary step to the analysis of intersubjectivity. To start with the latter would be to theorize from on high rather than working from the ground upwards. As Husserl employs it, analogy is not a metaphor, it is not the expression of a supposed likeness, but marks an "inductive" application of features from one level to those of another, higher level. Note also that analogies here are generally unidirectional, that is, extending from the relatively simple to the complex. See Nenon, "Husserl's Theory of the Mental," 232 concerning this "order of procedure"; though Nenon's remarks bear immediately on the unfolding of

Ideas II, they may be extended to Husserlian thought in general. On analogy in Husserl, see Klaus Hedwig, "Husserl und die Analogie," *Zeitschrift für philosophische Forschung* 36 (1982), 77–86. On the relationship between subjectivity and intersubjectivity, see Klaus Erich Kaehler, "Die Monade in Husserls Phänomenologie der Intersubjektivität," *Tijdschrift voor Filosofie* 59 (1995), 692–709.

89. On time and the eternal, see I, 1, 2, and 5 esp. the opening. Compare the relationship between distress and its alleviation touched on here to that between danger and its overcoming addressed in I, n. 64. See also I, n. 100 for Husserl's reference to a "static eschatology."

90. On the "ought" as "absolute ought" see Hart, *The Person and the Common Life*, esp. 296–300 and 320–24.

91. See James G. Hart, "The Entelechy and Authenticity of Objective Spirit: Reflections on Husserliana XXVII," *Husserl Studies* 9 (1992), 91–110; Mensch, *Intersubjectivity and Transcendental Idealism*, chap. 6; and Sepp, *Praxis und Theoria*, 247–79. See also Guillermo Hoyos, "Zum Teleologiebegriff in der Phänomenologie Husserls," in U. Claesges and K. Held, eds., *Perspektiven transzendentalphänomenologischer Forschung* (The Hague: Nijhoff, 1972), 61–84; and Ante Pazanin, "Teleologieproblem bei Husserl," in J.-E. Pleines, ed., *Teleologie. Ein philosophisches Problem in Geschichte und Gegenwart* (Würzburg: Königshausen & Neumann, 1994), 230–50.

92. Reason is what distinguishes man from other animals and even from himself as prehistorical man; see *Hua* XXIX, 384 n. 1, as well as "Wert des Lebens," 222–24. See CM, § 36, 108.

93. On the struggle to move from *doxa* to *epistêmê*, see Walter Biemel, "Zur Bedeutung von δόξα und ἐπιστήμη im Umkreis der Krisis-Thematik," in his *Gesammelte Schriften* I, 131–46.

94. Unlike Heidegger, Husserl does not speak of *Menschenwesen*. He does not think *Wesen* verbally, but rather substantively, thus as 'essence' or 'being' rather than as 'naturing'. Kohák asserts the primacy of the verbal sense of *Wesen* in Husserl (see Kohák, *Idea and Experience*, 9), but also translates it, e.g., as 'type' (13) as well as 'principle' and 'pattern' (15).

95. On such striving see Sepp, *Praxis und Theoria*, 92–97.

96. Although Husserl clearly uses Aristotelian concepts in the *Crisis* when elaborating on the definition of man and the teleology it entails, he parts radically with Aristotle already regarding the notion of the definition itself (see Aristotle's definition of the definition, *Met.* 1016^{a}33). In Aristotle each definition may be fulfilled, whereas in Husserl this is impossible for "spiritual" entities. And this has important consequences for Husserl's teleology. See I, n. 108.

97. See *VL*, 321–22/276. In this context Husserl refers to ideas as "intensional infinities" (322/276).

98. See *Crisis*, 275–76/341, as well as *PRS*, 339.

99. See *Crisis*, 275.32–33/341, as well as "Wert," 212: "My life is rational and I am practically rational whenever I will the best possible and perform to the best of my ability, and whenever I decide [*den Willen fassen*] not to let myself go along, [whenever I decide] to strive for, to do, to will the best possible, then I am rational not only regarded objectively and contingently, but rather am consciously rational; I live in the *ethos of reason,* and my life is itself of greater value by virtue of this ethos. This is the 'ethical'

consideration; it shows me the *form of rational life*. But I am ethical not by virtue of the mere cognition, but by virtue of free resolve."

100. See, however, the shift Husserl describes in a letter to Émile Baudin, dated May 26 and June 8, 1934: "The teleology of reason . . . takes the place of the teleology of religion, which gives sense to humanity and the world for everyone, for humanity as such" (Ms. E III 4, p. 39a). (Reinhold N. Smid cites this passage in his Introduction to *Hua* XXIX; however, it is not among those of Husserl's actual or drafted letters to Baudin published in *BW* 7, 13–22.) See Husserl's objection to the religious interpretation of his talk of teleology on *Hua* XXIX, 362. On the other hand, see his letters to Baudin. Cairns reports the following of Husserl (*Conversations*, 36; September 22, 1931), which points to a possible interpretation of Husserl's occasionally religiously charged language: "In addition to our common goal as human beings, we have, each of us, a special calling, *Beruf*, that we must hearken to. (Here and elsewhere the religious formulation is to be taken as a symbol.)" See the talk of the "great symbols" in his letter to Fink, cited in I, n. 70. A symbol helps to bring the regulative idea to intuition. Adelgundis Jaegerschmid ("Conversations," 58) reports a conversation with Husserl which took place on April 26, 1936, and which concluded with the topic of "the static eschatology of our earth." She reports him as saying: "Finitude, separated from God (infinity), strives to return to infinity. Grace is the freedom of God."

101. This should be clear already based on his remarks on the Middle Ages, which Husserl regards as having been "blindly traditionalistic." He apparently holds Catholicism responsible for the "darkness" of that age. Husserl seems to oppose it because he considers it to be insufficiently "free." Whereas he devotes the majority of his discussion of the crisis to the dangers of skepticism, Catholicism and other forms of religion—and not simply Christianity, for Husserl himself was a Lutheran of sorts—constitute the other pole he wishes to avoid—namely as forms of dogmatism. Like skepticism, it too obstructs man's teleology, and also due to a lack of self-understanding. Dogmatic religion, then, stresses belief but effectively misconstrues that belief. It seems to remain passive. Reason is still not the guiding maxim. Thus, although Husserl stresses only the dangers of skepticism in the *Crisis*, it and dogmatic religion are the Scylla and Charybdis through which he seeks to steer his phenomenology. (Consider Husserl's repeated reference to Dürer's "Knight, Death, and the Devil," where the latter two may be equated with Scylla and Charybdis. See I, n. 70.) Husserl points to the twin dangers of skepticism and dogmatism (specifically, dogmatic metaphysics) in passing on *Hua* VIII, 22.

102. See *Hua* XXIX, 374, on the 'anticipation' or *Vorhabe* of a goal.

103. Since his will to rationality is the will to the absolute, what Husserl says of philosophy also holds of man: "it is rationality that, discovering again and again its unsatisfying relativity, is driven on in its toils, in its will to attain the true and full rationality" (*Crisis*, 274/339). Although he does not speak of belief or presentiment, Rudolf Bernet does elaborate the teleological character of sensory perception, where *anticipation* of the adequate self-givenness of the thing plays the role of the belief of concern here. See his "Perception as Teleological Process of Cognition," *Analecta Husserliana* 9 (1979), 119–32. See also Antonio Aguirre, "Zum Verhältnis von modaler und praktischer Möglichkeit," *Phänomenologische Forschungen* 24/25 (1991), 150–82, here 164.

104. The German reads: *Vernichtungsbrand des Unglaubens*. An alternative translation is 'holocaust of unbelief'.

105. Cairns reports (*Conversations*, 27; August 28, 1931) a remark Husserl makes about the *Cartesian Meditations*, but that holds for all his "introductions" to transcendental phenomenology: "He [i.e., Husserl] is seeking a way from the everyday life that would motivate a going over into the transcendental sphere. . . ." See Husserl's estimation of his position relative to the tradition, which has significant implications for the reorientation of humanity (*Hua* XXIX, 401; August 1936/June–July 1937): "A philosopher had to come who became aware that the possession of the philosophical task from an adopted tradition, from a school or literary instruction, does not yet mean having insight into the possibility [*die einsichtige Möglichkeit*] of the task or, equivalently, the method that is first given through this insight; a philosopher [had to come] who thereby also became aware that philosophy as a personal anticipation [*Vorhabe*] can be something for which one is personally responsible and can be actualized solely through the personal, responsible deed, and again: A philosopher [had to come] who for this reason is motivated not only to distance himself critically from historical traditions (thus first of all performing an epoché with respect to them), but even before that [to distance himself] even from his own task, which governs his working life [*Berufsleben*]—for in that task, too, lies a prejudice that stems from tradition, in the capacity [*Vermöglichkeit*], and perhaps in the methodology that has perhaps already been employed and that itself certainly stems from the traditions."

106. If, as is the position guiding the present study, absolute reason and God are synonymous in Husserlian thought and Husserl's task is, on the one hand, to motivate one to enter into the transcendental sphere and then climb endlessly up towards God and, on the other hand, to perform a critique of reason—the said motivation being in fact bound up with this critique—then one is tempted to say that the critique of central importance to Husserl amounts to an ontological proof, albeit an indirect one. See the following passage from 1908 or 1909 (Ms. B I 4, p. 2, cited in Iso Kern, *Idee und Methode der Philosophie* [Berlin: de Gruyter, 1975], 338 n. 172): "But that it must be possible, according to the ideally normative laws, to produce a unitary and thus rational order of consciousness, that there must be a nature and a culture and a development of nature that makes culture possible, and a development of culture in the sense of ideal culture—none of this is <a priori> 'necessary.' Or are there peculiar sources of necessity for all that? That would mean demonstrating [the existence of] God."

107. See *VL*, 336/289: "Philosophy constantly has to perform its function within a European humanity as the archontic [function] for humanity in its entirety."

108. Although Husserl denies that the organic-biological figure of development fully captures his notion of teleology ("I mean that we feel . . . that an entelechy is inborn in our European humanness which holds sway throughout all the changing forms of Europe and accords to them the sense of a development towards an ideal form of life and Being as an eternal pole. Not that this is a case of one of those well known types of purposeful striving [*Zielstrebigkeiten*] that give organic beings their character in the physical realm; thus it is not something like a biological development from a seminal form [*Keimgestalt*] through stages of maturity with successive aging and perishing" [*VL*, 320/275]), he nevertheless uses terms that would be consonant with such explanation, terms that themselves present the very figure he wishes to reject, e.g., *Triebkraft* (in

botany this can be rendered as 'germinating power') and *aufkeimen* (to bud, burgeon, germinate, sprout).—Ullrich Melle suggests, rightly it seems, that while Husserl gives preference to geological metaphors, the most appropriate would actually be those taken from biology since of primary concern to him is a flux that best fits (biological) life. See Melle's illuminating "Husserls Phänomenologie des Willens," *Tijdschrift voor Filosofie* 54 (1992), 280–305, here 304.—Husserl's rejection of the organic model is likely motivated by his conviction that the life of spirit is an endless struggle; he continues: "There is, for essential reasons, no zoology of peoples. They are spiritual unities; they do not have, and in particular the supranational unity of Europe [*Übernationalität Europa*] does not have, a mature form that has never been reached or could be reached as a form that is regularly repeated"—as, e.g., in the case of a tree. "Psychic humanness has never been complete and never will be, and can never repeat itself. The spiritual telos of European humanness, in which the particular telos of particular nations and of individual men is contained, lies in the infinite, is an infinite idea towards which, in a hidden manner, the whole spiritual becoming aims, so to speak" (*VL*, 320–21/275). Husserl's writings are replete with such metaphors; see, e.g., *Hua* XXIX, 48.22–35, *Hua* XXVII, 195.15–18, and "Wert des Lebens," 222–23. His appeal to the infinite runs counter to the kind of completion proper to metaphysical accounts of teleology, here in particular counter to Aristotle's account (see I, n. 96). Although Husserl calls for the distinction of man, it is a perpetual distinction, a permanent revolution, as it were, that he has in mind. Unlike in metaphysics, here it is impossible for man to fulfill his definition or destiny.

109. See *Hua* XXIX, 363.

110. As Biemel reports in his Introduction to *Hua* VI, Husserl prefaced the publication of the first portion of the *Crisis* with the following remarks: "The work I am beginning with the present treatise, and shall complete in a series of further articles in *Philosophia*, makes the attempt, by way of a teleological-historical reflection upon the origins of our critical scientific and philosophical situation, to establish the unavoidable necessity of a transcendental-phenomenological reorientation [*Umwendung*] of philosophy" (*Crisis*, xiv n. 3/3 n. 1).

111. See *Ideas I*, 118, but also *Hua* XXIX, 406: "In exuberance, the individual philosopher may think he has put the plan 'philosophy' into action, thus that in his system he has set 'the' [true] philosophy on its course."

112. See *Hua* XXIX, 371.18–30. In a letter to Roman Ingarden, dated August 31, 1923, Husserl already expresses his belief that his method will transform humanity, and in fact by providing a new basis on the one hand and a new ethos on the other: "May Heaven give you the strength and the firm ethos [*Gesinnung*] for a new kind of the most radical and selfless philosophy that our epoch needs so desperately. We *must* have the courage for a new life and, first of all, for a new kind of scientific life. The passage to the 'Mothers' is the passage back and forward to an 'original' life, which, in everything and everyone, can support its right, its sense, its honesty through the clarity of the origin [*Ursprüngsklarheit*] and can be *understood* down to the last detail. Only humanity can redeem itself, and it can do so only if we, each of us and for himself, effect self-redemption, if we individuals find the courage and the great will to direct our *undivided* attention to self-clarification, self-knowledge, and then self-purification, and from there to prepare by way of clarification the idea of a universally united, genuine humanity [*Menschheit*], of a supranational Humanity [*Humanität*] (with *genuine* national particu-

larizations), purity, and right. You have been called; persist in love and do not fall prey to the world. I am counting on you" (*BW* 3, 218; Husserl's emphasis).

As Schuhmann notes (ibid., n. 86), the use of 'Mothers' is an allusion to Goethe's *Faust* II. They are goddesses who have neither time nor place. Mephistopheles says of them to Faust: "Nach ihrer Wohnung magst ins Tiefste schürfen; / Du selbst bist schuld, daß ihrer wir bedürfen." ("You may dig down to the deepest depths to their dwelling place; / you yourself are to blame that we need them.") See Hamburger Ausgabe III (Munich: Beck, 16th ed., 1996), 191 lines 6213ff. Husserl describes phenomenology as the "science of 'origins,' of the 'Mothers' of all knowledge," as well as the "soil [*Mutterboden*]" from which "all philosophical method" springs (see *Ideas III*, 80.26ff. and 105.13ff.). So fundamental is this "soil" that "all philosophical methods lead back to it and to the work in it." See also *PP*, 193.20. Hart discusses the "Mothers" in *The Person and the Common Life*, 1–5.

In Husserl's talk of *Gesinnung* (ethos), one should hear *Sinn* (sense). One has the *Ge-sinn-ung* of concern to Husserl only to the extent that one has been endowed with a sense (*ge-sinnt*) or rather has become aware of the sense in which each human being participates, whether knowingly or not. The ethos is *given* by the things themselves; the individual's responsibility is to summon up the courage and the will to persist in it and follow out the course it prescribes.

113. On the philosopher's vocation and his peculiar fate, see *Hua* XXIX, 410–11 and *Hua* VIII, chap. 1. See Husserl's letter to Adolf Grimme, dated February 4, 1933 (*BW* 3, 97): "In history there is only one kind of genuine, invincible realities: they are called idealities. The fall of European humanity is nothing but the fall of the belief in ideas such that the force of seizing upon them originally can no longer be unfolded vitally due to falsifying or trivializing phraseology. The old stock of ideas is also insufficient and is no longer naive seeing. A new, absolutely radical philosophy that illuminates everything by virtue of its absolute universality (i.e., illuminating all the dark caves of skepticism and mysticism) is necessary. My life's work has sought to establish the method and parameters of work for doing so. Unfortunately, this kind of thing cannot have an immediate effect." See also my "As Fate Would Have It: Husserl on the Vocation of Philosophy," *New Yearbook for Phenomenology and Phenomenological Philosophy* I (2000), 111–60.

114. Husserl's emphasis. *Hua* XXIX, 406: "But system follows system. Philosophies in the plural are not works belonging to one category; philosophy as an aim does not have a plural. All philosophies strive after *the* philosophy, which, according to its sense, is singular" (Husserl's emphasis). See I, 22 on philosophy's singularity.

115. In 1931 Husserl regards himself and his potential co-workers as "functionaries of eternity." See his letter to Ludwig Landgrebe from November 12, 1931 (*BW* 4, 276): "Precisely in our fateful age and world, or rather in their universally unitary fate of complete collapse, the call from eternity and infinity must be heard on our behalf, on behalf of the whole of humanity, to overcome finitude as free and genuine men and become functionaries of eternity.") The mathematician can become "the functionary of world-cognition" (*Hua* XXVII, 185.35).

116. See, e.g., the letter to Herbert Spiegelberg from June 19, 1935 (*BW* 2, 253.23).

117. See Elisabeth Ströker, "Edmund Husserls Phänomenologie: Philosophia Perennis in der Krise der europäischen Kultur," *Phänomenologische Forschungen* 22 (1989), 11–38.

118. Thus in the "Draft of an Introduction to *Ideas I* " from (roughly July) 1912, Husserl describes his endeavor as follows: "The aim of the following considerations is a leading upwards [*Emporleitung*] to the idea of pure phenomenology, of this science which is fundamental to philosophy and psychology and which only recently made its breakthrough. Such a leading upwards is badly needed. For phenomenology's proper province of inquiry does not lie within the endless horizon of cognition that the natural attitude of the inquiring regard of real Being comprehends" (*Hua* III/2, 530). In another fragmentary text from 1912 (this time, one probably from June) Husserl recounts the "course" he takes in *Ideas I* (see *Hua* III/2, 526–27). There it is clear that he constructs this book (or intends to do so) such that each successive step leads the reader ever higher, first towards the attainment of the idea of phenomenology and then onwards towards its fulfillment.

119. Husserl makes these remarks in his 1930 Afterword in retrospect on *Ideas I* from 1913. The same intention, the same ethos, permeates both writings, despite the seventeen years that separate them. See the following quotation in the body of our text from the latter work. See a parallel remark from 1929 in *FTL*, § 71, 161.

120. In this passage, as well as in the subsequent two quotations in the body of the text, the emphasis stems from Husserl. He describes himself, along with Meinong, as a traveler already in 1906 (*PN*, 296): "We are like two travelers in one and the same dark part of the world." For another instance of this Conradian motif, see Husserl's remarks to Grimme cited in I, n. 114.

121. See also *BW* 7, 222 (November 28–29, 1934): "Regarding the system of phenomenology—the necessary draft of the general 'map' of the transcendental continent—I have come farther; I still hope to make it to the border so that I can die in peace."

122. See Afterword, 551; see 560–61.

123. See Afterword, 550–51.

124. Afterword, 569: "die *Eine* Philosophie" (Husserl's emphasis).

125. See *Ideas I*, 1.

126. The crisis seems at first glance to be brought on by skepticism—and that is certainly the impression Husserl gives in the *Crisis*. However, insofar as the crisis is one of belief, or more precisely, of the *lack* of belief, it proves to be a crisis brought on by neutrality, which exceeds every skepticism insofar as it does not merely negate belief, as does skepticism, but annihilates belief altogether. There is no remainder that could simply be revalued—that is, reaffirmed and so reinstated. Rather, a new leap must be made. A new foundation must be secured into which one gains apodictic insight, which alone "conquers one's will." See the concluding remarks of the present introduction concerning belief and neutrality, as well as III, 157–80.

127. See his letter to Johannes Daubert from December 23, 1923 (*BW* 2, 80): "Everything is a pure consequence of our beginnings. I have grown ever more radical in the will to the ultimate honesty of thinking, in the will to push ruthlessly to the end, where the ultimate harmony and truth dwells. I have never spared myself and have had to give up, rethink, many things that were still half-baked, dogmatic, onesidedly-absolu-

tized. The air around me has become clearer, purer; I now live in the open, mountain air. Hopefully I shall be able to complete [*vollenden*] myself in the work that is needed."

128. See *FTL*, 13–14: "Any sense in which we philosophers ask about a sense of the world (the real world or whichever ideal one) presupposes the clarification of the transcendental origin and itself moves on the ground of transcendental science."

129. See the letter to W. P. Bell from December 13, 1922 (*BW* 3, 43–44).

130. See I, 12–13.

131. See *FTL*, 11–12: "By penetrating still more deeply, the insight presents itself that an actually philosophical logic, a theory of science that explicates every side of the essential possibility of a genuine science as such and is therefore able to guide the becoming of genuine science, can grow solely in the context of a transcendental phenomenology."

132. *BW* 7, 218.5: *Philosophie des Aufstiegs*. See ibid., 164.12 and Afterword, 551.

133. See his letter to Daniel Martin Feuling, O.S.B., dated March 30, 1933 (*BW* 7, 88): "Phenomenological philosophy as an idea that lies in the infinite *is*, of course, 'theology.' (To me that means: *genuine* philosophy is *eo ipso* theology.) But phenomenology in temporariness [*Zeitweiligkeit*], in historical vitality, is *dynamis*; it is in becoming, is 'method,' is the way to absolute and universal knowledge, and the latter: knowledge *on* the way. With every step, ascertainment and simultaneously prescription for new beings as the next task, for new steps, but ones that have their steadfastness in what is already fixed. The prescription provides 'guiding threads'; but only actually theoretical execution yields theoretical sentences, the actually proven, definite, legitimately delimited sense of Being. Without a preview [*Vorschau*], there is no moving forward; but preview is not theory. For that reason, the sentences in your paper which refer to God should not be taken as my theoretical *teachings* [Lehren]. Would that I were that far!" (Husserl's emphasis.) See likewise the letter to Erich Przywara, S.J., dated July 15, 1932 (ibid., 237.12–20) concerning Husserl's "atheological philosophizing" and his aim at a "'theological' conclusion." He follows these remarks by saying that God is for him a "methodological idea" (ibid., 238.2), which is to say, a regulative idea. Decisive for our purposes is not whether Husserl believed in a personal God, but whether his system has an uppermost limit. And clearly this limit is to be found only in his, admittedly vague, notion of God (see IV, 216–17). Husserl says to A. Jaegerschmid ("Conversations," 50; April 28, 1931): "Phenomenology as science is there for those who do not have the access to faith that you [A. J.] have." That is to say: "The churches want what I want: to lead humanity to *aeternitas*. It is my task to attempt this by means of philosophy. Everything that I have written thus far is only preparatory; those writings merely present methods. Unfortunately, in the course of one's life one never gets down to the core, to what is essential. It is so important that philosophy be led away from liberalism and rationalism to what is essential, to truth. The question concerning the ultimate Being, concerning truth, must be the object of every true philosophy. That is my life's work" (ibid., 53; December 31, 1934). And finally: "Human life is nothing but the path to God. I attempt to reach this goal without theological proofs, methods, and aids, namely to reach God without God. I must, as it were, eliminate God from my scientific existence to order to blaze the trail to God for human beings who, unlike you [A. J.], do not have the certainty of faith through the Church. I know that my way of proceeding could be dangerous for me were I myself not a man deeply bound to God and a believer in Christ" (ibid., 56; December 1935). Concerning the function Husserl aims to fulfill for the unbeliev-

ers, see A. Jaegerschmid, "Die letzten Jahre Edmund Husserls (1936–1938)," *Stimmen der Zeit* 199, no. 2 (1981), 129–38, here 130. Regarding the specification of the meaning of God in Husserl, see the work of James Hart, esp. *The Person and Common Life*, passim, and that of Mensch, esp. *After Modernity*, 57–78, and *Intersubjectivity and Transcendental Idealism*, 360–74 et passim.

134. See, e.g., Lauer, "Introduction," 5. He denies that Husserlian thought is a system, while nevertheless acknowledging its programmatic character. The question is, how is that program structured? The answer will be an articulation of Husserl's system in *his* sense of the term. Lauer's denial is all the more puzzling since it is found in the introduction to Lauer's translation of "Philosophy as Rigorous Science," the very text in which Husserl suggests—if only suggests—the system argued for in the present study. Its suggestion, however, rests on the demand for a firm ground, which, as will become clear, entails the trajectory from it as lowermost limit up towards the uppermost limit. Consider Husserl's characterization of phenomenology as "a systematic science" (*Ideas III*, 82).

135. See, e.g., *BW* 9, 459.23–27.

136. See *BW* 7, 88.23–24.

137. Husserl's personal goal, however, is completion and finitude. Consider, e.g., a remark that is echoed time and again in his late letters (ibid., 227.16–19; April 14, 1937): "I almost want to hope that I do indeed survive the fight for my life—which only was and is and continues if it is completed in the completion [*Vollendung*] of its vital sense." See, e.g., his letter of February 1, 1922, to Paul Natorp regarding his "inability to finitize [*verendlichen*]" himself (*BW* 5, 151–52), and I, nn. 54, 108, and 127.

138. Husserl implies this polarity, e.g., in a passage from the end of September 1912 on the "extension of the phenomenological reduction" (*Hua* III/2, 564): "Since thereby, too, everything has been excluded that is related to the ego and God as transcendently apperceived free deed, creation, etc., we now have excluded all possible individual transcendent actualities: which are ordered, so to speak, as polar opposites [*polar gegenübergeordnet*] with respect to consciousness: as world of appearance and as world of absolute subjectivity or world of freedom."

139. By contrast, Boeder is able to demonstrate the three terms that are constitutive of the whole of Husserlian thought in *Das Vernunft-Gefüge der Moderne*, 135–87. He articulates the structure of the integral positions or ratios of modernity by means of the terms 'destiny/determination' (*Bestimmung*), 'topic' (*Sache*), 'thinking' (*Denken*), terms that derive from Heidegger's phrase 'the determination of the topic of thinking' (*die Bestimmung der Sache des Denkens*). On Boeder's use of these terms in general, see *Seditions*, xiv–xvi.

The lack of a middle term in Husserl—again, on his self-understanding—is not surprising given his emphasis on immediacy, on direct access, on originariness, etc. The "principle of all principles" is a case in point. Mediacy plays only a very limited role in his thought. Put somewhat differently, in Husserlian thought, bipartite relations have precedence, whereas tripartite or many-termed relations come into view only to be subsumed under bipartite relations—a case in point being a many-rayed or polythetic synthesis, which must be converted into a monothetic synthesis in order to become the subject of predication; such a move is precisely a reduction to a bipartite structure. In fact there is no need for mediation where reflection has direct access to the things themselves; thinking takes care of itself here, as it were.

140. See I, nn. 80, 82, and 133.

141. Sokolowski identifies two main formal structures in Husserlian thought: "the contrast between empty and filled intentions, or between absence and presence, and the relationships between wholes and parts. Other formal structures, like that of an identity within a manifold, or the more specialized relationship of sign and the signified, are defined with the help of the first two" (*Husserlian Meditations*, 8). Later he notes: "The contrariety of parts and wholes is founded on the contrariety of empty and filled intentions; and, reciprocally, the latter is founded on the former" (57). Tom Nenon notes two modes of foundation in Husserl: ontological and epistemological; they are themselves ultimately nested or stand, in our terms, in a "telescopic" relation to one another, though neither perspective is absolute: each can found the other. See his "Two Models of Foundation in the *Logical Investigations*," in B. C. Hopkins, ed., *Husserl in Contemporary Context: Prospects and Projects for Phenomenology* (Dordrecht: Kluwer, 1997), 97–114. See also Timothy J. Stapleton, "The Logic of Husserl's Transcendental Reduction," *Man and World* 15 (1982), 369–82 and Thomas Prufer, "Husserlian Distinctions and Strategies in *The Crisis*," in *Recapitulations: Essays in Philosophy* (Washington, D. C.: Catholic University of America Press, 1993), 48–57.

142. See *PP*, Beilage 25, 483 on polarization: "To the ego-polarization corresponds, we can say, an endlessly multifarious object-polarization, the latter as a production [*Leistung*] effected by an identical ego in the manifold of synthetically organized life." See also "Wert des Lebens," 233, and *Hua* XXVIII, 218.

143. In "Husserls Phänomenologie des Willens," 300, Ullrich Melle notes the following polarities: "In addition to the opposition between receptivity and spontaneity, Husserl also speaks of the opposition between sensuousness and the understanding, between passivity and activity, between latent and patent consciousness, and between unthematic and thematic consciousness. These oppositions, which are by no means identical, serve Husserl as fundamental ordering principles for his analyses of consciousness." See also *Ideas I*, 233: "To every cogito there belongs a precisely corresponding counterpart such that its noema has its precisely corresponding counternoema in the parallel cogito." Concerning reason and unreason, see *Hua* XXV, 147.32ff.

144. Apparently following Husserl's clarification of his use of *prinzipiell* (principial) in the passage just cited—but also in keeping with Cairns's *Guide*—Kersten renders the word in his translation of *Ideas I* as 'essentially necessary'. However, this paraphrase not only ignores Husserl's distinction between 'universality' and 'necessity', but it also conceals the thought of 'principle' (*Prinzip, Anfang,* ἀρχή) operative in and of central importance to his usage. We cite once again Husserl's clarification: "We are using here, as throughout this writing, the word *prinzipiell* in a rigorous sense with reference to *the highest and thus most radical* essential universalities or essential necessities." To preserve the nuances of the term, then, it is translated as 'principial' throughout the present study.

145. See, e.g., his letter to Albrecht cited in I, n. 54.

146. See I, 16–17, 20–21, and I, n. 51 concerning the sense in which all subjectivity is latently rational.

147. See Nenon, "Husserl's Theory of the Mental," 225.

148. See, e.g., Landgrebe, "Husserls Phänomenologie und die Motive zu ihrer Umbildung," 9–39, but esp. 11: "The fundamental, driving motif in the entire develop-

ment of Husserl's phenomenology is his unique conception of intentionality." See also Oskar Becker, "Die Philosophie Edmund Husserls," *Kant-Studien* 35 (1930), 119–50, here 142.

149. See *Hua* XXVII, 118: "Just as the individual singular man has his inborn telos, an infinite idea born in him, that of his 'true' ego and his true life, which, once in him, even if at first unclearly, awakens, constitutes the categorical *imperative* of his subsequent life; in a firm ethos it is destined (as idea) to stamp his life with a new form, that of the life as it ought to be [*gesollt*] and as legitimated or even that of a life in the form of the actualization of the categorical idea, and in fact by virtue of an unerring will (the centeredness of the will in the idea of the categorical imperative)—likewise for a *humanity*, i.e., for the humanity that is active in the streaming unity of a communal and cultural life" (Husserl's emphasis). These ideas are not identical, but "stand in close relation" or are "analogous" to one another. They mirror one another.

150. See *Hua* XV, 590: "Thus my transcendental beginning and ending is contained within me, as a being now in the mode of present . . ."

151. Cairns, *Conversations*, 47; November 24, 1931.

152. Although her essay on "First Philosophy" is instructive, particularly concerning the "absolute" in Husserl's thought, Ströker fails to consider there the relation of the ground to its "opposite pole," not to mention the intermediate phases. She does focus on the unity of Husserl's intention to establish First Philosophy, but she neglects the whole in which this philosophy has its firstness, from which it derives its sense.

153. See Karl Schuhmann, "Husserls Idee der Philosophie," *Husserl Studies* 5 (1988), 235–56, esp. 240–41. See also his Introduction to Husserl's *Briefwechsel* (*BW* 10, 1–70, here 41–42). Husserl apparently drafted a plan for a large systematic work in 1930, which Iso Kern includes in his edition of *Hua* XV, xxxvi. The plan begins with a "Founding of the egological theory of consciousness" and ends with "The problems of teleology and God." These extremes are of central interest here, particularly since they remain essentially constant throughout Husserl's "transcendental" phase. The intermediate phases are less important not only because they vary, but especially because they lie within the whole delimited by the two extremes. Schuhmann discusses the candidates for inclusion in the whole and their order in his essay (see "Husserls Idee der Philosophie," 240). As late as 1937 (*BW* 7, 225–26), Husserl describes the unfolding of his thought in the *Crisis* as such a trajectory. It is a "gradual leading upward [*allmähliche Emporleitung*] from naive and closed traditionality . . . to the genuine autonomy of the 'transcendental reduction'—to the discovery of the 'transcendental Ego,'" then to "universal transcendental intersubjectivity," and finally to "absolute transcendental historicity and the transcendental teleology of the absolute."

154. Important exceptions are found in the work of Mensch, Sepp, and Hart.

155. See, e.g., Stephan Strasser, "Das Gottesproblem in der Spätphilosophie Edmund Husserls," *Philosophisches Jahrbuch* 67 (1959), 130–42 and "Monadologie und Teleologie in der Philosophie Edmund Husserls," *Phänomenologische Forschungen* 22 (1989), 217–35. See also Louis Dupré, "Husserl's Thought on God and Faith," *Philosophy and Phenomenological Research* 29 (1968–69), 201–15.

156. See, e.g., David Bell, "Phenomenology, Solipsism and Egocentric Thought," *Proceedings of the Aristotelian Society*, sup. vol. 62 (1988), 45–60.

157. See Preface, xv.

158. See Schuhmann, *Die Dialektik der Phänomenologie* II, and Edward G. Ballard, "On the Method of Phenomenological Reduction, Its Presuppositions, and Its Future," in L. Embree, ed., *Life-World and Consciousness* (Evanston, Ill.: Northwestern University Press, 1972), 101–23, here 103–4.

159. Biemel, "Die entscheidenden Phasen," 88.

160. Becker, "Die Philosophie Edmund Husserls," 139.

161. Martin Heidegger, *Aus der Erfahrung des Denkens*, Gesamtausgabe 13 (Frankfurt a. M.: Klostermann, 1983), 82: *in sein Gefüge eingeschwungen ist*. See Boeder, *Seditions*, 162 et passim.

162. So Husserl remarked, according to Cairns; see his *Conversations*, 2 (June 27, 1931).

163. Ibid., 3. This move from the *Cartesian Meditations* to *Ideas I* can be viewed as a progressive radicalization. This points one from the "heights" back to the ground, which is made most perspicuous by Husserl in *Ideas I* and in it alone.

164. On the significance of *Ideas I* to the remainder of Husserl's work, see Elisabeth Ströker, "Husserls Konzept einer reinen Phänomenologie und phänomenologischen Philosophie," in *Husserls Werk* (Hamburg: Meiner, 1992), 56ff.

165. See *Hua* VIII, 156: "*But it is, above all, positionality that belongs necessarily to life, and in every segment*" (Husserl's emphasis).

166. See *Crisis*, 8/10, 10/12, and 11/13, respectively.

167. See III, n. 82.

168. *Hua* XXVII, 117–18. See the letters to W. P. Bell, *BW* 3, 10–51, from the 1920s.

169. *Hua* XXVII, 118. See I, n. 70 on straying.

Chapter II. Phenomenological Propaedeutics

1. Throughout Chapters II–IV of this study, numbers in parentheses within the body of the text refer to the original pagination of *Ideas I*, which is noted in the margins of both the German edition and the English translation used here. For conventions employed in references, see the prefatory note to the Bibliography, below.

2. Modernity is meant here as an "epoch" subsequent to the modern era (*Neuzeit*), which concludes with Hegel. The former comprises the positions of Frege, Schlick, Kuhn (functional reason), Dilthey, Husserl, Wittgenstein (hermeneutic reason), and Marx, Nietzsche, Heidegger (apocalyptic reason). For the explication of the tectonic of their ratios and thus of the whole of modernity, see Boeder, *Das Vernunft-Gefüge der Moderne*. His *Seditions* provides much insight into the sense of 'modernity' as it is employed in the present study.

3. Husserl points out "the literal sense" of 'radical' when he speaks of the "radical failings of method" marring the psychology of his day (see *Ideas I*, 2). If he is to succeed in elevating "psychology to a higher scientific level" while also "extending its field of work," he must first get down to the roots that this discipline has thus far, i.e., until the advent of transcendental phenomenology, overlooked or taken for granted.

4. Much attention has been paid to the relationship between the *Logical Investigations* and *Ideas I*, though less in view of a unifying task than of problems and method.

See, among others, Mohanty, "The Development of Husserl's Thought," 53–63, as well as both volumes of Schuhmann's *Die Dialektik der Phänomenologie*, and Herman Philipse, "Transcendental Idealism," in B. Smith and D. W. Smith, eds., *The Cambridge Companion to Husserl* (Cambridge: Cambridge University Press, 1995), 239–322.

5. Although 'to exclude' is the common translation of *ausschalten*, the literal 'to switch off' is often more accurate, since no thing, state, or attitude is actually excluded; rather, a specific form of belief is "switched off." In that sense it is "excluded" from the doxic or judicative sphere. The former translation is acceptable only so long as one remembers both *what* is excluded thereby and from what. Husserl makes the proper sense clear in a manuscript penned at the end of September 1912: "The whole natural world has been excluded [*ausgeschaltet*] from the field of judgment, and what we have retained of it were the lived experiences and concatenations of lived experiences that bring about consciousness [*bewußtmachen*] of the natural world; and if we have this purity once, then we thereby have *eo ipso* the entire field of pure consciousness, we have gained the regard for the transcendental and follow its own guiding thread further" (Beilage 16, *Hua* III/2, 560–61). Either translation will be used here depending on the context.

6. See *EBA*, 295–96/174–75 for Husserl's use of 'propaedeutic'.

7. In a similar vein, Ballard ("On the Method of Phenomenological Reduction," 105) points to Husserl's "methodological anxiety evident at every step in this effort to achieve this complete awareness."

8. See Aristotle, *Posterior Analytics* 71^b33ff., *Physics* 184^a16ff., and *On Sophistical Refutations* 183^b22–27. Husserl explicitly invokes this distinction, e.g., in *Hua* XXIV, 212. See also Afterword, 557. Adler draws out the significance of Aristotelian motifs to Husserlian thought in "Prolegomena to Phenomenology," 7, 8, 10, 20, 23, and the relevant notes.

9. There is a sense in which Husserl seems to violate this rule in *Ideas I*. Namely, he begins by distinguishing between facts and essences. However, essences are nothing anyone living in the natural attitude encounters in his or her everyday dealings, even if, as Husserl says, "everyone sees 'ideas,' 'essences,' and does so, so to speak, continuously; they operate with them in thinking and also effect eidetic judgments—except that from their epistemological standpoint they interpret them away" (see *Ideas I*, 41). There is a sense in which Husserl imposes what is first by nature on the reader of *Ideas I* prematurely, that is, before sufficiently passing through what is first for us. And this may be the reason for his complaint about the fragmentary character of this work (see I, 28–29). However, this holds only partially, for Husserl does begin with the natural attitude and the facts of concern to it, and then proceeds to its sciences, and only then to essences and their corresponding sciences.

As for the violation of the "nature of the things" by starting with what is first by nature, it would occur were the investigator, or the one who makes a case for phenomenology, to fail to respect the attitude in which each prephenomenological individual finds him- or herself: the "natural attitude" in Husserl's terminology. It belongs among the things investigated by the phenomenologist no less than any specific act of consciousness or its correlate. See II, n. 18.

10. Husserl does not speak of 'sedimentation' in *Ideas I*, but rather in the *Crisis*. Nevertheless, his language here suggests this metaphor, for the "habits of thinking" obscure or cover over the origin sought after. For the later usage, see *Crisis*, 52/52. See I, 4 on 'boring', as well as II, 94–95 on 'destruction', which are predecessors of the idea of removing layers of sedimentation in order to get to the true foundation.

11. See II, 35–36 and n. 104 concerning the severing of ties with the world. As for Husserl's "doctrine of essence" or "ideas," he never developed it *expressis verbis* and, even where essence is thematized (such as in the Second Investigation or the first chapter of *Ideas I*) it is never dealt with *in extenso*. In *Ideas III*, e.g., he merely promises the future development of such a doctrine (see *Ideas III*, 86.13ff.). Thankfully, however, there are a number of helpful attempts to make sense of Husserl's views on essence, most notably: Gilbert T. Null, "Husserl's Doctrine of Essence," in J. N. Mohanty and W. R. McKenna, eds., *Husserl's Phenomenology: A Textbook* (Lanham: CARP and University Press of America, 1989), 69–105; James R. Mensch, "Essence and Existence in Thomas and Husserl," in *After Modernity*, 67–78; Sokolowski, *Husserlian Meditations*, 57–85; Ströker, *Husserls transzendentale Phänomenologie*, 80–94; J. N. Mohanty, "Individual Fact and Essence in Edmund Husserl's Philosophy," in *Phenomenology and Ontology* (The Hague: Nijhoff, 1970), 152–62; and Burt C. Hopkins, "Phenomenological Cognition of the A Priori: Husserl's Method of 'Seeing Essences' (*Wesenserschauung*)," in B. C. Hopkins, ed., *Husserl in Contemporary Context: Prospects and Projects for Phenomenology* (Dordrecht: Kluwer, 1997), 151–78. On the other hand, Husserl does develop a doctrine of essence insofar as his account of phenomenology itself can be regarded as such a doctrine, the premier eidetics.

12. Hence, like Ströker in *Husserls transzendentale Phänomenologie*, Bernet, Kern, and Marbach do well in discussing the reductions by first addressing the phenomenological reduction and only then taking up the eidetic reduction. See their *Edmund Husserl*, 56–74 and 74–84, respectively.

13. Note that the eidetic reduction is not thematized as such in *Ideas I* beyond its brief mention in the passage cited in the previous paragraph (ibid., 4). Rather, it is used, and continuously so. For an alternative to the account presented here of the distinction and relation of the eidetic and phenomenological reductions, see Ströker, *Husserls transzendentale Phänomenologie*, 87–88.

14. Throughout the present study *Erlebnis* will generally be translated as 'lived experience'. It is to be distinguished from *Erfahrung* (experience), however, which typically refers to external experience.

15. See Afterword, 552: "Since the reduction to the transcendental, and at the same time this further reduction [namely, the eidetic reduction] to the *eidos*, is the method of access to the new science's field of work, it becomes clear (and this must be sharply emphasized at the outset) that the proper beginning of the systematic inauguration of this science lies in the chapters that deal with the aforementioned reductions." As just noted, whereas the eidetic reduction and eidetic inquiry can be carried out both outside of and within the phenomenological sphere, it is only after the latter has been entered (by means of the epoché) that the eidetic reduction and eidetic inquiry become radical and thereby gain their proper sense. On account of this, a hierarchy between the two reductions may be discerned, wherein the transcendental-phenomenological reduction founds the eidetic reduction, i.e., provides the latter with its ground.

16. See Null, "Husserl's Doctrine of Essence," 69–90, for a presentation of the background (provided by both the *Logical Investigations* and the philosophical tradition) of the doctrine of essence developed in *Ideas I*.

17. Husserl alludes to this relationship in *Ideas III*, 22: "It is not what calls itself 'modern science' and not those who call themselves 'experts' that make the method, but rather the *essence* of the objects and the appurtenant essence of the possible experience of objects of the relevant category (that is, the Apriori of phenomenological constitution) *prescribes* everything that belongs principially to the method; and it characterizes the expert of genius that he grasps this intuitively (even if he does not capture it philosophically in rigorous concepts and formulated norms) and orients the particular problems and the particular methods in accordance with it. All the discoveries and inventions of experts move within the parameters of an absolutely nontransgressible Apriori that one cannot draw from their doctrines, but only from phenomenological intuition." This Apriori encompasses the essences to which genius gains access.

18. The sense of 'theory' operative here should become clearer in what follows (see esp. II, 53–54), but at this point at least three interrelated features of Husserl's understanding of theory may be noted: in its prephenomenological manifestations it is *dogmatic*, which means that it *approaches things with preconceptions*, and imposes these notions on those things. In other words, in asserting itself, theory (again, traditionally considered, on Husserl's view) violates the natural order and *subjects Being to thinking*, whereas properly phenomenological "theory" grows out of the things themselves (ideally) precisely as they give themselves; it takes its bearings solely by the things. It lets them be, and abides by their directives. Phenomenology thereby seeks to accord with its guiding insight into the priority of Being over thinking. On this priority, see the discussion of the "principle of all principles" on II, 54–56.

Concerning Husserl's notion of attitude, and in particular of the natural attitude, see Sebastian Luft, "Husserl's Phenomenological Discovery of the Natural Attitude," *Continental Philosophy Review* 31 (1998), 153–70, and Matthias Fischer, *Differente Wissensfelder – Einheitlicher Vernunftraum. Über Husserls Begriff der Einstellung* (Munich: Fink, 1985), esp. 14–20 and 55–92. Luft claims (154) that "Husserl never systematically worked out a full and consistent theory of the natural attitude," and that the latter therefore remains an "operative concept." Such a "theory," however, is rendered superfluous by Husserl's disclosure of *the* presupposition of the natural attitude—that is, the general thesis, which is certainly the heart of the matter. Without it there is no natural attitude. Husserl's account of the natural attitude in *Ideas I* is indeed sufficient, that is, sufficient for his purposes: insofar as it is his task to motivate the idea of phenomenology, and thereby to overcome the obstacles to entering into its sphere, he need only demonstrate—and hence thematize—the nature of those obstacles, which are summed up in the general thesis, or the mistaken belief that what is in fact contingent is absolute, necessary. Furthermore, one may wonder about the extent to which the natural attitude may be considered an operative concept in Husserlian thought, for after the performance of the epoché, the natural attitude cannot be "operative" in phenomenology, since it is excluded once its ground has been excluded. To accuse Husserl of shortcomings in these respects is to ignore his intention. (For the paradigmatic exposition of the distinction between 'operative' and 'thematic' concepts, see Eugen Fink, "Operative Begriffe in Husserls Phänomenologie," in *Nähe und Distanz* [Freiburg/Munich: Alber,

1976], 180–204. Note that, contrary to Luft's suggestion, Fink does not claim that the natural attitude remains an operative concept in Husserl. Rather, he states quite clearly that Husserl thematizes it and thereby shows its "operative vital presupposition." See ibid., 193. Ballard ["On the Method of Phenomenological Reduction," 105] is more careful in his appeal to Fink's notion.)

19. Husserl stresses (see *Ideas I*, 7 n.) that he is not telling "any stories" here. The natural attitude is original in the sense that it is the attitude in which we find ourselves immediately, that is, always already. It is the attitude into which we are born. Unless a modification is effected, it holds sway in all our dealings in and with the world

20. See *PP*, 63.22ff. concerning the relationship between theory and natural experience, which share the fundamental "presumption of horizon."

21. On the role of perception in Husserlian thought, see William R. McKenna, "Husserl's Theory of Perception," in J. N. Mohanty and W. R. McKenna, eds., *Husserl's Phenomenology: A Textbook* (Lanham: CARP and University Press of America, 1989), 181–212.

22. See *Ideas I*, 8: "Experiential sciences are 'factual' sciences." Kersten translates this as: "Sciences of experience are sciences of 'matters of fact.'" In what follows, preference will be given to 'natural science' instead of 'science of nature'; likewise to 'experiential' and 'factual science' instead of 'science of experience' and 'of facts', respectively. Wherever extra clarity seems to be afforded by the second formulation, however, it will be employed.

23. It is the insight into the gulf separating and the hierarchy existing between the contingent and the Apriori that motivates one to effect the eidetic reduction and ultimately the epoché. See in this connection *PP*, 71: "Every attempted transition to an Apriori in this determinate sense (an unconditional universality generated through seeing insight) demands liberation from the fact. In our case the fact is the world we experience as actual, factual with these factual, physical things." See Hopkins, "Phenomenological Cognition of the A Priori," esp. n. 14, and Sokolowksi, *Husserlian Meditations*, 104–5.

24. Here 'existence' renders *Bestand*. Elsewhere, following Kersten, 'existence' renders *Existenz*, whereas 'factual existence' renders *Dasein*. Concerning the latter term, however, wherever the context makes it clear that real existence is under discussion (as in the case of factual, physical, or spatiotemporal things), then the adjectival and adverbial forms will be replaced accordingly.

25. Husserl's usage of 'essence' and *eidos* suggests that the latter represents a maximal case of the former—that is, insofar as it is pure, the *eidos* is free to the greatest degree from factualness. On the other hand, in his Introduction to *Ideas I* (see 8), he distinguishes these two concepts merely terminologically and not "ontologically." Despite his introduction of this distinction, however, Husserl makes comparatively little use of the latter term, preferring instead the former. On *eidos* see Sokolowski, *Husserlian Meditations*, 62ff.

26. See, e.g., *Hua* XVIII, §62.

27. See *Ideas I*, 10: "To begin with, 'essence' denoted that which is to be found in the very own Being of an individuum as the latter's What. However, any such What can be 'transformed into an idea.'"

28. The individual participates in the essence in a determinate sense; it provides a "gateway," as it were, to its own essence. On the nature and role eidetic seeing in Husserl, see, again, Hopkins, "Phenomenological Cognition of the A Priori," and Sokolowski, *Husserlian Meditations*.

29. *Individuelle Anschauung*. This is to be understood not as an "individual" intuition, but rather as the "intuition of something individual." In his translation of *Ideas I*, Kersten uses the latter paraphrase. Similarly, in the present text 'eidetic intuition' and 'eidetic seeing' translate *Wesensanschauung* and *Wesensschauung*, respectively. The former is to be understood as the intuition of an essence, the latter as the seeing of an essence. However, wherever additional clarity is required, the extended formulations will be employed.

30. See Edward S. Casey, "Imagination and Phenomenological Method," in F. A. Elliston and P. McCormick, eds., *Husserl: Expositions and Appraisals* (Notre Dame, Ind.: University of Notre Dame Press, 1977), 70–82, esp. 75ff. (B).

31. What is decisive is the givenness in intuition, not the reality of what is given. See *Ideas I*, 13: "Just as any thinking, any making statements about requires experience for its justification . . . likewise thinking about pure essences as justifying bases requires . . . the seeing of essences."

32. Husserl's paradigmatic use of *metabasis* occurs in his *Prolegomena* (*Hua* XVIII, A/B 6). Use is also made of it on *Ideas I*, 115, where it still means the transgression of regional boundaries or the mixing of the cognitions of one sphere with those of another. The notion of *metabasis* can be widened to mean mixing things that do not belong together, that is, failing to observe essential distinctions. See I, n. 70 above concerning "straying from the path," which can also be considered a form of *metabasis*. Concerning the treatment of *metabasis* in the *Prolegomena*, see Adler, "Prolegomena to Phenomenology," 22–24, and in the later work, see Eckard Wolz-Gottwald, "Zur metábasis im Spätwerk Edmund Husserls," *Allgemeine Zeitschrift für Philosophie* 20 (1995), 111–30.

33. It should be borne in mind that *Satz* may be translated as, among other things, 'proposition', 'sentence', or 'positum'. It is the latter term that will be given priority below (see IV, 199–200). At this point, however, it suffices to employ the first term.

34. See IV, 203.

35. See *Ideas I*, 16: "The connection (*itself eidetic*) obtaining between individual object and essence . . . founds a corresponding interrelation between factual sciences and eidetic sciences."

36. See II, n. 17.

37. See *Ideas III*, § 14 concerning the manner in which phenomenology encompasses the various ontologies, and may even be said to be the wellspring of the latter. Phenomenology is to be "the great organon of all transcendental cognition" (ibid., 78).

38. In the final paragraphs of the first chapter of *Ideas I*, thus in § § 10–17, Husserl takes pains to refine his elaboration of the hierarchies obtaining between facts and essences, as well as between material and formal essences. Such hierarchies may be viewed as encased, nested, or telescopic structures, on the order of Chinese boxes. While these paragraphs would be crucial to an articulation of Husserl's "doctrine of essence," they cannot concern us here, for the guiding intention of the present study is not to take up every distinction or tool developed by Husserl, to say nothing of every-

thing in detail, but rather to trace the movement of his thought in view of its norm, which is his task. For an account of features of Husserl's "doctrine of essence" not covered here, see Null, "Husserl's Doctrine of Essence," as well as J. N. Mohanty, "Husserl's Formalism," in T. M. Seebohm et al., eds., *Phenomenology and the Formal Sciences* (Dordrecht: Kluwer, 1991), 93–105, esp. 100ff. (d).

39. Apparently there is only one idea, whereas there may be more than one phenomenology. The elucidation of the idea will determine which candidates for the status of "phenomenology" will earn that name. The chief criterion is the extent to which a given "phenomenology" seeks to fulfill the idea.

40. The negativity in question here is not merely imagined, but, for Husserl, characterizes the age in which phenomenology is born. As a consequence, he always thinks on the defensive in his efforts to establish the science of pure phenomenology. The negative may be said to form the underside of every positive account he puts forth. It is important to note, however, that although negativity drives Husserl's thought in a sense, it is by no means a motor as it was in the philosophical tradition, such as, e.g., in Hegel. This has to be the case inasmuch as the negativity of significance to Husserl lacks the prerequisite acknowledgment (*Anerkennung*) of the position negated. The negated position does not form a moment of the subsequent positive position; it plays no constitutive role in what follows the negation. No synthesis takes place, but only the exclusion of one position in favor of another. As will be seen, the justification of such exclusion is achieved by means of the principle that itself requires the exclusion in the first place. It is thoroughly consistent that the negated position not be accorded any acknowledgment, for at issue is the first principle, the starting point. And in Husserl's case, acknowledgment would presuppose that two positions had the same starting point, which they could not have at this stage.

41. Husserl refers here for the first time to the "philosophical ἐποχή." But in fact the principle here in question is, strictly speaking, not equivalent to the phenomenological epoché. As will be seen below, the demand that one take one's bearings by the things themselves as they give themselves in intuition is not a modification of consciousness in the same sense as that effected by the epoché, but rather a methodological norm. The demand requires the exclusion of theory, of preconceived notions, etc., and in fact the belief in all such things insofar as it brings one to assert them as the measure of all things. (Concerning the "philosophical epoché," see *Hua* III/2, 482 and 531.41ff.) The phenomenological epoché excludes something entirely different and ushers in a new attitude altogether. The demand in question is made within the same attitude as that in which the other sciences are practiced. Husserl's suggestion that this demand is equivalent to the epoché is misleading and can at best be taken metaphorically. A kind of abstinence (*Enthaltung*) is required here, it is true. But the abstinence required and the attitude in which each is carried out are literally a world apart. At best the demand might be equated with a phenomenological reduction; but that is not legitimate at this stage, for such can be effected only within the phenomenological attitude. Concerning this demand, which will be soon named the "principle of all principles," see II, 54–56. Concerning the epoché, see II, 57–75, esp. 62–68.

42. The full title of the work under investigation here, *Ideas Pertaining to a Pure Phenomenology and to a Phenomenological Philosophy*, already suggests that phenomenology and philosophy are not one and the same for Husserl. On his view, philosophy only becomes a legitimate enterprise as rigorous science, and this it becomes only by virtue of

the grounding pure phenomenology provides. Hence, it is not just philosophy, but *phenomenological* philosophy. Schuhmann attempts to clarify the relationship between the two sides of this title in his "trilogy" (see I, n. 22), but especially in *Die Dialektik der Phänomenologie* II.

43. See *Prolegomena* and *Crisis*. This remains the point of difference for Husserl throughout his career. It motivates his entire endeavor. The denial of "ideas," etc. is tantamount to the denial of reason.

44. On the skepticism of concern to Husserl, see Adler, "Prolegomena to Phenomenology," Karl Mertens, *Zwischen Letztbegründung und Skepsis* (Freiburg/Munich: Alber, 1996), and Gail Soffer, *Husserl and the Question of Relativism* (Dordrecht: Kluwer, 1991), 59–101.

45. See *Hua* XVIII, esp. 120.

46. Concerning the effects of such "blindness of the soul," see *Crisis*, Part I.

47. Though this must be qualified. See II, n. 62.

48. Friederike Rechtenwald (in *Die phänomenologische Reduktion bei Edmund Husserl* [Münster: Helios, 1929], 15) suggests the link between intuition as Husserl understands it and revelation. She says: "In the entire phenomenological attitude, the main emphasis is placed on intuition, on that which is 'originarily given' in consciousness, on the formations of 'pure consciousness,' which is a priori. But if in the analysis of pure consciousness we go so far back that we hit upon this intuitive, this original [something], this impetus [*Anstoß*] or this free ascent [*Aufsteigen*] cannot be grasped scientifically. This suggests the view that the intuitive is to be a kind of revelation of the 'essence,' which reigns unshakably in the phenomenological Heaven."

49. Extended to concepts, Husserl calls the method dictated by this principle "in the main the Socratic method" (*Ideas III*, 100.33).

50. Husserl notes that those prejudiced by theory tend to see what they want to see: "Prejudices are remarkably easy to satisfy regarding theories" (*Ideas I*, 41).

51. The distinction of attitudes will be treated shortly. See II, 59–60.

52. On the epoché, see II, 57–75.

53. Strictly speaking, every prephenomenological science and philosophy is either skeptical or dogmatic in character. On Husserl's view, it is only phenomenology, and especially transcendental phenomenology, that is nonskeptical and undogmatic. And it alone enables other sciences and philosophies to follow suit.

54. Husserl says that this principle demands "the exclusion of all assumptions that cannot be fully and completely realized phenomenologically" (*Hua* XIX/1, § 7, A 19). Procedurally, this results in investigations akin to those carried out especially in the opening chapter of *Ideas I*, although also throughout this work. In the *Logical Investigations*, abiding by the principle of presuppositionlessness means: "Every epistemological investigation must be carried out on a purely phenomenological ground. The 'theory' striven for in [the investigation] is after all nothing but the reflection on and evident clarification of what thinking and cognizing are in general, wherein its rightful claim to objectivity actually lies, which are the essential forms that belong to the idea of cognition, in particular to the idea of a priori cognition, in which sense the 'formal' laws grounded in these forms are laws of thought, and in which sense they delimit the ideal possibility of theoretical cognition and cognition in general."

55. Thus Oskar Becker is mistaken in projecting the transcendental reduction back into the *Logical Investigations*. See his "Die Philosophie Edmund Husserls," 127 and 129–30.

56. The principle of all principles, the epoché, and the phenomenological reductions are not identical. The distinctions between them will be drawn out in the course of the following analyses. But it should be noted that the key point of difference is always one of attitude.

57. In *Ideas III*, 80, e.g., Husserl says: "In the eidetics of space, of material nature, of spirit, etc., we do *dogmatic* science under the title of 'ontology'" (his emphasis). See also *Ideas III*, 94.21ff.

58. See *PRS*, 315: "The spell of primeval naturalism also consists in the fact that it makes it so difficult for us all to see 'essences,' 'ideas,' or rather, since we do indeed see them, so to speak, constantly, [it makes it difficult for us] to accept them in their specific peculiarity instead of countersensically naturalizing them."

59. Husserl's account of skepticism in *Ideas I* is for the most part "negative" and thus one-sided. However, such negativity need not be merely negative. In his 1923–24 lectures on First Philosophy (*Hua* VII), e.g., he treats at length the manner in which skepticism has been beneficial to philosophy, and thus productive, by awakening it from its "dogmatic slumber" and driving it onward. Consider also that Husserlian phenomenology is "originally" skeptical. See in this connection Mertens, *Letztbegründung und Skepsis*, 53ff. Furthermore, consider Husserl's view that every actionality can fall back into inactionality and its translation into the field of knowledge and practice: namely, every knowledge and every practice threatens to slip into the passivity of laming dogmatism.

60. See his allusion to this epoch in *PRS*, 289. In addition, see the Vienna lecture (esp. *VL*, 341/294), where he makes "the leap to the so-called modern era [*den Sprung zur sogenannten Neuzeit*]" from antiquity. See also *Crisis*, 5/8 for his account of the "turn against the medieval mode of existence" in the Renaissance. Admittedly, he does not speak directly about phenomenology there, but the philosophy of the modern era, as well as that of antiquity, is his own "admired example [*bewundertes Vorbild*]," and so can be regarded as the analog of his thought, especially in the present context. Following the passage just cited, Husserl also speaks of Greek philosophy. It intends to stay "free of the bonds of all myth and tradition" (ibid.). He regards phenomenology as the heir of the sense of those two modes of philosophy and thus of the ideal they pursued, even if in different ways. See James G. Hart, "The Study of Religion in Husserl's Writings," in M. Daniel and L. Embree, eds., *Phenomenology of the Cultural Disciplines* (Dordrecht: Kluwer, 1994), 265–96, here 284–85.

61. See, e.g., *VL*, 341.25/294.

62. Contrary to Husserl's claims, however, Adler ("Prolegomena to Phenomenology," esp. 39-48) has shown that Husserl does in fact use a form of argumentation in his refutations of skepticism—namely, he employs reflexive arguments in order to elicit the "pragmatic contradictions" of which the skeptic is guilty.

63. Although the distinction between these levels, as well as that between the epoché and the eidetic reduction, will be addressed below once the general thesis and its exclusion have been treated, at this point this much can be said: These three levels may be distinguished based on their respective degree of purity. Natural or naive inquiry is

immersed in or completely dependent upon the general thesis. Prephenomenological eidetic inquiry is purer, for it does not deal with contingent facts but with necessary essences; nevertheless, it remains "infected," as it were, by the general thesis. Only transcendental-phenomenological inquiry is pure, and in fact because of the exclusion of the general thesis as effected by the epoché. Following this purification, however, a "new eidetics" becomes possible, namely that which moves within the field of inquiry opened by the epoché. This new, pure eidetics is precisely transcendental phenomenology.

64. See II, n. 75.

65. Afterword, 564. Husserl repeats this time and again in his correspondence, especially to those of his students who have preferred to stick to the level of phenomenology of the *Logical Investigations*, that is, who prefer eidetic analysis to transcendental-phenomenologically purified analysis. Husserl considers the dogged attachment to the earlier stage of his work on the part of some of his students and readers to be a blatant disregard of his intention but also of phenomenology in its proper, i.e., most advanced form. And as a result of such disregard, their efforts cannot properly be called phenomenology on Husserl's view. Karl Schuhmann's argument for the legitimacy of the existence of various kinds of phenomenology given Husserl's notion of phenomenological ascent (*Emporsteigen*) does not undermine Husserl's view of such students and readers (see Schuhmann, *Die Dialektik der Phänomenologie* II, passim). Husserl speaks from the standpoint of transcendental phenomenology; he *sees* its necessity. And it is based on this necessity, on the compulsion of the will that results from having seen it, that he repeatedly demands of his students that they come to terms with the epoché, that they finally understand it, if they truly want to do work in phenomenology. For only based on such understanding will one see its necessity; as long as one sees in it a mere possibility, one will not rise to the level of genuine inquiry.

66. See Philip J. Bossert, "The Sense of 'Epoché' and 'Reduction' in Husserl's Philosophy," *Journal of the British Society for Phenomenology* 5 (1974), 243–55, here 247 col. 1 and n. 13. Although his paper is instructive, Bossert's use of 'epoché' is often imprecise.

67. It is important to note that Husserl is speaking from the standpoint of the natural attitude here. Thus *Wirklichkeit* means as much as 'reality' in this context—it is not distinguished from *Realität* (reality). Once consciousness has been distinguished into the natural and the phenomenological attitudes, however, *Wirklichkeit* (actuality) will also be accorded a different meaning, specifically with regard to the actuality of irrealities. It will be distinguished from *Realität*, and will be a feature of pure consciousness. Reality is bound up with factual existence; actuality need not be.

68. Of course, as was noted (see II, n. 18), there is a sense in which the natural attitude is indeed theoretical, namely insofar as it is dogmatic. But the sense of theory at issue in the present context is clearly that which results from reflection. Here theory is an intellectual construct.

69. Note here the distinction between consciousness and thinking. Consciousness precedes thinking; the former is experiential. Husserl says earlier of one's involvement with the environing-world (*Ideas I*, 48–49): "I can let my attention wander away . . . to all the Objects I 'know' just now to be here and there in the surroundings of which there is also immediate consciousness—a knowing that involves no conceptual thinking and

that changes into a clear intuiting only with the advertence of my attention, and even then only partially and for the most part quite imperfectly."

70. Therefore the performance of the epoché does not result in an "impoverishment" but rather an enrichment of our understanding of consciousness. See Bossert, "The Sense of 'Epoché' and 'Reduction'," 249 col. 2.

71. Liangkang Ni, e.g., suggests that the belief in the existence of the world can be disregarded because it is so basic; see his *Seinsglaube in der Phänomenologie Edmund Husserls* (Dordrecht: Kluwer, 1999), xvii–xviii; see also chap. VII. And yet in doing so, he covers over the central importance of foundedness in Husserl's thought and thus of the teleology, and by extension the system, and ultimately the *place* of these reflections within the *systematic whole* of Husserl's transcendental-phenomenological investigations. Furthermore, he misconstrues the effect of the epoché.

72. Husserl points to this indeterminacy of the world early on in his account of the natural attitude: "in a fixed order of Being, it [i.e., the world] reaches into the unlimited. What is now perceived, what is more or less clearly co-present and determinate (or at least somewhat determinate), is partly penetrated, partly surrounded by a horizon of indeterminate actuality of which there is vague consciousness" (*Ideas I*, 49). And shortly thereafter he notes: "Moreover, the indeterminate surroundings are infinite." He puts this slightly differently in *PP*, 63: "In itself our experiencing grasps, looks at, feels, etc. the whole of [*umgreift, umblickt, umtastet usw.*] the world itself as it itself, originally in certainty. Doubt as a breaking of certainty appears only in single instances as a transitory phase on the way to new, once again unbroken certainty within the universal parameters of a unified Being-certainty. Truth is true judgment, the decision of questions that have arisen. At the level of mere experience, doubt does indeed bear along with it another level of questioning and thus the intention towards decisions. But the world itself, the universe 'of' beings, never stands in question so long as we live along in natural experience." I.e., natural, as opposed to theoretical or philosophical, doubt never bears on the whole of the world at once, but only on aspects of the world—and always within "the one world of experience" (59). As the "factually existing world," it is always our "environing-world" (56).

73. Husserl's understanding and investigation of 'modification' as well as of 'belief' will be taken up in III; see esp. 142ff.

74. However, this does not mean that the phenomenological attitude is completely neutral, contrary to Henry Pietersma's claim (see his "Assertion and Predication in Husserl," *Husserl Studies* 2 [1985], 75–95, here 91), but rather selectively neutral—that is, it is neutral with regard to the general thesis. Not all belief is expunged by means of the epoché, but only the belief in the existence of the world.

75. See "Der cartesianische <und> der Weg der universalen phänomenologischen Psychologie <in die transzendentale Phänomenologie>" (1923), in *Hua* VIII, 275–301. See also Iso Kern, "Die drei Wege zur transzendental-phaenomenologischen Reduktion in der Philosophie Edmund Husserls," *Tijdschrift voor Filosofie* 24 (1962), 304–22, as well as Bernet, Kern, Marbach, *Edmund Husserl*, 62–72, and John J. Drummond, "Husserl on the Ways to the Performance of the Reduction," *Man and World* 8 (1975), 47–69. As becomes evident, the canonical way to the epoché is the Cartesian. The other ways Husserl pursued are "equally possible," but the fact remains that the Cartesian way is the first (see Afterword, 558). Every other way is taken on

analogy and in the attempt to make the epoché more accessible or secure its results. Due to its paradigmatic role, we shall focus here only on the "Cartesian way." Because the others are secondary and in fact derivative, we shall disregard them in the present study. Karl Mertens (in *Zwischen Letztbegründung und Skepsis*, 31) shares our position on the relative values of the different ways to reduction in all essentials, as does Paolo Volonté, *Husserls Phänomenologie der Imagination* (Freiburg/Munich: Alber, 1997), 64–66, esp. 66 n. 53. Drummond's argument for the interdependence of the Cartesian and ontological ways would correspond to our reading were one to take the former as the epoché and the latter as the subsequent, securing phenomenological reductions.

In *The Triumph of Subjectivity* (New York: Fordham, 1958), 50–57, Quentin Lauer identifies not ways to, but levels of reduction, and in fact no less than six of them. However, he equates the primary epoché with what is really the principle of all principles (see 50). The psychological reduction, as he calls it (51), seems to be the epoché proper, the one of concern to the present study. Lauer then identifies the eidetic reduction as a subsequent stage of reduction, though as noted above (II, 36) it is not peculiar to the transcendental sphere and is in fact effected prior to the epoché. The remaining four stages of reduction may be at work in Husserl's expositions, but it is not clear that they add anything to our understanding of what is at stake here. In *Ideas I*, at least, there are only two kinds of reduction (eidetic and phenomenological), the latter seem to be divisible only into two types: the inaugural epoché (which is applied to the general thesis) and the subsequent reductions (which can be applied to any thesis, though only as reminders). Elisabeth Ströker discusses (in "Das Problem der ἐποχή in der Philosophie Edmund Husserls," in *Phänomenologische Studien* [Frankfurt a. M.: Klostermann, 1987], 35–53, here 47–48) the "thematic reduction," but this is merely a new name for the reductions subsequent to the epoché. On these, see II, 68–70.

76. Unlike in Descartes, whose procedure is effected once and for all. (See First Meditation: "I realized that it was necessary, *once in the course of my life*, to demolish everything completely and start again right from the foundations if I wanted to establish anything at all in the sciences that was stable and likely to last." René Descartes, *Meditations on First Philosophy*, in *The Philosophical Writings of Descartes* II, trans. J. Cottingham, R. Stoothoff, and D. Murdoch [Cambridge: Cambridge University Press, 1984], 17; my emphasis.)

77. See, again, Husserl's remark: "Possibility is everywhere eidetic possibility . . ." (*Ideas III*, 83.9–10). See ibid., 83.19–25, as well as Ms. A VII 22, p. 7a (quoted in Costa, "Transcendental Aesthetic," 16): by inquiring into essences "we gain clarity on what belongs essentially to the possibility of any physical thing whatsoever, thus on that without which any physical thing whatsoever cannot be thought, without which it cannot be perceived and cannot be 'demonstrated' in an experiential context" (my translation). See also Mohanty, "Husserl on 'Possibility'."

78. The sense in which an act can be doubted, in this case an act of doubt, is bound up with the modifiability of acts.

79. This application of the principle of noncontradiction—as it concerns belief—will come into play again and again in Husserl's works. See especially his critique of skepticism in the *Crisis*, 3–17/3–18.

80. The latter part of this sentence may alternatively be translated (and this is how Kersten translates it) as "like the excluded outside the context of inclusion." As

has been noted, *ausschalten* is usually translated as 'to exclude', but literally as 'to switch off'. By the same token, *schalten* is to be read as 'to switch'. It is this figurative sense Husserl invokes here. The talk of 'exclusion' in connection with theses and the epoché should therefore not be confounded with 'annihilation' or 'elimination', but should be taken in the sense, e.g., of switching off a light.

81. See Nenon, "Husserl's Theory of the Mental," 225–26 and 230–35.

82. Volonté (*Husserls Phänomenologie der Imagination*, 66–67) errs in equating the epoché with doubt. This should be evident not only in light of the foregoing discussion of Descartes's attempt at universal doubt, from which Husserl sets off the epoché, but even more so in light of Husserl's analyses of modalization. On the latter see III, 152–57.

83. See, e.g., *EJ*, § 21a on the "Origin of Negation," as well as *Ideas I*, § 106 (which is discussed on III, 155–56). In the former work, Husserl refers to negation as a modality, whereas in the latter he seems to set off negation, along with affirmation, from the modalities.

84. See II, n. 72 above concerning the impossibility, e.g., of doubting the existence of the world.

85. It is striking that the phenomenological enterprise is based, in large part, on two kinds of neutrality modification: the *epoché* opens up its field of inquiry and *fantasy*, or the fiction it generates, is the "vital element" of that inquiry. Strangely, it is yet another neutrality modification that jeopardizes this enterprise. It will be addressed in III; see 161–62.

86. Again, Husserl does not *continue* any tradition but breaks with it radically. This he stresses time and again. He never changes his position on this point, despite any appearance to the contrary—for instance, when he appeals to the likes of Descartes, Hume, Kant, and Fichte as his predecessors. See, e.g., "Philosophy as Rigorous Science" for Husserl's views on the tradition and his relation to it.

87. Husserl added in Copy D: "better, refraining from belief." Thus 'belief' is more precise than 'judgment'. See *Hua* III/2, 485.

88. See *Crisis*, 140/137 concerning Husserl's description of the nature of the epoché and the leap it entails.

89. It is important that one pay special attention to his appeal to Descartes and other philosophers of the modern era, as well as of Greek antiquity. Husserl never takes them on their own terms but always instrumentalizes them for his own ends. He appeals to them as authorities, ones we accept in the natural attitude. Husserl wishes to lead his reader into transcendental phenomenology, and to do so he calls upon accepted ways of thinking, traditional examples, in order to motivate the leap needed to enter into phenomenology in his sense.

90. While the talk of annihilation is figurative, it is by no means inaccurate or hyperbolic, but thoroughly consistent with the results of Husserl's analyses; it is "misleading" only so long as one does not see that, terminologically, 'annihilation' is the polar opposite of 'existence'. This talk is in fact no less unusual than that of 'exclusion' or 'switching off', for how is one really to exclude or switch off the world?

91. Note that the shift between spheres is premised on the shift between modes of belief. The belief in the world and all it contains is excluded all at once. But the belief in the residual immanent sphere and all it contains remains in play.

92. See *Ideas I*, 108: "Now that we have received it [*i.e.*, pure consciousness] in our seeing regard, it is still useful to consider, *conversely*, what must remain excluded for the purpose of an investigation of pure consciousness and whether the necessary exclusion concerns only the sphere of nature."

93. The status and nature of the pure ego has been a point of controversy. See Eduard Marbach, *Das Problem des Ich in der Phänomenologie Husserls* (The Hague: Nijhoff, 1974), as well as Iso Kern, "Selbstbewußtsein und Ich bei Husserl," in G. Funke, ed., *Husserl-Symposion Mainz* (1989), 51–63, and Douglas Heinsen, "Husserl's Theory of the Pure Ego," in H. Dreyfus, ed., *Husserl, Intentionality, and Cognitive Science* (Cambridge, Mass.: MIT Press, 1982), 147–67. Nenon's "Husserl's Theory of the Mental" is indispensable for any attempt to come to terms with Husserl's understanding of the pure ego or the mental, as is Rudolf Bernet's "An Intentionality without Subject or Object?" *Man and World* 27 (1994), 231–55.

94. See, e.g., I, n. 80.

95. See *Ideas I*, 113: "At the same time we thereby acquire the explicit knowledge that a descriptive phenomenology is principially independent of all those disciplines."

96. See *Ideas I*, 113–14: "our intention is precisely to found phenomenology itself as an eidetic science, as the eidetic doctrine of transcendentally purified consciousness."

97. This phrase renders *Bewußtseinserlebnis überhaupt*. Note the subjective genitive in 'lived experience of consciousness'. This translation will be maintained throughout the present study.

98. See *Ideas I*, 60–61: "As the starting point, we take consciousness in a pregnant sense, which offers itself at first, one we can designate most simply by the Cartesian term 'cogito', by the phrase 'I think'. As is well known, 'cogito' was understood so broadly by Descartes that it includes every 'I perceive, I remember, I fantasy, I judge, feel, desire, will', and thus all egoic lived experiences that are at all similar to them, with their countless flowing particular formations. The ego itself, to which they are all related or which, in very different ways, 'lives' 'in' them actively, passively [*leidend*], or spontaneously, which 'comports' itself receptively and otherwise in them—and in fact the ego in every sense—we shall at first leave out of consideration."

99. See ibid.: "It then becomes evident that every lived experience in the stream that our reflective regard can fix upon has an essence of its own that can be seized upon intuitively, a 'content' that allows of being considered by itself in its peculiarity. Our concern is to seize upon this content of the cogitatio in its pure peculiarity and characterize it universally, thus by excluding everything that does not lie in the cogitatio with respect to what the cogitatio is in itself. Our aim is likewise to characterize the unity of consciousness that is required purely, and therefore necessarily required, by what belongs to the cogitationes as their own such that they could not exist without that unity."

100. For Husserl's full account, which we can only outline here, see *Ideas I*, 61–64 (§35).

101. See also III, 131–33. For overviews of Husserl's notion of intentionality, see J. N. Mohanty, *The Concept of Intentionality* (St. Louis: Warren H. Green, 1972), esp. 59–127, Bernet, Kern, Marbach, *Edmund Husserl*, 85–96, and Ronald McIntyre and David Woodruff Smith, "Theory of Intentionality," in J. N. Mohanty and W. R.

McKenna, eds., *Husserl's Phenomenology: A Textbook* (Lanham: CARP and University Press of America, 1989), 147–79. For a more general account of the phenomenological import of intentionality, see Sokolowski, *Introduction to Phenomenology*, 8–16.

102. See *Ideas I*, 70: "Can the unity of a whole exist other than through the agreement of the essence proper to its parts, and must not the latter therefore have some sort of community of essence instead of principial heterogeneity?" The whole in question is that made up of the parts 'world' and 'consciousness'. See also the Third Logical Investigation.

103. See *Ideas I*, 99: "A picture or a sign refers to something lying outside it that could 'itself' be seized upon were one to go over into a different mode of objectivation, into that of giving intuition. In its self, a sign or a picture does not 'make manifest' the designated (or depicted) self. But the physical thing as determined by physics is nothing alien to what appears sensuously-'bodily'; rather, it is something that makes itself manifest originarily in it, and in fact a priori (for indefeasible eidetic reasons) only in it."

104. Rudolf Bernet even speaks of the "subjugation of the world" as the consequence of transcendental-phenomenological method. See his "Husserl's Concept of the World," in A. Dallery and C. Scott, eds., *Crises in Continental Philosophy* (Albany, N.Y.: State University of New York Press, 1990), 3–21, here 5. He claims that the "annihilation of the world goes against the sense of intentionality, which always carries the subject to an interest in the entities of the world and their appearing" (ibid., 6). However, Bernet's objection would dissolve were he to have attended to the true target of that annihilation, which is belief. The world is annihilated insofar as I cease to believe in it. Such a lack of belief brings with it a lack of interest. See II, 93–96 on the "destruction of transcendence" and II, 96–98 on the "annihilation of the world," as well as III, 137.

105. This is, as it were, the "most superlative" of distinctions: *die kardinalste Unterschiedenheit.*

106. See *Ideas I*, 78: "It belongs to the essence of certain peculiarly structured kinds of lived experience, more precisely, to that of peculiarly structured concrete perceptions, that what is in them is meant as a spatial thing; to their essence belongs the ideal possibility of their changing into determinately ordered continuous manifolds of perception that can always be continued, thus that are never completed."

107. See *Ideas I*, 79: "Between perception on the one hand and pictorial-symbolic or significative-symbolic objectivation on the other is an unbridgeable essential difference. In the case of the latter kinds of objectivation, we intuit something in the consciousness that it depicts something else or indicates it significatively. . . ." Husserl then notes that such a consciousness is not present in perception.

108. Ludwig Landgrebe argues that "Husserl's break with Cartesianism" takes place only in the unfolding of his 1923–24 lecture course on First Philosophy, specifically on the "Theory of the Phenomenological Reduction" (see Landgrebe, "Husserls Abschied vom Cartesianismus," in *Der Weg der Phänomenologie*, 163–206; the lectures to which Landgrebe refers are to be found in *Hua* VIII). But in fact Husserl broke with Descartes and Cartesianism already by 1912, namely at the point at which he expressly confronted Cartesian thought and used the method of universal doubt only as the stepping stone to the epoché. See *Ideas I*, §31, as well as 82–89, above. On the other hand, the talk of "breaking with Cartesianism" is dubious, since it implies that Husserl stands

in the Cartesian "tradition." Regarding the question of Husserl's relation to the philosophical tradition, see I, 10–11 and I, n. 72, as well as I, 14 and I, n. 84.

109. On the method of free or imaginative variation, see *PP*, §9. and *EJ*, §87.

110. This law, which is the simple consequence of the claim of universality, is the basis for the analogy not just between two individual egos, but also between (individual) subjectivity and intersubjectivity. See I, n. 88 and V, 219 on this analogy.

111. See the previous note.

112. That the epoché does not eliminate *all* belief in Being (*Seinsglaube*), but only a specific kind of belief (*Weltglaube*, or the belief in the existence of the world), is indicated, e.g., by Husserl's remark on positing at *Ideas III*, 85.18–21: "positing a noema as existing does not mean positing the objectuality 'corresponding' to the noema, although it is the objectuality referred to [*bedeuten*] in the noema."

113. As for how Husserl was able to see this attitude in the first place, which would seem to be ruled out from the start by its unnaturalness, the claim is not that it is impossible to see the phenomenological attitude, but only that it is impossible to do so from the standpoint of the natural attitude—that is, as long as one lives along in it, oblivious to it. The latter impossibility consists in the fact that one living in the natural attitude would not be motivated to look for another attitude or standpoint. The motivation for such a quest would have to be, we suggest, a disruption of the natural attitude, such as the one Husserl experienced as the crisis of his age. See I, nn. 33 and 74.

114. Hence it marks an enrichment and not an impoverishment of consciousness.

115. This passage should make one hesitate to claim, on the one hand, that consciousness is not a "region of being" (as Mohanty does in "The Development of Husserl's Thought," 61) or, on the other hand, that for Husserl consciousness is equivalent to thinking. The latter claim would hold only under very specific circumstances—that is, at the level of speech.

116. Where others see endless distinctions, Husserl sees the "conceptual definiteness" of his exposition. There is a definite order to the account given so far, a logic of progression, and it will continue to be unfolded up through the "phenomenology of reason."

Chapter III. The Disclosure of the System's Lowermost Limit: Subjectivity

1. See, e.g., the Introduction to *Ideas I*, 3 (see II, 34–35). In the present context, Husserl points to the "ways of thinking that have been practiced for millennia" (see *Ideas I*, 120); these ways of thinking inhibit entry into the phenomenological sphere and hence must be broken.

2. Due to its concern with the familiar—which is to say, with the natural—the natural attitude necessarily if unknowingly excludes the phenomenological attitude, for it is something wholly unfamiliar, both regarding its method and its intention. On the other hand, the phenomenological attitude excludes the natural attitude as such by revaluing it and making it the subject of phenomenological analyses. Because the natural attitude is not familiar with the phenomenological attitude, it cannot name it, nor for that matter can the natural attitude name itself, for it is not familiar with itself as

such. Only as a result of the differentiation of attitudes is it named, and only then can it be investigated—though, of course, never as long as the investigator lives in the natural attitude. This is the achievement of phenomenology alone. Their exclusive relationship to one another is permanent: it does not cease after the epoché has been effected, but manifests itself thereafter as the struggle required by the phenomenologist to stay in the new attitude and not fall back into the natural attitude and its naiveté. Not only, Husserl notes, does it require great effort just to see the phenomenological attitude, but also to stay in it—the phenomenologist is always in danger of committing a *metabasis*. Even after he has entered the field of phenomenological inquiry, he must continue to be on guard against all such illegitimate transgressions, against mixing natural with phenomenological cognitions. By contrast, there is a sense in which these attitudes stand in an inclusive relationship to one another: the phenomenological attitude "includes" the natural attitude as its object of inquiry. But again, the natural attitude is no longer had in its original immediacy, but only as the object of reflection. Despite the subsequent inclusion, then, the initial exclusion remains primary. See II, nn. 18 and 113.

3. No deductive or inductive inference is possible that would enable a move from the natural to the phenomenological attitude. This would also seem to rule out the translatability of one into the other. J. N. Mohanty argues for the translatability of one world into another, even if one or more intermediary worlds are necessary so as to achieve the translation (see his "Phänomenologische Rationalität und die Überwindung des Relativismus," *Phänomenologische Forschungen* 19 [1986], 53–73, here 64ff.). However, if the natural and the phenomenological attitudes each has access to a world of its own, then we can speak at best here of a one-way translation, i.e., from the natural to the phenomenological attitude. How would it be possible to translate the latter attitude into the former, given that the phenomenological attitude lacks the naiveté of the natural attitude? One possible objection to our question, however, is that the phenomenologist is always threatened by the danger of falling back into the natural attitude. But can such a relapse be equated with a translation?

4. Insight into this disparateness, which of course entails insight into the existence of the phenomenological sphere, does not necessitate the performance of the epoché. To assert the contrary is to commit a fundamental error. Already Husserl's emphasis on what is required to "live in" something should make it clear that seeing something (as in reflection) is not the same thing as living in it. This holds as much of individual lived experiences as it does of attitudes. If this is right, then the usual objection to Husserl's analyses in the first two parts of *Ideas I*—that he has to have already performed the epoché in order to engage in those initial eidetic analyses, and thus falls prey to a vicious circularity or a *petitio principii*—is unfounded. The objection rests, so to speak, on an inverse *metabasis* or an inadmissible restriction of reflection. Furthermore, that would mean that there is no vicious circularity in Husserl's presentation.

5. Unlike in the previous note, where of concern is the distinction between the insight into the difference of regions (and in particular into the difference of the natural and phenomenological spheres), on the one hand, and the performance of the epoché, on the other, in the case of the performance and justification of the epoché itself there is definitely a circularity. The question remains, however, whether it is vicious.

6. Overlooking this distinction, i.e., equating two disparate regions, plunges one into countersense. One of the key strategies Husserl repeatedly employs in order to

evade the threat of countersense is to draw the distinction between regions. In his discussion in the *Prolegomena*, e.g., of the naturalization of thought, he makes it quite clear that failing to make such distinctions inevitably leads to a *metabasis*, which has to end in disaster.

7. Or, perhaps more accurately, recursively. See *Ideas I*, 170–71, where Husserl states that in phenomenology, to begin with, "all concepts or terms must remain in flux in a certain way"—the concretion of concepts occurs only in the course of inquiry, which consists of double-sided, spiral-like movement of progress and justification. "For the beginning, any expression is good—and especially any suitably chosen figurative expression—that is capable of directing our regard to a phenomenological occurrence that can be seized upon clearly. Clarity does not exclude a certain halo of indeterminacy. Its further determination or clarification is precisely the further task. . . ." Precisely because all clarity is surrounded by a halo of indeterminacy, Husserl has to conceive of his endeavor, i.e., the phenomenological enterprise, as infinite, incapable of ever being completed. And so it is inevitable that wherever one begins, e.g. where Husserl begins in order to establish transcendental phenomenology, there will always be inadequacies of expression—that is, conceptual inadequacies, indeterminacies that can only be corrected after one has gained some sort of systematic foothold. (Incidentally, this point alone should make it quite clear why pursuing Husserlian problems merely as such can never be fruitful; what made Husserl's thought productive was his task and his attempt—taken in general terms—to fulfill it, and not the details of that attempt, which have the infinity, so to speak, of the stream of lived experiences. This precisely is the chief danger of Husserl's thought: to lose oneself in the flux of approaches, investigations, and sundry details. The only way to avoid this quicksand is to bring *seinen Gedanken auf den Punkt*, and that requires first of all that one fix his task and then trace out the main lines of his attempt to fulfill it.)

8. This state of affairs mirrors that of the relation between having the presentiment of an essence and intuiting an essence partially; e.g., Husserl has the presentiment or the idea of phenomenology that guides his efforts to articulate this new science completely, but he does not yet have that science *in toto*. The apparent tension here between the two modes of having becomes problematic only when one fails to distinguish between them.

9. See in this connection Aristotle, *Metaphysics* Γ 3. There is a sense in which for Husserl the justification of method derives from the latter's efficacy or productivity. One is tempted to say that the end (or in this case the product) justifies the means, or "if it isn't broken, don't fix it."

10. See *Ideas I*, 124: "One must therefore be able to persuade oneself at any time in new reflections that the affair-complexes spoken of in the methodological statements may be given with perfect clarity, that the concepts used actually conform faithfully to what is given, etc."

11. Husserl indicates this order on *Ideas I*, 123: "It must bring into view occurrences of pure consciousness as examples, make them perfectly clear, analyze and seize upon their essences within the limits of that clarity, trace with insight the essential concatenations, capture what is seen in faithful conceptual expressions that allow their sense to be prescribed purely by what is seen or what one gains general insight into, etc."

12. The alleged sedimentations of metaphysical usage do not concern Husserl regarding the choice of terms. The only kind of sedimentation that is worrisome to him is that of traditional or metaphysical theories. Although in his Introduction he is careful to avoid terms weighed down with traditional connotations, at this point, at least, he does not seem to consider theory to be intertwined with terminology. Decisive for Husserl is the beginning and the *fiat* that enables it. As such the beginning is, in a sense, absolute. And it is for this reason also that Husserl will deny the importance of the nether reaches of consciousness in the constitution of meaning. See III, 131–32 and 171.

13. See *Ideas I*, 127–28: "intuitedness as such admits of continuous intensity-like differences under the heading of clarity that, like intensities, begin with zero but end with a fixed upper limit. One might say that the lower degrees indicate the latter in a certain manner; intuiting a color in a mode of imperfect clarity, we 'mean' the color as it is 'in itself' [*an sich selbst*]—that is, precisely as the color given with perfect clarity. Nevertheless, one should not let oneself be misled by the metaphor of indicating—as though one thing were a sign of another—nor should one speak here . . . of a presentation of the clear 'in itself' by means of the unclear, such that, for example, a physical property is 'presented,' i.e., adumbrated, in intuition by means of a sensation. Graduated differences in clarity are definitely those peculiar to the mode of givenness." In keeping with his guiding interest in achieving maximal clarity and thus the most certain knowledge, it is fitting that Husserl emphasizes the ascent towards the upper limit, or the increase in clarity, rather than the equally possible descent towards the lower limit, or the decrease in clarity.

14. See Casey, "Imagination and Phenomenological Method," 76 col. 1, and Mark P. Drost, "The Primacy of Perception in Husserl's Theory of Imagining," *Philosophy and Phenomenological Research* 50 (1990), 569–82.

15. The freedom Husserl has in view here, which we may call "eidetic freedom," is not limitless, not arbitrary, but bound through and through by essence. The "free" will moves always only within the parameters set by essence.

16. Further distinctions will be taken up in the context of Husserl's elaboration of the "doctrine of the neutrality modification" (III, 157–80).

17. In this context Husserl slides between 'category' and 'region'. In his thought the essential priority of (Being as) consciousness, this first substance, as it were, outbids every "doctrine of categories" from Aristotle on.

18. However, beginning with this "ground" does not require that one plumb its nether reaches. As will be seen shortly, Husserl is careful to point out that this is not necessary for his purposes here. The basis of his system is not provided by the obscure depths of consciousness, but rather by consciousness as it is productive, constitutive; thus of interest to Husserl is only secondarily the stuff or hyle that is given form by the ego's regard. See I, n. 16.

19. See *Ideas I*, 144: "With these new considerations we do not actually leave the problems of method behind."

20. The objection might be made that the field cannot be accessed in the first place if not by means of the method. And yet, Husserl would likely respond, it is the insight into—and thus intuition of—the "existence" of the field, or at least the possibility thereof, that motivates the attempt to access it. That the method must arise from the

region in which it is to be applied is consistent with Husserl's earlier remarks on the use of concepts and the reflexive movement of thought and justification of those concepts.

21. See *Ideas I*, 132, and III, 113.

22. For instructive accounts of Husserl's analysis of reflection, see Sokolowski, *Husserlian Meditations*, 186–91 and Ströker, *Husserls transzendentale Phänomenologie*, 95–106. On the various problems connected with Husserl's analysis, see, e.g., Burt C. Hopkins, "Husserl's Account of Phenomenological Reflection and Four Paradoxes of Reflexivity," *Research in Phenomenology* 19 (1989), 180–94, Thomas Damast, "Zum Problem einer Theorie der Reflection bei Husserl," in H. Busche et al., eds., *Bewußtsein und Zeitlichkeit* (Würzburg: Königshausen & Neumann, 1990), 199–212, and Thomas Seebohm, "Reflexion and Totality in the Philosophy of E. Husserl," *Journal of the British Society for Phenomenology* 4 (1973), 20–30.

23. The latter reason is, of course, the basis of the former. This corresponds to the essential relation between region and method. Consider the relationship between reflexive and bipolar structures in Husserl discussed on I, 24–26.

24. See *Ideas I*, § 79, esp. pp. 155–56.

25. Concerning the "argumentative" strategies Husserl employs in the *Prolegomena* to counter "naturalistic" or "psychologistic" skepticism, though also with regard to skepticism in its various forms, see Adler, "Prolegomena to Phenomenology."

26. Even the countersense that results from a *metabasis* can be reduced to this type. That this is so becomes evident when one sees that the attempt to reduce findings from the phenomenological sphere to those of the natural sphere, the attempt to reduce the transcendental to the empirical, always already presupposes the findings of the transcendental sphere. Again, a *metabasis* consists of an illegitimate transgression of regional boundaries and thereby a confounding of essential features of each of the regions in question. Wherever there is doubt about the possibility and efficacy of reflection, there is often a confusion between the empirical and eidetic spheres as well.

27. For the phenomenologist himself, the skeptical misgivings pose no real danger, for he has seen by means of "real work" that they are self-refuting—and hence unfounded. But they do threaten "future" phenomenologists, who have yet to be instructed in the method, etc. In this regard, the danger is to the establishment and expansion of phenomenology as First Science. However, despite its importance on a larger scale, the discussion of these misgivings remains secondary to Husserl's presentation at this point; his chief concern is to elaborate the basic features of consciousness—in this case, reflection.

28. Fink (in "Operative Begriffe," 185) discusses this distinction in terms of 'operative' and 'thematic' concepts, respectively. In his "Urbewußtsein und Reflexion bei Husserl," Ni overlooks the fact that the difference between living-in or lived experiencing (*Erleben*) and reflection lies in the manner in which consciousness is directed to its objectuality in each case.

29. Once again we find the same structure as in the case of degrees of clarity (consider the polarity of 0–1 discussed in I, 24–26). Here at issue, however, is a tripartite structure: retention and protention form the extremes and the Now mediates between them. And yet this mediation is not such that the mediating term can be considered simultaneously with the extremes, i.e., the Present Now cannot be thought simultaneously with the Past Now and Future Now. Rather, as soon as one standpoint is taken, as

soon as one moment is chosen, it acts as an extreme, which can be related to one of the other two. Whereas the passage of time is tripartite, the relation of moments in time is only bipartite. Now and Past, Now and Future, or Past and Future. There is no mediation here. Of course, there is the obvious point: Past and Future are such only with reference to a Now. The priority lies with the Now, as the determinative first over against its other.

30. 'Reference' translates *Bezogenheit* here. Its literal translation would read 'referredness' or 'relatedness'.

31. See *Ideas I*, 150: "It is by reflexively experiential acts alone that we know something of the stream of lived experiences and of the necessary reference of the stream to the pure ego. . . ." In this way also it is possible to gain a "presentiment" of the phenomenological sphere.

32. See *Ideas I*, 148: "every reflection, by its essence, emerges from changes in attitude, whereby a pregiven lived experience or lived experience datum (as unreflected) undergoes a certain transformation, precisely into the mode of reflected consciousness (or that of which there is consciousness)."

33. A distinction must be made, of course, between the character of the Object of the analyses and that of the analyses themselves. Clearly, Husserl's presentation is, by his standards, anything but naive, whereas the level on which he finds and discusses his Object is indeed "naive." This must be so, for we have yet to reach the level of (critical) phenomenology.

34. See *Ideas I*, 149: "Every lived experience is within itself a flux of becoming; it is what it is in an original generation of an invariant essential type; it is a continuous flux of retentions and protentions mediated by a phase of originariness that itself is in flux, a phase in which there is consciousness of the living Now of the lived experience in contradistinction to its 'before' and 'after.'"

35. Thus Husserl will say at *Ideas I*, 159: "The old ontological doctrine that the cognition of 'possibilities' must precede the cognition of actualities is, in my opinion, provided it is correctly understood and made useful in the right way, a great truth." Consider in this connection the necessity, as Husserl sees it, of beginning with the possibility of performing the epoché and only then taking up the necessity thereof.

36. *Leiden von*. It may be paraphrased as 'being acted upon'.

37. See Heinsen, "Husserl's Theory of the Pure Ego," 152–55 (sec. III) and 161.

38. The use of the figure of the stream in the talk of a "stream of lived experiences" is appropriate only in connection with an ego, for it is only by virtue of the ego's regard that a succession of lived experiences—as a series of temporal phases—becomes thinkable. Therefore, 'continuum' or 'horizon' are the best descriptors of the sphere of lived experiences when it is discussed in isolation. See *Ideas I*, 165: "The stream of lived experiences is an infinite unity, and the stream-form is a form that necessarily encompasses all the lived experiences *of* a pure ego—a form with various systems of forms."

39. The equality of or lack of distinction between lived experiences taken on their own (and therefore without reference to an ego) is akin, at least structurally, to the equal rank of essences gained by means of the eidetic reduction prior to the performance of the epoché. See II, 36.

40. The sense of fulfillment operative here is clearly distinct from that operative in the philosophical tradition. One must distinguish between two senses of fulfillment in

Husserl: on the one hand, the fulfillment proper to the stream (it is always already fulfilled, in itself) and, on the other, the fulfillment sought by the ego, i.e., the fulfillment of sense, which is, of course, measured against the primary fulfillment of the stream.

41. It should be noted that there are two ways of reading Husserl's remark on the duration of lived experiences: on the one hand, with respect to the isolated stream, in which case their duration is necessarily atemporal; on the other hand, with respect to the ego, in which case duration is temporal. In the present context, the "objective" direction of inquiry is taken, and so the former sense is emphasized.

42. See, e.g., *Ideas I*, 168, where Husserl notes that we can say of "every lived experience that comes into the view of possible reflection as an Object . . . that it is a temporal lived experience."

43. Strikingly, the indubitability of the stream for the pure ego is on a par with that of the world for the naive human being. Each provides the basis of life in the corresponding attitude; each exceeds one's grasp, despite its indubitability; neither can be perceived as a whole, but only piecemeal.

44. As we have sought to show above in the Introduction, Husserl certainly strives after God. If God were the ultimate absolute to which he refers in this context, then his God would seem not to lie in the heights (contrary to Husserl's usual assertion), but to provide the ground of conscious life. In view of the express aim of Husserl's striving, then, the movement of phenomenology would be circular, for reaching God in the heights would mean returning to the very ground of Being. The end would therefore be the beginning, and the beginning, the end. Husserl might then be seen to move away from God in order to reach him, which would accord, in a sense, with his remark that he is seeking the way to God without God (see I, n. 133). This gives rise to problems regarding reason, however, insofar as God may be considered absolute reason. On God as the ground, see I, n. 16; on God as reason, see 13, 23 and IV, 216–17.

45. See II, n. 101.

46. See *Hua* XXVII, 174.7–9. See Robert Sokolowski, *The Formation of Husserl's Concept of Constitution* (The Hague: Nijhoff, 1964), 137–38.

47. That it is not necessary to plumb the depths, but is instead admissible and even most fitting to pursue an investigation at higher levels is stressed by Husserl in *Hua* III/2, Beilage 22, p. 569.

48. On hyle, see *PP*, § 31. Hyletic Data are, as it were, invisible as such while being the medium through which other data are perceived. They lack "all consciousness-characteristics," but can become the "core contents" of "functional characteristics, which all have in common that by means of these core contents, and by enspiriting [*vergeistigen*] them, as it were, [the functional characteristics] give rise to consciousness of [*bewußt machen*] other objectualities."

49. See *Ideas I*, 172: "We find . . . those sensuous moments overlaid by a stratum that, as it were, 'animates,' that bestows sense (or essentially implies a sense-bestowal), a stratum by means of which precisely the concrete intentional lived experience arises from the sensuous, which has in itself no intentionality."

50. See A. P. Youschkevitch, "The Concept of Function up to the Middle of the 19th Century," trans. O. B. Sheynin, in *Archive for History of Exact Sciences* 16 (1976–77), 37–85, esp. 39, where he provides a basic definition of single-valued functions of one real variable.

51. Hence, one might express the Husserlian function as "the consciousness (C) of an objectuality (o) generates a sense (S)," or formally: C(o) = S.

52. Given the significance of constitution, it would seem that thinking has priority over Being. But the converse is the case. Objectualities are constituted not by thought, but by consciousness, which is first and foremost a region of *Being*. What it creates thereby is not Being, but sense. And only on the basis of sense does thinking become possible.

53. Once again, theory is the source of blindness to the essential relations. This is further testimony to the fact that Being, not thinking, is privileged by Husserlian phenomenology. Note that in the passage just cited intersubjectivity is linked to attitude: only those in the same attitude can access and scrutinize the same results. This suggests that those in one attitude would have difficulties, to say the least, communicating with those in another attitude.

54. The controversy surrounding Husserl's concept of the noema has reached immense proportions. Already several years ago, Denis Fisette counted over 300 publications on the noema; see his *Lecture frégéene de la phénoménologie* (Combas: Éditions de l'Eclat, 1994), 10. For an instructive survey and attempted solution of the tangled controversy, see Rudolf Bernet, "Husserls Begriff des Noema," in S. IJsseling, ed., *Husserl-Ausgabe und Husserl-Forschung* (Dordrecht: Kluwer, 1990), 61–80. B. Smith and D. W. Smith (Introduction, 22–27) also provide a useful overview of the debate. See also the works on the noema by, among others, Drummond, Føllesdal, McIntyre and Smith, Mohanty, and Sokolowski. In addition to Fisette's study, see the relevant essays in H. Dreyfus, ed., *Husserl, Intentionality, and Cognitive Science*, and J. Drummond and L. Embree, eds., *The Phenomenology of the Noema* (Dordrecht: Kluwer, 1992).

55. Given the possibility of engaging in either noetic or noematic analysis, this law must be commutative.

56. For someone as sensitive to the power of "symbols" as was Husserl, it can be no accident that in his elaboration of the fundamental constituents of intentionality and, ultimately, of knowledge, he employs the image of an apple tree, which, of course, is popularly considered the "tree of knowledge" as described in Genesis. For Husserl's reference to other symbols, see I, nn. 45 and 70.

57. See *Ideas I*, 182: "Perception, for example, has its noema, most basically its perceptual sense, that is, the perceived as such."

58. Regarding the noema viewed in accordance with the principle of all principles, see *Ideas I*, 182: "The noematic correlate, which here is called 'sense' (in a quite expanded significance), is everywhere to be taken exactly as it lies immanently in the lived experience of perception, judgment, liking, etc., that is, as it is offered to us [by the lived experience] when we examine this lived experience itself in a pure manner."

59. See *Ideas I*, 183: "In our phenomenological attitude we can and must ask the eidetic question: What is the 'perceived as such,' which essential moments does it harbor within itself as this perceptual noema? We receive the answer in pure devotion to what is given essentially; we can describe 'something appearing as such' faithfully, with perfect evidence."

60. This phrase translates *etwas "im Sinne haben"*, which may be literally rendered as 'to have something in the sense'.

61. The basic structure of lower and upper limits is maintained here. Consider the relation between subjectivity and reason. See I, 25.

62. As has been seen in the foregoing, Husserl always begins with what is familiar (what is first for us) and seeks to sharpen or correct the observations therein so as to grasp the phenomenon in question in its essence (and thereby what is first by nature).

63. The talk of appearance always implies the appearance of something *to* a consciousness.

64. Husserl reiterates this point later (*Ideas I*, 206–7) in slightly different terms: "in the stuffs themselves, according to their essence, the relation to the objective unity is not unambiguously predelineated; rather, the same material complex can undergo multiple interpretations that jump discretely [*ineinander überspringen*] into one another, [interpretations] by virtue of which different objectualities are intended. Is it not therefore already clear that essential distinctions lie in the animating interpretations themselves as moments of lived experiences and that are differentiated along with the accordant adumbrations and through the animation of which they constitute 'sense'?" See also *Hua* XI, 34 regarding doubt: "One and the same composition of hyletic data is the common basis for two interpretations that lie one on top of the other. Neither of them is crossed out during the doubt; they stand here in mutual conflict; each has in a way its strengths, each is motivated—as it were, supported—by the perceptions thus far and their intentional content."

65. Note that reflection is not specifically a modification (the proper sense of which will be clarified shortly), just as perception is not. What is new here is the *mode* of givenness.

66. See *Ideas I*, 209: "On the one hand, we have the simple reproductive modification, the simple representiation, which in its own essence, strangely enough, gives itself as the modification of something else. Representiation refers back to perception in its own phenomenological essence. . . ."

67. See the first frontispiece in this volume.

68. Boeder notes rightly that the belief Husserl has in mind is δόξα and not πίστις, that is, *doxa*, not faith. Thus it is more a passive belief, and certainly not "religious" belief. The latter is of a higher level and necessarily involves the will. See Boeder, *Das Vernunft-Gefüge der Moderne*, 174.

69. Note that this certainty is incipiently not a matter of decision, but is naive: "The original, normal perception has the primal mode 'existent, valid unqualifiedly; it is the unqualified, naive certainty" (*Hua* XI, 36).

70. See III, 140–41.

71. See Beilage 8 in *Hua* VIII, 363–68, esp. 365 on modalization as "devaluation."

72. The "first dimension of characterizations" is not first by nature, but only for us.

73. Husserl first speaks of only *one* modification (negation), noting its analog (affirmation) seemingly only in passing. As becomes clear in the course of his characterization of each, they are closely related, but opposite: the result of each is obviously opposite to that of the other—that is, opposite in sign.

74. That negation is not the expunction but rather the modification, the transformation, of a position becomes particularly evident in *Hua* XI, 31: "Here we are thus studying how the phenomenon of 'otherwise,' of 'annulment' [*Aufhebung*], nullity, or negation looks originally. We see that it is fundamentally essential that a suppression

take place whereby a new sense is laid upon a previously constituted sense; correlatively, we see in the noetic direction a formation of a second apprehending, apperception, which does not lie beside the first one, but rather lies on top of it and conflicts with it. Belief conflicts with belief, the belief possessing one sense-content and mode of intuition conflicts with one possessing another content in its mode of intuition." And further: "We can also say that the old sense is declared to be invalid and replaced with another that is regarded as valid" (*Hua* XI, 32). In *EJ*, § 21a, 96/89, Husserl describes the generation of a new Being-object by negation as a "doubling," which results in a new sense being overlaid on the preceding sense. The doubling does not leave the two senses, old and new, simply side by side, even though there is consciousness of each, but rather the old sense is "overlaid with the new and crossed out in the relevant moments." The new sense might be said to "subjugate" the old. All of this takes place on the doxic level—"belief conflicts with belief"—prior to all predication; see ibid., 97/90. The same holds of the modalizations discussed thus far; see ibid., 99–104/91–99.

75 See Bernet, "An Intentionality without Subject or Object?" 237. See also *Hua* XXVIII, 208–12.

76. As for why he does not consider them here, it may be connected with the fact that the product of affirmation has less intuitive force than that of negation—that is, unlike the negatum, the affirmatum is syntactically invisible. For example, the affirmation of 'existing' would effectively be 'yes-existing'. But the 'yes' typically falls to the side, and in everyday speech would seem strange. The reason the 'yes' disappears would seem to lie in a kind of double affirmation that occurs in expression, where belief is added to belief, yielding simply belief—or, at best, the emphasis of belief. This state of affairs may have motivated Frege, e.g., to introduce the judgment-stroke into his concept-script (see *Begriffsschrift*, ed. I. Angelelli [Hildesheim: Olms, 2d ed., 1964], 2). But as Wittgenstein points out, the assertion—the expression—is itself an affirmation or assertion. Hence his remark that Frege's judgment-stroke (Wittgenstein: 'assertion-sign'/*Behauptungszeichen*) is redundant (see *Philosophische Untersuchungen*, Werkausgabe 1 [Frankfurt a. M.: Suhrkamp, 2d ed., 1995], § 22). Yet Frege's intention clearly was to make explicit what takes place in expression, albeit without acknowledging what takes place in expression itself. Husserl's neglect of this issue would seem to imply as much, which would suggest that he and Wittgenstein agreed on this point.

77. This topic is addressed in passing in 1914; see *Hua* XXVIII, 124–25.

78. At this point in his exposition Husserl refers to Adolf Reinach's treatise, "On the Theory of the Negative Judgment," saying that it would be "instructive" to consider it "on the basis of the clarifications of the essence of doxic occurrences attempted in the previous paragraphs and to place its problematic in [the context of] our examination" (*Ideas I*, 219 n. 1). This reference is significant not only due to the potentially fruitful suggestion that the theory of negative judgment be investigated in connection with the doxic sphere and its modalizations, but also because it underscores the fact that the modifications discussed thus far belong to a family of sorts. On the other hand, it could be taken to reflect Husserl's view that his clarifications have been marked by a degree of conventionality insofar as they may accord more or less with traditional accounts of negative judgment. Be that as it may, the truly radical significance of Husserl's reference becomes clear only in retrospect, i.e., once he has begun his exposition of the "doctrine of the neutrality modification." Only then does one see that the mention of Reinach's

treatise marks a break with the familiar and announces, if laconically, the entry into *terra incognita*. This break is rendered even less conspicuous, however, by the fact that Husserl—as is his habit—does not "get right to the point," but instead first backtracks and supplements the foregoing analyses. The chief supplementation here concerns the iterability of the modifications encountered thus far, a feature that further underscores their community.

Reinach's paper, "Zur Theorie des negativen Urteils," may be found in *Münchener Philosophische Abhandlungen* (Leipzig: Barth, 1911), 196–254 (English: "On the Theory of the Negative Judgment," trans. Barry Smith, in B. Smith, ed., *Parts and Moments: Studies in Logic and Formal Ontology* [Munich: Philosophia, 1982], 315–77). For an account of the main themes of Reinach's work, see Smith's Introduction to his translation in ibid., 289–313. Concerning the negative judgment within the context of Husserlian phenomenology, see Dieter Lohmar, "Beiträge zu einer phänomenologischen Theorie des negativen Urteils," *Husserl Studies* 8 (1992), 173–204.

79. This figurative way of speaking should not lead one to forget that for Husserl negation is always of a *position* and never of affirmation.

80. Husserl's assertion here that the neutrality modification, in particular the universal neutrality modification, is of such importance would seem to be contradicted by the fact that he has hardly discussed it elsewhere. Important exceptions are found in *Ideas II*, 262–63/274–75, *Hua* XXIII, esp. 571–90, and *Hua* XXIX, 424–25. Although he employs the term 'neutrality modification' in each of these texts, it is actually the fantasy modification of which he speaks. This is without exception the case, as far as I have been able to determine. His concern with fantasy is, of course, ultimately methodological in character. The universal neutrality modification, by contrast, adds nothing to his system—and that is precisely the point. There are two possible reasons, then, for his relative neglect of this universal modification: on the one hand, his primary concern is to establish his system and to engage in investigations that contribute to that establishment; on the other hand, he is concerned with his system as such nowhere as much as he is in *Ideas I*. This is the only work in which he projects his system in its entirety. Consequently, the "leading upwards" (*Emporleitung*) to the uppermost limit is nowhere as evident as it is here—in systematic significance, namely. The universal neutrality modification comes into play precisely where the *ascent* becomes most crucial, just short of Husserl's ultimate goal: reason. Another possible source of its absence in his subsequent works is his remark that wherever positionality is addressed, his findings pertain necessarily to neutrality as well—which would mean that it is every bit as present, even if "operatively," in Husserl's later work on his system as it is in all explicitness in *Ideas I*. Since, as will be seen, neutrality is the shadow of positionality, one would be justified in maintaining that wherever Husserl speaks of positionality, neutrality is also present—as its shadow. The decisive reason for its presence, as well as its later (apparent) absence—see the concluding pages of our Introduction, above—is bound up with Husserl's articulation of his system.

81. See *Ideas I*, 222, where Husserl says that in the course of his investigation of the "universal modification of consciousness," he will also treat "a kind of genuine modification of belief that we still lack, one with which the new modification in question is easily confused. . . ." The modification Husserl is referring to is "that of assumptions

[*Annahmen*]." As for what makes this modification genuine as opposed to the "new modification," this will become clear in what follows.

82. See *Sich-in-das-Leisten-hineindenken* (thinking-oneself-into-the-producing). The phrase *sich in etwas hineindenken* has several nuances, the most important of which is 'doing as if' as in *sich in jemanden hineindenken* (to put oneself in someone's position). One imagines oneself in someone else's shoes without actually being in those shoes. Hence, one merely thinks; no genuine living-in takes place on this level.

Note that Eugen Fink's prize-winning dissertation from May 1928, *Vergegenwärtigung und Bild. Beiträge zur Phänomenologie der Unwirklichkeit* (the first part of which was published in *Jahrbuch für Philosophie und phänomenologische Forschung* 11 [1930], 239–309 and reprinted in his *Studien zur Phänomenologie 1930–1939* [The Hague: Nijhoff, 1966], 1–78), is his response to a competition announced in May of 1927 by the department of philosophy at the University of Freiburg, a competition that Fink won, together with H. Ropohl. The announcement specified the general topic of the competing studies: "The psychic phenomena captured in the ambiguous expressions 'to think as if [*sich denken als ob*]', 'merely to imagine something [*sich etwas bloß vorstellen*]', 'to fantasy' shall be differentiated and subjected to a purely phenomenological analysis." See ibid., 1 n. 1 and *BW* 4, 153. The formulation of the announcement recalls the foregoing list of modes of consciousness in which the neutrality modification plays a role, but also Hans Vaihinger's *Die Philosophie des Als-Ob* (Berlin: Reuther & Reichard, 1911); the 6th ed. was translated into English by C. K. Ogden under the title *The Philosophy of 'As if'* (New York: Harcourt, Brace, 2d ed., 1935). This work may well have been the impetus for Husserl's insight into the systematic import of neutrality and thus for his radicalization in *Ideas I* of the analyses he had presented in the Fifth Investigation (see III, n. 84). On Vaihinger see, e.g., Hubertus Busche, "Was ist keine Fiktion? Zeitlichkeit als Wurzel der imaginären Verfaßtheit alles empirischen Bewußtseins in Vaihingers *Philosophie des Als Ob*," in H. Busche et al., eds., *Bewußtsein und Zeitlichkeit* (Würzburg: Königshausen & Neumann, 1990), 173–97.

83. The oversight of this modification continues to be the norm, even in Husserl scholarship, despite his analysis of it in *Ideas I*, §§109–17. See III, n. 90.

84. Husserl does, of course, note that he has treated several aspects of the "doctrine of the neutralization modification" elsewhere: they "have already been penetrated in the main in the *Log. Inv.*, especially concerning [its] relationship to fantasy." However, even if several aspects of the doctrine were articulated in the Fifth Logical Investigation (*Hua* XIX/1, §§39ff.) for the first time, the neutrality modification was not named—which is one reason why he has to approach it "circumscriptively" here. It is articulated as such only in *Ideas I*; only in this work is it accorded its proper, *systematic* significance. Regarding his account of neutrality in the *Investigations*, Husserl remarks in *Ideas I* (274 n. 1): "We do not, of course, consider neutral having-as-'undecided' ['*Dahingestellt'-haben*] now, as we did there, to be a 'quality' (thesis) alongside other qualities, but rather a *modification* that 'mirrors' all qualities and therefore whole acts of whatever sort." The chief differences between the analyses in the *Investigations* and those in *Ideas I* will be seen to lie in the character and scope of the neutrality modification. As it is grasped in the latter work, neutrality is no longer held to be equivalent to indecision (see III, n. 86), nor to be one quality among others, nor to be specific. Although implicit in the *Investigations*, the universality of the neutrality modification is

drawn out here for the first time. Taken on its own, as it was in the Fifth Investigation, it seems to be just one modification of acts among others. The significance of its unique status and scope can be seen only within the frame of Husserl's system. Specifically, its import becomes clear only in view of its bearing on reason. That it obstructs the move to reason is *the* insight that sets off the analyses of neutrality presented in *Ideas I* from those of quality in the *Investigations*. (This further supports our thesis, incidentally, that *Ideas I* marks a radicalization of the project begun in the *Logical Investigations*, and in fact a radicalization of his grasp of the *system* of phenomenology.) For analyses of the Fifth Investigation, see Quentin Smith, "On Husserl's Theory of Consciousness in the Fifth Logical Investigation," *Philosophy and Phenomenological Research* 37 (1977), 482–97, and Daniel Lorca, "Husserl's Theory of Consciousness in the Fifth Logical Investigation," *Journal of the British Society for Phenomenology* 30 (1999), 151–65. Both authors remain at the level of the *Logical Investigations*, despite mention of *Ideas I*. Neither considers the radical significance of discovery here, which, again, can be seen only in the light of *Ideas I*. It alone makes visible the fundamental role of belief and the danger of its neutralization.

85. Note that 'positive' is not used here in contrast to 'negative', but rather to 'neutral'.

86. The indecision proper to doubt is not to be confused with that proper to neutrality. This becomes clear from a remark Husserl makes in his lectures on "passive synthesis" (*Hua* XI, 36): "The possibility of deciding, of solving, and perhaps actively doing so, belongs to the essence of doubt; in contrast to [negation], doubt itself means undecidedness; consciousness is undecided consciousness." Doubt can be decided, whereas neutrality does not allow of such decision. Neutrality leaves no alternatives between which one might choose, but instead annihilates the very ground of every alternative. That is, the belief or interest. Doubt is present only where there is interest in decision; otherwise, it is actually neutrality.

87. See Boeder, *Das Vernunft-Gefüge der Moderne*, 175.

88. Because the will is implied in them, the expressions in the preceding list cannot be simply adopted. A new one must be found for—and a complete characterization given of—the new modification.

89. See *PP*, Beilage 11 concerning the role interest plays in conscious life, specifically in action. In this connection Husserl contrasts "authentic actualization" with "inauthentic effect." The difference between the two lies in interest. Disinterested striving is at best an oxymoron. Interest presupposes belief. On belief see Sepp, *Praxis und Theoria*, 66–69, and on the central role of interest regarding action, ibid., 69–74.

A theory of the will must account for neutrality, for it represents the zero-point, the total absence of will—even if the neutrality was willed in the first place, such as in the case of the neutrality brought about by the epoché. This is a specific kind of neutralization, however. It remains open whether the neutrality generated by the universal neutrality modification can be willed—that is, if one can willfully perform this modification. Husserl himself says only that it need not be willed, but does not address the positive case, the active, willed neutralization. There is a sense in which the neutrality resultant upon the universal neutrality modification is a passive effect, but it is not possible to decide this matter on the basis of Husserl's writings, at least not on the basis of those published thus far. Ullrich Melle has clearly elaborated three forms of the will as

Husserl understands them: resolve (*Entschluß*), the *fiat*, the action-will (*Handlungswille*). All of these are based on a positing or belief, though this is not emphasized here. The will moves through the positing and beyond, towards the achievement of the willful intention. See Melle's "Husserls Phänomenologie des Willens," 292–95. In "Husserl's Phenomenology of Will in His Reflections on Ethics" (in N. Depraz and D. Zahavi, eds., *Alterity and Facticity* [Dordrecht: Kluwer, 1998], 121–38, here 127–29), Karl Mertens shows Husserl's understanding of the fundamental nature of belief with regard to the will. On this point see Husserl, "Wert des Lebens," 216. See also Hart, *The Person and the Common Life*, chap. 2, esp. §7, in which he outlines a Husserlian "Theory of the Will."

90. Concerning the epoché, see the exposition on II, 57–75. In Copy A (see *Hua* III/2, 510 [entry keyed to III/1, 248]) Husserl writes "no" opposite the phrase "closely akin." This would seem at first glance to call into question the relationship between the epoché and the neutrality modification. However, in view of their structural affinities, which we shall discuss shortly, his 'no' can only be taken as a warning. The phrase 'closely akin' threatens to obscure the distinction between the two modifications—a state of affairs attested sufficiently in Husserl scholarship. That his 'no' is not to be taken as a simple negation of the affinity is suggested by the fact that Husserl had already pointed to the "close kinship" between the epoché and 'merely thinking' in the early stages of his treatment of the former (see *Ideas I*, 55).

One is tempted to say that the "kinship" of the epoché and the neutrality modification have been noted so much in the secondary literature that the latter is not even seen, but instead identified with the former. This would explain why so little attention has been paid to the neutrality modification as such. But even when it has been mentioned, it is usually regarded as just another modification of consciousness among others. An example of the latter tendency is provided in Sokolowski, *The Formation of Husserl's Concept of Constitution*, 146. Of course, Sokolowski's intention is to give a genetic account of constitution in Husserlian thought and so cannot be concerned with all the details of a given text. Yet, one wonders how an adequate account of constitution in Husserl can be given without attending to the fundamental role of belief. And this is precisely what the "doctrine of the neutrality modification" reveals. But more important for now is the fact that treating the neutrality modification as just one among other modifications of consciousness runs counter to Husserl's express remark that this modification "occupies a completely isolated place, and thus by no means may be placed in the series of those modifications discussed above" (*Ideas I*, 222). More recently and more seriously, Volonté has failed to account for the uniqueness of the neutrality modification, even though he quotes the passage just cited; see his *Husserls Phänomenologie der Imagination*, 138–39. Despite Husserl's remarks to the contrary, Volonté presents neutralization in Husserl as something homogeneous. This may be because he has failed to see the pivotal role of belief in Husserlian thought, as well as the distinctions between the kinds of belief thematized therein. This would explain why, e.g., he does not address iteration in any detail. A modification that can be iterated is radically different from the neutrality modification, even if the former belongs to the family of neutrality modifications, as does fantasy.

As for the former misreading—the identification of the epoché and the neutrality modification—which is by far the most common in the literature, see, e.g., Ströker,

Husserls transzendentale Phänomenologie, 64–80, and Sepp, *Praxis und Theoria*, 103–5, esp. 104. It is instructive to consider Ströker's account more closely.

She rightly identifies the "inexplicit belief in Being [*Seinsglaube*]"—while initially not specifying the scope of such belief—as the target of the epoché, which must first become explicit in a reflexive turn as "belief" and thereby transformed into a thesis in order to be excluded (71); but she nevertheless goes on to identify the epoché with the universal neutrality modification, albeit only implicitly. In fact, she makes no explicit mention of the neutrality modification (nor ever acknowledges its existence in Husserl's analysis), but instead imports features of the latter into her discussion of the epoché. For instance, Ströker correctly points out that the epoché "brings into view co-givens [*Mitgegebenheiten*] that remain concealed to me in the natural attitude and makes them accessible to phenomenological investigation for the first time" (73), for all of the constituent features of consciousness indeed become accessible to phenomenological investigation first upon effecting the epoché and the consequent attainment of the absolute sphere of the pure ego. But then, in seeking to clarify the effect of the epoché, she imports language that will be used *only later* in the context of Husserl's analysis of belief and its modalization: "These are specifically the doxic object-characteristics or object-modes such as being-actual, being-possible, being-doubtful, being-fantasied with respect to the object intended, [characteristics or modes] to which correspond on the side of the act doxic-thetic or Being-intending moments as dependent component parts of the acts" (ibid.). Here Ströker errs in connecting these modes and characteristics so strictly to the kind of *Seinsglaube* that is made ineffective by this reduction: "Not only are singular Being-validities to be subjected to the epoché, but the 'general thesis' of the natural attitude is to be bracketed and the 'belief in the existence of the world' [*Weltglaube*] is to be inhibited altogether" (ibid.). But the reduction is universal *only* insofar as it brackets all theses that take part in the *Weltglaube*, i.e., that presuppose the existence of the world. However, the modes and characteristics discussed prior to the latter quotation come into question in Husserl's analysis only with regard to positings that no longer share in the *Weltglaube* and that thus are not affected by the epoché. These will be seen to be put out of action by the neutrality modification or, under very special circumstances, by fantasy or in aesthetic consciousness. But unlike the latter kindred modifications, and unlike the epoché, the universal neutrality modification can target *any and every* positing, and not just the general thesis (as in the case of the epoché) or a memorial thesis (as in fantasy).

It may perhaps be helpful to point out another manifestation of this second error, which encourages the neglect of the neutrality modification, an error that in this instance amounts to an imprecise use of terminology. Here our example stems from Fink, "Operative Begriffe in Husserls Phänomenologie." First: "By means of the obstruction of our effecting the positing, thus by means of the epoché with respect to the positing of Being, we transform (for ourselves) the Being into a 'phenomenon,' whereby 'phenomenon' does not mean anything that shows itself whatsoever, but rather a 'seeming' [*Schein*] that shows itself, as it were a 'neutralized' being, robbed of its thetic characteristics" (197). Fink goes on to speak of the general thesis and its "neutralization," but he fails to specify which thetic characteristics are subjected to the epoché, implying that all such characteristics are thereby affected and not just those bound up with the general thesis. Secondly, and most seriously: "In the horizon of naiveté, the neutrality modification is, after all, only possible as the suspension of our belief in Being [*Seinsglauben*] with respect to the Being of a singular, determinate being; [the modification] thus remains in a comprehensive field of unbroken belief; it remains based on the ground of the world [*Weltboden*]" (198–99). While the epoché is a kind of neutrality modification, as will be seen, it is not *the* universal neutrality modification of concern to Husserl in his "doctrine of the neutrality modification." Fink's talk of "the neutrality modification" as the setting-out-of-action of the general thesis promotes confusion because, in failing to acknowledge the existence of yet another kind of neutrality modification he leads one to believe that the epoché is the sole version thereof.

There are in fact a number of exceptions to the tendency to overlook this modification: first, a later text by Ströker, namely her "Husserls Konzept," in *Husserls Werk*, 51–69. She does not focus on the neutrality modification, but does accord it importance. Secondly, Eugen Fink, *Vergegenwärtigung und Bild*. Fink focuses on the neutrality modification, for which Husserl praises him (see Cairns, *Conversations*, 11), but not the universal neutrality modification. Instead, he examines and seeks to expand upon Husserl's treatment of fantasy and picture consciousness. This is a work of "original" phenomenology, even though it is based on Husserl's works. Due to its originality, it can provide little assistance to us here—and especially because Fink does not pursue a systematic intention, but engages in *particular* studies. Thirdly, and similarly to Fink, Ni (in *Seinsglaube in der Phänomenologie Edmund Husserls*) seeks to improve upon Husserl—though clearly without having understood him sufficiently; he takes up the neutrality modification as a *problem*, without regard to its proper place within *Ideas I*. It is a work that is more about its author than about Husserl, and so a fruitful confrontation is ruled out in light of our present concern: to understand Husserlian thought. Fourthly, Volonté's comprehensive work on "Husserl's phenomenology of imagination"—which must certainly be engaged by anyone investigating Husserl's understanding of imagination—offers a brief analysis of this modification, but one marred by his failure to grasp fully the pivotal differences between fantasy and the neutrality modification, which stems from his failure to accord belief its fundamental role in Husserlian thought; like Fink, he equates it primarily with the fantasy modification (see III, n. 95). The final exception to be mentioned here is found in Boeder, *Das Vernunft-Gefüge der Moderne*, 135–87, esp. 175–79. As far as I have been able to ascertain, his is the only discussion of the neutrality modification that accords it its rightful (i.e., systematic) place.

91. See III, 157–60.

92. Neutral consciousness lacks all seriousness; it is marked by disinterest, or better: indifference. Where something does not matter, there can be no genuine scrutiny—for such scrutiny does not matter, or makes do difference. On the import of seriousness, see Sepp, *Praxis und Theoria*, 86–87.

93. See *Hua* XXIX, 7: "Unreason is the negative mode of reason."

94. This "all" is in fact limited to a particular kind of lived experience, i.e., to memories. But since every lived experience may be transformed into a memory, the universality of fantasy still holds; for essential reasons, it must take a detour, as it were, through memory, whereas the universal neutrality modification need not do so. See III, 175–79 (4.8).

95. In *Ideas I*, § 111 ("The Neutrality Modification and Fantasy") alone, within the span of just over one page, he says as much twice: (1) "fantasy . . . must nevertheless be distinguished from the universal neutrality modification with its manifold formations that comply with all kinds of positing" (p. 224), and (2) "It is, however, of fundamental significance not to confuse this modification [i.e., fantasy] . . . with that neutrality modification with which we can confront every 'positing' lived experience" (p. 225). See also in § 114, p. 233: "It is not necessary to warn anew against the so obvious confusion of the modification at issue here with the fantasy modification, which likewise creates a counterpart, its fantasy image, for every lived experience." Volonté (in *Husserls Phänomenologie der Imagination*, 216–17) obscures the distinction between fantasy and universal neutralization. Through his oversight, he implies that the latter is not distinct from fantasy and the other kinds of neutralization.

96. See *Ideas I*, 225: "this modification, ideally possible at all times, which would convert any lived experience, even the fantasying lived experience itself, into precisely corresponding mere fantasy, or equivalently, into neutralized memory. . . ." See also ibid., 224: fantasy is "applicable to all lived experiences." See also the previous note.

97. See *Ideas I*, 225: "In this respect memory is a wholly specific positing lived experience."

98. Picture or aesthetic consciousness has been the topic of a number of studies, either directly or indirectly. In addition to Fink, *Vergegenwärtigung und Bild*, and Volonté, *Husserls Phänomenologie der Imagination*, 190–210, see, e.g., Alexander Haardt, "Bildbewußtsein und ästhetische Erfahrung bei Edmund Husserl," in J. Bloss et al, eds., *Intentionalität – Werte – Kunst (Husserl – Ingarden – Patocka)* (Prague: Filosofia, 1995), 223–33, and Hans-Joachim Pieper, "'Von Schonheit ist hier keine Rede'. Husserl und das Problem der ästhetischen Einstellung," *Phänomenologische Forschungen* n. s. 3 (1998), 3–33. The relation and distinction between picture- or aesthetic consciousness and the universal neutrality modification is not drawn out by these authors, though Pieper takes steps in this direction; see ibid., 20ff.

99. Were it a transforming operation, a new position would be produced, as perhaps occurs in the case of fantasy (as opposed to *mere* fantasy).

100. Two qualifications are in order here. First, the fantasy modification is iterable *insofar as* it is representiation. It is reproductive in a special sense, and hence iterable. As will be seen, the universal neutrality modification may also be said to be reproductive, but only in the sense that it generates the shadow or powerless reflection of what has been neutralized. Strictly speaking, it is not a member of the class of representiations. Secondly, the quotation marks surrounding 'operation' imply a qualification. In fact, neutralization is not an operation in the same sense as other modifications: it is not productive and thus not iterable. One could, of course, repeat the neutrality modification *in infinitim* if one liked, but that would be redundant. Neutrality is and remains neutrality; repeating the modification does not generate anything new. Casey notes ("Imagination and Phenomenological Method," 81 n. 25) that it is iterability that distinguishes the neutrality modification from fantasy, or "imagination" in his terminology. But he does not inquire into the significance of this difference.

101. See *Ideas I*, § 107, as well as III, 156–57.

102. Husserl does not clarify this point, nor is it addressed in the literature to my knowledge. However, in light of the fact that fantasy is re-productive and that it can be iterated, which means that it involves some kind of correlation between belief or interest and Being-object, the key to the relative positionality of fantasy must lie in memory. What in the memory is neutralized would seem to be, at the very least, the "existence" of the context from which it is wrested. The object of fantasy is unbound from its former connections on the one hand, and not granted the thesis of existence on the other hand. The object of fantasy has only quasi-existence. Casey points in this direction ("Imagination and Phenomenological Method," 75 col. 1): "In imagining, . . . the world as perceived or remembered does disappear; it forms no part of imagined content, which is confined to strictly imaginal presences." That something peculiar is at work here is underscored by Husserl's distinction between fantasy (the neutralization of memory) and *mere* fantasy (the neutralization of fantasy itself, though not by fantasy, but by the universal neutrality modification—not even fantasy is impervious to it!). Concerning the latter, see the passage from *Ideas I*, 225 cited in III, n. 95. For our purposes, chief among which is to draw out the unique status of the universal neutrality modification, it is enough to show the distinction of fantasy from the latter. A full clarification of fantasy in light of these distinctions will have to be left for a future study.

103. Even though the art historian's remarks, e.g., can be attached to theses after the manner of suppositions, the initial move into aesthetic consciousness (by means of the neutralization of perception) cannot be iterated. Any subsequent modification of the depicting picture-object would occur not in aesthetic consciousness, but in fantasy, which would require that the object had been accessed in memory.

104. The decisive distinction here with regard to predication is between *actual* and *quasi*-predication. They are mutually exclusive.

105. The "yielding" (*ergeben*) in question here is not to be confused with productivity in the proper sense of the word.

106. Note that inattention is not necessarily the same as disinterest or indifference. They can coincide, but need not. Rather, interest allows of gradation: the ego can be more interested in one thing than in another. The resultant attentive selection would not seem to dispense with the previous interest, but only reduce it.

107. Apparently Husserl changed 'actional'/*aktuell* here to 'actual'/*wirklich* in Copy A of *Ideas I* (see *Hua* III/2, 510 [keyed to III/1, 256]). This is indeed an improvement over the original text insofar as it helps to draw out the distinction between 'actual' and 'quasi', both of which can be targeted by actional or attentive regard.

108. The "idleness" of fantasy consciousness must, however, be distinguished from that of the (absolutely) neutral consciousness resultant upon the universal neutrality modification. This is necessary because, as has been noted, fantasy is productive in a special sense, namely it fabricates fictions, whereas (absolutely) neutral consciousness produces nothing whatsoever. Fantasy consciousness is idle from the standpoint of authentic or positional consciousness, since the productions of the latter can be directly subjected to rational scrutiny, while the productions of fantasy must be reintegrated into the sphere of belief by way of supposition. That is to say, without the addition of belief, fantasy remains unproductive in the only sense that matters to Husserl: it would not produce or contribute to the production of knowledge.

109. See *Ideas I*, 232: "The situation is . . . that the neutrality modification is not a specific modification attached to actional theses, which are the only ones that are actually theses, but is instead an eidetically fundamental peculiarity of any consciousness whatsoever, expressed in the behavior towards actional protodoxic positability or unpositability."

110. That is, not in the sense of a fluke. It is doubtful that Husserl considers flukes possible, since even what is usually called an anomaly is governed by an essence: essentially, an anomaly is just as possible as the common. This accords both with Husserl's understanding of essence as predelineating all possibilities and with his preference of bipolar structures. Thus the abnormal is the polar opposite of the normal, as the neutral is the polar opposite of the positional. Husserl's analyses of the relationship between normality (*Normalität*) and abnormality (*Anormalität*), which center on the essence of man, hold much in store for an analysis of the neutrality not just of an individual act, but of an individual and, above and beyond that, an entire community (see I, n. 40). See, e.g., CM, 154, *PP*, §20, *Hua* VIII, 92, and *Hua* XV, 148–70 and 227–36. See also Anthony Steinbock, "Phenomenological Concepts of Normality and Abnormality," *Man and World* 28 (1995), 241–60.

111. As Husserl points out in this context, the expressions 'shadow' (*Schatten*) and 'mirror-image' (*Widerspiegelung*), as he uses them, are not to be taken as meaning that there is anything illusory about neutralities. Already the possibility of illusion presupposes a doxic consciousness, which has been ruled out here.

112. In Husserlian phenomenology, positionality and actuality have priority; not only phenomenological inquiry but all science and all productivity depends ultimately on positionality. It is for this reason that 'authenticity' (*Eigentlichkeit*) has pride of place in Husserlian thought, so much so that one would be justified in calling his phenomenology a "philosophy of authenticity." By contrast, in Heidegger 'inauthenticity' (*Uneigentlichkeit*) is first (see §68 of *Sein und Zeit* [Tübingen: Niemeyer, 16th ed., 1986]; *Being and Time*, trans. John Macquarrie and Edward Robinson [New York: Harper & Row, 1962]). The difference between the two thinkers is not one of preference but rather of intention. Husserl is concerned to elucidate the precondition of knowledge and thus of science, which, again, is authenticity. This is not Heidegger's concern. His analysis of Da-sein seeks to determine "how it is" so as to prepare the way to "how it is not but is to be." Hence he privileges inauthenticity, which is the originary mode of Being for the They (*das Man*). Husserl will himself thematize "how it is" in the *Crisis*. In that context he does not speak of 'authenticity' but of 'seriousness', a synonym of the former term, and of the prevailing lack of belief in reason. He does not undertake an existential analysis, however; nor has he somehow come under Heidegger's influence in any other way. Rather, Husserl's remarks in the *Crisis* on "how it is" remain within the horizon of his thought as it had been sketched out no later than in *Ideas I*; they are still aimed at instilling the will to science—that is, to phenomenologically grounded science—in his audience. Heidegger's thought is expressly *un*-scientific; his fundamental ontology is not intended to be a First Science in Husserl's sense. In his *Vernunft-Gefüge der Moderne* (175), Boeder points to Heidegger's translation of Husserl's notion of 'authenticity'. Hart notes the significance of 'authenticity' in Husserl's writings. See his "Entelechy and Authenticity of Objective Spirit," 103–4, as well as *The Person and*

Common Life, 408 and 416, and "The Study of Religion," 266. See also Schuhmann, *Husserls Staatsphilosophie*, 158.

113. The difficulty with this example is admittedly that Oldenburg's "original" is not actually an original, but is already a copy. Hence, the "ghost" is the "shadow" of a copy. In other words, it marks an iteration of fantasy: the fantasy-modification of a preceding fantasy.

114. So belief does indeed have a "negative," i.e., polar opposite, with which it is paired: neutrality. See Pietersma, "Assertion and Predication in Husserl," 78.

115. The positability in question here is that proper to immanent perception or reflection. The ego can reflect on the neutralized lived experience or its correlate. But to engage in such reflection, it must exit neutral consciousness and reenter doxic consciousness, the originary mode of which is time consciousness.

116. See *Ideas I*, 236: "a belief, an actual belief, is 'aroused'; we believe already 'before we know it.' Likewise, at times the liking- or disliking-positings, desirings, even resolutions, are already alive before we 'live' 'in' them, before we effect the authentic cogito, before the ego is 'activated' judgingly, likingly, desiringly, willingly." 'Knowing' must be distinguished here, which was the point of the employment of the metaphor of the levels of acts in the foregoing. The key to the necessary distinction lies in Husserl's phrases "before we know it" and "before we 'live in' them," but also "before we effect the authentic cogito" and "before the ego is activated." The phrase 'before we know it' is not to be understood as referring to knowledge in the strict sense—namely, to that which arises through predicative acts. Rather, as the subsequent phrases make clear, the knowing involved here is that of explicitness, in other words: it is nothing but naive living. And thus it is not yet "logical" and so not rational, but at best the basis thereof. 'Knowing' merely designates 'explicitness' in this context and thus the active directedness of the ego's ray of regard.

117. See the final paragraph of section 4.7.1, above.

118. In Beilage 62 (*Hua* III/2, 614) from 1916, Husserl says of thetic hierarchies: "When we have emotional acts such as joy grounded in doxic acts, there again is something uppermost that is grounded in the substrata that 'serve' it." What is uppermost is in fact the archontic thesis: "But however much that [i.e., the interrelations of theses] may be differentiated: we nevertheless reach an uppermost positionality, and that is what was meant by 'archontic'." In the case of acts of belief, the archontic thesis is precisely the doxic positing. In such acts, the uppermost and lowermost limits coincide.

119. See the works of Sepp (esp. *Praxis und Theoria*), Hart (esp. *The Person and Common Life*), Spahn, and Melle, all of whom are concerned to elucidate the relationship between theory and praxis, though they do not stop there.

120. There are at least two main senses of 'inauthentic' in Husserlian thought: the symbolic and the neutral. In the latter case it of course signals a lack of belief.

121. See Pietersma, "Assertion and Predication in Husserl," for an attempt to come to terms with the relation between the doxic and language.

122. Fantasy would seem to mark an exception to these remarks, but it is not an objectivation. Rather, it is the modification of an objectivation. The productivity of fantasy becomes significant only once it can be scrutinized, which means, again, once it has been brought back into contact with or reintegrated into the doxic sphere.

123. Consider in this connection Frege's twelfth "core proposition on logic": "Logic first begins with the conviction that there is a difference between truth and

untruth." Cited from Gottlob Frege, "17 Kernsätze zur Logik," in *Nachgelassene Schriften*, H. Hermes, F. Karnbartel, and F. Kaulbach, eds. (Hamburg: Meiner, 2d ed., 1983), 190. Interestingly enough, Michael Dummett passes over the doxic basis of logic entirely in his comments on the "Kernsätze." See his *Frege and Other Philosophers* (Oxford: Clarendon, 1991), 65–78, here 75.

124. See III, 142–45.

125. On Husserl's view, in other words, speech does not *do* anything, that is, does not *produce* anything, but merely mirrors or re-presents the affair-complex. It works much like Wittgenstein's tableau vivant. In "Prolegomena to Phenomenology," Adler has convincingly demonstrated Husserl's "blindness" to the pragmatic dimension of language.

126. Interestingly enough, in this connection Husserl points to the relation between formal logic on the one hand and "the idea of a formal axiology and theory of praxis [*Praktik*]" on the other. Formal logic founds these other disciplines. See *Ideas I*, 250 n. 1.

127. On *Ideas I*, 254, Husserl remarks: "In that connection it is also, though not merely, a matter of obscurations." The "new dimension" he has sought to introduce here is that of the will, of its peculiar actionality, its spontaneity. At issue is, namely, actionality or activity as opposed to passivity. Husserl thematizes "modalities of effectuation." They may be marked by clarity or a lack thereof, of course, but that does not hit on the key role of the will.

128. Instead of 'pops up' (*auftauchen*), one could even say 'is aroused' in the sense of the previous discussion of acts that "are there before we know it."

129. This process is, of course, closely related to what, in reference to Dilthey and Heidegger, has been labeled the 'hermeneutic circle'. Husserl's account of the circle differs from each of theirs, however, precisely with regard to his elucidation of intentionality, specifically of intention and fulfillment. See Heidegger, *Sein und Zeit*, §32 and Wilhelm Dilthey, "Die Entstehung der Hermeneutik" (1900), in *Die geistige Welt. Einleitung in die Philosophie des Lebens*, Gesammelte Schriften V (Stuttgart: Teubner/ Göttingen: Vandenhoeck & Ruprecht, 1924; 3d ed., 1961), 317–38, here 330.

130. See J. N. Mohanty, "Husserl's Theory of Meaning," in F. A. Elliston and P. McCormick, eds., *Husserl: Expositions and Appraisals* (Notre Dame, Ind.: University of Notre Dame Press, 1977), 18–37.

131. Husserl has already distinguished between actual and quasi-predicates. See *Ideas I*, 229, as well as III, 166–67.

132. One must bear in mind that protodoxa corresponds to a Being and, in doing so, does not alter that Being in the slightest. The doxic itself does not effect modifications, but is the basis on which they are effected.

133. Note, however, that faithful and complete expression must of necessity maintain the differences it is to express. The requisite activation or appeal to the doxic does not reduce everything to the doxic. Recall that the doxic, like the logical, neither adds anything to nor takes anything away from what is thematized, on Husserl's view.

IV. Towards the System's Uppermost Limit: Reason

1. See J. N. Mohanty, "The 'Object' in Edmund Husserl's Phenomenology," in *Phenomenology and Ontology* (The Hague: Nijhoff, 1970), 138–51.

2. Concerning the mediation in question here, see J. N. Mohanty, "A Note on the Doctrine of Noetic-Noematic Correlation," *Analecta Husserliana* 2 (1972), 317–21, and David Woodruff Smith, "Mind and Body," in B. Smith and D. W. Smith, eds., *The Cambridge Companion to Husserl* (Cambridge: Cambridge University Press, 1995), 323–93, here 340.

3. In fact the core ultimately cannot be reduced to sense, but at this point in his analysis Husserl speaks of the two as if they were identical. They will be seen to differ with regard to completeness.

4. This may seem to contradict what was said in the opening paragraph of this section, where Husserl was quoted as identifying content with sense. However, 'sense' has in the meantime been refined; the starting point of the discussion was with the "usual equivocal talk of the content of consciousness." Note in the cited passage that Husserl places 'content', 'sense', and 'object' each in quotation marks. They still lack the precision at which his current analysis aims.

5. David Michael Levin, in his *Reason and Evidence in Husserl's Phenomenology* (Evanston, Ill.: Northwestern University Press, 1970), xviii, clearly misunderstands the sense of radicality in Husserl when he says that "Husserlian phenomenology is not, after all, radical in the sense that, abandoning the traditional ideal of reason, it denies the very endeavor to give knowledge some kind of absolute and indubitable foundation; nor is it radical in the sense that it *unerringly* sought for a foundation 'outside' the proper category of knowledge itself. The subsequent phenomenologies of Sartre and Merleau-Ponty are, in these respects, more radical enterprises, inasmuch as knowledge is shown to be grounded 'outside' itself, in the (philosophically prior) *lived* (simply experienced) acts of intentional meaning, whence our knowledge is constituted" (Levin's emphasis). 'Radicality' must be taken literally, thus as *radix*, 'root'. Furthermore, it must not be forgotten that for Husserl consciousness is a sphere of *Being* and, as a consequence, that all knowledge takes its bearings by Being; knowledge, like reason, is subsequent to Being. This means, then, that knowledge is indeed "grounded 'outside' itself"—contrary to Levin's claim, which is made all the more puzzling by the fact that Levin himself rightly notes that for Husserl consciousness has priority as *Being*; see Levin, *Reason and Evidence*, 11. On the inseparability of the ego from "intentional life," see *EBA*, 283.33ff./164. See also Bernet, "An Intentionality without Subject or Object?" 237.

6. In his *Dialektik der Phänomenologie* II, Schuhmann rightly notes that phenomenology and the critique of reason are "one and the same" (7), as well as that phenomenology and phenomenological philosophy are "mutually founding" (21), but he tends to lose sight of the hierarchical relationship between the two sides. They are not of equal rank; rather, phenomenology is always first, even if the findings of phenomenological philosophy might someday make it necessary to revise findings made in phenomenology. Pivotal here is the order of the disciplines, which for Husserl corresponds to the "natural order of the problems" (see I, 11). The hierarchy existing between these two sides is rigorously ordered; it extends from the ground (disclosed by phenomenology) up to the apogee of Being (which some part of phenomenological philosophy may one day reach). It is a *teleological* order.

7. See *FTL*, 16–17.

8. See Elisabeth Ströker, "Husserls Evidenzprinzip. Sinn und Grenzen einer methodischen Norm der Phänomenologie als Wissenschaft," in *Phänomenologische Studien* (Frankfurt a. M.: Klostermann, 1987), 1–34, here 8.

9. As seen above, actual or positional and neutral predication are equally possible.

10. See Antonio Aguirre, "Transzendentalphänomenologischer Rationalismus," in U. Claesges and K. Held, eds., *Perspektiven transzendentalphänomenologischer Forschung* (The Hague: Nijhoff, 1972), 102–28, here 103.

11. See Sepp, *Praxis und Theoria*, 139. This talk of reason echoes features of "the mental" noted by Nenon in his "Husserl's Theory of the Mental," 225.

12. Husserl employs *Vernunft* in this chapter predominantly in constructions such as *Vernunftbewußtsein*, *Vernunftcharakter*, and *Vernunftakt*. In them, *Vernunft* has an adjectival character; they are thus best rendered as 'rational consciousness', 'rational characteristic', and 'rational act', respectively. It rarely appears as an independent substantive. This suggests that even where it does appear as such, it is to be taken in the sense of a predicate. Consider, e.g., the talk of the "verdict of reason [*Rechtsprechung der Vernunft*]" above. Here reason is ascribed to something; this something is deemed rational. Reason itself is not an agent that engages in passing verdicts. Contrary to the usual assumptions, the genitive operative here is to be taken as objective rather than as subjective.

13. Levin comes very close to seeing that reason is a predicate in Husserl, but steers away from this determination in favor of his own distinction between reason as result or as process, whereby he favors the latter interpretation: "For this vision [i.e., of the reign of reason] can be conceived, on the one hand, as the demonstration that there truly exists a special privileged *kind* of evidence (knowledge), a truly 'rational' evidence, as the support and measure for all other kinds of evidence (knowledge); or, on the other hand, it can be conceived as affirming the primacy of a methodological value, animating a process of evidential clarification and justification which is, from a logical point of view, always incomplete and tentative. According to the first interpretation, we might say, reason is thoroughly *substantival*, a finished product, and truth is consequently treated as a peculiar kind of *property* (attribute), presumably qualifying either a privileged kind of insight, or else a somehow specially 'marked' kind of proposition. While according to the second, reason is instead *procedural*, essentially creative, always, as some philosophers are fond of saying, in a state of perpetual 'becoming' (phenomenological anticipation), and located, as it were, in the interstices, the evidential interconnections and interdependencies of the structure of knowledge. And here, then, truth is simply a matter of the contextual evaluation of the conditions which justify knowledge" (Levin, *Reason and Evidence*, 31; his emphasis). Levin does not see that reason itself is a property, which does not rule out its being a goal of inquiry, as in Levin's second sense of reason. Levin (31–32) claims that, of the two conceptions, Husserl adhered to the former in the *Logical Investigations* and *Cartesian Meditations*, but to the latter in *Ideas I* and *Formal and Transcendental Logic*. He comes close to speaking of it as a predicate on p. 116, for instance, but there uses it as an adverb and not as an adjective: "in a rationally compelling and satisfying way." But Levin does speak of reason as a subject or substance, and thus substantively, on p. 171, for instance: "that consciousness, as reason, will discern," "holding reason forever in thrall"; while also speaking of it as a norm: "the ideal of reason"; then, somewhat ambiguously, in "the demands of reason." As a substantive, see

also 207: "efficacy of reason." Levin himself is inconsistent in his talk of 'reason'. Husserl, by contrast, is nothing but consistent. Incidentally, much like Levin, R. A. Mall also distinguishes between two senses of reason—that is, reason as end or goal and reason as process—a thesis he has in turn from Ludwig Landgrebe; he makes no mention of Levin. See Mall's "Phenomenology of Reason," in U. Claesges and K. Held, eds., *Perspektiven transzendental-phänomenologischer Forschung* (The Hague: Nijhoff, 1972), 129–41.

14. Hence, as Biemel notes ("Die Idee der Phänomenologie bei Husserl," 170), "reason is an essential becoming," a sense that is already present in *Ideas I*, and not just in *Crisis*. On gradation see Ströker, "Husserls Evidenzprinzip," in her *Phänomenologische Studien*, 10–11. For discussions of the various problems connected with Husserl's notion of reason and evidence, see Ströker, ibid.; Levin, *Reason and Evidence*; Leo Bostar, "The Methodical Significance of Husserl's Concept of Evidence and Its Relation to the Idea of Reason," *Husserl Studies* 4 (1987), 143–67; and Henry Pietersma, "Truth and the Evident," in J. N. Mohanty and W. R. McKenna, eds., *Husserl's Phenomenology: A Textbook* (Lanham: CARP and University Press of America, 1989), 213–36.

15. Analogously to his understanding of reason in Husserl, Levin (*Reason and Evidence,* xx) identifies two kinds of apodicticity, one final, the other a goal guiding endless inquiry. But again, even granting Levin's reading, the two versions need not be mutually exclusive.

16. See Pietersma, "Truth and the Evident," 233ff.

17. See Dagfinn Føllesdal, "Rationalität in Husserls Phänomenologie," *Phänomenologische Forschungen* 19 (1986), 35–52. He seeks to thwart the founding function of logical reason in Husserl. Barry Smith and David Woodruff Smith stress in their Introduction that Husserl was committed to the classical distinction between the theoretical and the practical (3), whereby the latter is to found the former, but they do not admit a hierarchy between the theoretical subdisciplines, specifically between epistemology, ontology, and phenomenology, in their terms (13–14). It must at least be acknowledged, however, that pure logic founds these three. The question there would be: What is the relationship between the three subdisciplines in light or on the basis of the priority of pure logic? And then: Even if they are mutually supporting, which of the three would one want to articulate first, and why?

18. See Mohanty, "Husserl on 'Possibility'," 21–26.

19. Consider, once again, Husserl's formulation of the "principle of all principles," on II, 54–56.

20. See *Ideas I*, 301: "what occurs in the *eidos*, functions as an absolutely insurmountable norm for the fact."

21. At issue here is therefore not a correlation between reason and actuality, but rather between belief and Being. Evidence, and thus reason, is a distinguishing feature of the latter correlation, whether in the form of maximal evidence or a lesser grade, which depends again wholly on the character of the correlation. See Aguirre, "Transzendentalphänomenologischer Rationalismus," 111. See Bernet, "An Intentionality without Subject or Object?" 242–43.

22. Contrary to Levin, there is no "pre-thetic" consciousness, unless one were to identify it with doxic consciousness, which Levin does not do. See Levin, *Reason and Evidence*, 21. He suggests that when one reaches the level of prethetic consciousness

one has reached the ground: "We are confronted with the pure stream of experience in its immediate, primordial, sensuous temporality. Itself non-constituted, this experience is the ground of all genetic constitution." The dubiousness of this claim should have become clear no later than in the explication of Husserl's "doctrine of the neutrality modification" above. Levin's claim, which clearly stems from Merleau-Ponty, is rendered even less convincing by his confused talk of the thetic; see Levin, ibid., 66 n. 56. A case in point is his appeal to a "pre-thetic certitude" that is somehow, in its radicality, not doxic. In Husserl's terms, this would make no sense. Certitude is, after all, another name in Husserlian thought for protodoxa.

23. See *Ideas I*, 315: God is the "ideal representative of absolute knowledge"; and cf. Fink's remark, reported by Cairns in his *Conversations*, 14 (August 17, 1931): "The term God is used occasionally by Husserl in private conversations to mean the community of *transcendental egos* which 'creates' a world, but this is for Husserl a 'private opinion.'" Cairns also reports Husserl's remarks on this topic from August 22, 1931 (ibid., 22–23): "'The problem of transcendental constitution,' said Husserl in effect, 'is, as I have said to Herrn Dr. Fink, none other than the problem of how God created the absolute world, and continues to create it, even as the transcendental intersubjectivity creates the world.' The phenomenological form of the ontological argument is the conclusion from the absolute constitutive consciousness." See also Boyce Gibson's report of Husserl's remarks on the relationship between phenomenology and metaphysics in his diary entry of July 24, 1928 ("Freiburg Diary," 69 col. 2): "I gather that Metaphysics, as he [i.e., Husserl] conceives it is a special development of Phenomenology. The 'höchste Stufe' [highest level] of Phenomenology, dealing more specifically with the problems of 'Schicksal, Tod und Gott' [fate, death, and God]." In Husserlian thought, God seems first and foremost to be a Kantian idea, a regulative concept, the goal of all striving. It is on account of this that God can be identified with reason: it is the striving for a maximal condition. See *Hua* XV, 610 (early 1930s): "God is not himself the monad-all, but rather the entelechy lying in it, as the idea of the infinite telos of development, that of 'humanity' based on absolute reason, as necessarily regulating monadic Being, and regulating based on one's own free decision. This as an intersubjective [decision] is a necessarily expanding process, without which, despite the necessarily attendant events of decline, universal Being simply cannot be, etc."

24. See I, nn. 45, 100, and 127.

25. See III, n. 44.

26. In this connection, consider Sokolowski's distinction between adjectival and nominal essences in *Husserlian Meditations*, 67.

27. See Afterword, 561–62.

28. Or members of the "scientific army." See Boyce Gibson ("Freiburg Diary," 65 col. 1), where he reports Husserl as saying: "As philosophers our attention must be that of privates in the great *Wissenschafts-armee*; each of us disinterestedly contributes his quota." On a related note, see *EBA*, 301/179: "Thus phenomenology demands of the phenomenologist that he abstain from the ideal of a *philosophical* system and yet live as a modest worker in community with others for a *philosophia perennis*." It is important to bear in mind here that Husserl distinguishes his own system from philosophical systems.

Chapter V. The Phenomenological Movement

1. See CM, 182–83.

2. Letter to Dorion Cairns, March 21, 1930; *BW* 4, 23.15–28.

3. "It is difficult; the most difficult thing of all in philosophy is the phenomenological reduction, to penetrate and practice it" (Letter to Roman Ingarden, November 13, 1931; *BW* 3, 281). Concerning the selflessness with which rigorous science is to be engaged in, Husserl is reported as saying: "Martyrdom is the principle of the Church. . . . For science, too, martyrdom will become the solely passable road to salvation. Only heroes of spirit, radical people, can perhaps save science once more." (Jaegerschmid, "Conversations," 50–51.) See also Bossert, "The Sense of 'Epoché' and 'Reduction'," 251 col. 2 and 255 col. 1 on the indispensability of the phenomenological reduction.

4. See Cairns, *Conversations*, 43 (November 20, 1931): "He said that neither Heidegger nor Becker nor Kaufmann understood the phenomenological reduction. . . . But it is his conviction that the most important thing about his whole philosophy is the transcendental reduction. He repeated what Fink had told me before, that the phenomenological reduction is something which must be continually repeated in phenomenological work."

5. See Cairns, *Conversations*, 10 (August 13, 1931).

6. Letter to Friedrich Mittelsten Scheid, April 25, 1934; *BW* 7, 189. See his letter to Roman Ingarden, July 10, 1935; *BW* 3, 301.

7. Phenomenology is not entirely a *res nullius*, then, at least one cannot appropriate it just however one wants, on Husserl's view, but only in his specific sense—if one is to engage in authentic phenomenological inquiry, that is. Consider, e.g., *Ideas III*, 81: "Any investigation and any stock of knowledge, any gain in knowledge, can be called 'phenomenological' that belongs to phenomenology *in our specific sense*." And shortly thereafter Husserl distinguishes between phenomenology proper and its use: "That is an application of phenomenology, not phenomenology itself." The specific sense of Husserlian thought prescribes a system or systematic development: "Despite the limitation to the sphere of mere intuition and eidetic insight, phenomenology in our sense is thus a systematic science and now must also be carried out within this limitation" (*Ideas III*, 82). The limitation to the sphere is bounded, as we have sought to show, above and below by quite definite parameters, definite even if Husserl did not succeed in gaining full clarity on them. The definiteness and thus finitude of his position, of his phenomenology, seems to have escaped many scholars, for whatever reason. For instance, in their Introduction to *The Cambridge Companion to Husserl*, 9, Barry Smith and David Woodruff Smith make the puzzling claim that, on the one hand, "Husserl officially defined the science of phenomenology as the study of the essence of conscious experience, and especially of intentional experience" in *Ideas I*, and that, on the other hand, this "definition fits Husserl's work as well as that of his successors: Adolf Reinach, Max Scheler, Roman Ingarden, Alfred Schutz, Martin Heidegger, Maurice Merleau-Ponty, Jean-Paul Sartre, and recent analytic phenomenologists such as Dagfinn Føllesdal and Hubert Dreyfus." Not only does this definition not capture all that is decisive about Husserl's idea of phenomenology (as witnessed by the list of its adherents), but the claim is simply wrong regarding at least Heidegger and Merleau-Ponty. See the following sketch of the most obvious ways in which their "phenomenologies" differ from Husserl's.

8. See my Introduction to Boeder, *Seditions*, ix–x.

9. For an initial characterization of 'submodernity', see ibid., xxxvii–xxxviii, as well as "The Dimension of Submodernity," in ibid., 227–39.

10. See the paradigmatic example in Spiegelberg, *The Phenomenological Movement*.

11. See Martin Heidegger, "Mein Weg in die Phänomenologie," *Zur Sache des Denkens* (Tübingen: Niemeyer, 3d ed., 1988), 81–90; *On Time and Being*, trans. Joan Stambaugh (New York: Harper & Row, 1972), 74–82.

12. The focus on similarities is encouraged by the characterization of phenomenology as a "style" or an "accent" of thought. See, e.g., Jean-François Lyotard's "Introduction" to his *Phenomenology*, trans. Brian Beakley (Albany, N.Y.: State University of New York Press, 1991), §§1 and 6. See also Spiegelberg, "Movements in Philosophy," 284–85, where he stresses the unifying tenets of the "phenomenological movement," specifically the general agreement on the necessity of basing all knowledge claims on intuitive givenness and of exploring essences or essential characteristics by means of intuition.

13. Heidegger, "Mein Weg," 90/82. Note that Heidegger does not speak of 'phenomenology' but rather of 'phenomenological philosophy'. In light of the relationship between these two as defined by Husserl (consider the full title of *Ideas*), it becomes clear that Heidegger is not talking about phenomenology in Husserl's sense. And it is not immediately clear what is gained by lumping them together.

14. Ibid.

15. Maurice Merleau-Ponty, *Phénoménologie de la Perception* (Paris: Gallimard, 1945), i; *The Phenomenology of Perception*, trans. Collin Smith (London: Routledge & Kegan Paul, 1962), vii. The French is followed henceforth by the English pagination.

16. Maurice Merleau-Ponty, "An Unpublished Text by Maurice Merleau-Ponty: A Prospectus of His Work," trans. Arleen B. Dallery, in *The Primacy of Perception and Other Essays on Phenomenological Psychology*, ed. J. Edie (Evanston, Ill.: Northwestern University Press, 1963), 3–4.

17. *Phenomenology of Perception*, v/x–xi.

18. Prospectus, 5.

19. Prospectus, 6.

20. Maurice Merleau-Ponty, "The Primacy of Perception and Its Philosophical Consequences," trans. James M. Edie, in *The Primacy of Perception and Other Essays on Phenomenological Psychology*, ed. J. M. Edie (Evanston, Ill.: Northwestern University Press, 1963), 25.

21. For a characterization of Heidegger's and Merleau-Ponty's positions, see Boeder, *Seditions*, 183–98 and 228–33, respectively.

22. *Crisis*, 508/389: "Philosophy as science, as serious, rigorous, even apodictically rigorous science—the dream has been dreamed out." For Husserl the dream had most definitely not been dreamed out. See Biemel, "Zur Bedeutung von δόξα und ἐπιστήμη," 146. See also Orth, *Edmund Husserls "Krisis. . . .,"* 29–34.

Bibliography

Conventions of Citation

Unless otherwise noted, all works cited are by Edmund Husserl. All abbreviations of his works are provided below alongside the relevant work. All translations are mine, as is all emphasis, unless otherwise noted. Any translation I have consulted was modified as was deemed necessary and without notice. Translations have been cited primarily as an aid to the English-speaking reader; in such cases, the English pagination always follows the German. Wherever the original German pagination is provided in the margins of the English editions—and this is noted below, when relevant—only the reference to the original pagination is provided.

In order to demonstrate the steadfastness of Husserl's intention, the works cited are always the original published versions (the so-called A-versions); wherever his later interventions in a text are considered, they are either noted as such or are cited from subsequent editions. Wherever it has been thought worthwhile, line numbers have been cited; they are separated from page numbers by a period. Line numbers refer only to the German edition of the text in question.

In those cases in which a text is cited repeatedly within the body of the text, its abbreviation is provided only in the first instance. (The exception is in Chapters II–IV, in which only *Ideas I* is cited, and without preceding abbreviation.) Likewise, page references are provided only in the first instance of quotation; subsequent passages that fall on the same page will accordingly remain under the scope of the preceding reference. Wherever the conventions outlined here differ, the modifications are noted at the end of the corresponding bibliographic entry below.

Roman numerals appearing in the notes without a preceding title or abbreviation refer to the chapters of the present study; they are followed in each case by either page or note numbers.

I. Works by Edmund Husserl

Afterword — "Nachwort zu meinen 'Ideen zu einer reinen Phänomenologie und phänomenologischen Philosophie.'" In *Jahrbuch für Philosophie und phänomenologische Forschung* 11 (1930): 549–70. English translation: "Afterword to my *Ideas Pertaining to a Pure Phenomenology and to a*

Phenomenological Philosophy," trans. Marcus Brainard, in *Ideas Pertaining to a Pure Phenomenology and to a Phenomenological Philosophy. First Book: General Introduction to Pure Phenomenology* (Seattle: Noesis Press, Ltd., forthcoming 2002). (Original German pagination in margins.)

BW — *Briefwechsel*. Edited by Karl Schuhmann with Elisabeth Schuhmann. Husserliana Dokumente III. 10 vols. Dordrecht: Kluwer Academic Publishers, 1994. (The abbreviation will be followed by volume number and page reference.)

CM — *Cartesianische Meditationen und Pariser Vorträge*. Edited by S. Strasser. Husserliana I. The Hague: Martinus Nijhoff Publishers, 1950. English translation of the former text: *Cartesian Meditations: An Introduction to Phenomenology*, trans. Dorion Cairns (The Hague: Nijhoff, 1960). (Original German pagination in margins.)

Crisis — *Die Krisis der europäischen Wissenschaften und die transzendentale Phänomenologie*. Edited by Walter Biemel. Husserliana VI. The Hague: Martinus Nijhoff Publishers, 1954. English translation: *The Crisis of European Sciences and Transcendental Phenomenology*, trans. David Carr (Evanston, Ill.: Northwestern University Press, 1970).

Draft — "Entwurf einer 'Vorrede' zu den *Logischen Untersuchungen* (1913)." Edited by Eugen Fink. *Tijdschrift voor Filosofie* 1 (1939): 106–33 and 319–39. English translation: *Introduction to the Logical Investigations: A Draft of a Preface to the Logical Investigations (1913)*, ed. E. Fink, trans. Philip J. Bossert and Curtis H. Peters (The Hague: Nijhoff, 1975). (Original German pagination in margins.)

EBA — "Der Encyclopaedia Britannica Artikel." In *Phänomenologische Psychologie. Vorlesungen Sommersemester 1925*, 237–301 and 517–26. Edited by Walter Biemel. Husserliana IX. The Hague: Martinus Nijhoff Publishers, 1962. English translation: "The *Encyclopaedia Britannica* Article," in *Psychological and Transcendental Phenomenology and the Confrontation with Heidegger (1927–1931)*, ed. and trans. Thomas Sheehan and Richard E. Palmer (Dordrecht: Kluwer Academic Publishers, 1997), 83–196.

EJ — *Erfahrung und Urteil. Untersuchungen zur Genealogie der Logik* (1938). Edited by Ludwig Landgrebe. Hamburg: Claassen & Goverts, 1948. English translation: *Experience and Judgment: Investigations in a Genealogy of Logic*, trans. James S. Churchhill and Karl Ameriks (Evanston, Ill.: Northwestern University Press, 1973).

Fichte — "Fichtes Menschheitsideal (Drei Vorlesungen 1917)," in *Aufsätze und Vorträge (1911–1921)*, 267–93. Edited by Thomas Nenon and Hans Rainer Sepp. Husserliana XXV. Dordrecht: Martinus Nijhoff Publishers, 1986. English translation: "Fichte's Ideal of Humanity (Three Lectures, 1917)," trans. James G. Hart, in *Husserl Studies* 12 (1995): 111–33.

FTL *Formale und transzendentale Logik. Versuch einer Kritik der logischen Vernunft*. Edited by Paul Janssen. Husserliana XVII. The Hague: Martinus Nijhoff Publishers, 1974. English translation: *Formal and Transcendental Logic*, trans. Dorion Cairns (The Hague: Nijhoff, 1969). (Original German pagination in margins.)

Hua II *Die Idee der Phänomenologie. Fünf Vorlesungen*. Edited by Walter Biemel. Husserliana II. The Hague: Martinus Nijhoff Publishers, 1950. English translation: *The Idea of Phenomenology*, trans. William P. Alston and George Nakhnikian (The Hague: Nijhoff, 1964). (Original German pagination in margins.)

Hua III/1–2 *Ideen zu einer reinen Phänomenologie und phänomenologischen Philosophie. Erstes Buch: Allgemeine Einführung in die reine Phänomenologie*. Edited by Karl Schuhmann. Husserliana III/1–2. The Hague: Martinus Nijhoff Publishers, 1976. English translation of *Hua* III/1: *Ideas Pertaining to a Pure Phenomenology and to a Phenomenological Philosophy. First Book: General Introduction to a Pure Phenomenology*, trans. F. Kersten (Dordrecht: Kluwer Academic Publishers, 1983).

Hua VII *Erste Philosophie (1923/24). Erster Teil: Kritische Ideengeschichte*. Edited by Rudolf Boehm. Husserliana VII. The Hague: Martinus Nijhoff Publishers, 1956.

Hua VIII *Erste Philosophie (1923/24). Zweiter Teil: Theorie der phänomenologischen Reduktion*. Edited by Rudolf Boehm. Husserliana VIII. The Hague: Martinus Nijhoff Publishers, 1959.

Hua XI *Analysen zur passiven Synthesis. Aus Vorlesgungs- und Forschungsmanuskripten 1918–1926*. Edited by Margot Fleischer. Husserliana XI. The Hague: Martinus Nijhoff Publishers, 1966.

Hua XV *Zur Phänomenologie der Intersubjektivität. Texte aus den Nachlaß. Dritter Teil: 1929–1935*. Edited by Iso Kern. Husserliana XV. The Hague: Martinus Nijhoff Publishers, 1973.

Hua XVIII *Logische Untersuchungen. Erster Band: Prolegomena zur reinen Logik*. Edited by Elmar Holenstein. Husserliana XVIII. The Hague: Martinus Nijhoff Publishers, 1975. Includes A and B versions. English translation of the latter: *Logical Investigations*, trans. J. N. Findlay (New York: Humanities Press, 1970), vol. I, 41–247.

Hua XIX/1 *Logische Untersuchungen. Zweiter Band, Erster Teil. Untersuchungen zur Phänomenologie und Theorie der Erkenntnis*. Edited by Ursula Panzer. Husserliana XIX/1. The Hague: Martinus Nijhoff Publishers, 1984. Includes A and B versions. English translation of the latter: *Logical Investigations*, trans. J. N. Findlay (New York: Humanities Press, 1970), vol. I, 248–432 (First and Second Investigations) and vol. II, 435–659 (Third through Fifth Investigations)

Hua XIX/2 — *Logische Untersuchungen. Zweiter Band, Zweiter Teil. Untersuchungen zur Phänomenologie und Theorie der Erkenntnis*. Edited by Ursula Panzer. Husserliana XIX/2. The Hague: Martinus Nijhoff Publishers, 1984. Includes A and B versions. English translation of the latter: *Logical Investigations*, trans. J. N. Findlay (New York: Humanities Press, 1970), vol. II, 661–851 (Sixth Investigation).

Hua XXIII — *Phantasie, Bildbewußtsein, Erinnerung. Zur Phänomenologie der anschaulichen Vergegenwärtigungen. Texte aus dem Nachlaß (1898–1925)*. Edited by Eduard Marbach. Husserliana XXIII. The Hague: Martinus Nijhoff Publishers, 1980.

Hua XXIV — *Einleitung in die Logik und Erkenntnistheorie. Vorlesungen 1906–1907*. Edited by Ullrich Melle. Husserliana XXIV. Dordrecht: Kluwer Academic Publishers, 1984.

Hua XXVII — *Aufsätze und Vorträge (1922–1937)*. Edited by Thomas Nenon and Hans Rainer Sepp. Husserliana XXVII. Dordrecht: Kluwer Academic Publishers, 1989.

Hua XXVIII — *Vorlesungen über Ethik und Wertlehre 1908–1914*. Edited by Ullrich Melle. Husserliana XXVIII. Dordrecht: Kluwer Academic Publishers, 1988.

Hua XXIX — *Die Krisis der europäischen Wissenschaften und die transzendentale Phänomenologie. Ergänzungsband. Texte aus dem Nachlaß*. Edited by Reinhold N. Smid. Husserliana XXIX. Dordrecht: Kluwer Academic Publishers, 1993.

Hu-Chr. — *Husserl-Chronik. Denk- und Lebensweg Edmund Husserls*, by Karl Schuhmann. Husserliana Dokumente I. The Hague: Martinus Nijhoff Publishers, 1977.

Ideas I — *Ideen zu einer reinen Phänomenologie und phänomenologischen Philosophie. Erstes Buch: Allgemeine Einführung in die reine Phänomenologie*. In *Jahrbuch für Philosophie und phänomenologische Forschung* 1 (Halle/Saale: Max Niemeyer Verlag, 1913): 1–323. English translation: *Ideas Pertaining to a Pure Phenomenology and to a Phenomenological Philosophy. First Book: General Introduction to Pure Phenomenology*, trans. Marcus Brainard (Seattle: Noesis Press, Ltd., forthcoming 2002). (Original German pagination in margins.)

Ideas II — *Ideen zu einer reinen Phänomenologie und phänomenologischen Philosophie. Zweites Buch: Phänomenologische Untersuchungen zur Konstitution*. Edited by Marly Biemel. Husserliana IV. The Hague: Martinus Nijhoff Publishers, 1952. English translation: *Ideas Pertaining to a Pure Phenomenology and to a Phenomenological Philosophy. Second Book: Studies in the Phenomenology of Constitution*, trans. Richard Rojcewicz and André Schuwer (Dordrecht: Kluwer Academic Publishers, 1989).

Ideas III — *Ideen zu einer reinen Phänomenologie und phänomenologischen Philosophie. Drittes Buch: Die Phänomenologie und die Fundamente der Wissenschaften.* Edited by Marly Biemel. Husserliana V. The Hague: Martinus Nijhoff Publishers, 1952. English translation: *Ideas Pertaining to a Pure Phenomenology and to a Phenomenological Philosophy. Third Book: Phenomenology and the Foundations of the Sciences*, trans. Ted E. Klein and William E. Pohl (Dordrecht: Kluwer Academic Publishers, 1980).

LL — "Phänomenologische Methode und phänomenologische Philosophie" (London Lectures, 1922). Edited by Berndt Goossens. *Husserl Studies* 16 (2000): 200–54.

PN — "Persönliche Aufzeichnungen." Edited by Walter Biemel. *Philosophy and Phenomenological Research* 16 (1956): 293–302. English translation: "Personal Notes," ed. W. Biemel, trans. Marcus Brainard, in *New Yearbook for Phenomenology and Phenomenological Philosophy* I (2001), 319–29. (Original German pagination in margins.)

PP — *Phänomenologische Psychologie. Vorlesungen Sommersemester 1925.* Edited by Walter Biemel. Husserliana IX. The Hague: Martinus Nijhoff Publishers, 1962. English translation of the main text of the lecture course (*Hua* IX, 1–234): *Phenomenological Psychology*, trans. John Scanlon (The Hague: Nijhoff, 1977). (Original German pagination in margins.)

PRS — "Philosophie als strenge Wissenschaft." In *Logos. Internationale Zeitschrift für Philosophie der Kultur* 1 (1910–11): 289–341. English translation: "Philosophy as Rigorous Science," trans. Marcus Brainard, in *New Yearbook for Phenomenology Phenomenological Philosophy* II (forthcoming 2002). (Original German pagination in margins.)

SGM — "Statische und genetische Methode." In *Hua* XI, 336–45. English translation: "Static and Genetic Method," trans. Anthony Steinbock, in *Continental Philosophy Review* 31 (1998), 135–42.

VL — "Die Krisis des europäischen Menschentums und die Philosophie." In *Hua* VI, 314–48. English translation: "Philosophy and the Crisis of European Humanity," trans. David Carr, in *The Crisis of European Sciences and Transcendental Phenomenology*, 269–99. This text, also known as the "Vienna Lecture," has also been translated by Quentin Lauer under the title "Philosophy and the Crisis of European Man" and included in Edmund Husserl, *Phenomenology and the Crisis of Phenomenology* (New York: Harper & Row, 1965), 149–92. Carr's translation is cited here.

Wert — "Wert des Lebens. Wert der Welt. Sittlichkeit (Tugend) und Glückseligkeit <Februar 1923>." Edited by Ullrich Melle. *Husserl Studies* 13 (1996): 206–35.

II. Works by Others

Adler, Pierre. "Prolegomena to Phenomenology: Intuition or Argument?" *Graduate Faculty Philosophy Journal* 16 (1992): 3–76.

Aguirre, Antonio. *Genetische Phänomenologie und Reduktion. Zur Letztbegründung der Wissenschaft aus der radikalen Skepsis im Denken E. Husserls*. Phaenomenologica 38. The Hague: Martinus Nijhoff Publishers, 1970.

———. "Transzendentalphänomenologischer Rationalismus." In U. Claesges and K. Held, eds. *Perspektiven transzendentalphänomenologischer Forschung*, 102–28. Phaenomenologica 49. The Hague: Martinus Nijhoff Publishers, 1972.

———. "Zum Verhältnis von modaler und praktischer Möglichkeit." *Phänomenologische Forschungen* 24/25 (1991): 150–82.

Allen, Jeffner. "What is Husserl's First Philosophy?" *Philosophy and Phenomenological Research* 42 (1982): 610–20.

Ayer, A. J. *Central Questions of Philosophy*. London: Weidenfeld & Nicolson, 1973.

Baldwin, Thomas. "Phenomenology, Solipsism and Egocentric Thought." *Proceedings of the Aristotelian Society*. Supplementary volume 62 (1988): 27–43.

Ballard, Edward G. "On the Method of Phenomenological Reduction, Its Presuppositions, and Its Future." In L. E. Embree, ed. *Life-World and Consciousness: Essays for Aron Gurwitsch*, 101–23. Evanston, Ill.: Northwestern University Press, 1972.

Becker, Oskar. "Die Philosophie Edmund Husserls." *Kant-Studien* 35 (1930): 119–50.

Bell, David. *Husserl*. New York: Routledge, 1990.

———. "Phenomenology, Solipsism and Egocentric Thought." *Proceedings of the Aristotelian Society*. Supplementary volume 62 (1988): 45–60.

Bernet, Rudolf. "Endlichkeit und Unendlichkeit in Husserls Phänomenologie der Wahrnehmung." *Tijdschrift voor Filosofie* 40 (1978): 251–69. English version: "Perception as Teleological Process of Cognition," *Analecta Husserliana* 9 (1979): 119–32.

———. "Husserls Begriff des Noema." In S. IJsseling, ed. *Husserl-Ausgabe und Husserl-Forschung*, 61–80. Phaenomenologica 115. Dordrecht: Kluwer Academic Publishers, 1990.

———. "Husserl's Concept of the World." In A. B. Dallery and C. E. Scott, eds. *Crises in Continental Philosophy*, 3–21. Albany, N.Y.: State University of New York Press, 1990.

———. "An Intentionality without Subject or Object?" Translated by Michael Newman. *Man and World* 27 (1994): 231–55.

———. "Logik und Phänomenologie in Husserls Lehre von der Wahrheit." *Tijdschrift voor Filosofie* 43 (1981): 35–89.

———. "Phenomenological Reduction and the Double Life of the Subject." Translated by François Renaud. In T. Kisiel and J. van Buren, eds. *Reading Heidegger from the Start: Essays in His Earliest Thought*, 245–67. Albany, N.Y.: State University of New York Press, 1994.

———. "Zur Teleologie der Erkenntnis: Eine Antwort an Rudolf Boehm." *Tijdschrift voor Filosofie* 40 (1978): 662–68.

Bernet, Rudolf, Iso Kern, and Eduard Marbach. *Edmund Husserl. Darstellung seines Denkens*. Hamburg: Felix Meiner Verlag, 1989.

Biemel, Walter. *Gesammelte Schriften*. 2 vols. Stuttgart: frommann-holzboog, 1996.

Blumenberg, Hans. *Paradigmen zu einer Metaphorologie*. Frankfurt a. M.: Suhrkamp Verlag, 1998.

Boeder, Heribert. "Die conceptuale Vernunft in der Letzten Epoche der Metaphysik." *Abhandlungen der Braunschweigischen Wissenschaftlichen Gesellschaft* 43 (1992): 345–60.

———. *Seditions: Heidegger and the Limit of Modernity*. Edited, translated, and with an introduction by Marcus Brainard. Albany, N.Y.: State University of New York Press, 1997.

———. *Das Vernunft-Gefüge der Moderne*. Freiburg/Munich: Verlag Karl Alber, 1988.

———. *Topologie der Metaphysik*. Freiburg/Munich: Verlag Karl Alber, 1980.

Boehm, Rudolf. *Vom Gesichtspunkt der Phänomenologie. Husserl-Studien*. Phaenomenologica 26. The Hague: Martinus Nijhoff Publishers, 1968.

———. *Vom Gesichtspunkt der Phänomenologie* II: *Studien zur Phänomenologie der Epoché*. Phaenomenologica 83. The Hague: Martinus Nijhoff Publishers, 1981.

Bossert, Philip J. "The Sense of 'Epoché' and 'Reduction' in Husserl's Philosophy." *Journal of the British Society for Phenomenology* 5 (1974): 243–55.

Bostar, Leo. "The Methodical Significance of Husserl's Concept of Evidence and Its Relation to the Idea of Reason." *Husserl Studies* 4 (1987): 143–67.

Boyce Gibson, W. R. "From Husserl to Heidegger: Excerpts from a 1928 Freiburg Diary." Edited by H. Spiegelberg. *Journal of the British Society for Phenomenology* 2 (1971): 58–83. (Bracketed additions to this text are mine.)

Brainard, Marcus. "As Fate Would Have It: Husserl on the Vocation of Philosophy." *New Yearbook for Phenomenology and Phenomenological Philosophy* I (2001): 111–60.

———. Introduction (ix–xlix) to *Seditions: Heidegger and the Limit of Modernity*, by Heribert Boeder. Edited, translated, and with an introduction by M. Brainard. Albany, N.Y.: State University of New York Press, 1997.

Buckley, R. Philip. *Husserl, Heidegger and the Crisis of Philosophical Responsibility*. Phaenomenologica 125. Dordrecht: Kluwer Academic Publishers, 1992.

———. Review of James G. Hart, *The Person and the Common Life*. Phaenomenologica 126 (Dordrecht: Kluwer Academic Publishers, 1992). In *Husserl Studies* 13 (1997): 169–77.

Busche, Hubertus. "Was ist keine Fiktion? Zeitlichkeit als Wurzel der imaginären Verfaßtheit alles empirischen Bewußtseins in Vaihingers *Philosophie des Als Ob*." In H. Busche, G. Heffernan, and D. Lohmar, eds. *Bewußtsein und Zeitlichkeit. Ein Problemschnitt durch die Philosophie der Neuzeit*, 173–97. Würzburg: Verlag Königshausen & Neumann, 1990.

Cairns, Dorion. *Conversations with Husserl and Fink*. Phaenomenologica 66. The Hague: Martinus Nijhoff Publishers, 1976.

———. *Guide for Translating Husserl*. Phaenomenologica 55. The Hague: Martinus Nijhoff Publishers, 1973.

Carr, David. "Intentionality." In E. Pivcevic, ed. *Phenomenology and Philosophical Understanding*, 17–36. Cambridge: Cambridge University Press, 1975.

Casey, Edward S. "Imagination and Phenomenological Method." In F. A. Elliston and P. McCormick, eds. *Husserl: Expositions and Appraisals*, 70–82. Notre Dame, Ind.: University of Notre Dame Press, 1977.

Costa, Vincenzo. "Transcendental Aesthetic and the Problem of Transcendentality." In N. Depraz and D. Zahavi, eds. *Alterity and Facticity: New Perspectives on Husserl*, 9–27. Phaenomenologica 148. Dordrecht: Kluwer Academic Publishers, 1998.

Damast, Thomas. "Zum Problem einer Theorie der Reflection bei Husserl." In H. Busche, G. Heffernan, and D. Lohmar, eds. *Bewußtsein und Zeitlichkeit. Ein Problemschnitt durch die Philosophie der Neuzeit*, 199–212. Würzburg: Verlag Königshausen & Neumann, 1990.

Descartes, René. *The Philosophical Writings of Descartes*. Translated by John Cottingham, Robert Stoothoff, and Dugald Murdoch. 2 vols. Cambridge: Cambridge University Press, 1984–85.

Diemer, Alwin. *Edmund Husserl. Versuch einer systematischen Darstellung seiner Phänomenologie*. 2d ed. Meisenheim: Verlag Anton Hain, 1965.

———. "Die Phänomenologie und die Idee der Philosophie als strenge Wissenschaft." *Zeitschrift für philosophische Forschung* 13 (1959): 243–62.

Dilthey, Wilhelm. *Die geistige Welt. Einleitung in die Philosophie des Lebens*. Edited by Georg Misch. *Gesammelte Schriften* V. Stuttgart: Teubner and Göttingen: Vandenhoeck & Ruprecht, 1924; 3d ed., 1961.

Dreyfus, Hubert L. "Husserl's Perceptual Noema." In H. D., ed. *Husserl, Intentionality, and Cognitive Science*, 96–123. Cambridge, Mass.: MIT Press, 1982.

Drost, Mark P. "The Primacy of Perception in Husserl's Theory of Imagining." *Philosophy and Phenomenological Research* 50 (1990): 569–82.

Drummond, John J. "From Intentionality to Intensionality and Back." *Études phénoménologiques* 14 (1998): 89–126.

———. "Husserl on the Ways to the Performance of the Reduction." *Man and World* 8 (1975): 47–69.

———. *Husserlian Intentionality and Non-Foundational Realism: Noema and Object*. Contributions to Phenomenology 4. Dordrecht: Kluwer Academic Publishers, 1990.

———. "The 'Spiritual' World: The Personal, the Social, and the Communal." In T. Nenon and L. Embree, eds. *Issues in Husserl's "Ideas II,"* 237–54. Dordrecht: Kluwer Academic Publishers, 1996.

Ducat, Philippe. "Rationalism, Idealism, Nationalism." In N. Depraz and D. Zahavi, eds. *Alterity and Facticity: New Perspectives on Husserl*, 87–102. Phaenomenologica 148. Dordrecht: Kluwer Academic Publishers, 1998.

Dummett, Michael. *Frege and Other Philosophers*. Oxford: Clarendon Press, 1991.

———. *Origins of Analytic Philosophy*. Cambridge, Mass.: Harvard University Press, 1993.

———. "Thought and Perception: The Views of Two Philosophical Innovators." In D. Bell and N. Cooper, eds. *The Analytic Tradition: Meaning, Thought and Knowledge*, 83–101. Oxford: Basil Blackwell, 1990.

Dupré, Louis. "Husserl's Thought on God and Faith." *Philosophy and Phenomenological Research* 29 (1968–69): 201–15.

Eley, Lothar. *Die Krise des Apriori in der transzendentalen Phänomenologie Edmund Husserls*. Phaenomenologica 10. The Hague: Martinus Nijhoff Publishers, 1962.

Ellis, Ralph D. "Afferent-Efferent Connections and 'Neutrality-Modifications' in Perceptual and Imaginative Consciousness." *Man and World* 23 (1990): 23–33.

Elveton, R. O. *The Phenomenology of Husserl: Selected Critical Readings*. 2d ed. Seattle: Noesis Press, Ltd., 2000.

Evans, J. Claude. "The Myth of Absolute Consciousness." In A. B. Dallery and C. E. Scott, eds. *Crises in Continental Philosophy*, 35–44. Albany, N.Y.: State University of New York Press, 1990.

Findlay, J. N. "Phenomenology and the Meaning of Realism." In E. Pivcevic, ed. *Phenomenology and Philosophical Understanding*, 143–58. Cambridge: Cambridge University Press, 1975.

Fink, Eugen. *Nähe und Distanz*. Freiburg/Munich: Verlag Karl Alber, 1976.

———. *Studien zur Phänomenologie 1930–1939*. Phaenomenologica 21. The Hague: Martinus Nijhoff Publishers, 1966.

Fischer, Matthias. *Differente Wissensfelder – Einheitlicher Vernunftraum. Über Husserls Begriff der Einstellung*. Munich: Wilhelm Fink Verlag, 1985.

Fisette, Denis. "The Horizon of the Self: Husserl on Indexicals." In D. Zahavi, ed. *Self-Awareness, Temporality, and Alterity*, 119–35. Contributions to Phenomenology 34. Dordrecht: Kluwer Academic Publishers, 1998.

———. *Lecture frégéene de la phénoménologie*. Combas, France: Éditions de l'Eclat, 1994.

Føllesdal, Dagfinn. "Husserl on Evidence and Justification." In R. Sokolowski, ed. *Edmund Husserl and the Phenomenological Tradition: Essays in Phenomenology*, 107–29. Studies in Philosophy and the History of Philosophy 18. Washington, D.C.: Catholic University of America Press, 1988).

———. "Husserl's Notion of the Noema." *Journal of Philosophy* 66 (1969): 680–87. Reprinted in H. L. Dreyfus, ed. *Husserl, Intentionality, and Cognitive Science*, 73–80. Cambridge, Mass.: MIT Press, 1982.

———. "Husserl's Theory of Perception." In H. L. Dreyfus, ed. *Husserl, Intentionality, and Cognitive Science*, 93–96. Cambridge, Mass.: MIT Press, 1982.

———. "Noema and Meaning in Husserl." *Philosophy and Phenomenological Research* 50 (1990): 263–71.

———. "Rationalität in Husserls Phänomenologie." *Phänomenologische Forschungen* 19 (1986): 35–52.

Frege, Gottlob. *Begriffsschrift und andere Aufsätze*, edited by I. Angelelli. 2d ed. Hildesheim: Georg Olms Verlag, 1964.

———. *Kleine Schriften*, edited by I. Angelelli. Hildesheim: Georg Olms Verlag, 1967.

———. *Nachgelassene Schriften*, edited by H. Hermes, F. Kambartel, and F. Kaulbach. 2d ed. Hamburg: Felix Meiner Verlag, 1983.

Freud, Sigmund. *Fragen der Gesellschaft / Ursprünge der Religion*, edited by A. Mitscherlich, et al. Freud-Studienausgabe IX. 7th ed. Frankfurt a. M.: S. Fischer Verlag, 1994.

Gurwitsch, Aron. "Husserl's Theory of Intentional Consciousness." In H. L. Dreyfus, ed. *Husserl, Intentionality, and Cognitive Science*, 59–71. Cambridge, Mass.: MIT Press, 1982.

———. "Perceptual Coherence as the Foundation of the Judgment of Predication." In F. Kersten and R. Zaner, eds. *Phenomenology: Continuation and Criticism. Essays in Memory of Dorion Cairns*, 62–89. Phaenomenologica 50. The Hague: Martinus Nijhoff Publishers, 1973.

Haardt, Alexander. "Bildbewußtsein und ästhetische Erfahrung bei Edmund Husserl." In J. Bloss, W. Strózewski, and J. Zumr, eds. *Intentionalität – Werte – Kunst (Husserl – Ingarden – Patocka)*, 223–33. Prague: Filosofia, 1995.

Hall, Harrison. "Husserl's Realism and Idealism." In J. N. Mohanty and W. R. McKenna, eds. *Husserl's Phenomenology: A Textbook*, 429–44. Lanham: The Center for Advanced Research in Phenomenology and University Press of America, 1989.

Hart, James G. "Agent Intellect and Primal Sensibility in Husserl." In T. Nenon and L. Embree, eds. *Issues in Husserl's "Ideas II,"* 107–34. Dordrecht: Kluwer Academic Publishers, 1996.

———. "Axiology as the Form of Purity of Heart: A Reading of Husserliana XXVIII." *Philosophy Today* (Fall 1990): 206–21.

———. "The Entelechy and Authenticity of Objective Spirit: Reflections on Husserliana XXVII." *Husserl Studies* 9 (1992): 91–110.

———. "Entelechy in Transcendental Phenomenology." *American Catholic Philosophical Quarterly* 66 (1992): 189–212.

———. "From *mythos* to *logos* to Utopian Poetics: An Husserlian Narrative." *International Journal for Philosophy of Religion* 25 (1989): 147–69.

———. "Genesis, Instinct, and Reconstruction: Nam-In Lee's *Edmund Husserls Phänomenologie der Instincte." Husserl Studies* 15 (1998): 101–23.

———. "Husserl and Fichte: With Special Regard to Husserl's Lectures on 'Fichte's Ideal of Humanity.'" *Husserl Studies* 12 (1995): 135–63.

———. "I, We, and God: Ingredients of Husserl's Theory of Community." In S. IJsseling, ed. *Husserl-Ausgabe und Husserl-Forschung*, 125–49. Phaenomenologica 115. Dordrecht: Kluwer Academic Publishers, 1990.

———. *The Person and the Common Life: Studies in a Husserlian Social Ethics*. Phaenomenologica 126. Dordrecht: Kluwer Academic Publishers, 1992.

———. "A Précis of an Husserlian Philosophical Theology." In S. W. Laycock and J. G. Hart, eds. *Essays in Phenomenological Theology*, 89–168. Albany, N.Y.: State University of New York Press, 1986.

———. "The Study of Religion in Husserl's Writings." In M. Daniel and L. Embree, eds. *Phenomenology of the Cultural Disciplines*, 265–96. Contributions to Phenomenology 16. Dordrecht: Kluwer Academic Publishers, 1994.

Harvey, Charles. "Husserl's Complex Concept of the Self and the Possibility of Social Criticism." In A. B. Dallery and C. E. Scott, eds. *Crises in Continental Philosophy*, 47–55. Albany, N.Y.: State University of New York Press, 1990.

Hedwig, Klaus. "Husserl und die Analogie." *Zeitschrift für philosophische Forschung* 36 (1982): 77–86.

Heidegger, Martin. *Aus der Erfahrung des Denkens*. Gesamtausgabe 13. Frankfurt a. M.: Vittorio Klostermann, 1983.

———. *Sein und Zeit*. 16th ed. Tübingen: Max Niemeyer Verlag, 1986. English translation: *Being and Time*, trans. John Macquarrie and Edward Robinson (New York: Harper & Row, 1962).

———. *Vorträge und Aufsätze*. 6th ed. Pfullingen: Verlag Günther Neske, 1990. Several essays contained therein have been translated by William Lovitt and published in *The Question Concerning Technology and Other Essays* (New York: Harper & Row, 1977).

———. *Zur Sache des Denkens*. 3d ed. Tübingen: Max Niemeyer Verlag, 1988. English translation: *On Time and Being*, trans. Joan Stambaugh (New York: Harper & Row, 1972).

Heinsen, Douglas. "Husserl's Theory of the Pure Ego." In H. L. Dreyfus, ed. *Husserl, Intentionality, and Cognitive Science*, 147–67. Cambridge, Mass.: MIT Press, 1982.

Henrich, Dieter. "Über die Grundlagen von Husserls Kritik der philosophischen Tradition." *Philosophische Rundschau* 6 (1958): 1–26.

Hopkins, Burt C. "Husserl's Account of Phenomenological Reflection and Four Paradoxes of Reflexivity." *Research in Phenomenology* 19 (1989): 180–94.

———. "Phenomenological Cognition of the A Priori: Husserl's Method of 'Seeing Essences' (*Wesenserschauung*)." In B. C. Hopkins, ed. *Husserl in Contemporary Context: Prospects and Projects for Phenomenology*, 151–78. Contributions to Phenomenology 26. Dordrecht: Kluwer Academic Publishers, 1997.

Hoyos Vásquez, G. *Intentionalität als Verantwortung. Geschichtsteleologie und Teleologie der Intentionalität bei Husserl*. Phaenomenologica 56. The Hague: Martinus Nijhoff Publishers, 1976.

———. "Zum Teleologiebegriff in der Phänomenologie Husserls." In U. Claesges and K. Held, eds. *Perspektiven transzendentalphänomenologischer Forschung*, 61–84. Phaenomenologica 49. The Hague: Martinus Nijhoff Publishers, 1972.

Hülsmann, Heinz. "Der Systemanspruch der Phänomenologie E. Husserls." *Salzburger Jahrbuch für Philosophie* 7 (1963): 173–86.

Ingarden, Roman. *On the Motives which led Husserl to Transcendental Idealism*. Translated by Arnór Hannibalsson. Phaenomenologica 64. The Hague: Martinus Nijhoff Publishers, 1975.

Jaegerschmid, Adelgundis. "Gespräche mit Edmund Husserl 1931–1936." *Stimmen der Zeit* 199, no. 1 (1981): 48–58. English translation, which includes both parts of Jaegerschmid's record (see next entry for second part): "Conversations with Edmund Husserl, 1931–1938," trans. Marcus Brainard, in *New Yearbook for Phenomenology and Phenomenological Philosophy* I (2001), 331–50. (Original German pagination in margins.)

———. "Die letzten Jahre Edmund Husserls (1936–1938)." *Stimmen der Zeit* 199, no. 2 (1981): 129–38. (See preceding entry for English translation.)

Janssen, Paul. *Geschichte und Lebenswelt. Ein Beitrag zur Diskussion von Husserls Spätwerk*. Phaenomenologica 35. The Hague: Martinus Nijhoff Publishers, 1970.

Kaehler, Klaus Erich. "Descartes und die transzendentale Phänomenologie." In C. Hubig, ed. *Cognitio humana – Dynamik des Wissens und der Werte*, 423–32. Berlin: Akademie Verlag, 1997.

———. "Die Monade in Husserls Phänomenologie der Intersubjektivität." *Tijdschrift voor Filosofie* 59 (1995): 692–709.

Kern, Iso. "Die drei Wege zur transzendental-phaenomenologischen Reduktion in der Philosophie Edmund Husserls." *Tijdschrift voor Filosofie* 24 (1962): 303–49.

———. *Idee und Methode der Philosophie. Leitgedanken für eine Theorie der Vernunft*. Berlin: Walter de Gruyter, 1975.

———. "Selbstbewußtsein und Ich bei Husserl." In G. Funke, ed. *Husserl-Symposion Mainz* 27.6.–4.7.1988, Akademie der Wissenschaften und der Literatur, Abhandlungen der geistes- und sozialwissenschaftlichen Klasse no. 3 (1989): 51–63.

Kersten, Fred. "Husserl's Doctrine of Noesis-Noema." In F. Kersten and R. Zaner, eds. *Phenomenology: Continuation and Criticism. Essays in Memory of Dorion Cairns*, 114–44. Phaenomenologica 50. The Hague: Martinus Nijhoff Publishers, 1973.

———. "The Occasion and Novelty of Husserl's Phenomenology of Essence." In P. J. Bossert, ed. *Phenomenological Perspectives: Historical and Systematic Essays in Honor of Herbert Spiegelberg*, 61–92. Phaenomenologica 62. The Hague: Martinus Nijhoff Publishers, 1975.

———. "Zur transzendentalen Phänomenologie der Vernunft." *Perspektiven der Philosophie* 1 (1975): 57–84.

Klein, Ted. "'Essences and Experts': Husserl's View of the Foundations of the Sciences." In T. Nenon and L. Embree, eds. *Issues in Husserl's "Ideas II,"* 67–80. Dordrecht: Kluwer Academic Publishers, 1996.

Kohák, Erazim. *Idea and Experience: Edmund Husserl's Project of Phenomenology in "Ideas I."* Chicago: University of Chicago Press, 1978.

Kottukapully, J. "Husserl's Critique of his Cartesian Way." *International Philosophical Quarterly* 22 (1982): 145–56.

Krysztofiak, Wojciech. "Phenomenology, Possible Worlds, and Negation." *Husserl Studies* 8 (1992): 205–20.

Küng, Guido. "The Phenomenological Reduction as Epoché and Explication." In F. A. Elliston and P. McCormick, eds. *Husserl: Expositions and Appraisals*, 338–49. Notre Dame, Ind.: University of Notre Dame Press, 1977.

Kuspit, Donald B. "Fiction and Phenomenology." *Philosophy and Phenomenological Research* 29 (1968): 16–33.

Landgrebe, Ludwig. *Der Weg der Phänomenologie. Das Problem einer ursprünglichen Erfahrung*. Gütersloh: Gütersloher Verlagshaus Gerd Mohn, 1963.

Lauer, Quentin. Introduction to *Phenomenology and the Crisis of Philosophy*, by Edmund Husserl, 1–68. New York: Harper & Row, 1965.

———. *The Triumph of Subjectivity. An Introduction to Transcendental Phenomenology*. New York: Fordham University Press, 1958.

Lee, Nam-In. *Edmund Husserls Phänomenologie der Instinkte*. Phaenomenologica 128. Dordrecht: Kluwer Academic Publishers, 1993.

Levin, David Michael. "Husserl's Notion of Self-Evidence." In E. Pivcevic, ed. *Phenomenology and Philosophical Understanding*, 53–78. Cambridge: Cambridge University Press, 1975.

———. *Reason and Evidence in Husserl's Phenomenology*. Evanston, Ill.: Northwestern University Press, 1970.

Lohmar, Dieter. "Beiträge zu einer phänomenologischen Theorie des negativen Urteils." *Husserl Studies* 8 (1992): 173–204.

Lorca, Daniel. "Husserl's Theory of Consciousness in the Fifth Logical Investigation." *Journal of the British Society for Phenomenology* 30 (1999): 151–65.

Luft, Sebastian. "Husserl's Phenomenological Discovery of the Natural Attitude." *Continental Philosophy Review* 31 (1998): 153–70.

Lyotard, Jean-François. *La phénoménologie*. 10th ed. Paris: Presses Universitaires de France, 1986. English translation: *Phenomenology*, trans. Brian Beakley (Albany, N.Y.: State University of New York Press, 1991).

Mackie, J. L. "Problems of Intentionality." In E. Pivcevic, ed. *Phenomenology and Philosophical Understanding*, 37–52. Cambridge: Cambridge University Press, 1975.

Mall, R. A. "The God of Phenomenology in Comparative Contrast to that of Philosophy and Theology." *Husserl Studies* 8 (1991): 1–15.

———. "Phenomenology of Reason." In U. Claesges and K. Held, eds. *Perspektiven transzendental-phänomenologischer Forschung*, 129–41. Phaenomenologica 49. The Hague: Martinus Nijhoff Publishers, 1972.

Marbach, Eduard. "Ichlose Phänomenologie bei Husserl." *Tijdschrift voor Filosofie* 35 (1973): 518–59.

———. *Das Problem des Ich in der Phänomenologie Husserls*. Phaenomenologica 59. The Hague: Martinus Nijhoff Publishers, 1974.

Marx, Werner. *Die Phänomenologie Edmund Husserls*. Munich: Wilhelm Fink Verlag, 1987.

McGill, V. J. "Evidence in Husserl's Phenomenology." In F. Kersten and R. Zaner, eds. *Phenomenology: Continuation and Criticism. Essays in Memory of Dorion Cairns*, 145–66. Phaenomenologica 50. The Hague: Martinus Nijhoff Publishers, 1973.

McIntyre, Ronald, and David Woodruff Smith. "Husserl's Identification of Meaning and Noema." In H. L. Dreyfus, ed. *Husserl, Intentionality, and Cognitive Science*, 81–92. Cambridge, Mass.: MIT Press, 1982.

———. "Theory of Intentionality." In J. N. Mohanty and W. R. McKenna, eds. *Husserl's Phenomenology: A Textbook*, 147–79. Lanham: The Center for Advanced Research in Phenomenology and University Press of America, 1989.

McKenna, William R. *Husserl's "Introductions to Phenomenology": Interpretation and Critique*. Phaenomenologica 89. The Hague: Martinus Nijhoff Publishers, 1982.

———. "Husserl's Theory of Perception." In J. N. Mohanty and W. R. McKenna, eds. *Husserl's Phenomenology: A Textbook*, 181–212. Lanham: The Center for Advanced Research in Phenomenology and University Press of America, 1989.

Meier, Heinrich. *Die Lehre Carl Schmitts. Vier Kapitel zur Unterscheidung Politischer Theologie und Politischer Philosophie*. Stuttgart/Weimar: J. B. Metzlersche Verlagsbuchhandlung, 1994. English translation: *The Lesson of Carl Schmitt: Four Chapters on the Distinction between Political Theology and Political Philosophy*, trans. Marcus Brainard (Chicago: University of Chicago Press, 1998).

Melle, Ullrich. "Husserls Phänomenologie des Willens." *Tijdschrift voor Filosofie* 54 (1992): 280–305.

———. Introduction to "Wert des Lebens. Wert der Welt. Sittlichkeit (Tugend) und Glückseligkeit <Februar 1923>," by Edmund Husserl. *Husserl Studies* 13 (1997): 201–5.

———. "Objektivierende und nicht-objektivierende Akte." In S. IJsseling, ed. *Husserl-Ausgabe und Husserl-Forschung*, 35–49. Phaenomenologica 115. Dordrecht: Kluwer Academic Publishers, 1990.

———. "Die Phänomenologie Edmund Husserls als Philosophie der Letztbegründung und radikalen Selbstverantwortung." In H. R. Sepp, ed. *Edmund Husserl und die phänomenologische Bewegung*, 45–59. Freiburg/Munich: Verlag Karl Alber, 1988.

Mensch, James Richard. *After Modernity: Husserlian Reflections on a Philosophical Tradition*. Albany, N.Y.: State University of New York Press, 1996.

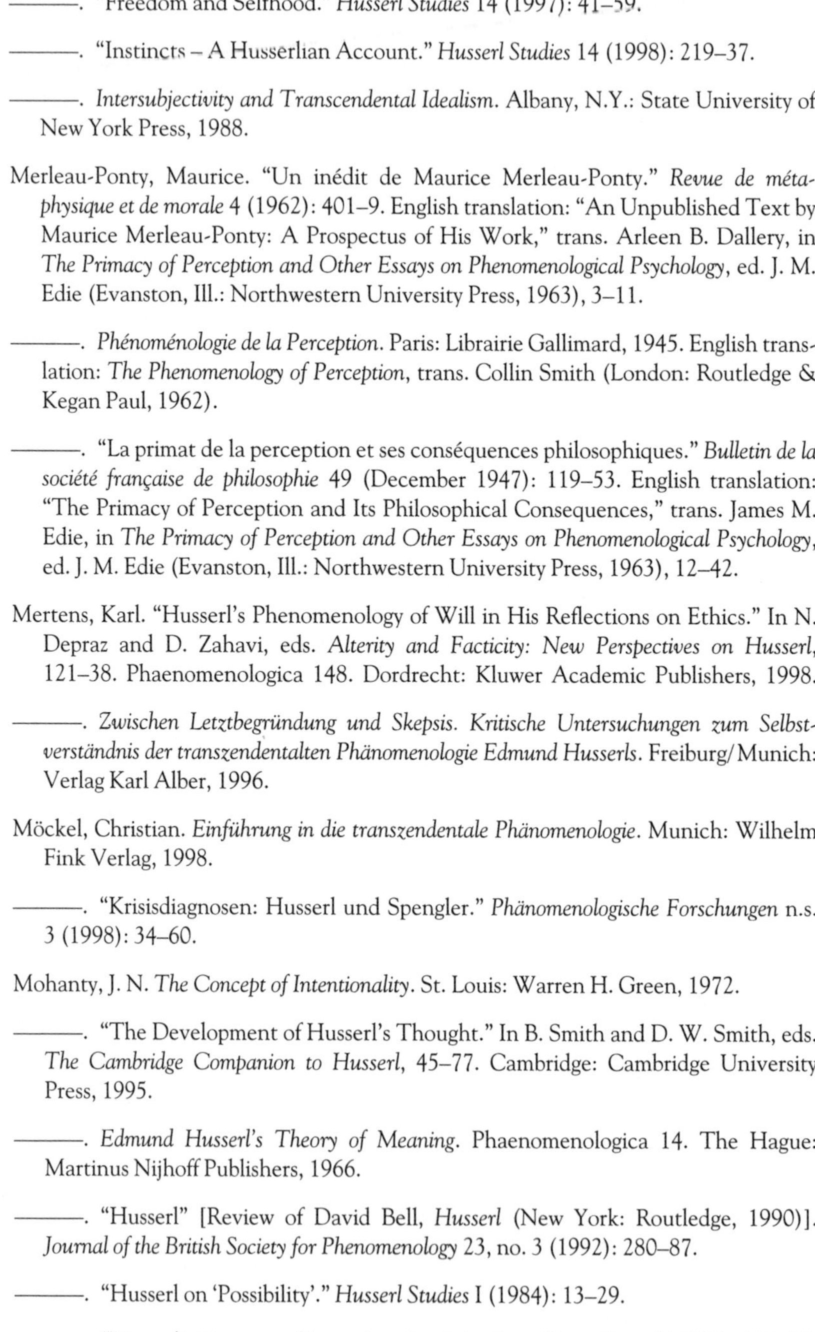

———. "Freedom and Selfhood." *Husserl Studies* 14 (1997): 41–59.

———. "Instincts – A Husserlian Account." *Husserl Studies* 14 (1998): 219–37.

———. *Intersubjectivity and Transcendental Idealism*. Albany, N.Y.: State University of New York Press, 1988.

Merleau-Ponty, Maurice. "Un inédit de Maurice Merleau-Ponty." *Revue de métaphysique et de morale* 4 (1962): 401–9. English translation: "An Unpublished Text by Maurice Merleau-Ponty: A Prospectus of His Work," trans. Arleen B. Dallery, in *The Primacy of Perception and Other Essays on Phenomenological Psychology*, ed. J. M. Edie (Evanston, Ill.: Northwestern University Press, 1963), 3–11.

———. *Phénoménologie de la Perception*. Paris: Librairie Gallimard, 1945. English translation: *The Phenomenology of Perception*, trans. Collin Smith (London: Routledge & Kegan Paul, 1962).

———. "La primat de la perception et ses conséquences philosophiques." *Bulletin de la société française de philosophie* 49 (December 1947): 119–53. English translation: "The Primacy of Perception and Its Philosophical Consequences," trans. James M. Edie, in *The Primacy of Perception and Other Essays on Phenomenological Psychology*, ed. J. M. Edie (Evanston, Ill.: Northwestern University Press, 1963), 12–42.

Mertens, Karl. "Husserl's Phenomenology of Will in His Reflections on Ethics." In N. Depraz and D. Zahavi, eds. *Alterity and Facticity: New Perspectives on Husserl*, 121–38. Phaenomenologica 148. Dordrecht: Kluwer Academic Publishers, 1998.

———. *Zwischen Letztbegründung und Skepsis. Kritische Untersuchungen zum Selbstverständnis der transzendentalten Phänomenologie Edmund Husserls*. Freiburg/Munich: Verlag Karl Alber, 1996.

Möckel, Christian. *Einführung in die transzendentale Phänomenologie*. Munich: Wilhelm Fink Verlag, 1998.

———. "Krisisdiagnosen: Husserl und Spengler." *Phänomenologische Forschungen* n.s. 3 (1998): 34–60.

Mohanty, J. N. *The Concept of Intentionality*. St. Louis: Warren H. Green, 1972.

———. "The Development of Husserl's Thought." In B. Smith and D. W. Smith, eds. *The Cambridge Companion to Husserl*, 45–77. Cambridge: Cambridge University Press, 1995.

———. *Edmund Husserl's Theory of Meaning*. Phaenomenologica 14. The Hague: Martinus Nijhoff Publishers, 1966.

———. "Husserl" [Review of David Bell, *Husserl* (New York: Routledge, 1990)]. *Journal of the British Society for Phenomenology* 23, no. 3 (1992): 280–87.

———. "Husserl on 'Possibility'." *Husserl Studies* I (1984): 13–29.

———. "Husserl's Concept of Intentionality." *Analecta Husserliana* I (1970): 100–32.

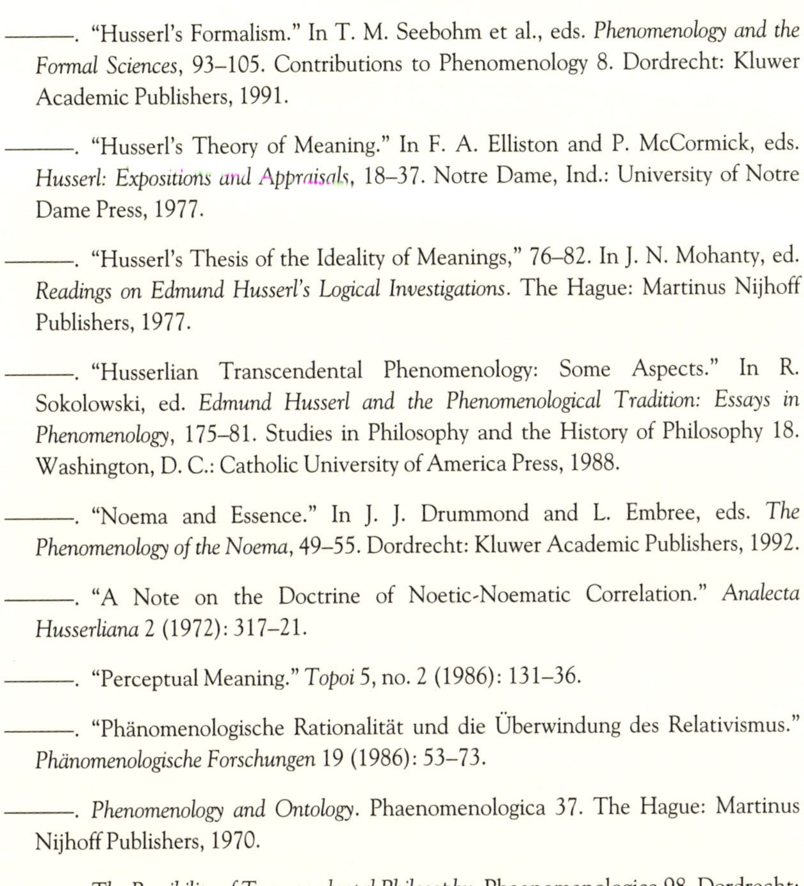

———. "Husserl's Formalism." In T. M. Seebohm et al., eds. *Phenomenology and the Formal Sciences*, 93–105. Contributions to Phenomenology 8. Dordrecht: Kluwer Academic Publishers, 1991.

———. "Husserl's Theory of Meaning." In F. A. Elliston and P. McCormick, eds. *Husserl: Expositions and Appraisals*, 18–37. Notre Dame, Ind.: University of Notre Dame Press, 1977.

———. "Husserl's Thesis of the Ideality of Meanings," 76–82. In J. N. Mohanty, ed. *Readings on Edmund Husserl's Logical Investigations*. The Hague: Martinus Nijhoff Publishers, 1977.

———. "Husserlian Transcendental Phenomenology: Some Aspects." In R. Sokolowski, ed. *Edmund Husserl and the Phenomenological Tradition: Essays in Phenomenology*, 175–81. Studies in Philosophy and the History of Philosophy 18. Washington, D. C.: Catholic University of America Press, 1988.

———. "Noema and Essence." In J. J. Drummond and L. Embree, eds. *The Phenomenology of the Noema*, 49–55. Dordrecht: Kluwer Academic Publishers, 1992.

———. "A Note on the Doctrine of Noetic-Noematic Correlation." *Analecta Husserliana* 2 (1972): 317–21.

———. "Perceptual Meaning." *Topoi* 5, no. 2 (1986): 131–36.

———. "Phänomenologische Rationalität und die Überwindung des Relativismus." *Phänomenologische Forschungen* 19 (1986): 53–73.

———. *Phenomenology and Ontology*. Phaenomenologica 37. The Hague: Martinus Nijhoff Publishers, 1970.

———. *The Possibility of Transcendental Philosophy*. Phaenomenologica 98. Dordrecht: Kluwer Academic Publishers, 1985.

Natorp, Paul. "Husserls 'Ideen zu einer reinen Phänomenologie'." *Die Geisteswissenschaften* 1 (1914): 420–26 and 448–51.

Nenon, Thomas. "Husserls phänomenologischer Cartesianismus. Zum Verhältnis von Selbstbewußtsein und Selbstverantwortung in seiner phänomenologischen Transzendentalphilosophie." *Phänomenologische Forschungen* n. s. 2 (1997): 177–88.

———. "Husserl's Theory of the Mental." In T. Nenon and L. Embree, eds. *Issues in Husserl's "Ideas II,"* 218–31. Contributions to Phenomenology 24. Dordrecht: Kluwer Academic Publishers, 1996.

———. "Two Models of Foundation in the *Logical Investigations*." In B. C. Hopkins, ed. *Husserl in Contemporary Context: Prospects and Projects for Phenomenology*, 97–114. Contributions to Phenomenology 26. Dordrecht: Kluwer Academic Publishers, 1997.

Ni, Liangkang. *Seinsglaube in der Phänomenologie Edmund Husserls*. Phaenomenologica 153. Dordrecht: Kluwer Academic Publishers, 1999. (This is a revised version of his "Das Problem des Seinsglauben in der Phänomenologie Edmund Husserls. Ein Versuch mit Husserl." Dissertation Freiburg i. Br. 1990.)

———. "Urbewußtsein und Reflexion bei Husserl." *Husserl Studies* 15 (1998): 77–99.

Null, Gilbert T. "Husserl's Doctrine of Essence." In J. N. Mohanty and W. R. McKenna, eds. *Husserl's Phenomenology: A Textbook*, 69–105. Lanham: The Center for Advanced Research in Phenomenology and University Press of America, 1989.

Orth, Ernst Wolfgang. *Edmund Husserls "Krisis der europäischen Wissenschaften und die transzendentale Phänomenologie." Vernunft und Kultur*. Darmstadt: Wissenschaftliche Buchgesellschaft, 1999.

———. "Interkulturalität und Inter-Intentionalität. Zu Husserls Ethos der Erneuerung in seinen japanischen Kaizo-Artikeln." *Zeitschrift für philosophische Forschung* 47 (1993): 333–51.

Overvold, Gary E. "Husserl and the Tradition." *Analecta Husserliana* 60 (1998): 13–23.

Patzig, Günther. "Kritische Bemerkungen zu Husserls Thesen über das Verhältnis zwischen Wahrheit und Evidenz." *Neue Hefte für Philosophie* 1 (1971): 12–32.

Pazanin, Ante. "Teleologieproblem bei Husserl." In J.-E. Pleines, ed. *Teleologie. Ein philosophisches Problem in Geschichte und Gegenwart*, 230–50. Würzburg: Verlag Königshausen & Neumann, 1994.

Pérez-Paoli, Ubaldo R. "Husserl und die Aufgabe der Philosophie." *Mitteilungen der TU Braunschweig* 24, no. 3 (1989): 46–50.

Philipse, Herman. "Psychologism and the Prescriptive Function of Logic." *Grazer Philosophische Studien* 29 (1987): 13–33.

———. "Transcendental Idealism." In B. Smith and D. W. Smith, eds. *The Cambridge Companion to Husserl*, 239–322. Cambridge: Cambridge University Press, 1995.

Pieper, Hans-Joachim. "'Von Schonheit ist hier keine Rede.' Husserl und das Problem der ästhetischen Einstellung." *Phänomenologische Forschungen* n. s. 3 (1998): 3–33.

Pietersma, Henry. "Assertion and Predication in Husserl." *Husserl Studies* 2 (1985): 75–95.

———. "Husserl's Concept of Existence." *Synthese* 66 (1986): 311–28.

———. "Truth and the Evident." In J. N. Mohanty and W. R. McKenna, eds. *Husserl's Phenomenology: A Textbook*, 213–36. Lanham: The Center for Advanced Research in Phenomenology and University Press of America, 1989.

Prufer, Thomas. *Recapitulations: Essays in Philosophy*. Studies in Philosophy and the History of Philosophy 26. Washington, D.C.: Catholic University of America Press, 1993.

Rechtenwald, Friederike. *Die phänomenologische Reduktion bei Edmund Husserl*. Münster: Helios-Verlag, 1929.

Reinach, Adolf. "Zur Theorie des negativen Urteils." *Münchener Philosophische Abhandlungen*, 196–254. Leipzig: Verlag von Johann Ambrosius Barth, 1911. English translation: "On the Theory of the Negative Judgment," trans. Barry Smith, in B. Smith, ed., *Parts and Moments: Studies in Logic and Formal Ontology* (Munich: Philosophia Verlag, 1982), 315–77.

Ryle, Gilbert. *Collected Papers*. 2 vols. New York: Barnes & Noble, 1971.

Scheier, Claus-Artur. "Die Grenze der Metaphysik und die Herkunft des gegenwärtigen Denkens." *Abhandlungen der Braunschweigischen Wissenschaftlichen Gesellschaft* 46 (1995): 189–96.

Schuhmann, Karl. *Die Dialektik der Phänomenologie* I: *Husserl über Pfänder*. Phaenomenologica 56. The Hague: Martinus Nijhoff Publishers, 1973.

———. *Die Dialektik der Phänomenologie* II: *Reine Phänomenologie und phänomenologische Philosophie. Historisch-analytische Monographie über Husserls "Ideen I."* Phaenomenologica 57. The Hague: Martinus Nijhoff Publishers, 1973.

———. *Die Fundamentalbetrachtung der Phänomenologie. Zum Weltproblem in der Philosophie Edmund Husserls*. Phaenomenologica 42. The Hague: Martinus Nijhoff Publishers, 1971.

———. "Husserls Idee der Philosophie." *Husserl Studies* 5 (1988): 235–56. English version: "Husserl's Concept of Philosophy," *Journal of the British Society for Phenomenology* 21 (1990): 274–83.

———. *Husserls Staatsphilosophie*. Freiburg/Munich: Verlag Karl Alber, 1988.

———. Introduction to *Briefwechsel* by Edmund Husserl. Husserliana Dokumente III/1–10. Edited by K. Schuhmann with E. Schuhmann. Dordrecht: Kluwer Academic Publishers, 1994. Vol. 10: 1–70.

———. "Malvine Husserls 'Skizze eines Lebensbildes von E. Husserl.'" *Husserl Studies* 5 (1988): 105–25.

———. "Markers on the Road to the Conception of the Phenomenological Movement: Appendix to Spiegelberg's Paper." *Philosophy and Phenomenological Research* 43 (1983): 299–306.

———. "'Phänomenologie': Eine begriffsgeschichtliche Reflexion." *Husserl Studies* I (1984): 31–68.

Seebohm, Thomas. "Apodiktizität. Recht und Grenze." In G. Funke, ed. *Husserl-Symposion Mainz* 27.6.–4.7.1988. Akademie der Wissenschaften und der Literatur, Abhandlungen der geistes- und sozialwissenschaftlichen Klasse no. 3 (1989): 65–99.

———. "Reflexion and Totality in the Philosophy of E. Husserl." *Journal of the British Society for Phenomenology* 4 (1973): 20–30.

Sepp, Hans Rainer. "Husserl über Erneuerung. Ethik im Schnittfeld von Wissenschaft und Sozialität." In H.-M. Gerlach and H. R. Sepp, eds. *Husserl in Halle. Spurensuche im Anfang der Phänomenologie*, 111–30. Frankfurt a. M.: Peter Lang, 1994.

———. "Intentionalität und Schein." In J. Bloss, W. Strózewski, and J. Zumr, eds. *Intentionalität – Werte – Kunst (Husserl – Ingarden – Patocka)*, 54–58. Prague: Filosofia, 1995.

———. *Praxis und Theoria. Husserls transzendentalphänomenologische Rekonstruktion des Lebens*. Kontexte 1. Freiburg/Munich: Verlag Karl Alber, 1997.

———, ed. *Edmund Husserl und die phänomenologische Bewegung*. Freiburg/Munich: Verlag Karl Alber, 1988.

Smith, Barry. "Introduction to Adolf Reinach, 'On the Theory of the Negative Judgment.'" In B. Smith, ed., *Parts and Moments: Studies in Logic and Formal Ontology*, 289–313. Munich: Philosophia Verlag, 1982.

———, and David Woodruff Smith. Introduction to their edition of *The Cambridge Companion to Husserl*, 1–44. Cambridge: Cambridge University Press, 1995.

Smith, David Woodruff. "Mind and Body." In B. Smith and D. W. Smith, eds. *The Cambridge Companion to Husserl*, 323–93. Cambridge: Cambridge University Press, 1995.

Smith, Quentin. "On Husserl's Theory of Consciousness in the Fifth Logical Investigation." *Philosophy and Phenomenological Research* 37 (1977): 482–97.

Soffer, Gail. *Husserl and the Question of Relativism*. Phaenomenologica 122. Dordrecht: Kluwer Academic Publishers, 1991.

Sokolowski, Robert. *The Formation of Husserl's Concept of Constitution*. Phaenomenologica 18. The Hague: Martinus Nijhoff Publishers, 1964.

———. *Husserlian Meditations: How Words Present Things*. Evanston, Ill.: Northwestern University Press, 1974.

———. "Husserl's Protreptic." In L. Embree, ed. *Life-World and Consciousness: Essays for Aron Gurwitsch*, 55–82. Evanston, Ill.: Northwestern University Press, 1972.

———. "Intentional Analysis and the Noema." *Dialectica* 38 (1984): 113–29.

———. *Introduction to Phenomenology*. Cambridge: Cambridge University Press, 2000.

———. "Ontological Possibilities in Phenomenology: The Dyad and the One." *Review of Metaphysics* 29 (1976): 691–701.

———. *Pictures, Quotations, and Distinctions: Fourteen Essays in Phenomenology*. Notre Dame, Ind.: University of Notre Dame Press, 1992.

———. "The Structure and Content of Husserl's *Logical Investigations*." *Inquiry* 14 (1971): 318–47.

Solomon, Robert C. "Husserl's Concept of the Noema." In F. A. Elliston and P. McCormick, eds. *Husserl: Expositions and Appraisals*, 168–81. Notre Dame, Ind.: University of Notre Dame Press, 1977.

Sommer, Manfred. "Husserl on 'Ground' and 'Underground'." *Phänomenologische Forschungen*. Supplementary volume (1998): 131–49.

Spader, Peter H. "Phenomenology and the Claiming of Essential Knowledge." *Husserl Studies* 11 (1994): 169–99.

Spahn, Christine. "Der ethische Impuls der husserlschen Phänomenologie." *Analecta Husserliana* 60 (1998): 25–81.

———. *Phänomenologische Handlungstheorie. Edmund Husserls Untersuchungen zur Ethik*. Würzburg: Verlag Königshausen & Neumann, 1996.

Spiegelberg, Herbert. "'Epoché' without Reduction: Some Replies to My Critics." *Journal of the British Society for Phenomenology* (1974): 256–61.

———. "Is the Reduction Necessary for Phenomenology? Husserl's and Pfänder's Replies." *Journal of the British Society for Phenomenology* 4 (1973): 3–17.

———. "Movements in Philosophy: Phenomenology and its Parallels." *Philosophy and Phenomenological Research* 43 (1983): 281–97.

———. *The Phenomenological Movement. A Historical Introduction*. Phaenomenologica 5–6. 3d rev. ed. with the collaboration of K. Schuhmann. Dordrecht: Martinus Nijhoff Publishers, 1982.

Stapleton, Timothy J. "The Logic of Husserl's Transcendental Reduction." *Man and World* 15 (1982): 369–82.

Steinbock, Anthony J. "Husserl's Static and Genetic Phenomenology: Translator's Introduction to Two Essays." *Continental Philosophy Review* 31 (1998): 127–34.

———. "The New 'Crisis' Contribution: A Supplementary Edition of Edmund Husserl's *Crisis* Texts." *Review of Metaphysics* 57 (1994): 557–84.

———. "Phenomenological Concepts of Normality and Abnormality." *Man and World* 28 (1995): 241–60.

Strasser, Stephan. "Der Gott des Monadenalls." *Perspektiven der Philosophie* 4 (1978): 361–77.

———. "Das Gottesproblem in der Spätphilosophie Edmund Husserls." *Philosophisches Jahrbuch* 67 (1959): 130–42.

———. "History, Teleology, and God in the Philosophy of Husserl." Translated by Philip Lawton. *Analecta Husserliana* 9 (1979): 317–33.

———. "Monadologie und Teleologie in der Philosophie Edmund Husserls." *Phänomenologische Forschungen* 22 (1989): 217–35.

Ströker, Elisabeth. "Edmund Husserls Phänomenologie: Philosophia Perennis in der Krise der europäischen Kultur." *Phänomenologische Forschungen* 22 (1989): 11–38.

———. *Husserls transzendentale Phänomenologie*. Frankfurt a. M.: Vittorio Klostermann, 1987.

———. *Husserls Werk. Zur Ausgabe der Gesammelten Schriften*. Hamburg: Felix Meiner Verlag, 1992.

———. *Phänomenologische Studien*. Frankfurt a. M.: Vittorio Klostermann, 1987.

———. "Phenomenology as First Philosophy: Reflections on Husserl." In R. Sokolowski, ed. *Edmund Husserl and the Phenomenological Tradition: Essays in Phenomenology*, 249–63. Studies in Philosophy and the History of Philosophy 18. Washington, D. C.: Catholic University of America Press, 1988.

Ströker, Elisabeth, and Paul Janssen. *Phänomenologische Philosophie*. Freiburg/Munich: Verlag Karl Alber, 1989.

Trappe, Tobias. "Phänomenologie als Geometrie des Bewußtseins?" *Allgemeine Zeitschrift für Philosophie* 20 (1995): 211–31.

Vaihinger, Hans. *Die Philosophie des Als-Ob*. Berlin: Reuther & Reichard, 1911. An English translation of the 6th ed. by C. K. Ogden was published under the title *The Philosophy of 'As if': A System of the Theoretical, Practical and Religious Fictions of Mankind* (New York: Harcourt, Brace and Co., 2d ed., 1935).

Volonté, Paolo. *Husserls Phänomenologie der Imagination. Zur Funktion der Phantasie bei der Konstitution der Erkenntnis*. Kontexte 2. Freiburg/Munich: Verlag Karl Alber, 1997.

Welton, Donn. "Der andere Husserl." *Phänomenologische Forschungen* 24/25 (1991): 116–48.

———. "Structure and Genesis in Husserl's Phenomenology." In F. A. Elliston and P. McCormick, eds. *Husserl: Expositions and Appraisals*, 54–69. Notre Dame, Ind.: University of Notre Dame Press, 1977.

Wilton, Andrew. "Symbolism in Britain." In A. Wilton and R. Upstone, eds. *The Age of Rossetti, Burne-Jones & Watts: Symbolism in Britain 1860–1910*, 11–33. London: Tate Gallery Publishing, Ltd., 1997.

Wittgenstein, Ludwig. *Philosophische Untersuchungen*. Werkausgabe 1. 2d ed. Frankfurt a. M.: Suhrkamp Verlag, 1995.

Wolz-Gottwald, Eckard. "Zur metábasis im Spätwerk Edmund Husserls." *Allgemeine Zeitschrift für Philosophie* 20 (1995): 111–30.

Zahavi, Dan. "Horizontal Intentionality and Transcendental Intersubjectivity." *Tijdschrift voor Filosofie* 59 (1997): 304–21.

Zaner, Richard M. "On the Sense of Method in Phenomenology." In E. Pivcevic, ed. *Phenomenology and Philosophical Understanding*, 125–42. Cambridge: Cambridge University Press, 1975.

Index of Names

rationalist followers) despised the productions of imagination and the utterances of sense, so they dismissed much of what had traditionally been thought of as correct. But doesn't the Cartesian well-grounded certainty actually make the claim of being correct, or yielding correctness – correctness to the nature of the world as science conceives it? If Cartesian certainty, then, gives us, in the end, another variant of correctness, it cannot be excluded from the essence of truth.

Contributions, no. 212, "Truth as Certainty," lays stress on the self-reflective character of certainty, exemplified by the Cartesian *cogito.* Modernity itself and the modern doctrine of reason derive from this, inasmuch as the self-certain ego can transfer the certainty that it gained of itself to every field of objects under its purview. Heidegger traces the progeny of such reason through Kant and German Idealism to the technological fabrications of later modernity. The question posed by the title of this section, however, is what such certainty has to do with truth. The section does not tell us that, and is no more forthcoming regarding the texts of modern philosophy than earlier ones had been regarding the ancients: it seems Heidegger is assuming the treatment he gives them in *AWP* and *N.*

Leibniz on Grounding

The natural philosophy or natural science of modernity is not an aimless, unmotivated charting of random phenomena in the world. Instead, through observing the bodies of animals and plants, reason is able to discover a correlation or correspondence between their teleology and the constitution of reason itself in the observer. When we grasp that the gills of fishes admit oxygen into the organism, we can grasp that these facts of life also have their transcending reasons. While some philosophers in modernity drew a line between truths of reason and matters of fact, that dichotomy did not govern the actual work of observing reason. The facts of nature are the modern embodiment of truth because they have a correspondence or adequation to reason.

It would seem useful here to divert our attention to another philosopher – Leibniz, an examination of whose thought is found in lectures given in 1955–56, *The Principle of Reason* (*SG*).[157] Leibniz gave perfect expression to the seventeenth-century spirit. In the fourth chapter of *SG,* Heidegger undertakes an analysis of Leibniz's words and reasoning in a number of his treatises devoted to what we call in English the "principle of sufficient reason," *nihil est sine ratione.* Earlier, Heidegger had called attention to the strange spectacle of history, that a principle seemingly so basic to science and philosophy had never received recognition until the middle of the seventeenth century, through Leibniz, two millennia after the onset of philosophy. Leibniz called history a *principium grande,* a mighty principle because it regulated everything. *Ratio est in Natura, cur aliquid potius existat quam nihil* (Heidegger *SG,* p. 52). And for Leibniz, Nature was no limited domain – this Reason, *Ratio,* governed mankind and history and the universe – and also God, whose existence was, for Leibniz, one of the consequences of this principle. The magnitude or power of the principle is expressed in what Heidegger sees as the full and accurate wording of it: *principium reddendae rationis* (in later texts, e.g., the *Monadology* no. 32, the word *sufficientis* is added). This means that only if its reason can be assigned by a representing thought can an entity be. Leibniz did not think of this only as an axiom for our subjective cognition – the principle rules the world itself (p. 54). Our representation of an entity is adequate and true only if it also represents its grounding – that is what the sciences do – and because this principle actually prevails in the world, the objects of the world are indeed grounded, and are solid and secure (p. 56).

Leibniz also says (on p. 44 of *SG* Heidegger quotes the late treatise *Specimen inventorum*) that the principle of grounding has its own grounding in the principle of truth, that "for every truth [i.e., true proposition] the grounding can be assigned." Earlier, in the *Primae Veritates,*[158] Leibniz argued that the essence of truth, as accord of subject and predicate, or their identity, rendered the principle of grounding necessary.

We can also cite Hegel here as a historian, a witness to the period from the Renaissance onward that showed an embodiment of reason in the world. And I believe Heidegger has characterized this modernity in much the same way that Hegel did, for instance, in his chapter on Reason, *Vernunft,* in the *Phenomenology of Spirit.*[159] Reason is for Hegel "the certainty of consciousness that it is all reality" (M 233). While the ascetic clergy of medieval times (at least as Hegel saw them) cultivated contempt for worldly reality, now in modernity the environing world is not foreign to us but is our own: in research and science, there is nothing that is essentially hidden or secret. We assume the right to dissect cadavers and to chart the moons of Jupiter, and when the things become revealed they will be in correspondence with the notions or thoughts in the mind. The first figure treated in this chapter is called "Observing Reason." What will reason do once it possesses the certainty that the world really is one with it, that the world belongs to it and it to the world? It will begin to explore the world, seeking to find itself in all the manifold there. It looks for its objective correlative, reason incarnate in nature, an experience of truth that finds its guarantee not in God but in sufficient reason.

Hegel on Certainty

Here we may consult "Hegel and the Greeks" (*HG*),[160] an address by Heidegger from 1958. It begins by surveying the current diminished state of philosophy, which apparently is submerged in "logistic" and social science, and then turns back to the heroic age of Hegel, when philosophy had no doubts about its proper concern (*Sache*): the process whereby subjectivity became capable of truth. *HG* also expresses in its conclusion the relationship of several variant forms of truth to the primordial *Alētheia*, so it is valuable to the present study.

The essay is devoted mainly to explaining how Hegel understood Greek philosophy as forming the initial stage of abstract thinking, focused on *being*; then how he treats the particular philosophers of Greece. As we read on in *HG*, we do see complexities in the relationship between *Alētheia* and truth. First of all, Hegel grasped truth as certainty, *die Gewissheit*, of the self-knowing absolute subject. He did *not* comprehend it as *Alētheia*, and indeed his philosophy had no grasp of *Alētheia* in any form at all. Yet Heidegger pursues this matter: **"Is not precisely certainty in its essence referred to [*angewiesen auf*] *Alētheia* … granted that we carefully ponder the latter as disclosure [*Entbergung*]?"** (267/332). What grounding does Heidegger have for that claim? There are two main points. First, given that for Hegel, being is the first and abstract theme of philosophy, the very emergence of being can only occur under the regime of unconcealedness: a manifestation and disclosedness of being. Second, if for Hegel the completeness of philosophy is the self-reconciliation and self-recognition of spirit, then disclosure or unconcealedness must be at play there at the end, as well as in every intermediate stage of the phenomenology of spirit (267–8/332). Two pages later (270/334), we see an explicit parallel. First, if *Alētheia* is at work in being and its manifestation, then being is referred to (*angewiesen auf*) unconcealment, and not vice versa, and being has to do with (*hat zu tun mit*) unconcealedness, but not vice versa. Second, i truth, according to its essence, is determined as certainty, or as correctness, and these can only subsist within the domain of unconcealedness, then truth has to do with (*hat zu tun mit*) *Alētheia*, but not *Alētheia* with truth. Moreover, the relationship is described here as a relationship of essence: *das Wesen der Wahrheit* that has come into force both as *Richtigkeit* and as *Gewissheit* can only subsist in the domain of *Alētheia* (270/334); that kind of attachment is *why* truth has to do with *Alētheia*. It is the *essence* of truth that served to express the connection of certainty with unconcealedness.

9. Attunement in *WW* 5

WW, chapter 5, corresponds to Section II(b)(i) of 1930, which we treated in Part I, Unit 8, and, like it, prepares the transition from the Second to the Third Arc without actually executing it. It begins by combining the two factors that constitute the essence of truth: the freedom that emerged in the First Arc, and the unconcealedness that emerged in the Second. We are to understand that all human conduct and *Vor-stellen* are conditioned by our letting-be, and also that every being is conditioned by the totality of beings. For both those reasons, our *Vor-stellen* and statements are *attuned, abgestimmt,* by the totality of beings that, in our freedom, we let be. This positive conclusion from the earlier stages of the pathway is what explains the title of chapter 5, "The Essence of Truth." It is not as if the argument had come to a conclusion – it continues in chapters 6 and 7, introducing the two variants of untruth, that is, concealment and erring. Rather, there is a pause at this juncture, to acknowledge the provisional essence of truth at which we have arrived. The attuning of conduct and *Vor-stellen* by the world totality yields a kind of according between the human being and the world that fulfils an elementary sense of truth. Yet that must be followed by the deeper probe of untruth required by the essence.

In chapter 5, Heidegger notes two limitations that condition this "accord" or "attunement." First of all, the human being is not able to sense or feel the attunement. This is the same point that we noticed in Part I, Unit 8, which we took to be a criticism of Max Scheler. It is not the "life," or the "soul," or the "feelings" that are attuned; it is our existence. The implication is that the attunement is strictly a matter that *thinking* must discern. Second, we are to avoid the temptation of supposing that the world-whole is just the sum total of all the singular beings. We have already seen, in Part I, Unit 8, that Heidegger works with two senses of totality – a primordial World (revealed to our *Verstehen*) and the sum total of what is known (accessed by *Auslegung,* interpretation). In 1949 he continues to stress the recessiveness and darkness of the first, primordial whole, but even more strongly the vacuity of the sum-total-world that has become interpreted by all our sciences and cognitions:

> **Precisely in the levelling and planing of this omniscience, this mere knowing, the openedness of beings gets flattened out into the apparent nothingness of what is no longer even a matter of indifference, but rather is simply forgotten.**

The 1930 text was clearly affirming the superiority of the ancients' exposure to the primordial whole, even while they lacked detailed information about beings, but the 1949 text, noting the modern indifference to the primordial whole, also assigns a futility to the accumulation of scientific knowledge. Thus, this chapter engages directly with the rationalists, the scientists, and their "world-order." For the scholarly, scientific mind, the primordial or Aboriginal revelation of the whole of the World only has the status of a "primitive," "mythical," "pre-logical" consciousness. It cannot be brought into any connection with the "everyday calculations and preoccupations" of a modern humanity that has forgotten and abandoned its attunement. What does this humanity require, that is, a humanity raised up by science and rationalism? It must now be introduced to darkness and deception. There are indistinct hints, at the end of chapter 5, of the Corner that must now be turned, of the necessary role of concealment, *die Verborgenheit,* in the essence of truth. But we shall take this point up in the next Unit.

(C) The Present Age: En-owning and Mystery

10. A Reversal in Thinking

Heidegger will be turning now to a discussion of our own day and its interest in truth, but this will require turning a Corner more difficult to negotiate than any of the previous ones, as we enter the Third Arc of thinking. The 1943–49 text introduced *die Verbergung* at the end of chapter 5, and this is followed by chapter 6, titled "Untruth as Concealment" *(Die Unwahrheit als die Verbergung)*. But at an unknown date (perhaps before 1949), he entered a marginal note to the 1943 edition, acknowledging that we could approach the topic of concealment only if, in our thinking, we could accomplish a very particular leap (*Sprung*); the words of this marginal note require some detailed explanation. Then, in Unit 11, we shall study chapter 6 itself. To quote the note and its printed translation:

> **Zwischen 5. und 6. der Sprung in die (im Ereignis wesende) Kehre.**
> **Between 5 and 6 the leap into the turning (whose essence unfolds in the event of appropriation).**

Thus, only with the accomplishing of the leap would the reader be able to understand the argument about concealment that follows in chapter 6. What is the background for this? The terminology of this inscription is largely foreign to the language of this part of *WW* – it reflects the 1936–38 *Contributions to Philosophy.* [161] This work, composed between 1936 and 1938 (*GA* 65), is regarded by many, including its editor, F.-W. von Herrmann, as Heidegger's second *magnum opus* after *SZ*, yet many readers have found it not easily intelligible. We now have expositions of it in English that have proved helpful to me and other readers, by Kenneth Maly,[162] by Richard Polt[163] and by Daniella Vallega-Neu.[164] In addition, we now have a full-scale rereading of Heidegger by Thomas Sheehan that interprets Heidegger's entire work by using the main idea of the *Contribution*, the *Ereignis*, as a key to open up the whole.[165] I am going to treat *GA* 65 below in the light of *WW*, and in that way attempt a way of reading it that takes it out of its isolation and places it together with lectures or with published texts that have already communicated well to the readership. The scholar Neumann, who edited the 1930 texts we quoted in Part I [Günther Neumann, in "Der Weg ins Ereignis nach Heideggers Vortrag 'Der Satz der Identität'"],[166] offers an exemplary reading of this nature. What such studies accomplish is indicated as well by the title and contents of F.-W. von Herrmann's book, *Pathways into the Ereignis*,[167] hitherto untranslated. Instead of quoting below from one of the translations of the *Contributions*, I shall just be referring from time to time to one of more of its paragraphs, offering a précis that connects the argument to the immediate context in my own manuscript. I believe that an exposition of *WW*, chapter 6, can help us grasp some of the difficult ideas of the *Contributions*, a suggestion that must prove itself in this exposition. *WW* can be read without interruptions, even though the whole meditation is constituted by twists and leaps of thinking. This movement from chapter 5 to chapter 6 goes to a new and higher attunement that is mentioned only indirectly in the 1949 text: the footnoted *Ereignis*. So if the corresponding chapters in *WW* are guided by something from the *Contributions*, it will be one of my aims to show that there is light cast in the other direction, the *Contributions* elucidated through *WW*.

GA 45 and 65 show how the very beginning of Western history and Western thinking was defined by an experience of *alētheia*, and how this history has now, in our time, come to its decisive end.[168] We are without power to return our thinking back to their world. That is our fate in (post) modernity. But Heidegger's principal hypothesis here is the possibility of a second beginning (*ein anderer Anfang*), for which his work aims to be a preparation, as we read in a number of prominent locations.[169] The destiny that had been ordained for the Greeks was twofold: (a) to inaugurate thinking, and thereby (b) to discover and express the matter (*Sache*) of thinking: the question of beings in their being (*GA* 45, p. 129). It was their special destiny in thought to seize upon these beings and their being within a basic mood of adoration or amazement (*thaumazein*, pp. 165–81), and the special character of their thought was to apprehend the beings and their being within a primordial unconcealment, *alētheia* (pp. 108–37); this was a character not of the thought itself (still less of statements) but of the beings themselves and their being. Now, after the ending of the Greek epoch, we are obliged still to ask about our future. There is a necessity we confront. Amazement and adoration are no longer possible for us, but what *is* necessary for us (if we do not lose sight of the Greeks and our *Geschichte*) is to ask: what constitutes unconcealedness? What are the grounds for *alētheia*? (pp. 124–7). Now it is necessary to renew the question of the essence of truth (pp. 142–4). All of these themes are at work in the Third Arc of *WW*. The need for a second beginning of thought does not proceed *only* from the narrative history in which we locate archaic Greek thinking. We have come to this juncture by a pathway of thought that belongs to the present essay – a pathway that has given a philosophical genesis of *alētheia* that accompanies the narrative history.

Now, to return to the "leap" that is required. It is more than just another Corner to be turned in thinking. Since thinking is an expression of our existence (*Da-sein*), calling for a leap is actually appealing to a venture of our existence. We are to be changed. Yet Heidegger's text does not read as a sermon, an exhortation, or a Kierkegaardian "upbuilding discourse." Rather, the text proposes a leap, or reversal, in thinking that will *indicate* a possible leap in our existence, one that may be open to us, or may summon us.[170] The merely discursive reversal in thinking does, however, allow us to understand (discursively) the existential consequences of the leap in existence. In *WW*, this leap is away from the position of the human being that concluded the Second Arc, standing in the unconcealedness of the world. And, looking at Heidegger's philosophy as a whole, the leap is also away from the Cartesian Ego, the Leibnizian Reason, and the Hegelian Spirit, all of which experienced truth as certainty. For the contemporary reader, on the other hand, this is a leap into our own existence (*Da-sein*) and thereby a leap away from our conventional singular identity (name, nationality, gender). This given identity is to be put aside, that is, put behind a veil of ignorance, as we realize our identity as *Da-sein. Contributions to Philosophy* offers the reason for this leap.

Experience in modern times is imbued with technological ambition as well as a metaphysical framework. Modern scientists and philosophers rebelled against the obscurity they saw in traditional thought and science, and they provided a standard of clarity and distinctness that could be operationalized in the many forms of newly emergent science, industry, and technology. No more *Erstaunen*! Where science and industry can reach inside the material things, and replicate them in effect, this expresses the metaphysics of modernity. In this climate, what has become of the being of beings? It has gone down utterly into the things – it is their reality. Heidegger calls it *Machenschaft*: the very business of fabrication and control.[171] Where philosophy is confined to this setting, it will no longer maintain a focus on being; the latter is no longer a *noumenon*. It is gone.[172] Philosophy once focused on the being of beings, taking it as "being-ness," a general character; the revolution of modernity has transformed being itself into *Machenschaft*, fabrication, so that it has lost any transcendence over the beings, and merged into them. Philosophy has become *Technik*, no longer content to understand the world but determined to change it. Heidegger's effort now is to find grounds whereby thinking could cease that kind of interrogation. So the metaphysical drive to interrogate and know being on the basis of beings must be abandoned.[173]

Throughout *AWP*, Heidegger refers to the twin phenomena of modern science and machine technology as governing the modern age. We read, for example:

> **In the planetary imperialism of technically organized man the subjectivism of man reaches its highest point, from which it will descend to the flatness of organized uniformity and there establish itself. The uniformity becomes the surest instrument of the total, i.e., technological dominion over the earth.** (*AWP*, p. 84)

It is clear enough that we occupy a place in a world constructed by technology, with its system of producing, disseminating, and pricing everything as resources; this all plays out within an ontological framework (sometimes Heidegger calls it the *Ge-stell*, sometimes *Machenschaft*) that represents the final outcome of the metaphysics that was created in the first beginning of thought.

For Heidegger, the technology of a given age (and he is interested in our own) constitutes an integrated worldwide system, one that enlists physics and other sciences, that recruits builders and the entire population, that implements all our powers of design, representation, getting, and spending – all in the service of a mechanism that has no goals external to itself, to its own maintenance and development. In the best-known and most eloquent treatment, an address from 1953, "The Question Concerning Technology" (*T*),[174] Heidegger outlines the ontology that he sees as effective in our world, whereby there cease to be objects and everything has been redefined as "resources" (*Bestand*), reaching right up to the human being, now understood as "human resources" or personnel (*Menschenmaterial*). Alive to the ontological difference, he argues that this formation of beings is owing to the technological cast or *Geschick* of being itself – as *das Ge-Stell*: the synthesis of many forms of *stellen* (setting forth) – ordering (*bestellen*), representing (*vorstellen*), adjusting (*nachstellen*), and so on, by which the resources are commanded. This work and related essays should not be read merely as cultural criticism, for Heidegger maintains, at the conclusion of the address, that the technological *Ge-Stell* is an embodiment of truth, the truth that is effective in our age.

We cannot even *perform* the leap into the new thinking through our own powers. Only if we are *summoned* into this thinking, after the veiling and the vanishing of beings and their being, can we exercise it. We are drawn into this leap because of an experience in philosophy, because philosophy led to the unworthy claims to its own mastery, for instance, such as Heidegger experienced between 1930 and 1933. His early pathway of thinking remained attuned to the impulses governing modern phenomenology and modern philosophy generally. While Heidegger's pathway was hardly typical of modern thought, there were certain features of it that were not thought through, that were merely carried forward by the trajectory of academic life and politics: certain aspects of his philosophy, his philosophy of science, and his thoughts on truth, led to his hybristic adventure. But a similar experience will arise with materialist philosophy and Marxism, with empiricist philosophy and scientism, with vitalist philosophy and Nietzsche.

If the metaphysical drive to interrogate being on the basis of beings must be abandoned, the question we confront is how, in the second beginning, any thinking at all may be prompted. Beyng is now to be thought in a new connection to ourselves, to *Da-sein,* the connection he calls the *Ereignis.*[175] One meaning of this word is that it induces selfhood in us, in our *Da-sein;* if it enables us to be "our own," it can be called "en-owning."[176] When Heidegger changed the spelling for "being" to *Seyn,* it was because he wished to speak *not* of an *object* of thought, *noumenon,* but of what might prompt thought and give rise to it after the concealment of all the beings. That is to think beyng *qua Ereignis,* en-owning.

Heidegger's 1957 lecture "The Principle of Identity"[177] offers what is, to my mind, the most compelling account of "en-owning," seen as the counterpart, in the second beginning, to the principle of identity ("A is A") that was the highest law of thought in the first beginning. It is inspired by his reinterpretation of Parmenides's Fragment 3, *to gar auto noein estin te kai einai,* now understood to mean that thinking *belongs* to being and that being *belongs* to thinking; they reach out to each other, converging in a mediated identity.[178] The modern form taken by this identity is the "constellation" of man and being that prevails as the essence of modern technology, the *Ge-Stell.* The *Ge-Stell,* with its manifold energies of ordering, positing, pricing, representing, pursuing, making, delivering, commanding, and conscripting, assigns the conditions under which anything in this world can *be;* and likewise it governs the daily work and nightly leisure of everyone now in the world. But according to Heidegger (*GA* 11, pp. 39–45), the destiny of this modern constellation is to be revealed and overcome (*verwunden*), because behind the human being who labours there is the human essence, *Da-sein* or existence, and behind the technical devices that take up the foreground there is being (*Seyn*), to which our *Da-sein* responds and to which it belongs. Heidegger's lecture calls upon us to make the leap into the deeper constellation where being "en-owns" our *Da-sein;* indeed, the en-owning has already been at work even in the technological constellation.

The leap of thinking comes about because our own essence or *Wesen* as human beings and as *Da-sein* belongs together with the original wholeness (world) and with the retreating *alētheia.* Our *Da-sein* is attuned, but the attuning is concealed. As beings as a whole and *alētheia* go into concealment and retreat, we are dragged along with them, and our thinking too is called upon: we belong to that which is withdrawing. This is how *Da-sein* becomes en-owned (appropriated) by being itself, or what Heidegger called beyng when it is withdrawn from the beings that attune us. This belonging is accomplished by the *Verstehen* that, in our comment on Attuning in Part I, we showed was primordial in relation to any interpretation, *Auslegung,* of the world. Thereby *Da-sein* is summoned to give the grounding for beyng, now that no beings are available, in metaphysical style, for that function. And that is the Turning (*die Kehre*) in the *Ereignis.* If concealment and mystery enter into the constitution of *Da-sein* and shape all its activity, its action and thought, this is one element of the *Ereignis.* But the other is the Turning or reversal – that *Da-sein* affords a grounding for the en-owning.

Though in thinking this we might seem to be pushing out beyond the technological world, this is not due to our own powers of transcendence, or any metaphysical impulse. *Da-sein* is summoned by the retreating *alētheia* because its own essence belongs there. We find the parallel point in *Contributions* (e.g., no. 133): beyng has need of the human being in accord with its own essence and thereby makes its appeal, *Zuruf,* to *Da-sein.* This is the turning or *Kehre* that belongs to the *Ereignis,* in which our own projective thinking is called forth, or *ereignet.* In our freedom, though it has been evoked, we do project and comprehend our world. So *Da-sein* in its own essence belongs to beyng and grounds it (*Contributions,* no. 255). *Da-sein* is made to be a self through the prompting or appeal of beyng, even as beyng is delivered over to *Da-sein.* Their reciprocal joining is the *Ereignis,* and the Turning in the *Ereignis* is our taking on the grounding function for being.

Thinking that escapes metaphysics will not submit beyng to the ontological difference. The background for this point can be seen in *Contributions,* no. 266, "Beyng and the Ontological Difference." Here Heidegger is accounting for the place of the ontological difference in his work. It is not a doctrine of ontology; rather, it marks a transition, *Übergang,* which thought makes out of metaphysics, to a second beginning. Traditionally, thought sought to determine beings, and it did so through an indirect hypothesis of the *being* of beings. So while thought was determined by the ontological difference, no philosophy ever grasped it explicitly. Identifying it (postulating being over against beings) is an unstable work of thought that will lead it away from its guiding interest in beings and bring into view the question of the truth of being itself. In this circumstance, a question is posed for thought: what was the origin of the ontological difference in the first place? It arose out of the prompting from beyng. Thought, awakened by the *Ereignis* of beyng, came to understand nature, *physis*, grasping vaguely the distinct things around as instances or embodiments of *physis*, and also, equally vaguely, the universal indwelling power: *physis* itself. Heidegger works out the mechanics of this thinking, and pays some attention here and in the preceding Section 265 to the role played by logic in this origin. In *WW* **9.1** Heidegger speaks as if *Seyn* were the difference itself, but the argument depends on the account of *Contributuions*: that *Seyn* was the originating, energizing *Ereignis* that brought forth all thinking.

11. The Concealment of *Alētheia: WW* 6.1

Now Heidegger must correct his own course too. We shall proceed to the correction of the faulty course to which 1930 committed him – what led, for example, to 1933: when we make a second beginning we aren't commanding anything or marshalling any resources – our posture is restrained (*die Verhaltenheit*). This will involve thinking renouncing its claim to investigate beings. This is signified in *WW* by an invasion of concealment into *alētheia* itself. Here the concealment serves to cover up or disable the beings that philosophy and science had thematized. Thinking lets the beings go. With beings retreating from view, the interrogation and determining of beings is put out of operation.

In the 1930 text, our conduct was attuned by the totality of beings. *Da-sein* was engaged in letting the totality of beings be, and while those beings were not concealed from such letting-be, the *sein* of *Da-sein* itself, the being of the exister, was concealed, operating in the dark. Thus *Da-sein* confronted a unity of concealment and unconcealment, and this was called mystery, "the authentic Non-essence of truth." All these aspects of concealment and mystery are reaffirmed in the 1949 version, but they are supplemented by a radical new thesis – the concealment of *alētheia* itself.

In the publications of 1943 and 1949, the first two paragraphs of chapter 6, "Untruth as Concealing," inject material not found in 1930 that mostly shows the influence of work from the 1930s. In *WW* **6.1** it is beings as a whole that are concealed, and it is from *Da-sein* that they are concealed, and now this is magnified to the highest degree. Heidegger adds in a footnote in the 1940 version (p. 421) that the concealment covers up being, or beyng (*Seyn*), not just beings. We may think of being spelled in the usual way, or spelled with a "y," but in either case we must recognize two points: (1) that here Heidegger acknowledges that being too, and not just beings, is subject to concealment; and (2) that this also holds for the being of the exister, *das Sein des Da-seins.* Moreover, the *Sein* of *Seinlassen* falls under concealment as well. In chapter 6, the subject of sentence after sentence is *die Verborgenheit,* and the effect of these prose incantations is the overwhelming impact of *Verborgenheit.* All the sentences of **6.1** invoke the primacy, the agency, and the power of this concealment, but none so much as the very first sentence.[179] It is hurled at us, defying comprehension, and my interpretation renders some of its meaning but not its style. This impossible sentence might be rendered by an expanded translation in three clauses:

> **The *Da-sein* of the human being is overshadowed by a concealment, wherein *alētheia* is unable to accomplish disclosure.**
>
> **This barrier is not just the privation or delay of an eventual disclosure.**
>
> **The concealment has put itself forth and entered into the *alētheia* itself.**[180]

How can we understand this? This material is not only difficult to understand – more than that, it seems to elevate concealment to such a degree that any chance of unconcealment will be lost. But therewith the pathway that sought to explore truth would end up by abandoning it altogether. Is there any pointer away from that conclusion?[181]

We already spoke of mystery in Part I, à propos 1930 – but now it takes on a greater role in the second beginning, in *WW*, chapters 6 and 7. Our letting-be, even as it discloses something, *also* has an essential relationship to concealment, Heidegger said in 1930, and he says it here too at **6.1.** He introduces mystery, *das Geheimnis,* as a form of the concealment of the concealed, so we need to ask what he adds in giving it this name. While the concealment *is*, to be sure, the mystery, what is specific to mystery is that it is the *unity* of concealment with unconcealment. For that reason, Heidegger will say in the coming paragraphs that the human vocation is to acknowledge and preserve the mystery: it is the concealment that we are able to know.

This mystery has been identified as the initial form of untruth, but Heidegger's further claim, expressed in *WW* 1949, chapter 6, is that this concealment or mystery is essential to *truth*: it belongs to the essence of truth in the manner of a *Pre*-essence (*vor-wesendes Wesen*).

> **The proper non-essence of truth is the mystery. Here non-essence does not have the sense of inferiority to essence in the sense of what is general**

> **[*koinos, genos*], its *possibilitas* and the ground of its possibility. Non-essence is here what in such a sense would be a pre-essential essence.** (tr. J. Sallis; *Pathmarks*, p. 148)

In calling this the Pre-essence, Heidegger has said it *is* the precondition for the essence of truth. Thus we can say that a research program that set out to abolish concealment, and make war on it, would be one initiative lacking this requisite untruth; so such an initiative falls into the deformation that Heidegger calls here on the same page the Non-essence of truth in the derivative sense. Heidegger says in chapter 6 that *Da-sein*, insofar as it ek-sists, always preserves the mystery, always guards it as the Pre-essence of truth.

Other writings of Heidegger speak of the mystery in just this way; I single out one passage from the address "Gelassenheit" that he delivered in Messkirch in 1955:

> ***The meaning of the technological world conceals itself.* But if we keep it specifically, permanently, in mind that in the technological world we are touched by a hidden meaning, then we shall be standing in the domain of something that is concealed from us and yet is concealed precisely because it approaches us. Showing itself in this way and at the same time withdrawing is the basic character of what we call mystery. The posture by which we can keep ourselves open for the concealed meaning of the technological world is what I call *openness for the mystery.***[182]

This says that the mystery is something that can speak to us – we do not think it up but encounter it, and as it addresses us we experience in it a withdrawal. What is withdrawn is meaning or sense, in this case of the technological world, but with the intimation nevertheless that a meaning or sense really is there though not within our ken. We never encounter mystery all by itself or absolutely – it is a mystery *of* something, in this case of the technological world.

That which approaches us yet withdraws was also described more fully in "A Dialogue on Language, between a Japanese and an Inquirer,"[183] in which the interlocutors sought to express in the German language certain qualities of Japanese works of art that had traditionally been spoken of in the Japanese language, especially in the term *iki*. The special quality of this art is summed up with such phrases as:

> **The delight that ensnares and carries away into stillness ... the hint that beckons on ... the message of the veiling that opens up.**[184]

Heidegger and his visitor move on to find that this same quality is ascribed by the Japanese to language itself, and at the end of their dialogue they are ready to understand *all* language and all saying – Eastern and Western – in these terms, finding here the appropriate expression for "... an insight into the untouchable which is veiled from us by the mystery of Saying, *das Geheimnis des Sage.*"[185]

So there is a withdrawal or concealment at work *within* the mystery that nevertheless reaches us and addresses us. Mystery is what is now left for thinking in the second beginning: it has taken the place of the *alētheia* that cannot shine for us as it did for the ancients. Heidegger is inviting us into a form of thinking, in the second beginning, that exercises sufficient restraint so as to be open to the mystery that inhabits all saying, and that we can encounter in all modes of experience, in the comprehensive experience of things. We recognize mystery in several guises: we can recognize (a) that there is a general hiddenness of beings as a whole, for example, the world has a meaning though we do not apprehend it; and (b) that in the face of the other person we confront an inaccessible fact of their being, for example, what it is like to be that person, that is, what their own understanding of their being is. Our philosophical thinking no longer makes a claim to determine beings.

Heidegger contrasts the usual human experiences with the truth of being, that is, the mystery or concealedness. The normal human being does not have the restraint that a respect for the mystery would induce:

> **Our bearing towards concealing conceals itself in letting a forgottenness of the mystery take precedence and disappear ... If the human being sets out to extend, change, newly assimilate, or secure the openedness of the beings pertaining to the most various domains of his activity and interest, then he still takes his directives from the sphere of readily available intentions and needs.**

In mystery (*das Geheimnis*), there is not merely something unknown, but also something in some way known but that hides its truth. Heidegger repeats in **6.5** the well-known points about the human predilection for what is tangible, concrete, ontic, and manageable; Parmenides already said the same thing in the Fragment 6 of his B-series in the collection by Diels. Through our turning away from the mystery, the ex-sistent *Da-sein* has become, instead, in-sistent, and falls into Erring (chapter 7).

Now we proceed further into chapter 6. With a hesitation that is not characteristic of him, Heidegger concludes **6.2** by acknowledging that his variations on Essence and Non-essence might seem too arcane for his readers, so he will let the matter drop. Yet he does add a further comparison that is helpful as we ponder the place of chapter 6 within the essay:

> **But surely for those who know about such matters the "non-" of the originary Non-essence of truth, as un-truth, points to the still unexperienced domain of the truth of being (not merely of beings).**

This comparison places the non-essence of truth, the untruth that we know as concealment and mystery, on a level with the truth of being. Later (in **9.3** – see below) Heidegger will clarify that in this essay the question of the truth of being, and not merely of beings, was left intentionally undeveloped. He says here in chapter 6 that we lack the "experience" of the domain of the truth of being; here he is recognizing that hitherto philosophical thinking had been confined to the "first beginning" that grasped only the being of beings, proceeding metaphysically to think being on that basis. We find this contrast all over the later Heidegger: it is the "truth of being" that was not accessible in this first beginning. Many such statements can be found.[186]

But the domain of the truth of being that Heidegger has mentioned is governed by a "not," namely the Non-essence of truth, precisely in modern or postmodern times where being is *withdrawn* from beings. This is the very same circumstance that we recorded as the invasion of concealment into *alētheia*, bringing an eclipse of *alētheia*. But it opens a pathway for a new way of thinking being. Just as we in our times must accept mystery as our substitute for *alētheia*, so we must attempt, in the second beginning, to rethink being, and in particular to think it in its truth. To think it now as beyng signifies its removal from beings, no longer immanent, not indwelling. To free beyng from beings requires a leap.

When we consider how the *Da-* of *Da-sein*, that is, the Open or the *Lichtung*, is shaped by the *Ereignis*, we can take some guidance from our studies in *WW*, particularly the role of concealment or mystery. Confronted with such a sentence as opens chapter 6, we do not need to be told by a footnote that a leap is called for. The philosophical thinking that was paying heed to the *alētheia* of the ancient Greeks is now rebuked by a concealment that will permit no light to radiate from any *alētheia*. Since the original wholeness of the world will now be hidden from *Da-sein*, it will of course be inaccessible to ourselves as human beings, and therefore to our thinking too. We cannot encounter such a concealment without a leap away from the thinking inaugurated by the Greeks, away from "the first beginning of thinking."[187] In the third clause above, Heidegger has said that what pertains most intimately to concealment, its *Eigenstes*, has now become the distinguishing mark, the characteristic property, *das*

Eigentum, of *alētheia*. This occurrence, the invasion of concealment into *alētheia*, calls for a new kind of thinking that, in *GA* 45 and 65, Heidegger calls the "second beginning of thinking."

As an appendix to our discussion, we can refer the reader to chapter 7 of the 1949 text, on Un-truth as Erring – it is very close indeed to the 1930 version, so it needs no additional discussion here. But the subject of erring has also come up in Heidegger's earlier lectures on Plato, particularly the treatment of untruth in the *Theaetetus*, so we add a brief comment on those lectures.

The matter of untruth is raised by Plato himself while his characters are exploring the claim that knowledge is judgment or belief, *doxa*, and in particular *true* judgment, true belief. So the question arises, How can there be false judgment? (187 d to 201 b). Heidegger's investigation aims to elicit from Plato's text the *essence* of untruth, and by his hypothesis, this essence will also exhibit the manner in which untruth is inwardly connected to truth. The soul is like a tablet of wax that may be hard or soft, pure or impure (*Theaet.* 191 c–195 b); so it receives impressions and remembers them more accurately or less (**31–32,** pp. 292–3; **33–34**, pp. 255–8). So when you see somebody on the street, you can think it is Socrates when it is really Theaetetus because your original impression was of poor quality, or it has faded. Since the present stimulus can become associated with a content of memory that is not germane, we can err. That is what Heidegger calls our bifurcation: the convergence of present stimulus with recollected content. But, for Heidegger, the point is that all truth and recognition also depend on the bifurcation: Truth and untruth have the same conditions. The key point is that untruth has now been shown to pertain to the bifurcated human constitution itself, and does not arise by accident (**31–32**, 295–7; **33–34**, p. 258).

The simile of the aviary (*Theaet.* 196 c–199 c) is intended by Plato to show that we have only an insecure hold on much of our mental content: yes, we have plenty of information, but we often do not implement it, apply it, or grasp it thoroughly. It is one thing to have a vague representation of virtue; quite another to aim at exact and differentiated knowledge of it, as Socrates demanded of himself and his interlocutors. The difference between possessing a kind of picture of it, and holding it firmly, does not apply to the perception of someone on the street, but rather to the broader field of the content of memory. But the vagueness of your grasp of this content is the ground for the confusions that occur in false judgment. In **31–32**, pp. 292–318, he accommodated Plato's point quite exactly by differentiating "different kinds of holding," *verschiedene Weisen des Behaltens* (p. 302), that corresponded to the differentiation Plato made between mere possession (*ktēsis*) and the active grasping that he called *hexis*. He builds on the point that untruth has now been traced, along with truth, to the human constitution. Our question is whether, through this reading of *Theaetetus*, Heidegger can show the deep and wide reach of the essence of untruth. Are error and falsity sufficiently profound phenomena to secure Heidegger's point? If Heidegger is following Socrates and Plato in discovering the grounds of possibility of *to pseudos* in false judgments, we wonder whether that will suffice to illuminate the full essence. Both lecture courses promise in their titles of Part II to treat the essence of untruth. Is the *pseudēs doxa*, false judgment, perhaps too derivative an offshoot of Erring? What we want to find is some Platonic counterpart to the deeper essence, *das Irren*, that Heidegger found at the root of all the variety of mistakes, falsehoods, and so on. Heidegger notes that Plato shows that false judgment is possible through an investigation of the soul – a deep-seated terrain where the possibility of erring has lodged itself. There are indications in the *Theaetetus*-lectures of the deeper roots of *to pseudos*. Plato's similes for being-in-the-world and for the inner constitution of the soul do exhibit a deeper resonance. Untruth, we are told in *WW*, embraces the duality of concealment and erring. *But it also incorporates – within the essence! – all the derivatives and offshoots such as false judgment*. Therefore the treatment of *to pseudos* can be germane to the question of the essence of untruth.

12. The Truth of Being: The Clearing for Its Concealment – *WW* 8 and 9

Chapter 8 contains the material that constituted the end of the pathway in 1930, stressing the opposition of philosophy to common sense, and introducing the quotation from Kant that celebrated the utter autonomy of philosophy. Yet now these points become qualified and historicized. The resistance of common sense to the question of being only became historically important through the Sophists of antiquity, who opposed the philosophizing of Plato. And Heidegger has learned that he cannot any longer endorse a Kantian autonomy of philosophy – rather, he places Kant historically at the beginning of the end of metaphysics: Kant made the ultimate affirmation of subjectivity that wanted to guard the laws of truth, but had yet to learn that this "subject" was itself guarded and kept by truth.

The last paragraph of chapter 8 offers a first retrospective summary of the essay. We see that the essay had two main divisions. It began from the correctness of statements, and found the grounding for them in the "ek-sistent freedom of letting-be"; then, in the second part, this grounding had its own further grounding in concealment and in erring. He explores this further in another retrospective in chapter 9.

> **In its decisive steps, which lead from truth as correctness to ek-sistent freedom, and from the latter to truth as concealing and as erring, [the essay] accomplishes a change in the questioning that belongs to the overcoming of metaphysics.**[188]

Both retrospectives indicate that the essay on the essence of truth was ultimately destined to lead to another question: as he puts it in chapter 8, to ask whether the question of the essence of truth does not resolve itself into this other question – into the truth of essence. This suggestion is left unexplained here, except for this addition: "**But in the concept of 'essence' philosophy thinks being.**" Chapters 8 and 9 together offer a study of the intertwining of these two questions, but we must see that this study is no longer seeking to *answer* either of them. How then does Heidegger treat these questions here?

Chapters 8 and 9 of *WW* look back over the whole pathway that has been traversed in the essay, seeking to characterize the thinking that was practised there. We may take guidance from the very last sentence of the essay:

> **The course of the questioning is intrinsically the path of a thinking that, instead of furnishing representations and concepts, experiences and tests itself as a transformation of its relatedness to being.**

The pathway was an exercise in which thinking put itself to the test, transforming the relation in which thinking stands to being. The address only wanted to think on the basis of the grounding of thinking in *Da-sein*. The transformation of thinking replaces concepts with a new nearness of *Da-sein* to being. Thinking is not representing it, but responding to it. Our *Da-sein* has been related to being, not objectifying it discursively, but "**preparing a nearness to the truth of being**" – "**the truth of being sought as the ground of a transformed historical position.**" It is "**every kind of anthropology and all subjectivity of the human being,**" to which our usual representations and concepts are traceable. Throughout the pursuit of the essence of truth, we did *not* undertake to thematize being, or the truth of being. We left that untouched as the horizon that was encompassing the study of the essence of *truth*. Thought's relation to being, its essential nearness, is an *experience* (*wesentliche Erfahrung*) that belongs to *Da-sein* and to thinking, but this has not been an *inquiry* into the truth of being, even though such an inquiry would ultimately belong as a coping stone to the completed inquiry into the essence of truth. And in chapter 9, where Heidegger talks about the question of truth and the question of being, it is still not mainly with the intent of providing answers. Chapters 8 and 9 are treating the questions *as questions*, the thinking *as thinking* – not to answer them, but to understand how they express the posture of our *Da-sein*.

To treat the questions *as questions*, the thinking *as thinking*, means to bring to the fore the questioner, the thinker, that is, to see the grounding of the questioning in *Da-sein*. In chapter 9, Heidegger will offer a wider retrospective over his whole journey of thought, saying that the present question of the essence of truth actually arose for him out of his questioning of the truth of being, or the truth of essence. Looking at the whole of the last paragraph of chapter 9, **9.3** (which dates from 1943), we can see how it expresses the relationship between the question of the essence of truth, and the question of the truth of essence (i.e., of being): Heidegger says that one question was "deliberately left undeveloped" and that was the question concerning the truth of being, as distinct from the truth of beings or that-which-is. That is the question that he was invoking earlier behind the autonomous moral laws of Kantian subjectivity, but we should also note that the second paragraph of chapter 6, already in 1943, also ended by anticipating this question in all its subtlety. Then he offers the second retrospective over *WW* that we just quoted. Heidegger says, in **9.2**, that the question of the truth of essence was to be studied, though it cost him much trouble: he had attempted, but failed, to supplement *WW* with another essay, "On the Truth of Essence." He adds that a passage in the *Letter on Humanism* (1947) would explain what difficulty had hindered him. He is referring to the passage (*Wegmarken*, p. 159; *Pathmarks*, pp. 249–50) where he explains why *SZ* had remained incomplete, without its proposed third Division, "Time and Being." There was to be a turning (*Kehre*) in the thinking as it entered into this third Division, but, he says, "**thinking failed in the adequate saying of this turning and did not succeed with the help of the language of metaphysics**." Evidently he means, here in **9.2,** that the same difficulty hindered the writing of "On the Truth of Essence." But then, in *HB*, he adds a point of great interest to us: "**The lecture 'On the Essence of Truth,' thought out and delivered in 1930 but not printed until 1943, provides a certain insight into the thinking of [this] turning.**"[189] So on the one hand, *WW* did not get its companion essay; but even so, the existing text will throw some light on the turning that was required in Heidegger's thinking. If we remember that *HB* appeared in 1947, we realize that it is referring back to the first publication of *WW* in 1943. What could Heidegger have had in mind here? What is the relevant aspect of *WW*?

It is the two retrospectives that give some insight into the necessary turning of Heidegger's thought. Thought took a first step from correctness of statements to ek-sistent freedom, and then pursued the latter to its own further grounding in concealing and erring. This has begun to take us out of metaphysics (now understood in its modern form as the transcendental-horizonal framework that was still operating in the language of *SZ*). We might pull these retrospectives together at this point, and offer a retrospective of the whole that will show us the active role of the mystery of *Da-seyn* in the pathway of thinking, and thereby provide a clue to the other question motivating Heidegger, as to the truth of essence, or being.

If we look more deeply in a retrospective way into the specific role of essence, *Wesen*, in the pathway of thinking, we can see just how the questioning and the thinking have been guided by it. We have followed a *Denkweg*, but the corners of that pathway were not imposed by the movements of *Denken*; rather, thought was forced to turn the corners in response to the structure of the essence itself. What appears in this retrospect is the commanding power of the essence of truth over the questioning and thinking that move on the pathway. Essence has the directive power, generating and collecting the many mutations of truth, which thinking follows.

Thus, the Platonic ascent to the essence of truth articulated in the Introduction was made to turn in a contrary direction, ending up assigning truth to human freedom in chapter 3, not because *Denken* chose to move in that direction, but because of the diverse strata of essence itself: in the first instance, the essence was the quiddity or "What" (and that was the adequation of intellect and thing), but the deeper grounding for the quiddity was what made it *possible* – possibility was a deeper stratum of essence – and this led still deeper to the grounding for that possibility, which proved to be freedom. This of course is not an *attribute* of the human being, but the opening into which our *Da-sein* is admitted, the freedom that possesses us. While the initial appearance of essence here was – as Heidegger tells us at the opening of *WW*, chapter 9 – a mere quiddity that might seem to preside over an array of instances of truth, that initial appearance was immediately superseded in chapter 2. There is a necessary deflection of thought induced by the architecture of the essence.

In the course of executing this arc, thought also discovered that what made truth possible also made statements possible – the essence of the statement was also open-standing conduct, that is, the conduct of *das Da-seyn*. But thought was forced to ask after the essence of freedom – another essence intertwined with the essence of truth; and indeed in exploring this, we discovered in chapter 4 the essence of the human being: *Da-seyn*. That insight resulted from exploring the essence of freedom, which proved to be letting-be. So in this architecture we have an essential bonding of many members. The further result of chapter 4 was to posit the historical essence (or *Geschick*) of truth – as unconcealedness, in fusion with freedom. But this led to assigning a subsidiary status, attached to the essence of truth, to both correctness and certainty: not elements in the essence, but not separated either.

We saw earlier that the "objects" of our presentation and statement had an original identity as "things" lying in the Open, and that the unity of their identity was to be beings, *Seiende*, to which *Da-sein* gained access through letting-be. This puts us squarely before the question concerning being, or the truth of being itself. Though Heidegger has told us that *WW* did not intend to discuss that question directly, we see nevertheless that the present chapter 9 is the point from which such a questioning could proceed.

After the meditation granted in chapter 5 the attunement of *Da-seyn* (and therefore of human being and thinking) by beings as a whole (or the world), thought turned the most radical and difficult corner: to introduce untruth into the essence. There is concealment, the Non-essence that counts as a pre-essence; and there is erring, the Counter-essence of truth. They stand in a different relation to truth than do, for example, correctness and certainty. The climax of the pathway of thought is the discovery of philosophy itself, the most essential embodiment of truth, which arises through the union of concealment and erring.

The essence that led thinking through so many mutations of truth is a single power that in its dynamism leads thinking to one form of truth, then another, and another. But in this work, it is itself hidden. The unconcealments achieved here are the truth of essence. The retrospective summary allows us to give that name to the active, powerful role of essence in this meditation.

Looking back into the first beginning, we ask: How was unconcealedness bestowed upon beings? How was the clearing originally given? Aristotle told us (*Metaphysics, Theta,* 10) that truth or unconcealment was given with their very being. That is the metaphysical clearing. But, for us, beyng itself does not appear in this clearing. This clearing, the *Lichtung*, covers up beyng. But on the other hand, its very concealment, which seems to be its absence, does appear in the clearing. Any subject that utterly conceals itself is not to be known or understood, or to constitute a suitable subject for thinking – such a subject rebuffs us utterly. Yet there remains the other possibility. Such a subject may invite inquiry if its self-concealment has become manifest, if its self-concealment itself has entered into the clearing.[190] Such a subject, in fact, is that which invites questioning. How can there be a clearing for that which is self-concealing? The union of concealment with the Open is the truth of being or essence, and depends on the Open in which both the concealment of being and the lighting for that concealment can occur. In this new conjuncture envisaged by Heidegger in **9.1**, after metaphysics, truth is re-redefined: it is no longer the correspondence of knowledge with its object; it would have to be a sheltering that clears (*lichtendes Bergen*), or a clearing for self-concealment (*Licht des verbergenden Entzugs*).

The present essay has taught us to approach *Da-sein* in the light of concealment, mystery and erring, and, in view of all Heidegger's writing in the 1930s, we can express that by way of the new spelling, *das Seyn*. It is *das Seyn des Da-seyns* that is the mystery. Chapter 6 spoke formally about mystery, as pertaining to the essence of truth – but here we deformalize the theme, and recognize the mystery as *das Seyn*, beyng, specifically in one relationship: *das Seyn des Da-seyns*. As for *das Seyn des Da*-seyns, the essential grounding of humanity is hidden from our gaze, and cannot become our *noumenon* – yet its very hiddenness is manifest to us, so that we are never convinced by materialist reductions that absorb us into a generalized economy of entities.

When we make a second beginning with the *Ereignis*, we aren't commanding anything or marshalling any resources – our posture is restrained (*die Verhaltenheit*).

13. Philosophy among the Disciplines

We have been dealing with Heidegger's correction of his own course of thought, and now we shall see how this brings a further correction – of the relationship of his thinking to all the other ventures of human intelligence and research, especially those that are practised in the university. In departing from metaphysics; in becoming unbound by the ontological difference; in concentrating on mystery; in submitting to the *Ereignis*; in seeking a close intimacy with being – how does the thinker find a place within the community of study and research? My claim will be that the later Heidegger exercises restraint in relation to all of these disciplines, a convincing exercise of "letting them be."

At the beginning of this study, I noted that Heidegger's introduction to *WW* began by enumerating many disciplines, all affording us access to "truths" of some description. Heidegger was resolute in separating his question concerning the essence of truth from all those inquiries, and while he gained some clarity for himself thereby, the lurking danger later came into full view in the rectoral address: if other disciplines can attain truth in their respective domains, it is the philosopher alone who can say what truth is, and the others have nothing to contribute on that score. That is what opens the door to the coercive pretensions we heard in the address: the philosopher is to tell them what the truth is, and what the knowledge is, that they think they are pursuing. His period in the rectorate was a low point in the modern history of universities.

Heidegger resigned as rector in April 1934, and we know he distanced himself from Nazism in the succeeding years (how far he did so remains a subject of dispute, as I indicated in the Intermission). But more germane to my study is to look at Heidegger's work after 1934 to see what relations exist between philosophy and the other inquiries and disciplines he had once sought to govern as rector. I offer the briefest summary of the ways in which Heidegger, in his later period, that of the "second beginning," characterizes the thinker in his relations to the sciences and the arts. Centrally, it is the work of the thinker to engage them in conversation or dialogue (*Gespräch*): to ask questions that are genuinely open, to listen, to interpret, and that may well mean to penetrate to a level that is unfamiliar to them. Above all, the thinker is to cooperate with other scholars and scientists in unveiling nature and the word, and to allow the veil to show itself.

On the Arts

In *The Origin of the Work of Art*, the thinker acknowledges that art is a separate source of truth, and attempts to engage the arts in conversation.[191] At the start of the essay,[192] Heidegger leads us through a phenomenology of the work of art, noting how we are surrounded on every side by works of all descriptions; then he undertakes a phenomenological meditation upon these apparently familiar things, choosing as the focus for his thought one of the paintings of van Gogh. Heidegger never discusses the painting's formal features of design, or whatever might be original in its colour-work, or any of the art-historical references to the modern tradition of oil painting in the Netherlands or elsewhere. He responds to what has been *disclosed* by the painting:

> **What happens here? What is at work in the work? Van Gogh's painting is the disclosure of what the equipment, the pair of peasant shoes, *is* in truth. The entity emerges into the unconcealedness of its being. The Greeks called the unconcealedness of beings *alētheia*. We say "truth" and think little enough in using this word. If there occurs in the work a disclosure of a particular being, disclosing what and how it is, then here there is an occurring, a happening of truth at work.** (*PLT*, p. 36)

The painting has the status of a bearer or conductor of truth, just as surely as any statement or any perception does. The painting does more than take on the status of truth-bearer, at least the equivalent of a statement – it takes us even beyond the unconcealedness of an object, and beyond the unconcealedness of the world of the object. It discloses the very event of disclosure. We come to grasp what the turbulent power of unconcealing itself is: the appearing of the shoes, the happening of truth, *das Geschehen der Wahrheit:*

> **That is how self-concealing being is illuminated. Light of this kind joins its shining to and into the work. This shining, joined in the work, is the beautiful. Beauty is one way in which truth *occurs* as unconcealedness.** (*PLT*, p. 56)

But when Heidegger treats the disclosive power of art, he brings to the fore the power of *concealment* that has to accompany that:

> **Truth is present only as the conflict between lighting and concealing in the opposition of world and earth. Truth wills to be established in the work as the conflict of world and earth.** (*PLT*, p. 62)

The earth is the dimension of concealment that belongs to every art work and to its very function of unconcealing:

> **But as a world opens itself the earth comes to rise up ... Earth, bearing and jutting, strives to keep itself closed and to entrust everything to its law ... [T]his being itself occupies the Open of truth. This occupying, however, can happen only if what is to be brought forth, the rift, entrusts itself to the self-secluding factor that juts up in the Open. The rift must set itself back into the heavy weight of stone, the dumb hardness of wood, the dark glow of colours.** (*PLT*, p. 63)

The work of earth as concealment is well stated in another paragraph:

> **[Earth] shows itself only when it remains undisclosed and unexplained. Earth thus shatters every attempt to penetrate into it. It causes every merely calculating importunity upon it to turn into a destruction. This destruction may herald itself under the appearance of mastery and of progress in the form of the technical-scientific objectivation of nature, but this mastery nevertheless remains an impotence of will. The earth appears openly cleared as itself only when it is perceived and preserved as that which is by nature undisclosable, that which shrinks from every disclosure and constantly keeps itself closed up.** (*PLT*, p. 47)

On German Poetry

On German poetry, we have all of Heidegger's essays, so well discussed, for example, by Beda Allemann.[193] Through our art and poetry, we participate in unconcealedness, but therefore also concealment. Several essays of Heidegger offer us a picture of the role of concealment in the poetic work of art. The essay "Remembrance" is devoted to Hölderlin's poem of the same name,[194] and, like it, evokes the Mardi Gras that is celebrated in the month of March in the south of France – Hölderlin wants to find in this celebration hints for the vocation of future poets, German ones, who have to leave their homeland to journey in southern climes and learn the celebrations of the South. Poetry is the festival of language. One line of the poem speaks of *the month of March, / When night and day are equal* … The poets have to learn from this what a celebration is. The very heart of a festival is the time of its preparation, the preceding night, the festival eve:

> **The month of March is the month of the holiday.**
> ***When night and day are equal.***

> **Usually we use the word sequence day and night. We first call out the day as being something "positive." We let follow it the night, which is its disappearance. Night is the absence of day. But for Hölderlin the night which precedes the day is the sheltering profusion of the day, even though still indeterminate. Night is the mother of day. Insofar as the holy comes in the breaking of day, and the advent of the gods is given, the night is the time of god-lessness. The word does not mean here the mere lack or even the naked absence of gods. The time of god-lessness contains what is indecisive about what is yet to be decided. Night is the time of the sheltering of the *gods of the past* and of the concealment of the gods that are coming. Because the night, in such sheltering-concealing darkness, is not nothing, it also has its own vast *clarity* and the *peacefulness* of the silent preparation for something which is coming. To the latter belongs its own vigil, not that sleeplessness that needs sleep, but rather that which keeps watch over and protects the night.** (*GA* 4, p. 104; *EHP*, pp. 132–3)

> ***But someone pass me,***
> ***Full of dark light,***
> ***The fragrant cup …***

> **The wine is named the *dark light* … The poet of course sees an illumination which comes to appearance through its darkness. The dark light does not**

deny clarity; rather, it is the excess of brightness which, the greater it is, denies sight all the more decisively. The all-too-flaming fire does not just blind the eyes; rather, its excessive brightness also engulfs everything that shows itself and is darker than darkness itself. Sheer brightness is a greater danger to the poet's presentation, because the brightness leads to the illusion that in its appearance alone there can be sight. The poet asks for the gift of the dark light in which the brightness is tempered and softened. But this softening does not weaken the light of the brightness. For the darkness permits the appearance of that which conceals, and thus in its appearing preserves what is concealed within. (*GA* 4, pp. 119–20; *EHP*, pp. 141–2)

Academic Science

As for the researches of *academic science,* Heidegger led many discussions that were interrogative in character, as in his 1938 seminar, "Begründung des neuzeitlichen Weltbildes durch die Metaphysik," and *The Time of the World-Picture.*[195] Thinking engages the scientific practitioner in conversation.

I may note that there are cases where we must seek a positive connection between correctness and unconcealedness. In scientific research, mentioned at the opening of *WW,* the ambiguity of truth, as a hybrid of correctness and unconcealedness, shows up with special force. Science is an international, institutionalized practice, and these features express its achievements as *correct.* Our current research results can be called "correct" when they have been put through the procedure of replication and verification in the practice of scientific experiments; their theses have been verified – that is, sharply identified, separated from collateral information, and then correlated with the new evidence. What Heidegger's *WW* does contribute to this discussion is the interaction between correctness and unconcealedness, two facets of truth. The latter is not what is verified in some replicating experiment – rather, it opens the broad horizons in which particular theses or doctrines are located; it is the ontological portion of science and is subject to quite different standards from the correct research results. Major doctrines such as evolution, relativity, and quantum physics belong in this category of truths.

This is also how thinking becomes realized in its interaction with *technology, and technological researches,* as we see in the concluding pages of the essay "Die Frage nach der Technik." *Die Technik* itself is an occasion of truth and a preliminary guide to the *Ereignis.* This essay belongs together with the group of addresses offered in Bremen,[196] which have been well discussed by Mitchell, the translator,[197] and in a number of essays by Babette Babich.[198]

On Psychology

We have the Zollikon Seminars,[199] where Heidegger interacts with psychiatrists and psychologists, often of a Freudian disposition, in meetings arranged by Medard Boss.

God and Theology

The last avenue of truth Heidegger mentioned at the opening of *WW* 1949 was "cultic faith," *kultisches Glauben*, that is, religion (his own phrase is less esoteric in German, where *Kultus* signifies any form of worship – and was historically used to signify culture – and does not carry the suspicious overtones of "cult"). In acknowledging here a religious access to truth (in 1943 and 1949), Heidegger is departing from the anticlerical and anti-Christian tone of much of what he wrote in the 1930s. But this does not signify a rapprochement between faith and philosophy – it is the faith that has freed itself from metaphysics that can experience its own truth. We now have an excellent study of Heidegger that treats this subject particularly well.[200]

Heidegger did not write very much about religion, but in these later years he would say that religious faith can be assured of its relationship to God without the aid or mediation of philosophy. The bond that links the believer to his God has its own kind of truth, one that is not unconcealedness and not correctness. A few years after 1949, he sketched a kind of "cultic faith" that has repudiated the Scholastic and metaphysical kind of theology:

> ***Causa sui*** **[is] the appropriate philosophical name for God. To this God one can neither pray nor bring offerings. Man cannot get down on his knees in reverence before the *Causa*, and he cannot make music and dance before this God.**[201]

In the Preface to the 1930 address in Marburg on the essence of truth,[202] which was furnished with the extra title, "Philosophizing and Faith," Heidegger said that his address would be dealing centrally with faith in the only manner that was appropriate for philosophy in approaching this subject – which was to remain silent about it! No philosophical theology! But no materialist atheism either! There are no defences that shield the philosopher from the claims that religion makes upon every human being. The philosopher's silence on faith is the silence of recognition and restraint.

Chapter 4 will explore the Open, which is already indicated in the chapter title, "The Essence of Freedom." It introduces the term *das Da-sein* for "the concealed essential ground of the human being." In *WW*, *Da-sein* is not a replacement term for "human being," as it was in *SZ*. The human being is sustained by *Da-sein*, and the *Da-* of *Dasein* is the Open that we have been treating. *Da-sein* is something bigger than ourselves and possesses us. Likewise, freedom is not a human characteristic or endowment, but something that possesses us: it is the *Da* or the Open. As human beings belonging to *Da-sein*, we are perpetually displaced into the Open, the *Da*, and fated to discover there that which is manifest or present there.

Later in Heidegger's career, this "Open" will be given the name of *die Lichtung*. It has been shown by Capobianco that this later word involves a spatial metaphor signifying "clearing" or "openness," rather than a metaphor of light, involving *das Licht*,[146] so it is a direct descendent of the "Open" of *WW*. Capobianco has also shown that *SZ* had employed the term *Lichtung* in a different sense that *was* based on a metaphor of light, so there it meant illumination.[147] But *SZ* did not yet separate *Da-sein* from the human being, in the manner of *WW*. What we shall see instead in chapter 4 is the sharp differentiation of function, within *Da-sein*, between the *Da-* (the Open) and the *-sein* (active penetration into the Open, expressed in human conduct). Although *WW* has moved away from the fundamental ontology of *Da-sein*, it still accords considerable import to human conduct within the structure of truth, and notably within the form of untruth called "erring."

Let us put together the comments that Heidegger made in **4.3** on the unconcealed with what he said about *Da-sein* in **4.5–4.6.** The Open that he has been studying in *WW* was already comprehended by the ancients, he tells us, as *ta alēthea*, the unconcealed. All the *Seiende* displayed themselves in it. And, besides, he encourages us still today to rethink truth in the light of that ancient word. Can we now grasp that deconcealedness, *die Entborgenheit* of *Seiendes*? In part, we do so already – that is, in practice – for in letting *Seiende* be, we are thrust out into the midst of them, exposed to their disclosures. Such venturing-out is given with our very mode of being. Our essential ground, our *Da-sein*, leads us into this exposure, and that has major consequences for the argument: it is our **"ek-sistent engagement through which the openness of the open region, i.e., the '*Da-*,' is what it is"** (4.4).

Although this *Da-* is the very same as the Open, and the same as *ta alēthea*, we should not assert that *Da-sein* as such is identical with the Open or *ta alēthea*. Rather, our *Da-sein* brings us, through our ek-sistence, to *belong* to the *Da-*, or to the open region. While the *Da-* is the vast openness in which beings show themselves – it is their truth; and while we are in the *Da-*, the *Da-* is also in us, in our *Da-sein*, as our *freedom*. The *sein* of *Da-sein* pushes the human being out into the Open, into the unconcealed, bringing liberation. But the *sein* of *Da-sein* retreats from our consciousness, as a hidden ground. There are also passages of the *Contributions* that discuss this relationship, though often with different terms, and with a more elusive style than *WW*. Often we read here of the clearing, *die Lichtung*, a later word for the Open and the Unconcealed.[148] How do the *Contributions* relate it to *Da-sein* and the *Da*? We can look at no. 173, titled "*Das Da-sein*," and no. 175, titled "*Das Da-sein und das Seiende im Ganzen.*" From the first cited section, we quote:

> ***Da-sein* is a way to be which "is" the *Da-* (taking "is" in an active-transitive sense, so to speak) such that in accord with *this* preeminent being and as this being itself, *Da-sein* is a unique being (that which essentially occurs in the essential occurrence of beyng).**[149]

We may treat the second text in the form of a paraphrase: Since the *Da* is the *Lichtung* for the being that conceals itself, we have to separate *Da-sein* from the human being – because the *Da* endures the truth of being. So *Da-sein* is the between that can become the open site for beings that protrude into it.[150]

My attention was drawn to these texts by several posts that Lawrence Berger entered on the Heidegger Circle Forum, 10 and 28 November and 3 December 2015, as part of a discussion he conducted with Thomas Sheehan on the question of how *Da-sein* was related to the *Lichtung* in the *Contributions*. I find his conclusion convincing, that here *das Da-* does seem to coincide with (or be identical to) *die Lichtung*, but that that is not true of *das Da-sein* as such. (Sheehan's views appeared in *Making Sense*, pp. 136–9.) This conclusion is confirmed by *WW*, chapter 4.

(B) Governance and Certainty

7. Medieval Philosophy and Its Continuing Influence: *WW* 1.5–1.6

There is a further, major addition in the 1943 and 1949 versions of *WW*, a lengthy excursus on the medieval theological presuppositions of the *adaequatio*-theory, taking up two full pages of text, chapter 1, paragraphs 5 and 6. The scope of the point reaches through medieval and modern philosophy, but the details Heidegger cites are found in the very same treatise of Aquinas that he always cites for the traditional definition, the *Disputed Questions on Truth.* Here Aquinas speaks both of truth in the intellect and the truth of things; he also introduces the divine intellect as the term of reference for the truth found in things, thus confirming the double movement of adequation.[151]

At the end of chapter 1, Heidegger observed that there was an account of truth still more ancient than Aquinas's – he quotes Aristotelian language – but he does not take the opportunity to explore any relations between the ancient and the medieval viewpoints. That history was one he had explored very thoroughly in earlier years, from 1914 to 1924, where he saw philosophical questions interlinked with Christian faith and Christian theology. There are many sources one could explore in grasping Heidegger's early views on ancient thought in contrast to the medieval, especially lecture courses from the early 1920s. There is the course "Augustine and Neoplatonism" from summer 1921,[152] and, from just one year later, *Phenomenological Interpretations of Aristotle: Introduction to Phenomenological Research.*[153] But in the 1930s and 1940s he did not generally include medieval history in his analysis. Still, that history was an unexpressed operative factor in the *Seinsgeschichte* that Heidegger *did* treat, and that is why the medieval source still has relevance for the rectified phenomenology of *WW* 2, 3, and 4.

Translation of *WW*, beginning at **1.4**:

The dual character of the accord is brought to light by the traditional definition of truth: *veritas est adaequatio rei et intellectus.* This can be taken to mean: truth is the correspondence [*Angleichung*] of the matter to knowledge. But it can also be taken as saying: truth is the correspondence of knowledge to the matter. Admittedly the above definition is usually stated only in the formula *veritas est adaequatio intellectus ad rem.* Yet truth so conceived, propositional truth, is possible only on the basis of material truth [*Sachwahrheit*], of *adaequatio rei ad intellectum.* Both concepts of the

essence of *veritas* have continually in view a conforming to ... [*sich richten nach* ...], and hence think truth as *correctness* [*Richtigkeit*]. Nevertheless, the one is not the mere inversion of the other. On the contrary, in each case *intellectus* and *res* are thought differently. In order to recognize this we must trace the usual formula for the ordinary concept of truth back to its most recent (i.e., the medieval) origin. *Veritas* as *adaequatio rei ad intellectum* does not imply the later transcendental conception of Kant – possible only on the basis of the subjectivity of the human essence – that "objects conform to our knowledge." Rather, it implies the Christian theological belief that, with respect to what it is and whether it is, a matter, as created [*ens creatum*], is only insofar as it corresponds to the *idea* preconceived in the *intellectus divinus*, i.e., in the mind of God, and thus measures up to the idea (is correct) and in that sense is "true." The *intellectus humanus* too is an *ens creatum*. As a capacity bestowed upon human beings by God, it must satisfy its *idea*. But the understanding measures up to the idea only by accomplishing in its propositions the correspondence of what is thought to the matter, which in its turn must be in conformity with the *idea*. If all beings are "created," the possibility of the truth of human knowledge is grounded in the fact that matter and proposition measure up to the idea in the same way and therefore are fitted to each other on the basis of the divine plan of creation. *Veritas* as *adaequatio rei (creandae) ad intellectum (divinum)* guarantees *veritas* as *adaequatio intellectus (humani) ad rem (creatam)*. Throughout, *veritas* implies *convenientia*, the coming of beings themselves, as created, into agreement with the Creator, an "accord" with regard to the way they are determined in the order of creation.

To interrupt the quotation at this point, we can recognize one feature of the Scholastic view that reaches beyond the ancient treatment either of unconcealedness or correctness. Heidegger has noted that the created entity stands in agreement with the divine idea, and that the human intellect has the possibility of entering into accord with that entity. Thus of course the true human judgment will accord with the divine idea, but the further point is that the human intellect itself is an *ens creatum*, just as surely regulated by *its* idea in the mind of God as is any other created thing. The human being with his intellect is embraced by the divine benevolence.

But this order, detached from the notion of creation, can also be represented in a general and indefinite way as a world-order. The theologically conceived order of creation is replaced by the capacity of all objects to be planned by means of a worldly reason [*Weltvernunft*] that supplies the law for itself

and thus also claims that its procedure is immediately intelligible (what is considered "logical").[154]

So the medieval definition of truth can outlast its original theological inspiration. Modern philosophy can abandon the doctrine of creation and eventually even the very idea of God, but can still adhere to the formula of *adaequatio.* This detheologizing of truth is a major Curve or Corner in this meditation, and in the following Unit, on the course of modern philosophy, we will treat the juxtaposition of modernity with Scholasticism.

8. The Rational World-Order

We have read (*WW* **1.6**) that modern philosophy has replaced God with a "world-reason," *Weltvernunft,* that plays a role equivalent to that of the divine author, and that is responsible for a new kind of "world-order," *Weltordnung.* **"It supplies the law for itself and thus also claims that its procedure is immediately intelligible (what is considered 'logical')."** Heidegger does not cite any author to document this reading, but in fact his intention is to characterize a whole period in post-medieval philosophy, giving voice to a general idea that was expressed by many authors of the Renaissance period and the Enlightenment. Though he does not follow up this idea in *WW* 1949, it is an integral part of the *Seinsgeschichte* that he has outlined in many other writings both earlier and later.

Descartes on Certainty

A number of Heidegger's lectures and essays introduce a point that bears on the theme of truth but does not appear in any version of *WW* or in any of the lectures we have discussed hitherto: his claim that in modern philosophy, from Descartes onwards, truth (*die Wahrheit*) became interpreted as certainty (*die Gewissheit*). We find this first in "The Age of the World Picture" (*AWP,* 1938),[155] in the notes of the *Contributions* from the same period, and in the 1940 lectures on Nietzsche called *European Nihilism (N)*;[156] the point became a commonplace in many later works of the 1940s and 1950s.

Descartes propounded the metaphysics that was needed for modern times and modern science. It grasped the human mind as the *res cogitans,* that is, as the reflective subject that independently secures its own being. (*N,* p. 168). Thereby knowledge was to be reformed under the guidance of clear and distinct ideas. It is when an object's essence and properties are reduced to the mathematical determinations that are prescribed by method that it can be said to be truly known or understood. Thus, philosophy grasped the field of nature as the projected space-time continuum in which the motions of bodies could be calculated mathematically (*N*, p. 169). What such methodical knowing has achieved is a certainty, *Gewissheit* – equivalent to the certainty whereby the ego established itself (*N*, pp. 168–70). For Descartes, such certainty is what we mean by truth (*N*, pp. 169–70). The unshakeable foundation of truth (*fundamentum inconcussum veritatis*) is method (*AWP*, p. 81). That means that determining the mathematical properties of objects will be the vehicle of truth. Is there some way of proving metaphysically that what is in accord with this certainty is true?

N.B. we see (*N*, p. 169) that Descartes did *not* adopt this principle of certainty in opposition to the traditional definition of truth as *adaequatio intellectus et rei.* Rather, the principle of certainty has assimilated the old definition to the new context in which merely adventitious and empirical phenomena are set aside until they can be recast in the form of science; it is just that now the *intellectus* and the *res* have been newly determined metaphysically. Adequation now holds between them under their new mathematical, methodical description. Thus the fundamental Ego-certainty achieved by method is just as much the foundation for adequation in physics as was the divine governance for the Scholastics. This Cartesian interpretation of truth as certainty is an important guide to Heidegger in his readings of modern philosophy up through Leibniz, Kant, and Hegel.

While Descartes has preserved the tradition of adequation, he has *not* preserved the more ancient doctrine of unconcealedness. This is one point of Heidegger's running contrast of Descartes with a typical Greek thinker, Protagoras, who still preserved the ancient Greek idea:

> **Representing is no longer the apprehending of what presences within whose unconcealment the apprehending itself belongs, belongs indeed, as its own kind of presence to the things that are unconcealedly present. Representation is no longer the self-disclosure for … but rather the laying hold and grasping of …** (*AWP*, p. 82)

This may explain why the Cartesian definition received no discussion in any of the versions of *WW*: it was just too far removed from what Heidegger was presenting as the essence of truth. But before we draw too firm a line between Heidegger's study and Descartes's, we ought to ask whether Descartes has proved able to preserve in his account of truth one of the descendants of the ancient definition of the essence of truth, namely, the concept of correctness. Certainly, Descartes (and his

CONCLUSION

Against Self-Expression

I shall conclude by indicating briefly how Heidegger's study of truth would apply to everyday speech, drawing especially on his earlier and later versions of "Un-truth as Erring."

Modern dramatists have shown us how a speech, while seeming to say one thing, often communicates something unsaid – a complaint, for instance: "This is what I had to endure," an unstated grievance, a need in the self. Or a speech can engage in subterranean boasting: "This is what I accomplished; see how they envy me," an undiluted assertion of self behind the apparent meaning. Another effect can be heard at times when an opinion or point of view seems to be endowed with complete certainty: "Here are the true facts of the case – quite indubitable." Here too we sometimes detect an unstated level – the certainty originally attaches to the speaker himself: it is his rock-like conviction, the solidity of his being, that gives grounding to the "indubitable facts of the case." It is because *he* says it that the case is so certain. But then, when it is the speaker who authenticates the facts, we may begin to doubt: the case may not speak for itself after all. Many of us share the desire to be certain of things, and especially to *appear* to be certain of them.

These are different cases: a need in the self that a speech betrays, an assertion of the self, an air of certainty bestowed on an opinion – yet we often think about such cases in a common way, with the vocabulary of "self-expression." We may express an opinion, yet we may also express a need, or an emotion, or a will; we think that all of these are somehow "inherent" in the self and then find utterance in speech (and of course in gestures and deeds). Our society and law, and our educational practice, set a high value on self-expression, whose exercise is rigorously defended. The value of an expression of self is not, as such, affected by truth; if we encourage someone to express feelings and even opinions, we do not condemn them if they are not true. Rather, what we expect is that they be sincere, what we really think, and what we really feel.

But already in *SZ* and in his early lectures in Freiburg and Marburg, Heidegger submitted this idea of "expression," *Ausdruck*, to a phenomenological critique. This early work comes to a head in *SZ*, Section 33, which shows how the statement is a derivative mode of interpretation – meaning that its character as predication, expression, and communication is subordinate to its fundamental achievement: apophansis, letting-be-seen, revealing, disclosing, letting-*X*-show-itself. Only that is compatible with the ontology of *Da-sein*, being-in-the-world. That ontology releases our thought from the snares of "selfhood," from a view of language and speech as expressing a self. And if *Da-sein* is first of all an opening upon the world, its speech is first of all the revealing of the world and what is in the world. Though our speech is enshrouded with selfhood and Erring, these have not utterly effaced our *Da-sein* and its truth. The practice of thinking is an exemplary recovery of truth, even as it is shadowed by untruth, because its most characteristic act is questioning. It is the opposite of the rock-like claim of being certain. I mean to suggest that Heidegger's texts, which practise a visible questioning, are particularly valuable for an age like ours in which questioning is rare, in which we want to exhibit our certainty, and are embarrassed when we seem to lack it. Moreover, the sciences do not undertake the mission of inducing questioning in the public. But to be able to ask a question is an important achievement – it means a capacity to live, to exist, in the uncertain, the undetermined.

Notes

Introduction

1 Martin Heidegger, "*Vorträge: Teil 1:*1915–1932," in Heidegger, *Gesamtausgabe (GA)*, vol. 80.1, ed. Günther Neumann (Frankfurt am Main: Klostermann, 2016), 327–428.

2 *Vom Wesen der Wahrheit (WW)* (Frankfurt am Main: Klostermann, 1949); The essay reappeared in *Wegmarken (W)* (Frankfurt am Main: Klostermann, 1967); and then in Heidegger's *GA*, vol. 9, with Klostermann, 1976.

3 Martin Heidegger, *Basic Writings*, ed. D. Krell (New York: Harper, 1977); Martin Heidegger, *Pathmarks (P)*, ed. W. McNeill (Cambridge: Cambridge University Press, 1998).

4 *Der Ursprung des Kunstwerkes*, published in *Holzwege*, now *GA* 5. It's available in two English translations, in *Poetry, Language, Thought* (*PLT*), ed. A. Hofstadter (New York: Harper & Row, 1971); and in *Off the Beaten Track*, trans. J. Young (Cambridge: Cambridge University Press, 2002).

5 Martin Heidegger, *Sein und Zeit* (Tübingen: Niemeyer, 1927), now in Heidegger, *Gesamtausgabe* (*GA*), vol. 2 (Frankfurt am Main: Klostermann, 1977); revised translation by J. Stambaugh (Albany: SUNY Press, 2010).

6 This reading of Section 44 is given in detail in my article, "Truth as a Phenomenon," *The Review of Metaphysics* 68 (June 2015): 803–32.

7 Daniel Dahlstrom, *Heidegger's Concept of Truth* (Cambridge: Cambridge University Press, 2001).

8 Martin Heidegger, *Logic. Die Frage nach der Wahrheit*, ed. Walter Biemel, in Heidegger, *Gesamtausgabe (GA)*, vol. 21 (Frankfurt am Main: Klostermann, 1976); Translated by Thomas Sheehan (Bloomington: Indiana University Press, 2010).

9 *Platon. Sophistes, GA* 19 (Frankfurt am Main: Klostermann, 1992), ed. Ingeborg Schüssler; translated by R. Rojcewicz and A. Schuwer (Bloomington: Indiana University Press, 1997).

10 See G. Nicholson, "On the Manifold Meaning of Truth in Aristotle," in *The Multidimensionalaity of Hermeneutic Phenomenology*, ed. B. Babich and D. Ginev (Heidelberg: Springer, 2014), 227–42.

11 The chronology is found in *Heidegger-Jahrbuch I. Heidegger und die Anfänge seines Denkens*, ed. A. Denker, H.H. Gander, and H. Zaborowski (Freiburg and Munich: Alber, 2004), 491–5. Heidegger also offered this address in Dresden in 1932. More information on the Karlsruhe and Marburg versions will be found in T. Kisiel, *The Genesis of Heidegger's "Being and Time"* (Berkeley: University of California Press, 1993), 468 (with notes); and G. Schneeberger, *Nachlese zu Heidegger* (Bern, 1962): 9–13.

12 *WW* (Frankfurt am Main: Klostermann, 1943). This edition was translated by R.F.C. Hull and A. Crick and published in Heidegger, *Existence and Being*, ed. W. Brock (Chicago: Regnery, 1949).

13 Martin Heidegger, *Gesamtausgabe* (*GA*), vol. 80.1 *Vorträge. Teil 1: 1915–1932*, ed. Günther Neumann (Frankfurt am Main: Klostermann, 2016), 327–428. It does not print the Marburg and Freiburg versions of December separately, since it seems they were word-for-word the same, except for the title announced to the Marburg theologians, "Philosophizing and Believing," and a short preface in Marburg that I treat at the very end of Part II.

14 *Vom Wesen der Wahrheit. Zu Platons Höhlengleichnis und Theätet*, *GA* 34 (Frankfurt am Main: Klostermann, 1988); translated by T. Sadler (London: Continuum Books, 2002). I'll refer to it as **31–32**, giving reference to pages in the German edition.

15 The 1933–34 lecture course had the familiar title *Vom Wesen der Wahrheit*; it is published as the second part of *Sein und Wahrheit*, a volume including the lectures from summer 1933 as well as winter 1933–34, in *GA* 36–7 (Frankfurt am Main: Klostermann, 2001); now published in English translationas *Being and Truth 1933–34*, trans. G. Fried and R. Polt (Bloomington: Indiana University Press, 2010). I'll refer to it as **33–34**, mentioning the German pages.

16 *Platons Lehre von der Wahrheit*, published in 1942 and eventually in *Wegmarken* (Frankfurt am Main: Klostermann, 1967); now *GA* 9; Translated by T. Sheehan in *Pathmarks*, ed. W. McNeill (Cambridge: Cambridge University Press, 1998).

17 *Beiträge zur Philosophie. Vom Ereignis* (*GA* 65), ed. F.W. von Herrmann (Frankfurt am Main: Klostermann, 1989); two translations: *Contributions to Philosophy (From Enowning)*, trans. K. Maly and P. Emad (Bloomington: Indiana University Press, 1999); and *Contributions to Philosophy*, trans. R. Rojcewicz and D. Vallega-Neu (Bloomington: Indiana University Press, 2012).

18 F.W. von Herrmann, *Wahrheit – Freiheit – Geschichte. Eine Systematische Untersuchung zu Heideggers Schrift "Vom Wesen der Wahrheit"* (Frankfurt am Main: Klostermann, 2002).

19 Ibid., 214–15; see also 1, 10, 46.

20 Overviews can be found in all of the following excellent studies: William Richardson, *Heidegger: Through Phenomenology to Thought* (The Hague: Nijhoff, 1965): Otto Päggeler, *Martin Heidegger's Path of Thinking* (Atlantic Highlands: Humanities Press, 1982); Kisiel, *The Genesis*; von Herrmann, *Wahrheit*; *Becoming Heidegger: On the Trail of His Early Occasional Writings*, ed. Theodore Kisiel and Thomas Sheehan (Evanston: Northwestern University Press, 2007); Thomas Sheehan, *Making Sense of Heidegger* (London and New York: Rowman & Littlefield, 2015).

21 "… unter Beibehaltung des Ansatzes, der Grundstellung und des Aufbaus …," *GA* 80.1, 428.

22 Ekkehard Fräntzki, *Die Kehre. Heideggers Schrift "Vom Wesen der Wahrheit"* (Pfaffenweiler: Centaurus Verlagsgesellschaft, 1985).

Part I: The Early Pathway of Thinking: Freiburg, December 1930

23 All versions of the text begin with those words.

24 The outline of the published essay is thoroughly articulated in F.W. von Herrmann, *Wahrheit*. The course of the argument was also treated by Walter Biemel, "Heideggers Schrift 'Vom Wesen der Wahrheit,'" *Symposion, III* (Freiburg, 1952), and in his *Martin Heidegger: An Illustrated Study*, trans. J.L. Mehta (New York: Harcourt Brace Jovanovich, 1976), ch. 5.

25 John Sallis, "Deformatives: Essentially Other Than Truth," in *Reading Heidegger*, ed. J. Sallis (Bloomington: Indiana University Press, 1993), 29–46, has a good description of the dynamic, moving character of the addresses and the essay. His text was marked by a few deconstructive flourishes that were criticized by Walter Biemel, "Marginal Notes on Sallis's Peculiar Interpretation of Heidegger's 'Vom Wesen der Wahrheit,'" in *The Path of Archaic Thinking: Unfolding the Work of John Sallis*, ed. Kenneth Maly (Albany: SUNY Press, 1995), 221–39; but the deconstructive motifs were interesting and do not diminish the value of the description.

26 Von Herrmann, 101 ff.

27 Karl Marx and Frederick Engels, *Selected Works in One Volume* (New York: International Publishers, 1968), 28.

28 V.I. Lenin, "'Left-wing' Communism – an Infantile Disorder [1920]," in Lenin, *Selected Works* (Moscow: Progress Publishers, 1968), 519.

29 R.J.B. Bosworth, *Mussolini* (London: Arnold, 2002), 104.

30 *GA* 9, 103; *Pathmarks*, 82.

31 *GA*, 104; *Pathmarks*, 82–3.

32 *GA* 9, 121; *Pathmarks*, 95.

33 Heidegger, *Reden und Andere Zeugnisse eines Lebensweges* (*GA* 16), ed. Hermann Heidegger, 372–94; translated by Lisa Harries, *Martin Heidegger*

and National Socialism, ed. Günther Neske and Emil Kettering (New York: Paragon House, 1990), 15–32.

34 GA 16, 652–83. Translated by William J. Richardson, *Heidegger: The Man and the Thinker*, ed. Thomas Sheehan; the quotation appears there on page 47.

35 *Facts and Thoughts*, paragraphs 3 and 4.

36 *GA* 9, 121; *Pathmarks*, 95.

37 M. Heidegger, *Grundprobleme der Phänomenologie* (*GA* 24) (Frankfurt am Main: Klostermann, 1975); translated by A. Hofstadter (Bloomfield: Indiana University Press, 1982).

38 *Disputed Questions on Truth*, I, 2, translated by Mulligan, McGlynn, and Schmidt (Chicago: Regnery, 1952).

39 Edmund Husserl, *Logische Untersuchungen, II Teil, Kapitel VI. Das Ideal der Adäquation. Evidenz und Wahrheit*, 1st ed. 1901, translated by J.N. Findlay (London: Routledge Kegan Paul, 1970).

40 Bertrand Russell, *An Inquiry into Meaning and Truth* (London: Pelican Books, 1962), ch. 21.

41 *Logik. Die Frage nach der Wahrheit* (*GA* 21); translation by Thomas Sheehan, *Logic: The Question of Truth* (Bloomington: Indiana University Press, 2010).

42 Heinrich Maier, *Die Syllogistik des Aristoteles*, 2 vols. (Tübingen: Lauffschen Buchhandlung, 1896). Maier was a leading proponent of psychologism.

43 "Der Satz ist definiert mit Rücksicht auf Wahrheit und nicht umgekehrt,Wahrheit kommt vom Satz her."

44 *Aufweisend sehen lassen (Aussage) ist nur das Reden, darin das Entdecken oder Verdecken vorkommt*, 132. Several variants of this point appear on pages 133–5.

45 Heidegger, *Vom Wesen des Grundes* [1929], in *Wegmarken* (*GA*, 9), 131; translated by W. McNeill, in Heidegger, *Pathmarks*, ed. W. McNeill (Cambridge: Cambridge University Press, 1998), 103–4.

46 The reader will recognize in this example the view of Tarski that such an external correlation is all the philosopher is able to hope for in this domain.

47 Martin Heidegger, *Hegels Phänomenologie des Geistes, GA* 32, ed. I. Görland (Frankfurt am Main: Klostermann, 1980); translated by K. Maly and P. Emad (Bloomington: Indiana University Press, 1988).

48 Heidegger, *Hegels Phänomenologie des Geistes*, 90–3; trans. 63–6.

49 Heidegger, *Hegels Phänomenologie des Geistes*, 91; trans. 65.

50 I translate from Section 35 of the German translation by G.F. Meier (Halle, 1783). "… *die innerliche Möglichkeit einer Sache ist das Wesen.*" In context, beginning from Section 18, Baumgarten has been treating grounds, or *ratio*, based on Leibniz's principle of sufficient reason.

51 Christian Wolff, *philosophia prima sive ontologia* [1736], now edited by Jean Ecole (Hildesheim: Olms Verlagsbuchhandlung, 1962), 126; the whole section devoted to essence and existence, the possible and the impossible, runs from Sections 79 to 178.

52 *GA,* vol. 3. My page references are to the second edition (Frankfurt am Main: Klostermann, 1951).

53 See, e.g., F.H. Jacobi, "Open Letter to Fichte," in *Philosophy of German Idealism,* ed. E. Behler (New York: Continuum, 1987), 122.

54 *David Hume,* in Jacobi, *Werke,* II (Leipzig: Fleischer, 1812–25), 99.

55 *Vom Wesen des Grundes,* which eventually appeared in *Wegmarken,* 1967, and then in *GA* 9, 1976; translated by W. McNeill, in *Pathmarks,* ed. McNeill (Cambridge: Cambridge University Press, 1998), 97–135.

56 "... Rein vergessen muss ich alle Bewegung, und mir gerade dies Vergessen ... am angelegentlichsten *sein lassen.*" From *Über das Unternehmen des Kritizismus. Die Vernunft zu Verstande zu Bringen,* Jacobi, *Werke,* vol. III, 147.

57 *Martin Luthers Evangelien-Auslegung,* ed. E. Mülhaupt (Göttingen: Vandenhoeck & Ruprecht, 1954), vol. IV, 3.

58 *Vom Wesen der Menschlichen Freiheit* (*GA* 31); translated by Ted Sadler: *The Essence of Human Freedom* (London: Continuum, 2002). See von Herrmann, *Wahrheit,* 93–101.

59 See "On the Manifold Meaning of Truth in Aristotle," 227–42.

60 Paul Friedländer, *Platon,* Band I (Berlin: de Gruyter, 1954); translated by H. Meyerhoff (New York: Harper, 1958), 222–3.

61 Ernst Heitsch, "Die nicht-philosophische *alētheia,*" *Hermes* 90 (1962): 24–33.

62 For instance, Heribert Boeder, "Der frühgriechische Wortgebrauch von Logos und Ale¯theia," *Archiv für Begriffsgeschichte* 4 (1959): 82–112.

63 *Platon. Dritte Auflage,* vol. I (Berlin: de Gruyter, 1964). Not yet translated.

64 *Ta alēthea* can be found in Hesiod, and the later historians and tragedians, e.g., Aeschylus, *Seven Against Thebes,* 710, 943, and is commonly translated as "reality."

65 See Heidegger's discussion in "*Alētheia* (Heraklit, Fragment 16)," *Vorträge und Aufsätze* (1954): 257–82.

66 See Diels on Heraclitus, Section A, "Attributions": e.g., Sextus Empiricus, adv. Math. VII, 126 ff.

67 I treated this in the paper "Truth as a Phenomenon," 803–32.

68 See my paper, "Truth and Unconcealedness," in *Gatherings: Annual of the Heidegger Circle* 4 (2014): 70–85, where I argue that in his very latest work Heidegger did not retract his interpretation of truth as unconcealedness, as some critics have alleged.

69 Bernard Williams, *Truth and Truthfulness* (Princeton: Princeton University Press, 2002), "Endnote. The Vocabulary of Truth: An Example."

70 Now in *Wegmarken* 1967, 2–3 (*GA* 9).

71 *The Fundamental Concepts of Metaphysics, GA* 29/30; translated by William McNeill and Nicholas Walter (Bloomington: Indiana University Press, 1995), 242.

72 The term "exister" was often used by Kierkegaard in the *Concluding Unscientific Postscript*, though not by Heidegger.

73 For instance, Werner Marx, *Heidegger and the Tradition* (Evanston: Northwestern University Press, 1971), 251.

74 Von Herrmann, *Wahrheit*, 135–44.

75 See especially Scheler, *Wesen und Formen der Sympathie*, published 1923 in Husserl's *Jahrbuch für Philosophie und Phänomenologische Forschung.*

76 Ernst Tugendhat, *Der Wahrheitsbegriff bei Husserl und Heidegger* (Berlin: de Gruyter, 1967), 370–6.

77 This is emphasized in the 1940 written version in a footnote on page 421, which spells *Seyn* with a *y*.

78 Academy edition, vol. 4, 425.

79 *Kant und das Problem der Metaphysik* (*GA* 3) (Klostermann, 1991); translated by Richard Taft (Bloomington: Indiana University Press, 1997).

80 Heidegger, *Der Zeitbegriff in der Geschichtswissenschaft. Frühe Schriften* (*GA* 1), 416.

81 *Phänomenologie und Theologie, GA* 9, 48; *Pathmarks*, 41.

82 *GA* 9, 48, *Pathmarks*, 42.

83 *Phänomenologische Interpretation von Kants Kritik der reinen Vernunft* (*GA* 25), ed. Ingtraud Görland (Frankfurt: Klostermann, 1977); translated by Kenneth Maly and Parvis Emad (Bloomington: Indiana University Press, 1997).

84 *GA* 9, 131; "On the Essence of Ground," in, *Pathmarks*, 103.

85 Ibid.

86 Ibid., 134; *Pathmarks*, 105.

87 Ibid., 135; *Pathmarks*, 106.

Intermission: Political Storms

88 In the volume *The Heidegger Case*, ed. Tom Rockmore and Joseph Margolis (Philadelphia: Temple University Press, 1992), 133.

89 In Thomas Sheehan, *Heidegger: The Man and the Thinker* (Chicago: Precedent Publishing, 1981), 46.

90 The account by Hugo Ott, *Martin Heidegger: Unterwegs zu seiner Biographie* (Frankfurt am Main: Campus Verlag, 1988); translated by A. Blunden as *Martin Heidegger: A Political Life* (New York: Basic Books, 1993) has been widely accepted as the most authoritative.

91 *GA* 16 "*Die Selbstbehauptung der deutschen Universität*; translation by Karsten Harries, *Review of Metaphysics* 38 (1985): 467–87.

92 See K.A. Moehling, *Martin Heidegger and the Nazi Party*, thesis, Northern Illinois University, 1972, 264, 265.

93 See "The Rectorate: Facts and Thoughts," published only posthumously.

94 Now published in the *Heidegger-Jahrbuch*, 4, ed. A. Denker and H. Zaborowski (Freiburg: Alber, 2009); translated by G. Fried and R. Polt,

Nature, History, State, 1933–34 (London: Bloomsbury, 2013). Before it was published, this was reported by Emmanuel Faye in his book *Heidegger. L'introduction du nazisme dans la philosophie* (Paris: Éditions Albin Michel, 2005), 195 ff.

95 Also reported by Faye, in ibid., 349 ff.

96 Now available in English: *On Hegel's "Philosophy of Right,"* ed. Peter Trawny; translated by Andrew J. Mitchell (New York: Bloomsbury, 2014).

97 *Reden und Andere Zeugnisse eines Lebensweges 1910–1976* (*GA* 16), ed. Hermann Heidegger (Frankfurt: Klostermann, 2000).

98 Guido Schneeberger, *Nachlese zu Heidegger* (Bern, 1962), after page 144.

99 *GA* 16, no. 103, 188–9. Heidegger issued a second statement on 11 November, largely overlapping in content, which is no. 104 in this collection.

100 *GA* 94, 530.

101 Peter Trawny, *Heidegger and the Myth of a Jewish World-Conspiracy,* trans. Andrew J. Mithell (Chicago: University of Chicago Press, 2016).

102 The volume, *Heidegger und der Antisemitismus,* was edited by Walter Homolka and Arnulf Heidegger (Freiburg: Herder, 2016).

103 I borrow the title of the book edited by Margolis and Rockmore.

104 Victor Farias, *Heidegger et le Nazisme* (Paris: Verdier, 1987).

105 Graeme Nicholson, "Two Faces of Heidegger," in *Dialectic and Narrative,* ed. T.R. Flynn and D. Judovitz (Albany: SUNY Press, 1993), 47–55.

106 See M. Heidegger, "Sprache und Heimat," in *Dauer im Wandel,* a festschrift for Carl Burckhardt, ed. H. Rinn and M. Rychner (Munich: Callwey, 1961), 174–93.

Part II: Later Work: The Pathway Rectified

107 *Hölderlins Hymnen "Germanien" und "der Rhein,"* ed. Suzanne Ziegler (Frankfurt am Main: Klostermann, 1980 – *GA* 39), 27; translated by W. McNeill (Bloomington: Indiana University Press, 2009).

108 *Vorträge und Aufsätze* (*GA* 7), 93–8.

109 My article, "Truth and Unconcealedness," 70–85, treated this.

110 *Platons Lehre von der Wahrheit* appeared in *Geistige Überlieferung* (Berlin, 1942), then in book form, along with the "Letter on Humanism" (Bern: Francke, 1947); then in *Wegmarken* (1967), reappearing in *GA* 9. Translation by Thomas Sheehan and William McNeill in *Pathmarks,* 1998. See *Wegmarken,* pp. 227–30; *Pathmarks,* 174–8.

111 *Das Ende der Philosophy und die Aufgabe des Denkens* (1964), in *Zur Sache des Denkens* (*GA* 14), 87–8; translated by J. Stambaugh, in Heidegger, *Basic Writings,* 447.

112 See, for example, "The Question Concerning Technology," (1953) (*GA* 7); English translation by W. Lovitt, in Krell, *Basic Writings*, 325.
113 *GA* 9, 226; *Pathmarks*, 172.
114 *GA* 9, 228; *Pathmarks*, 174–5.
115 GA 9, 227–8; *Pathmarks*, 175.
116 GA 9, 226; *Pathmarks*, 174.
117 *GA* 9, 229; *Pathmarks*, 176.
118 See now especially Francisco Gonzalez, *Plato and Heidegger: A Question of Dialogue* (University Park: Pennsylvania State University Press, 2009). He has full documentation of the Heidegger material and the secondary literature.
119 Ibid., 147–61.
120 Likewise, **33–34** mostly adheres to this accurate account of the yoke: see Section 27, with its visual schema. There is, however, one careless passage in **33–34**, Section 29(c), in which Heidegger refers to the objects of *nous* as "truth," thus connected by a yoke to *nous* – very likely a passage added extemporaneously and in haste – and it is unfortunate that Gonzalez jumped on this, ignoring all the other more careful passages.
121 GA 9, 232; *Pathmarks*, 178.
122 In Units 2 and 3 I have re-translated some lines of *WW* 1949 for emphasis. But in later units of Part II I have relied on the translation published by John Sallis.
123 F.-W. von Herrmann, *Wahrheit – Freiheit – Geschichte: Eine Systematische Untersuchung zu Heideggers Schrift "Vom Wesen der Wahrheit"* (Frankfurt am Main: Klostermann, 2002), pp. 76–8.
124 Martin Heidegger, *Die Lehre vom Urteil im Psychologismus. Ein kritisch-positiver Beitrag zur Logik*, now in Heidegger, *Gesamtausgabe* (*GA*), vol. 1, ed. F.W. von Herrmann (Frankfurt am Main: Klostermann, 1978). In the dissertation, Heidegger was following in the direction pioneered by Husserl's critique of psychologism in the first volume of his *Logical Investigations* of 1900.
125 Von Herrmann thinks Heidegger had Husserl in mind: *Wahrheit*, 86–7.
126 Tugendhat, *Der Wahrheitsbegriff.*
127 *Die Folge ist, dass das Offenbare selbst zum Mass wird*, 376.
128 See the volume *Truth*, ed. George Pitcher (Englewood Cliffs: Prentice-Hall, 1964), containing the two articles by our authors, both entitled "Truth."
129 See, for example, *GA* 45, 156–7.
130 Many texts of Heidegger affirm this – see, e.g., **31–32**, 51.
131 Sheehan, *Making Sense.*
132 Repeated often – see *Making Sense*, pp. 23, 32.
133 Richard Capobianco, *Engaging Heidegger* (Toronto: University of Toronto Press, 2010); idem, *Heidegger's Way of Being* (Toronto: University of Toronto Press, 2014).
134 Sheehan, *Making Sense*, xii.

135 Ibid., xii; see also pp. 10, 23, 115, 127–8.

136 The phenomenology of *SZ* is treated in my paper, "Truth as a Phenomenon," 803–32.

137 Repeated often – see pp. 23, 32.

138 *Vom Wesen der Menschlichen Freiheit,* Summer semester 1930; *GA* 31, ed. Hartmut Tietjen (Frankfurt am Main: Klostermann, 1982), 20–6.

139 See the volume of Isaiah Berlin, *Four Essays on Liberty* (London: Oxford University Press, 1969).

140 *GA* 31, 20–6.

141 See the dialogue, 4 June 2017, with contributions from Richard Capobianco, Thomas Sheehan, and Richard Polt, among others; the debate was prompted by other Heidegger texts, notably the 1949 Introduction to "What Is Metaphysics?"

142 Here he never refers to the active verb *alētheuō,* which he had often cited in past years from Aristotle's writings: see his *Plato's Sophist* (*GA* 19), 23–64; and *SZ,* 219.

143 Sheehan, *Making Sense.*

144 *GA* 9, 188; *Pathmarks,* 144.

145 Sheehan, *Making Sense,* 61. See similar remarks on pp. 71, 73, 78.

146 See *Engaging Heidegger,* 94–101.

147 Ibid., 88–91.

148 *WW* employs the term *Lichtung* only in ch. 9, in the first paragraph added in the 1949 edition.

149 Das Da-sein ist eine Weise zu sein, die, indem sie das Da "ist" (aktiv-transitiv gleichsam), gemäß *diesem* ausgezeichneteen Sein und als dieses Sein selbst ein einzigartiges Seiendes ist (das Wesende der Wesung des Seyns)." *GA* 65, 296.

150 "Allein schon die Besinnung auf das Da als die Lichtung für die Sichverbergung (das Seyn) muss ahnen lassen, wie entscheidend der Bezug des Da-seins zum Seienden im Ganzen ist – weil das Da die Wahrheit des Seins aushält. In dieser Richtung gedacht rückt das Da-sein – selbst nirgendwo unterbringbar – weg vom Bezug zum Menschen und enthüllt sich als das 'Zwischen' das vom Seyn selbst entfaltet wird als der offene Hereinragungsbereich für das Seiende" *GA* 65, 17–25.

151 Thomas Aquinas, *Disputed Questions on Truth.*

152 It is the second part of *Phänomenologie des religiösen Lebens,* ed. Claudius Strube (*GA* 60, 1995).

153 Edited by Walter Bröcker and Käte Bröcker-Oltmanns (*GA* 61, 1985).

154 *GA* 9, 180–1; translated by John Sallis in *Pathmarks,* 138–9.

155 *Die Zeit des Weltbildes,* in *Holzwege* (1950), now *GA* 5, ed. F. W. von Herrmann (Frankfurt am Main: Klostermann, 1977); translated by J. Young, in Heidegger, *Off the Beaten Track,* ed. J. Young and K. Haynes (Cambridge: Cambridge University Press, 2002).

156 The edition of *Nietzsche* (2 vols.), Pfullingen: Neske, 1961, prepared for publication by Heidegger himself, and now reissued in *GA* 6.1 and 6.2, ed. B. Schillbach (Frankfurt am Main: Klostermann, 1996–7), can now be compared with the re-edited texts of the original lectures in *GA* 43, 44, 46, 47, and 48 (this last volume corresponds to our text on European nihilism). My references are to the 1961 text, vol. 2.

157 See Heidegger, *Der Satz vom Grund* (Pfullingen: Neske, 1957), *GA* 10; translation by Reginald Lilly, *The Principle of Reason* (Bloomington: Indiana University Press, 1991).

158 Heidegger treated this in the first section of *WG* in 1928.

159 G.W.F. Hegel, *Phänomenologie des Geistes*, 1807. I cite the English translation by A.V. Miller (Oxford: Oxford University Press, 1977), which numbers the different paragraphs of the text, and which I cite as "M – " followed by the paragraph number.

160 From *Wegmarken*, now in *GA* 9, ed. F.W. von Herrmann (Frankfurt am Main: Klostermann, 1976), 255–72; English translation by R. Metcalf, J. Sallis, and W. McNeill, in Heidegger, *Pathmarks*, ed. W. McNeill (Cambridge: Cambridge University Press, 1998), 323–36.

161 Von Herrmann, *Wahrheit*, 145–9, 215–17.

162 Kenneth Maly, *Heidegger's Possibility: Language, Emergence – Saying Being* (Toronto: University of Toronto Press, 2008).

163 Richard Polt, *The Emergency of Being: On Heidegger's Contributions to Philosophy* (Ithaca: Cornell University Press, 2006).

164 Daniella Vallega-Neu, *Heidegger's Contributions to Philosophy* (Bloomington: Indiana University Press, 2003).

165 Sheehan, *Making Sense.*

166 *Heidegger Studies* 25 (2009): 157–89.

167 *Wege Ins Ereignis* (Frankfurt am Main: Klostermann, 1994).

168 The lecture course from 1937–38, *Basic Questions of Philosophy: Selected "Problems" of "Logic" (Grundfragen der Philosophie: Ausgewählte "Probleme" der "Logik"* *GA* 45), ed. F.W. von Herrmann, trans. R. Rojcewicz and A. Schuwer (Bloomington: Indiana University Press, 1994), was delivered at the same time as Heidegger was composing the *Beiträge*; the two works express the same view of history, and these lectures can contribute substantially towards grasping the more esoteric work on this and on many other topics.

169 *Beiträge* no. 81; *Grundfragen* (*GA* 45), 1–6, 108–18; see von Herrmann, *Wahrheit*, 198–203.

170 The leap is described most fully in *GA* 65, Sections 115, 122, 128, 130–5.

171 This is described particularly in the division of *GA* 65 called *Anklang*, Sections 50–80.

172 See Heidegger, *Zur Seinsfrage* (*GA* 9), where being survives only in crossed-out form, or under erasure.

173 See the 1949 Bremen Lectures (*GA* 79), which are more focused and powerful than the *Contributions.*

174 *Die Frage nach der Technik,* in *VA* (*GA* 7), English translation in W. Lovitt, *The Question of Technology and Other Essays* (New York: Harper & Row, 1977).

175 See Sheehan, *Making Sense;* von Herrmann, *Wege ins Ereignis;* Vallega-Neu, *Heidegger's Contributions;* Polt, *The Emergency of Being.* I have been particularly indebted to Sheehan's many studies of *Ereignis* and *Kehre,* both in the book cited and in many articles and posts. I am also most indebted to von Herrmann's, *Wahrheit,* 214–30, for his account of the *Ereignis* does link it to the argument of *WW.*

176 The present translation of the word was pioneered by Parvis Emad and Kenneth Maly in their 1999 translation of the *Beiträge.*

177 Now published in *GA* 11 *Identität und Differenz,* ed. F.W. von Herrmann (2006), with many illuminating marginal corrections from Heidegger's hand.

178 *GA* 11, 36–8.

179 "Die Verborgenheit versagt der *alētheia* das Entbergen und läßt sie noch nicht als *sterēsis* (Beraubung) zu, sondern bewahrt ihr das Eigenste als Eigentum."

180 The text of 1940 says that concealment is denying the alpha-privative of *alētheia,* denying its character as privation. It may be that the second clause above should be rendered: "*Alētheia* would not be permitted even if it were just the *sterēsis* (privation) of concealment." But we'll persevere here with the first version.

181 Fräntzki, *Die Kehre,* 110–12, has a peculiar interpretation of this difficult sentence, seeing in it a triumph of unconcealedness over concealment, which supposedly manifests the "metaphysical" bias of the 1949 version and distorts the original insight into the finitude of truth. But on the contrary, the primacy of concealment is clear in this sentence!

182 Heidegger, *Gelassenheit* (Pfullingen: Neske, 1959), 26; *GA* 16.

183 The dialogue was first published in *Unterwegs zur Sprache (US)* (Pfullingen: Neske, 1959), *GA* 12; *On the Way to Language* (*OWL*), trans. Peter Hertz (New York: Harper & Row, 1971). As Heidegger tells us in his documentation at the end of the book, the dialogue was written in 1953–54, occasioned by a visit from Professor Tezuka of Tokyo.

184 *US,* 141; *OWL,* 44.

185 *US,* 148; *OWL,* 50.

186 See, for example, "Time and Being," *GA* 14, embarking on the thinking of being that does not ground it in beings.

187 On this, see the entire opening section of the *Contributions,* titled the Preview, *Vorblick.* This is also elucidated by the lectures in *GA* 45, which we shall cite at the end of Unit 12 below.

188 *Wegmarken,* 97; *Pathmarks,* 154.

189 Von Herrmann has a valuable discussion of the chronology here, *Wahrheit,* 207–23.

190 This point is particularly well developed in the three appendices found in *GA* 45.

191 See Andrew Mitchell, *Heidegger among the Sculptors* (Stanford: Stanford University Press, 2010).

192 *Holzwege* [1950], 60; now in *GA* 5. *Off the Beaten Track,* 45–6. I shall be quoting from the translation by Albert Hofstadter that appears in the collection he edited, *Poetry, Language Thought, PLT* (New York: Harper & Row, 1971).

193 Beda Allemann, *Hölderlin und Heidegger* (Freiburg: Atlantis, 1954).

194 Heidegger, "Andenken," in *Erläuterungen zu Hölderlins Dichtung, GA* 4 (Frankfurt am Main: Klostermann, 1981); idem, *Elucidations of Hölderlin's Poetry,* trans. K. Hoeller (Amherst: Humanity Books, 2000). Page references are first to *GA* 4, then to the translation.

195 See Trish Glazebrook, *Heidegger on Science* (Albany: SUNY Press, 2012); and many essays by Babette Babich (e.g., "Towards a Critical Philosophy of Science," *International Journal of the Philosophy of Science* 24, no. 4 [2010]: 343–91). J. Kockelmans, *Heidegger and Science* (Washington, D.C.: University Press of America, 1985), is a classic in this field, as are the works of Patrick Heelan and Robert Crease.

196 See M. Heidegger, *Bremen and Freiburg Lectures* (*GA* 79, ed. Petra Jäger), translated by Andrew Mitchell (Bloomington: Indiana University Press, 2012).

197 Andrew Mitchell, *The Fourfold* (Evanston: Northwestern University Press, 2015).

198 See, for example, Babette Babich, "Constellating Technology: Heidegger's *Die Gefahr/The Danger,*" in *The Multidimensionality of Hermeneutic. Phenomenology,* ed. B. Babich and D. Ginev (Heidelberg: Springer, 2014).

199 Martin Heidegger, *Zollikon Seminars* (Evanston: Northwestern University Press, 2001).

200 Judith Wolfe, *Heidegger and Theology* (London: Bloomsbury, 2014).

201 Heidegger, *Identität und Differenz* (Pfullingen: Neske, 1957), 70.

202 *GA* 80.1, 379.

Index

New Studies in Phenomenology and Hermeneutics

General Editor: Kenneth Maly

Gail Stenstad, *Transformations: Thinking after Heidegger*

Parvis Emad, *On the Way to Heidegger's "Contributions to Philosophy"*

Bernhard Radloff, *Heidegger and the Question of National Socialism: Disclosure and Gestalt*

Kenneth Maly, *Heidegger's Possibility: Language, Emergence – Saying Be-ing*

Robert Mugerauer, *Heidegger and Homecoming: The Leitmotif in the Later Writings*

Graeme Nicholson, *Justifying Our Existence: An Essay in Applied Phenomenology*

Ladelle McWhorter and Gail Stenstad, eds, *Heidegger and the Earth: Essays in Environmental Philosophy*, Second, Expanded Edition

Richard Capobianco, *Engaging Heidegger*

Peter R. Costello, *Layers in Husserl's Phenomenology: On Meaning and Intersubjectivity*

Friedrich-Wilhelm von Herrmann, *Hermeneutics and Reflection: Heidegger and Husserl on the Concept of Phenomenology*, translated by Kenneth Maly. Published in German as *Hermeneutik und Reflexion. Der Begriff der Phänomenologie bei Heidegger und Husserl*

Richard Capobianco, *Heidegger's Way of Being*

Janet Donohoe, *Husserl on Ethics and Intersubjectivity: From Static to Genetic Phenomenology*

Miles Groth, *Translating Heidegger*

Graeme Nicholson, *Heidegger on Truth: Its Essence and Its Fate*